Real-Time Data Analysis Exercises

Up-to-date macro data is a great way to engage in and understand the usefulness of macro variables and their impact on the economy. Real-Time Data Analysis exercises communicate directly with the Federal Reserve Bank of St. Louis's FRED® site, so every time FRED posts new data, students see new data.

End-of-chapter exercises accompanied by the Real-Time Data Analysis icon 🌐 include Real-Time Data versions in **MyEconLab**.

Select in-text figures labeled **MyEconLab** Real-Time Data update in the electronic version of the text using FRED data.

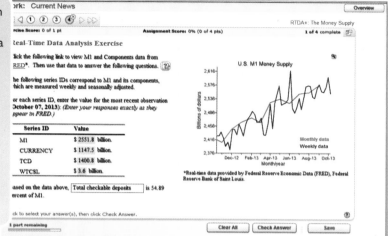

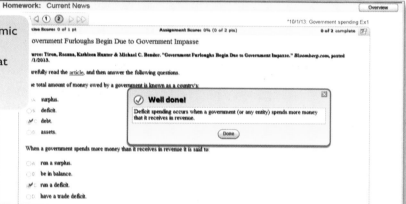

Current News Exercises

Posted weekly, we find the latest microeconomic and macroeconomic news stories, post them, and write auto-graded multi-part exercises that illustrate the economic way of thinking about the news.

Interactive Homework Exercises

Participate in a fun and engaging activity that helps promote active learning and mastery of important economic concepts.

Pearson's experiments program is flexible and easy for instructors and students to use. For a complete list of available experiments, visit *www.myeconlab.com*.

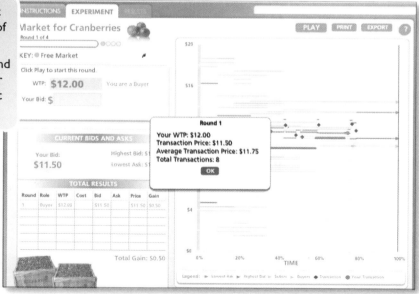

PEARSON **Choices** Providing Options and Value in Economics

Digital

Complete **Digital** Experience

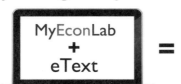

= Allow your students to save by purchasing a stand-alone MyEconLab directly from Pearson at **www.myeconlab.com**. Pearson's industry-leading learning solution features a **full Pearson eText** and course management functionality. Most importantly, MyEconLab helps you hold students accountable for class preparation and supports more active learning styles. Visit **www.myeconlab.com** to find out more.

Students can purchase a three-hole-punched, full-color version of the text via myeconlab.com at a **significant discount delivered right to their door.** →

Instant eText Access

= The **CourseSmart eBookstore** provides instant, online access to the textbook and course materials students need at a lower price. CourseSmart's eTextbooks are fully searchable and offer the same paging and appearance as the printed texts. You can preview eTextbooks online anytime at **www.coursesmart.com**.

Homework and Tutorial Only

= Same great assessment technology without the **Pearson eText**.

Students can purchase a three-hole-punched, full-color version of the text via myeconlab.com at a **significant discount delivered right to their door.** →

Digital + Print

Great Content + Great **Value**

= Package our premium bound textbook with a MyEconLab access code for the most enduring student experience. Find out more at **www.myeconlab.com**.

Great Content + Great **Price**

= Save your students money and promote an active learning environment by offering a Student Value Edition—a three-hole-punched, full-color version of the premium textbook that's available at a 35% discount—→packaged with a MyEconLab access code at your bookstore.

Custom

Customized Solutions

= Customize your textbook to match your syllabus. Trim your text to include just the chapters you need or add chapters from multiple books. With no unused material or unnecessary expense, Pearson Learning Solutions provides the right content you need for a course that's entirely your own. **www.pearsonlearningsolutions.com**

Contact your Pearson representative for more information on Pearson Choices.

ALWAYS LEARNING   **PEARSON**

2nd Edition

Macroeconomics
Policy and Practice

Frederic S. Mishkin
Columbia University

PEARSON

Boston Columbus Indianapolis New York San Francisco Upper Saddle River
Amsterdam Cape Town Dubai London Madrid Milan Munich Paris Montreal Toronto
Delhi Mexico City São Paulo Sydney Hong Kong Seoul Singapore Taipei Tokyo

Macroeconomics Matters: The Latest Economic Events and Policy Responses

	APPLICATIONS apply the analysis in each chapter to explain important real-world situations.	**POLICY AND PRACTICE** cases explore specific examples of policies and how they were executed.	**MACROECONOMICS IN THE NEWS** boxes introduce relevant news articles and data from the daily press and explain how to read them.
Chapter 2 Measuring Macroeconomic Data		• Can GDP Buy Happiness? • Policy and Overstatements of the Cost of Living	• Unemployment and Employment • Interest Rates
Chapter 3 Aggregate Production and Productivity	• Why Are Some Countries Rich and Others Poor? • Explaining Real Wage Growth • Oil Shocks, Real Wages, and the Stock Market		
Chapter 4 Saving and Investment in Closed and Open Economies	• How the United States Became the Largest Net Debtor in the World • The Twin Deficits	• Government Policies to Stimulate Saving • Crowding Out and the Debate over the 2009 Fiscal Stimulus Package	• Balance of Payments Accounts
Chapter 5 Money and Inflation	• Testing the Quantity Theory of Money • Testing the Fisher Effect	• The Zimbabwean Hyperinflation	• The Monetary Aggregates
Chapter 5 Appendix The Money Supply Process	• Quantitative Easing and the Money Supply 2007–2013		
Chapter 6 The Sources of Growth and the Solow Model	• Evidence on Convergence, 1960–2012 • U.S. Growth Rates in the Postwar Period	• China's One-Child Policy and Other Policies to Limit Population Growth	
Chapter 7 Drivers of Growth: Technology, Policy, and Institutions	• Does Population Growth Improve Living Standards?	• Government Measures to Increase Human Capital • The World Bank's *Doing Business* • Does Foreign Aid Work?	
Chapter 8 Business Cycles: An Introduction			• Leading Economic Indicators
Chapter 9 The *IS* Curve	• The Vietnam War Buildup, 1964–1969	• The Fiscal Stimulus Package of 2009	
Chapter 10 Monetary Policy and Aggregate Demand		• Movements Along the *MP* Curve: The Rise in the Federal Funds Rate Target, 2004–2006 • Shifts in the *MP* Curve: Autonomous Monetary Easing at the Onset of the 2007–2009 Financial Crisis	
Chapter 11 Aggregate Supply and the Phillips Curve		• The Phillips Curve Tradeoff and Macroeconomic Policy in the 1960s	
Chapter 12 The Aggregate Demand and Supply Model	• The Volcker Disinflation, 1980–1986 • Negative Demand Shocks, 2001–2004 • Negative Supply Shocks, 1973–1975 and 1978–1980 • Positive Supply Shocks, 1995–1999 • Negative Supply and Demand Shocks and the 2007–2009 Financial Crisis • The United Kingdom and the 2007–2009 Financial Crisis • China and the 2007–2009 Financial Crisis		

	APPLICATIONS apply the analysis in each chapter to explain important real-world situations.	**POLICY AND PRACTICE** cases explore specific examples of policies and how they were executed.	**MACROECONOMICS IN THE NEWS** boxes introduce relevant news articles and data from the daily press and explain how to read them.
Chapter 13 Macroeconomic Policy and Aggregate Demand and Supply Analysis	• The Great Inflation • Nonconventional Monetary Policy and Quantitative Easing	• The Federal Reserve's Use of the Equilibrium Real Interest Rate, r^* • The Activist/Nonactivist Debate Over the Obama Fiscal Stimulus Package • The Fed's Use of the Taylor Rule • Abenomics and the Shift in Japanese Monetary Policy in 2013	
Chapter 14 The Financial System and Economic Growth	• The Tyranny of Collateral • Is China a Counter-Example to the Importance of Financial Development to Economic Growth?		
Chapter 15 Financial Crises and the Economy	• The Mother of All Financial Crises: The Great Depression • The Global Financial Crisis of 2007–2009	• Was the Fed to Blame for the Housing Price Bubble? • The Federal Reserve's Nonconventional Monetary Policies and Quantitative Easing During the Global Financial Crisis • Japan's Lost Decade, 1992–2002 • Debate Over Central Bank Response to Bubbles	
Chapter 16 Fiscal Policy and the Government Budget		• The Entitlements Debate: Social Security and Medicare/Medicaid • The European Sovereign Debt Crisis • Tax Smoothing • The 2009 Debate Over Tax-Based Versus Spending-Based Fiscal Stimulus • Two Expansionary Fiscal Contractions: Denmark and Ireland • The Debate Over Fiscal Austerity in Europe • The Bush Tax Cuts and Ricardian Equivalence	
Chapter 17 Exchange Rates and International Economic Policy	• The Global Financial Crisis and the Dollar • Why Are Exchange Rates So Volatile? • How Did China Accumulate Over $3 Trillion of International Reserves?	• Will the Euro Survive? • The Collapse of the Argentine Currency Board	• Foreign Exchange Rates
Chapter 18 Consumption and Saving	• Consumer Confidence and the Business Cycle • Housing, the Stock Market, and the Collapse of Consumption in 2008 and 2009	• The 2008 Tax Rebate • Behavioral Policies to Increase Saving	• The Consumer Confidence and Consumer Sentiment Indices
Chapter 19 Investment	• Stock Market Crashes and Recessions	• U.S. Government Policies and the Housing Market	
Chapter 20 The Labor Market, Employment, and Unemployment	• Why Has Labor Force Participation of Women Increased? • Why Are Income Inequality and Returns to Education Increasing? • Why Are European Unemployment Rates Generally Much Higher Than U.S. Unemployment Rates?	• Unemployment Insurance and Unemployment • Minimum Wage Laws	
Chapter 21 The Role of Expectations in Macroeconomic Policy	• The Consumption Function • A Tale of Three Oil Price Shocks	• The Political Business Cycle and Richard Nixon • The Demise of Monetary Targeting in Switzerland • Ben Bernanke and the Federal Reserve Adoption of Inflation Targeting • The Appointment of Paul Volcker, Anti-Inflation Hawk	

Editor in Chief: Donna Battista
Executive Acquisitions Editor: Adrienne D'Ambrosio
Acquisitions Editor: Christina Masturzo
Program Manager: Carolyn Philips
Editorial Assistant: Patrick Henning
Executive Marketing Manager: Lori DeShazo
Managing Editor: Jeff Holcomb
Project Manager: Alison Eusden
Operations Specialist: Carol Melville
Senior Art Director: Jonathan Boylan
Cover Art: Pal Teravagimov/Shutterstock
MyEconLab Content Project Manager: Noel Lotz
Executive Media Producer: Melissa Honig
Associate Project Manager, Rights and Permissions: Samantha Graham
Full-Service Project Management and Composition: Cenveo® Publisher Services
Printer/Binder: R.R. Donnelley/Harrisonburg
Cover Printer: R.R. Donnelley
Text Font: Palatino LT Std

Credits and acknowledgments borrowed from other sources and reproduced, with permission, in this textbook appear on the appropriate page within text.

FRED® is a registered trademark and the FRED® logo and ST. LOUIS FED are trademarks of the Federal Reserve Bank of St. Louis, http://research.stlouisfed.org/fred2/

Microsoft® and Windows® are registered trademarks of the Microsoft Corporation in the U.S.A. and other countries. Screen shots and icons reprinted with permission from the Microsoft Corporation. This book is not sponsored or endorsed by or affiliated with the Microsoft Corporation.

Many of the designations by manufacturers and sellers to distinguish their products are claimed as trademarks. Where those designations appear in this book, and the publisher was aware of a trademark claim, the designations have been printed in initial caps or all caps.

Cataloging-in-Publication Data is on file at the Library of Congress

10 9 8 7 6 5 4 3

ISBN 10: 0-13-342431-6
ISBN 13: 978-0-13-342431-7

To My Mom

Brief Contents

Contents

Chapter 4 Web Appendix
SAVING AND INVESTMENT IN LARGE OPEN ECONOMIES
GO TO THE COMPANION WEBSITE, www.pearsonhighered.com/mishkin

Chapter 5

Chapter 10

Chapter 10 Appendix

Chapter 12 Web Appendix A
THE TAYLOR PRINCIPLE AND INFLATION STABILITY
GO TO THE COMPANION WEBSITE, **www.pearsonhighered.com/mishkin**

Chapter 12 Web Appendix B
THE EFFECTS OF MACROECONOMIC SHOCKS ON ASSET PRICES
GO TO THE COMPANION WEBSITE, **www.pearsonhighered.com/mishkin**

Chapter 12 Web Appendix C
THE ALGEBRA OF THE AGGREGATE DEMAND AND SUPPLY MODEL
GO TO THE COMPANION WEBSITE, **www.pearsonhighered.com/mishkin**

Chapter 13
**MACROECONOMIC POLICY AND AGGREGATE
DEMAND AND SUPPLY ANALYSIS**

Chapter 16 Web Appendix
OTHER MEASURES OF THE GOVERNMENT BUDGET DEFICIT
GO TO THE COMPANION WEBSITE, www.pearsonhighered.com/mishkin

Chapter 17
EXCHANGE RATES AND INTERNATIONAL ECONOMIC POLICY

Chapter 18 Web Appendix
INCOME AND SUBSTITUTION EFFECTS: A GRAPHICAL ANALYSIS
GO TO THE COMPANION WEBSITE, www.pearsonhighered.com/mishkin

Chapter 19

Chapter 19 Web Appendix
A MODEL OF HOUSING PRICES AND RESIDENTIAL INVESTMENT
GO TO THE COMPANION WEBSITE, www.pearsonhighered.com/mishkin

Chapter 20
THE LABOR MARKET, EMPLOYMENT, AND
UNEMPLOYMENT. 544

Chapter 22
MODERN BUSINESS CYCLE THEORY

Chapter 22 Web Appendix
THE NEW CLASSICAL MODEL

GO TO THE COMPANION WEBSITE, **www.pearsonhighered.com/mishkin**

Epilogue
POLICY AND PRACTICE: WHERE DO MACROECONOMISTS AGREE AND DISAGREE?

Web Chapter

FINANCIAL CRISES IN EMERGING MARKET ECONOMIES

GO TO THE COMPANION WEBSITE, **www.pearsonhighered.com/mishkin**

PREVIEW

DYNAMICS OF FINANCIAL CRISES IN EMERGING
MARKET ECONOMIES

Stage One: Initiation of Financial Crisis

Stage Two: Currency Crisis

Stage Three: Full-Fledged Financial Crisis

APPLICATION: Crisis in South Korea, 1997–1998

Financial Liberalization/Globalization Mismanagement

Perversion of the Financial Liberalization/Globalization Process: Chaebols and the South Korean Crisis

Stock Market Decline and Failure of Firms Increase Uncertainty

Aggregate Selection and Moral Hazard Problems Worsen, and Aggregate Demand Falls

Currency Crisis Ensues

Final Stage: Currency Crisis Triggers Full-Fledged Financial Crisis

Recovery Commences

APPLICATION: The Argentine Financial Crisis, 2001–2002

Severe Fiscal Imbalances

Adverse Selection and Moral Hazard Problems Worsen

Bank Panic Begins

Currency Crisis Ensues

Currency Crisis Triggers Full-Fledged Financial Crisis

Recovery Begins

When an Advanced Economy Is Like an Emerging Market Economy:
The Icelandic Financial Crisis of 2008

POLICY AND PRACTICE: Preventing Emerging Market Financial Crises

Beef Up Prudential Regulation and Supervision of Banks

Encourage Disclosure and Market-Based Discipline

Limit Currency Mismatch

Sequence Financial Liberalization

SUMMARY

KEY TERMS

REVIEW QUESTIONS AND PROBLEMS

Preface

There has never been a more exciting time to teach macroeconomics. The recent world-wide financial crisis cast a spotlight on macroeconomics and prompted instructors worldwide to rethink their teaching of the course. Students today enter the intermediate macroeconomics course knowing the relevance of the business cycle—it impacts what is happening in their world *right now*, in the aftermath of the most severe recession since World War II. The silver lining of these trying economic times lies in our ability to draw on this familiarity and the rich tapestry of recent economic events to enliven macroeconomic theory.

Macroeconomics: Policy and Practice, Second Edition, focuses on the policy issues currently debated by the media and the public at large. Building on my expertise in macroeconomic policy making at the Federal Reserve, I highlight the techniques used by policy makers in practice. I ground this applied approach to intermediate macroeconomics with a careful, step-by-step development of all models.

What's New in the Second Edition

In addition to the expected updating of data through 2013 whenever possible, major new material has been added in every part of the text.

Enhanced Pearson e-text with Mini-Lectures: A New Way of Learning MyEconLab

The Enhanced Pearson e-text in MyEconLab for the second edition is available online from MyEconLab textbook resources. Instructors and students can highlight the text, bookmark, search the glossary, and take notes. More importantly, the e-text provides a new way of learning that is particularly useful to today's students. Not only are students able to read the material in the textbook but, by a simple click on an icon, they are able to watch over 100 mini-lectures presented by the author—one for every analytic graph in the text. These mini-lectures build each graph step-by-step and explain the intuition necessary to fully understand the theory behind the graph. The mini-lectures are an invaluable study tool for students who typically learn better when they see and hear economic analysis rather than read it.

Real-Time Data

A high percentage of the in-text data is labeled *MyEconLab Real-Time Data*. This label indicates that students can view the latest data using the e-text to access the Federal Reserve Bank of St. Louis's FRED database. In addition, each chapter now has a whole new class of problems that make use of real-time data analysis. These problems, marked with ⬤, ask students to download data from the Federal Reserve Bank of St. Louis's FRED website and then use that data to answer questions about current issues in macroeconomics.

In MyEconLab, these easy-to-assign and automatically-graded Real-Time Data Analysis exercises are linked directly to the FRED site, so that every time FRED posts new data, students can see it. As a result, Real-Time Data Analysis exercises offer a no-fuss solution for instructors who want to make the most recent data a central part of their macroeconomics course. These exercises will help students understand macroeconomics better and enable them to see the real-world relevance of their study of macroeconomics.

Nonconventional Monetary Policy and the Zero Lower Bound

In recent years, monetary policy makers have entered a brave new world in which they have had to resort to nonconventional monetary policy because the policy interest rate, the federal funds rate in the United States, has hit a floor of zero, the so-called "zero lower bound." The policy rate cannot be driven lower than this bound, making conventional monetary policy infeasible. Nonconventional monetary policy at the zero lower bound, such as quantitative easing, is very controversial and stimulates a lot of interest among students. The second edition contains extensive discussion of this topic, with the following new material:

- A new Application, "Quantitative Easing and the Money Supply, 2007–2013" (Chapter 5)
- A new section on monetary policy at the zero lower bound, which uses the dynamic aggregate demand and aggregate supply model to explain how the zero lower bound affects the conduct of monetary policy (Chapter 13)
- A new Policy and Practice case, "Abenomics and the Shift in Japanese Monetary Policy in 2013" (Chapter 13)
- A new Policy and Practice case, "Nonconventional Monetary Policy and Quantitative Easing During the Global Financial Crisis" (Chapter 15)
- A new section on fiscal multipliers at the zero lower bound that explains why fiscal multipliers are likely to be larger at the zero lower bound (Chapter 16)
- A new section on nominal GDP targeting (Chapter 21)

New Material on Business Cycle Analysis

This edition has substantial new material on business cycle analysis, to make it easier for students to understand the dynamic aggregate demand and aggregate supply model. This new material includes:

- A new section on the alternative view of the business cycle, which distinguishes the long-run trend from deviations in this trend and introduces the concept of the output gap (Chapter 8)
- New material that integrates the concept of financial frictions into the dynamic aggregate demand and aggregate supply model at the outset, by naming financial frictions as an additional factor that shifts the *IS* curve (Chapter 10) and the *AD* curve (Chapter 12)
- A new section that clarifies the difference between movements along the *MP* curve and shifts in the *MP* curve, with two new Policy and Practice cases to illustrate the difference: "Movement Along the *MP* Curve: The Rise in the Federal Funds Rate Target, 2004–2006" and "Shifts in the *MP* Curve:

Autonomous Monetary Easing at the Onset of the 2007–2009 Financial Crisis" (Chapter 10)
- A new box, "What Does *Autonomous* Mean?" (Chapter 12)
- A new box, "The Relationship of the Phillips Curve and the Short-Run Aggregate Supply Curve" (Chapter 11)
- A new box, "The Difference Between the Taylor Rule and the Taylor Principle" (Chapter 13)

The Euro Crisis

The Euro crisis has been a continuing drama since 2010, and so this edition includes the following new material.

- A new section on sovereign debt crises that explains the dynamics of these crises (Chapter 16)
- A new Policy and Practice case, "The European Sovereign Debt Crisis" (Chapter 16)
- A new Policy and Practice case, "The Debate Over Fiscal Austerity in Europe" (Chapter 16)
- A new Policy and Practice case, "Will the Euro Survive?" (Chapter 17)

Economic Growth

To better motivate the discussion of the Solow model, Chapter 6 now begins with an introductory section that examines economic growth around the world. Also, Chapter 6 has been reorganized so that growth accounting is discussed at the end of the chapter, in order to better motivate Chapter 7 on the drivers of economic growth. New figures have been added to Chapter 6 to show how output per worker changes over time when there is a change in the saving rate, population growth, or technology.

Links Between the Microeconomic Foundations of Macroeconomics and the Dynamic Aggregate Demand/Aggregate Supply Model

To illustrate the links between the microeconomic material in Part 7 of the text and the dynamic aggregate demand/aggregate supply model, I have added the following new material:

- A new Application, "Consumer Confidence and the Business Cycle" (Chapter 18)
- A new Application, "Stock Market Crashes and Recessions" (Chapter 19)
- A new section on the role of the natural rate of unemployment in the *AD/AS* model (Chapter 20)

Hallmarks

The five distinguishing characteristics of *Macroeconomics: Policy and Practice*, Second Edition, are: (1) its emphasis on policy and practice, (2) its dynamic approach to macroeconomics, (3) its focus on the interaction between finance and macroeconomics, (4) its focus on economic growth, and (5) its international perspective.

Policy And Practice

This book emphasizes policy and practice in macroeconomics by providing theoretical frameworks that are geared to discussing the most exciting, current, major policy debates in the macroeconomics field. The best way to teach macroeconomics is by continually exposing the student to cases and applications so that he or she *really* understands the underlying theory.

Over 30 in-chapter Applications show students how to apply economic theory to real-world examples. These Applications include discussions of the Great Inflation from 1965 to 1982, the 2007–2009 financial crisis, the impact of oil prices on real wages and the stock market, why income inequality has been growing over time, and why some countries are rich and others are poor. In addition, over 30 Policy and Practice cases explore specific examples of actual policies and how they were executed. These cases include such topics as how the Federal Reserve uses the Taylor rule, the use of nonconventional monetary policy during the 2007–2009 financial crisis, the political business cycle and Richard Nixon, the question of whether the Euro will survive, and China's one-child policy. These Applications and Policy and Practice cases provide critically important perspectives on current events, domestic and global issues, and historical episodes.

A Dynamic Approach To Macroeconomics

Analyzing today's hot-button policy issues requires approaching macroeconomic theory using the models that researchers and policy makers employ. The central modeling element in *Macroeconomics: Policy and Practice*, Second Edition, is a powerful, dynamic aggregate demand and supply (*AD/AS*) model that highlights the interaction of inflation and economic activity. In this model, inflation (as opposed to the price level) is plotted on the vertical axis.

Given the vital importance of this model, I build it step-by-step across Chapters 9–13:

- Chapter 9 develops the first building block of the aggregate demand and supply model, the *IS* curve.
- Chapter 10 describes how monetary policy makers set real interest rates with the *monetary policy (MP) curve*, which describes the relationship between inflation and real interest rates. The chapter then uses the *MP* curve and the *IS* curve to derive the aggregate demand curve.
- Chapter 11 uses the Phillips curve to derive the aggregate supply curve.
- Chapter 12 assembles the building blocks from preceding chapters to develop the aggregate demand and supply model, and then puts this model to immediate use with Applications that analyze business cycle fluctuations in the United States and abroad.
- Chapter 13 shifts perspective by showing how the aggregate demand and supply model can help us understand the issues policy makers confront when they attempt to stabilize inflation and output fluctuations.

The aggregate demand and supply model, with inflation on the vertical axis, therefore serves as the sole engine for the analysis of short-run fluctuations. Students benefit from this exclusive focus and the careful development of a single model: Reliance on the dynamic *AD/AS* model continually reinforces their understanding of the model and provides a unified framework for all analysis.

WHY THE DYNAMIC *AD/AS* FRAMEWORK? The dynamic *AD/AS* model includes many of the essential elements of the *ISLM* model. It develops the *IS* curve (Chapter 9) and illustrates the determination of interest rates in the money market through the interaction of money demand and supply (Chapter 10). However, the dynamic *AD/AS* model has several very important advantages over *ISLM* and traditional aggregate demand/aggregate supply frameworks:

- The dynamic *AD/AS* framework focuses on the interaction between *inflation* and output, which is exactly what the media and policy makers focus on. In contrast, traditional aggregate demand/aggregate supply analysis focuses on the interaction between the *price level* and output.
- The dynamic *AD/AS* framework characterizes monetary policy easing or tightening as a change in the *interest rate*, which is exactly the way central banks conduct monetary policy. In contrast, the *ISLM* and traditional aggregate demand/aggregate supply model frameworks characterize monetary policy as a change in the *money supply*. No central bank in the world today conducts monetary policy in this way.
- The dynamic *AD/AS* framework is consistent with modern macroeconomic analysis as it is treated in the academic literature.
- The dynamic *AD/AS* framework allows for a simple analysis of current monetary policy issues, such as nonconventional monetary policy and the zero-lower-bound problem. In addition, it allows for a modern treatment of such topical policy issues as the recent shift in monetary policy in Japan, referred to as Abenomics, and why fiscal multipliers have become larger in recent years.
- Finally, although the *AD/AS* framework is a change from the way macroeconomics has been taught in the past, it actually makes it easier for students to learn because they have to master only one model rather than three, as was the case with more traditional approaches that include separate developments of the *ISLM* model, traditional aggregate demand/aggregate supply, and the Phillips curve.

The Interaction of Finance and Macroeconomics

The financial crisis that hit the world economy from 2007 to 2009 made abundantly clear the interaction between finance and macroeconomics. Two full chapters on finance and macroeconomics provide a coherent approach to key topics such as financial system dynamics and asymmetric information, and demonstrate their relevance in macroeconomic analysis. Chapter 14, "The Financial System and Economic Growth," shows how a well-functioning financial system promotes economic growth. This chapter develops the tools that are then used in Chapter 15, "Financial Crises and the Economy," to examine how disruptions to the financial system affect aggregate demand and the economy, with a particular emphasis on the root causes of, effects of, and policy responses to the financial crisis of 2007–2009. An additional Web chapter, "Financial Crises in Emerging Market Economies," expands the analysis of economic fluctuations to economies that have recently opened up their markets to the outside world.

Focus On Economic Growth

The explosion of research on economic growth in recent years is an exciting development in the macroeconomics field, with direct relevance to the question of why some countries suffer slow economic growth and remain poor, while others enjoy rapid economic growth and prosper. I discuss the Solow model in detail in Chapter 6, and present endogenous growth theory and the importance of institutions to economic growth in Chapter 7. As mentioned previously, Chapter 14 includes additional material on economic growth.

An International Perspective

Topical coverage and applications integrate an international dimension throughout *Macroeconomics: Policy and Practice*, Second Edition. For example, Chapter 4's analysis of the interaction of saving and investment discusses open and closed economies together, rather than in separate chapters. International trade and the impact of net exports on aggregate demand are discussed immediately as part of the *AD/AS* model in Part 4, as opposed to in a separate chapter, and the textbook applies the aggregate demand and supply model to analyze the impact of the 2007–2009 financial crisis in the United Kingdom, Ireland, and China. The Web chapter on emerging market economies provides further international perspective.

A Flexible Structure

Macroeconomics: Policy and Practice, Second Edition, offers a highly flexible structure with many different paths that instructors can take to tailor the book to their course needs. Most instructors will begin by assigning Chapters 1–4. For a long-run emphasis, instructors can then assign Chapters 5–7. Instructors wishing to cover the short run first can instead proceed directly to Part 4.

The core chapters that most instructors will teach in their courses, Chapters 1–13, make up the first four parts of the book. Instructors can assign subsequent chapters as they choose or skip them entirely, allowing them to focus on the particular areas of macroeconomics that match their course goals. Suggested outlines for semester-long courses with varying emphases follow. (Quarter-long courses would typically use three or four fewer of the optional chapters.)

- *Course Starting with Long-Run Analysis:* Chapters 1–13, and up to six of the remaining eleven chapters.
- *Course Starting with Micro Foundations and Long-Run Analysis:* Chapters 1–3, 18–20, 4–13, and up to three of the remaining eight chapters.
- *Course Starting with Short-Run Analysis:* Chapters 1–5, 8–13, 6–7, and up to six of the remaining eleven chapters.
- *Course Starting with Micro Foundations and Short-Run Analysis:* Chapters 1–3, 18–20, 4–5, 8–13, 6–7, and up to three of the remaining eight chapters.
- *Course Focusing on the Micro Foundations of Modern Business Cycle Analysis:* Chapters 1–3, 18–20, 4–5, 8–13, 21–22, and up to two of the remaining ten chapters.
- *Course with International Focus:* Chapters 1–13, 17, Web chapter on emerging market economies, and up to four of the remaining nine chapters.
- *Course with Finance Focus:* Chapters 1–15, and up to four of the remaining seven chapters.

Interest-Generating Features

Motivating the study of macroeconomics means bringing it to life through a wide variety of pedagogical features.

Previews at the beginning of each chapter tell students where the chapter is heading, why specific topics are important, and how they relate to other topics in the book.

Applications apply the analysis in each chapter to explain important real-world situations.

Policy and Practice cases explore specific examples of actual policies and how they were executed.

Macroeconomics in the News boxes introduce students to relevant news articles and data that are reported daily in the press, and explain how to read them.

Boxes highlight interesting material, including historical episodes and recent events.

Summary tables are useful study aids that recap key points.

Key statements are important points set in boldface italic type so that the student can easily find them for later reference.

Graphs with detailed captions demonstrate the interrelationship of the variables and are central to the illustrations of policy analysis. Innovative color-blended arrows guide students' analysis of the meanings of shifting curves.

Mini-Lectures, presented by the author for all of the analytic graphs in the text, are accessible through the e-text, which is available online from MyEconLab textbook resources. The mini-lectures provide a step-by-step discussion of the analysis.

A **Summary** at the end of each chapter lists the main points covered.

Key terms, which are important words or phrases, are boldfaced when they are defined for the first time and listed by page number at the end of each chapter.

End-of-chapter Review Questions, Problems, and Real-Time Data Analysis Problems guide students' mastery of the material, with a particular emphasis on real-world applications.

Supplemental Resources Simplify Teaching and Learning

A variety of comprehensive supplemental resources for professors and students accompany this book.

MyEconLab is the premier online assessment and tutorial system, pairing rich online content with innovative learning tools. The MyEconLab course for *Macroeconomics: Policy and Practice*, Second Edition, includes all the review questions and problems from the textbook. As a special feature, all Policy and Practice cases and Applications are also offered in MyEconLab, along with three to four assessment questions to test students' understanding of the key concepts. Look for these exercises within each chapter in a separate section called "Applications."

STUDENTS AND MYECONLAB The MyEconLab online homework and tutorial system puts students in control of their own learning through a suite of study and practice tools correlated with the online, interactive version of the textbook and other media tools. Within MyEconLab's structured environment, students practice what they learn, test their understanding, and then pursue a study plan that MyEconLab generates for them based on their performance on practice tests.

INSTRUCTORS AND MYECONLAB MyEconLab provides flexible tools that allow instructors to easily and effectively customize online course materials to suit their needs. Instructors can create and assign tests, quizzes, or homework assignments. MyEconLab saves time by automatically grading questions and tracking results in an online grade book. After registering for MyEconLab, instructors also have access to downloadable supplements.

ADDITIONAL MYECONLAB FEATURES

- **Weekly News Updates**. Each week, a relevant and current article from a newspaper or journal is posted, along with discussion questions.

For more information and to register, please visit **www.myeconlab.com**.

ADDITIONAL INSTRUCTOR RESOURCES **The Instructor's Manual**, an online supplement prepared by Martin Pereyra of the University of Missouri and the author, offers chapter overviews, outlines and objectives, and answers to the end-of-chapter questions and problems including solutions to the Data Analysis problems by Aaron Jackson of Bentley University. Additionally, the Instructor's Manual includes resources for each chapter that tie into the Applications and Policy and Practice features of the chapter, including discussion questions that professors can use in class with students, references to interesting outside materials such as newspaper and journal articles and macroeconomic data, and references to websites containing related real-world examples. The Instructor's Manual is available at **www.pearsonhighered.com/irc** in Microsoft Word and PDF formats.

The **PowerPoint Presentations**, prepared by Jim Lee of Texas A&M University–Corpus Christi, provide all figures and tables from the text, as well as brief lecture notes that follow the structure and sequence of the text. They include coverage of the main topics of the chapter, organized by A-head, the key terms and equations from the chapter, and the Applications and Policy and Practice features in the chapter.

Animated PowerPoint Presentations, created by the author, are also available at **www.pearsonhighered.com/irc**. These PowerPoint slides provide the analytical figures and are completely manipulable by the user. Instructors can custom design their PowerPoint lectures with step-by-step animations of all key text figures.

The **Test Item File**, originally prepared by Paul Kubik of DePaul University, Victor Valcarcel of Texas Tech University, and Brian Trinque of the University of Texas–Austin, and updated for the second edition by Brian Trinque, provides 75 multiple-choice questions and 10 short-answer questions for each chapter. The questions provide a mix of numerical, graphical, and conceptual approaches for all chapter topics. In addition, the questions are MyEconLab-compatible and follow the Association to Advance Collegiate Schools of Business (AACSB) tagging procedures. The Test Item File is available at **www.pearsonhighered.com/irc** electronically in Microsoft Word format and as computerized TestGen-format files that can be used with TestGen test-generating software. This test-generating program permits instructors to edit, add, or delete questions from the test bank; analyze test results; and organize a database of tests and student results, allowing for flexibility and ease of use.

ADDITIONAL STUDENT RESOURCES **The Companion Website,** located at **www.pearsonhighered.com/mishkin**, features Web appendices on a wide variety of topics, as well as a Web chapter, "Financial Crises in Emerging Market Economies."

Acknowledgments

There are many people to thank on this project. I have been blessed with three extraordinary editors on this project: Noel Seibert, my original acquisitions editor; Adrienne D'Ambrosio, my current acquisitions editor; and Rebecca Ferris-Caruso, my development editor. Many thanks as well to members of the production, editorial, and marketing teams at Pearson: Kathryn Dinovo, Alison Eusden, Carolyn Philips, David Theisen, Lori DeShazo, and Kathleen McLellan. I also want to thank Neil Mehrotra, Ozge Akinci, and Jorge Mejia Licona for very helpful research assistance, and Daniel Sorid for giving me the student's perspective while providing me with invaluable editing. I have also received insightful comments from my colleagues Marc Giannoni and Mark Gertler.

This book has been thoroughly accuracy checked through several rounds. I would like to thank the accuracy reviewer, Jim Eaton, for his extraordinary efforts and attention to detail. In addition, I have received thoughtful comments from outside reviewers, editorial board members, focus group participants, community call participants, and class testers, who are listed below.

Reviewers:

Gilad Aharonovitz, *Washington State University*
S. Nuray Akin, *University of Miami*
Lian An, *University of North Florida*
S. Boragan Aruoba, *University of Maryland*
Elizabeth Asiedu, *University of Kansas*
Nursel Aydiner-Avsar, *University of Utah*
Lance Bachmeier, *Kansas State University*
Mina Baliamoune, *University of North Florida*
David Beckworth, *Texas State University*
Cihan Bilginsoy, *University of Utah*
Nicola Borri, *Boston University*
David Bunting, *Eastern Washington University*
Michael Carew, *Baruch College of CUNY*
Joel D. Carton, *Florida International University*
Marcelle Chauvet, *University of California*
Darian Chin, *California State University–Los Angeles*
Olivier Coibion, *College of William and Mary*
Firat Demir, *University of Oklahoma*
James Devine, *Loyola Marymount University*
John Dogbey, *Ohio University*
Fred Donatelli, *Binghamton University*
Abdunasser Duella, *California State University–Fullerton*
Quentin Duroy, *Denison University*

Amitava Krishna Dutt, *University of Notre Dame*
Jim Eaton, *Bridgewater College*
Ryan Edwards, *Queens College*
Sharon Erenburg, *Eastern Michigan University*
Alexander Field, *Santa Clara University*
Todd Fitch, *University of California–Berkeley*
Hamilton Fout, *Kansas State University*
Jean Gauger, *The University of Tennessee*
Ronald D. Gilbert, *Texas Tech University*
George Heitmann, *Muhlenberg College*
Kolver Hernandez, *University of Delaware*
Adam Honig, *Amherst College*
Yu Hsing, *Southeastern Louisiana University*
Ralph D. Husby, *University of Illinois at Urbana–Champaign*
Kim Huynh, *Indiana University–Bloomington*
Murat Iyigun, *University of Colorado–Boulder*
Aaron L. Jackson, *Bentley University*
Vivekanand Jayakumar, *University of Tampa*
Barry Jones, *Binghamton University*
Bryce Kanago, *University of Northern Iowa*
Cem Karayalcin, *Florida International University–University Park*
Arthur Kartman, *San Diego State University*
John Keating, *University of Kansas*
Todd Keister, *Rutgers University*
Elizabeth Sawyer Kelly, *University of Wisconsin–Madison*

Focus Group Participants:

Francis Ahking, *University of Connecticut*
Serife Nuray Akin, *University of Miami*
Lian An, *University of North Florida*
James Arias, *Georgia College and State University*
Nursel Aydiner-Avsar, *University of Utah*
Michael D. Bauer, Economist, *Federal Reserve Bank of San Francisco*
David Beckworth, *Texas State University*
Emma Bojinova, *Canisius College*
Mark Brady, *San Jose State University*
Michael Buckley, *Fordham University*
Susanne Buesselmann, *Wayne State University*
Bolong Cao, *Ohio University*
Piyaphan Changwatchai, *University of Utah*
Adhip Chaudhuri, *Georgetown University*
May Collins, *Mira Costa College*
William Craighead, *Wesleyan University*
Chetan Dave, *New York University–Abu Dhabi*
Stephen Davis, *Southwest Minnesota State*
Dennis Debrecht, *Carroll University*
Justin Dubas, *Texas Lutheran University*
Dennis Edwards, *Coastal Carolina University*
Noha Emara, *Barnard College, Columbia University*
Merton Finkler, *Lawrence University*
Layton Franko, *Queens College*
Lise Frulio, *Northwest Arkansas Community College*
Tim Fuerst, *Bowling Green State University*
Sarah Ghosh, *University of Scranton*
Satyajit Ghosh, *University of Scranton*
Chris Gingrich, *Eastern Mennonite University*
Vance Ginn, *Texas Tech University*
Roy Gobin, *Loyola University*
Nick Gomersall, *Luther College*
Michael J. Gootzeit, *University of Memphis*
Steven Greenlaw, *University of Mary Washington*
Alan Gummerson, *Florida International University*
Marwa Hassan, *Rutgers University*
Scott Hegerty, *Canisius College*
Kolver Hernandez, *University of Delaware*
Kim Huynh, *University of Indiana*
Miren Ivankovic, *Anderson University*
Brian Jacobsen, *Wisconsin Lutheran College*

Louis Johnston, *College of Saint Benedict Saint John's University*
Jason Jones, *Furman University*
Lillian Kamal, *University of Hartford*
Bryce Kanago, *University of Northern Iowa*
Leonie Karkoviata, *University of Houston*
Ben Kim, *University of Nebraska–Lincoln*
Ruby Kishan, *Texas State University–San Marcos*
Todd Knoop, *Cornell College*
Gregory Krohn, *Bucknell University*
Krishna Kumar, *Duke University*
Kenneth Kuttner, *Williams College*
Susan Laury, *Georgia State University*
Jim Lee, *Texas A&M–Corpus Christi*
Jialu Liu, *Indiana University–Bloomington*
Gregory Lubiani, *Southwest Tennessee Community College*
Guangyi Ma, *Texas A&M University*
Karen Maguire, *University of Colorado–Boulder*
John McArthur, *Wofford College*
Shahriar Mostashari, *Campbell University*
Kanda Naknoi, *Purdue University*
Esen Onur, *California State University–Sacramento*
Biru Paksha Paul, *State University of New York at Cortland*
Nate Peach, *Colorado State University*
William Perkins, *Manhattanville College*
Reza Ramazani, *Saint Michael's College*
John Rasmus, *Diablo Valley Community College*
Luisa Blanco Raynal, *Pepperdine University*
Malcolm Robinson, *Thomas More College*
Jack Russ, *San Diego State University*
Subarna Samanta, *College of New Jersey*
Mike Sandberg, *University of Florida*
Amy Schmidt, *Saint Anselm College*
Andrei Shevchenko, *Michigan State University*
Fahlino Sjuib, *Framingham State College*
Rachael Small, *University of Colorado–Boulder*
Bill Smith, *University of Memphis*
Issoufou Soumaila, *Texas Tech University*
Mark Steckbeck, *Campbell University*
Herman Steckler, *George Washington University*
Paul Stock, *University of Mary Hardin–Baylor*

Ellis Tallman, *Oberlin College*

Wendine Thompson-Dawson, *Monmouth College*

Jay Tontz, *Diablo Valley College*

Raúl Velázquez, *Manhattan College*

Bhavneet Walia, *Nicholls State University*

Anne Wenzel, *San Francisco State University*

Grace Yan, *Oklahoma State University–Tulsa*

Chenygu Yang, *University of Central Florida*

Mark A. Yanochik, *Georgia Southern University*

Janice Yee, *Worcester State College*

Elizabeth Anne York, *Meredith College*

Class Testers:

Michael Buckley, *Fordham University*

Michael Carew, *Baruch College of CUNY*

Jim Eaton, *Bridgewater College*

Jean Gauger, *The University of Tennessee*

Aaron L. Jackson, *Bentley University*

Jason Jones, *Furman University*

Susan Laury, *Georgia State University*

John McArthur, *Wofford College*

Shahriar Mostashari, *Campbell University*

Kanda Naknoi, *Purdue University*

Ellis Tallman, *Oberlin College*

Victor Valcarcel, *Texas Tech University*

Finally, I want to thank my extended family, who enable me to be so productive because they give me so much joy: my wife, Sally; my two children, Matthew and Laura; Matthew's wife Kim; my goddaughters, Alba, Glenda, and Norma; their husbands, Isaac, Andy, and Sergio; and their six children, Robbie, Sophie, Adrian, Sam, Sarah, and Olivia.

I dedicate this book to my mother, who was still sharp as a tack and a lot of fun when she passed away in 2012 at age ninety-one.

Frederic S. Mishkin

About the Author

Frederic S. Mishkin is the Alfred Lerner Professor of Banking and Financial Institutions at the Graduate School of Business, Columbia University. He is also a research associate at the National Bureau of Economic Research and past president of the Eastern Economics Association. Since receiving his Ph.D. from the Massachusetts Institute of Technology in 1976, he has taught at the University of Chicago, Northwestern University, Princeton University, and Columbia. He has also received an honorary professorship from the People's (Renmin) University of China. From 1994 to 1997, he was executive vice president and director of research at the Federal Reserve Bank of New York and an associate economist of the Federal Open Market Committee of the Federal Reserve System. From September 2006 to August 2008, he was a member (governor) of the Board of Governors of the Federal Reserve System.

Professor Mishkin's research focuses on monetary policy and its impact on financial markets and the aggregate economy. He is the author of more than twenty books, including *The Economics of Money, Banking, and Financial Markets*, Tenth Edition (Pearson, 2013); *Financial Markets and Institutions*, Eighth Edition (Pearson, 2015); *Monetary Policy Strategy* (MIT Press, 2007); *The Next Great Globalization: How Disadvantaged Nations Can Harness Their Financial Systems to Get Rich* (Princeton University Press, 2006); *Inflation Targeting: Lessons from the International Experience* (Princeton University Press, 1999); *Money, Interest Rates, and Inflation* (Edward Elgar, 1993); and *A Rational Expectations Approach to Macroeconometrics: Testing Policy Ineffectiveness and Efficient Markets Models* (University of Chicago Press, 1983). In addition, he has published more than 200 articles in such journals as *American Economic Review*, *Journal of Political Economy*, *Econometrica, Quarterly Journal of Economics, Journal of Finance, Journal of Money, Credit and Banking,* and *Journal of Monetary Economics.*

Professor Mishkin has served on the editorial board of *American Economic Review* and has been an associate editor at *Journal of Business and Economic Statistics, Journal of Applied Econometrics, Journal of Economic Perspectives,* and *Journal of Money, Credit and Banking*; he also served as the editor of the Federal Reserve Bank of New York's *Economic Policy Review*. He is currently an associate editor (member of the editorial board) at five academic journals, including *International Finance; Finance India; Review of Development Finance; Borsa International Review;* and *Emerging Markets, Finance and Trade*. He has been a consultant to the Board of Governors of the Federal Reserve System, the World Bank, and the International Monetary Fund, as well as to many central banks throughout the world. He was also a member of the International Advisory Board to the Financial Supervisory Service of South Korea and an advisor to the Institute for Monetary and Economic Research at the Bank of Korea. Professor Mishkin was a Senior Fellow at the Federal Deposit Insurance Corporation's Center for Banking Research and was an academic consultant to and serves on the Economic Advisory Panel of the Federal Reserve Bank of New York.

Part 1

Introduction

Part 1 Introduction

We begin with an introduction to the study of macroeconomics. Chapter 1 describes the questions that macroeconomists seek to answer and the data they seek to explain, raising key policy questions that will be the focus of the remaining chapters of this book: How can poor countries get rich? Is saving too low? Do government budget deficits matter? How costly is it to reduce inflation? How can we make financial crises less likely? How active should stabilization policy be? Should macroeconomic policy follow rules? Are global trade imbalances a danger? Chapter 2 examines how economists define and measure the most important macroeconomic data.

In keeping with our focus on key policy issues and the techniques policymakers use in practice, we will analyze the following specific examples in Policy and Practice cases:

- "Can GDP Buy Happiness?"
- "Policy and Overstatements of the Cost of Living"

The Policy and Practice of Macroeconomics

1

Preview

What are your career plans after graduation? Many factors beyond your grades and choice of a major affect the ultimate path you take. When you graduate from college, will jobs be plentiful or will a high unemployment rate (as occurred in the aftermath of the 2007–2009 recession) make it a challenge to find work? Will overall prices be rising rapidly, so you will need more money to pay for your expenses next year? Will the value of the U.S. dollar decline so that it will be more expensive to travel abroad? Should you worry about the current high government budget deficits? Jumping ahead, will the economy grow rapidly over the next thirty years, so your children will be better off than you? We will address the economics underlying the answers to these questions throughout this book.

In this chapter, we set the stage for your exploration of the policy and practice of macroeconomics. We start the chapter by examining what macroeconomists do and what data they seek to explain. We then preview the policy issues that we explore throughout this book.

The Practice of Macroeconomics

In formal terms, **macroeconomics** is the study of economic activity and prices in the overall economy of a nation or a region. Macroeconomic research draws heavily on **microeconomics,** which looks at the behavior of individual firms, households, or markets.[1]

The Process: Developing Macroeconomic Models

Macroeconomists try to explain how the overall economy works by using an **economic theory,** a logical framework to explain a particular economic phenomenon. Economic theory involves developing an **economic model,** a simplified representation of the

---

[1]We will explore the microeconomic foundations of macroeconomics in Chapters 18 to 20 of this book.

economic phenomenon that takes a mathematical or graphical form. The development of an economic theory or model typically involves five steps:

1. Identify an interesting economic question. For example, a macroeconomist might want to understand why the unemployment rate rises or falls over time, or why workers' wages in real terms (in terms of the goods and services they can actually buy) rise more rapidly during certain periods, but not others.

2. Specify the variables to be explained by the model, as well as the variables that explain them. A variable that a macroeconomist wants to explain is referred to as an **endogenous variable,** because it is explained *inside* the model he or she is building (and thus has the *endo* prefix). She would then identify a set of factors, called **exogenous variables,** that are used to explain the endogenous variable, but are taken as given and thus are viewed as determined *outside* the model. (This is why they have the *exo* prefix.)

   For example, in explaining the endogenous variable (the unemployment rate), the macroeconomist might specify consumer optimism or government spending as exogenous variables that are taken as given. Or if he or she were interested in explaining real wage growth, the endogenous variable, the macroeconomist might choose the rate of technological progress or the power of unions as the exogenous variables. The schematic diagram in Figure 1.1 illustrates the relationship between endogenous and exogenous variables in an economic model.

3. Posit a set of equations or graphical analysis to connect movements in the exogenous variables to the endogenous variables. For example, we might create a formula showing how, all else being equal, a 10% increase in government spending would change the unemployment rate. This formula is our model.

4. Compare the conclusions of the model with what actually happens. For example, if the model is designed to explain the unemployment rate, we

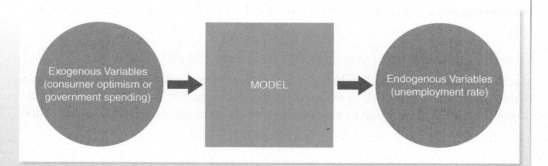

FIGURE 1.1

Variables in Macroeconomic Models

The model is a set of equations or a graphical analysis that explains movements in the endogenous variables—variables that are explained by the model—as a result of changes in the exogenous variables—given factors not determined by the model.

Exogenous Variables (consumer optimism or government spending)

MODEL

Endogenous Variables (unemployment rate)

would compare the model's predictions to actual unemployment data in prior years. If the conclusions do not match this historical data, return to step 2 and change the model.

5. If the data are well explained, use the model to make further predictions, say on where the unemployment rate will head a year from now, and suggest policies to lower it.

The iterative process of comparing a model to actual data, making improvements along the way, raises new economic questions and advances knowledge in macroeconomics. We will look at the interaction of data and macroeconomic models as we proceed through this book, highlighting how the field of macroeconomics has evolved over time. We will also see how well macroeconomic models explain the data by looking at numerous applications featuring the U.S. and world economies throughout every chapter.

The Purpose: Interpreting Macroeconomic Data

Macroeconomists, and in turn macroeconomic models, focus in particular on three economic data series: *real GDP*, the *unemployment rate*, and the *inflation rate*. We look at each in turn.

REAL GDP. **Real Gross Domestic Product (GDP)** measures the output of actual goods and services produced in an economy over a fixed period, usually a year. As we will see in Chapter 2, real GDP also equals the total amount of real income of every person and firm in the economy.

Figure 1.2 shows real GDP per person in the U.S. economy from 1900–2013 and has two important attributes. (To account for changes in the purchasing power of a dollar, we treat all goods and services as if they were sold at prices from the year 2011.) First,

MyEconLab Real-time data

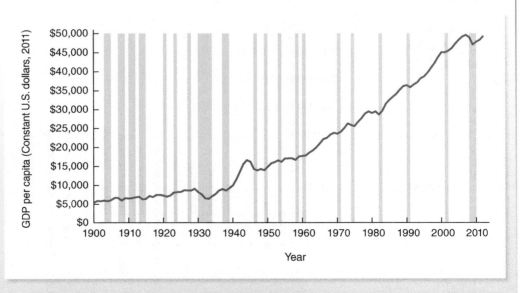

FIGURE 1.2

U.S. Real GDP Per Capita, 1900–2013

Due to business cycle fluctuations, real GDP per person has grown substantially but not smoothly, over time. We represent recessions with the shaded areas. Depressions are severe declines in real GDP, the most notable being the Great Depression (1929–1933).

Sources: Federal Reserve Bank of St. Louis, FRED Database. http://research.stlouisfed.org/fred2/; and for data before 1960, Maddison, Angus. *Historical statistics*. http://www.ggdc.net/maddison/

notice in Figure 1.2 that real GDP per person has grown substantially over time. In 1900, the average U.S. person earned nearly $5,000. Today, this number has risen by more than a factor of nine, to nearly $50,000. U.S. citizens today have far more income than their great grandparents did, and have been getting richer and richer over time. What explains this rise in income? Economic growth, the subject of Chapters 6, 7, and 14 of this book, is one of the most important topics in macroeconomics.

Second, notice in Figure 1.2 that real GDP grows unevenly over time and fluctuates around a trend. Fluctuations in real GDP are called a **business cycle,** which represents recurrent up and down movements in economic activity that differ in how regular they are. When economic activity declines and real GDP per person falls, there is a **recession.** In Figure 1.2, recession periods are marked by the shaded areas—and are frequent phenomena. When the decline in real GDP is severe, a recession is classified as a **depression.** The most notable of these is the Great Depression that lasted from 1929 until 1933. What causes recessions and particularly depressions is another of the most-studied questions in macroeconomics. We study short-run fluctuations in economic activity in Chapters 8–13.

So far we have only looked at real GDP per person in the United States. Figure 1.3 compares real GDP per person in a number of countries. As you can see, there are huge differences from country to country. Rwanda has a real GDP per person of just over $600, which is less than one-eighteeth of U.S. real GDP. Macroeconomists study factors that affect real GDP over time. South Korea, for example, in 1960 had a real GDP per person of $1,500 that was actually lower than that of Bolivia. Today, Bolivia remains poor, while South Korea has moved into the rich countries' club, with its ranking of per person real GDP in the top quarter of all nations. South Korea turned around its prospects through very high economic growth rates. We focus on why some countries are so rich and others so poor, and how countries can improve their prospects, in Chapters 6, 7, and 14.

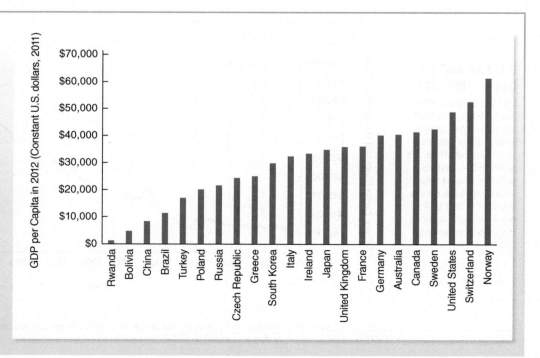

FIGURE 1.3

Cross-Country Comparison of Real GDP per Capita in 2012

Real GDP per person varies widely across countries. Rwanda has a real GDP per person of just over $600, which is less than one-eighteeth of U.S. real GDP, which is nearly $50,000.

Source: World Bank. *World development indicators.* http://data .worldbank.org/indicator/

UNEMPLOYMENT RATE. The **unemployment rate** measures the percentage of workers looking for work, but who do not have jobs, at a particular point in time. When unemployment is high, households suffer a loss of income and may even find themselves unable to meet basic needs for food and shelter.

Figure 1.4 shows the U.S. unemployment rate from 1929–2013. Notice that the unemployment rate always remains well above zero, indicating that even during good times, there is always some unemployment. In addition, in Figure 1.4 the unemployment rate fluctuates substantially and rises sharply in the shaded areas denoting recessions. In 1933, during the Great Depression, the unemployment rate climbed to 25%. The most recent recession from 2007–2009, which has been dubbed the "Great Recession," although not nearly as severe as the Great Depression, still resulted in the largest rise in unemployment in the post–World War II period, with the unemployment rate rising by six percentage points, peaking at over 10%. What happens in labor markets to drive up unemployment during contractions in economic activity? We will seek answers to this question in Chapters 9–12 and 20.

Figure 1.5 compares the average unemployment rates over the past decade for different countries. Greece's over 12% unemployment rate is more than four times that of Switzerland, indicating the wide variation across countries. We will study the characteristics of labor markets that lead to high average unemployment rates in some countries but not others in Chapter 20.

INFLATION. **Inflation** or the **inflation rate** tells us how rapidly the overall level of prices is rising. Notice in Figure 1.6 that up until World War II, the inflation rate was on average about zero, and was often negative, a situation referred to as **deflation.** In the late 1960s, inflation rose and remained quite high for an extended period of time through the early 1980s, a period economists often refer to as the Great Inflation. We will address the causes of inflation and its historical peaks in Chapters 9–13.

MyEconLab Real-time data

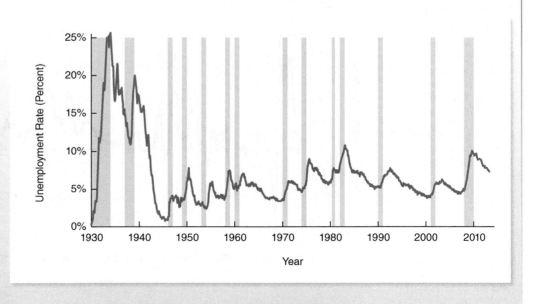

FIGURE 1.4

U.S. Unemployment Rate, 1929–2013

The unemployment rate always remains well above zero, has substantial fluctuations, and rises sharply during recessions, denoted by the shaded areas.

Sources: Federal Reserve Bank of St. Louis, FRED Database. http://research .stlouisfed.org/fred2/; and data prior to 1948, National Bureau of Economic Research. *Macro history database, income and employment.* www.nber.org/ databases/ macrohistory/ contents/chapter08.html

FIGURE 1.5

Cross-Country Comparison of Average Unemployment Rates, 2003–2013

The average unemployment rates over the past decade for a number of countries show much variation. For example, Greece's over 12% unemployment rate is four times higher than Switzerland's 3.1% unemployment rate.

Source: International Monetary Fund. http://www.imf.org/external/data.htm

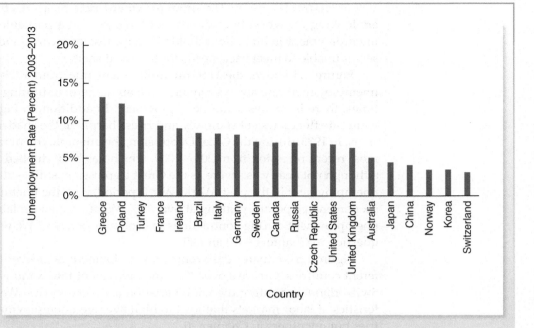

MyEconLab Real-time data

FIGURE 1.6

U.S. Inflation Rate, 1910–2013

Up until World War II, the average inflation rate was near zero. In the late 1960s, inflation rose and remained quite high for an extended period of time through the early 1980s, the period of the Great Inflation.

Source: Federal Reserve Bank of St. Louis, FRED Database. http://research.stlouisfed.org/fred2/

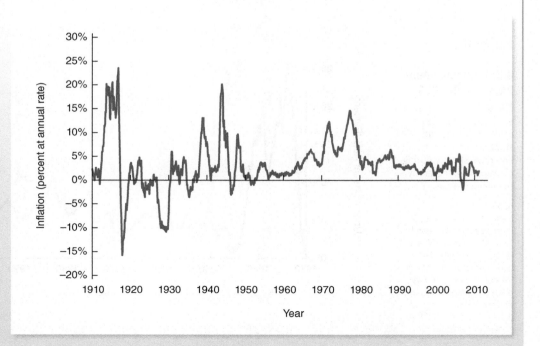

FIGURE 1.7

Cross-Country Comparison of Average Inflation Rates, 2003–2013

Countries' average inflation rates over the past decade have differed, with most countries having inflation rates averaging less than 5% at an annual rate, but some, such as Turkey and Russia, with inflation rates well above that.

Source: International Monetary Fund. http://www.imf.org/external/data.htm

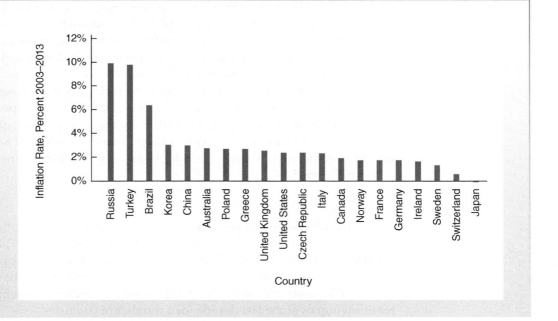

A changing price level complicates decision making for consumers, businesses, and government, and this uncertainty can hamper economic growth. Consider a shop owner who finds that he or she can raise prices and make more profit. The owner might conclude that demand for his or her goods is rising and invest in expanding the store. If the overall price level is rising and demand for his or her goods hasn't changed, the decision to expand the shop could backfire.

Figure 1.7 shows that the average inflation rates over the past decade for a number of countries have differed substantially. What makes some countries more prone to inflation than others? Some countries have experienced super high inflation rates, which we refer to as **hyperinflation.** Zimbabwe (not shown in the figure) is the most recent extreme example, with its inflation rate soaring to over two million percent at an annual rate. Why do some countries experience hyperinflation? We will pursue these questions in Chapters 5 and 16.

 # Macroeconomic Policy

The careful work necessary to develop economic models and analyze key data is not simply an academic exercise: the underlying goal is to determine what policies can produce better macroeconomic outcomes. We will look at numerous specific examples of how macroeconomic policy is practiced in the Policy and Practice cases that appear throughout the text. We now set the stage by previewing several policy issues that are of particular concern to macroeconomists.

How Can Poor Countries Get Rich?

It's a simple insight that high economic growth enables poor countries to become rich. Nonetheless, designing policies to achieve economic growth is one of the greatest challenges facing macroeconomists. If it were easy to raise growth rates in poor countries, policymakers could eliminate much of world poverty. Doing so might even help create a more stable world in which the threat of terrorism would diminish.

Numerous questions are central to growth-stimulating policies. What institutions in a country foster economic growth? Will policies to encourage the development of a more efficient financial system significantly raise economic growth rates? What role does education play in economic growth? How important are policies to encourage research and development in fostering economic growth? While there are not always clear-cut answers to these questions, we will see in Chapters 6, 7, and 14 that macroeconomics has a lot to say about policies aimed at achieving high economic growth.

Is Saving Too Low?

As Figure 1.8 shows, the percentage of income saved by U.S. citizens—known as the U.S. personal saving rate—fell sharply between 1975 and 2007, but rose during the financial crisis and 2007–2009 recession. Most countries have appreciably higher saving rates than the United States, with some countries like China having very high rates, above 50%. Figure 1.9 compares average national saving rates (which includes government saving) over the last decade for a number of countries.

We will see in Chapters 4, 6, and 16 that higher saving rates translate into higher investment, which boosts economic growth and the long-run level of real GDP. When households have very low saving, they lack a cushion to cope with severe economic downturns. During the most recent recession, many U.S. households had so little savings that they found themselves unable to pay their bills and were forced to declare bankruptcy.

We will see in Chapters 4 and 18 that households will save more if the amount they earn on their savings is high. Tax policy is one way to increase the returns to saving. For

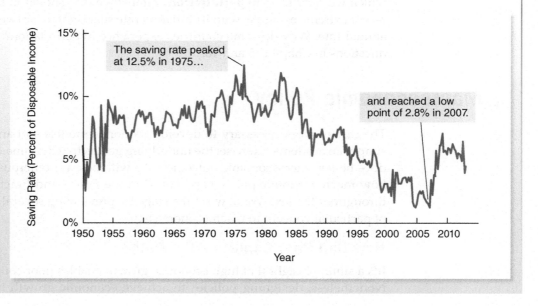

FIGURE 1.8

U.S. Personal Saving Rate, 1960–2013

The U.S. saving rate fell sharply between 1975 and 2007, but rose during the financial crisis and 2007–2009 recession

> The saving rate peaked at 12.5% in 1975…

> and reached a low point of 2.8% in 2007.

Source: Federal Reserve Bank of St. Louis, FRED Database. http://research.stlouisfed.org/fred2/

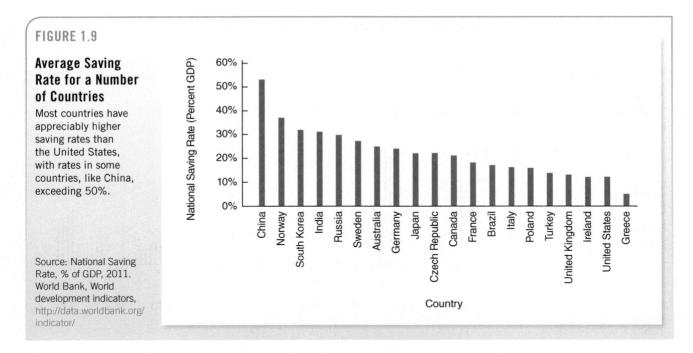

FIGURE 1.9

Average Saving Rate for a Number of Countries

Most countries have appreciably higher saving rates than the United States, with rates in some countries, like China, exceeding 50%.

Source: National Saving Rate, % of GDP, 2011. World Bank, World development indicators, http://data.worldbank.org/indicator/

example, governments can lower income taxes for households that put money into saving vehicles such as 401(k)s. Alternatively, governments can make consumption more costly through national sales taxes, or give tax breaks to businesses that contribute to employee pensions.

Do Government Budget Deficits Matter?

Government budget deficits, an excess of government spending relative to revenue, widened to over 10% of GDP after the 2007–2009 recession, their highest levels since World War II, as shown in Figure 1.10. The sea of red ink since has caused many commentators to worry about the future of America and propose drastic actions. Will budget deficits lead the government to go broke? Will they burden future generations with higher taxes to repay debt issued to fund these deficits? Will the government print money to finance its profligate spending and cause runaway inflation?

To cut the deficit, some propose tightening **fiscal policy** (policymakers' decisions to raise taxes, cut government spending, or both). Others say the budget deficit doesn't pose a danger and warn that tighter fiscal policy can do more harm than good. Are drastic actions required to get deficits under control? Massive recent U.S. government budget deficits—matched in many other countries throughout the world—have raised the stakes on the debate about government budget deficits. We will address the issue in Chapter 16.

How Costly Is It to Reduce Inflation?

By the end of the 1970s, the inflation rate in the United States and many other countries exceeded 10%, a period often referred to as the Great Inflation. Some macroeconomists proposed policies to fight the inflation; many others argued that these steps would be too painful, reducing output and triggering high unemployment rates. During the

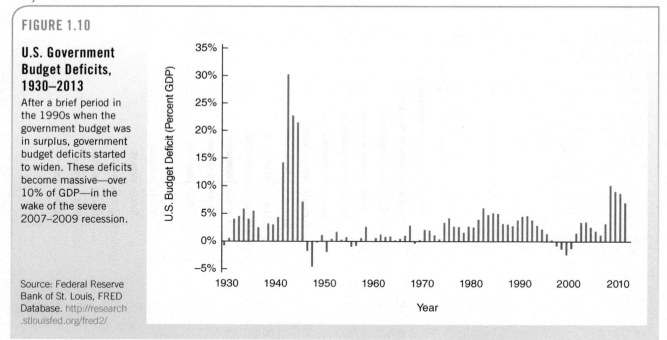

FIGURE 1.10

U.S. Government Budget Deficits, 1930–2013

After a brief period in the 1990s when the government budget was in surplus, government budget deficits started to widen. These deficits become massive—over 10% of GDP—in the wake of the severe 2007–2009 recession.

Source: Federal Reserve Bank of St. Louis, FRED Database. http://research .stlouisfed.org/fred2/

Great Recession of 2007–2009, the inflation rate fell to zero. But many were concerned that the price level could soar when the economy started to recover.

The job of keeping inflation in check is core to the mission of U.S. Federal Reserve and other **central banks,** the government agencies that oversee banking systems. Central banks also conduct **monetary policy,** the management of the amount of money in the economy and interest rates. Given the challenges of fighting inflation, central bankers spend a great deal of time investigating monetary policy frameworks to control the price level. We will examine the issue of how costly it is to keep inflation low and how to conduct monetary policy to contain inflation in Chapters 13 and 22 of this book.

How Can We Make Financial Crises Less Likely?

Starting in 2007, the United States and many other countries throughout the world experienced a major **financial crisis,** a large-scale disruption in financial markets characterized by sharp declines in the prices of **assets** (property that includes bonds, stocks, art, land, etc.) and business failures. Financial crises are always accompanied by sharp economic downturns, as we saw in the Great Recession of 2007–2009. We discuss the roots of financial crises and actions to make them less likely in Chapter 15.

How Active Should Stabilization Policy Be?

An important goal for macroeconomic policy is to minimize business cycle fluctuations and stabilize economic activity, commonly referred to as **stabilization policy.** One group of economists, known as *activists*, advocates the use of policies to eliminate excessive unemployment whenever it develops. In contrast, another group of economists, known as *nonactivists*, argues that the economy has a self-correcting mechanism that will quickly restore an economy in recession to a healthy condition. Activist policies, nonactivists say, could kick in at the wrong time, producing undesirable fluctuations in economic activity and inflation. For their part, activists think that doing nothing will leave too many people out of work for too long.

When recessions occur, as happened in 2007–2009, the debate between activists and nonactivists becomes very heated. We examine this issue in detail in Chapters 13, 21, and 22.

Should Macroeconomic Policy Follow Rules?

Another dimension of the debate on stabilization policy is whether policymakers should conduct policy in a *discretionary manner*—that is, react as they see fit as the situation evolves—or with *rules*—a binding plan that specifies in advance how policy will respond to data on variables such as inflation and unemployment. As we will analyze in Chapter 21 on the role of expectations in macroeconomic policy, discretionary policy can lead to a set of short-run policies that produce bad long-run outcomes, such as high inflation. Rule-determined policy can avoid these bad outcomes by making sure that policy accounts for appropriate long-run considerations, making good long-run outcomes more likely. However, rules can put policymakers in a straightjacket, and changes in the structure of the economy may make a rule obsolete. Are rules made to be broken?

The long-standing debate over rules versus discretion in macroeconomics is an important focus of Chapters 21 and 22 of this book.

Are Global Trade Imbalances a Danger?

In the 2000s, the U.S. economy was running large trade deficits in which it was purchasing far more goods and services from abroad than foreigners were buying from it. Massive amounts of capital flowed into the United States to fund U.S. spending, especially from China, which was running large trade surpluses. These global trade imbalances left the United States increasingly indebted to foreigners and provided the capital inflows that helped fuel a boom in housing purchases. The subsequent bust in the housing market after 2006 was a key factor in the Great Recession of 2007–2009.

We will explore what causes global trade imbalances in Chapters 4 and 16, and see what government policies can be used to reduce them. We will also see, in Chapter 15, why these imbalances can be dangerous and can help fuel financial crises like the one in the 2007–2009 period.

 # How We Will Study Macroeconomics

I hope that the policy questions in this chapter have piqued your interest and have convinced you that studying macroeconomics will be a worthwhile enterprise.

Emphasis on Policy and Practice

This textbook will introduce you to the policy and practice of macroeconomics by developing several macroeconomic models to help you understand how the aggregate economy works. Because theory without practice is inherently sterile, this book will emphasize the policy and practice of macroeconomics, both by using the models developed here in a large number of applications, which are separately broken out in the text, and with the Policy and Practice cases mentioned earlier. This exposure to real-world examples will help you appreciate that economics is far more than abstract theories: it is a powerful way of thinking that can help you understand the world—and your own economic options—better.

Concluding Remarks

I have been a practicing macroeconomist for over thirty years now. I fell in love with macroeconomics as an undergraduate in a similar course to the one you are taking here (taught by the famous Robert Solow, mentioned prominently in this book). I have had the privilege of applying my knowledge to policy and practice as a Federal Reserve official in exciting periods: from 1994 to 1997, when I was an executive vice president and director of research at the Federal Reserve Bank of New York, and from 2006 to 2008, when I was a governor of the Federal Reserve System. I hope that your progress through the chapters in this book will help you understand what is happening in the overall economic environment, and perhaps foster the enthusiasm for this subject that I have had for most of my life.

SUMMARY

1. The practice of macroeconomics involves examining macroeconomic data and then developing an economic theory or model to explain it. The key economic data series that macroeconomists try to explain are real GDP, the unemployment rate, and inflation.

2. Several policy issues that receive the most attention from macroeconomists are as follows: Is saving too low? How can we help poor countries to get rich? Do government budget deficits matter? How costly is it to reduce inflation?

How can we prevent financial crises? How active should stabilization policy be? Should macroeconomic policy follow rules? What can be done about global trade imbalances? We will address all of these policy issues in the coming chapters.

3. This textbook will introduce you to the policy and practice of macroeconomics by developing several macroeconomic models and applying them to real-world examples and data.

KEY TERMS

assets, p. 12
business cycles, p. 6
central banks, p. 13
deflation, p. 7
depression, p. 6
economic model, p. 3
economic theory, p. 3
endogenous variables, p. 4

exogenous variables, p. 4
financial crisis, p. 12
fiscal policy, p. 11
government budget deficits, p. 11
hyperinflation, p. 9
inflation, p. 7
inflation rate, p. 7
macroeconomics, p. 3

microeconomics, p. 3
monetary policy, p. 12
Real Gross Domestic Product (GDP), p. 5
recession, p. 6
stabilization policy, p. 12
unemployment rate, p. 7

REVIEW QUESTIONS

All Questions are available in MyEconLab *for practice or instructor assignment.*

Preview

1. What macroeconomic conditions, issues, and events can shape your future?

The Practice of Macroeconomics

2. What is the distinction between endogenous variables and exogenous variables in economic models?

3. What is the five-step process for developing macroeconomic models?

4. What three macroeconomic data series are of particular interest to macroeconomists? Why?

5. What is the business cycle? Which part of the business cycle is of particular concern to macroeconomists? Why?

6. What happens to the overall level of prices during periods of inflation and deflation?

Macroeconomic Policy

7. What is a nation's saving rate and why is it an important concern for macroeconomists?

8. What is a government budget deficit? Why are macroeconomists concerned with budget deficits?

9. Explain the difference between fiscal policy and monetary policy. What are some of the reasons these macroeconomic policies are used?

10. What is stabilization policy? What two important debates occur among macroeconomists regarding its use, and who are the parties to these debates?

11. What are global trade imbalances and why do economists focus on them?

PROBLEMS

All Problems are available in MyEconLab *for practice or instructor assignment.*

The Practice of Macroeconomics

1. Sciences other than economics also use models to explain the behavior of endogenous variables based on assumptions about the environment and changes in exogenous variables. Suppose you have to design a model that links childhood obesity and diabetes.
   a) Which one would be the exogenous variable? Which one would be the endogenous variable?
   b) Can you think of other exogenous variables?

2. Suppose your model predicts that overweight children have an 80% higher risk of suffering from diabetes in their adult life. If data show that overweight children do not suffer from diabetes as predicted by your model (i.e., data show a lower than 80% probability), what would your next step be?

3. The following table shows Spain's (annualized) quarterly real GDP growth rates for the 2007–2012 period. (Roman numbers refer to quarters.)

Variable	2007 I	2007 II	2007 III	2007 IV	2008 I	2008 II
Real GDP	7.6	7.3	6.5	6.4	5.6	4.6

Variable	2008 III	2008 IV	2009 I	2009 II	2009 III	2009 IV
Real GDP	3.1	0.5	−0.1	−4.1	−4.5	−3.3

Variable	2010 I	2010 II	2010 III	2010 IV	2011 I	2011 II
Real GDP	−1.5	−0.2	0.0	0.4	0.5	0.5

Variable	2011 III	2011 IV	2012 I	2012 II	2012 III	2012 IV
Real GDP	0.6	0.0	−0.7	−1.4	−1.6	−1.9

   a) Plot real GDP growth rate in a graph. Can you identify a trend in the data?
   b) Based on the data shown, can you identify the beginning (i.e., the year and the quarter) of the current recession?

4. Unemployment is a very important topic in macroeconomics. A high unemployment rate means that a lot of individuals willing to work cannot find a job. This is bad for the economy, as some resources (i.e., labor) remain idle. Comment on the effects that being unemployed have on an individual.

Macroeconomic Policy

5. During the 1970s, most Latin American countries ran huge budget deficits. As their governments resorted to printing money (increasing the money supply) to pay for these deficits, very high inflation rates resulted. As a consequence, real GDP declined or remained constant during the 1980s. Comment on the relationship between budget deficits, inflation, and real GDP growth.

6. Assume that a civil war erupts in a given country, creating chaos and destroying most of the economy's infrastructure (e.g., roads, businesses, and telecommunications).
   a) What would be the effect on economic growth?
   b) How do you think a civil war affects incentives to invest in that country?
7. The recent global financial crisis is a good example of how important the financial system is for the performance of any economy. Usually the immediate effects of a financial crisis include a decrease in asset prices, business failures, and more difficult access to credit for both firms and households. Comment on the consequences that a financial crisis will have on unemployment and economic growth.
8. The United States has been experiencing very low or even negative savings rates during the recent past. If this situation persists, what does it means for future generations?
9. A Council of Economic Advisers post on January 15, 2010, stated that "The American Recovery and Reinvestment Act [...] was the boldest countercyclical fiscal action in American history. [...] the Administration is committed to taking every responsible mea-sure to spur job creation." Comment on the characteristics of the Obama administration's economic policy at that time. Is it an activist or a nonactivist policy?

10. The Federal Reserve took swift action to help restore the United States financial system after the global financial crisis started in fall 2007. The various instruments used by the Federal Reserve were highly criticized for fueling expectations of higher inflation rates. What is the effect of monetary policy on expectations about inflation?
11. Consider the difficult task of raising children. One of the most widely recognized challenges of this task is to properly balance rules and ad-hoc decisions. Constantly breaking rules might send the wrong message to a kid, while strictly enforcing rules every time might result in excessive punishments. The debate about the conduct of macroeconomic policy is not significantly different from this example.
    a) Comment on the American Recovery and Reinvestment Act of 2009. Can this Act be characterized as discretionary policy?
    b) Is it possible for this set of policies to affect the incentives of financial intermediaries or other major economic agents?

DATA ANALYSIS PROBLEMS

The Problems update with real-time data in MyEconLab and are available for practice or instructor assignment.

1. For each of the following pairs of variables, pull the data from the St. Louis Federal Reserve FRED database and create a scatterplot graph of the two variables using Excel. For each pair, name the exogenous variable relative to the endogenous variable, and indicate whether the variables are unrelated.
   a) Personal Income (PINCOME) and Personal Consumption Expenditures (PCEC), quarterly data since 1980 Q1.
   b) Total Nonfarm Payrolls (PAYEMS) and M1 money supply (M1SL), monthly data since January 2000.
   c) Personal Saving Rate (PSAVERT) and the 10-year US Treasury Rate (GS10), monthly data since January 1980.
2. Go to the St. Louis Federal Reserve FRED database, and calculate the GDP growth rate and inflation rate. For GDP, use (GDPC1).

For the inflation rate, use the personal consumption expenditure price index (PCECTPI). For each series, change the units to *Percent Change from Year Ago* and download using data since 2000 Q1. Note that quarters in which the US was officially in a recession are 2001 Q2 to 2001 Q4, and 2008 Q1 to 2009 Q2.
   a) Which period had the highest inflation rate? The lowest inflation rate? When, if at all, did deflation occur?
   b) Which period had the highest growth rate of GDP? The lowest growth rate of GDP?
   c) What relationship, if any, is there among GDP growth, the inflation rate, and recessions?
3. Go to the St. Louis Federal Reserve FRED database, and pull data on annual

unemployment rates for the following countries, starting in 2000: United States (USAURNAA), Canada (CANURNAA), United Kingdom (GBRURNAA), Japan (JPNURNAA), and Germany (DEUURNAA). Graph the data for all five countries on one graph by using the *Add Data Series* function, and download the data into an Excel table. Note that the United States experienced a recession in 2001 and in 2008–2009.

 a) Which country experienced the highest unemployment rate, and when? Which country experienced the lowest unemployment rate, and when?

 b) Calculate the average unemployment rates for the U.S. during years of recession and when not in recession. How do they compare? Is this what you would expect?

 c) Look at the graph of unemployment rates. Which countries seem to show similar trends? Which seem to behave differently than the rest?

4. Go to the St. Louis Federal Reserve FRED database, and pull data on a common measure of standard of living, real GDP per capita, in 2011 U.S. dollars. Choose the following countries: United States (USARGDPC), Japan (JPNRGDPC), United Kingdom (GBRRGDPC), and South Korea (KORRGDPC). Download the data since 1990 into an Excel spreadsheet. For your last country, choose China. For China, real GDP per capita will have to be constructed by using nominal GDP per capita and a measure of prices. To do this, download nominal GDP per capita for China (PCAGDPCNA646NWDB) and a measure of the price level in China (CHNCPIALLAINMEI). Once the Chinese data are downloaded onto a spreadsheet, create a column for real GDP per capita, which will be nominal GDP per capita divided by the price level; then multiply by 100. Place all of the data for the five countries in a single spreadsheet, and then create one graph showing all five series, from 1990 until the present day.

 a) Which country among these five currently has the highest standard of living? Which has the lowest?

 b) How has South Korea's standard of living changed in comparison to that of Japan and the United Kingdom over this time period?

 c) How has China's standard of living changed in comparison with the standard of living in the other countries since 1990?

Measuring Macroeconomic Data

Preview

It is easy to take macroeconomic data for granted, especially when print and electronic media bombard us with economic facts and figures. When the most recent recession started in 2007, the latest releases of economic statistics quickly indicated that the economy was weakening. In contrast, when the Great Depression of the 1930s began, economists did not have immediate access to data indicating the severity of the situation. Economists recognized that better data were needed, to both inform the public and guide policymakers. Economists like Simon Kuznets, with his colleagues at the U.S. Department of Commerce, developed the National Income and Product Accounts in the 1930s. What became known as *national income accounting* may not sound very exciting—after all, who ever thinks that accounting is exciting—but it has been called one of the great inventions of the twentieth century.[1] In 1971, Simon Kuznets was awarded a Nobel Prize for his role in inventing national income accounting.

In this chapter, we examine how economists define and measure the most important data in macroeconomics, areas of study critical to your gaining a full understanding of macroeconomics. In this chapter, we will examine the following questions: How do we measure economic activity, and specifically *gross domestic product*, a broad measure of economic activity? What are the key components of gross domestic product? How do we measure inflation, and does it tell us how rapidly the cost of living is rising? What is unemployment and how do we measure it? What are interest rates, and which measures of interest rates are the most important in macroeconomics?

Measuring Economic Activity: National Income Accounting

Gross domestic product (GDP), the total value of goods and services produced in an economy, is the broadest measure of economic activity. We add up the value of all the goods and services produced in one year—say, from cell phones, automobiles, textbooks, DVDs, computers, haircuts, and rock concerts—to determine GDP. The U.S. Bureau of

---

[1]See Paul Samuelson and William Nordhaus, "GDP: One of the Great Inventions of the Twentieth Century," *Survey of Current Business* (January 2000): 6–9.

Economic Analysis (part of the U.S. Commerce Department) calculates GDP on a quarterly basis with data provided by other government agencies such as the Census Bureau and the Bureau of Labor Statistics. U.S. GDP is currently around $15 trillion, that is, nearly $50,000 per person.

There are several alternate definitions and approaches for measuring GDP. Our initial definition of GDP is given in terms of goods and services produced. We will also define GDP in terms of expenditure and income: GDP is the total income of everyone in the economy, and it is also the total amount of expenditure for goods and services in the economy. These various GDP definitions are equivalent because the total income in an economy must equal the total amount of expenditure, which equals total production. This reasoning makes intuitive sense because there is a buyer and a seller for every good or service produced in the economy. When you pay $15 for a haircut at your local barbershop, your $15 expenditure is $15 of income for the barber, who has produced the $15 haircut.

National income accounting, an accounting system to measure economic activity and its components, shows the relationship among the expenditure, income, and production methods of measuring GDP. We express national income accounting in the **fundamental identity of national income accounting:**

$$\text{Total Production} = \text{Total Expenditure} = \text{Total Income} \qquad (1)$$

Equation 1 says that any of the three approaches—production, expenditure, or income—should give the same answer when computing GDP. Let's calculate GDP with each of these approaches to refine our definitions of GDP.

Measuring GDP: The Production Approach

In the **production approach,** we define GDP as the current *market value* of all *final* goods and services *newly produced* in the economy during a *fixed period* of time. Each of these italicized phrases indicates key principles that we will examine in detail.

Market Value

An economy produces countless goods and services. This fact raises the age-old question, "How do we compare apples with oranges?" If the economy produces one billion apples and two billion oranges, would it be just as successful if it instead produced two billion apples and one billion oranges? If the economic value of apples and oranges is the same, the answer is yes: the total number and value of apples and oranges produced is the same amount, three billion. Because prices of various goods and services are rarely identical, we use national income accounting, which bases the economic value of a good or service on its market value, that is, the price it sells for. To calculate the value of output in the economy, you weigh each good and service by its current market price and add the results. In the case of apples and oranges, GDP would be as follows:

$$\text{GDP} = (\text{price of apples} \times \text{quantity of apples}) \\ + (\text{price of oranges} \times \text{quantity of oranges})$$

If apples and oranges each sold for $1, then total output for apples and oranges would indeed be the same in both cases, $3 billion (2 billion × $1 + 1 billion × $1 =

1 billion × \$1 + 2 billion × \$1). But if apples sold for 50 cents and oranges for \$2, then the total output of apples and oranges would differ in the two cases. In the first case, total output would be \$3 billion (2 billion × \$0.50 + 1 billion × \$2), while in the second, it would be \$4.5 billion (1 billion × \$0.50 + 2 billion × \$2).

NONMARKET GOODS AND SERVICES. Unfortunately, for the ease of computing accurate measures of GDP with national income accounting, not all goods and services produced in the economy are sold in markets that provide a market price. Some of these nonmarket goods and services are left out of measures of GDP by necessity. Many household services that are produced within a family or by friends—cleaning, cooking, child care—would be included if it were easier to measure them.

UNDERGROUND ECONOMY. Goods and services produced in the *underground economy* are also not counted in GDP. In the **underground economy,** goods and services produced are hidden from the government, either because they are illegal (drugs or prostitution) or because the person producing the goods and services is avoiding paying taxes on the income he or she receives (the carpenter who is paid in cash and does not declare it on his or her tax return). In some countries, the underground economy (also sometimes referred to as the "black market economy") is very large, and as a percentage of the total economy it differs substantially among countries. Italy, an example among rich countries, is notorious for tax avoidance, so its GDP is likely to be understated relative to other countries because of the large size of its underground economy.

IMPUTED VALUES FOR NONMARKET GOODS AND SERVICES. Many other nonmarket goods and services lacking a market price are counted in GDP by determining an **imputed value,** an estimate of what the price of the good or service would be if it were traded in a market. For example, an important component of GDP is housing services. When you rent your college apartment, there is a market price that you pay and so it is easy to include it in GDP. But what if, instead, you owned the apartment? A homeowner is getting housing services, just as a renter is. To impute the value of these services, the Department of Commerce, which computes GDP, assumes that in effect the homeowner is paying rent to him- or herself. A homeowner's imputed value is the rental price of comparable housing in the market.

The existence of nonmarket goods and services suggests that GDP is an imperfect measure of output produced in the economy. An especially large component of GDP that is not traded in the market is goods and services provided by the government, such as national defense, police protection, firefighting, and education. The standard practice is to value these services at the cost of providing them. The imputed value of a police officer giving out traffic tickets, for example, is the wages he or she is paid when doing traffic duty.

Final Goods and Services

Production of goods and services typically occurs in stages. We classify goods and services into two types: **intermediate goods and services** are used up entirely in the stages of production, whereas **final goods and services** are the end goods in the production process.

To illustrate, suppose that Intel produces $400 of microprocessors to go into the Mac that Apple sells for $1,500, and it costs $50 to ship the Mac to the computer store where you buy it. The $400 of microprocessors is an intermediate good, the $50 of shipping is an intermediate service, and the $1,500 Mac is a final good. Would it make sense to include all these goods and services in GDP? No. We include only the $1,500 Mac, the final good, in GDP. Otherwise, there would be double counting because the costs of the intermediate goods and services used in producing the Mac are already included in the price for the final good. That is, GDP should include only the market value of final goods and services.

VALUE-ADDED TECHNIQUE AND GDP. One important technique for calculating the value of all final goods and services produced in the economy is with **value added,** the value of a firm's output minus the cost of the intermediate goods and services purchased by the firm. By adding up the value added for each firm, we get the final value of the goods and services produced. In our Mac example, the value added for the producer of microprocessors is $400, while the value added for the shipping firm is $50 (assuming that it did not use any intermediate goods). The value added for Apple is the final price of the Mac minus the cost of the intermediate inputs: $1,500 minus the $400 cost of the microprocessors and the $50 cost of shipping, that is, $1,050. The sum of the value-added items for each of these firms—$1,050 plus $400 plus $50—is $1,500, the same value as the final good, the Mac. Now imagine adding up all the value added in the economy to determine the total value of final goods and services in the economy. This approach is likely to include all final goods and services in the economy, but appropriately excludes intermediate goods and services.

CAPITAL GOODS AND GDP. There are some subtleties as to when to classify goods as intermediate versus final goods. Suppose a robot is manufactured to install windshields in new automobiles. Is it an intermediate good or a final good? Although the robot is used to help produce new cars, it is not used up in producing the car and will keep on installing windshields for many years. The robot is a **capital good,** a good that is produced in the current period to be used in the production of other goods and that is not used up in the stages of production. We classify new capital goods as final goods and thus include them in GDP because they are not included in spending on other final goods and yet their production is certainly part of economic activity.

INVENTORY INVESTMENT AND GDP. Inventories—firms' holdings of raw materials, unfinished goods, and unsold finished goods—are another type of good that is not used up in the current period. The change in inventories over a given period of time, say a year, is referred to as **inventory investment.** We include inventory investment in GDP for the same reason that we include capital goods: an increase in the level of inventories means that there has been an increase in economic activity. For example, suppose that at the beginning of the year, Apple has $1 billion of microprocessors and $1 billion of finished Mac computers on hand, for a total of $2 billion of inventories. At the end of the year, it has $1.5 billion of microprocessors and $1.5 billion of finished Macs in stock. Its level of inventories has increased from $2 billion to $3 billion, an increase of $1 billion. This $1 billion increase in inventories is the inventory investment for that year, and we add it into GDP.

Newly Produced Goods and Services

GDP should include only goods and services that are newly produced in the current period; it excludes those that were produced in previous periods. If you buy a three-year-old car from a used car lot, there is no increase in production of automobiles: the cost of the used car is *not included* in *GDP*. The car was already counted in GDP when its original owner purchased it new. However, the value of the services provided by the car dealership that sold you the used car is included in GDP.

Fixed Period of Time

We calculate GDP over a fixed period of time, such as a quarter or a year. For example, GDP for the year 2014 tells us the value of final goods and services produced over the course of 2014. GDP is a **flow,** an amount *per* a given unit of time, in contrast to a **stock,** a quantity *at* a given point in time. (Note that the *stock* concept is not to be confused with the term *common stock*, such as a share of IBM.) The concept of stocks versus flows is vitally important in economics and is discussed in the box, "Stocks Versus Flows."

Although we see from the discussion in this section that the technical difficulties in measuring GDP are serious, there is an even deeper question of whether GDP provides an appropriate measure of how well an economy is doing, as the following Policy and Practice case indicates.

Policy and Practice

Can GDP Buy Happiness?

You won't find Bhutan anywhere near the top of the list of wealthiest nations. But in 1972, the king of Bhutan said his tiny South Asian nation would rank much higher if its wealth were measured not by gross domestic product but by "gross national happiness," incorporating factors such as spirituality and culture. At the time, his idea sounded ludicrous to most economists. But over the years, many governments began to acknowledge that GDP is an inadequate—albeit highly useful—measure of well-being.

Starting in 1990, the United Nations began to rank countries on a so-called "human development index": a combination of life expectancy, education, literacy, educational participation, and GDP. By this measure, in 2012 the United States ranked third behind Norway and Australia, countries whose GDP per person is well below that of the United States. (Bhutan ranked 140.) In 2008, a French economic commission led by Nobel Prize winner Joseph Stiglitz called for significant modifications to GDP and the development of a new generation of national statistics to measure factors such as political freedom, physical safety, and work–life balance. The proposal was taken up by the Organization for Economic Cooperation and Development, a body of the world's richest countries. In spite of these efforts, per-capita GDP remains the most broadly accepted measurement of national well-being.

Stocks Versus Flows

Throughout this book, we will discuss many macroeconomic variables, some of which are stocks and the others flows. Understanding the difference between them is critical to avoiding confusion when we study macroeconomics.

To see the difference between a stock and a flow, consider the classic example of a bathtub, shown in Figure 2.1. Stocks and flows are clearly related: a stock is often an accumulation of flows over time. If the faucet has been running for a half hour with a *flow* of one gallon per minute and the tub was initially empty, then the *stock* of water in the tub will be thirty gallons, that is, thirty minutes times the flow of one gallon per minute. The most important flow variable we have discussed in this chapter is GDP, which always has to be thought of as an amount produced *per year* or *per quarter*. Examples of stocks and flows that are related include the following: inventory investment, a flow, which accumulates into the stock of inventories;

saving, a flow, which accumulates into a person's wealth; and fixed investment, a flow, which accumulates into the economy's capital stock.

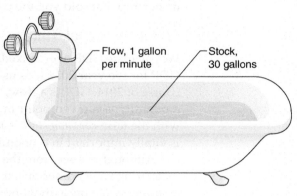

FIGURE 2.1

Stocks Versus Flows

The water coming out of the faucet is a *flow* (one gallon per minute), while the amount of water in the tub is a *stock* (thirty gallons).

Measuring GDP: The Expenditure Approach

We now turn to our second technique for computing GDP: with the **expenditure approach,** GDP is the total spending on currently produced final goods and services in the economy. The expenditure approach allows us to get information on the different components of spending that add up to GDP. The national income accounts divide spending into four basic categories: *consumption expenditure, investment, government purchases (spending),* and *net exports,* each of which we will discuss in turn. The national income accounts add up these four categories of spending to determine GDP in the **national income identity,**

$$Y = C + I + G + NX \tag{2}$$

where

$$Y = \text{GDP} = \text{total production (output)}$$
$$C = \text{consumption expenditure}$$
$$I = \text{investment}$$
$$G = \text{government purchases of goods and services}$$
$$NX = \text{net exports} = \text{exports} - \text{imports}$$

TABLE 2.1	GDP AND ITS COMPONENTS, 2012		
		Billions of Dollars	**Percent of GDP**
Personal consumption expenditure (C)		**11,286**	**68.7**
Consumer durables		1,231	7.5
Nondurable goods		2,595	15.8
Services		7,459	45.4
Investment (I)		**2,500**	**15.2**
Fixed investment		2,018	12.3
Inventory investment		13	0.14
Residential investment		469	2.9
Government purchases (G)		**3,151**	**19.2**
Federal		1,275	7.8
State and local		1,875	11.4
Net exports (NX)		**− 516**	**− 3.1**
Exports		2,214	13.5
Minus imports		2,730	16.6
Total = GDP (Y)		**16,420**	**100.0**

Source: Bureau of Economic Analysis. Table 1.1.5. www.bea.gov/national/nipaweb/SelectTable.asp?Selected=Y

Note: Numbers may not add up to the totals due to rounding.

Equation 2 is one of the most fundamental equations in macroeconomics, and we will make use of it many times throughout this book. Table 2.1 provides 2012 data from the U.S. economy on these four components and some subcomponents.

Consumption Expenditure

Consumption expenditure (also referred to as **personal consumption expenditure** and **consumption**) is the total spending for currently produced consumer goods and services. Consumption expenditure is by far the largest component of GDP and was 68.7% of GDP in 2012 (see Table 2.1). We can break it down into three basic categories:

1. *Consumer durables* are goods purchased by consumers that last a long time (are *durable*), such as automobiles, electronic goods, and appliances.

2. *Nondurable goods* are short-lived consumer goods such as food, housing services (but not purchases of houses, which are part of investment), gasoline, and clothing.

3. *Services* are purchased by consumers; examples include haircuts, education, medical care, air travel, and financial services.

Investment

Investment is spending on currently produced capital goods that are used to produce goods and services over an extended period of time. Investment was 15.2% of GDP in 2012. We can break it down into three basic categories:

1. *Fixed investment*, also referred to as *business fixed investment*, is spending by businesses on equipment (machines, computers, furniture, and trucks) and structures (factories, stores, and warehouses).

2. *Inventory investment* is the change in inventories held by firms. If inventories are increasing, inventory investment is positive, but if they are decreasing, inventory investment is negative.

3. *Residential investment* is household purchases of *new* houses and apartments. (We do not include purchases of existing housing in GDP because it was produced in earlier periods.) Houses and apartments are capital goods for households because they produce a service (a roof over our heads) over an extended period of time. Indeed, for most of us, housing is the most important purchase we ever make in our lives.

Government Purchases

Government purchases is spending by the government—whether federal, state, or local—on currently produced goods and services. Government purchases were 19.2% of GDP in 2012. Although most of the media attention focuses on federal spending, as you can see from Table 2.1, more spending is done by state and local governments than by the federal government.

GOVERNMENT CONSUMPTION VERSUS GOVERNMENT INVESTMENT. Government purchases that appear in GDP include purchases of goods (highways, military equipment, and computers) and services (rangers for national parks, police protection, health care, and education). We refer to government purchases for short-lived goods and services like health care and police protection as **government consumption**, whereas spending for capital goods like buildings and computers represents **government investment**.

TRANSFERS AND GDP. Government payments for Social Security, Medicare, and unemployment insurance benefits are **transfers** from one segment of society—healthy, working people—to another segment—the elderly, sick, and jobless. Because they are

Meaning of the Word *Investment*

Economists use the word *investment* somewhat differently than other people do. When noneconomists say that they are making an investment, they are normally referring to the purchase of common stocks or bonds, purchases that do not necessarily involve newly produced goods and services. But when economists speak of investment spending, they are referring to the purchase of physical assets such as *new* machines or new houses—purchases that add to GDP.

not payments in exchange for currently produced goods and services, they are not included in government purchases, G, or GDP. Interest payments on government debt are also not made in exchange for goods and services, so we exclude them from government purchases, G, and GDP.

Net Exports

Net exports are exports minus imports: that is, the value of currently produced goods and services exported, or sold to other countries, minus the value of goods and services imported, or purchased from abroad. It is easy to see why exports should be included in GDP. But why must we subtract imports out to get a correct measure of GDP? The answer is that spending on imports is included in consumption expenditure, investment, and government purchases, but imports are not produced in the United States.[2]

Net exports have been quite negative in recent years, –3.1% of GDP in 2012, because U.S. citizens buy more foreign goods and services than foreigners buy U.S. goods and services. For example, exports at 13.5% of GDP in 2012 were substantially less than imports at 16.6% of GDP. We also refer to net exports as the **trade balance;** the negative trade balance in 2012 is often discussed in the media by saying that the United States has been running a large trade deficit.

Changes in the Spending Components of GDP over Time

Figure 2.2 shows how the different expenditure components as a percentage of GDP have changed over the last sixty-three years. Four interesting facts are apparent from looking at Figure 2.2.

1. Consumption expenditure grew steadily as a share of GDP from 1970 to 2013, rising from 63% of GDP to close to 70%. Why the consumption expenditure share showed this positive trend is one of the questions that macroeconomics seeks to explain, which we will turn to in Chapter 18.

2. Investment is much more volatile than other components of GDP. We will explain why this occurs in Chapter 19 on investment. Because of its high volatility, even though the average size of investment relative to GDP is only a third that of consumption expenditure, investment plays a very large role in explaining fluctuations in economic activity.

---

[2]Another way to see why imports have to be subtracted from exports, giving net exports as a component of GDP, is to recognize that domestic output equals consumption, investment, and government purchases on domestically produced goods, marked with a subscript d, plus foreign spending on domestically produced goods, that is, exports, EX:

$$Y = C_d + I_d + G_d + EX$$

Total consumption expenditure, investment, and government purchases have an additional component of foreign produced goods, i.e., imports, denoted by an im subscript, so adding in these terms and then subtracting them again means that we can rewrite GDP as follows:

$$Y = (C_d + C_{im}) + (I_d + I_{im}) + (G_d + G_{im}) + EX - (C_{im} + I_{im} + G_{im})$$

Then, since we can write total consumption expenditure, investment, and government purchases as $C = (C_d + C_{im})$, $I = (I_d + I_{im})$, and $G = (G_d + G_{im})$, while total imports is $IM = (C_{im} + I_{im} + G_{im})$, we can use substitution to write

$$Y = C + I + G + EX - IM$$

which, since net exports equals exports minus imports (i.e., $NX = EX - IM$), we can rewrite as

$$Y = C + I + G + NX$$

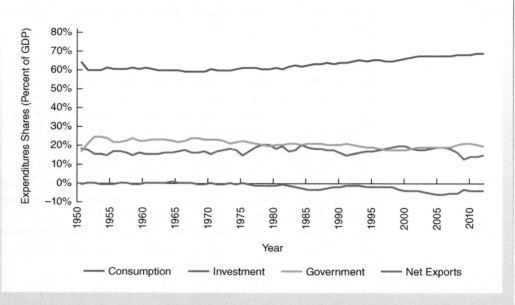

FIGURE 2.2

Expenditure Components of U.S. GDP, 1950–2013

Over the past sixty-three years, U.S. consumption expenditure rose steadily as a share of GDP, and investment was much more volatile than other components of GDP. Government purchases remained quite stable over the past sixty-three years at around 20% of GDP, while net exports were near zero or negative, with the trade deficit worsening over time.

Source: Federal Reserve Bank of St. Louis, FRED Database. http://research.stlouisfed.org/fred2/

3. Despite claims that the government has expanded in size, government purchases have actually remained quite stable at around 20% of GDP over the past sixty-year period. Transfer payments, which are not included in government purchases, have grown relative to government purchases, giving the impression that the government has expanded in size.

4. In most years, net exports have been negative and the United States has been running a trade deficit. Just a few years ago, the trade deficit climbed to over 5% of GDP.

Different countries have different sizes of expenditure components relative to GDP, as the box entitled "An International Comparison of Expenditure Components" suggests.

 ## Measuring GDP: The Income Approach

The third way of measuring GDP, the **income approach,** involves adding up all the incomes received by households and firms in the economy, including profits and tax revenue to the government.

Categories of Income

Table 2.2 (on page 30) shows the major categories of U.S. income in 2012. We will discuss each major category in turn.

1. *Compensation of employees* includes both the wages and salaries of employees (excluding the self-employed) and employee benefits, which include

payments for health insurance and retirement benefits. As Table 2.2 indicates, employee compensation is the largest category of income, 53.2% of GDP in 2012. Although wages and salaries have been declining relative to GDP, total compensation relative to GDP has stayed nearly constant over time because the declining share of wages and salaries has been offset by increasing employee benefits.

2. *Other income* includes income of the self-employed, income that individuals receive from renting their properties (which includes royalty income on books and music), and the net interest earned by individuals from businesses and foreign sources (interest income minus the interest that they pay).

An International Comparison of Expenditure Components

Other countries have very different shares of consumption, investment, government purchases, and net exports relative to GDP, as Figure 2.3 indicates. The United States differs from other countries in the figure by having the highest share of GDP going to consumption, a low share of GDP going to investment, and a negative share going to net exports. China stands out by having the lowest share of consumption and the highest share of investment.

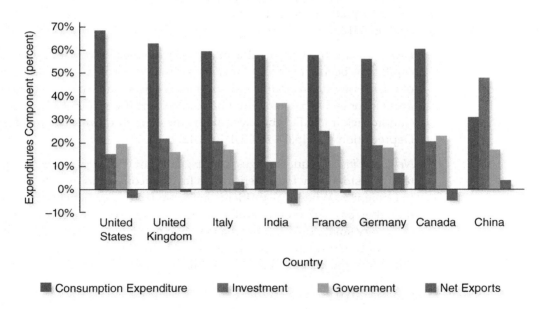

FIGURE 2.3

Shares of Expenditure Components for Different Countries

The United States differs from other countries by having the highest share of GDP going to consumption, a low share of GDP going to investment, and a negative share going to net exports. China has the lowest share of consumption and the highest share of investment.

Source: OECD and for China estimates from *National Bureau of Statistics*. The data are for the year 2010.

TABLE 2.2	INCOME APPROACH TO GDP, 2012		
		Billions of Dollars	**Percent of GDP**
Compensation of employees		8,787	53.2
Other income		3,370	20.4
Corporate profits		2,047	12.4
Total = National income		**14,204**	**86.0**
Depreciation		2,575	15.6
Total = Gross national product (GNP)		**16,779**	**101.6**
Net factor income		−257.0	−1.6
Total = Gross domestic product (GDP)		**16,420**	**100.0**

Source: Bureau of Economic Analysis. Tables 1.12 and 1.7.5. www.bea.gov/national/nipaweb/SelectTable.asp?Selected=Y

Note: Numbers do not add up to the totals because the statistical discrepancy is ignored.

In addition, the other income category includes indirect business taxes like the sales tax because these taxes need to be added to net income of business to yield their total income. Other income was 20.4% of GDP in 2012.

3. *Corporate profits* is made up of the profits of corporations. It was 12.4% of GDP in 2012.

4. *Depreciation* is the loss of value of capital from wear and tear or because capital has been scrapped because it is obsolete. To obtain the net income of businesses, depreciation was subtracted out, so in order to compute gross income, we have to add it back into GDP. If we do not add depreciation back into GDP, then we call the measure **net domestic product.** Depreciation was 15.6% of GDP in 2012.

5. *Net factor income* equals wages, profits, and rent (called *factor income*) paid to U.S. residents by foreigners minus factor income paid by U.S. residents to foreigners. When U.S. residents get more factor payments from abroad than they pay out, their overall income goes up. Net factor income is typically very small. In 2012, it was a negative number, −1.6% of GDP, indicating that U.S. residents received less income from foreigners than they paid out to foreigners, and so made a negative contribution to GDP.

Income Measures

By adding up the various items in Table 2.2, we get several measures of income reported in the national income accounts. We add up the first three items to obtain **national income.** We then add depreciation to obtain **gross national product (GNP),** which measures the total income earned by U.S. residents.[3] However, some of this income is

---

[3]We have ignored *statistical discrepancy,* which is the difference between the production-based measure of GDP and the income-based measure of GDP, because the statistical discrepancy item is usually small. In 2012, the statistical discrepancy was $101.7 billion, 0.6% of GDP.

not produced domestically, but rather is earned from wages, rents, and profits from production abroad. To get a domestically produced measure of gross product, gross *domestic* product (GDP), we have to add net factor income, which is negative, to gross *national* product (GNP), as Table 2.2 indicates. In 2012, U.S. GDP was $16.4 trillion.

Private disposable income, the amount of income the private sector has available to spend, is another important income measure that is a key determinant of the level of private sector spending. **Private disposable income** equals the income received by the private sector, plus payments made to the private sector by the government, minus taxes paid to the government. More precisely,

$$
\begin{aligned}
\text{Private Disposable Income} = \ & \text{GDP} \\
& + \text{net factor income} \\
& + \text{transfer payments received from the government} \\
& + \text{interest payments on government debt} \\
& - \text{taxes}
\end{aligned} \tag{3}
$$

The government also has disposable income available to spend, **net government income,** which equals the following:

$$
\begin{aligned}
\text{Net Government Income} = \ & \text{taxes} \\
& - \text{transfers} \\
& - \text{interest payments on government debt}
\end{aligned} \tag{4}
$$

Adding Equations 3 and 4 together, we see that private disposable income plus net government income equals GDP plus net factor payments from foreigners, which is gross national product, GNP.

Real Versus Nominal GDP

Now that we have established how macroeconomists determine GDP, let's examine how to use this data for analysis. Refining the GDP data involves separating changes in economic activity from changes in prices.

Nominal Variables

So far, all of the income, expenditure, and production variables we have been discussing are measured at current market (*nominal*) prices and are referred to as **nominal variables.** Market prices allow us to sum up different goods and services to get a measure of GDP, which more accurately should be called **nominal GDP.** However, nominal variables, such as nominal GDP, have one huge disadvantage: they don't tell us what is happening to economic activity over time if prices are changing. If, for example, all prices of goods and services in the economy doubled, then nominal GDP would as well, but the actual quantity of goods produced, and hence economic activity, would be unchanged. When you see an increase in nominal GDP, it could be rising because the quantities of goods and services are rising, or alternatively because the prices of goods and services are rising, or both.

Real Variables

A measure of an economic variable in terms of quantities of actual goods and services is called a **real variable.** The measure of GDP that tells us how economic activity is changing over time is *real GDP*. Real GDP is the value of goods and services produced using constant prices rather than current prices, as is the case for nominal GDP. In other words, real GDP is the GDP measure that is adjusted for changes in the average level of prices in the economy, referred to as the **price level.** Real GDP tells us the total amount of output (actual goods and services) produced in an economy. We can write the relationship between real GDP and nominal GDP as follows:

$$\text{Real GDP} = \frac{\text{Nominal GDP}}{\text{Price Level}} \tag{5}$$

or

$$\text{Nominal GDP} = \text{Price Level} \times \text{Real GDP} \tag{6}$$

To calculate real GDP for the year 2014, let's return to the example of an economy that produces only apples and oranges. We can calculate GDP with all prices set at the values they had in a given year, called a *base year*, say, the year 2005:

Real GDP in 2014 = (price of apples in 2005 × quantity of apples in 2014)
+ price of oranges in 2005 × quantity of oranges in 2014

If apples sold for 50 cents and oranges for $2 in 2005, with 1 billion of each produced in 2014, the calculation of real GDP would be as follows:

Real GDP in 2014 = ($0.50 × 1 billion) + ($2 × 1 billion) = $2.5 billion

If the quantity of apples produced rose to 2 billion and the number of oranges produced rose to 1.5 billion, then real GDP for 2015 would be as follows:

Real GDP in 2015 = (price of apples in 2005 × quantity of apples in 2015)
+ (price of oranges in 2005 × quantity of oranges in 2015)
= ($0.50 × 2 billion) + ($2 × 1.5 billion) = $4.0 billion

Because we kept prices in these calculations at their base-year values, we see that changes in real GDP can occur only if quantities of goods and services produced change. This relationship is exactly what we would want if a measure of GDP is to be an accurate measure of economic activity: changes in *real* GDP provide information on whether economic well-being is improving, while *nominal* GDP frequently does not. Economists quote real GDP in terms of base-year prices. For example, we would say that real GDP in 2015 is $4 billion in 2005 dollars.

If you just looked at the raw data on GDP, you might conclude that every winter the economy goes into recession, when in reality output tends to fall in cold and snowy months. To get a clearer assessment, economic statistics are **seasonally adjusted,** which means economists adjust the data to subtract out the usual seasonal fluctuations using advanced statistical techniques.

Chain-Weighted Measures of Real GDP

If prices of some important goods changed dramatically relative to prices of other goods, using a fixed base year for prices when calculating real GDP can produce misleading results. Between 2005 and 2011, for instance, computer prices fell far more rapidly than prices of other goods. Using the prices for computers from a base year of 2005 would weigh computers too heavily in real GDP calculations relative to using a more recent year as a base year. In 1996, the Bureau of Economic Analysis decided to fix this problem by switching to **chain-weighted measures** of GDP, in which the base year is allowed to change continuously. This means that percentage change in real GDP over a year, say from 2014 to 2015, is calculated with average prices for goods and services for the 2014–2015 period: that is, the base year is the average of 2014–2015. Then for 2015–2016, the change in real GDP is calculated using a base year that is the average of 2015–2016. Thus every year, the base year is advanced by one year. After calculating these growth rates, we "chain" them together—that is, the level of real GDP is increased each year by the growth rate calculated in this way, so that the level of real GDP can be compared for any two dates. This process in effect updates the relative prices of goods and services every year so that their prices don't get too far out of date.[4]

Measuring Inflation

Inflation, a topic we introduced in Chapter 1, is one of the most important variables that macroeconomists study. Measuring inflation involves different measures of the price level that we refer to as **price indexes.** We first look at the GDP deflator because it comes directly out of our calculation of real GDP. We then discuss the PCE deflator and the *consumer price index*, which is the most widely reported price index in the media.

GDP Deflator

From either Equation 5 or Equation 6, notice that we can write the price level as the ratio of nominal GDP to real GDP:

$$\text{Price Level} = \frac{\text{Nominal GDP}}{\text{Real GDP}} \tag{7}$$

Nominal GDP divided by real GDP is known as the **GDP deflator** or the **implicit price deflator for GDP.** The name *deflator* comes from the fact that, as we see in Equation 7, this measure *deflates* nominal GDP to obtain real GDP.

The GDP deflator is always calculated so that it equals 100 in the base year. We thus calculate the GDP deflator for a given year as follows:

$$\text{GDP deflator for year } y = 100 \times \frac{\text{Nominal GDP in year } y}{\text{Real GDP in year } y} \tag{8}$$

---

[4]For nominal GDP and the pre-1996 procedure for calculating real GDP, the national income identity, $Y = C + I + G + NX$, holds exactly. The real components of chain-weighted real GDP, however, don't add up exactly to real GDP. If you are interested in looking at the share of these GDP components, you should do the calculation with nominal measures. If you are interested in how economic activity in each category of spending is increasing, then you should look at the real, chain-weighted measures.

For example, if nominal GDP in 2015 is $15 trillion and real GDP in 2005 dollars is $12 trillion, then the GDP deflator for 2015 is $100 \times (\$15 \text{ trillion}/\$12 \text{ trillion}) = 125$, which means that the price level as measured by the GDP deflator has risen 25% from 2005 to 2015.

PCE Deflator

Another widely used measure of the price level, particularly by the Federal Reserve, is the **personal consumption expenditure (PCE) deflator,** which we calculate in the same way as the GDP deflator, but only for the personal consumption expenditure component of GDP.

$$\text{PCE deflator for year } y = 100 \times \frac{\text{Nominal PCE in year } y}{\text{Real PCE in year } y} \tag{9}$$

Because the PCE is based on the prices of consumer goods, it is closer to measuring what the consumer price index measures, which we will discuss next.

Consumer Price Index

The **consumer price index (CPI)** is a measure of the average prices of consumer goods and services. Think of it as a cost of living index. The Bureau of Labor Statistics (part of the U.S. Department of Labor) calculates the CPI monthly. In contrast, the GDP deflator is calculated quarterly by the Bureau of Economic Analysis, while the PCE deflator is calculated monthly by the same organization.

DETERMINING THE BASKET OF GOODS. The Bureau of Labor Statistics collects prices on thousands of consumer goods and services. How does it average all these prices to get a price index? A simple average would be inaccurate because the prices of some goods and services are far more important to a consumer's budget than others. For example, the average consumer spends a lot more on gas than he or she does on other items such as apples. The solution is that the Bureau of Labor Statistics determines what people actually buy with an expenditure survey and then compiles a "basket of goods" that the average urban consumer buys. For example, the Bureau might determine that the average urban consumer buys ten gallons of gas per week and two apples. It multiplies each quantity by each current price and then compares this calculation to one done with prices from a base year, which, by definition, has an index of 100.

CALCULATING CPI. To illustrate, let's assume that the basket of goods for the average consumer consists of ten gallons of gas and two apples. The calculation of the CPI for 2014 with a base year of 2005 would then be as follows:

$$\text{CPI for 2014} = 100 \times \frac{(10 \times \text{price of gas per gallon in 2014}) + (2 \times \text{price of apples in 2014})}{(10 \times \text{price of gas per gallon in 2005}) + (2 \times \text{price of apples in 2005})}$$

Although the consumer price index attracts much attention in the media, it can seriously overstate the cost of living, causing important policy implications.

Policy and Practice

Policy and Overstatements of the Cost of Living

The CPI is used in most labor contracts and in determining some government payments, such as Social Security benefits. Substantial measurement errors in the CPI could have important policy implications, particularly if increases in the CPI overstate increases in the cost of living. Consider three scenarios.

1. Suppose the government indexes payments to the CPI, so that payments automatically rise by the same percentage as the CPI. If increases in the CPI overstate increases in the cost of living, there could be substantial overpayments.

2. If the CPI inflation rate overstates the true inflation rate, policymakers may take steps to reduce CPI inflation more than is necessary, say, by overly tightening monetary policy by raising interest rates.

3. If the CPI overstates the increase in the cost of living, households' real income will be understated. The CPI may indicate that families are doing worse than is really the case, which could lead to policy actions such as redistributing income through the tax system.

A 1995 government commission headed by Michael Boskin of Stanford University investigated the accuracy of CPI inflation measures. The commission's 1996 report concluded that increases in the CPI might overstate increases in the cost of living on the order of one percentage point, and maybe a little higher. How could this be? For one, consumers can find substitutes for goods that become suddenly more expensive. Second, price increases often reflect quality improvements in goods, a fact the CPI often ignores. And third, the introduction of new goods can improve consumer choice and reduce the cost of living without showing up in CPI. For example, in the 1980s, a family of six might have needed to buy two cars. With the introduction of the minivan, it could spend less on one car.

In response to the Boskin commission's findings, the Bureau of Labor Statistics changed the way it constructs the CPI to reduce both substitution and quality adjustment bias. Nonetheless, researchers still estimate that the bias in the CPI inflation rate is still on the order of $\frac{1}{2} - 1\%$ per year.[5]

Inflation Rate

We define the *inflation rate* precisely as the percentage rate of change of the price level over a particular period. We can write it as follows:

$$\pi_t = \frac{P_t - P_{t-1}}{P_{t-1}} = \frac{\Delta P_t}{P_{t-1}} \tag{10}$$

[5]See David Lebow and Jeremy Rudd, "Measurement Error in the Consumer Price Index: Where Do We Stand?" *Journal of Economic Literature* (March 2003): 159–201; and Robert J. Gordon, "The Boskin Commission Report: A Retrospective One Decade Later," NBER Working Paper No. 12311, June 2006.

where

$$\pi_t = \text{inflation rate in period } t$$

$$P_t = \text{price level at time } t$$

$$P_{t-1} = \text{price level at time } t{-}1$$

If the price level—whether we measure it with a price index like the GDP deflator, the PCE deflator, or the CPI—rises from 100 to 102 over a year, then the inflation rate is $2\% = (102 - 100)/100 = 0.02$. If it rises to 103 the next year, then the inflation rate for that year is $1\% = (103 - 102)/102 = 0.01$.

Different price indices do sometimes lead to different inflation rates, as Figure 2.4 shows for the 1950–2013 time period in the United States. However, inflation rates using these different measures do move pretty closely together and tell similar stories, showing a sharp rise in inflation in the 1970s and early 1980s, which was subsequently reversed thereafter.

Percentage Change Method and the Inflation Rate

Alternatively, we can obtain the inflation rate using the fact that ***the percentage change of a product of a number of variables is approximately equal to the sum of the percentage changes of each of these variables.*** In the case of the product of two variables, we write this fact as follows:

$$\text{Percentage Change in}(x \times y) = (\text{Percentage Change in } x) \\ + (\text{Percentage Change in } y) \tag{11}$$

MyEconLab Real-time data

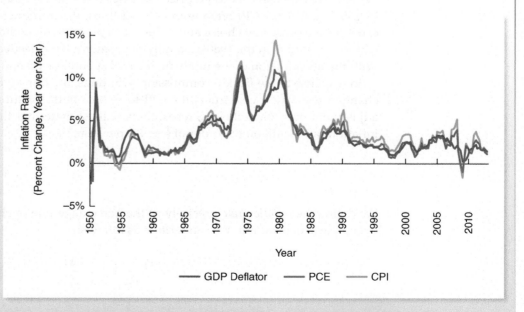

FIGURE 2.4

U.S. Inflation Rates with Different Price Indexes, 1950–2013

The GDP deflator, the PCE deflator, and CPI sometimes lead to different inflation rates. However, inflation rates using these different measures do move pretty closely together and tell similar stories, showing a sharp rise in inflation in the 1970s and early 1980s and a downward trend from the late 1980s onward.

Source: Federal Reserve Bank of St. Louis, FRED Database. http://research.stlouisfed.org/fred2/

Applying this fact to Equation 6, which stated that nominal GDP equals the price level times real GDP, leads to the following:

$$\text{Percentage Change in Nominal GDP} = (\text{Percentage Change in the Price Level}) + (\text{Percentage Change in Real GDP})$$

The percentage change in the price level is the inflation rate, while the percentage changes in nominal and real GDP are the growth rates of these variables. As a result, we can rewrite the preceding equation as follows:

$$\text{Growth Rate of Nominal GDP} = (\text{Inflation Rate}) + (\text{Growth Rate of Real GDP}) \tag{12}$$

If the growth rate of real GDP is 3% and the inflation rate is 2%, then the growth rate of nominal GDP is approximately 5%. Alternatively, by rearranging and subtracting the growth rate of real GDP from both sides of Equation 12, we obtain the following:

$$\text{Inflation Rate} = (\text{Growth Rate of Nominal GDP}) - (\text{Growth Rate of Real GDP}) \tag{13}$$

By calculating growth rates of both nominal and real GDP, we can determine the inflation rate in terms of the GDP deflator. In the example, we can calculate the inflation rate of 2% as the 5% growth rate of nominal GDP minus the 3% growth rate of real GDP.

Measuring Unemployment

The *unemployment rate* is one of the most closely followed economic statistics because it provides an indication of what is happening in the labor market and how well the economy is utilizing its resources—in this case, labor.

The unemployment rate (or civilian unemployment rate) is the percentage of people in the civilian population (which excludes those in the military or in prison) who want to work but who do not have jobs and are thus unemployed. The Bureau of Labor Statistics computes the unemployment rate every month from a survey of about 60,000 households (see the Macroeconomics in the News box, "Unemployment and Employment," on page 39). The survey classifies each adult (age 16 and over) in one of three categories.

1. *Employed*, if the person is working, either full time or part time, during the past week, or was temporarily away from his or her job because of illness, vacation, or the inability to get to work because of bad weather.

2. *Unemployed*, if the person did not work during the past week, but had looked for a job over the previous four weeks, or was waiting to return to a job from which he or she had been laid off.

3. *Not in the labor force*, if the person did not work during the past week and had not looked for a job over the previous four weeks.

Those not in the labor force are of two types. Those who would like to work but have given up looking are **discouraged workers.** The other type is those who voluntarily have left the labor force—such as full-time students, retirees, or people who have chosen to stay at home, either raising children or taking care of the household.

The **labor force** (civilian) is as follows:

$$\text{Labor Force} = \text{Number of Employed} + \text{Number of Unemployed} \tag{14}$$

The unemployment rate is then calculated as follows:

$$\text{Unemployment Rate} = \frac{\text{Number of Unemployed}}{\text{Labor Force}} \tag{15}$$

Although this measure of unemployment is the standard one reported in the media, measuring the unemployment rate is far from straightforward. The standard way of reporting the unemployment rate described previously does not give a full picture of what is happening in labor markets. Workers who have dropped out of the labor force because they have been unable to get a job are not counted as being unemployed, even though they want to work and are clearly suffering. Similarly, other workers are counted as employed even if they have only been able to get a part-time (less than forty hours a week) job when they would have preferred to work full time. A case can be made to view these types of workers as unemployed. As a result, the Bureau of Labor Statistics has calculated additional measures of unemployment that count as unemployed discouraged workers, marginally attached workers, and part-time workers, and finds that this measure of the unemployment rate (denoted by U-6) is often much higher than the most commonly reported unemployment rate. For example, in June 2013, the conventionally measured unemployment rate averaged 7.8%, but the broader U-6 measure averaged 14.3%, painting a far direr picture of the situation in labor markets.

Two other important statistics are the **labor-force participation rate,** the percentage of the adult civilian population in the labor force,

$$\text{Labor-Force Participation Rate} = \frac{\text{Labor Force}}{\text{Adult Population}} \tag{16}$$

and the **employment ratio,** the percentage of the adult civilian population employed,

$$\text{Employment Ratio} = \frac{\text{Employed}}{\text{Adult Population}} \tag{17}$$

The pie chart in Figure 2.5 breaks the June 2013 adult civilian population into the three categories. From these data, we can calculate the labor force, the unemployment rate, the labor-force participation rate, and the employment ratio in June 2013.

Labor Force	$= 144.8 + 12.3 = 157.1 \text{ million}$
Unemployment Rate	$= 12.3/157.1 = 7.8\%$
Labor-Force Participation Rate	$= 157.1/245.6 = 64.0\%$
Employment Ratio	$= 144.8/245.6 = 59.0\%$

MyEconLab Real-time data

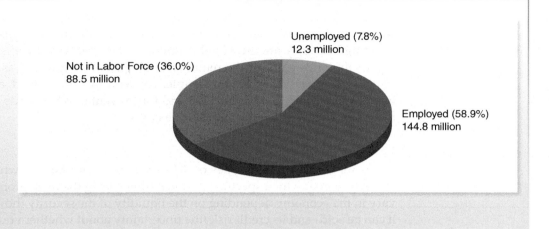

FIGURE 2.5

Unemployment in the Adult Civilian Population, 2013

The pie chart divides the U.S. adult civilian population into the three categories in June 2013, based on employment status.

Source: Federal Reserve Bank of St. Louis, FRED Database. http://research .stlouisfed.org/fred2/

Unemployed (7.8%)
12.3 million

Not in Labor Force (36.0%)
88.5 million

Employed (58.9%)
144.8 million

The data thus tell us that 64.0% of the population were in the labor force, 59.0% were employed, and 7.8% were unemployed. As we will see in Chapter 20, there have been dramatic changes in the labor markets over the past fifty years, with the labor-force participation rates falling over time for men but increasing for women.

MACROECONOMICS IN THE NEWS

Unemployment and Employment

The Bureau of Labor Statistics releases a report called *The Employment Situation* (found at www.bls.gov/news.release/empsit.nr0.htm) with data on the labor force, employment, and the unemployment rate, every month. This report presents statistics by age and race, so that we can calculate unemployment rates for different segments of the population, using two different surveys.

The unemployment rate that is reported in the media and is described in the text is based on the *household survey* of 60,000 households. An alternative survey, the *establishment survey*, collects responses from approximately 150,000 business *establishments* on employment, average hourly and weekly earnings, and hours worked. Sometimes these two surveys give a very different picture of what is happening in the labor market. For example, according to the establishment survey, the first year and a half after the 2001 recession ended constituted a "jobless recovery," with employment declining by one million jobs. In contrast, the household survey indicated that employment rose by over one million jobs during the same period.

Why do the two surveys sometimes give a different picture of conditions in the labor market? One reason is that the household survey counts *workers*, not jobs, while the establishment survey does the opposite. If a worker holds two jobs, he or she is counted twice in the establishment survey, but not in the household survey. Another reason is that the household survey counts the self-employed as working, while the establishment survey does not. A third reason is that the establishment survey is more extensive than the household survey: it covers more workers. The difference in the results from the two surveys illustrates that economic statistics can never be completely accurate and that we must always interpret them carefully.

Measuring Interest Rates

Interest rates are another prominent variable that macroeconomists study, so understanding how they are measured is important. An **interest rate** is the cost of borrowing, or the price paid for the rental of funds (usually expressed as a percentage of the rental of $100 per year). If, for example, you lend $100 to a friend, and he or she agrees in one year's time to pay you $105—$5 for the rental of the funds and $100 for repayment of the loan—then the interest rate is 5%.

Types of Interest Rates

There are many different types of debt securities, with **bonds,** which make payments on a regular basis for a specified period of time, being the most prominent. Interest rates vary in the economy depending on the liquidity of the security (how easily and quickly it can be sold) and its credit risk (the uncertainty about whether you will get paid back). We describe some of the most important interest rates that you read about in the newspaper in the Macroeconomics in the News box, "Interest Rates." Luckily, except in very unusual times, most interest rates move together, so throughout this book we usually treat all interest rates as being identical. We therefore talk about only one interest rate, *the* interest rate.

**MACROECONOMICS
IN THE NEWS**

Interest Rates

There are a number of interest rates that receive a lot of media attention. The most important ones are:

Prime rate: The base rate on corporate bank loans to "prime" (credit-worthy) borrowers. It is a good indicator of the cost of business borrowing from banks.

Federal funds rate: The interest rate charged on overnight loans between banks (referred to as federal funds because the loans are of deposits that are held at the Federal Reserve). The Federal Reserve targets this rate to conduct monetary policy.

London Inter-Bank Offered Rate (LIBOR): The interest rate that banks in London offer each other for inter-bank loans. It is a good indicator of short-term interest rate developments in international markets.

Treasury bill rate: The interest rate on U.S. Treasury bills (government bonds with maturities of less than one year). Interest rates on Treasury bills are a general indicator of short-term interest rate movements.

Ten-year Treasury bond rate: The interest rate on U.S. Treasury bonds with ten years to maturity. It is a general indicator of long-term interest rate movements.

Federal Home Loan Mortgage Corporation rate: The interest rate on Federal Home Loan Mortgage Corporation guaranteed mortgages, often called conforming mortgages. It is an indicator of the cost of financing residential mortgages.

These interest rates are reported daily in newspapers such as the *Wall Street Journal.* For historical data on these series, see the Federal Reserve Bank of St. Louis's FRED database (http://research.stlouisfed.org/fred2/).

Real Versus Nominal Interest Rates

An interest rate you read about in the newspaper is a **nominal interest rate** because it makes no allowance for inflation. The **real interest rate** is the amount of extra purchasing power a lender must be paid for the rental of his or her money. Hence, the real interest rate is the interest rate that is adjusted by subtracting expected changes in the price level (inflation) to accurately reflect the real cost of borrowing. This definition of the real interest rate is more precisely referred to as the *ex ante real interest rate* because it is adjusted for *expected* changes in the price level. The ex ante real interest rate is the interest rate that is most relevant to economic decisions, and typically is what economists mean when they make reference to the "real" interest rate. The interest rate that is adjusted for *actual* changes in the price level is called the *ex post real interest rate*. It describes how well a lender has done in real terms *after the fact*.

FISHER EQUATION. The **Fisher equation,** named for Irving Fisher, one of the great monetary economists of the twentieth century, defines the real interest rate in precise terms by stating that the nominal interest rate i equals the real interest rate plus the expected rate of inflation π^e:[6]

$$i = r + \pi^e \tag{18}$$

Rearranging terms, we find that the real interest rate equals the nominal interest rate minus the expected inflation rate:

$$r = i - \pi^e \tag{19}$$

To see why this definition makes sense, let us first consider a situation in which you have made a one-year loan with a 4% interest rate ($i = 4\%$) and you expect the price level to rise by 6% over the course of the year ($\pi^e = 6\%$). As a result of making the loan, at the end of the year you will have 2% less in real terms—that is, in terms of real goods and services you can buy. In this case, the Fisher definition indicates that the interest rate you have earned in terms of real goods and services is as follows:

$$r = 4\% - 6\% = -2\%$$

As a lender, you are clearly less eager to make a loan in this case, because in terms of real goods and services you have actually earned a negative interest rate of 2%. By contrast, as the borrower, you fare quite well because, at the end of the year, the amounts you will have to pay back will be worth 2% less in terms of goods and services—you as the borrower will be ahead by 2% in real terms. **When the real**

---

[6]The Fisher equation in Equation 18 is actually an approximation. A more precise formulation of the Fisher equation is as follows:

$$i = r + \pi^e + (r \times \pi^e)$$

because

$$1 + i = (1 + r)(1 + \pi^e) = 1 + r + \pi^e + (r \times \pi^e)$$

Subtracting 1 from both sides gives us the first equation in the footnote. For small values of r and π^e, the term $(r \times \pi^e)$ is so small that we can ignore it in Equation 18 in the text.

interest rate is low, there are greater incentives to borrow and invest, but fewer incentives to lend.

The Important Distinction Between Real and Nominal Interest Rates

The real interest rate, which reflects the real cost of borrowing, is likely to be a better indicator of the incentives to borrow, invest, and lend than the nominal interest rate. That is, real interest rates appear to be the best guide as to how people will be affected by what is happening in **credit markets,** the markets in which households and businesses get funds (credit) from each other. Figure 2.6, which presents estimates from 1955 to 2013 of the real (*ex ante*) and nominal interest rates on three-month U.S. Treasury bills (a short-term Treasury security with three months until maturity), shows that nominal and real rates often do not move together. (This is also true for nominal and real interest rates in the rest of the world.) In particular, when U.S. nominal rates were high in the 1970s, real rates were actually extremely low—often negative. By the standard of nominal interest rates, you would have thought that credit market conditions were tight in this period, because it was expensive to borrow. However, the estimates of the real rates indicate that you would have been mistaken. In real terms, the cost of borrowing was actually quite low.

Learning definitions and learning how data are measured are not always the most exciting of pursuits. Nonetheless, the work we have done in this chapter is crucial to understanding the macroeconomic phenomena that we examine in the rest of the book.

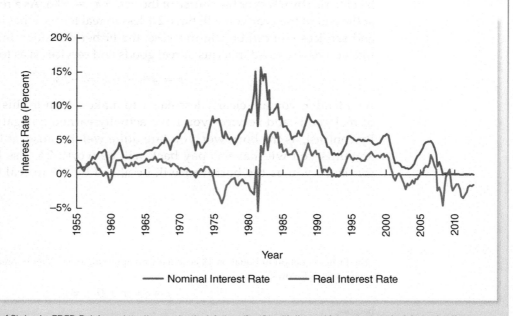

FIGURE 2.6

Real and Nominal Interest Rates (Three-Month Treasury Bill), 1955–2013

Nominal and real interest rates often do not move together. When U.S. nominal rates were high in the 1970s, real (ex ante) rates were actually extremely low—often negative.

Source: Federal Reserve Bank of St. Louis, FRED Database. http://research.stlouisfed.org/fred2/; with the real interest rate calculated using the procedure outlined in Mishkin, Frederic S. 1981. The real interest rate: An empirical investigation. *Carnegie-Rochester Conference Series on Public Policy* 15: 151–200.

SUMMARY

1. Gross domestic product (GDP) is the total market value of all final goods and services newly produced in the economy. We measure GDP in three ways: the production approach, the expenditure approach, and the income approach.

2. The production approach measures GDP by adding up the market value of all *final* goods and services that are *newly produced* in the economy over a *fixed period* of time.

3. The expenditure approach measures GDP by adding up the total spending on currently produced final goods and services in the economy. With this approach there are four basic categories of expenditure: consumption expenditure, investment, government purchases, and net exports. The fundamental identity of national income accounting says that GDP equals the sum of consumption expenditure, investment, government purchases, and net exports, that is, $Y = C + I + G + NX$.

4. The income approach measures GDP by adding up all the incomes received by households and firms in the economy, including profits and tax revenue to the government. In this approach, there are eight categories of income: compensation of employees, self-employment income, rental income, net interest income, indirect business taxes, corporate profits, depreciation, and net factor income.

5. Interpreting GDP requires distinguishing between real and nominal GDP. Real GDP provides the most information about the level of economic activity and equals nominal GDP adjusted for changes in the price level.

6. The inflation rate is the percentage rate of change of the price level, measured by a price index, over a particular period of time. The most popular price indexes are the consumer price index (CPI), the GDP deflator, and the personal consumption expenditure (PCE) deflator. There is a link between inflation, nominal GDP, and real GDP: the growth rate of nominal GDP equals the sum of the inflation rate and the growth rate of real GDP.

7. The unemployment rate is the percentage of people in the civilian population who want to work but are unemployed. The labor-force participation rate is the percentage of the adult civilian population in the labor force, and the employment ratio is the percentage of the adult civilian population that are employed.

8. The real interest rate is the nominal interest rate minus the expected rate of inflation, that is, $r = i - \pi^e$. It is a better measure of the incentives to borrow, invest, and lend than the nominal interest rate, and it is a more accurate indicator of the tightness of credit market conditions than the nominal interest rate.

KEY TERMS

bond, p. 40
capital good, p. 22
chain-weighted measures, p. 33
consumer price index (CPI), p. 34
consumption, p. 25
consumption expenditure, p. 25
credit markets, p. 42
discouraged workers, p. 37
employment ratio, p. 38
expenditure approach, p. 24
final goods and services, p. 21
Fisher equation, p. 41
flow, p. 23

fundamental identity of national income accounting, p. 20
GDP deflator, p. 33
government consumption, p. 26
government investment, p. 26
government purchases, p. 26
gross domestic product (GDP), p. 19
gross national product (GNP), p. 30
implicit price deflator for GDP, p. 33
imputed value, p. 21

income approach, p. 28
interest rate, p. 40
intermediate goods and services, p. 21
inventories, p. 22
inventory investment, p. 22
investment, p. 26
labor force, p. 38
labor-force participation rate, p. 38
national income, p. 30
national income accounting, p. 20

REVIEW QUESTIONS

All Questions are available in MyEconLab *for practice or instructor assignment.*

Measuring Economic Activity: National Income Accounting

1. What is the fundamental identity of national income accounting? What is its significance?

Measuring GDP: The Production Approach

2. How is GDP defined in the production approach to measuring economic activity? Explain how economists at the U.S. Department of Commerce's Bureau of Economic Analysis account for the production of goods and services that are not sold in markets, the production of intermediate goods and services, and the purchase of used goods and imported goods and services.

3. Distinguish between a flow measure and a stock measure. Which type of measure is GDP?

4. Why are capital goods and inventories treated differently from intermediate goods in the production approach to measuring GDP?

Measuring GDP: The Expenditure Approach

5. Identify the four major expenditure components in the national income identity and discuss the major subcategories of each component.

Measuring GDP: The Income Approach

6. What are the main types of income included in national income? Why doesn't national income equal GDP?

Real Versus Nominal GDP

7. How do macroeconomists distinguish between nominal and real values of variables? Does nominal GDP or real GDP provide a better picture of changes in economic activity and economic well-being? Why?

8. Describe the GDP deflator and the personal consumption expenditure deflator.

Measuring Inflation

9. What is the consumer price index, who calculates it, and how is it calculated and used to measure the inflation rate?

Measuring Interest Rates

11. Explain the differences between nominal and real interest rates and between ex ante and ex post real interest rates.

Measuring Unemployment

10. What does the unemployment rate measure, who calculates it, and how is it calculated?

PROBLEMS

All Problems are available in MyEconLab *for practice or instructor assignment.*

Measuring Economic Activity: National Income Accounting

1. Is it correct to assume that total income equals total expenditure for a household? What about for the whole economy?

Measuring GDP: The Production Approach

2. The inhabitants of Pandora value their natural environment (e.g., forests, springs, breathable air, etc.) twice as much as the inhabitants of Utopia. Suppose that the value added for all goods and services increases by the same amount in both countries, but has a negative effect on the environment (e.g., pollution).
   a) According to the production approach to the measurement of GDP, is this good or bad?

   b) Are both countries necessarily better off? Which country benefits more for sure?
   c) The inhabitants of Utopia are very concerned about income distribution, which is not that important for the inhabitants of Pandora. If the increase in value added results in further wealth concentration, how will this affect your answers to part (b)?

Measuring GDP: The Expenditure Approach

3. Consider the expenditure approach to the measurement of GDP. For each of the following situations, decide if the transaction will affect GDP and, if so, in which expenditure category will it be included.
   a) A household purchase of a home built in 2005.
   b) A household purchase of a newly built dishwasher.

   c) A farmer purchases a new tractor to work his or her field.
   d) A disabled individual receives a transfer from the U.S. government.
   e) The U.S. Department of Defense buys ten helicopters just built in Brazil.

Measuring GDP: The Income Approach

4. Use the following table, based on BEA data from the first quarter of 2013 (billions of dollars), to calculate items (a) and (b):
   a) Other income
   b) Net factor income

Compensation of employees	8,737
Corporate profits	2,021
National income	**14,313**
Gross domestic product	16,535
Gross national product	**16,772**
Factor income to the rest of the world	237

Real Versus Nominal GDP

5. Mario and Lucia are discussing current economic data printed in the morning newspaper. Mario is quite happy about the fact that nominal GDP has increased at a steady rate for the last two years and asserts that this is very good news, since it means they are better off than a few years ago. Lucia warns Mario about his conclusions and suggests that she has observed a steady increase in many prices during the same period, which might undermine Mario's conclusion. Based on this information:
   a) Who do you think is right? Explain why.
   b) Is it possible that Mario and Lucia could be worse off than two years ago?

Measuring Inflation

6. Based on surveys conducted by the BLS, the CPI basket assigns a weight of approximately 15% to transportation spending. Suppose you walk to your workplace every day and you do not use any other means of transportation.
   a) With everything else the same, if the price of transportation services increases by 10%, by how much would the CPI increase?
   b) Is the CPI measuring the true change in your cost of living?

7. Suppose that Apple Inc. manufactures a new generation of iPhones that can ascertain whether your interlocutor is lying. Assuming that the price of this good will be higher than that of the currently marketed iPhone, comment on the CPI's capability to correctly measure the corresponding change in the cost of living.

Measuring Unemployment

8. Use the accompanying table to calculate the following statistics for Brazil:
   a) Labor force
   b) Labor-force participation rate
   c) Unemployment rate

Adult Population (millions)	140
Unemployed (millions)	7
Employed (millions)	88

9. Refer to the previous exercise for data and assume that three million unemployed individuals become "discouraged" and decide not to look for a job anymore. Calculate the new unemployment rate for Brazil.

Measuring Interest Rates

10. Suppose you take out a loan at your local bank and the nominal interest rate is 12%. The bank expects the inflation rate to be 4% during the life of your loan.
    a) What is the bank's ex ante real interest rate?
    b) What is the bank's ex post real interest rate if the inflation rate happens to be larger than 4% during the life of this loan?
    c) As a borrower, would you benefit from a higher or lower actual inflation rate?

DATA ANALYSIS PROBLEMS

The Problems update with real-time data in MyEconLab and are available for practice or instructor assignment.

1. Go to the St. Louis Federal Reserve FRED database, and find the most recent values for Gross Domestic Product (GDP) and Gross National Product (GNP).
   a) Calculate net factor income using the most recent values.
   b) Based on the most recent values, explain whether foreign production by U.S. firms is larger than U.S. production by foreign firms, or vice versa.

2. Go to the St. Louis Federal Reserve FRED database and find the most recent values, and values from one year earlier, for nominal GDP (GDP) and real GDP (GDPC1).
   a) Compute the GDP price deflator for the most recent period and for one year prior to the most recent period. Express your answer relative to 100 in the base year.
   b) Using your answer to part (a) above, calculate the year-over-year inflation rate over the last year.
   c) Now, calculate the growth rate in real GDP and the growth rate in nominal GDP over the same one-year period. How do these values relate to your answer in part (b) above?

3. Go to the St. Louis Federal Reserve FRED database and find the most recent values of the unemployment rate (UNRATE), the labor force participation rate (CIVPART), and the labor force (CLF16OV). Using these values, calculate the number of people not in the labor force, the number of unemployed, the number of employed, and the employment ratio.

4. The U.S. Treasury issues some bonds as *Treasury Inflation Indexed Securities,* or *TIIS,* which are bonds adjusted for inflation: hence the yields can be roughly interpreted as real interest rates. Go to the St. Louis Federal Reserve FRED database and find the data on the following TIIS bonds to compare these yields with their nominal counterparts for the most recent available data, and answer the questions below.
   - 5 year U.S. treasury (DGS5) and 5 year TIIS (DFII5)
   - 7 year U.S. treasury (DGS7) and 7 year TIIS (DFII7)
   - 10 year U.S. treasury (DGS10) and 10 year TIIS (DFII10)
   - 20 year U.S. treasury (DGS20) and 20 year TIIS (DFII20)
   - 30 year U.S. treasury (DGS30) and 30 year TIIS (DFII30)
   a) Following the Great Recession of 2007–2009, the 5, 7, 10, and even the 20 year TIIS yields became negative for a period of time. How is this possible?
   b) For each of the bond pairs above, calculate the difference between the bonds (DGS5 – DFII5, etc.). What does this difference represent?
   c) Based on your answer to part (b) above, are there significant variations in the differences in the bond pairs? Interpret the magnitude of the variation in differences among the pairs.

Part 2

Macroeconomic Basics

Part 2 Macroeconomic Basics

We will now turn to constructing some basic frameworks that will serve as building blocks for our analysis in the rest of the book. Chapter 3 provides a framework for understanding production and thus the productive capacity of an economy. Chapter 4 and its appendix describe the relationship between saving and investment and how it affects the amount of wealth in the economy and real interest rates. Chapter 5 examines the links among money, inflation, and nominal interest rates, and discusses why inflation is costly. Its appendix outlines how the money supply is determined.

We will examine applications in each chapter to make the critical connection between theory and real-world practice:

- "Why Are Some Countries Rich and Others Poor?"
- "Explaining Real Wage Growth"
- "Oil Shocks, Real Wages, and the Stock Market"
- "How the United States Became the Largest Net Debtor in the World"
- "The Twin Deficits"
- "Testing the Quantity Theory of Money"
- "Testing the Fisher Effect"
- "Quantitative Easing and the Money Supply, 2007–2013"

In keeping with our focus on key policy issues and the techniques policymakers use in practice, we will also analyze the following specific examples in Policy and Practice cases:

- "Government Policies to Stimulate Saving"
- "Crowding Out and the Debate over the 2009 Fiscal Stimulus Package"
- "The Zimbabwean Hyperinflation"

3 Aggregate Production and Productivity

Preview

Traveling abroad, you will find stark differences in standards of living. Europeans and Americans live similarly well—yet if you travel to sub-Saharan Africa, you will see abject poverty and people living without the necessities of shelter, health care, and nutritious food. The average American produces over fifteen times that of a Nigerian, despite Nigeria's oil wealth. Why are Americans wealthy while Nigerians are poor? To answer questions like this, we first need to understand why some nations produce more than others. An economy's productive capacity—its ability to create goods and services—is central to the well-being of its citizens.

This chapter provides a framework for understanding production in the overall (aggregate) economy. After examining the fundamental *factors* of production, we will look at what determines their prices and the income they generate, as well as their share of national income.

Determinants of Aggregate Production

As you learned in Chapter 2, real gross domestic product (GDP) measures the amount of goods and services produced in an economy. Real GDP is determined by 1) the amount of inputs, or **factors of production,** that go into the production process, and 2) the *production function*, which tells us how much is produced from given quantities of the factors of production.

Factors of Production

In modern economies, the two most important factors of production are *labor* and *capital*. Economists measure **labor** by summing the numbers of hours people work, or person-hours, which we will denote by L. However, to simplify our discussion throughout the chapter, we will assume that the hours each person works are constant, so that we can use the number of workers as the unit for the labor input. **Capital** is the quantity of structures and equipment—such as factories, trucks, and computers—that workers use to produce goods and services, which we will denote by K. It is measured by the value of the capital stock in real terms, that is, in constant dollars. For now, we will overlook other factors of production—raw materials, energy, and land—so that we can first establish a basic framework.

Economists often put bars over letters in models to signify that the quantity is exogenous, that is, it is taken as given, a convention that we will use throughout this book. In this chapter we will assume that the quantity of capital and labor available in the economy is fixed, so

$$K = \overline{K}$$
$$L = \overline{L}$$

In later chapters, we will relax this assumption and treat these quantities as endogenous variables whose values vary over time. For simplicity, we will also assume for now that all of the capital and labor in the economy is fully utilized. We will see later on that factors of production are not fully utilized when people lose their jobs and factories sit idle.

Production Function

Given the quantities of labor and capital, how much output can an economy produce? The answer is provided by the **aggregate production function** (also referred to as the **production function**), which is a description of how much output, Y, is produced for any given amounts of factor inputs, such as K and L. We present the production function as follows:

$$Y = F(K, L) \tag{1}$$

with the F representing the function that translates K and L into a quantity of real output.

Cobb-Douglas Production Function

We can build on the basic idea of a production function by making two observations. First, an efficient, developed economy will generally produce more with the same quantity of capital and labor than an inefficient, primitive economy. Second, the shares of labor and capital income in the U.S. economy have remained relatively constant over time at about 70% labor and 30% capital, an observation we'll explore in more depth later.[1] The **Cobb-Douglas production function** incorporates both of these ideas:

$$Y = F(K, L) = AK^{0.3}L^{0.7} \tag{2}$$

The A variable describes **productivity** or, more precisely, **total factor productivity,** telling us how *productive* capital and labor are. In other words, it tells us how much output an economy can produce given one unit of capital and one unit of labor. If total factor productivity, A, goes up by 5%, then for the same amount of labor and capital, the total amount of goods and services produced in the economy increases by 5% under the Cobb-Douglas function.

---

[1]The more general form of the Cobb-Douglas production function is written as $Y = F(K, L) = AK^{\alpha}L^{1-\alpha}$. As will be demonstrated later in the chapter, the α exponent on K is equal to the capital share of national income, while the $1 - \alpha$ exponent on L is the labor share of national income. The choice of the value of $\alpha = 0.3$ is based on researchers' estimates from historical data.

We can also view productivity from the perspective of an economy's workers. We define **labor productivity** as the amount of output produced per unit of labor. Economists measure labor productivity by dividing measured output by the amount of labor input. This straightforward process leads the media to rely on labor productivity rather than total factor productivity. But it has drawbacks. For example, labor productivity can rise even when the productivity of labor and capital together are falling. For example, if Microsoft placed super-automatic espresso machines in every cubicle, its workers might produce slightly more software than before. It would be hard, however, to argue that the espresso machines were an efficient use of capital for producing software. Unlike labor productivity, total factor productivity takes into account how productive labor and capital are together. Throughout the text, when we discuss productivity, we will always be referring to total factor productivity.

We can directly measure the real level of output (Y), capital (K), and labor (L). The same is not true of total factor productivity, A. Thankfully, with the help of algebra, we can solve for A when given values for Y, K, and L, by dividing both sides of Equation 2 by $K^{0.3}L^{0.7}$ to yield the following:[2]

$$A = \frac{Y}{K^{0.3}L^{0.7}} \qquad (3)$$

Suppose that an economy has output, in constant (real) dollars (Y), of \$10 trillion, capital (K) of \$10 trillion, and labor (L) of 100 million workers. We then calculate A as follows:

$$A = \frac{10}{10^{0.3}100^{0.7}} = 0.20$$

The production function is then:

$$Y = 0.20 \times K^{0.3}L^{0.7} \qquad (4)$$

Application

Why Are Some Countries Rich and Others Poor?

The production function is a powerful concept that will have many uses in our study of macroeconomics. Here we use it to start answering a fundamental question: Why are some countries so rich and others so poor?

We measure how rich or poor a country is by its per capita income. For simplicity, we will assume that every citizen works, so that per capita income is the same as average income (output) per worker, Y/L. (We make this simplifying assumption because, although not everyone works, differences in income per worker provide a fair measure of the differences

[2]As we will discuss in Chapter 6, this measure of total factor productivity is referred to as a "Solow residual."

in per capita income.) We find income per worker, denoted by y, by dividing both sides of the Cobb-Douglas production function in Equation 2 by L:[3]

$$y = \frac{Y}{L} = \frac{AK^{0.3}L^{0.7}}{L} = \frac{AK^{0.3}}{L^{0.3}} = Ak^{0.3} \tag{5}$$

where $k = K/L =$ capital per worker.

Equation 5 thus tells us that income per worker equals the total factor productivity term A multiplied by the capital per worker, raised to the power 0.3. Assuming that the workers and population are the same, the production function then indicates that there are two sources of differences in per capita income:

1. the productive efficiency of the economy, represented by the total factor productivity term A, and

2. the amount of capital per person, represented by k.

Equation 5 thus motivates the study of long-run economic growth you will find in the next part of this book. Chapter 6 examines what determines the amount of capital per person, while Chapter 7 examines how technology and institutions affect the productive efficiency of the economy.

To make a country richer, the production-function analysis suggests that policymakers should increase productive efficiency and capital per person. But which should be the higher priority?

Table 3.1 allows us to distinguish between the effects of productivity and capital levels on an economy's relative wealth. It shows the per capita income of ten countries relative to the United States (with all values for the United States set to 1.00). As column 2 shows, the value of k of 1.05 for Japan indicates that Japan has 5% more capital per person than the United States. Column 3 indicates that if the United States and Japanese economies were equally productive (so that we can assume $A = 1.00$ for both countries and so y would equal $k^{0.3}$), we would expect Japan with $k^{0.3} = 1.01$ to have a 1% greater per capita income than the United States. But, as the fourth column shows, total factor productivity, A, in Japan is actually 70% of U.S. productivity. As a result, Japan's actual per capita output in column 5, as calculated from Equation 5, $y = Ak^{0.3}$, is 0.71—that is, 29% less than the United States. In other words, Japan's per capita income is lower than that of the United States due to the lower productivity of its economy, not its quantity of capital per person.

The poorer countries at the top of Table 3.1 tell a somewhat different story. China, for example, has substantially less capital per person, at only 26% of the U.S. level. This fact partially explains why China is poorer than the United States. But productivity also plays a big role. As the third column shows, Chinese per capita income would be 67% of the U.S. level if China were just as productive. In fact, per capita income in China is only 19% of United States per capita income, since Chinese total factor productivity is just 28% of the U.S. level.

Notice in Table 3.1 that column 4 is typically a smaller fraction than column 3, indicating that lower per capita income stems more from low total factor productivity than from low

---

[3]Note that $y = Y/L$ is also labor productivity and so Equation 5 not only provides information about the sources of per capita income growth, it also tells us about the sources of labor productivity growth. Equation 5 thus demonstrates that labor productivity can increase either because total factor productivity, A, increases, or because capital per worker, k, increases.

TABLE 3.1	PER CAPITA INCOME RELATIVE TO THE UNITED STATES FOR DIFFERENT COUNTRIES			
Country	Capital per Person	$k^{0.3}$	Total Factor Productivity, A	Per Capita Income, $y = Ak^{0.3}$
Nigeria	0.02	0.31	0.18	0.05
India	0.06	0.44	0.19	0.08
China	0.26	0.67	0.28	0.19
Brazil	0.25	0.66	0.33	0.22
Argentina	0.36	0.74	0.46	0.34
Italy	0.93	0.98	0.70	0.68
Japan	1.05	1.01	0.70	0.71
France	0.81	0.94	0.79	0.74
United Kingdom	0.61	0.86	0.88	0.76
Germany	0.83	0.94	0.86	0.81
United States	1.00	1.00	1.00	1.00

Source: Penn World Tables in Federal Reserve Bank of St. Louis, FRED Database. http://research.stlouisfed.org/fred2. The data are for the year 2011. Capital calculated as last period capital net of depreciation plus investment starting in 1960. Initial capital calculated by perpetual inventory method. Capital per person is taken as the ratio relative to the United States. Per capita income is GDP per capita relative to the United States. TFP is per capita income divided by capital raised to 0.3 (column 3).

capital. The conclusion from our analysis of Table 3.1 is therefore a striking one: *the short-fall of per capita income in other countries relative to the United States is due more to lower productivity than it is to lower amounts of capital per person.*

Cobb-Douglas Production Function Characteristics

The Cobb-Douglas production function has two particularly attractive characteristics that give it a prominent role in the study of macroeconomics: 1) it displays *constant returns to scale*, and 2) it has *diminishing marginal product*. We explain each of these points in turn and examine them with historical data.

CONSTANT RETURNS TO SCALE. The Cobb-Douglas production function displays **constant returns to scale**: if you increase all the factor inputs by the same percentage, then output increases by exactly the same percentage. Put simply, doubling the inputs doubles the output, which makes intuitive sense. If a company can build 1,000 vehicles a month with one fully staffed factory, it should be able to produce 2,000 vehicles a month with two identical fully staffed factories.

We can verify that constant returns to scale are true for the Cobb-Douglas production function by substituting $2\overline{K}$ and $2\overline{L}$ into Equation 4:

$$Y = F(2\overline{K}, 2\overline{L}) = 0.20(2\overline{K})^{0.3}(2\overline{L})^{0.7}$$

$$= 0.20 \times (2^{0.3}2^{0.7}) \times \overline{K}^{0.3}\overline{L}^{0.7} = (2^{(0.3+0.7)}) \times F(\overline{K}, \overline{L})$$

$$= (2^{1.0}) \times F(\overline{K}, \overline{L}) = 2 \times F(\overline{K}, \overline{L})$$

DIMINISHING RETURNS. The Cobb-Douglas production function also has **diminishing marginal product,** which means that as the amount of one factor input increases, holding other inputs constant, the increased amount of output from an extra unit of the input (its **marginal product**) declines. To illustrate, let's write down the production function for a given amount of labor input, say, 100 million workers.

$$Y = 0.20 \times K^{0.3}(100)^{0.7} = 0.20 \times K^{0.3}(25.1) = 5.0 \times K^{0.3} \tag{6}$$

Figure 3.1 plots the production function F relating output to capital. Notice that the production function is upward sloping: as capital increases, output goes up. Further, as capital increases, the slope, $\Delta Y/\Delta K$, falls. For example, going from point 1 to point 2, the capital stock rises from \$5 to \$6 trillion for a change, ΔK, of \$1 trillion. This rise in capital then leads to output rising from \$8.1 trillion to \$8.6 trillion, for a change of \$0.5 trillion. The slope at point 1 is then 0.5 ($\Delta Y/\Delta K = 0.5/1.0$). Now let's look at the slope at point 3, where the capital stock is \$9 trillion and output is \$9.7 trillion. In going to point 4, where the capital stock rises by \$1 trillion, output rises to \$10 trillion. The slope at point 3 is then $\Delta Y/\Delta K = 0.3/1.0 = 0.3$, which is less than the 0.5 slope at point 1.

The slope of the production function $\Delta Y/\Delta K$, the **marginal product of capital (MPK),** indicates how much output increases for each additional unit of capital, holding other inputs constant. Thus another way to describe the slope of the production function is that *as the capital stock increases, the marginal product of capital declines.* In other words, there is diminishing marginal product of capital.

MyEconLab Mini-lecture

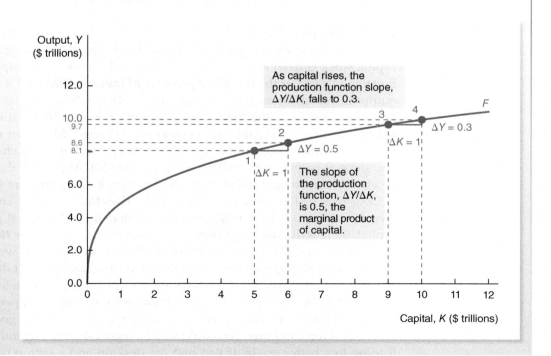

FIGURE 3.1

Production Function Relating Output and Capital

The production function for an amount of labor = 100 million workers. It is upward sloping—as capital increases, output goes up—and it displays diminishing marginal product of capital—as capital increases, the slope, $\Delta Y/\Delta K$, falls.

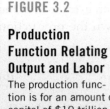

FIGURE 3.2

Production Function Relating Output and Labor

The production function is for an amount of capital of $10 trillion. It is upward sloping—as labor increases, output goes up—and it displays diminishing marginal product of labor—as labor increases, the slope, $\Delta Y/\Delta L$, falls.

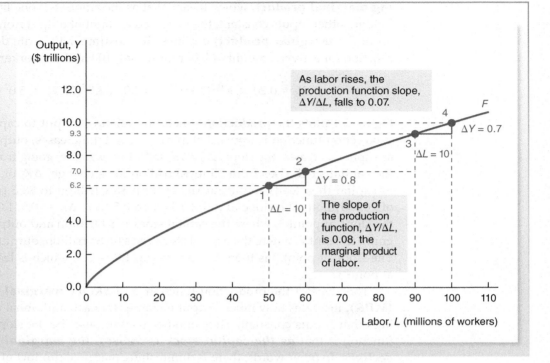

We can demonstrate the same effect when the other input, labor, increases. We write down the production function for a given amount of capital, say $10 trillion.

$$Y = 0.20(10)^{0.3} L^{0.7} = 0.20(2.0) L^{0.7} = 0.4 L^{0.7} \tag{7}$$

which is plotted in Figure 3.2.

Figure 3.2 shows the production function F that relates output to labor when the capital stock is fixed at $10 trillion. As Figure 3.2 shows, the slope of the production function, $\Delta Y/\Delta L$, is the **marginal product of labor (MPL),** and it indicates how much output increases for each additional unit of labor, holding capital constant at $10 trillion. For example, going from point 1 to point 2, it's evident that the amount of labor rises from fifty to sixty million workers for a change, ΔL, of ten million. This rise in labor then leads to output rising from $6.2 to $7.0 trillion, for a change of $0.8 trillion. The slope at point 1 is then 0.08 ($\Delta Y/\Delta L = 0.8/10$). At point 3, the amount of labor is ninety million workers and output is $9.3 trillion. In going to point 4, where the amount of labor rises by ten million workers, output rises to $10 trillion. The slope at point 3 is then $\Delta Y/\Delta L = 0.7/10 = 0.07$, which is less than the 0.08 slope at point 1. Just as with capital, there is diminishing marginal product of labor, that is, **as the amount of labor input increases, the marginal product of labor declines.** As we add more of either input, while holding the other one constant, its marginal product decreases.

To illustrate, think about what happens if you have to write a term paper with very little capital, say, just a pen and paper. Because handwriting a paper is time-consuming, you might have little time to research and produce a not-very-good five-page paper. With a desktop computer, you could write a higher-quality paper that's ten pages long, leading to a better grade. If you had the desktop and a laptop computer, you could be even more productive, since you could type your great thoughts even when away from home and might write a twelve-page paper. Notice how adding the first computer allowed you to write five more pages, while adding the second computer increased the paper's size by only two pages. The marginal product of capital is still positive, but it will have fallen, just as the production function indicates.

CALCULATING THE MARGINAL PRODUCT OF CAPITAL AND LABOR. We can calculate the marginal product of capital and labor from Equations 6 and 7 with a little bit of calculus.[4] The marginal product of capital and labor is as follows:[5]

$$MPK = 0.3\,Y/K \tag{8}$$

and

$$MPL = 0.7\,Y/L \tag{9}$$

Changes in the Production Function: Supply Shocks

So far we have been assuming that an economy's production function remains constant over time. The production function can shift, however, which we refer to as a **supply shock,** a change in the output an economy can produce from the same amount of capital and labor. In other words, a supply shock involves a change in A, total factor productivity. **Positive (or favorable) supply shocks** result in an increase in the quantity of output produced for given combinations of capital and labor, while **negative (or adverse) supply shocks** lead to a decline in the quantity of output produced from given quantities of capital and labor. Negative shocks are less common, but can occur if, for example, burdensome government regulations make the economy less productive.

TYPES OF SUPPLY SHOCKS. Supply shocks come in several varieties that we will discuss in turn.

1. Technology Shocks: Technological advances, such as the development of a faster computer chip, can raise total factor productivity so that the A parameter in the production function rises.

---

[4]Equation 8 comes directly from differentiating Equation 6 with respect to K.
$$\mathrm{d}Y/\mathrm{d}K = 0.3 \times 5.0K^{(0.3-1)} = 0.3 \times 5.0/K^{0.7} = 0.3 \times 5.0\,Y/(5.0K^{0.3}K^{0.7})$$
$$= 0.3 \times Y/K$$
Equation 9 comes directly from differentiating Equation 7 with respect to L.
$$\mathrm{d}Y/\mathrm{d}L = 0.7 \times 0.4L^{(0.7-1)} = 0.7 \times 0.4/L^{0.3} = 0.7 \times 0.4Y/(0.4L^{0.7}L^{0.3})$$
$$= 0.7 \times Y/L$$
[5]These calculations can be used to show how marginal products change with changes in A, K, or L. Substituting for Y using the production function from Equation 2, $MPK = 0.3AK^{0.3}L^{0.7}/K = 0.3A\,L^{0.7}/K^{0.7}$. As K goes up, the denominator rises and so the marginal product of capital, MPK, necessarily falls, showing that there is diminishing marginal product of capital. On the other hand, if A or L rises, then the numerator rises and so the marginal product of capital rises. Similarly, $MPL = 0.7AK^{0.3}L^{0.7}/L = 0.7A\,K^{0.3}/L^{0.3}$. As L goes up, the denominator increases and the marginal product of labor, MPL, also falls, indicating that there is diminishing marginal product of labor. If A or K rises, then the numerator rises and so the marginal product of labor rises.

FIGURE 3.3

Response of the Production Function to a Negative Supply Shock

A negative supply shock shifts the production function downward from F_1 to F_2 in both panels (a) and (b). At any given level of capital, say, K_1, the slope of the production function in panel (a), the marginal product of capital, declines when the production function shifts from F_1 to F_2. At any given level of labor, say, L_1, the slope of the production function in panel (b), the marginal product of labor, declines when the production function shifts from F_1 to F_2.

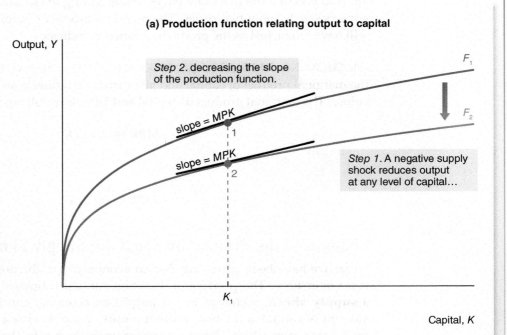

(a) Production function relating output to capital

Output, Y

Step 2. decreasing the slope of the production function.

slope = MPK
1

slope = MPK
2

F_1

F_2

Step 1. A negative supply shock reduces output at any level of capital…

K_1

Capital, K

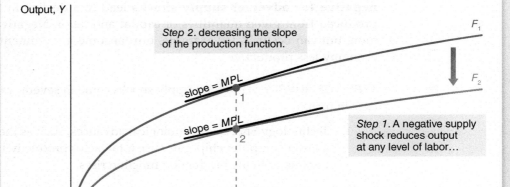

(b) Production function relating output to labor

Output, Y

Step 2. decreasing the slope of the production function.

slope = MPL
1

slope = MPL
2

F_1

F_2

Step 1. A negative supply shock reduces output at any level of labor…

L_1

Labor, L

2. Natural Environment Shocks: Blizzards, droughts, floods, earthquakes, and hurricanes can slow construction activity to a grind, reducing output for a given level of capital and labor. An unusually warm winter may have the opposite effect.

3. Energy Shocks: Energy is an important factor of production separate from capital or labor. When energy supplies are disrupted—for example, when OPEC cuts back on the production of oil to raise prices—firms use less energy, causing the amount of output the economy produces to fall for a given quantity of capital and labor.

EFFECT OF A SUPPLY SHOCK. We can clearly see the effect of a supply shock on the aggregate production function by considering a Middle Eastern war that disrupts global oil supplies. This negative supply shock reduces output for any given level of capital and labor and so causes A to fall. As a result, in panels (a) and (b) of Figure 3.3, the production function shifts downward from F_1 to F_2. In addition, as you can see in Figure 3.3, for any given quantities of labor or capital, say K_1 and L_1, when moving from point 1 to point 2, the slope of the production function also declines—that is, the marginal product of both capital and labor fall.[6] When the negative supply shock causes the level of output to fall for a given quantity of capital and labor, the decline in the numerators in both Equations 8 and 9 means marginal product of capital and labor both fall.

Supply shocks therefore have the following impact: ***a negative supply shock causes the aggregate production function to shift downward and also causes the marginal products of capital and labor to fall.*** Reversing the reasoning, we have the following: ***a positive supply shock causes the aggregate production to shift upward and raises the marginal products of capital and labor.***

Determination of Factor Prices

The production function enables us to make some interesting predictions about the level of wages and rental costs of capital. This will also help us to see how the economy distributes national income to workers and capital owners. We conduct this analysis under a *classical framework*, assuming the economy has *perfect competition* and is at its long-term equilibrium level. By **perfect competition,** we mean that firms take market prices as given because they are not large or powerful enough to charge more than the market price for their goods or services. Also, firms are not powerful enough to pay their workers less than the market wage, nor are groups of workers, such as unions, powerful enough to get wages above the market wage. By long-run equilibrium, we mean here that everyone who wants work can find it, and all factories and other capital

---

[6]We can also confirm this downward slope directly from Equations 8 and 9, which show that because Y is in the numerators of both equations, as Y falls when the production function shifts downward, the marginal products of capital and labor also fall.

are utilized, so that quantity of labor and capital supplied equals quantity demanded. These assumptions, of course, may not hold at every moment in every country, but they serve as useful benchmarks to understand how factor prices are determined.

Demand for Capital and Labor

The more capital and labor employed by firms, the more they can produce and sell. But adding capital and labor adds costs, reducing profit.

ECONOMIC PROFITS. **Economic profits** are the revenue from selling goods and services, minus the costs of the inputs.[7] Key components of economic profit include the following:

1. *The revenue from selling goods and services* is the average level of the prices of goods and services, P, times the amount of goods and services sold, Y: using the production function, the revenue $P \times Y$ is $P \times F(K, L)$.

2. *The cost of using capital* is the price paid to rent the capital, often referred to as the **rental price of capital,** R, times the amount of capital, K, that is, RK.[8]

3. *The cost of labor* is the price of labor, the **wage rate,** W, times the amount of labor, L, that is, WL.

We write nominal economic profits (or cost) as follows:

$$P \times F(K, L) - RK - WL$$

However, what firms and households care about are profits in terms of what they can buy, that is, real economic profits. We divide the preceding expression by the price level, P, to get real economic profits, Π:

$$\Pi = F(K, L) - (R/P)K - (W/P)L$$

We define the **real rental price (or cost) of capital,** r_c, as the rental price of capital in terms of goods and services, which is the nominal rental price of capital divided by the price level—that is, $r_c = (R/P)$. Similarly, the **real wage rate** is the wage in term of goods and services, which can be written as the nominal wage rate divided by the price level, $w = (W/P)$.[9] Hence the expression for real economic profits can be written as:

$$\Pi = F(K, L) - r_cK - wL \tag{10}$$

---

[7]Note that economic profits differ from accounting profits because most firms own their own capital and so we add the capital bill, RK, to economic profits to determine accounting profits.

[8]The concept of the rental price of capital is intuitively thought of as the rental payments that the owner of a unit of capital receives each period from the person or business that uses the capital. For example, the rent that a student pays for his or her apartment is the rental price of capital for the apartment. Similarly, the wage rate is the rent that a worker receives from supplying his or her labor each period.

[9]We denote the real rental cost of capital as r_c to distinguish it from r, the real rate of interest, which is the notation used elsewhere in the text, because although they are related, they do differ.

We can maximize the real profit function subject to choices about K and L through calculus[10] or intuition; here we take the intuitive route. Profit maximization implies first that ***firms will want an amount of capital that will make the marginal product of capital equal to the real rental price of capital:***

$$MPK = r_c \qquad (11)$$

Maximizing profits also implies that ***firms will hire an amount of labor that will make the marginal product of labor equal to the real wage rate:***

$$MPL = w \qquad (12)$$

Let's first examine the result in Equation 11. When firms have too little capital—consider firms in a poor African country with rudimentary factories—they can produce and sell significantly more by outfitting their factories with machines and other capital. The boost in revenue vastly outweighs the cost of the capital itself. Or, as an economist might say, the marginal product of capital exceeds the real rental cost of capital, $MPK > r_c$, so that adding more capital raises profits. As firms continue to add more capital, the effect of the diminishing marginal product of capital kicks in, so that each additional unit of capital boosts revenue by less and less. Eventually, as more capital is added, the marginal product of capital just equals the real rental cost of capital and $MPK = r_c$. At this point, firms will stop adding capital, because doing so would reduce profit.

What if firms kept adding capital even after this point, so that there was a surplus of capital in the economy? At this point, the marginal product of capital will be very low and below the real rental cost of capital $MPK < r_c$. Firms could increase their profits by reducing the amount of capital, since the cost is above the extra revenue it produces. Firms will therefore keep cutting the amount of capital until the marginal product of capital, MPK, rises up to the real rental price of capital r_c and Equation 11 holds.

The same type of argument explains why the condition in Equation 12 also holds. If firms have very little labor in their factories, the marginal product of labor will be higher than the real wage rate, $MPL > w$. Adding workers increases profits since the additional revenue from the output they produce will exceed their wage cost. Firms will then keep adding workers until the marginal product of labor falls to the real wage rate and Equation 12 holds where $MPL = w$. Similarly, if the marginal product of labor is below the real wage rate, $MPL < w$, then firms would rationally lay workers off because the revenue the extra workers generate is below their wage cost. Firms will shed enough workers to raise the marginal product of labor MPL to the level of the real wage w.

---

[10]To get the first-order conditions, we partially differentiate the profit function in Equation 10 with respect to K and L and set the partial derivatives to zero. Doing this for capital,

$$\partial\Pi/\partial K = \partial Y/\partial K - r_c = MPK - r_c = 0$$

Rearranging terms, the first-order condition for capital is as follows:

$$MPK = r_c$$

Going through the same computation for labor,

$$\partial\Pi/\partial L = \partial Y/\partial L - w = MPL - w = 0$$

Rearranging terms, the first-order condition for labor is as follows:

$$MPL = w$$

We can summarize the conclusion from the profit-maximizing conditions in Equations 11 and 12 in a slightly different way: ***firms demand additional quantities of each factor of production (labor and capital) until the marginal product of that factor falls to its real factor price.***

DEMAND CURVE ANALYSIS. In panels (a) and (b) of Figure 3.4, we plot the marginal products of both labor and capital. The MPL and MPK curves are downward sloping: as the quantity of the factor increases, diminishing marginal product implies that the marginal product for that factor falls. Since the quantity of the factor demanded occurs at the point where the marginal product equals the real factor price, the marginal product curves indicate the quantity of the input demanded for any given real factor price. Hence the marginal product of labor curve is also the demand curve for labor, and we therefore mark it as both MPL and D^L in panel (a), while the marginal product of capital curve is the demand curve for capital, and we label it as MPK and D^K in panel (b).

Supply of Capital and Labor

Now that we've established the quantity of capital and labor firms will demand and plotted the demand curves, we consider the supply side of the picture.

Recall that a supply curve shows the relationship between the quantity of the factor supplied and any given real factor price. As we mentioned earlier, we will assume that the quantity of capital and labor are given at fixed values, $\overline{L}$ and $\overline{K}$. The quantity supplied of each of these factors then remains unchanged for any given factor price. We portray the supply curves for labor and capital, marked as S^L and S^K in Figure 3.4 panels (a) and (b), as vertical lines at $\overline{L}$ and $\overline{K}$, respectively.

Factor Market Equilibrium

As you'll recall from your principles of economics course, with a supply and a demand curve, we can now study the *market equilibrium*, in which the amount that firms are willing to buy (*demand*) equals the amount that the owners of the factors of production are willing to sell (*supply*) at a given price. In the factor markets, market equilibrium is achieved when the quantity of the factor demanded equals the quantity of the factor supplied. Equilibrium in the market for labor means

$$D^L = S^L \tag{13}$$

And in the capital market, it means

$$D^K = S^K \tag{14}$$

In Figure 3.4 panels (a) and (b), the equilibrium in both markets occurs at point E, at which the real wage rate is w^* and the real rental price of capital is r_c^*.

EXCESS SUPPLY. The concept of market equilibrium is useful because there is a tendency for the market to head toward it. In panels (a) and (b) of Figure 3.4, notice what happens when we have a real factor price that is above the equilibrium price: the quantity demanded of the factor at point A is less than the quantity supplied at point B. We call this situation where the quantity demanded of a factor is less than the quantity supplied a condition of **excess supply.** Because the owners of the factors want to sell more

MyEconLab Mini-lecture

FIGURE 3.4

Supply and Demand Analysis of the Factor Markets

The marginal product curves for both labor and capital are downward sloping and are the same as the demand curves for labor and capital. Equilibrium in panels (a) and (b) occurs at point E, where the quantity of the factor demanded equals the quantity of the factor supplied. The equilibrium real wage rate in panel (a) is w^* and the equilibrium real rental price of capital in panel (b) is r_c^*. When the real factor price is above the equilibrium price, the quantity supplied at point B is greater than the quantity demanded at point A, and the resulting condition of excess supply causes the factor price to fall, as shown by the downward arrow. When the real factor price is below the equilibrium price, the quantity supplied at point C is less than the quantity demanded at point D, and the resulting condition of excess demand causes the factor price to rise, as shown by the upward arrow.

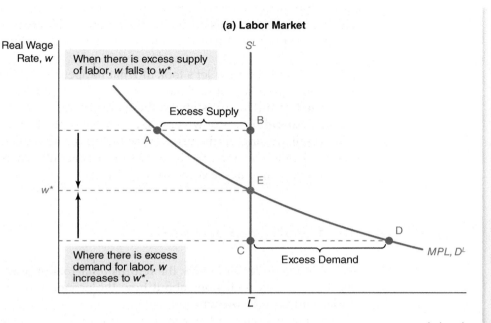

(a) Labor Market

When there is excess supply of labor, w falls to w^*.

Excess Supply

Where there is excess demand for labor, w increases to w^*.

MPL, D^L

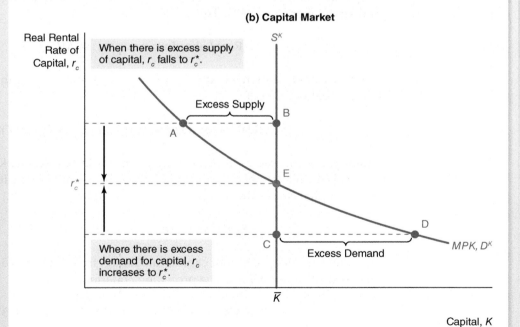

(b) Capital Market

When there is excess supply of capital, r_c falls to r_c^*.

Excess Supply

Where there is excess demand for capital, r_c increases to r_c^*.

MPK, D^K

of them than firms demand, their price will fall, which is why the downward arrows are drawn in panels (a) and (b) of Figure 3.4. As long as the factor price remains above the equilibrium price, there will continue to be an excess supply of the factor, and the price will continue to fall. This decline will stop only when the factor price has reached the equilibrium price of w^* and r_c^* in Figure 3.4 panels (a) and (b).

EXCESS DEMAND. Now let's look at what happens when the factor price is below the equilibrium price at points C and D in panels (a) and (b) of Figure 3.4. The quantity demanded of the factor is above the quantity supplied, so we are in a condition of **excess demand.** Firms now want to buy more of the factor than owners of the factors want to sell, driving up the price of the factors, as illustrated by the upward arrows in Figure 3.4 panels (a) and (b). The price stops rising only when the excess demand for the factor is eliminated at the equilibrium price.

Distribution of National Income

Now that we understand how the returns to factors of production are determined, we can draw some conclusions about how the economy distributes national income to workers and capital owners.

The income paid to labor in real terms, real labor income, is the real wage times the quantity of labor. As we have shown previously, the real wage equals the marginal product of labor, $w = MPL$. Thus,

$$\text{Real Labor Income} = wL = MPL \times L$$

We know from Equation 9 that $MPL = 0.7\ Y/L$ and, substituting this for MPL in the preceding equation, we get

$$\text{Real Labor Income} = 0.7\ (Y/L) \times L = 0.7Y \tag{15}$$

Similarly, the income paid to owners of capital in real terms, known as real capital income, is the real rental price of capital times the quantity of capital, $r_c K$. The real rental price of capital equals the marginal product of capital, $r_c = MPK$, so

$$\text{Real Capital Income} = r_c K = MPK \times K$$

From the marginal product of capital calculation from Equation 8, $MPK = 0.3\ Y/K$, we can substitute in for MPK in the preceding equation,

$$\text{Real Capital Income} = 0.3\ (Y/K) \times K = 0.3Y \tag{16}$$

As you might expect, adding real labor and capital income together yields $Y\ (= 0.7Y + 0.3Y)$, the total amount of output produced in the economy, which we saw in Chapter 2, equals national income, the sum of real labor income and real capital income. Therefore,

$$\text{National Income} = Y = 0.7Y + 0.3Y = \text{Real Labor Income} + \text{Capital Income} \tag{17}$$

National income is thus divided between payments to labor and payments to capital, with the size and quantities of these payments determined by the marginal products of labor and capital.

Another way of looking at how income is distributed to capital and labor is to look at the shares of national income, which involves dividing Equations 15 and 16 by Y:

$$\text{Labor Income Share} = wL/Y = 0.7Y/Y = 0.7 \tag{18}$$

$$\text{Capital Income Share} = r_cK/Y = 0.3\,Y/Y = 0.3 \tag{19}$$

The labor income share of 0.7 is the value of the exponent on labor in the Cobb-Douglas production function that we defined in Equation 2, while the capital income share of 0.3 is the value of the exponent on capital in the production function. Most importantly, if the Cobb-Douglas production function is correct, then **the shares of labor income and capital income in national income do not change even as the total level of income rises and falls.** This prediction from the Cobb-Douglas production function is exactly what we see in the data: labor's share in national income has been remarkably steady at around 70% of national income over the last sixty years.

The Cobb-Douglas production function has the sensible property that aggregate production displays constant returns to scale. In addition, it is consistent with the empirical fact that the shares of national income going to capital and labor have remained pretty constant despite an economy that has grown substantially over the last sixty years. As the following two applications show, the Cobb Douglas production function can also help explain real wage growth and the effect of oil price shocks on the stock market.

Application

Explaining Real Wage Growth

While the wages of American workers have risen over the decades, the rate of change has varied quite considerably over time. As Table 3.2 indicates, real wages—including nonsalary compensation such as health and pension benefits—on average grew 2.3% per year from 1959 to 1973, but only 0.7% over the next twenty-two years. Since then, from 1995 to 2012, real wage growth accelerated, averaging 1.3% per year. What explains the changing trend rate of growth in real wages?

Our analysis of factor price determination provides the answer. As shown by Equation 9, real wages are determined by the marginal product of labor: $w = MPL = 0.7\,(Y/L)$. The term Y/L, output per unit of labor, is labor productivity,[11] and the fact that real wages are proportional to labor productivity implies that real wages and labor productivity should grow at close to the same rate. Indeed, the numbers in Table 3.2 bear out this relationship. Notice the very close correspondence between the growth rate of real wages and the growth rate of labor productivity. As labor productivity growth slowed from 2.9% to 1.4% after 1973, real wage growth

---

[11]To keep things simple, we have used the number of workers as the unit of labor. However, because the amount of hours that people work has changed over time, it is more accurate to define the quantity of labor as the total number of hours worked, which equals the number of workers times the average number of hours they work. In this case, the unit of labor used to compute labor productivity is hours worked, so that labor productivity is measured as output per hours worked.

TABLE 3.2	GROWTH IN LABOR U.S. PRODUCTIVITY AND REAL WAGES	
Period	**Growth Rate of Labor Productivity (%)**	**Growth Rate of Real Wages (%)**
1959–1973	2.9	2.3
1973–1995	1.4	0.7
1995–2012	2.5	1.3

Source: Bureau of Labor Statistics. http://www.bls.gov/data/

declined from 2.3% to 0.7%. As labor productivity growth climbed from 1.4% to 2.5% after 1995, real wage growth jumped from 0.7% to 1.3%.

Economists debate the causes of the labor productivity growth slowdown after 1973. One possible factor is the sharp rise in energy prices that occurred around that time. After 1995, productivity gains from personal computers and information technology seem to have fueled productivity growth. Although we are not entirely sure what shaped the trend in labor productivity growth, changes in the trend rate of growth of real wages are clearly related to the trend rate of growth of labor productivity.

Application

Oil Shocks, Real Wages, and the Stock Market

The U.S. economy has experienced three oil price shocks in the last forty years. After each, both real wages and stock market prices fell. Our supply and demand analysis of factor prices can help explain why a sudden rise in oil prices could trigger these outcomes.

Earlier we saw that a negative supply shock reduces the marginal product of labor for any given level of labor and capital (Figure 3.3). Hence, the demand curve for labor shifts down and to the left from D_1^L to D_2^L, as shown in panel (a) of Figure 3.5. With labor supply fixed at $\bar{L}$, equilibrium in the labor market moves from point 1 to point 2, and the real wage rate falls from w_1 to w_2. This prediction of our supply and demand analysis is borne out in the data. In the aftermath of the first oil price shock in 1973–1974, real wages fell 1.9%. When the second oil price shock hit in 1979–1980, real wages again fell, by 1.1%. The most recent oil price shock in 2007–2008 was followed by a decline in real wages of 2.4%.

Negative supply shocks also reduce the marginal product of capital, so the demand curve for capital shifts down and to the left, from D_1^K to D_2^K, in Figure 3.5 panel (b). With the supply of capital fixed in the short term, we would expect the real rental price of capital to fall from r_{c1} to r_{c2}. Think of common stocks as a claim on the income generated by firms' capital: the decline in the real rental price of capital suggests that stock prices will fall when the rental income from capital has fallen. Indeed, this is exactly what happened. From 1973 to 1975, after the first oil shock, stock prices declined by around 25%. After the second oil shock in 1979–1980, the stock market declined again, falling by 7% from 1980 to 1981. The most recent oil shock in 2007–2008 coincided with a 50% decline in the stock market from

MyEconLab Mini-lecture

FIGURE 3.5

Effect of a Negative Supply Shock on Real Wage and the Real Rental Price of Capital

A negative supply shock reduces the marginal product of labor for any given level of labor and capital. In panel (a), the demand curve for labor shifts down and to the left from D_1^L to D_2^L and the real wage rate falls from w_1 to w_2 at the new equilibrium of point 2. A negative supply shock also leads to a decline in the marginal product of capital, shifting the demand curve for capital down and to the left from D_1^K to D_2^K in panel (b). At the new equilibrium, point 2, the real rental price of capital falls from r_{c1} to r_{c2}, leading to a stock market decline.

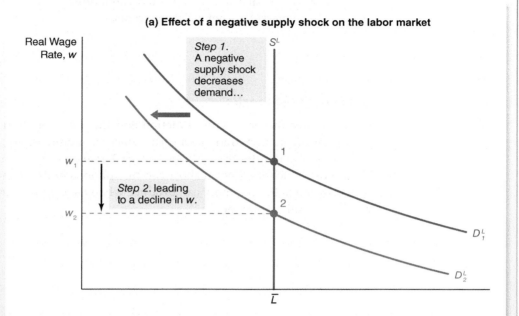

(a) Effect of a negative supply shock on the labor market

Step 1. A negative supply shock decreases demand...

Step 2. leading to a decline in w.

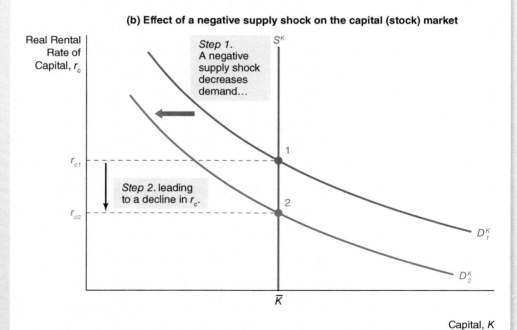

(b) Effect of a negative supply shock on the capital (stock) market

Step 1. A negative supply shock decreases demand...

Step 2. leading to a decline in r_c.

2007 to 2009. While a financial crisis in that period contributed to the sharp decline in stock prices, the oil shock may have exacerbated the losses.

If you are an investor or a worker—and you'll probably soon be both—negative supply shocks in the oil market are not welcome events.

Concluding Remarks

Our analysis of the production function and the determination of factor prices paves the way for an examination of long-run macroeconomic issues, including the relative wealth and growth rates of countries, in Part 3. It also is a basic building block for Part 4 of this book, which focuses on short-run fluctuations in the economy. The analysis will tell us how much the economy can produce when its resources are fully utilized, that is, when it is at full employment.

SUMMARY

1. The aggregate production function tells us how much output an economy produces for given amounts of factor inputs, capital and labor. The Cobb-Douglas production function, $Y = F(K, L) = AK^{0.3}L^{0.7}$, displays constant returns to scale: when all the factor inputs increase by the same percentage, aggregate output increases by exactly the same percentage. The Cobb-Douglas production function also displays diminishing marginal product: as the amount of a specific factor input increases, holding other inputs constant, its marginal product decreases. Positive supply shocks result in an increase in the quantity of output and marginal products of factors for any given combination of capital and labor, while negative supply shocks do the opposite.

2. Profit maximization indicates that firms demand a quantity of each factor of production (labor and capital) up until the marginal product of that factor falls to its real factor price, that is, $MPK = R/P = r_c$ and $MPL = W/P = w$. Hence, the marginal product curves for each factor are also the demand curves for each factor. Factor prices are determined at the intersection of the demand and supply curves for each factor.

3. National income is divided between payments to capital and payments to labor, with the sizes of these payments determined by the marginal products of capital and labor. Capital and labor income shares of national income do not change even as the level of income grows over time.

KEY TERMS

adverse supply shock, p. 57

aggregate production function, p. 51

capital, p. 50

Cobb-Douglas production function, p. 51

constant returns to scale, p. 54

diminishing marginal product, p. 55

economic profits, p. 60

excess demand, p. 64

excess supply, p. 62

factors of production, p. 50

favorable supply shock, p. 57

labor, p. 50

labor productivity, p. 52

marginal product, p. 55

marginal product of capital, p. 55

marginal product of labor, p. 56

negative supply shock, p. 57

perfect competition, p. 59

positive supply shock, p. 57

production function, p. 51

productivity, p. 51

real rental price (cost) of capital, p. 60

real wage rate, p. 60

rental price (cost) of capital, p. 60

supply shock, p. 57

total factor productivity, p. 51

wage rate, p. 60

REVIEW QUESTIONS

All Questions are available in MyEconLab *for practice or instructor assignment.*

Determinants of Aggregate Production

1. What relationship does the aggregate production function portray? Which of the production function's variables are endogenous and which are exogenous?

2. How does total factor productivity differ from labor productivity?

3. Explain each symbol or term in the Cobb-Douglas production function. Which element in the production function cannot be measured directly? How is it measured?

4. Explain the two characteristics of the Cobb-Douglas production function that make it particularly useful to macroeconomists.

5. What are supply shocks and from what sources can they arise? Distinguish between positive and negative supply shocks.

Determination of Factor Prices

6. What are factor prices? What classical assumptions are used in explaining how they are determined?
7. Explain each term in the profit function for a firm.
8. What rule do firms follow to determine how much of each input to hire in order to maximize profits?

9. Why do the factor demand and supply curves have their particular slopes?
10. Explain how an equilibrium factor price is established in a factor market if there is either an excess demand for the factor or an excess supply of the factor.

Distribution of National Income

11. What determines the distribution of national income between payments to labor and payments to capital?

PROBLEMS

All Problems are available in MyEconLab *for practice or instructor assignment.*

Determinants of Aggregate Production

1. Consider the following production function:
   $Y = F(K, L) = A(2K + 3L)$. Does this production function exhibit constant returns to scale? (Hint: Replace K and L by $2K$ and $2L$, respectively, and check if $F(2K, 2L) = 2F(K, L)$.)
2. Consider the following production function:
   $Y = F(K, L) = AK^{0.4}L^{1.0}$.
   a) Calculate the marginal product of labor.
   b) Does this production function exhibit diminishing marginal product of labor?
3. Suppose Equation 2 represents the production function of both Mexico and Spain. Use the following information to answer the next questions.

Country	L = Population (millions)	K = Capital (trillion)	Y = Output (trillion)
Mexico	105	0.18	1.0
Spain	45	0.74	1.7

   a) Calculate total factor productivity for both countries using Equation 3.
   b) Calculate per capita income for both countries.
   c) Explain the difference in per capita income.

4. The figure below represents the production function relating output to capital in the United States. Suppose unusual weather conditions result in a higher than expected crop yield in the midwestern states.
   a) Draw the new production function in the same graph.
   b) What is the effect on the marginal product of capital?

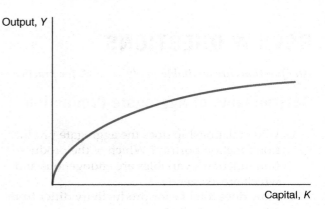

Output, Y

Capital, K

Determination of Factor Prices

5. A manufacturer of toys is employing fifty workers and using fifteen pieces of equipment to assemble toys. Currently, the marginal product of labor is $5 and the marginal product of capital is $25. Assuming the market prices for labor and capital are $12 and $20 respectively, answer the following:
   a) Is this firm maximizing its profit?
   b) What should this firm do with respect to its employees and its use of equipment?

6. Assume that the marginal product of labor is given by the following expression: $MPL = \dfrac{52}{L^{0.3}}$

   (L is measured in millions).
   a) What is the marginal product of labor when $L = 80$ million?

b) Determine the equilibrium real wage if the labor supply equals 100 million workers ($\bar{L} = 100$).

7. Assume that the marginal product of capital is given by the following expression:

   $$MPK = \frac{60}{K^{0.7}} \ (K \text{ is measured in trillions}).$$

   a) Graph the demand curve for capital and find the equilibrium real rental rate of capital if capital supply is ten trillion.
   b) Suppose a positive supply shock hits the economy, and now $MPK = \dfrac{70}{K^{0.7}}$. Draw the new demand curve and calculate the new equilibrium real rental rate of capital.

Distribution of National Income

8. Suppose an economy has total income of $8 trillion, where total labor income equals $6 trillion and capital income equals $2 trillion. Which are the values of the exponents on labor and capital using a Cobb-Douglas production function?

9. Suppose that you work at the statistical office of a given country. The graph plots estimates of the labor and capital income shares for that country over time.

Your boss suggests that a Cobb-Douglas production function could be a good representation of that country's income. Is your boss right?

10. Suppose that the following Cobb-Douglas production function represents the economy of Chile: $Y = F(K, L) = AK^{0.4}L^{0.6}$. Assuming Chile's national income equals $170 billion, calculate real labor income and real capital income.

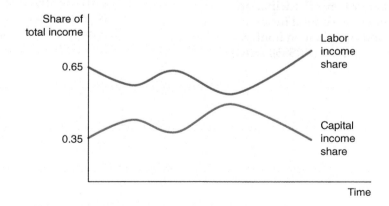

DATA ANALYSIS PROBLEMS

The Problems update with real-time data in MyEconLab *and are available for practice or instructor assignment.*

1. Go to the St. Louis Federal Reserve FRED database, and find data on nominal wages (COMPNFB) and prices using the consumer price index (CPIAUCSL). Convert the data series to annual data by using the "frequency" setting on the website, and choose the units as "percent change from a year ago" for both data series.

   a) Calculate the average percentage change in nominal wages per year and the average CPI inflation rate since 1980. How has inflation affected purchasing power over that period?

   b) Calculate the average real wage growth per year using your answer to part (a).

   c) Download a measure of labor productivity, output per person (PRS85006163), using the annual frequency setting and "percent change from a year ago" units, and calculate the average growth rate of labor productivity per year since 1980. Compare your results to part (b) above and Table 3.2, and comment on the relationship between labor productivity growth and real wage growth.

2. GDP per capita can be expressed as GDP/ Population = GDP/Worker × Workers/ Population, or GDP per capita = Labor Productivity × Labor Force Participation Rate. Go to the St. Louis Federal Reserve FRED database, and find data on nonfarm business output per person (PRS85006163) and the labor force participation rate (CIVPART).

   a) Calculate the total percentage change in output per person using (PRS85006163) and the percentage point change in the labor force participation rate (CIVPART) from 2000 up until the latest available data.

   b) Based on the behavior of the two data series, what are the implications for growth in GDP per capita?

3. Although they are distinctly different, the marginal product of labor, MPL, and labor productivity are closely related and should behave similarly. Go to the St. Louis Federal Reserve FRED database, and find data on output per hour (OPHNFB) and real compensation per hour (COMPRNFB) in the nonfarm business sector. Plot both data series on the same graph by using the *Add Data Series* function.

   a) Generally, how does the labor productivity measure (OPHNFB) behave during recessions and during expansions? Generally, how does the real compensation measure (COMPRNFB) behave during recessions and during expansions?

   b) Assuming output per worker is a good proxy for the marginal product of labor, is your answer to part (a) consistent with how you would expect the labor market to behave? Briefly explain.

Saving and Investment in Closed and Open Economies

Preview

In recent years, U.S. workers have saved little of what they earned. Indeed, in 2013, the U.S. *private saving rate*, the percentage of income Americans tuck away each year, sank to nearly the lowest level in the postwar period. U.S. households are in good company with their limited saving habits: the U.S. government has been spending far more than it receives from tax revenue, leading to large government budget deficits and severely negative *government saving rates*. What do these low saving rates and government budget deficits mean for the U.S. economy? Will living beyond our means make the country poorer in the future? If so, how might the government encourage more private saving? Should we worry that government budget deficits will shrink the capital stock and generate large imbalances in foreign trade?

In this chapter, we answer these questions by tracing the relationship between saving and investment. We take a long-run perspective in which wages and prices are flexible. We will see that lower saving leads to lower investment, slowing the growth of the capital stock and indeed making the United States poorer in the future. We will also see that lower saving leads to greater borrowing from foreigners, requiring future debt payments that will reduce the wealth of Americans.

Relationship Between Saving and Wealth

Any child with an allowance and a piggy bank intuitively knows that *income, saving,* and *wealth* are intimately related. Over time, even a child with a very low allowance can fill up a piggy bank with quarters by spending less on comic books and candy, and saving more.

Similarly, in the adult world, financial success is about more than income. We also need to consider **wealth,** a person's holdings of assets (such as bonds, stocks, houses, and fine art) minus his or her liabilities, the amount he or she owes (such as mortgages, car loans, and credit card balances). A lawyer fresh out of law school who earns a $150,000 salary at a top law firm but is saddled with student loans is surely not as well off as a rich kid with a $2 million trust fund who brings in $125,000 per year in income.

What is true for a child, adult, or household is also true for a country. To paint a full picture of a country's economy, we need to know a country's income, or GDP, over a specific period, as well as its **national wealth,** a country's holdings of assets minus its liabilities at a particular point in time. Just as with the child and the piggy bank, a country with a high saving rate will amass national wealth over time. We begin with a look at three national saving measures that figure prominently in macroeconomics.

Private Saving

Private saving equals private disposable income minus consumption expenditure. We calculate private disposable income, Y_D, as GDP, Y, minus net taxes, T (taxes minus government transfers minus interest payments on the debt):

$$Y_D = Y - T \tag{1}$$

Thus we can write private saving, S_P, as disposable income, $Y - T$, minus consumption expenditure, C:

$$S_P = Y - T - C \tag{2}$$

We subtract consumption expenditure from disposable income because it represents spending for current needs that does not produce higher income in the future and so will not add to wealth. The other component of private spending, investment, includes purchases of capital goods that do add to future income and wealth. Therefore, we do not subtract investment from disposable income.

The **private saving rate** is the proportion of private disposable income that is saved, S_P/Y_D. As you can see in Figure 4.1, the private saving rate has declined dramatically since the 1980s, creating serious macroeconomic issues that we will study later in the book.

Government Saving

Government purchases consists of two components: **government investment,** I_G, which is spending on capital goods like highways and schools that add to the capital stock and promote economic growth, and **government consumption,** C_G, which is government spending on current needs. In other words,

$$G = C_G + I_G$$

Government saving equals net government income less government consumption. For all practical purposes, we can think of net government income as taxes net of transfers, T, so we can write government saving as follows:

$$S_G = T - C_G$$

Deciding what is government consumption versus government investment is not clear cut. For example, the government's purchases of military equipment for war could be viewed as an investment in the nation's long-term prosperity, or as short-term spending on current needs with little long-term benefit. Hence, before 1996, the national income accounts lumped government consumption and investment into government purchases, G. Because of these ambiguities, throughout this book, we will use the "old" definition of government saving that subtracts government purchases from net taxes:

$$S_G = T - G \tag{3}$$

FIGURE 4.1

Three Measures of the Saving Rate in the United States, 1955–2013

The private saving rate declined dramatically from the 1980s through the mid-2000s, and remains low. Starting in the early 2000s, the government has been dissaving at a very high rate, leading to a decline in the national saving rate.

Source: Federal Reserve Bank of St. Louis, FRED Database. http://research .stlouisfed.org/fred2/

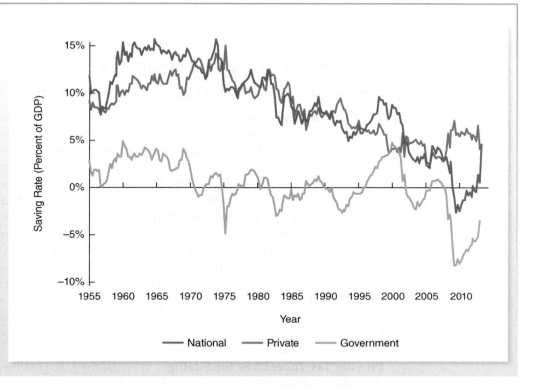

The government's tax receipts minus its outlays equals its **budget surplus,** $T - G$. This amount is identical to government saving. When government outlays are greater than government receipts, we say the government budget is in deficit and, as Equation 3 indicates, the government is also dissaving so that $S_G < 0$. Notice in Figure 4.1 that from 2001 to 2013, the government has been dissaving at a high rate.

National Saving

We calculate **national saving** by summing private saving and government saving. Adding Equations 2 and 3 together causes the T terms to cancel out, so national saving, S, is:

$$S = S_P + S_G = Y - C - G \tag{4}$$

In other words, national saving equals GDP minus spending on current needs, which include consumption expenditure and government purchases. The **national saving rate** is the share of national income saved by the government and households, or S/Y. Because both private saving and government saving have been decreasing relative to income, the national saving rate has fallen as well, as Figure 4.1 shows. To keep the terminology simple throughout the rest of the chapter, unless we are describing a particular type of saving, when we use the term *saving*, S, we are referring to national saving.

Many governments have worried that their countries' low saving rates will make them poorer in the future, an issue we discuss in the following Policy and Practice case.

Policy and Practice

Government Policies to Stimulate Saving

Governments stimulate saving through four main methods.

Tax Consumption.   A high tax on consumption encourages consumers to spend less and save more, thereby amassing wealth. But how do you tax consumption? A straightforward way is to impose a national sales tax. If, for example, you have to pay a 5% tax on every item that you buy, you will think twice about your purchases and may decide to save more. Most U.S. states impose a sales tax, but there is no national sales tax. Similar to a sales tax is a **value-added tax,** which is a tax that is paid by a producer on the difference between what it receives for its goods and services minus the costs. As we saw in Chapter 2, the sum of all the value added on a good is the final value of that good. Consequently, a value-added tax on all firms has the same effect as a tax on the price a consumer pays for that good, and so should encourage saving in exactly the same way. Most European countries, as well as Canada, have value-added taxes, which is one reason why they have higher saving rates than the United States. Many economists who believe that the U.S. national saving rate is too low are supporters of a value-added or national sales tax.

Provide Tax Incentives for Saving.   In 1974, the U.S. government created tax-sheltered accounts known as Individual Retirement Accounts (IRAs) to provide households a tax break for depositing money into a savings account. The income a household deposits into these accounts is exempt from income taxes, thereby lowering the household's tax bill. This tax break thus encourages the household to save more, increasing national saving. The effectiveness of these tax breaks on overall saving is controversial. If a household would have saved the amount even without a tax shelter like an IRA, then the IRA tax incentive would not substantially affect national saving.

Increase Return on Saving.   Measures that increase the return on assets like common stock increase the incentives for households to save. In 2003, for example, the Bush administration proposed legislation that was subsequently passed that lowered the tax that investors pay on capital gains, the difference between the sale and purchase price of an asset like a stock or a house. In addition, the Bush administration lowered the income tax rate on certain classes of dividends paid on common stock.

Reduce Budget Deficits.   Reducing budget deficits increases national saving—but in recent years, the opposite has occurred. Budget deficits have skyrocketed in many countries throughout the world because politicians have not restrained government spending.

Uses of Saving

Where does saving go? We can find the answer using the national income identity discussed in Chapter 2, $Y = C + I + G + NX$. Substituting $C + I + G + NX$ for Y in Equation 4 results in the following:

$$S = (C + I + G + NX) - C - G = I + NX \tag{5}$$

We refer to Equation 5 as the **uses-of-saving identity,** which tells us that saving either goes into investment—acquiring capital goods and boosting the capital stock—or, alternatively, into net exports—selling goods to foreigners in exchange for foreign currency assets. In other words, a nation that saves can invest in its capital stock or acquire assets from foreigners.

By subtracting I from both sides of Equation 5, we can rewrite the identity as follows:

$$
\begin{aligned}
S - I &= NX \\
\text{Net Capital Outflow} &= \text{Trade Balance}
\end{aligned}
\tag{6}
$$

NET CAPITAL OUTFLOW. We refer to the $S - I$ term, the difference between saving and investment, as **net capital outflow** (or *net foreign investment*), so Equation 6 is the **net capital outflow identity.** If saving is greater than investment, then the excess saving is invested abroad and so constitutes a net capital outflow, that is, more capital flows from the domestic economy to foreigners than flows into the domestic economy from abroad. If, on the other hand, investment is greater than saving, the excess of investment over saving is financed by borrowing abroad. We can say that net capital outflow is negative, or that there is a capital inflow.

TRADE BALANCE. We also refer to the net exports NX term of Equation 6 as the *trade balance*.[1] When NX is positive, the trade balance is positive and we say that the country is running a **trade surplus.** If China sells more goods and services abroad than it buys, the net capital flow identity in Equation 6 tells us that it is sending capital abroad that finances foreigners' net purchases of Chinese goods and services. If, on the other hand, NX is negative, as has been true in the United States for many years, we say the country is running a **trade deficit.** Americans buy more goods and services from abroad than foreigners buy from us, creating a negative trade balance. For Equation 6 to hold, we must have a net capital inflow, which finances these purchases by borrowing from abroad. The trade balance is reported periodically in the **balance of payments accounts,** a bookkeeping system for recording all receipts and payments that have a direct bearing on the movement of funds between a nation (private sector and government) and foreign countries (see the Macroeconomics in the News box, "Balance of Payments Accounts").

EXAMPLE: LINK BETWEEN NET CAPITAL OUTFLOWS AND THE TRADE BALANCE. To illustrate the relationship between net capital outflows and the trade balance from the net capital outflow identity of Equation 6, let's consider what happens when Apple

---

[1]The trade balance is closely related to another concept that you hear reported in the media, the *current account balance*. The current account balance is the trade balance plus net factor payments to domestic residents from foreigners and net unilateral transfers. Because net factor payments and net unilateral transfers are quite small, we can treat the current account balance and the trade balance as the same thing.

Computer sells an iPod to a British consumer for 100 pounds. At the current exchange rate, say $2 per pound, the iPod is valued at $200. U.S. net exports and the U.S. trade balance now go up by $200, while Apple finds that it has an extra 100 pounds in its bank account in the UK. Consider Apple's following options:

1. *Apple keeps the 100 pounds in the British bank.* Apple is in effect making a loan to the British bank of the 100 pounds (worth $200) and so the net capital outflow is $200, as the net capital outflow identity in Equation 6 suggests.

2. *Apple, in search of a higher return, uses the 100 pounds to buy a share of stock in a British company like Rolls-Royce.* Apple's money is now being used to finance Rolls-Royce's activities, which is another form of a net capital outflow.

3. *Apple uses the proceeds to help set up an Apple store in the UK.* Apple thus adds to its holdings of British assets, which creates a net capital outflow.

4. *Apple deposits the 100 pounds in a British branch of its local American bank.* There will still be a net capital outflow—the U.S. bank will do something with the 100 pounds, like making a loan to a British company.

In all four scenarios, the net capital outflow identity holds: the increase in net exports of $200 is matched by an increase in capital outflows of $200.

The Link Between Saving and Wealth

The uses-of-saving and net capital outflow identities in Equations 5 and 6 are important because they show how saving is linked to wealth. As we already noted, saving can either finance investment or net exports. When saving finances net exports, the net capital outflow identity of Equation 6 shows that there is a net capital outflow, and Americans have increased their holdings of foreign assets by more than foreigners have increased their holdings of U.S. assets. The net holdings of foreign assets (American-owned foreign stocks, bonds, bank accounts, factories, etc., minus foreign-owned U.S. assets) is called **net foreign assets,** and an increase in net foreign assets is clearly an increase in wealth.

Although there is a direct link between saving and wealth, wealth can change even if there is no saving. We saw in Figure 4.1, for example, that Americans have had very

MACROECONOMICS IN THE NEWS

Balance of Payments Accounts

The Bureau of Economic Analysis (BEA), a division of the U.S. Department of Commerce, produces quarterly data on the balance of payments accounts. The BEA releases data around two and a half months after the end of the quarter and revises data every year in June to incorporate more complete and accurate information. You can find this data on the BEA website, www.bea.gov, by clicking on "Balance of Payments" under the "International" heading.

Although the BEA produces the complete balance of payments only quarterly, it produces and releases the trade balance data monthly, about a month to a month and a half after the month reported on. Because net exports are an important component of GDP and also tell us what is happening to net capital outflows, the announcement of trade balance data often receives a lot of media attention.

MyEconLab Real-time data

FIGURE 4.2

Ratio of U.S. Wealth to Income, 1955–2013

Wealth is highly influenced by values of asset holdings: from 2001 to 2007, despite a low private saving rate, the stock market and housing booms increased Americans' wealth-to-income ratio, while the crisis from 2007–2009 led to a sharp decline in wealth, with a subsequent moderate rise when the stock market recovered.

Source: Federal Reserve Bank of St. Louis, FRED Database. http://research.stlouisfed.org/fred2/

low private saving rates in recent years. Does this mean that personal wealth has not increased in the United States? The answer is no, as Figure 4.2 indicates. Despite low private saving rates from 2001 to 2007, Americans' wealth relative to disposable income rose steadily. Indeed, sometimes the opposite occurs. For example, in 2008, Americans' net worth plummeted, and yet the private saving rate jumped up.

What explains these movements in wealth that are not associated with saving? The answer is that the valuation of assets fluctuates substantially in the short run. In the very low saving years from 2001 to 2007, both the stock market and the housing market boomed, so that the value of Americans' holdings of stocks and houses increased dramatically. Thus wealth increased substantially even though Americans saved very little. On the other hand, in 2008, both the stock market and the housing market collapsed, leading to over a 20% decline in Americans' personal wealth even though the American private saving rate started to increase. The evidence from the 2000s suggests that changes in wealth can affect saving, a link we will discuss further in Chapter 18 when we examine what determines consumption.

Application

How the United States Became the Largest Net Debtor in the World

Up until the 1980s, the United States was the largest net creditor in the world, with Americans owning far more foreign assets than foreigners owned of U.S. assets. However, as Figure 4.3 indicates, starting in the late 1970s, net foreign assets relative to U.S. GDP began to fall at a fairly steady pace. By 2012, net foreign debt—U.S. debt to foreigners minus foreign debt

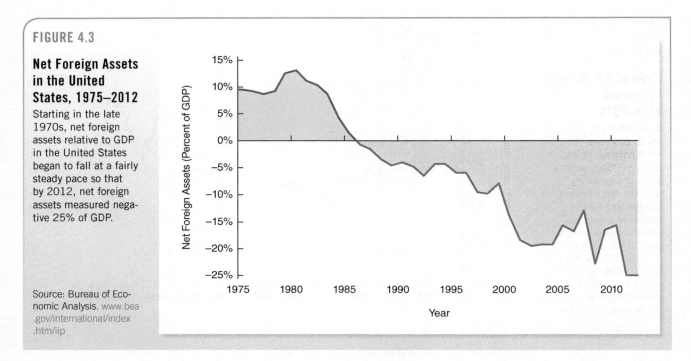

FIGURE 4.3

Net Foreign Assets in the United States, 1975–2012

Starting in the late 1970s, net foreign assets relative to GDP in the United States began to fall at a fairly steady pace so that by 2012, net foreign assets measured negative 25% of GDP.

Source: Bureau of Economic Analysis. www.bea.gov/international/index.htm/iip

to Americans, which is the opposite of net foreign assets—was $3.9 trillion, or 25% of GDP. How did the United States go from being the largest net creditor in the world to the largest net debtor?

The net capital outflow identity provides insights. Specifically, Equation 6 indicates that the trade balance, NX, is equal to net capital outflows, $S - I$. Figure 4.4 shows trends in the U.S. national saving, investment, and trade balance from 1960 to 2013. From 1960 until the mid-1970s, saving and investment generally moved closely together. Saving generally remained above investment, so that the trade balance was in surplus, as we can see in Figure 4.4. Starting in the early 1980s, U.S. national saving began to fall dramatically, from levels near 10% of GDP to levels below zero after 2009, while investment fell by far less. The trade balance went sharply into deficit, reaching a peak of 6.1% in 2005.

The net capital outflow identity indicates that the large trade deficits starting in the 1980s triggered substantial capital inflows into the United States, sending Americans' holdings of net foreign assets lower. Figure 4.3 supports this relationship: net foreign assets turned negative in 1986, and continued to decline thereafter. The trade deficit has finally begun to shrink in recent years, as Figure 4.4 shows—yet because the trade balance is still negative, net foreign assets continue to fall. When this decline will turn around is anyone's guess. It is clear, though, that the United States is going to be a net debtor to the rest of the world for a very long time.

MyEconLab Real-time data

FIGURE 4.4

U.S. National Saving, Investment, and the Trade Balance, 1960–2013

The trade balance was in surplus from the 1960s to the 1970s, with the saving rate slightly higher than investment. The trade surplus turned into a deficit starting in the early 1980s, when U.S. national saving began to fall dramatically, from levels near 10% of GDP to levels near zero after 2007, while investment fell by far less.

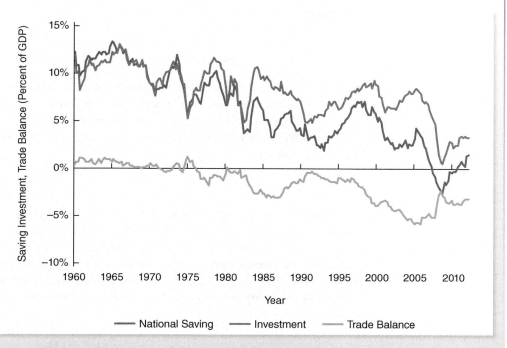

Source: Federal Reserve Bank of St. Louis, FRED Database. http://research.stlouisfed.org/fred2/

Saving, Investment, and Goods Market Equilibrium in a Closed Economy

We now look at the link between saving and investment in the long run, when all prices are flexible and have fully adjusted to exogenous shocks, so that aggregate output is determined by the production function in Chapter 3. We examine the link between saving and investment by asking what happens when the goods market is in equilibrium. To keep things simple, we start with a **closed economy,** an economy that is closed to international trade with zero net exports $(NX = 0)$.

Saving and Investment Equation

Because net exports are zero in a closed economy, there are three components of GDP: consumption expenditure, C, investment, I, and government purchases, G. The total demand for goods and services in a closed economy is $C + I + G$. If the goods market is in equilibrium, this demand will equal the amount of goods and services produced, Y. Goods market equilibrium therefore occurs when

$$Y = C + I + G \tag{7}$$

When we subtract C and G from both sides of Equation 7 and recognize that national saving S from Equation 4 is $Y - C - G$, we can rewrite the condition for goods market equilibrium as follows:

$$\underset{\text{Saving}}{S} \underset{=}{=} Y - C - G = \underset{\text{Investment}}{I} \tag{8}$$

The real interest rate, the inflation-adjusted cost of borrowing, keeps the market for saving and investment in equilibrium. This rate, which also describes the real benefit of saving, adjusts to maintain an equilibrium at which desired saving equals desired investment. We now look separately at saving and investment to see how they relate to the real interest rate.

Saving

We will explore the factors that determine consumption expenditure in detail in Chapter 18. For now, we will assume that the amount consumers want to spend is a function of three factors: disposable income $(Y - T)$, the real interest rate (r), and **autonomous consumption** $(\overline{C})$, the amount of consumption expenditure that is unrelated to either disposable income or the real interest rate. We can write the relationship of consumption expenditure to disposable income and the real interest rate as follows:

$$C = \overline{C} + C(\underset{+}{Y} - \underset{-}{T}, r) \tag{9}$$

The plus sign below $Y - T$ indicates that as disposable income increases, consumption expenditure rises, while the minus sign below r indicates that as real interest rates rise, consumption expenditure falls. As disposable income rises, consumers have more income to spend, increasing their desired amount of consumption expenditure. Rising real interest rates encourage consumers to save more and spend less, since they can earn a higher return on their saving.

We treat government fiscal policy as an exogenous variable, meaning it is determined by political considerations, which is beyond the scope of our model.

$$G = \overline{G} \tag{10}$$

$$T = \overline{T} \tag{11}$$

For simplicity, we also treat the level of capital and labor as exogenous, fixed at $\overline{K}$ and $\overline{L}$. We can input those factors into the production function described in Chapter 3 to determine the level of long-run aggregate output. Long-run aggregate output is therefore also an exogenous variable, which we fix at $\overline{Y}$. Putting this together,

$$Y = F(\overline{K}, \overline{L}) = \overline{Y} \tag{12}$$

Recognizing that saving $S = Y - C - G$ and substituting in from Equations 9–12, we can describe the desired amount of saving as follows:

$$S = \overline{Y} - \overline{C} - C(\overline{Y} - \overline{T}, r) - \overline{G} \tag{13}$$

We've now built a fully functioning economic model for desired saving, with four exogenous variables—$\overline{Y}$, $\overline{C}$, $\overline{T}$, and $\overline{G}$—and four endogenous variables—the real interest

FIGURE 4.5

The Saving-Investment Diagram: Equilibrium in the Goods Market

Goods market equilibrium occurs at point E, the intersection of the saving and investment curves, where the real interest rate is r^*. At the interest rate r_2, desired investment at point A is less than desired saving at point B: potential investors want to borrow less than savers want to lend, and so the real interest rate will fall to r^*. Similarly, if the real interest rate is r_1, then desired investment at point D is greater than desired saving at point C: investors will want to borrow more than savers are willing to lend and the real interest rate will rise to r^*.

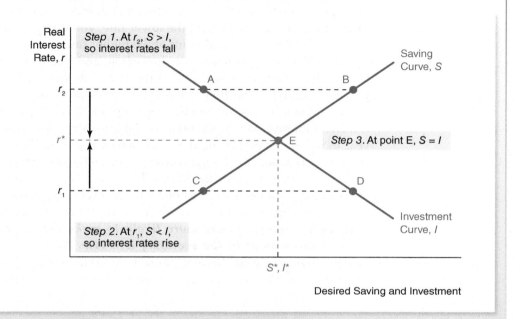

rate, r, consumption, C, desired investment, I, and desired saving, S. Notice also how changes in r change the level of C, which in turn affects the saving rate. If r rises, consumption expenditure falls. Lower consumption means higher saving. Thus, we can say that r is negatively correlated with C, and C is negatively correlated with saving. Hence, r is positively correlated with saving. With this model in hand, we plot desired saving against the real interest rate. The positive relationship between saving and the real interest rate produces the upward-sloping saving curve S shown in Figure 4.5. The slope of S matches our intuition about how interest rates affect saving by making consumption more costly.

Investment

As we concluded from our discussion of marginal product of capital in Chapter 3, firms and households will make investments as long as they expect to earn more from the investment than the rental cost of capital, that is, the interest cost of the loan to finance the investment. We think of both the benefits and interest costs in terms of the value of real goods and services, and so the interest rate that is most relevant to investment decisions is the real interest rate. For example, suppose Ford is thinking about buying a $100,000 car-painting robot that will increase profits by $10,000 per year in real terms. If it faces a 6% real interest rate on the $100,000 loan to finance the purchase of the robot, it will pay $6,000 per year in interest. The net gain is $4,000 per year. It makes sense for Ford to make the investment, and so it will go ahead and buy the robot. On the other hand, if the real interest rate is 15%, then the cost per year of financing the purchase is $15,000. The $10,000 in profits won't cover this amount, so Ford won't make the investment. Similarly, suppose you are thinking about buying a $100,000 house. You are more likely to buy the house when real interest rates are relatively low, say at 6%, than when they are at 15%. At the lower rate, you'd pay $6,000 per year in real terms, versus $15,000 a year in real terms at the higher rate.

Do real interest rates matter to household and firm investment decisions even if the households and firms have surplus funds and do not need to borrow? The answer is yes. For example, what if Ford has the $100,000 and doesn't need to take out a loan to purchase the robot? Instead of buying the robot, it could purchase an asset like a bond. If the real interest rate for the bond is high, say, 15%, then Ford would earn $15,000 per year in real terms by buying the bond, which is greater than the $10,000 it would earn from the robot. So, as before, it would not make the investment. Alternatively, if the real interest rate were 6%, then the $10,000 Ford would earn by purchasing the robot exceeds the $6,000 it would earn on the bond, and so it will now make the robot investment.

The conclusion from our analysis is the following: *as real interest rates fall, households and firms are more likely to make investments, and so the desired level of investment in the economy will rise.* We represent the increasing level of desired investment as the real interest rate falls with the downward-sloping curve marked by I in Figure 4.5, which can be written as the investment function:

$$I = \bar{I} + I(r)$$
$$\underset{-}{}$$

(14)

where $\bar{I}$ is **autonomous investment** (investment unrelated to the real interest rate) and the minus sign below r indicates that as the real interest rate increases, investment falls.

Goods Market Equilibrium

The goods market equilibrium condition, $S = I$, occurs at point E at the intersection of the saving and investment curves in Figure 4.5, which we refer to as the **saving-investment diagram**. The real interest rate that keeps the goods market in equilibrium is r^*. If the interest rate is above r^*, say at r_2, then desired investment at point A is less than desired saving at point B, and the goods market will not be in equilibrium. Under these conditions, potential investors are willing to borrow less than savers are willing to lend, and so lenders will be willing to lower rates to make more loans. The real interest rate will therefore fall, as the downward arrow indicates. Similarly, if the real interest rate is less than r^* at r_1, then desired investment at point D is greater than desired saving at point C, and so investors will want to borrow more than savers are willing to lend and the real interest rate will rise, as the upward arrow indicates. Only when the real interest rate is at r^* at point E will the goods market be in equilibrium and the real interest rate remain unchanged.

Response to Changes in Saving and Investment in a Closed Economy

How does the economy respond to changes in saving and investment? To examine this question, we look at changes in saving and investment levels graphically. As you learned in your principles of economics course when you studied supply and demand, it is always important to distinguish movements along a curve from shifts in the curve.

Only shifts in curves produce a change in the equilibrium quantities and price. This insight is also true in our analysis of saving and investment.

We have seen that the desired amount of saving is determined by $\overline{Y}$, $\overline{C}$, $\overline{T}$, $\overline{G}$, and r. Because the level of aggregate output $\overline{Y}$ in the long run is determined by the amount of capital and labor in the economy and the technology available, we take $\overline{Y}$ as given. Changes in desired saving when the real interest rate changes is a *movement along* the saving curve and does not cause the saving curve to shift. However, changes in $\overline{C}$, $\overline{T}$, and $\overline{G}$ can affect the amount of desired saving and thus *shift* the saving curve. We begin by looking at what happens when autonomous consumption changes.

Changes in Saving: Autonomous Consumption

If consumers become more optimistic, say, they think their job prospects will be better in the future, they might decide to spend more regardless of the real interest rate or disposable income. As a result, autonomous consumption expenditure $\overline{C}$ would rise. Alternatively, a change in their preferences might cause households to become reckless and extravagant, so autonomous consumption might rise and consumers will save less at any given real interest rate. The saving curve will then shift to the left from S_1 to S_2 in panel (a) of Figure 4.6, and the equilibrium will move from point 1 to point 2. The rise in autonomous consumption will then cause the amount of saving and investment to fall to S_2 and I_2, and the equilibrium real interest rate will rise to r_2.

On the other hand, if consumers become more pessimistic or become more conservative and so want to save more, then autonomous consumption will fall and saving will rise at any given real interest rate. In this case, the saving curve will shift rightward from S_1 to S_2 in panel (b) of Figure 4.6: saving and investment will rise to S_2 and I_2, and the equilibrium real interest rate will fall to r_2. We thus have the following result: *a rise in autonomous consumption causes saving and investment to fall and the real interest rate to rise in the long run, while a fall in autonomous consumption causes saving and investment to rise and the real interest rate to fall.*

Changes in Saving: Effects of Fiscal Policy

Changes in fiscal policy—such as a change in taxes $\overline{T}$ or government purchases $\overline{G}$—can also affect the amount of desired saving at any given real interest rate and thus shift the saving curve.

CHANGES IN TAXES. If the government raises taxes, then households will have less income to spend and so will consume less at any given real interest rate. The result is that saving, $S = Y - C - G$, will increase at any given real interest rate and the saving curve will shift to the right from S_1 to S_2 in panel (b) of Figure 4.6. The equilibrium will then move from point 1 to point 2. The rise in taxes will cause the amount of saving and investment to rise to S_2 and I_2, and the equilibrium real interest rate will fall to r_2. On the other hand, if the government lowers taxes, then households will have more disposable income and so will spend more, decreasing saving at any given real interest rate. In this case, the saving curve will shift leftward from S_1 to S_2 in panel (a) of Figure 4.6: saving and investment will fall to S_2 and I_2, and the equilibrium real interest rate will rise to r_2. The result is the following: *a rise in taxes causes saving and investment to rise and the real interest rate to fall in the long run, while a fall in taxes causes saving and investment to fall and the real interest rate to rise.*

CHANGES IN GOVERNMENT PURCHASES. Now suppose that the government decides to increase its purchases. The rise in government spending will result in a fall in saving

MyEconLab Mini-lecture

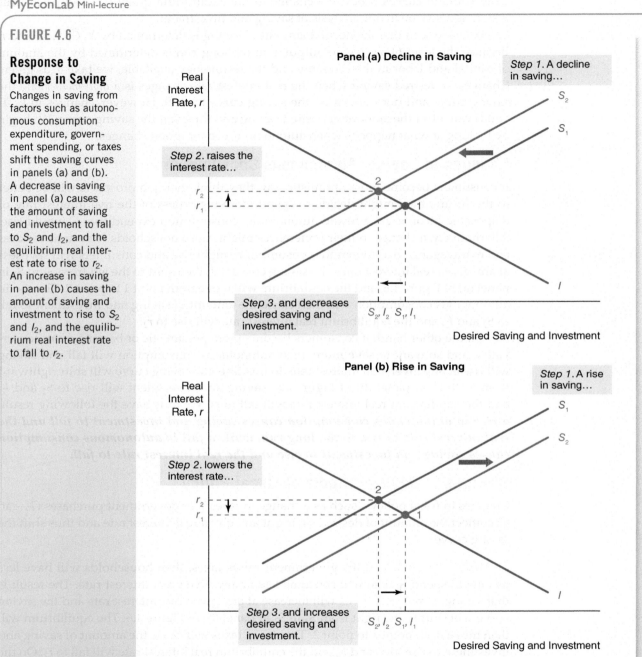

FIGURE 4.6

Response to Change in Saving

Changes in saving from factors such as autonomous consumption expenditure, government spending, or taxes shift the saving curves in panels (a) and (b). A decrease in saving in panel (a) causes the amount of saving and investment to fall to S_2 and I_2, and the equilibrium real interest rate to rise to r_2. An increase in saving in panel (b) causes the amount of saving and investment to rise to S_2 and I_2, and the equilibrium real interest rate to fall to r_2.

Panel (a) Decline in Saving

Step 1. A decline in saving…

Real Interest Rate, r

S_2

S_1

Step 2. raises the interest rate…

r_2

r_1

2

1

Step 3. and decreases desired saving and investment.

S_2, I_2 S_1, I_1

I

Desired Saving and Investment

Panel (b) Rise in Saving

Step 1. A rise in saving…

Real Interest Rate, r

S_1

S_2

Step 2. lowers the interest rate…

r_2

r_1

2

1

Step 3. and increases desired saving and investment.

S_2, I_2 S_1, I_1

I

Desired Saving and Investment

at any given real interest rate because $S = Y - C - G$, so that the saving curve will shift to the left, as in panel (a) of Figure 4.6. Saving and investment will then fall to S_2 and I_2, and the equilibrium real interest rate will rise to r_2. We call this result from our saving-investment analysis **crowding out** because the rise in government spending causes private investment to fall as government spending increases. If, on the other hand, the government cuts spending, then the saving curve will shift to the right, as in panel (b) of Figure 4.6: saving and investment will rise and the equilibrium interest rate will fall. We then have the following conclusion: *a rise in government spending causes saving and investment to fall and the real interest rate to rise in the long run, while a decline in government spending causes saving and investment to rise and the real interest rate to fall.*

CHANGES IN GOVERNMENT SAVING. Another way to see the effect of changes in fiscal policy is to recognize that government saving is $S_G = T - G$, which is identical to the budget surplus. Hence a rise in the budget surplus, either from a rise in taxes or a decrease in government spending, leads to higher government saving and higher national saving S.[2] A higher budget surplus therefore shifts the saving curve to the right, as in panel (b) of Figure 4.6, leading to a rise in saving and investment and a fall in the real interest rate. A decline in taxes or a rise in government spending that leads to a budget deficit, on the other hand, causes government saving to fall, as illustrated by panel (a) of Figure 4.6. The saving curve shifts to the left and saving and investment fall, while the real interest rate rises. We summarize the results on fiscal policy as follows: *increases in government budget deficits (government dissaving) cause saving and investment to fall in the long run and real interest rates to rise.*

Because government budget deficits can lead to crowding out of private investment and higher real interest rates, attempts to use fiscal policy to stimulate the economy are very controversial, as the following Policy and Practice case indicates.

Policy and Practice

Crowding Out and the Debate over the 2009 Fiscal Stimulus Package

Early in 2009, the Obama administration proposed and Congress passed a $787 billion fiscal stimulus package to promote economic recovery from the recession that started in 2007. Since the weakened economy was already generating lower tax revenue, the increased spending pushed up budget deficits to over $1 trillion. As a result, the deficit level relative to GDP reached a fifty-year high. Critics of the fiscal stimulus package worried that the huge government budget deficits would lead to a rise in interest rates and a decline in investment. They feared that the slow capital stock growth would reduce the future productive capacity of the American economy and make the nation as a whole poorer.

Although the 2009 fiscal stimulus package had potential benefits in terms of increasing employment and output (see Chapters 9 and 13), our saving-investment

---

[2]Although a rise in taxes increases government saving, $S_G = T - G$, it lowers private saving, $S_P = Y - T - C$. However, government saving rises one-for-one with taxes, while private saving falls by less than one-for-one because the rise in taxes causes consumption to fall, so $(T + C)$ rises by less than the increase in T. An increase in government saving at any given real interest rate therefore leads to a rise in national saving, $S = S_G + S_P$.

analysis indicates that we should take these criticisms seriously. If the fiscal stimulus package produces ongoing, huge government budget deficits and government dis-saving, it will generate a leftward shift of the saving curve, as in panel (a) of Figure 4.6, which will lead in the long run to a crowding out of investment and higher real interest rates. Even if the Obama fiscal stimulus package were successful in stimu-lating the U.S. economy in the short run (a topic we will discuss in later chapters), it could have important negative long-run consequences for the U.S. economy if it leads to continuing large budget deficits. Saving-investment analysis suggests that governments must not forget about the long-run consequences of budget deficits in thinking about the use of fiscal stimulus packages to manage the economy.

Changes in Autonomous Investment

Changes in desired investment as the real interest rate changes are movements along the investment curve that do not change the equilibrium level of real interest rates. However, changes in desired investment that are unrelated to real interest rates, that is, autonomous investment, $\bar{I}$, do cause the investment curve to shift, which leads to a change in equilibrium real interest rates.

There are several reasons that autonomous investment and the investment curve could shift. First, businesses might become more optimistic about the future and so expect higher returns from their investments. Then at any given interest rate, they would be more likely to find investments that are profitable, and desired investment

MyEconLab Mini-lecture

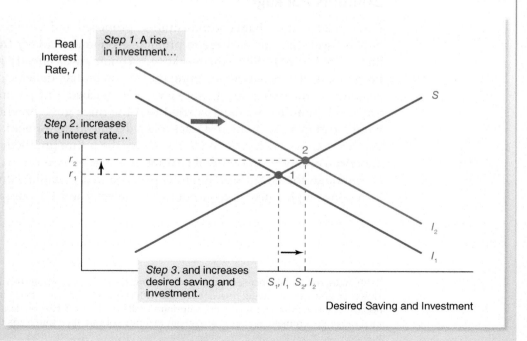

FIGURE 4.7

Response to a Rise in Investment

A rise in investment (either because of an increase in business optimism or a change in the tax code that encourages investment) shifts the investment curve to I_2, moving the equilibrium to point 2, increasing desired sav-ing and investment to S_2 and I_2, and raising the equilibrium real interest rate to r_2.

would rise. The result would be a rightward shift of the investment curve from I_1 to I_2 in Figure 4.7. Alternatively, changes in the tax code, such as an **investment tax credit,** which gives businesses a tax break when they make an investment in physical capital, encourage businesses to expand investment at any given real interest rate and also shift the investment curve to the right.

Notice in Figure 4.7 that the rightward shift of the investment curve causes the equilibrium to move from point 1 to point 2. Saving and investment will then rise, respectively, to S_2 and I_2, and the equilibrium real interest rate will also rise to r_2. ***An increase in business optimism or a change in the tax code that increases autonomous investment causes saving, investment, and the real interest rate to rise.*** Similar reasoning indicates that ***when businesses become more pessimistic or the government raises taxes on investment, lowering autonomous investment, the investment curve will shift to the left, and so saving, investment, and the real interest rate will fall.***

Saving, Investment, and Goods Market Equilibrium in an Open Economy

Now we are ready to modify our saving-investment diagram to analyze what happens in **open economies,** which are open to trade and flows of capital across their borders.

Perfect Capital Mobility and the Open Economy

We will assume that the open economy does not have any restrictions on flows of capital between domestic and foreign residents or vice versa, a situation we describe as **perfect capital mobility.** With perfect capital mobility, the domestic real interest rate, r, must be the same as the **world real interest rate,** r^w, the real interest rate found in world markets.

$$r = r^w \tag{15}$$

If the domestic real interest rate r were above the world real interest rate r^w, then with no barriers to capital flows, domestic residents (which include the government) would just borrow abroad at the world real interest rate r^w. Alternatively, if the domestic real interest rate were below the world real interest rate, domestic residents would only lend to foreigners and earn the world interest rate r^w. Since borrowing or lending would only occur at the world real interest rate r^w, the domestic real interest rate would not deviate from the world real interest rate, as in Equation 15.

Goods Market Equilibrium in an Open Economy

In an open economy with international trade, net exports NX will no longer be zero. The total demand for goods and services in an open economy is therefore now equal to $C + I + G + NX$. If the goods market is in equilibrium, this demand will equal the amount of goods and services produced, Y. Goods market equilibrium therefore occurs when:

$$Y = C + I + G + NX \tag{16}$$

By subtracting C and G from both sides of Equation 16 and again recognizing that national saving S from Equation 4 is $Y - C - G$, we can rewrite the condition for goods market equilibrium in an open economy as follows:

$$S \quad = Y - C - G = \quad I \quad + \quad NX$$
$$\text{Saving} \quad = \quad \text{Investment} \quad + \quad \text{Net Exports}$$
(17)

By subtracting I from both sides, we can write the goods market equilibrium condition alternatively as follows:

$$NX \quad = \quad S \quad - \quad I$$
$$\text{Net Exports} \quad = \quad \text{Saving} \quad - \quad \text{Investment}$$
(18)

which looks like the net capital flow identity of Equation 6, but is now an equilibrium condition.

Saving, Investment, and the Trade Balance in a Small Open Economy

We will now look at a **small open economy,** an economy that is open to trade and to flows of capital across its borders and that is "small" relative to the world economy, so that whatever happens in this economy has no effect on the world real interest rate. For a small open economy, we can take the world real interest rate, denoted by r^w, as given.

We start with the small open economy because the analysis is relatively straightforward and because many of the results carry over to **large open economies,** like the United States or the Eurozone (the European countries that have adopted the euro as their currency), which are open to trade and capital flows, but are sufficiently large that their saving and investment decisions do influence the world real interest rate. We will discuss large open economies later in the chapter and in an appendix available on the Companion Website.

Goods Market Equilibrium in a Small Open Economy

We begin by identifying saving and investment when the goods market is in equilibrium in a small open economy. Figure 4.8 uses a saving-investment diagram similar to the one we used for a closed economy, with the same saving and investment curves as in Figure 4.5. Recognize that equilibrium does not occur when saving equals investment, as in the closed economy. Instead, it occurs when desired saving *minus* desired investment equals net exports, as in Equation 18.

GOODS MARKET EQUILIBRIUM: TRADE SURPLUS. Suppose that the world real interest rate in Figure 4.8 is at r_1^w, which is above where the saving and investment curves intersect at r_E, the real interest rate if the economy were closed. With the domestic real interest rate equal to r_1^w, desired saving at point B is higher than desired investment at point A, and the difference between the two is a positive value of net exports.

FIGURE 4.8

Saving-Investment Diagram in a Small Open Economy

Equilibrium occurs when desired saving minus desired invest-ment equals net exports at the world real inter-est rate. At the world real interest rate r_1^w, desired saving at point B is higher than desired investment at point A: the difference between the two is a positive value of net exports. Equilibrium in the goods market in a small open economy then occurs at a real interest rate of r_1^w, where the

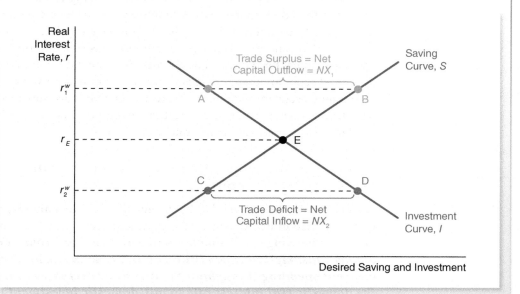

economy is running a trade surplus of NX_1. At the world real interest r_2^w, investment now rises to point D and is greater than saving at point C, and net exports equals NX_2, a negative number: there is a net capital inflow and a trade deficit.

Equilibrium in the goods market in a small open economy then occurs at a real interest rate of r_1^w, where the economy is running a trade surplus of NX_1. The domestic residents are lending to foreigners, so there is a net capital outflow because saving exceeds invest-ment. The net capital outflow and the lending to foreigners mean that domestic resi-dents are increasing their wealth by acquiring more net foreign assets.

To better understand goods market equilibrium in the small open economy, let's compare what is happening in the small open economy to a closed economy. In a closed economy, the real interest rate would have been driven down to r_E to equate saving and investment because the excess saving would have no place to go. In the small open economy, however, the domestic real interest rate cannot fall below r_1^w because domestic residents would not be willing to lend at a lower interest rate than they can get abroad. Instead, domestic residents would lend the excess saving, the trade surplus of NX, to foreigners, as Figure 4.8 indicates.

GOODS MARKET EQUILIBRIUM: TRADE DEFICIT. But what if the world real interest rate in Figure 4.8 falls to r_2^w, which is below r_E, so that the domestic real interest rate falls to r_2^w? Investment now rises to point D and is greater than saving at point C, and so $S - I$, which equals NX, is a negative number, meaning that the economy is running a trade deficit. Domestic residents now need to borrow the amount of the trade deficit to fund the excess investment the economy is engaged in, so there is a net capital inflow. When domestic residents borrow abroad and there is a net capital inflow, net foreign assets are falling and the country's wealth will decrease.

What could cause world real interest rates to fall from r_1^w to r_2^w? The answer lies in our analysis of the closed economy. Think of the economy of the world as a whole as a closed economy: the goods market is in equilibrium for the world economy when desired world saving equals desired world investment. Thus the analysis in Figures 4.5 through 4.7 applies to the world economy, so changes in autonomous consumption expenditure, investment, and fiscal policy for the world as a whole determine the real interest rate. The analysis for the closed economy therefore tells us that a rise in world saving—from a decline in world autonomous consumption expenditure, a decline in government spending throughout the world, or a rise in world taxes—or alternatively a decline in world investment, would lead to a fall in the world real interest rate from r_1^w to r_2^w.

Connection Between the World Economy and the Small Open Economy

Because Figure 4.8 shows that the decline in world real interest rates from r_1^w to r_2^w leads to an increase in investment and a decline in net exports and net capital outflows, we have the following result: ***increases in world saving (from a decline in world autonomous consumption expenditure, an increase in world taxes, or a decline in government spending throughout the world) or decreases in world investment cause the domestic real interest rate to fall, domestic investment to rise, and net capital outflows (net exports) to fall.*** What goes on in the rest of the world is therefore an important determinant of a country's investment, trade balance, and capital flows.

Response to Changes in Saving and Investment in a Small Open Economy

Now that we understand how to determine saving, investment, and the trade balance, we can examine what happens when there is a change in domestic saving or investment.

Changes in Domestic Saving

As we saw in our analysis of the closed economy, a decline in autonomous consumption expenditure or a rise in government saving (resulting from a rise in taxes or a decline in government spending) causes the saving curve to shift to the right from S_1 to S_2 in Figure 4.9. With world and, hence, domestic real interest rates unchanged at r_1^w, the amount of desired saving increases from point B_1 to point B_2. The distance between point A and point B_2 is larger than the distance from point A to point B_1, so $S - I$ has increased, thereby raising net exports from NX_1 to NX_2 and increasing the trade surplus. The higher amount of excess saving leads to an increase in lending to foreigners, so net capital outflow increases, as do net foreign assets. The result is the following: ***an increase in saving in the small open economy (from a decrease in autonomous consumption expenditure, a rise in government saving from a rise in taxes, or a decline in government spending) leads to a higher trade balance (an increase in the trade surplus or a shrinkage of the trade deficit) and an increase in net capital outflows.*** Similar reasoning indicates that ***a decrease in saving leads to a decline in the trade balance (a shrinkage in the trade surplus or an increase in the trade deficit) and a decrease in net capital outflows.***

FIGURE 4.9

Response to a Rise in Saving in a Small Open Economy

A rise in saving (either from a decline in autonomous consumption expenditure or a rise in government saving) shifts the saving curve from S_1 to S_2. With the world and hence the domestic real interest rate unchanged at r_1^w, the amount of desired saving increases from point B_1 to point B_2. At NX_2, net exports rise, increasing the trade surplus and net capital outflows.

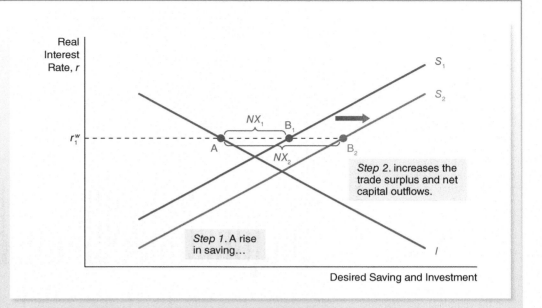

How does the response to a shift in the saving curve differ from what happens in the closed economy? In the closed economy, an increase in saving represented by a rightward shift in the saving curve, for example, leads to a fall in the real interest rate and a rise in investment. In the small open economy, the domestic and world real interest rates do not change. As a result, the rightward shift in the saving curve does not lead to a change in investment; instead, the excess saving spills over to an increase in net exports and a greater net capital outflow. However, in both the closed and open economies, the increase in saving leads to an increase in wealth. In the closed economy, the increase in investment from the increase in saving leads to a higher capital stock, which increases the productive capacity of the economy and so makes the country richer; in the small open economy, it leads to an increase in net foreign assets, which also makes the country richer.

Application

The Twin Deficits

From 1979 to 1983, U.S. government saving declined sharply because the budget deficit for combined government (federal, state, and local) went from under 2% of GDP to nearly 6% of GDP (the red bars in Figure 4.10). Starting in 1979, the defense buildup that began under President Jimmy Carter led to an increase in federal government spending. Then the Reagan administration's Economic Recovery Act of 1981 sharply cut income tax rates, leading to a 2% decline in tax revenue. What impact would the resulting government budget deficit have on the trade deficit?

MyEconLab Real-time data

FIGURE 4.10

The Twin Deficits, 1970–2013

U.S. government saving declined sharply from 1979 to 1983 when the government budget deficit went from under 2% of GDP to nearly 6% of GDP (the red bars). At the same time, the U.S. economy began to display a large trade deficit (the purple bars), leading to the twin deficits. However, in the late 1990s during the Clinton administration, both the federal and the combined government budget went into surplus, and yet the trade deficit continued to rise.

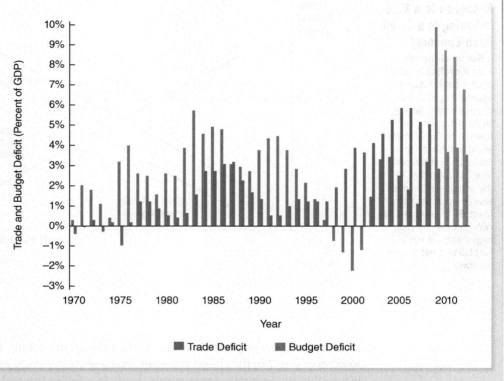

Source: Federal Reserve Bank of St. Louis, FRED Database. http://research.stlouisfed.org/fred2/

Our analysis in Figure 4.9 indicates that this decline in government saving would lead to a decrease in saving represented by a leftward shift of the saving curve and hence a decline in the trade balance. Sure enough, the U.S. economy began to display a large trade deficit, as we can see in Figure 4.10.

Economists call the phenomenon of a simultaneous trade deficit and government budget deficit **twin deficits,** and our saving-income analysis explains why they occur. However, the twin deficit phenomenon is not the only explanation for trade deficits. For example, we see in Figure 4.10 that in the late 1990s and early 2000s, during the Clinton administration, both the federal and the combined government budget went into surplus, and yet the trade deficit continued to rise. Our analysis suggests that other factors, such as consumers' willingness to spend and invest, also affect the trade balance. Indeed, private saving declined while investment surged during the boom of the late 1990s. Our model, however, suggests that the budget surpluses at that time kept the trade deficit from growing even larger.

Changes in Investment

Suppose that businesses become more optimistic and so autonomous investment rises. The investment curve shifts to the right from I_1 to I_2 in Figure 4.11. At the unchanged domestic and world real interest rate of r_1^w, desired investment increases from point A_1

MyEconLab Mini-lecture

FIGURE 4.11

Response to a Rise in Investment in a Small Open Economy

If optimistic businesses decide to increase investment, the investment curve shifts to the right from I_1 to I_2. Desired investment increases from point A_1 to point A_2, and the difference between saving and investment now decreases, leading to a decline in net exports from NX_1 to NX_2 and a decrease in net capital outflows.

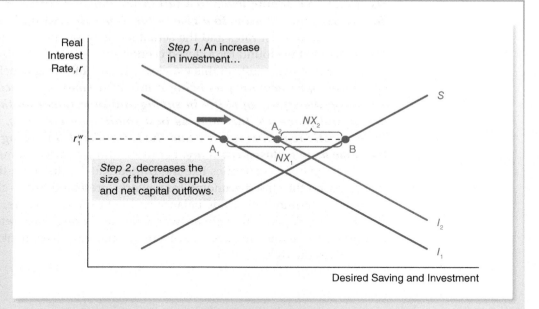

to point A_2, and so the difference between saving and investment now decreases, leading to a decline in net exports from NX_1 to NX_2. The smaller amount of excess saving and smaller trade surplus mean that domestic residents have less to lend to foreigners and so net capital outflows decrease. **An increase in autonomous investment causes a decline in the trade balance (the trade surplus to shrink or the trade deficit to increase) and lowers net capital outflows.** Net capital outflows decrease in this case, but wealth does not decline: although holdings of net foreign assets are lower than they otherwise would be, they are offset by the higher domestic capital stock that results from the increase in investment.

Large Versus Small Open Economies

Our analysis of the small open economy ignores the possible effects of changes in saving and investment in a large open economy, like the United States, on world interest rates. The saving-investment analysis for large open economies is more complicated than the analysis we have done so far for closed and small open economies, so here we will examine the differences in the effects of shifts in the saving and investment curves in a large versus a small open economy. (A full treatment of the impact of saving and investment in large open economies can be found in an appendix to this chapter that is available on the book's Companion Website at www.pearsonhighered.com/mishkin.)

The difference between the small and large economy frameworks is that shifts in saving and investment *do* affect the domestic real interest rate in a large open economy, but *not* in a small open economy. The reason for this difference is that the world interest rate *is* affected by shifts in domestic saving and investment in a large open economy, but is *not* affected by such shifts in a small open economy. ***In a large open economy, a rise in desired saving leads to a fall in the domestic interest rate, while a rise in desired investment leads to a rise in the domestic real interest rate.*** This effect on domestic real interest rates and the actual levels of saving and investment is therefore similar to what we found for a closed economy.

Looking at the results in this way leads to the following conclusion. ***We can think of a large open economy as being a mix of a small open economy and a closed economy: the effects of shifts in saving and investment on the trade balance and net capital flows are the same as in a small open economy, while the effects on the domestic real interest rate and the actual levels of saving and investment are the same as in a closed economy.*** For this reason, many economists discuss what happens in large open economies like the United States using both the simple small open economy and the closed economy frameworks presented in this chapter. When analyzing what determines the trade balance and net capital outflows, the small open economy framework gives the right answer; when analyzing what determines the domestic real interest rate and the actual levels of saving and investment, the closed economy model gives the right answer.

SUMMARY

1. Three saving measures figure prominently in macroeconomics: private saving ($S_P = Y - T - C$), government saving ($S_G = T - G$), and national saving ($S = Y - C - G = S_P + S_G$), which is the sum of the other two. The uses-of-saving identity indicates that saving is linked to wealth because it either goes into investment, which adds to physical capital, or into net capital outflow, which adds to a country's net foreign assets. The net capital outflow identity says that net capital outflow, the difference between saving and investment, equals net exports: $S - I = NX$.

2. In a closed economy, the goods market is in equilibrium when saving equals investment, $S = I$, at the intersection of the saving and investment curves.

3. An increase in saving (from a decrease in autonomous consumption, a decrease in government purchases, or an increase in taxes) shifts the saving curve to the right and leads to a lower real interest rate and higher saving and investment. An increase in autonomous investment shifts the investment curve to the right

and leads to a rise in investment, saving, and the real interest rate.

4. In an open economy, the domestic real interest rate equals the world real interest rate. Goods market equilibrium occurs when net exports equals saving minus investment: $NX = S - I$.

5. Increases in world saving or decreases in world investment cause the domestic real interest rate to fall, domestic investment to rise, and net capital outflows (net exports) to fall.

6. An increase in saving in a small open economy leads to a higher trade balance and an increase in net capital outflows. An increase in desired investment causes a decline in the trade balance and lowers net capital outflows.

7. A large open economy is a mix of a small open economy and a closed economy: the effects of shifts in saving and investment on the trade balance and net capital flows are the same as in a small open economy, while the effects on the domestic real interest rate and the actual amounts of saving and investment are the same as in a closed economy.

KEY TERMS

autonomous consumption, p. 82

autonomous investment, p. 84

balance of payments accounts, p. 77

budget surplus, p. 75

closed economy, p. 81

crowding out, p. 86

government consumption, p. 74

government investment, p. 74

government saving, p. 74

investment tax credit, p. 89

large open economy, p. 90

national saving, p. 75

national saving rate, p. 75

national wealth, p. 74

net capital outflow, p. 77

net capital outflow identity, p. 77

net foreign assets, p. 78

open economy, p. 89

perfect capital mobility, p. 89

private saving, p. 74

private saving rate, p. 74

saving-investment diagram, p. 84

small open economy, p. 90

trade deficit, p. 77

trade surplus, p. 77

twin deficits, p. 94

uses-of-saving identity, p. 77

value-added tax, p. 76

wealth, p. 73

world real interest rate, p. 89

REVIEW QUESTIONS

All Questions are available in MyEconLab *for practice or instructor assignment.*

Relationship Between Saving and Wealth

1. Describe the two components of national saving and explain how saving affects national wealth.

Saving, Investment, and Goods Market Equilibrium in a Closed Economy

2. What determines the desired amounts of national saving and investment? What relationship between desired saving and desired investment is required for goods market equilibrium, and how is this condition reached?

Response to Changes in Saving and Investment in a Closed Economy

3. What causes desired saving to increase? What effects will an increase in desired saving have in a closed economy?

4. What is crowding out?

Saving, Investment, and Goods Market Equilibrium in an Open Economy

5. Distinguish between a closed and an open economy. How do the conditions required for goods market equilibrium differ in the two types of economies?

6. What determines the world real interest rate? Why must the domestic real interest rate be the same as the world rate?

Saving, Investment, and the Trade Balance in a Small Open Economy

7. How does a small open economy differ from a large open economy?
8. What determines whether a small open economy will have a trade surplus or a trade deficit?

9. What happens in a small open economy if there is an increase in domestic saving?

Response to Changes in Saving and Investment in a Small Open Economy

10. What is the effect of an increase in domestic saving or domestic investment on the trade balance and net capital outflows?

Large Versus Small Open Economies

11. How are the effects of changes in domestic saving and investment for large open economies similar to those for small open economies and closed economies?

PROBLEMS

All Problems are available in MyEconLab *for practice or instructor assignment.*

Relationship Between Saving and Wealth

1. Suppose Japan has a GDP of $5 trillion, and that its national savings rate is 25%.
   a) Calculate Japan's national saving.

   b) Calculate Japan's government saving if private saving is $800 billion.

Saving, Investment, and Goods Market Equilibrium in a Closed Economy

2. Assume that you have saved $20,000 and that you are considering a couple of options. One of them is to use these funds as a down payment on a newly built house. The other one is to buy a U.S. savings bond.

   a) Which option will add to the economy's capital stock, and which one will not? Explain why.
   b) How would a decrease in the real interest rate affect your decision?

Response to Changes in Saving and Investment in a Closed Economy

3. Consider the (rather implausible) scenario in which the U.S. government phases out all Social Security transfers to retirees. Assuming the goods market is in equilibrium, graph the new saving curve and comment on the effects on the level of saving, investment, and the real interest rate.

4. The financial crisis that hit the United States first and then the world economy starting in fall 2007 meant that the future prospects of many firms looked gloomy at best for some time. Comment on the effect of a recession on the investment curve (only) and on the level of savings, the level of investment, and the equilibrium real interest rate. Show your answers using a saving-investment diagram.

5. On March 23, 2010, President Obama signed into law a major overhaul of the U.S. healthcare system. The Congressional Budget Office estimated that this legislation will reduce the U.S. government budget deficit by around $140 billion for the next ten years. Comment on the effect of this legislation on the saving curve (graph the new equilibrium).

Saving, Investment, and Goods Market Equilibrium in an Open Economy

6. Suppose Japan has a GDP of $5 trillion, and that its national savings rate is 25%. Assuming Japan is an open economy,
   a) calculate Japan's investment if net exports are 1% of GDP.
   b) calculate Japan's exports if imports are valued at $650 billion.

7. Consider the following diagram of a small open economy:
   a) Calculate net exports and the capital outflow when the world real interest rate is 7%.
   b) Calculate net exports and the capital outflow when the world real interest rate is 5%.

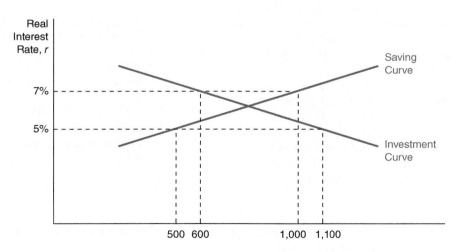

Desired Saving and Investment (in billions of dollars)

Response to Changes in Saving and Investment in a Small Open Economy

8. Consider a small open economy that is currently running a trade surplus. Answer the following questions using a graphical representation of desired saving and investment in the small open economy:
   a) Is the world real interest rate higher or lower than the real interest rate that would prevail if this were a closed economy?

   b) What would be the effect of an autonomous decrease in investment on the trade balance?

9. Comment on the effect of a decrease in autonomous investment on wealth when the economy can be considered a
   a) closed economy.
   b) small open economy.

Large Versus Small Open Economies

10. Comment on the effect of an increase in the government budget surplus (or a decrease in the government budget deficit) on the real interest rate, desired saving, and net exports for a

   a) large open economy.
   b) small open economy.

DATA ANALYSIS PROBLEMS

The Problems update with real-time data in MyEconLab *and are available for practice or instructor assignment.*

1. Go to the St. Louis Federal Reserve FRED database, find data on Gross Private Saving (GPSAVE) and Gross Saving (GSAVE), and download the data.
   a) How have these variables changed from 5 years earlier to the latest available data?
   b) Calculate Gross Government Savings for the latest available data and for the data from 5 years earlier.
   c) Based on your answer to part (b), is the government currently running a deficit, a surplus, or a balanced budget? What about 5 years ago?

2. Go to the St. Louis Federal Reserve FRED database, and find data on exports (BOPXGS) and imports (BOPMGS).
   a) Calculate net exports for the most current period available. Is the United States currently running a trade balance, surplus, or deficit?
   b) When was the last time the United States ran a trade surplus? (To answer this question, you will need to

download the data and take the difference between the two series.) Since that time, have there been net capital inflows to or net capital outflows from the United States?

3. Go to the St. Louis Federal Reserve FRED database and find data on government saving (GGSAVE).
   a) Describe what has happened to government saving from 2005 to the most current data available.
   b) Based on your answer to part (a), what do you expect should happen to real interest rates? Why? Use a saving-investment diagram to explain.
   c) One way to measure real interest rates is through Treasury Inflation-Indexed Securities, or *TIIS*. Download the 10-year TIIS (DFII10). How has the real interest rate (DFII10) behaved since 2005? Is this consistent with what you expected in part (b)? If not, explain why it may not be consistent.

An online appendix, "Saving and Investment in Large Open Economies," is available at the Companion Website, www.pearsonhighered.com/mishkin

Money and Inflation

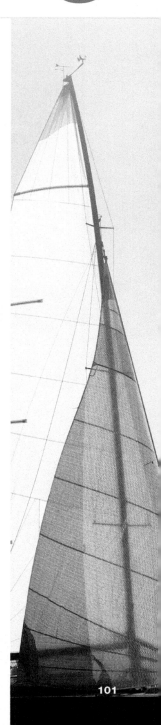

5

Preview

My first car, a Toyota Corolla, cost a little over $3,000 in 1976, while today a Toyota Corolla runs at a price of about $15,000. Today's $10 movie went for less than $2 in 1976, and for $10 you could have purchased the movie, a buttered popcorn, a soft drink, and even some dinner beforehand. Today's higher costs result from *inflation*, a general rise in the price level.

In graphical form, the swings in the inflation rate over the last half-century look like a roller coaster. Long stretches of moderate price level changes in the 1960s gave way to periods of soaring inflation rates over the next two decades. The inflation rate climaxed at over 13% in 1980, a period known as the Great Inflation, but has tempered since then. In 2009, the price level fell so quickly that inflation actually became negative for a time.

What explains these swings in the inflation rate? How can policymakers stop the price level's roller-coaster ride? Over fifty years ago, economist Milton Friedman famously proposed that "inflation is always and everywhere a monetary phenomenon."[1] Central banks, he argued, could prevent high-inflation episodes by controlling the *quantity of money*.

In this chapter, we will see that the growth rate of the quantity of money does explain inflation in the long run—when prices fully adjust to an equilibrium level—but not very well in the short run. We start the chapter by developing precise definitions of money and describing how it is currently measured. We then examine the link between money, inflation, and interest rates, and then discuss the costs of inflation for households and businesses.

[1]Milton Friedman, *Dollars and Deficits* (Upper Saddle River, NJ: Prentice Hall, 1968), 39.

What Is Money?

To avoid confusion, we must clarify how economists' use of the word *money* differs from conventional usage.

Meaning of Money

When people talk about money, they usually refer to **currency,** the bills and coins in our pockets. If a sketchy character approaches you and says, "Your money or your life," you would probably hand over all your currency. An economist, on the other hand, might reply, "What exactly do you mean by 'money'?" (And this response might have dire consequences.)

Economists define **money** as an asset that is generally accepted as payment for goods and services or in the repayment of debts. Because checks are also accepted as payment for purchases, deposits in checking accounts are also considered money. Even deposits in savings accounts can function as money if they can quickly and easily be converted into currency or checking account deposits. As you can see, there is no single, precise definition of money for economists.

To complicate matters further, the word *money* is frequently used synonymously with *wealth*. When people say that Donald Trump is rolling in money, they don't just mean he has a high balance in his checking account. They're also referring to his stocks, bonds, houses, and hotels. Economists would say "the Donald" has a great deal of **wealth,** the total collection of property that serves as a store of value. Wealth includes money and other assets, including property such as bonds, common stock, art, land, furniture, cars, and houses.

People also use the word *money* to describe what economists call *income*, as in the sentence, "Hortense would be a wonderful catch; she has a good job and earns a lot of money." Returning to the terminology we discussed in Chapter 2, **income** is a *flow* of earnings per unit of time. Money by contrast is a *stock*: It is a certain amount at a given point in time. If Hortense tells you that her income is $10,000, you cannot tell whether she earns a lot or a little without knowing whether she earns this $10,000 per year, per month, or per day. But if she told you she had $10,000 in small, unmarked bills in her briefcase, you would know exactly what she meant.

Functions of Money

Whether shells, rocks, gold, or paper (see the box, "Unusual Forms of Money"), money has three primary functions in any economy: as a *medium of exchange*, as a *unit of account*, and as a *store of value*. Of the three, its function as a medium of exchange best distinguishes money from other assets such as stocks, bonds, and houses.

MEDIUM OF EXCHANGE. In almost all market transactions in our economy, money in the form of currency and checks is a **medium of exchange;** it is used to pay for goods and services. The use of money as a medium of exchange promotes economic efficiency by minimizing **transaction costs,** the time and money spent exchanging goods or services. Without money, people would *barter*, or exchange goods and services directly for other goods and services. This process is highly inefficient, since all trades would need

Unusual Forms of Money

The need for money is so strong that almost every society beyond the most primitive invents it, and many seemingly strange objects have been used as money. American Indians used strings of beads called *wampum* as money, while early American colonists used barrels of tobacco and whisky as money because currency from the mother country, England, was unavailable. The residents on the island of Yap exchanged big stone wheels, up to twelve feet in diameter, as money. Prisoners of war in a POW camp during World War II found barter so inefficient that they made cigarettes their money in the conduct of all trades.* The diversity of the forms of money that have developed over the years is a testament to the inventiveness of the human race and to the development of tools and language.

*See the classic and entertaining article on the development of money in trying circumstances by R.A. Radford, "The Economic Organization of a P.O.W. Camp," *Economica* 12 (November 1945); 189–201.

to satisfy a "double coincidence of wants." An economics professor, for instance, would have to locate an intellectually curious farmer with whom to exchange food for a lesson on supply and demand, or else grow her own food. With money from teaching, the professor can visit any farmer (or his representative at the supermarket) to buy food. Money, therefore, promotes economic efficiency by eliminating transaction costs and allowing people to specialize in what they do best. Money is an essential lubricant for a smoothly running economy.

UNIT OF ACCOUNT. Just as we measure weight in pounds and distance in miles, we measure the value of goods and services in terms of money. Money provides a **unit of account,** or measure of value in the economy. It is far more convenient to indicate the price of all goods or services in terms of money than in terms of other goods and services. How confusing would it be if economics lectures were priced in terms of a number of hamburgers, while hamburgers were priced in terms of a number of apples? Suppose a professor, who doesn't like hamburgers but does like apples, wants to know how many apples he or she could buy after giving one lecture. The professor would need to go through a complicated calculation that might make that hamburger appealing after all.

STORE OF VALUE. Money also functions as a **store of value;** it is a repository of purchasing power that lasts over time. A store of value saves purchasing power from the time income is received until the time it is spent. This function of money is useful because most of us do not want to spend our income immediately upon receiving it, but rather prefer to wait until we have time or the desire to shop.

Stocks, bonds, property, and jewelry also store wealth, and many such assets can appreciate in value over time. Nevertheless, money is still desired as a store of value because of its use as a medium of exchange. This makes money the most **liquid** of all assets, which means it does not have to be converted into a medium of exchange in order to make purchases.

The Federal Reserve System and the Control of the Money Supply

We now go on to conduct a brief look at how the amount of money in the economy, also known as the **money supply,** is determined (with a more detailed discussion in the appendix to this chapter). But before we do, we need to discuss the key player in the money supply process, the central bank of the United States, which is officially known as the **Federal Reserve System** (or more commonly as the **Fed**). It is comprised of the twelve *Federal Reserve banks* and the *Board of Governors of the Federal Reserve System*.[2] Besides conducting monetary policy, the Fed's duties include issuing currency, clearing checks, and providing supervisory oversight of the financial system.

Federal Reserve Banks

The Federal Reserve System is divided into twelve districts. Each district has one main Federal Reserve bank, which may have branches in other cities in the district. We show the locations of these districts, the Federal Reserve banks, and their branches in Figure 5.1.

   The twelve Federal Reserve banks are involved in monetary policy in two key ways: five of the twelve bank presidents each have a vote in the **Federal Open Market Committee (FOMC),** which directs open market operations (the purchase and sale of government securities that affect both interest rates and the amount of liquidity in the banking system). The Federal Reserve Bank of New York always has a vote in the

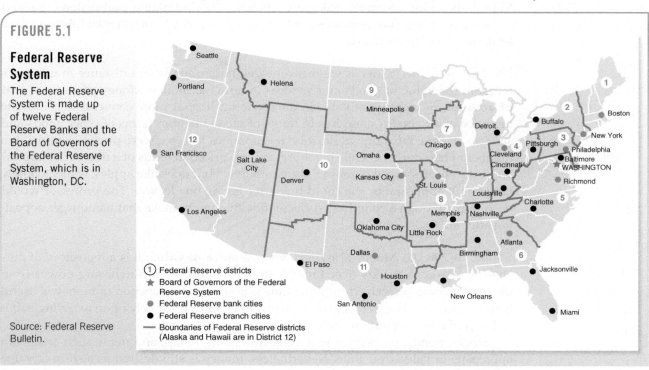

FIGURE 5.1

Federal Reserve System

The Federal Reserve System is made up of twelve Federal Reserve Banks and the Board of Governors of the Federal Reserve System, which is in Washington, DC.

Source: Federal Reserve Bulletin.

① Federal Reserve districts
★ Board of Governors of the Federal Reserve System
● Federal Reserve bank cities
● Federal Reserve branch cities
— Boundaries of Federal Reserve districts (Alaska and Hawaii are in District 12)

[2]For more detail on the structure of the Federal Reserve System and the European Central Bank, see Chapter 13, "Central Banks and the Federal Reserve System," in Frederic S. Mishkin, *The Economics of Money, Banking and Financial Markets*, 10th ed. (Boston: Addison-Wesley, 2013), 315–343.

FOMC, making it the most important of the banks. The other four votes allocated to the district banks rotate annually among the remaining eleven presidents.

Board of Governors of the Federal Reserve System

At the head of the Federal Reserve System is the seven-member **Board of Governors of the Federal Reserve System**, headquartered in Washington, DC. Each governor is appointed by the president of the United States and confirmed by the Senate. The chairperson of the Board of Governors serves a four-year, renewable term.

The Board of Governors is actively involved in decisions concerning the conduct of monetary policy. All seven governors are members of the FOMC and vote on the conduct of open market operations. Because there are only twelve voting members on this committee (seven governors and five presidents of the district banks), the Board has the majority of the votes. The chairperson of the Board, currently Ben Bernanke, advises the president of the United States on economic policy, testifies in Congress, and represents the Federal Reserve System in the media. The chairperson and other governors may also represent the United States in negotiations with foreign governments on economic matters. The Board has a staff of professional economists (larger than those of individual Federal Reserve banks) that provides economic analysis to inform the Board's decisions.

Federal Open Market Committee (FOMC)

The FOMC usually meets eight times a year (about every six weeks) and makes decisions regarding the conduct of open market operations that influence the money supply and interest rates. Indeed, the FOMC is often referred to as the "Fed" in the press: when the media say that the Fed is meeting, they actually mean that the FOMC is meeting. The committee consists of the seven members of the Board of Governors, the president of the Federal Reserve Bank of New York, and the presidents of four other Federal Reserve banks. The chairperson of the Board of Governors also presides as the chairperson of the FOMC. Even though only the presidents of five of the Federal Reserve banks are voting members of the FOMC, the other seven presidents of the district banks attend FOMC meetings and participate in discussions. Hence they have some input into the committee's decisions.

Up until recently, the Federal Reserve System had no rivals in terms of its importance in the central banking world. However, that situation changed in 1999 with the start-up of the European Central Bank, described in the box, "The European Central Bank."

The European Central Bank

Europe patterned its system of central banks after the Federal Reserve System. The *European Central Bank (ECB)*, housed in Frankfurt, Germany, is run by an Executive Board similar in structure to the Board of Governors of the Federal Reserve. Its six members, including a president and a vice president, are appointed to eight-year, nonrenewable terms. The *National Central Banks (NCBs)* have similar functions to the Federal Reserve Banks. And a *Governing Council*, composed of the Executive Board and the presidents of the National Central Banks, is similar to the FOMC. The Council meets monthly to make decisions on monetary policy. Each country appoints the president of its own National Central Bank, although the Executive Board members are selected by a committee of heads of state of all the European Monetary Union countries.

Control of the Money Supply

We will discuss the Fed's role in monetary policy in detail in Chapters 10 and 13. For now, we will provide a bit of intuition about how the Federal Reserve controls the amount of money in the economy. The Fed carries out this task primarily through the purchase and sale of government bonds in **open market operations.** A more detailed discussion of how the Federal Reserve controls the money supply is discussed in the appendix to this chapter, but for now, we will provide just a bit of intuition for the process. When the Fed buys a government bond from a bank, it pays for the bond with dollars, increasing the amount of dollars in the bank. Armed with this additional liquidity, banks can make additional loans to households and businesses that are deposited into checking accounts, increasing the level of checkable deposits. Since these deposits are included in the money supply, an open market purchase increases the money supply. Similar reasoning indicates that when the Fed sells government bonds, it takes in dollars from the public and reduces the money supply.

Measuring Money

Our previous discussion of the functions of money suggests that money is defined by people's behavior. Money is what people *believe* others will accept for payment. This behavioral definition does not tell us which assets in our economy we should consider money. To measure money, we need a precise definition that tells us exactly which assets to include.

The Federal Reserve's Monetary Aggregates

The Fed relies on two measures of the money supply, called **monetary aggregates** (see Table 5.1), that it evaluates over time to reflect available financial products.

M1. The Fed's narrowest measure of money, **M1,** includes only the most liquid assets: currency, traveler's checks, demand deposits, and checking account deposits. Table 5.1 shows the components of M1 for June 2013. The *currency* component of M1 includes only paper money and coins in the hands of the nonbank public: it does not include cash that is held in ATMs or bank vaults. Surprisingly, there is over $3,000 cash in circulation for each U.S. citizen (see the box, "Where Is All the U.S. Currency?"). The *demand deposits* component includes business checking accounts that do not pay interest as well as traveler's checks issued by banks. The traveler's checks component includes those issued by nonbanks. The *other checkable deposits* item covers the remainder of checking accounts, such as interest-bearing checking accounts held by households. These assets are clearly money because individuals can use them directly as a medium of exchange.

M2. The **M2** monetary aggregate includes all of M1 plus several less liquid asset types, such as money market deposit accounts and money market mutual fund shares with check-writing features. It also includes savings deposits, which can be taken out of the bank at any time, as well as certificates of deposit in denominations of less than $100,000. Certificates of deposit (CDs) are referred to as time deposits, since they can be redeemed without penalty only at a fixed maturity date. Table 5.1 shows the value of M2 for June 2013.

Where Is All the U.S. Currency?

The $1,123 billion in outstanding U.S. currency in 2013 is enough for every U.S. citizen to hold $3,600 in cash. That's a surprisingly large number, since currency is bulky, can be easily stolen, and pays no interest. Do you know anyone who carries $3,600 in his or her pockets? We have a puzzle: Where are all these dollars, and who is holding them?

Criminals are one group that holds a lot of dollars. If you were engaged in an illegal activity, you would not conduct your transactions with traceable checks that are a potentially powerful piece of evidence against you. That explains why the TV mobster Tony Soprano had so much cash in his backyard. Some businesses like to retain a lot of cash because operating as a cash business helps them avoid declaring income (an illegal activity) on which they would have to pay taxes.

Foreigners are the other group who routinely hold U.S. dollars. In many countries, people do not trust their own currency because their countries often experience high inflation, which erodes the value of that currency; these people hold U.S. dollars to protect themselves against this inflation risk. Lack of trust in the ruble, for example, has led many Russians to hoard enormous amounts of U.S. dollars. Russians, Argentines, Chinese, and Kazakhs hold the largest numbers of dollars outside the United States.

The Fed's Use of M1 Versus M2 in Practice

But which measure of the money supply—M1 or M2—does the Fed use to inform policy decisions? It's not obvious which monetary aggregate is a better measure of money, and Table 5.1 indicates that there is a significant difference ($8.1 trillion dollars) between the two measures. But if M1 and M2 tend to move in parallel, the Fed could use trends in

TABLE 5.1   **MEASURES OF THE MONETARY AGGREGATES**

		Value as of June 2013 ($ billions)
M1 = Currency		$ 1,123.0
+Traveler's checks		$ 3.7
+Demand deposits		$ 944.9
+Other checkable deposits		$ 451.0
Total M1	=	$ 2,522.6
M2 = M1		
+Small-denomination time deposits		$ 567.7
+Savings deposits and money market deposit accounts		$ 6,857.1
+Money market mutual fund shares (retail)		$ 651.5
Total M2	=	$10,598.9

Source: Components of M1 and M2, seasonally adjusted, June 2013. Federal Reserve Economic Database (FRED), Federal Reserve Bank of St. Louis, http://research.stlouisfed.org/fred2/

MACROECONOMICS IN THE NEWS

The Monetary Aggregates

Every week on Thursday, the Federal Reserve publishes the data for M1 and M2 in its H-6 release, and these numbers are often reported on in the media. The H-6 release can be found at www.federalreserve.gov/releases/h6/ current/h6.htm.

either monetary aggregate to predict future economic performance and conduct policy. Figure 5.2 plots the growth rates of M1 and M2 from 1960 to 2013. Notice how the two monetary aggregates rise and fall in tandem through the 1980s, and show a higher average growth rate during the Great Inflation of the 1970s than in the more moderate 1960s. Yet there are some glaring discrepancies where the movements of these aggregates regularly diverge. Contrast M1's high rates of growth from 1992 to 1994 with the much lower growth rate of M2. Also notice that from 2004 to 2007, M2's growth rate increased slightly, while M1 sharply decelerated and went negative. In 2009, M1 growth surged to over 15% from near zero the year before, while M2 growth rose only slightly. Given how different a story the two aggregates tell about the course of monetary policy in recent years, the Federal Reserve focuses on interest rates rather than money supply in conducting monetary policy.

MyEconLab Real-time data

FIGURE 5.2

Growth Rates of M1 and M2, 1960–2013

The graphs of the rise and fall of the growth rates of M1 and M2 are roughly similar. There are, however, periods, such as 1992–1994 and 2004–2007, during which they move in opposite directions, providing conflicting information about the course of monetary policy.

Source: Federal Reserve Economic Database (FRED). Federal Reserve Bank of St. Louis. http://research.stlouisfed.org/fred2/categories/25.

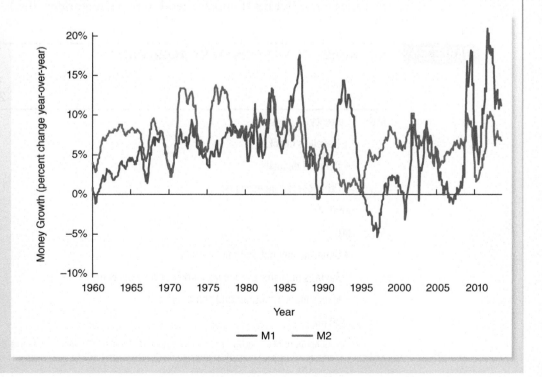

Quantity Theory of Money

Now that we have a clear understanding of money and the money supply, we will examine how changes in the money supply affect the economy over both short and long periods of time. We begin with a look at the long run and utilize the *quantity theory of money*, which links a country's total income to its supply of money. This theory is the product of the **classical economists,** also known as **classicals,** who assumed that wages and prices are completely flexible—that is, they completely and quickly adjust to the long-run equilibrium at which supply equals demand.

American economist Irving Fisher gave the clearest exposition of this theory in his influential book, *The Purchasing Power of Money*, published in 1911. Fisher examined the link between the total quantity of money M (the money supply) and the total amount of spending on final goods and services produced in the economy, $P \times Y$, where P is the price level and Y is aggregate output (income). (Recall from Chapter 2 that total spending $P \times Y$ is the same as aggregate nominal income for the economy, nominal GDP.)

Velocity of Money and the Equation of Exchange

The concept that provides the link between M and $P \times Y$ is called the **velocity of money** (also more simply referred to as *velocity*), the average number of times per year that a dollar is spent, or turns over, in buying goods and services produced in the economy. We calculate velocity V by dividing total spending $P \times Y$ by the quantity of money M:

$$V = \frac{P \times Y}{M} \tag{1}$$

If, for example, nominal GDP ($P \times Y$) in a year is \$10 trillion and the quantity of money is \$2 trillion, then velocity is 5, meaning that the average dollar bill is spent five times in purchasing final goods and services in the economy.

By multiplying both sides of Equation 1 by M, we obtain the **equation of exchange,** which relates nominal income to the quantity of money and velocity:

$$M \times V = P \times Y \tag{2}$$

The equation of exchange states that the quantity of money multiplied by the number of times the money is spent in a given year must equal nominal income (the total nominal income spent on goods and services in that year).[3]

---

[3]Fisher actually first formulated the equation of exchange in terms of the nominal value of transactions in the economy, PT:

$$MV_T = PT$$

where
$$P = \text{average price per transaction}$$
$$T = \text{number of transactions conducted in a year}$$
$$V_T = PT/M = \text{transactions velocity of money}$$

Because the nominal value of transactions T is difficult to measure, the quantity theory has been formulated in terms of aggregate output Y so that $T = vY$, where v is a constant of proportionality. Substituting vY for T in Fisher's equation of exchange yields $MV_T = vPY$, which we can rewrite as Equation 2 in the text, in which $V = V_T/v$.

As it stands, Equation 2 is nothing more than an identity—a relationship that is true by definition. It does not tell us, for instance, that when the money supply M changes, nominal income $P \times Y$ changes in the same direction. A rise in M, for example, could be offset by a fall in V that leaves $M \times V$ and therefore $P \times Y$ unchanged. Converting the equation of exchange, an *identity*, into a *theory* of how to determine nominal income requires an understanding of the factors that determine velocity.

DETERMINANTS OF VELOCITY. Irving Fisher reasoned that velocity is determined by the institutions in an economy that affect the way individuals conduct transactions. For example, the introduction of credit cards allowed millions of U.S. shoppers to use plastic instead of cash, requiring less money in the economy. With less money needed for the same level of nominal income, M fell relative to $P \times Y$ and velocity $(P \times Y)/M$ increased. Conversely, if it is more convenient for purchases to be paid for with cash or checkable deposits (both of which are money), more money is used to conduct the transactions generated by the same level of nominal income, and velocity falls. Fisher took the view that the institutional and technological features of the economy change velocity only gradually, so he expected velocity to be reasonably constant over long periods of time.

THE DEMAND FOR MONEY. Another way of interpreting Fisher's quantity theory is in terms of the **demand for money,** the quantity of money that people want to hold.

Because the quantity theory of money tells us how much money is held for a given amount of nominal spending, it is in fact a theory of the demand for money. To illustrate, let's first divide both sides of the equation of exchange by V to yield the following:

$$M = \frac{1}{V} \times PY$$

When the money market is in equilibrium, money supply equals money demand, so we can replace M in the equation by M^d. In addition, since in the quantity theory of money velocity is assumed to be constant, we can replace $1/V$ with a constant k. Substituting k for $1/V$ and M^d for M and then dividing both sides of the equation by P leads to the quantity theory of money demand:

$$\frac{M^d}{P} = k \times Y \tag{3}$$

This equation tells us that the demand for *real money balances*, that is, the quantity of money that people want to hold in terms of the goods and services that it can purchase, is proportional to income.

From the Equation of Exchange to the Quantity Theory of Money

Fisher's view that velocity is fairly constant over long periods of time, so that $V = \overline{V}$, transforms the equation of exchange into the **quantity theory of money,** which states that nominal income (spending) is determined solely by movements in the quantity of money M.

$$P \times Y = M \times \overline{V} \tag{4}$$

The quantity theory equation above indicates that when the quantity of money M doubles, $M \times \overline{V}$ doubles and so must $P \times Y$, the value of nominal income. To illustrate, let's assume that velocity is 5, nominal income (GDP) is initially $10 trillion, and the money supply is $2 trillion. If the money supply doubles to $4 trillion, the quantity theory of money tells us that nominal income will double to $20 trillion (= 5 × $4 trillion).

The Classical Dichotomy

Because classical economists (including Irving Fisher) viewed wages and prices as flexible, they believed that prices of goods and services and factor prices would fully adjust to the levels that equate the supply and demand for each good or service in the long run. As we saw in Chapter 3, this would mean that the level of output produced in the economy would be solely determined by the aggregate production function and the quantities of factors available. Consequently, the amount of goods and services produced in an economy in the long run is not affected by the price level—and this is also true for real factor prices, such as real wages and the real rental cost of capital. This view is known as the **classical dichotomy** because it indicates that in the long run there is a complete separation (*dichotomy*) between the real side of the economy and the nominal side (which changes with the price level).

Quantity Theory and the Price Level

The classical dichotomy tells us that we can take aggregate output as given, so we assign Y in the quantity theory of money, Equation 4, the constant value of $\overline{Y}$. Dividing both sides of Equation 4 by $\overline{Y}$, we can then write the price level as follows:

$$P = \frac{M \times \overline{V}}{\overline{Y}} \tag{5}$$

The quantity theory of money as represented by Equation 5 implies that if M doubles, P must also double in the short run because $\overline{V}$ and $\overline{Y}$ are constant. In our example, if aggregate output is $10 trillion, velocity is 5, and the money supply is $2 trillion, then the price level equals 1.0.

$$P = 1.0 = \frac{\$2 \text{ trillion} \times 5}{\$10 \text{ trillion}} = \frac{\$10 \text{ trillion}}{\$10 \text{ trillion}}$$

When the money supply doubles to $4 trillion, the price level must also double to 2.0 because

$$P = 2.0 = \frac{\$4 \text{ trillion} \times 5}{\$10 \text{ trillion}} = \frac{\$20 \text{ trillion}}{\$10 \text{ trillion}}$$

Classical economists relied on the quantity theory of money to explain movements in the price level. In their view, ***changes in the quantity of money lead to proportional changes in the price level.***

According to the quantity theory analysis, a country's central bank determines the general price level in the long run because it controls the supply of money. Furthermore, a central bank's work in adjusting the money supply changes only the price level and has no impact on real variables, an implication economists refer to as the **neutrality of money.** However, as we will see later in Part 4, many economists reject the neutrality of money in the short run.

Quantity Theory and Inflation

We now transform the quantity theory of money into a theory of inflation. Using the helpful mathematical fact we discussed in Chapter 2 that the percentage change (%Δ) of a product of a number of variables is approximately equal to the sum of the percentage changes of each of these variables, we can rewrite the equation of exchange as follows:

$$\%\Delta M + \%\Delta V = \%\Delta P + \%\Delta Y$$

Subtracting %ΔY from both sides of the preceding equation, and recognizing that the inflation rate, π, is the growth rate of the price level, that is, %ΔP,

$$\pi = \%\Delta P = \%\Delta M + \%\Delta V - \%\Delta Y$$

Since we assume velocity is constant, its growth rate is zero, and so the quantity theory of money is also a theory of inflation:

$$\pi = \%\Delta M - \%\Delta Y \tag{6}$$

Because the percentage change in a variable at an annual rate is the same as the growth rate of that variable, this equation can also be stated in words: ***the quantity theory of inflation indicates that, in the long run, the inflation rate equals the growth rate of the money supply minus the growth rate of aggregate output.*** For example, if the aggregate output is growing at 3% per year and the growth rate of money is 5%, then inflation is 2% (= 5% − 3%). If the Federal Reserve increases the money growth rate to 10%, then the quantity theory of inflation in Equation 6 indicates that the inflation rate will rise to 7% (= 10% − 3%).

Application

Testing the Quantity Theory of Money

Now that we have fully outlined the quantity theory of money, let's put it to the test with actual data over the long and short runs.

The Quantity Theory of Money in the Long Run. The quantity theory of money provides a long-run theory of inflation because it is based on the assumption that wages and prices are flexible. Figure 5.3 panel (a) plots ten-year averages of U.S. inflation rates against the ten-year average rate of U.S. money growth ($M2$) from 1870 through 2000. Since the growth rate of aggregate output Y over ten-year periods does not vary very much, Equation 6 indicates that the ten-year inflation rate should be the ten-year money growth rate minus a constant (the rate of aggregate output growth). Thus there should be a strong positive relationship between inflation and money growth rates—and this relationship is borne out in panel (a) of Figure 5.3. Decades with higher growth rates of the U.S. money supply typically see higher average inflation rates.

FIGURE 5.3

Relationship Between Inflation and Money Growth

In panel (a), decades with higher money growth rates (the 1910s, the 1940s, and the 1970s) typically have a higher average inflation rate. This relationship also holds in panel (b), where we examine the ten-year inflation and money growth rates from 2002–2012 for various countries.

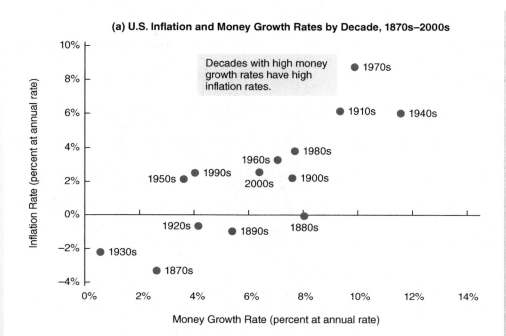

(a) U.S. Inflation and Money Growth Rates by Decade, 1870s–2000s

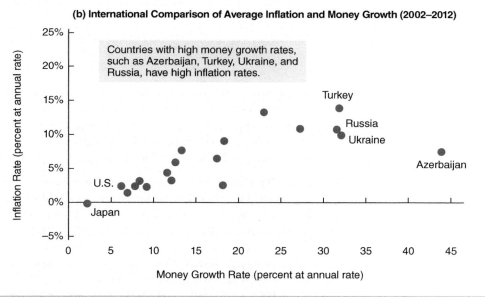

(b) International Comparison of Average Inflation and Money Growth (2002–2012)

Sources: For panel (a), Milton Friedman and Anna Schwartz, *Monetary trends in the United States and the United Kingdom: Their relation to income, prices, and interest rate, 1867–1975*, Federal Reserve Economic Database (FRED), Federal Reserve Bank of St. Louis, http://research.stlouisfed.org/fred2/. For panel (b), International Financial Statistics. International Monetary Fund. http://www.imf.org/external/data.htm

FIGURE 5.4

Annual U.S. Inflation and Money Growth Rates, 1965–2013

Plots of the annual U.S. inflation rate against the annual money (*M2*) growth rate from two years earlier (to allow for lag effects from money growth to inflation) do not support a short-run link between inflation and money growth. There are many years (such as 1963–1967, 1983–1985, and 2003–2005) during which money growth is high, yet inflation is low.

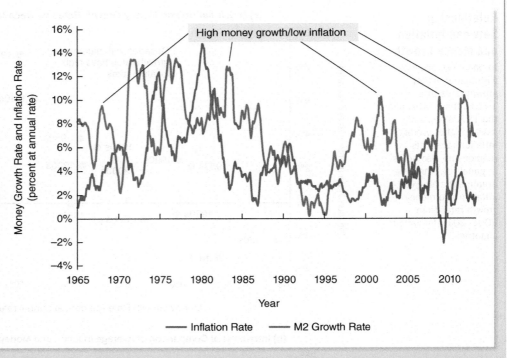

Sources: FRED, Federal Reserve Economic Data, Federal Reserve Bank of St. Louis; Bureau of Labor Statistics, http://research.stlouisfed.org/fred2/.

Does the quantity theory also explain differing long-run inflation rates across countries? It certainly does. Panel (b) of Figure 5.3 plots the average inflation rate over the ten-year period from 2002 to 2012 against the ten-year money growth rate for several countries. Note that countries with high money growth, such as Azerbaijan, Turkey, Ukraine, and Russia, tend to have higher inflation.

The Quantity Theory of Money in the Short Run. Does the quantity theory of money provide a good explanation of short-run inflation fluctuations as well? Figure 5.4 provides evidence on the link between money growth and inflation in the short run by plotting the annual U.S. inflation rate from 1965 to 2013 against the annual money (*M2*) growth rate. (The money supply lags by two years to allow for the time it takes for changes in money growth to affect inflation.) The relationship between inflation and money growth on an annual basis is not strong at all. There are many years—such as 1963–1965, 1983–1985, 2003–2005, 2008–2009, 2011–2013—during which money growth is high, but inflation is low. Indeed, it is hard to see a positive correlation at all between money growth and inflation in Figure 5.4.

The conclusion is that ***Milton Friedman's statement that "inflation is always and everywhere a monetary phenomenon" is accurate in the long run, but is not supported by the data for the short run.*** This insight tells us that the classical assumption that wages and prices are completely flexible may not be a good assumption for short-run fluctuations in inflation and aggregate output. For this reason, we relax this assumption in Part 4 of the book when we develop models of short-run inflation and output fluctuations.

Hyperinflation

Periods of extremely rapid price increases of more than 50% per month (over 1,000% per year) are called periods of **hyperinflation.** Many economies—both poor and developed—have experienced hyperinflation over the last century, but the United States has been spared such turmoil. One of the most extreme examples of hyperinflation throughout world history occurred recently in Zimbabwe in the 2000s, and it is discussed in the Policy and Practice case that follows.

Policy and Practice

The Zimbabwean Hyperinflation

The source of high money supply growth that causes hyperinflation to occur is typically fiscal imbalances, a topic that we will discuss in more detail in Chapter 16, and the hyperinflation in Zimbabwe that started in the early 2000s is no exception. After the expropriation of farms, which were redistributed to supporters of Robert Mugabe, the president of the country, agricultural output plummeted, and along with it tax revenue. The result was that the government's expenditures now greatly exceeded revenues. The government could have obtained revenues to cover its expenditures by raising taxes, but given the depressed state of the economy, generating revenue in this way was both hard to do and would have been politically unpopular. Alternatively, the government could have tried to finance its expenditure by borrowing from the public, but given the public distrust of the government, this was not an option. There was only one route left: the printing press. The government could pay for its expenditures simply by printing more currency (increasing the money supply) and using it to make payments to individuals and businesses. This is exactly what the Zimbabwean government did, and the money supply began to increase rapidly.

As predicted by the quantity theory, the surge in the money supply led to a rapidly rising price level. In February 2007, the Reserve Bank of Zimbabwe, the central bank, outlawed price increases on many commodities. Although this tactic has been tried many times before by governments in countries experiencing hyperinflation, it has never worked: criminalizing inflation cannot stop inflation when the central bank keeps on printing money. In March 2007, the inflation rate hit a record of over 1,500%. By 2008, Zimbabwe's official inflation rate was over two million percent (but unofficially over ten million percent). In July of 2008, the Zimbabwean central bank issued a new $100 billion bank note. That's a lot of zeros, but don't be too impressed. One of those bills could not even buy a bottle of beer. Zimbabwean currency became worth less than toilet paper.

In 2009, the Zimbabwean government allowed the use of foreign currencies like the dollar for all transactions, but the damage had already been done. The hyperinflation wreaked havoc on the economy, and an extremely poor country became even poorer.

Inflation and Interest Rates

As we discussed in Chapter 2, the Fisher equation states that the nominal interest rate i equals the real interest rate r plus the expected rate of inflation π^e,

$$i = r + \pi^e \tag{7}$$

Under the classical dichotomy, real variables like r are unaffected by inflation or expected inflation. Indeed, as we saw in Chapter 4, in the long run, when wages and prices are flexible, the real interest rate is determined by the interaction of saving and investment. So in the long run, when the classical view of inflation holds and the level of the real interest rate is given, we would expect that nominal interest rates would move one-for-one with expected inflation, as the Fisher equation suggests. For example, if the real interest rate is 2% and expected inflation is 3%, then the nominal interest rate should be 5%. If expected inflation rises to 10%, then the nominal interest rate would rise to 12%.

The Fisher equation and the classical dichotomy produce a theory of interest rates called the **Fisher effect:** when expected inflation rises, interest rates will rise. Irving Fisher was the first economist to point out the relationship between expected inflation and interest rates.

Application

Testing the Fisher Effect

How accurately does the prediction from the Fisher analysis describe trends in the United States and abroad? Notice in Figure 5.5 panel (a) that expected U.S. inflation over the coming year and the (nominal) interest rate on three-month Treasury bills have moved together since 1955. As expected inflation rose from the 1950s to the early 1980s, the three-month Treasury bill rate climbed from the 2% level to peak at 15%. When expected inflation declined to the 2–3% level in the mid-1990s, the interest rate on three-month Treasury bills also came down, to around the 5% level. The pattern holds in most, but not all, periods. For example, from 1981 to 1983, expected inflation fell precipitously without a corresponding drop in the Treasury bill rate. In addition, during the period from the early 1990s until the mid-2000s, inflation was much steadier than the Treasury bill rate. The U.S. evidence thus demonstrates that *the Fisher effect prediction that nominal interest rates rise along with expected inflation is accurate in the long run, but over shorter time periods, expected inflation and nominal interest rates do not always move together.*

The support for a strong Fisher effect relationship in the long run is further borne out by Figure 5.5 panel (b), which represents a selection of countries. The chart plots each country's average nominal interest rate over the ten-year period from 2002 to 2012 against the average inflation rate over the same ten-year period. (The ten-year average is a fair approximation of expected inflation over the same period.) There is a reasonably close association between the two, with high-inflation countries such as Indonesia also displaying high nominal interest rates.

Since nominal interest rates are determined by inflation expectations, they, too, are a monetary phenomenon. The quantity theory of inflation suggests that for a central bank to keep nominal interest rates low, it needs to prevent the money supply from growing at too rapid a rate. No wonder that financial market participants who bet on the level of interest rates keep a close eye on the Federal Reserve to see whether it will pursue policies to control inflation.

FIGURE 5.5

Expected Inflation and the Nominal Interest Rate

In panel (a), the long-run trend is consistent with the Fisher effect, but there are short-run periods when the Treasury bill rate does not track movements in expected inflation. Panel (b) also supports the long-run relationship in plots of average nominal interest rates and inflation rates over the ten-year period from 2002–2012 across a number of countries.

Sources: For panel (a), FRED, Federal Reserve Economic Data, Federal Reserve Bank of St. Louis; Board of Governors of the Federal Reserve System; http://research.stlouisfed.org/fred2/; the estimated expected inflation rate is estimated using the procedure outlined in Mishkin, Frederic S. 1981. The real interest rate: An empirical investigation. *Carnegie-Rochester Conference Series on Public Policy* 15: pp. 151–200. This procedure involves estimating expected inflation as a function of past interest rates, inflation, and time trends. For panel (b), International Monetary Fund. International Financial Statistics. www.imfstatistics.org/imf/

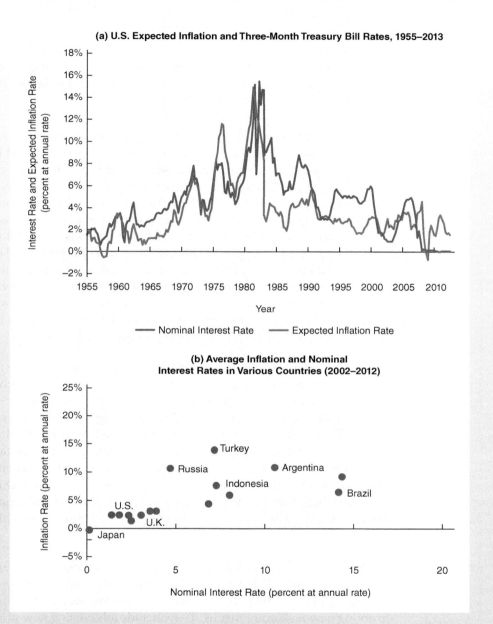

(a) U.S. Expected Inflation and Three-Month Treasury Bill Rates, 1955–2013

Nominal Interest Rate — Expected Inflation Rate

(b) Average Inflation and Nominal Interest Rates in Various Countries (2002–2012)

The Cost of Inflation

So far in this chapter, we have focused on the causes of inflation. But we have to ask, what are its consequences? Inflation imposes two types of costs on the economy: costs from anticipated inflation and costs from unanticipated inflation. We look at each in turn.

Costs of Anticipated Inflation

Suppose that inflation has been running at a steady but high rate of 10% for a long period of time, so that the 10% inflation rate is fully anticipated by the public. At first glance, why should there be any costs from the 10% inflation rate? Although prices on the things you buy will be going up every year at a 10% rate, you will expect your employer to pay you at least 10% more each year, which will prevent your real wage from declining and allow you to purchase the same quantities of goods and services. What about your savings? The Fisher effect analysis indicates that nominal interest rates should rise to compensate for the increase in the price level every year, and so the real interest rate on your savings account should also be unaffected.

In a world in which the classical dichotomy holds and inflation has no effect on the real side of the economy, fully anticipated inflation should not affect your well-being. However, even in the long run, the classical dichotomy may not be completely correct, so a perfectly anticipated inflation can be costly for five reasons:

SHOE-LEATHER COSTS. When inflation is high, nominal interest rates rise to compensate for the increase in the price level. As a result, it is more costly for you to hold cash in your pocket because it doesn't earn any interest. For example, say inflation increases nominal interest rates from 7% to 12%. Cash kept in your wallet can now earn an additional 5% in interest if you put it in, say, a savings account at a bank, which might prompt you to make a trip to the bank to put the cash into this account. The time and fuel spent on these trips are called **shoe-leather costs** by economists, because they bring to mind that too many trips can wear out your shoes. During hyperinflations, firms pay their workers more than once a day, and households shop far more frequently than they otherwise would. This inefficiency can impose very high shoe-leather costs on the economy.

MENU COSTS. High inflation, even if perfectly anticipated, requires that firms change prices frequently. Higher anticipated inflation therefore leads to costs associated with changing prices, which are referred to as **menu costs.** Menu costs cover more than printing new restaurant menus. They include advertising new prices to customers, relabeling goods with new price tags, and informing salespeople.

TAX DISTORTIONS. In practice, tax rates do not adjust fully to anticipated inflation, creating a cost for investors. To illustrate, suppose the price level doubles and your $1,000 of Apple stock doubles in value to $2,000. You are no better off when you sell it because the goods and services you can buy with the proceeds are unchanged. Nonetheless, you would pay a 15% capital gains tax, or $150, on the appreciation of the stock. This tax distortion might discourage investment when inflation is high.

INCREASED VARIABILITY OF RELATIVE PRICES. Because firms competing in the same market do not always change prices at the same time, higher inflation can cause high variability in relative prices. This high variability creates inefficiencies in the economy, because relative prices are more likely to be higher or lower than they should be in the absence of inflation. For example, say that Louis Vuitton updates prices for its handbags only in November, and Christian Dior updates them only in January. In a year of high inflation, the relative prices of the two brands of handbags would become severely misaligned in the month of December, so that few consumers would buy a Louis Vuitton bag in that month. When the timing of purchases is distorted by high inflation, there is an inappropriate allocation of resources in the economy.

LOSS OF THE DOLLAR YARDSTICK. When prices fluctuate, businesses and households have a tough time comparing the relative costs of goods and services. If a Toyota Corolla's price increases from $15,000 to $16,500, while a Dell computer's price jumps from $800 to $880, which is now a relatively better deal? Not everybody will immediately see that the prices of both goods went up by 10%—and some consumers might mistakenly think that relative prices have changed and therefore make poor spending decisions. A constant price level provides a *dollar yardstick*: a simplified price comparison wherein a change in the price of a good is a change in its real price. The consistent length of a yardstick makes it easy to compare the sizes of different items. Similarly, having low inflation keeps the dollar yardstick the same length and enables consumers to readily compare the prices of goods and services, benefiting firms and households.

Costs of Unanticipated Inflation

Although the costs of anticipated inflation might be substantial, the costs of inflation that is a surprise are likely to be even higher. There are several costs from unanticipated inflation.

INCREASED UNCERTAINTY. Inflation that turns out to be different than what you anticipated is likely to lead to incorrect investment and savings decisions that are costly to both you and the economy. To illustrate, let's begin by looking at the costs of unanticipated inflation with the case of lower-than-anticipated inflation. Suppose you expect the inflation rate to be 10% next year, but in fact it turns out to be less, say, 5%. Consider two financial transactions:

1. Purchase a certificate of deposit. If your certificate of deposit was paying you 12%—10% for the expected inflation adjustment and 2% for the real interest rate—you would end up with a windfall. Instead of earning 2% in real terms, you now earn 7% (= 12% − 5%). If you had known you would earn such a high return, you would have saved even more. Your inability to foresee the lower inflation was costly.

2. Take out a car loan. If you took out a car loan at 12% and the inflation rate turned out to be 5% instead of 10%, the real cost of the loan is now 7% (= 12% − 5%), not 2% (= 12% − 10%) as you expected. If you knew that the cost of the loan was going to be that high, you might have decided not to borrow and instead deferred your car purchase.

Now let's examine the case of higher-than-anticipated inflation. Suppose the inflation rate turns out to be higher than expected, say, 15%.

1. Purchase a certificate of deposit. You would have earned a negative 3% return in real terms on the certificate of deposit (= 12% − 15%) and you would wish you had saved less.

2. Take out a car loan. The car loan would now have a very low cost in real terms, negative 3% (= 12% − 15%), so you would regret not borrowing and investing more money.

Unanticipated inflation can also distort decisions about how much to work and how much labor a firm should employ. Suppose you and your boss expect the inflation rate to increase by 10% over the coming year. You receive a 10% pay hike to compensate for the expected price increase. The inflation rate increase turns out to be 5%, so you have received an unanticipated increase in your real wage of 5% and are eager to increase your work hours. Your boss, who has ended up paying 5% more in real terms than she expected, would prefer to reduce your hours, or might regret hiring you at all.

Unanticipated inflation therefore can lead to costly decisions on savings, investment, and the amount of labor that is supplied or demanded, leading to a less efficient economy. Furthermore, most people dislike uncertainty, so unanticipated fluctuations in inflation make both you and your boss worse off.

INCREASED VARIABILITY OF RELATIVE PRICES. We already have seen that anticipated inflation can lead to increased variability of prices, which makes the economy less efficient. This problem can be even worse when inflation is unanticipated. When inflation is anticipated, firms that set prices infrequently find that the relative prices of their products get more out of line over time. But because they expect a certain amount of inflation, they have some ability to devise plans for minimizing the resulting cost. If, on the other hand, inflation is unanticipated, firms may have trouble recognizing when the prices they have set are changing relative to other prices. For example, suppose the 15% inflation rate is 5% *greater* than the 10% rate a firm expected. When it raises prices by 10%, it may find that the demand for its product is temporarily higher than expected and may increase production. However, in reality, the long-run demand for the product did not go up—instead the relative price fell temporarily by 5%—and so demand will fall back down again. If the firm had understood this, it might not have ramped up production. Thus inflation that is higher than expected could lead to overproduction.

Now suppose the inflation rate is 5%, which is 5% *lower* than the 10% the firm expected. When the firm raises prices by 10%, it will find that demand is falling off and may cut production. But the long-run demand for the product actually did not decrease; instead, the relative price of the firm's product rose temporarily, unbeknownst to the firm. The firm again may make the wrong production decision. Unanticipated inflation therefore has the potential to sharply increase the variability of relative prices, creating inefficiency in the economy and a substantial misallocation of resources.

INFLATION UNCERTAINTY IS HIGHER WHEN THE LEVEL OF INFLATION IS HIGH. Historical data indicate that when inflation is high, the variability of inflation rises as well. Economists are not completely sure why this is the case, but it may be that higher levels of inflation increase uncertainty in the economy and lead to large swings in unanticipated inflation. We have seen that high uncertainty and big fluctuations in unanticipated inflation impose high costs on the economy. Thus a higher level of inflation raises these costs and can be very burdensome on the economy.

SUMMARY

1. Money is anything that is generally accepted as payment for goods and services or in the repayment of debts, and has three functions: a medium of exchange, a unit of account, and a store of value.

2. The Federal Reserve System consists of twelve regional Federal Reserve banks and the Board of Governors of the Federal Reserve System. The Federal Open Market Committee (FOMC), which meets about every six weeks, makes the decisions about monetary policy. The Federal Reserve controls the money supply primarily through the purchase and sale of government bonds, which is called open market operations. An open market purchase puts dollars into the hands of the public and so increases the money supply, while an open market sale does the opposite.

3. M1 is the narrowest measure of money and includes currency, traveler's checks, demand deposits, and other checkable deposits. M2 adds to M1 other assets that are not quite as liquid: small-denomination time deposits, savings deposits, money market deposit accounts, and money market mutual fund shares. Different measures of money tend to move together, but there are periods during which this is not the case.

4. The quantity theory of money as expressed by the equation of exchange, $M \times V = P \times Y$, indicates that nominal spending is determined solely by movements in the quantity of money. The classical dichotomy indicates that, in the long run, changes in the money supply and the price level do not affect real variables, so that there is a complete separation between the real and nominal sides of the economy. The quantity theory indicates that 1) changes in the quantity of money lead to proportional changes in the price level, because $P = (M \times \overline{V})/\overline{Y}$, and 2) the inflation rate is the growth rate of the money supply minus the growth rate of aggregate output—that is, $\pi = \%\Delta M - \%\Delta Y$. These implications of the quantity theory are borne out by the data in the long run, but not in the short run.

5. Hyperinflations have happened to many countries over the last hundred years, with the recent Zimbabwean hyperinflation being one of the most severe in history.

6. The Fisher equation, $i = r + \pi^e$, and the classical dichotomy lead to the conclusion that when expected inflation rises, interest rates rise along with it. This prediction holds true in the long run, but over shorter time periods, expected inflation and nominal interest rates do not always move together.

7. There are five costs from anticipated inflation: shoe-leather costs, menu costs, tax distortions, increased variability of relative prices, and the loss of the dollar yardstick. The costs of unanticipated inflation are likely to be even higher and include increased uncertainty and increased variability of relative prices. When the level of inflation is higher, the inflation uncertainty is higher as well.

KEY TERMS

REVIEW QUESTIONS

All Questions are available in MyEconLab *for practice or instructor assignment.*

What Is Money?

1. Describe the three primary functions money performs in an economy.

Measuring Money

3. What are the M1 and M2 monetary aggregates?

Quantity Theory of Money

4. What key assumption of classical economists provides the basis for their analysis of the relationship between money and other economic variables?
5. What is the relationship between velocity and the equation of exchange?

Hyperinflation

8. What is hyperinflation? What has been the main cause of hyperinflation episodes?

Inflation and Interest Rates

9. What is the Fisher effect? What is its significance?

The Federal Reserve System and the Control of the Money Supply

2. What are open market operations? What open market operation can the Federal Reserve conduct to increase the money supply?

6. What are the classical dichotomy, the quantity theory of money, and the neutrality of money?
7. How is the quantity theory of money converted into a theory of inflation? According to this theory, what determines the inflation rate?

The Cost of Inflation

10. What are the costs of anticipated and unanticipated inflation?

PROBLEMS

All Problems are available in MyEconLab *for practice or instructor assignment.*

What Is Money?

1. In the movie *The Count of Monte Cristo* (2002), a scene shows the main character paying for an estate in France using a wagon full of silver and gold coins. During the 1800s, it was not common for people to pay for a house using this method, but gold and silver pieces were quite extensively used as a means of payment.

   a) What method of payment do you think was most probably used to buy a house, even in the 1800s?
   b) Why do you think we do not use silver and gold coins as the preferred mean of payment anymore?

2. It is not unusual to find a business that displays a sign reading "no personal checks, please." Based on this observation, comment on the relative degree of liquidity of a checking account and currency.

3. Most of the time it is quite difficult to separate the three functions of money. Money performs its three functions at all times, but sometimes we can stress one in particular. For each of the following situations, identify which function of money is emphasized.
   a) Brooke accepts money in exchange for performing her daily tasks at her office, since she knows she can use that money to buy goods and services.
   b) Tim wants to calculate the relative value of oranges and apples, and therefore checks the price per pound of each of these goods quoted in currency units.
   c) Maria is currently pregnant. She expects her expenditures to increase in the future and decides to increase the balance in her savings account.

Measuring Money

4. Consider the following table with data about monetary aggregates (billions of dollars, seasonally adjusted data):

Date	M1	M2
May 2012	2,262.6	9,870.3
Nov. 2012	2,405.5	10,298.3
Feb. 2013	2,477.9	10,424.7
May 2013	2,534.7	10,598.9

   Source: Federal Reserve System (H.6)

   a) Calculate the annualized growth rate of M1 and M2 for the following periods: May 2012–May 2013 (one year), Nov. 2012–May 2013 (six months), and Feb. 2013–May 2013 (three months).
   b) Comment on the growth rates of these monetary aggregates.

5. Assume that you are interested in earning some return on idle balances you usually keep in your checking account and decide to buy some money market mutual fund shares by writing a check. Comment on the effects of your action (everything else being the same) on M1 and M2.

Quantity Theory of Money

6. Inhabitants of Pandora use stone beads as money. On average, every stone bead is used five times per year to carry out transactions. The total supply of beads is forty million.
   a) What is the level of aggregate spending in Pandora according to the quantity theory of money?
   b) Suppose the inhabitants of Pandora start using less money to conduct the same number of transactions (i.e., each individual carries fewer beads). What is the effect on the velocity of money?

7. Plot the following table on a graph showing average money growth rates on the horizontal axis and average inflation rates on the vertical axis (data is for the period 2002–2012, from the International Monetary Fund. International Financial Statistics). Inflation is measured using the CPI, and the monetary aggregate under consideration is M2.

	Argentina	Bolivia	Chile	Mexico
Inflation rate	10.88%	5.59%	3.20%	4.36%
Money growth rate	27.92%	34.12%	12.76%	11.44%

   Do these data support the quantity theory of money?

The Cost of Inflation

8. Currently, many banks offer online services that save customers a trip to the bank. In addition, ATMs and debit cards allow depositors twenty-four-hour access to their balances. Comment on the effects of online banking and ATMs on shoe-leather costs.

9. These days many firms post their catalogs or their product prices on the Internet. In addition, most retailers have adopted bar codes to keep track of their inventories and implement price changes. Comment on the effect of these technologies on menu costs.

10. Suppose Alex earned $500 (nominal capital gain) from selling stock he bought ten years ago. During the last ten years, prices increased significantly, which means that Alex's real capital gain is only $300. If the tax applied to capital gains is 35%,
    a) calculate Alex's real after-tax capital gain if the tax is applied to his nominal capital gain.
    b) calculate Alex's real after-tax capital gain if the tax is applied to his real capital gain.

DATA ANALYSIS PROBLEMS

The Problems update with real-time data in MyEconLab *and are available for practice or instructor assignment.*

1. Go to the St. Louis Federal Reserve FRED database, and find data on the M1 Money Stock (M1SL), M1 Money Velocity (M1V), and Real GDP (GDPC1). Convert the M1SL data series to "quarterly" using the *frequency* setting, and for all three series, use the "Percent Change From Year Ago" setting for *units*.
    a) Calculate the average percentage change in real GDP, the M1 money stock, and velocity since 2000:Q1.
    b) Based on your answer to part (a), calculate the average inflation rate since 2000 predicted by the quantity theory of money.
    c) Now, use the GDP Deflator price index (GDPDEF) and download the data using the "percent change from year ago" setting. Calculate the average inflation rate since 2000. Comment on the value relative to your answer in part (b).

2. Go to the St. Louis Federal Reserve FRED database, and find data on the 1-Year Treasury Rate (GS1) and the GDP Deflator price index (GDPDEF). For (GS1), choose the *frequency* setting as "quarterly"; for (GDPDEF), set the *units* setting to "Percent Change From Year Ago"; and download both data series. For the questions below, assume inflation is a good proxy for inflation expectations.
    a) From the current period of data available, compare inflation and the interest rate to what it was in 2005:Q1. Does the Fisher effect hold? Why or why not?
    b) From the current period of data available, compare inflation and the interest rate to what it was in 1980:Q1. Does the Fisher effect hold? Why or why not?
    c) (Advanced) Use the "scatterplot" function in Excel to create a scatterplot of inflation on the horizontal axis and the interest rate on the vertical axis. Use data from 1954:Q1 to the current available data. On the scatterplot, graph a fitted (regression) line of the data (there are several ways to do this; however, one chart layout has this option built in). Based on the fitted line, does the Fisher effect hold? Explain.

An online appendix, "The Great Depression Bank Panics and the Money Supply, 1930–1933," is available at the Companion Website, www.pearsonhighered.com/mishkin

The Money Supply Process

In response to the global financial crisis, the Federal Reserve established lending and large-scale-asset purchase programs that more than quadrupled the size of the Fed's balance sheet. Many commentators predicted that this massive expansion of the Fed's balance sheet would lead to rapid growth in the money supply, which in turn would lead to high inflation. Yet this did not occur, with the money supply growing only moderately and inflation actually falling. Why didn't the money supply surge once the Fed embarked on expanding its balance sheet? What policies did the Fed pursue that prevented this from happening?

To answer these questions and better understand how the Federal Reserve controls the money supply, this appendix outlines the money supply process.

 ## The Fed's Balance Sheet

We start our discussion of the money supply process by seeing how a central bank, in this case the Federal Reserve, changes its balance sheet, composed of assets and liabilities. Here we discuss a simplified balance sheet that includes four items that are essential to our understanding of the money supply process.

Federal Reserve System

Assets	Liabilities
Securities	Currency in circulation
Discount loans	Reserves

Liabilities

Currency in circulation and reserves are often referred to as *monetary liabilities* on the Fed's balance sheet. Increases in either will lift the size of the money supply, all else being equal. The sum of the Fed's monetary liabilities and the U.S. Treasury's monetary liabilities (Treasury currency in circulation, primarily coins) is the **monetary base.** When discussing the monetary base, we will focus only on the Fed's monetary

liabilities because the monetary liabilities of the Treasury account for less than 10% of the base.

1. *Currency in circulation.* The Fed issues currency (those green-and-gray pieces of paper in your wallet that say "Federal Reserve Note" at the top). Currency in circulation is the amount of currency in the hands of the public. Currency held by depository institutions is also a liability of the Fed, but is counted as part of the reserves.

2. *Reserves.* All banks have an account at the Fed in which they hold deposits. **Reserves** consist of deposits at the Fed plus currency that is held in bank vaults, known as *vault cash*. Reserves are assets for the banks but liabilities for the Fed, because the banks can demand payment on them at any time and the Fed is required to satisfy its obligation by paying Federal Reserve notes. An increase in reserves leads to an increase in the level of deposits and hence in the money supply.

Total reserves fall into two categories: reserves that the Fed requires banks to hold (**required reserves**) and any additional reserves the banks choose to hold (**excess reserves**). For example, the Fed might require that for every dollar of deposits at a depository institution, a certain fraction (say, ten cents) must be held as reserves. This fraction (10%) held as reserves is called the **required reserve ratio** and is denoted as *rr*.

Assets

Changes in the asset items lead to changes in reserves and consequently to changes in the money supply. The two key asset items in the Fed's balance sheet are as follows:

1. *Securities.* This category of assets covers the Fed's holdings of securities (bonds), most of which are issued by the U.S. Treasury. The Fed provides reserves to the banking system by purchasing securities, thereby increasing its holdings of these assets. An increase in securities held by the Fed leads to an increase in the money supply.

2. *Discount loans.* The Fed provides reserves to the banking system by making discount loans to banks. Banks refer to the discount loans they take out as *borrowings from the Fed* or, alternatively, as *borrowed reserves*. These loans appear as a liability on banks' balance sheets. An increase in discount loans can also be the source of an increase in the money supply. The **discount rate** is the interest rate the Fed charges banks for these loans.

 # Control of the Monetary Base

The *monetary base* (also called **high-powered money**) equals currency in circulation, *C*, plus the total reserves in the banking system, *R*. We express the monetary base *MB* as

$$MB = C + R$$

The Federal Reserve exercises control over the monetary base through its purchases or sales of securities in the open market, called **open market operations,** and through its extension of discount loans to banks.

Federal Reserve Open Market Operations

The Fed changes the monetary base primarily through its open market operations. A purchase of bonds by the Fed is called an **open market purchase,** and a sale of bonds by the Fed is called an **open market sale.**

To illustrate an open market purchase, suppose the Fed purchases $100 of bonds from a bank and pays for them with a $100 check. To analyze this transaction, we use a tool called a **T-account,** a simplified balance sheet, with lines in the form of a T, that lists only the changes that occur in assets and liabilities starting from some initial balance sheet position. Just like a balance sheet, both sides of the T-account must balance. The bank will either deposit the check in its account with the Fed or cash it in for currency, which will be counted as vault cash. Either action means that the bank will find itself with $100 more reserves and a $100 reduction in its holdings of securities. The T-account for the banking system, then, is as follows:

Banking System

Assets		Liabilities
Securities	−$100	
Reserves	+$100	

The Fed, meanwhile, finds that its liabilities have increased by the additional $100 of reserves, while its assets have increased by the additional $100 of securities that it now holds. Its T-account is as follows:

Federal Reserve System

Assets		Liabilities	
Securities	+$100	Reserves	+$100

This open market purchase increases reserves by $100, the amount of the open market purchase. Because there has been no change of currency in circulation, the monetary base has also risen by $100, so we see that the monetary base changes one-for-one with the Fed's holdings of securities.

Shifts from Deposits into Currency

Even if the Fed does not conduct open market operations, a shift from deposits to currency will affect the reserves in the banking system. However, such a shift will have no effect on the monetary base.

Let's suppose that Alicia (who opened a $100 checking account at the First National Bank) finds tellers abusive in all banks and closes her account by withdrawing the $100 balance in cash, vowing never to deposit it in a bank again. The effect on the T-account of the nonbank public is as follows:

Nonbank Public

Assets		Liabilities
Checkable deposits	−$100	
Currency	+$100	

The banking system loses $100 of deposits and hence $100 of reserves:

Banking System

Assets		Liabilities	
Reserves	−$100	Checkable deposits	−$100

For the Fed, Alicia's action means that there is an additional $100 of currency circulating in the hands of the public, while reserves in the banking system have fallen by $100. The Fed's T-account is as follows:

Federal Reserve System

Assets		Liabilities	
		Currency in circulation	+$100
		Reserves	−$100

The net effect on the monetary liabilities of the Fed is a wash; the monetary base is unaffected by Alicia's disgust at the banking system. But reserves are affected. Random fluctuations of reserves can occur as a result of random shifts into currency and out of deposits, and vice versa. The same is not true for the monetary base, making it a more stable variable than reserves.

Discount Loans

So far we have examined changes in the monetary base that occur solely as a result of open market operations. However, the monetary base is also affected when the Fed makes a discount loan to a bank. When the Fed makes a $100 discount loan to the First National Bank, the bank is credited with $100 of reserves from the proceeds of the loan. The following T-accounts illustrate the effects on the balance sheets of the banking system and the Fed:

Banking System				Federal Reserve System			
Assets		**Liabilities**		**Assets**		**Liabilities**	
Reserves	+$100	Discount loans (borrowings from the Fed)	+$100	Discount loans (borrowings from the Fed)	+$100	Reserves	+$100

The monetary liabilities of the Fed have now increased by $100, and the monetary base, too, has increased by this amount. However, if a bank pays off a loan from the Fed, thereby reducing its borrowings from the Fed by $100, the T-accounts of the banking system and the Fed are as follows:

Banking System				Federal Reserve System			
Assets		**Liabilities**		**Assets**		**Liabilities**	
Reserves	+$100	Discount loans (borrowings from the Fed)	+$100	Discount loans (borrowings from the Fed)	−$100	Reserves	−$100

The net effect on the monetary liabilities of the Fed, and hence on the monetary base, is a reduction of $100. We see that the monetary base also changes one-for-one with the change in the borrowings from the Fed.

Overview of the Fed's Ability to Control the Monetary Base

We have established that two primary factors determine the monetary base: open market operations and discount lending. The Fed completely controls the amount of open market purchases or sales by placing orders in the bond markets. Banks, however, decide how much to borrow from the discount window, although the Fed does influence their decision by setting the discount rate.

Therefore, we can split the monetary base into two components: one that the Fed can control completely and another that is less tightly controlled. The less tightly controlled component is the amount of the base that is created by discount loans from the Fed. The remainder of the base, called the *nonborrowed monetary base*, is under the Fed's control, because it results primarily from open market operations. The **nonborrowed monetary base** is the monetary base minus banks' borrowing from the Fed (discount loans), which we refer to as **borrowed reserves.**

Multiple Deposit Creation: A Simple Model

When the Fed supplies the banking system with $1 of additional reserves, deposits increase by a multiple of this amount—a process called **multiple deposit creation.** Because the money supply is made up of currency plus deposits, multiple deposit creation shows how increases in the monetary base lead to a multiple expansion of the money supply.

Deposit Creation: The Single Bank

Suppose that the $100 open market purchase described earlier was conducted with the First National Bank. After the Fed has bought the $100 bond from the First National Bank, the bank finds that it has an increase in reserves of $100. To analyze what the bank will do with these additional reserves, assume that the bank does not want to hold excess reserves because it does not earn enough interest on them. We begin the analysis with the following T-account:

First National Bank

Assets		Liabilities
Securities	−$100	
Reserves	+$100	

Because the bank has no increase in its checkable deposits, required reserves remain the same, and the bank finds that its additional $100 of reserves has increased excess reserves by $100. Let's say that the bank decides to make a loan equal in amount to the $100 increase in excess reserves. When the bank makes the loan, it sets up a checking account for the borrower and puts the proceeds of the loan into this account. In this way, the bank alters its balance sheet by increasing its liabilities with $100 of checkable deposits and at the same time increasing its assets with the $100 loan. The resulting T-account looks like this:

First National Bank

Assets		Liabilities	
Securities	−$100	Checkable deposits	+$100
Reserves	+$100		
Loans	+$100		

The bank has created checkable deposits by its act of lending. Because checkable deposits are part of the money supply, the bank's act of lending has, in fact, created money.

In its current balance sheet position, the First National Bank still has excess reserves and so might want to make additional loans. However, these reserves will not stay at the bank for very long. The borrower took out a loan not to leave $100 idle at the First National Bank but to purchase goods and services from other individuals and corporations. When the borrower makes these purchases by writing checks, they will be deposited at other banks, and the $100 of reserves will leave the First National Bank. ***A bank cannot safely make loans for an amount greater than the excess reserves it has before it makes the loan.***

The final T-account of the First National Bank is as follows:

First National Bank

Assets		Liabilities
Securities	−$100	
Loans	+$100	

First National Bank converted the $100 increase in reserves into additional loans of $100 plus an additional $100 of deposits that have made their way to other banks. (Borrowers deposit all the checks written on accounts at the First National Bank in banks rather than converting them into cash, because we are assuming that the public does not want to hold any additional currency.) Now let's see what happens to these deposits at the other banks.

Deposit Creation: The Banking System

To simplify the analysis, let us assume that the $100 of deposits created by the First National Bank's loan is deposited at Bank A, and that this bank and all other banks hold no excess reserves. Bank A's T-account becomes

Bank A

Assets		Liabilities	
Reserves	+$100	Checkable deposits	+$100

If the required reserve ratio, rr, is 10%, this bank will now find itself with a $10 increase in required reserves, leaving it $90 of excess reserves. Because Bank A (like the First

National Bank) does not want to hold on to excess reserves, it will make loans for the entire amount. Its loans and checkable deposits will then increase by $90. When the borrower spends the $90 of checkable deposits, the checkable deposits and the reserves at Bank A will decrease by this same $90 amount. The net result is that Bank A's T-account will look like this:

Bank A

Assets		Liabilities	
Reserves	+$10	Checkable deposits	+$100
Loans	+$90		

If the money spent by the borrower to whom Bank A lent the $90 is deposited in another bank, such as Bank B, the T-account for Bank B will be as follows:

Bank B

Assets		Liabilities	
Reserves	+$90	Checkable deposits	+$90

　　The checkable deposits in the banking system have increased by another $90, for a total increase of $190 ($100 at Bank A plus $90 at Bank B). In fact, the distinction between Bank A and Bank B is not necessary to obtain the same result on the overall expansion of deposits. If the borrower from Bank A writes checks to someone who deposits them at Bank A, the same change in deposits would occur. The T-accounts for Bank B would just apply to Bank A, and its checkable deposits would increase by the total amount of $190.

　　Bank B will want to modify its balance sheet further. It must keep 10% of $90 ($9) as required reserves and has 90% of $90 ($81) in excess reserves available for loans. Bank B will make an $81 loan to a borrower, who spends the proceeds from the loan. Bank B's T-account will be as follows:

Bank B

Assets		Liabilities	
Reserves	+$ 9	Checkable deposits	+$90
Loans	+$81		

The $81 spent by the borrower from Bank B will be deposited in another bank (Bank C). Consequently, from the initial $100 increase of reserves in the banking system, the total increase of checkable deposits in the system so far is $271 (= $100 + $90 + $81).

　　Following the same reasoning, if all banks make loans for the full amount of their excess reserves, further increments in checkable deposits will continue (at Banks C, D, E, and so on), as depicted in Table 5A1.1. Therefore, the total increase in deposits from the initial $100 increase in reserves will be $1,000: the increase is tenfold, the reciprocal of the 10% (0.10) required reserve ratio.

| **TABLE 5A1.1** | **CREATION OF DEPOSITS (ASSUMING A 10% RESERVE REQUIREMENT AND A $100 INCREASE IN RESERVES)** |

Bank	Increase in Deposits ($)	Increase in Loans ($)	Increase in Reserves ($)
First National	0.00	100.00	0.00
A	100.00	90.00	10.00
B	90.00	81.00	9.00
C	81.00	72.90	8.10
D	72.90	65.61	7.29
E	65.61	59.05	6.56
F	59.05	53.14	5.91
.	.	.	.
.	.	.	.
.	.	.	.
Total for all banks	1,000.00	1,000.00	100.00

If the banks choose to invest their excess reserves in securities, the result is the same. If Bank A had taken its excess reserves and purchased securities instead of making loans, its T-account would have looked like this:

Bank A

Assets		Liabilities	
Reserves	+$10	Checkable deposits	+$100
Securities	+$90		

When the bank buys $90 of securities, it writes a $90 check to the seller of the securities, who in turn deposits the $90 at a bank, such as Bank B. Bank B's checkable deposits increase by $90, and the deposit expansion process is the same as before. ***Whether a bank chooses to use its excess reserves to make loans or to purchase securities, the effect on deposit expansion is the same.***

As you can see, a single bank creates deposits only up to the amount of its excess reserves. But as each bank makes a loan and creates deposits, the reserves find their way to another bank, which uses them to make additional loans and create additional deposits. This process continues until the initial increase in reserves results in a multiple increase in deposits.

Critique of the Simple Model

Though our model of multiple deposit creation seems to imply that the Federal Reserve exercises complete control over the level of checkable deposits, in reality it does not, for two reasons:

1. If loan proceeds are held as cash and never deposited in a bank, then the loan will not cause multiple deposit expansion and the money supply will not increase as our model predicts.

2. If banks choose not to lend or buy securities to the capacity of their excess reserves, the full expansion of deposits predicted by the simple model of multiple deposit creation again does not occur.

The preferences of depositors and banks have a clear influence on the level of deposits and therefore the money supply that our simple model does not address.

Factors that Determine the Money Supply

Our critique of the simple model indicates the need to expand our analysis to discuss all the factors that affect the money supply. Let's look at changes in each factor in turn, holding all other factors constant.

Changes in the Nonborrowed Monetary Base

We have established that the Fed's open market purchases increase the nonborrowed monetary base (MB_n), and its open market sales decrease it. Holding all other variables constant, an increase in MB_n arising from an open market purchase increases the amount of the monetary base and reserves, so that multiple deposit creation occurs and the money supply increases. Similarly, an open market sale that decreases MB_n shrinks the amount of the monetary base and reserves, thereby causing a multiple contraction of deposits and the money supply to decrease. **We have the following result: the money supply is positively related to the nonborrowed monetary base MB_n.**

Changes in Borrowed Reserves from the Fed

An increase in discount loans from the Fed provides additional borrowed reserves, and thereby increases the amount of the monetary base and reserves, so that multiple deposit creation occurs and the money supply increases. If banks reduce the level of their discount loans, all other variables held constant, the monetary base and amount of reserves fall, and the money supply decreases. The result is that **the money supply is positively related to the level of borrowed reserves, BR, from the Fed.**

Changes in the Required Reserve Ratio

If the required reserve ratio on checkable deposits increases while all other variables, such as the monetary base, stay the same, there is less multiple deposit expansion, and hence the money supply falls. If, on the other hand, the required reserve ratio falls, multiple deposit expansion is higher and the money supply rises.

We now have the following result: **the money supply is negatively related to the required reserve ratio rr.** In the past, the Fed sometimes used reserve requirements to affect the size of the money supply. In recent years, however, reserve requirements have become a less important factor in the determination of the money multiplier and the money supply.

Changes in Currency Holdings

As shown before, checkable deposits undergo multiple expansion while currency does not. Hence, when borrowers convert checkable deposits into currency, holding the monetary base and other variables constant, there is a switch from a component of the money supply that undergoes multiple expansion to one that does not. The overall level of multiple expansion declines, and the money supply falls. On the other hand, if currency holdings fall, there is a switch into checkable deposits that undergo multiple deposit expansion, so the money supply rises. This analysis suggests that **the money supply is negatively correlated to currency holdings.**

Changes in Excess Reserves

When banks increase their holdings of excess reserves, reserves are no longer being used to make loans, ceasing multiple deposit creation and causing a contraction of the money supply. If, on the other hand, banks choose to hold less excess reserves, loans and multiple deposit creation will go up and the money supply will rise. **The money supply is therefore negatively correlated to the amount of excess reserves.**

Overview of the Money Supply Process

We now have a model of the money supply process in which all three of the players—the Federal Reserve System, depositors, and banks—directly influence the money supply.

As a study aid, Table 5A1.2 shows the money supply response to the five factors discussed previously and gives a brief synopsis of the reasoning behind them. We group the variables by the player or players who are the primary influence behind the variable. The Federal Reserve, for example, influences the money supply by controlling the first three variables (called "tools of the Fed"). Depositors influence the money supply through their decisions about their holdings of currency, while banks influence the

---

TABLE 5A1.2 | **MONEY SUPPLY RESPONSE**

Note: Only increases (↑) in the variables are shown. The effects of decreases on the money supply would be the opposite of those indicated in the "Money Supply Response" column.

Player	Variable	Change in Variable	Money Supply Response	Reason
Federal Reserve System	Nonborrowed monetary base	↑	↑	More *MB* for deposit creation
	Borrowed reserves	↑	↑	More *MB* for deposit creation
	Required reserve ratio	↑	↓	Less multiple deposit expansion
Depositors	Currency holdings	↑	↓	Less multiple deposit expansion
Depositors and banks	Excess reserves	↑	↓	Less loans and deposit creation

money supply by their decisions about excess reserves. However, because depositors' behavior influences bankers' expectations about deposit outflows, which as we will see affects banks' decisions to hold excess reserves, we also list depositors as a player in determining excess reserves.[1]

The Money Multiplier

Our analysis thus far is sufficient for you to understand how the money supply process works. For those of you who are more mathematically inclined, we can derive all of the results using a concept called the **money multiplier,** denoted by m, which tells us how much the money supply changes for a given change in the monetary base. The relationship between the money supply, M (in this case, the M1 definition), the money multiplier, m, and the monetary base, MB, is as follows:[2]

$$M = m \times MB \tag{1}$$

The money multiplier m tells us what multiple of the monetary base is transformed into the money supply. Because the money multiplier is larger than 1, the alternative name for the monetary base, *high-powered money*, is logical: a \$1 change in the monetary base leads to more than a \$1 change in the money supply.

Deriving the Money Multiplier

Let's assume that the desired holdings of currency, C, and excess reserves, ER, grow proportionally with checkable deposits, D. In other words, we assume that the ratios of these items to checkable deposits are constants in equilibrium, as the braces in the following expressions indicate:

$$c = \{C/D\} = \text{currency ratio}$$

$$e = \{ER/D\} = \text{excess reserves ratio}$$

We will now derive a formula that describes how the currency ratio desired by depositors, the excess reserves ratio desired by banks, and the required reserve ratio set by the Fed affect the multiplier m. We begin the derivation of the model of the money supply with the following equation:

$$R = RR + ER \tag{2}$$

This equation states that the total amount of reserves in the banking system, R, equals the sum of required reserves, RR, and excess reserves, ER.

---

[1]Another interesting application of the concepts here can be found in the Web appendix to this chapter, "The Great Depression Bank Panics and the Money Supply, 1930–1933," which is available at the Companion Website, www.pearsonhighered.com/mishkin.

[2]For a derivation of the money multiplier for the M2 definition of money, see the Web appendix to Chapter 14 in Frederic S. Mishkin, *The Economics of Money, Banking and Financial Markets*, 10th edition, which can be found at http://wps.aw.com/wps/media/objects/13761/14091673/appendixes/ch14apx2.pdf

The total amount of required reserves equals the required reserve ratio, rr, times the amount of checkable deposits, D:

$$RR = rr \times D$$

Substituting $rr \times D$ for RR in Equation 2 yields an equation that links reserves in the banking system to the amount of checkable deposits and excess reserves they can support:

$$R = (rr \times D) + ER$$

A key point here is that the Fed sets the required reserve ratio rr to less than 1. Thus \$1 of reserves can support more than \$1 of deposits, and the multiple expansion of deposits can occur.

Let's see how this works in practice. If excess reserves are held at zero ($ER = 0$), the required reserve ratio is set at $rr = 0.10$, and the level of checkable deposits in the banking system is \$800 billion, then the amount of reserves needed to support these deposits is \$80 billion ($= 0.10 \times$ \$800 billion). Multiple deposit creation enables the \$80 billion of reserves to support ten times this amount in checkable deposits.

Because the monetary base, MB, equals currency, C, plus reserves, R, we can generate an equation that links the amount of the monetary base to the levels of checkable deposits and currency by adding currency to both sides of the equation:

$$MB = R + C = (rr \times D) + ER + C$$

This equation reveals the amount of the monetary base needed to support the existing amounts of checkable deposits, currency, and excess reserves.

To derive the money multiplier formula in terms of the currency ratio $c = \{C/D\}$ and the excess reserves ratio $e = \{ER/D\}$, we rewrite the last equation, specifying C as $c \times D$ and ER as $e \times D$:

$$MB = (rr \times D) + (e \times D) + (c + D) = (rr + e + c) \times D$$

We next divide both sides of the equation by the term inside the parentheses to get an expression linking checkable deposits, D, to the monetary base, MB:

$$D = \frac{1}{rr + e + c} \times MB \tag{3}$$

Using the M1 definition of the money supply as currency plus checkable deposits ($M = D + C$) and again specifying C as $c \times D$,

$$M = D + (c \times D) = (1 + c) \times D$$

Substituting into this equation the expression for D from Equation 3, we have

$$M = \frac{1 + c}{rr + e + c} \times MB \tag{4}$$

We have derived an expression in the form of our earlier Equation 1. As you can see, the ratio that multiplies MB is the money multiplier, which tells us how much the money supply changes in response to a given change in the monetary base (high-powered money). The money multiplier m is thus

$$m = \frac{1 + c}{rr + e + c} \tag{5}$$

It is a function of the currency ratio set by depositors (c), the excess reserves ratio set by banks (e), and the required reserve ratio set by the Fed (rr).

Intuition Behind the Money Multiplier

To get a feel for what the money multiplier means, let us construct a numerical example with realistic numbers for the following variables:

rr = required reserve ratio = 0.10
C = currency in circulation = \$400 billion
D = checkable deposits = \$800 billion
ER = excess reserves = \$0.8 billion
M = money supply $(M1)$ = $C + D$ = \$1,200 billion

From these numbers we can calculate the values of the currency ratio c and the excess reserves ratio e:

$$c = \frac{\$400 \text{ billion}}{\$800 \text{ billion}} = 0.5$$

$$e = \frac{\$0.8 \text{ billion}}{\$800 \text{ billion}} = 0.001$$

The resulting value of the money multiplier is as follows:

$$m = \frac{1 + 0.5}{0.1 + 0.001 + 0.5} = \frac{1.5}{0.601} = 2.5$$

The money multiplier of 2.5 tells us that, given the required reserve ratio of 10% on checkable deposits, and the behavior of depositors as represented by $c = 0.5$ and of banks as represented by $e = 0.001$, a \$1 increase in the monetary base leads to a \$2.50 increase in the money supply (M1).

Note that the money multiplier is less than the multiple deposit expansion of 10 in the simple model. Although there is multiple expansion of deposits, there is no such expansion for currency. Thus, if some portion of the increase in high-powered money finds its way into currency, this portion does not undergo multiple deposit expansion. In our simple model earlier in the chapter, we did not allow for this possibility, and so the increase in reserves led to the maximum amount of multiple deposit creation. However, in our current model of the money multiplier, the level of currency does increase when the monetary base MB and checkable deposits D increase, because c is greater than zero. As previously stated, any increase in MB that goes into an increase in currency is not multiplied, so only part of the increase in MB is available to support checkable deposits that undergo multiple expansion. The overall level of multiple deposit expansion must be lower, meaning that the increase in M, given an increase in MB, is smaller than the simple model from earlier in the chapter indicated.[3]

---

[3]Another reason why the money multiplier is smaller is that e is a constant fraction greater than zero, indicating that an increase in MB and D leads to higher excess reserves. The resulting higher amount of excess reserves means that the amount of reserves used to support checkable deposits will not increase as much as it otherwise would. Hence the increase in checkable deposits and the money supply will be lower, and the money multiplier will be smaller. However, often e is tiny—around 0.001; the impact of this ratio on the money multiplier can be quite small. But there are periods, such as the Great Depression and the current period, during which e is much larger and so has a more important role in lowering the money multiplier.

Money Supply Response to Changes in the Factors

To complete our analysis, we need to recognize that the monetary base can be divided into two components: the sum of the nonborrowed base, MB_n, and borrowed reserves, BR— that is, $MB = MB_n + BR$. We can rewrite Equation 1 as follows:

$$M = m \times (MB_n + BR) \qquad (6)$$

Now we can show algebraically all the results given in Table 5A1.2, which shows the money supply response to the changes in the factors.

As you can see from Equation 6, a rise in MB_n or BR raises the money supply M by a multiple amount because the money multiplier m is greater than one. We determine how a rise in the required reserve ratio lowers the money supply by calculating what happens to the value of the money multiplier using Equation 5 in our numerical example, in which r increases from 10% to 15% (leaving all other variables unchanged). The money multiplier then falls from 2.5 to

$$m = \frac{1 + 0.5}{0.15 + 0.001 + 0.5} = \frac{1.5}{0.651} = 2.3$$

which, as we would expect, is less than 2.5.

Similarly, we can see in our numerical example that a rise in currency lowers the money supply by calculating what happens to the money multiplier when c is raised from 0.50 to 0.75. The money multiplier then falls from 2.5 to

$$m = \frac{1 + 0.75}{0.1 + 0.001 + 0.75} = \frac{1.75}{0.851} = 2.06$$

Finally, we can see that a rise in excess reserves lowers the money supply by calculating what happens to the money multiplier when e is raised from 0.001 to 0.005. The money multiplier declines from 2.5 to

$$m = \frac{1 + 0.5}{0.1 + 0.005 + 0.5} = \frac{1.5}{0.605} = 2.48$$

Note that although the excess reserves ratio has risen fivefold in this example, there has been only a small decline in the money multiplier. This decline is small because e is assumed to be quite small (a reasonable assumption for much of U.S. monetary history), and so changes in it have only a small impact on the money multiplier. However, there have been times, particularly during the Great Depression and the recent period, when this ratio has been far higher, and its movements have had a substantial effect on the money supply and the money multiplier.

The examples above show that the money multiplier decreases following increases in the required reserve ratio, the currency ratio, or the excess reserves ratio. Therefore, other things remaining constant, the money supply will decline in each case.

Application

Quantitative Easing and the Money Supply, 2007–2013

When the global financial crisis began in the fall of 2007, the Fed began lending and large-scale-asset purchase programs to bolster the economy. By June 2013, these purchases of securities led to a quadrupling of the Fed's balance and 287% increase in the monetary base. These lending and asset purchase programs, which resulted in a huge expansion of the monetary base, were given the name "quantitative easing." Quantitative easing is discussed further in Chapter 13. As our analysis in this appendix indicates, the massive expansion of the monetary base could potentially lead to a large expansion of the money supply. However, as shown in Figure 5A1.1, when the monetary base increased by more 276%, the M1 money supply rose by less than 90%. How does our money supply model explain this?

Figure 5A1.2 shows currency held by the public relative to checkable deposits (the currency ratio, c) and banks' holdings of excess reserves relative to checkable deposits (the excess reserves ratio, e) for the 2007–2013 period. We see that the currency ratio fell during this period, which our money supply model suggests would raise the money multiplier and the money supply because it would increase the overall level of deposit expansion. However, the effects of the decline in c were entirely offset by the extraordinary rise in the excess reserves ratio e, which climbed by a factor of 1,000 during this period.

What explains this substantial increase in the excess reserves ratio, e? The Fed's actions created far more reserves than were needed for banks to meet their reserve requirements. In order for banks to be willing to hold this huge increase in reserves, market interest rates had to be sufficiently low so that holding excess reserves was costless for them. In fact, once the Fed began paying interest on these reserves, starting in 2008, the interest rate on reserves often exceeded the rate at which the banks could lend them out in the federal funds market.

MyEconLab Real-time data

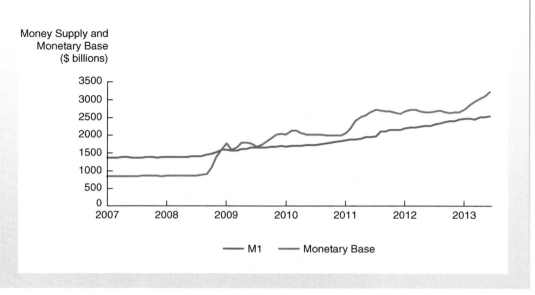

FIGURE 5A1.1

M1 and the Monetary Base, 2007–2013

The money supply rose by less than 90% despite an increase in the monetary base of over 270%.

Source: Federal Reserve Bank of St. Louis, FRED Database. http://research.stlouisfed.org/fred2/

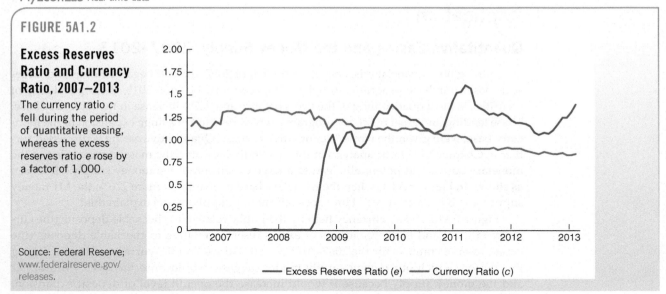

FIGURE 5A1.2

Excess Reserves Ratio and Currency Ratio, 2007–2013

The currency ratio c fell during the period of quantitative easing, whereas the excess reserves ratio e rose by a factor of 1,000.

Source: Federal Reserve; www.federalreserve.gov/releases.

Banks were therefore willing to have a much higher excess reserves ratio e. As our money supply model predicts, the huge increase in e would lower the money multiplier, and so the money supply would expand only slightly, despite the huge increase in the monetary base.

SUMMARY

1. There are three players in the money supply process: the central bank, banks (depository institutions), and depositors.

2. Four items in the Fed's balance sheet are essential to our understanding of the money supply process: the two liability items, currency in circulation and reserves (which together make up the monetary base), and the two asset items, securities and discount loans.

3. The Federal Reserve controls the monetary base through open market operations and the extension of discount loans to banks, and has better control over the monetary base than over reserves.

4. A single bank can make loans up to the amount of its excess reserves, thereby creating an equal amount of deposits. The banking system can create a multiple expansion of deposits, because as each bank makes a loan and creates deposits, the reserves find their way to another bank, which uses them to make loans and create additional deposits. In the simple model of multiple deposit creation, in which banks do not hold on to excess reserves and the public holds no currency, the multiple increase in checkable deposits equals the reciprocal of the required reserve ratio.

5. The simple model of multiple deposit creation has serious deficiencies. Decisions by deposi-

tors to increase their holdings of currency or by banks to hold excess reserves result in a smaller expansion of deposits than the simple model predicts. All three players—the Fed, banks, and depositors—are important in the determination of the money supply.

6. The money supply is positively correlated to the nonborrowed monetary base MB_n, which is determined by open market operations, and the level of borrowed reserves (discount loans) from the Fed, BR. The money supply is negatively correlated to the required reserve ratio, rr, holdings of currency, and excess reserves. The model of the money supply process takes into account the behavior of all three players in the money supply process: the Fed through open market operations, discount lending, and setting of the required reserve ratio; depositors through their decisions about their holdings of currency; and banks through their decisions about excess reserves, which are also influenced by depositors' decisions about deposit outflows.

7. The monetary base is linked to the money supply using the concept of the money multiplier, which tells us how much the money supply changes when there is a change in the monetary base.

KEY TERMS

REVIEW QUESTIONS AND PROBLEMS

All Questions and problems are available in MyEconLab *for practice or instructor assignment.*

1. What is the monetary base? How does the Federal Reserve influence its size?

2. Suppose the Fed buys U.S. Treasury securities from Bank of America. According to the simple model of multiple deposit creation, how does this open market purchase affect the money supply? What are the two basic assumptions of the simple model you have described?

3. Identify the five factors that determine the money supply. For each factor, explain which player(s) in the money supply process—the Federal Reserve, depositors, and banks—control or influence it, and how and why it affects the money supply.

4. Use the following information to determine the Fed's balance sheet and calculate the Fed's monetary liabilities:
   - Currency in circulation = $750 billion
   - Reserves of the banking system = $850 billion
   - Securities held by the Fed = $450 billion
   - Discount loans = $1,150 billion

5. Use the Fed and the banking system T-accounts to describe the effects of a Fed sale of $200 million worth of government bonds to a bank that pays with part of its reserves held at the Fed. What would be the effect of this transaction on the Fed's monetary liabilities?

6. Some developing countries have suffered banking crises in which depositors lost part or all of their deposits (in some countries there is no deposit insurance). This type of crisis decreases depositors' confidence in the banking system. What would be the effect of a rumor about a banking crisis on checkable deposits in such a country? What would be the effect on reserves and the monetary base?

7. The Federal Reserve announced the closing of many lending facilities, like the term auction facility (TAF), that were originally created to extend loans to financial intermediaries during the most difficult years of the recent global financial crisis. What would be the effect of closing these facilities on the monetary base?

8. Suppose the Federal Reserve conducts an open market purchase for $100 million. Assuming the required reserves ratio is 10%, what would be the effect on the money supply in each of the following situations?
   a) There is only one bank, and the bank decides not to make a loan with its excess reserves.
   b) There is only one bank, and the bank decides to make a loan for the full amount of its excess reserves.
   c) There are many banks, all of which make loans for the full amount of their excess reserves.

9. Under very particular conditions, banks would like to borrow from the Fed and, rather than use these borrowed funds to make loans, keep them in the form of excess reserves. What would be the effect on the monetary base and the money supply of an increase in discount loans that are kept in the form of excess reserves?

10. Calculate the money multiplier for the following values of the currency, excess reserves, and required reserves ratios (i.e., complete the following table), and explain why the money multiplier decreases when the currency or excess reserves ratio increases:

Currency deposit ratio	0.5	0.7	0.5
Excess reserves ratio	0.01	0.01	0.9
Required reserves ratio	0.08	0.08	0.08
Money multiplier			

11. During the Great Depression years of 1930–1933, bank panics led to a dramatic rise in the currency and excess reserves ratios, while the monetary base rose by 20%. Explain how banks' and depositors' behavior led to the sharp increase in the currency and excess reserves ratio, and explain using the money multiplier model why the money supply actually fell by 25% during that period despite the 20% rise in the monetary base.

DATA ANALYSIS PROBLEMS

The Problems update with real-time data in MyEconLab and are available for practice or instructor assignment.

1. Go to the St. Louis Federal Reserve FRED database and find the most currently available data on Currency (CURRNS), Total Checkable Deposits (TCDSL), Total Reserves (RESBALNS), and Required Reserves (RESBALREQ).

   a) Calculate the value of the currency deposit ratio, c.

   b) Use RESBALNS and RESBALREQ to calculate the amount of excess reserves, then calculate the value of the excess reserve ratio, er.

   c) Assuming the required reserve ratio, rr, is equal to 11%, calculate the value of the money multiplier m.

2. Go to the St. Louis Federal Reserve FRED database and find data on the M1 Money Stock (M1SL) and the Monetary Base (AMBSL).

   a) Calculate the value of the money multiplier using the most recent data available, and the data from five years prior.

   b) Based on your answer to part (a), how much would a $100 million open market purchase of securities affect the M1 money supply today versus five years ago?

Part 3

Long-Run Economic Growth

Part 3 Long-Run Economic Growth

This part of the book explores one of the most central questions of macroeconomics: why do some countries experience slow economic growth and stay poor, while others enjoy rapid economic growth and prosper? Chapter 6 and its appendices develop the *Solow growth model*, the basic model used in all modern research on economic growth. Chapter 7 delves into the sources of economic growth by examining in detail how advances in technology and the development of institutions promote economic growth.

We will examine applications in each chapter to make the critical connection between theory and real-world practice:

- "Evidence on Convergence, 1960–2012"
- "U.S. Growth Rates in the Postwar Period"
- "Does Population Growth Improve Living Standards?"

In keeping with our focus on key policy issues and the techniques policymakers use in practice, we will also analyze the following specific examples in Policy and Practice cases:

- "China's One-Child Policy and Other Policies to Limit Population Growth"
- "Government Measures to Increase Human Capital"
- "The World Bank's *Doing Business*"
- "Does Foreign Aid Work?"

6

The Sources of Growth and the Solow Model

Preview

Laptop-toting students in South Korea's gleaming capital city, Seoul, would hardly recognize the country their grandparents knew. In 1960, South Korea was an economic basket case, and Seoul was a poor and congested city lined with scrap-wood shantytowns. The average worker earned today's equivalent of $5 a day. Western economists concluded that Korea's hopes for revitalization were bleak. Today, we know that assessment couldn't have been farther off the mark. Over the next fifty years, South Korea transformed itself into one of the world's richest nations, and is now a member of the exclusive club of trillion-dollar economies. South Koreans earn over ten times what their predecessors did in 1960, drive expensive sedans, and work in air-conditioned offices.

The United States has also experienced extraordinary economic growth. The average U.S. citizen in 1870 lived in what we would consider abject poverty, without indoor plumbing or electric lighting. In 1870, U.S. per capita income in today's dollars was under $3,000, while today it has grown to over $40,000.

The pace of economic growth in South Korea and the United States is highly atypical. Consider Haiti, which in 1960 had around the same GDP as South Korea. Today, Haitians actually earn less than they did fifty years ago, after adjusting for inflation. Discovering why countries like South Korea and the United States thrive while countries like Haiti stagnate is one of the most important goals of macroeconomics. As Nobel Prize winner Robert Lucas put it, "The consequences for human welfare involved in questions like these [about economic growth] are simply staggering."[1]

We start the chapter by looking at economic growth around the world. We then explore the *Solow growth model,* the basis of all modern research on economic growth, and its limitations. Finally, we discuss *growth accounting*, which suggests that we go beyond the Solow model to look in more detail at the roles of technology and institutions in promoting economic growth, topics we analyze in Chapter 7.

[1]Robert Lucas, Jr., "On the Mechanics of Economic Development," *Journal of Monetary Economics* 22 (1988): 5.

Economic Growth Around the World

Figure 6.1 shows the level of real GDP per person since 1960 in ten countries in different parts of the world: North America, Europe, Africa, Asia, Latin America, and the Caribbean. The following facts are drawn from this figure.

- During the entire period, the United States has remained the richest country and has had a steady average economic growth rate.
- Almost all countries have experienced economic growth, with the exception of Haiti.
- The two European countries that started with the highest level of real GDP per person—France and the United Kingdom—have been catching up to the United States. This phenomenon is referred to as **convergence**, that is, countries with different initial levels of per capita income gravitate to a similar level of per capita income.
- The Asian countries of Japan, China, South Korea, and, more recently, India have experienced what is referred to as "convergence big time," with very rapid economic growth that has more than doubled their per capita income relative to that of the United States. These "growth-miracle" countries have been able to

MyEconLab Real-time data

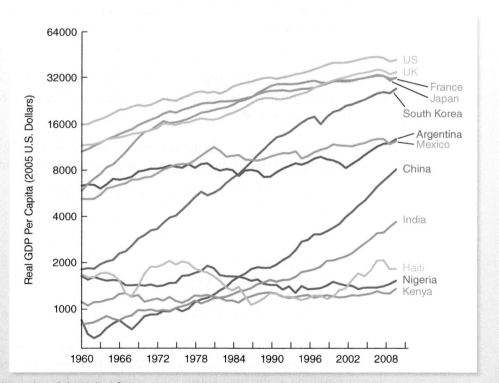

FIGURE 6.1

Real Per Capita GDP in Ten Countries

All countries except for Haiti have experienced positive economic growth from 1960 to 2010, with France, the United Kingdom, Japan, South Korea, and India displaying convergence to the U.S. level of real per capita GDP. The rest of the countries have not experienced convergence: Mexico and Argentina's income per person has remained about the same relative to that of the United States, while Kenya, Nigeria, and particularly Haiti have experienced growth disasters in which their real income per capita has fallen relative to that of the United States.

Note: The vertical axis in this figure is a ratio scale in which equal distances reflect the same percentage change, so that the slope of a curve indicates how fast an economy is growing.

Source: Penn World Tables in Federal Reserve Bank of St. Louis, FRED Database. http://research.stlouisfed.org/fred2/

remove over a billion people from deep poverty (income of less than one dollar per day), an extraordinary achievement.

- The Latin American countries of Mexico and Argentina have not experienced convergence, with Mexico and Argentina's per capita income level staying nearly the same relative to that of the United States.
- The two African countries of Kenya and Nigeria, although they have had some economic growth since 1960, have experienced what is referred to as a "growth disaster," with their income relative to that of the United States falling by more than half.
- The Caribbean country of Haiti has experienced the worst growth disaster of all, with the level of real GDP per person actually lower in 2011 than in 1960.

The Solow Growth Model

Our discussion of Figure 6.1 raises several questions about economic growth. How can we explain why most countries experience economic growth over time? Why do some countries display convergence, while others do not? Why do some countries have growth miracles, while others have growth disasters? The starting point for answering these questions is the **Solow growth model**, which explains how saving rates and population growth determine capital accumulation, which in turn determines economic growth. Robert Solow developed the model over fifty years ago, and earned a Nobel Prize for his work.[2]

Building Blocks of the Solow Growth Model

The Solow model has several building blocks: the production function, the investment function, the capital accumulation equation, and the description of the steady state. We look at each of these in turn.

PRODUCTION FUNCTION. The Solow model starts with the Cobb-Douglas aggregate production function with constant returns to scale, as discussed in Chapter 3:

$$Y_t = F(K_t, L_t) = AK_t^{0.3}L_t^{0.7} \tag{1}$$

where

$$
\begin{aligned}
Y_t &= \text{Output at time } t \\
K_t &= \text{capital stock at time } t \\
L_t &= \text{labor at time } t \\
A &= \text{available technology (measured by total factor productivity)}
\end{aligned}
$$

Equation 1 shows us how much output Y we can generate from given levels of factors of production and available technology. Notice that we introduce a new type of notation in Equation 1, the time subscript t, where the subscript t indicates the value of a variable at time t. Time subscript notation is important because what happens over time

---

[2]See Robert M. Solow, "A Contribution to the Theory of Economic Growth," *Quarterly Journal of Economics* (February 1956): 65–94.

is central to discussing economic growth. We discuss this notation in more detail in the box, "Time Subscripts."

The Solow model looks at the economy in per-worker terms. If output at time t is Y_t, then output per worker is Y_t/L_t, which we will represent with the lowercase y_t. In the same way, consumption expenditure per worker is $c_t = C_t/L_t$, and investment per worker is $i_t = I_t/L_t$. The amount of capital per worker, $k_t = K_t/L_t$, which we will refer to as the **capital-labor ratio**, plays a very prominent role in the Solow model. To convert Equation 1 into a per-worker production function, we divide both sides by L_t.

$$y_t = \frac{Y_t}{L_t} = \frac{AK_t^{0.3}L_t^{0.7}}{L_t} = \frac{AK_t^{0.3}}{L_t^{0.3}} = Ak_t^{0.3} \tag{2}$$

The Solow model assumes that A is exogenous, or given, so it does not say anything about how technology changes over time.

Figure 6.2 is a graphical representation of the per-worker production function. Notice how the per-worker production function slopes upward, indicating that as capital per worker rises, each worker produces more. The bowed-out shape of the curve tells us that the gains from a higher capital-labor ratio tend to diminish. These attributes of the per-worker production function are similar to those of the aggregate production function we studied in Chapter 3.

INVESTMENT FUNCTION. To simplify our analysis of the demand for goods and services, we will assume that the economy is closed and that government spending is zero. In per-worker terms, this means that the total demand for output is equal to consumption per worker plus investment per worker:

$$y_t = c_t + i_t \tag{3}$$

In developing his model, Solow assumed that consumers save a fixed fraction s, the **saving rate**, of their income each year, so that saving per worker, $y - c$, is

$$y_t - c_t = sy_t \tag{4}$$

Since, from Equation 3, $i_t = y_t - c_t$, we can substitute to get

$$i_t = sy_t \tag{5}$$

Time Subscripts

The subscripts t, $t - 1$, or $t + 1$ tell us in which time period something is happening. In previous chapters we have represented variable factors such as capital, labor, and aggregate output by K, L, and Y, without specifying exactly when these factors occurred. The time subscript allows us to be more specific about the timing of these factors. K_t, L_t, and Y_t, for example, are the capital, labor, and level of aggregate output that occurred during a specific time period t, which could be, for example, a year, a quarter of a year, or a month.

MyEconLab Mini-lecture

FIGURE 6.2

Per-Worker Production Function

The per-worker production function is upward sloping. As the capital-labor ratio increases, the slope of the production function declines because there is diminishing marginal product of capital.

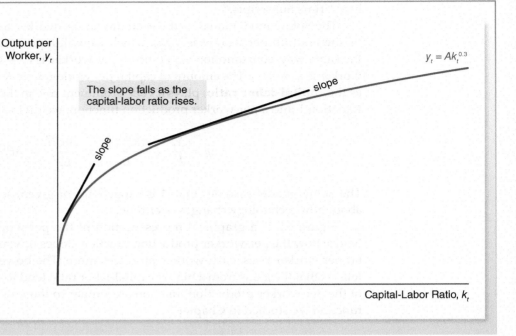

which is the familiar result that investment equals saving in a closed economy that we saw in Chapter 4. This equation tells us that investment is proportional to output, with s as the fraction of output that goes into investment.

Substituting the per-worker production function, $y_t = Ak_t^{0.3}$, into Equation 5, we get the **investment function**, which reveals the relationship between per-worker investment and the per-worker capital stock when investment equals saving.[3]

$$i_t = sAk_t^{0.3} \tag{6}$$

We show the plot of the investment function—that is, we plot i_t against k_t—in Figure 6.3. The graph has a bowed-out shape similar to the graph of the production function in Figure 6.2, and it is always below the production function because the saving rate is always between zero and one.

CAPITAL ACCUMULATION. Two forces determine changes in the capital stock: *investment* and *depreciation*. **Investment** is the purchase of new factories and machines that adds to the capital stock. **Depreciation** is the loss of capital from the wearing out of machines and factories over time. The Solow model assumes that a constant fraction δ of capital called the **depreciation rate** wears out each year. For example, if on average a unit of capital lasts twenty years, then the economy's depreciation rate is 5% per year and δ is 0.05. Because we assume the amount of depreciation is a constant fraction of the capital stock, depreciation per worker equals δk_t. When we plot depreciation per worker against capital per worker, k_t, it is a straight line with a slope of δ, as shown in Figure 6.3.

[3]The investment function in this chapter differs from the one in Chapters 4 and 9 because it assumes that the goods market is in equilibrium when saving equals investment.

FIGURE 6.3

The Solow Diagram

The steady-state level of the capital-labor ratio occurs at the intersection of the investment function and the depreciation line at point S. If capital per worker is initially at k_1, capital per worker rises over time to k^*. If capital per worker is initially at k_2, capital per worker falls over time to k^*.

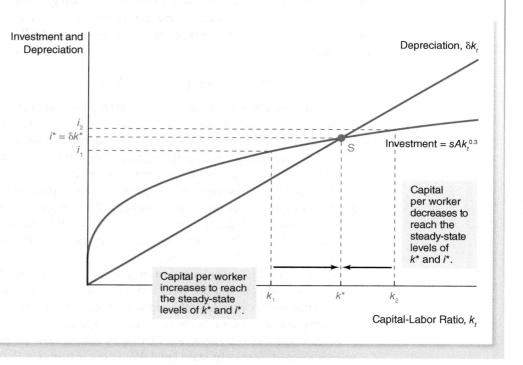

Capital accumulation—the change in the capital stock per worker, $\Delta k_t = k_{t+1} - k_t$—equals new capital investment, i_t, minus the loss in terms of wear and tear of old capital, or depreciation, δk_t:

$$\begin{array}{ccccc}
\Delta k_t & = & i_t & - & \delta k_t \\
\text{Change in capital stock} & = & \text{Investment} & - & \text{Depreciation} \\
\text{per worker} & & \text{per worker} & & \text{per worker}
\end{array} \quad (7)$$

Equation 7, which states that the change in the capital stock equals investment minus depreciation, is the **capital-accumulation equation**. Substituting in for investment from the investment function, we can rewrite this equation as follows:

$$\Delta k_t = sAk_t^{0.3} - \delta k_t \quad (8)$$

THE STEADY STATE. The **steady state**, the point at which capital per worker k_t comes to rest and stops changing, occurs when $\Delta k_t = 0$:

$$0 = sAk_t^{0.3} - \delta k_t$$

By adding δk_t to both sides of the preceding equation, we derive the condition that describes when the steady state occurs:

$$\begin{array}{ccc}
sAk_t^{0.3} & = & \delta k_t \\
\text{Investment} & = & \text{Depreciation}
\end{array} \quad (9)$$

In other words, when the capital stock per worker is in its steady state, investment and depreciation are identical. We show this relationship graphically by plotting the investment function and depreciation line. At the point of intersection, capital per worker is at its steady state. We label this point k^* in Figure 6.3, which is also known as the **Solow diagram**.

Dynamics of the Solow Growth Model

If an economy invests more than it loses through depreciation, its capital stock will grow. On the other hand, if an economy's capital stock depreciates more than the economy invests, the capital stock will decline. This intuitive relationship between investment, depreciation, and capital helps to explain how the capital-labor ratio reaches its steady state k^*.

Suppose an economy's initial capital-labor ratio is at k_1, which is less than k^*. As Figure 6.3 shows, investment at i_1 is greater than depreciation at δk_1, so Δk_t is greater than zero and k_t rises. Capital per worker will increase each period, as the rightward arrows indicate, until Δk_t returns to zero. This occurs when investment, $sAk_t^{0.3}$, equals depreciation, δk_t, or where the investment function and the depreciation line intersect at $k_t = k^*$.

Now suppose the initial amount of capital per worker is at k_2, which is greater than k^*. Investment at i_2 is smaller than depreciation at δk_2, so Δk_t is less than zero and k_t falls. Capital per worker k_t will keep on falling, as the leftward arrows indicate, until Δk_t returns to zero when investment equals depreciation at $k_t = k^*$.

We can take the analysis a step further by asking how output per worker changes as k_t moves toward its steady-state level. We know intuitively that if k_t is below the steady-state level, capital per worker will rise toward its steady state over time. With more capital per worker, total output per worker will rise as well. As k_t reaches its steady state, output per worker, y_t, will reach its own steady state.

We show this relationship graphically in Figure 6.4 by adding the production function $y_t = Ak_t^{0.3}$ to the Solow diagram. If capital per worker is initially at k_1, output per worker is at $y_1 = Ak_1^{0.3}$ at point 1. However, since $k_1 < k^*$, capital per worker rises to k^*, and over time output rises to $y^* = Ak^{*0.3}$ at point S (for "steady state").

What about consumption per worker? Because $y_t = c_t + i_t$, consumption per worker is the difference between the output curve and the investment function, as shown in Figure 6.4. As income rises to y^*, notice that consumption also rises. We can see this relationship even more directly by recognizing that, since $i_t = y_t - c_t = sy_t$,

$$c_t = (1 - s)y_t.$$

Thus as y_t rises, consumption per worker, c_t, rises until it gets to the steady state when $y_t = y^*$ and $c^* = (1 - s)y^*$. If, on the other hand, capital per worker is initially at k_2, where output per worker is $y_2 = Ak_2^{0.3}$ at point 2, capital per worker now falls. Over time, output falls to y^*. Similarly, consumption per worker c^* falls until it reaches $(1 - s)y^*$.

The dynamics of the Solow model give us a full understanding of the steady state. *The steady state at k^*, c^*, and y^* is where the economy will move to and stay if it initially starts away from the steady state at $k_t = k^*$. In other words, the steady state is where the economy converges in the long run and so is the long-run equilibrium for the economy.* We provide some further intuition about the steady state in the box, "The 'Bathtub Model' of the Steady State."

FIGURE 6.4

Output and Consumption in the Solow Model

The steady-state level of k^* is reached at the intersection of the investment function $i_t = sAk_t^{0.3}$ and the depreciation line δk_t. At this level of k^*, the steady-state level of output per capita, y^*, is at point S and the steady-state level of consumption per capita is c^*.

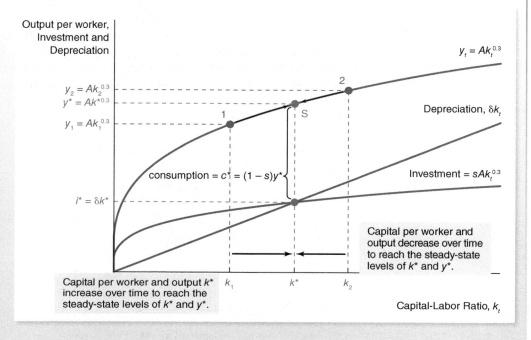

Output per worker, Investment and Depreciation

$y_t = Ak_t^{0.3}$

$y_2 = Ak_2^{0.3}$
$y^* = Ak^{*0.3}$

$y_1 = Ak_1^{0.3}$

Depreciation, δk_t

consumption = $c^* = (1 - s)y^*$

Investment = $sAk_t^{0.3}$

$i^* = \delta k^*$

Capital per worker and output decrease over time to reach the steady-state levels of k^* and y^*.

Capital per worker and output k^* increase over time to reach the steady-state levels of k^* and y^*.

k_1 k^* k_2

Capital-Labor Ratio, k_t

Convergence in the Solow Model

If multiple economies have the same aggregate production function, the same ratio of workers to the total population, and the same saving rate, the Solow model suggests that even if those economies start with different capital-labor ratios, they will tend to converge to the steady state and end up with similar levels of per capita income. Similar economies will thus experience **convergence**—that is, countries with different initial levels of per capita income will gravitate to a similar level of per capita income. Countries with low initial levels of capital and output per worker, $k_t < k^*$ and $y_t < y^*$, will grow rapidly because k_t and y_t will rise until they are both at their steady-state values of k^* and y^*.

The "Bathtub Model" of the Steady State

In Chapter 2, we used the analogy of a bathtub to illustrate the difference between stocks and flows. The same analogy is very useful in understanding the steady state in the Solow model.

In using the bathtub analogy to describe the Solow model, the flow into the bathtub is the amount of investment, $sAk_t^{0.3}$, which is represented by the flow from the faucet in Figure 6.5.

The flow out of the bathtub is depreciation, δk_t, which is represented by the flow from the drain. The amount of water in the tub is the stock of capital per worker, k_t. As the capital-accumulation equation (Equation 8) indicates, when investment is greater than depreciation, $sAk_t^{0.3} > \delta k_t$, the flow into the tub is greater than the flow out, so the water level, k_t, is rising. Similarly, when investment is smaller than depreciation, $sAk_t^{0.3} < \delta k_t$ the inflow is less than the outflow, and so the water level, k_t, is falling. Only when investment equals depreciation, $sAk_t^{0.3} = \delta k_t$, so that the water flowing into the tub equals the water flowing out of the tub, does the water level stop falling or rising to reach a steady state at $k_t = k^*$.

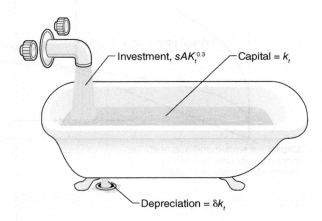

Investment, $sAK_t^{0.3}$

Capital = k_t

Depreciation = δk_t

FIGURE 6.5

"Bathtub Model" of the Steady State

The inflow from the faucet into the bathtub is the amount of investment, $sAk_t^{0.3}$, while the outflow from the drain is depreciation, δk_t. The water in the tub is the stock of capital per worker, k_t, and it reaches a steady state, k^*, at which it is neither rising nor falling, when the outflow equals the inflow—that is, when $sAk_t^{0.3} = \delta k_t$.

Application

Evidence on Convergence, 1960–2012

Let's test the theory of convergence by examining two groups of countries from 1960 to 2012: a subset of wealthy nations and a large mix of rich and poor nations. Panel (a) of Figure 6.6 displays strong evidence of convergence among the wealthy nations that belong to the Organization of Economic Cooperation and Development (OECD). Countries that had very high GDP per capita in 1960, such as Switzerland and the United States, tended to have low growth rates from 1960 to 2012. Countries such as Japan, South Korea, Greece, and Portugal, which had low per capita income in 1960, have high growth rates. Convergence is especially vivid after devastating destruction from wars, as the box, "War, Destruction, and Growth Miracles," suggests.

However, when we extend the analysis to a group of 105 rich and poor countries in panel (b) of Figure 6.6, evidence of convergence breaks down. We can see almost no relationship between the initial level of per capita income and growth rates from 1960 to 2012.

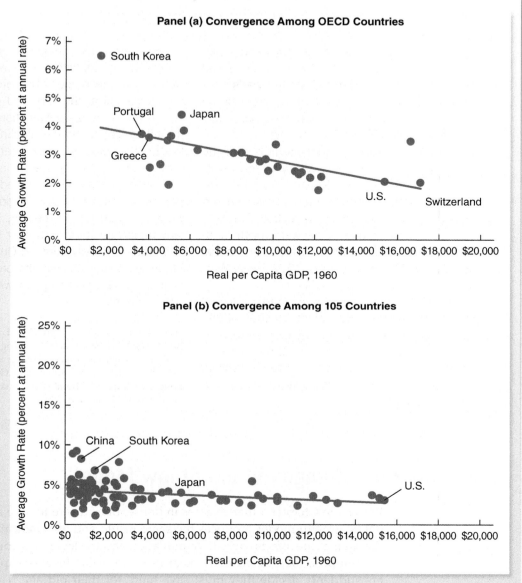

FIGURE 6.6

Evidence on Convergence, 1960–2012

Panel (a) provides strong evidence of convergence in the OECD countries. Countries that had very high GDP per capita in 1960, such as Switzerland and the United States, tend to have low growth rates from 1960 to 2012, while countries such as Japan, South Korea, Greece, and Portugal, which had low per capita income in 1960, have high growth rates. Panel (b) seeks to identify convergence in a larger group of 105 countries. There is almost no relationship between the initial level of real GDP per capita and growth rates from 1960 to 2012.

Sources: Penn World Tables. http://pwt.econ. upenn.edu/php_site/ pwt_index.php; and The World Bank. World Development Indicators. http://data.worldbank.org/ data-catalog

Panel (a) Convergence Among OECD Countries

Panel (b) Convergence Among 105 Countries

Many countries, such as Haiti, start out very poor and stay very poor. Others, such as Japan and South Korea, start out poor but get rich. Something else besides a movement toward the same steady state must explain these outcomes. The answer is that many economies are not similar, and as we will see in detail in Chapter 7, the difference mostly has to do with differences in productivity, which the Solow model treats as identical across countries.[4]

[4]The convergence concept applies to "similar" economies that have the same production function, population growth rate, and saving rate. If economies have different production functions, population growth rates, and saving rates, then the Solow model still indicates that each country will move to a steady state, but the steady state will differ among the countries. Another way of describing this is that the Solow model predicts conditional convergence for dissimilar economies—that is, these economies will converge to a particular steady state that is determined by their production functions, population growth rates, and saving rates.

War, Destruction, and Growth Miracles

World War II left the cities of Germany and Japan completely destroyed, with citizens destitute and the capital stock eviscerated. At the war's conclusion, Germans had less than a quarter of the income of Americans, while Japanese per capita income was just 15% of the U.S. level.

The Solow growth model predicts that the capital stock of economies with very low levels of capital per worker will rise very rapidly toward its steady state, boosting income per worker. History supports this prediction, as both Germany and Japan went through post–war growth miracles. Japan's per capita GDP grew at an annual rate of over 8% from 1948 to 1972, while West Germany's grew at nearly a 6% rate.

By 1972, both economies had achieved per capita income very close to that of the United States, suggesting that they were near their steady-state level. Just as the Solow model predicts, their economies then began to grow at a slower level, closer to the rates of growth in other rich countries.

Research also suggests that convergence occurs in regions within a country. One graphic example is the nuclear bombing of Hiroshima and Nagasaki at the very end of World War II. Given the immense devastation in these cities, the cities' capital stocks declined sharply relative to other parts of Japan. Yet within fifteen to thirty years, both cities experienced very rapid economic growth and converged in both size and per capita income to other regions of Japan that were less damaged in the war. There were similarly rapid rates of growth after the Vietnam War in Vietnam's heavily bombed Quang Tri province. Thirty years after the war, the province's per capita income had reached parity with that of the rest of the country.*

*See Donald R. Davis and David Weinstein, "Bones, Bombs and Break Points: The Geography of Economic Activity," *American Economic Review* 92 (December 2002): 1269–89; and Edward Miguel and Gerard Roland, "The Long-Run Impact of Bombing Vietnam," NBER Working Paper No. 11954, January 2006.

Saving Rate Changes in the Solow Model

We saw in Chapter 4 that changes in households' desire to save affect investment. The Solow growth model produces the same result, and also indicates how the change in the saving rate affects capital accumulation and the level of output.

Suppose the U.S. economy is at its steady-state level of capital k_1^* when consumers suddenly decide they must save more for their old age. The increased desire to save raises the saving rate parameter from s_1 to s_2 and, as we see in Figure 6.7 panel (a), shifts the investment function up from $s_1 A k_t^{0.3}$ to $s_2 A k_t^{0.3}$. Now, at an initial level of k_1^*, investment is greater than depreciation, so Δk_t is positive and capital per worker k_t begins to rise. As the rightward arrows indicate, k_t will keep on rising until it reaches k_2^*, where investment is again equal to depreciation, so the economy has reached its steady state. With a higher level of capital per worker, output per worker eventually rises to $y_2^* = A k_2^{*0.3}$. ***The increase in saving results in higher steady-state levels of capital and output per worker.***[5]

[5]Although a higher saving rate leads to a higher level of output per worker, consumption per worker does not always rise as the saving rate rises. There is a level of the saving rate that produces the highest level of consumption per worker, as is discussed in a Web appendix to this chapter, "The Golden Rule Level of the Capital-Labor Ratio," found at www.pearsonhighered.com/mishkin.

MyEconLab Mini-lecture

FIGURE 6.7

Response to an Increase in the Saving Rate

In panel (a), an increase in the saving rate from s_1 to s_2 shifts the investment function upward from $s_1Ak_t^{0.3}$ to $s_2Ak_t^{0.3}$. At an initial level of k_1^*, investment is greater than depreciation, so capital per worker k_t rises until it reaches k_2^*, where investment is now equal to depreciation, so the economy has reached its steady state. Panel (b) shows the corresponding movements of the capital-labor ratio and output per worker over time. At time 0, both k_t and y_t begin to rise, but as they increase, they grow at a slower rate. Finally, when $k_t = k_2^*$ and $y_t = s_2Ak_2^{*0.3}$, both the capital-labor ratio and output per worker stop growing because they have reached their steady state.

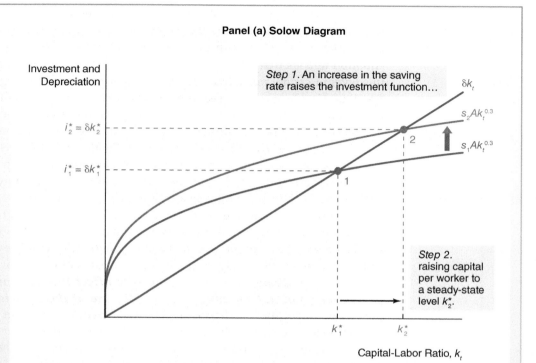

Panel (a) Solow Diagram

Investment and Depreciation

Step 1. An increase in the saving rate raises the investment function…

δk_t

$s_2Ak_t^{0.3}$

$s_1Ak_t^{0.3}$

$i_2^* = \delta k_2^*$

$i_1^* = \delta k_1^*$

Step 2. raising capital per worker to a steady-state level k_2^*.

k_1^* k_2^*

Capital-Labor Ratio, k_t

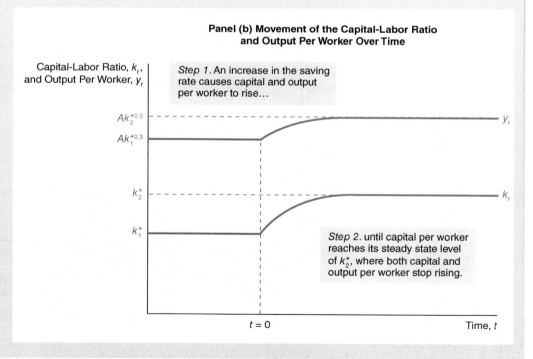

Panel (b) Movement of the Capital-Labor Ratio and Output Per Worker Over Time

Capital-Labor Ratio, k_t, and Output Per Worker, y_t

Step 1. An increase in the saving rate causes capital and output per worker to rise…

$Ak_2^{*0.3}$

$Ak_1^{*0.3}$

y_t

k_2^*

k_1^*

k_t

Step 2. until capital per worker reaches its steady state level of k_2^*, where both capital and output per worker stop rising.

$t = 0$

Time, t

Panel (b) of Figure 6.7 illustrates another way to see what is happening to the capital-labor ratio and output per worker over time when the saving rate rises from s_1 to s_2 at time 0, marked in the figure. At time 0, capital per worker is at k_1^* and output per worker is at $Ak_1^{*0.3}$. With the rise in the saving rate to s_2, the capital-accumulation equation tells us that $\Delta k_t = s_2 A k_t^{0.3} - \delta k_t$ is positive because, as shown in panel (a), at this level of capital per worker the investment function, $s_2 A k_t^{0.3}$, is above the depreciation line, δk_t. Hence, as we see in panel (b), both k_t and y_t begin to rise. However, as k_t rises, panel (a) shows that the distance between the investment function, $s_2 A k_t^{0.3}$, and the depreciation line, δk_t, shrinks, and so Δk_t declines, with the result that k_t and y_t rise at a slower rate, as can be seen in panel (b). Finally, when k_t gets to k_2^*, the investment function, $s_2 A k_t^{0.3}$, and the depreciation line, δk_t, intersect as shown in panel (a). Now, Δk_t declines to zero and k_t no longer rises. Hence, in panel (b), k_t stays at k_2^* and y_t stays at $Ak_2^{*0.3}$ because they are at their steady states.

Although the Solow growth analysis indicates that the growth rates of capital and output per worker will rise *temporarily* while the economy is moving toward the steady state, it does not indicate that these growth rates will rise *permanently*. Once the economy reaches its steady state, the growth rates of capital and output per worker return to zero. **Changes in the saving rate affect the level of capital and output per worker, but not the long-run growth rate of these variables.** In other words, the Solow model shows a *level effect*, but not a *growth effect*, from changes in the saving rate. This characteristic is due to the diminishing marginal product of capital. As capital rises, it becomes less productive: after the saving rate changes, the economy settles into a steady state in which the capital-labor ratio remains constant.

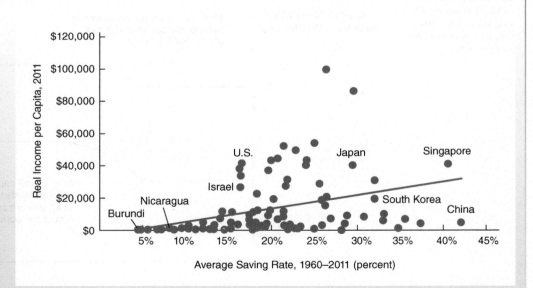

FIGURE 6.8

International Evidence on the Relationship of Per Capita Income and the Saving Rate

The plot of income per capita against the saving rate for nearly one hundred countries supports the prediction from the Solow model that countries that save more have higher per capita income. Countries like Singapore and South Korea, which have high saving rates, also have high per capita income, while countries like Nicaragua and Burundi have both a low saving rate and low per capita income.

Sources: Penn World Tables in Federal Reserve Bank of St. Louis, FRED Database. http://research.stlouisfed.org/fred2/; and The World Bank. World Development Indicators. http://data.worldbank.org/data-catalog

Assuming that the ratio of workers to the population is similar across countries, we would expect that ***the higher a country's national saving rate and hence the higher its level of investment relative to income, the higher its per capita income.*** Figure 6.8 plots income per capita against the saving rate for nearly one hundred countries. Note that Nicaragua has a very low saving rate and very low income, while Singapore has a very high saving rate and high income. As the theory predicts, countries with high national saving rates generally have high per capita income.[6]

Population Growth in the Solow Model

In the Solow framework we've developed, economies that reach the steady state stop growing. Yet since modern times, economic growth has persisted almost everywhere in the world. It must be that our model is not yet complete. In this section, we will add labor force growth into the Solow model, and in the next section we will add technology growth.

Population Growth and the Steady State

Population growth increases the size of the labor force over time, fueling economic growth. We assume that the ratio of workers to the population stays constant, so that the number of workers in the labor force grows at the same rate as the overall population, at a constant rate of n. In the United States, n equals around 1%.

When the number of workers is growing and the capital stock is kept constant, there is **capital dilution**, growth in the labor force that leads to less capital per worker. For example, if the number of workers is growing at 1% per year, the number of machines must grow at 1% per year to keep the capital-labor ratio constant. In other words, net investment would have to be 1% of the capital stock. If net investment were zero, then the capital stock per worker would fall by 1% of the capital stock per year.

We can show this effect by subtracting capital dilution nk_t from the capital-accumulation formula in Equation 8:[7]

$$\Delta k_t = sAk_t^{0.3} - \delta k_t - nk_t = sAk_t^{0.3} - (\delta + n)k_t \qquad (10)$$

Population growth affects capital accumulation in much the same way as depreciation. Depreciation lowers k_t because the capital stock is used up from wear and tear, while population growth lowers k_t by increasing the number of workers per unit of capital.

The steady-state equation changes only slightly. First, we replace the depreciation rate δ with $\delta + n$ in the analysis. Hence, we replace the depreciation term δk_t with a term reflecting depreciation *and* capital dilution, $(\delta + n)k_t$, in the Solow diagram. The modified Solow diagram in Figure 6.9 shows that the steady-state level of the capital-labor

[6]Although the evidence in Figure 6.8 supports the prediction from the Solow model, the positive correlation between the saving rate and income per capita could be the result of reverse causality: wealthy populations that earn well above subsistence levels of income are able to save more.

[7]We can derive this equation formally by using calculus. The rate of change of the capital-labor ratio is $dk/dt = d(K/L)/dt$. Using the chain rule of calculus, $dk/dt = (1/L)dk/dt - (K/L^2)dL/dt$. Given that $dk/dt = I - dK$ and $(dL/dt)/L = n$, suitable algebraic manipulation yields Equation 10.

FIGURE 6.9

Solow Diagram with Population Growth

The steady-state level of the capital-labor ratio k^* is at point S, the intersection of the investment function and the $(\delta + n)k_t$ line. If the capital-labor ratio is below k^* at k_1, then investment is greater than $(\delta + n)k_t$ and so k_t rises. If the capital-labor ratio is above k^* at k_2, then investment is below $(\delta + n)k_t$ and k_t falls.

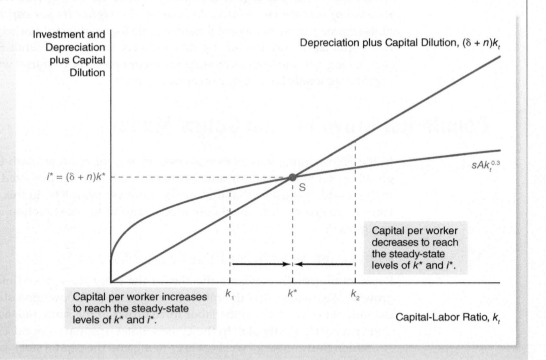

ratio k^* is now at the intersection of the investment function and the $(\delta + n)k_t$ line. As before, the economy always moves toward the steady-state value of k^*:

1. If the capital-labor ratio is below k^*, say, at k_1, then investment is greater than $(\delta + n)k_t$ and so k_t rises.

2. If the capital-labor ratio is above k^*, say, at k_2, then investment is below $(\delta + n)k_t$ and so k_t falls.

At the steady state, k_t is constant, but output, capital, and labor are all growing over time at a rate of n. As the number of workers grows at rate n, the capital stock also grows at rate n, so that the amount of capital per worker stays constant. With both capital and labor growing at n, output also grows at this same rate.[8]

The addition of population to the Solow model helps explain how economies can sustain growth in total output, but it does not explain why output *per person* keeps growing. Even with population growth, the capital-labor ratio eventually reaches a steady-state value of k^*, and output per worker also goes to a steady-state value of $y^* = Ak^{*0.3}$.

---

[8]To see that capital and output grow at the same rate as labor, that is, at rate n, recognize that capital per worker $k_t = K_t/L_t$, where L_t is labor. With k_t constant at the steady state at k^*, the numerator, K_t, must grow at the same rate as the denominator, L_t, that is, at the rate n. Similarly, with k_t constant at the steady state at k^*, $y_t = Y_t/L_t$ is also constant at y^*, so the numerator, Y_t, must also grow at the same rate as as the denominator, L_s, that is, at the rate n.

Changes in Population Growth

What happens to per-capita output when the population growth suddenly rises? Since the economy will have more workers with the same amount of capital, each worker has less capital with which to work. As a result, output per worker falls. The Solow model suggests, then, that high population growth lowers the average person's standard of living.

We show this result in Figure 6.10. When population growth rises from n_1 to n_2, it shifts up the depreciation and capital dilution line in panel (a) from $(\delta + n_1)k_t$ to $(\delta + n_2)k_t$. At the previous steady state k_1^*, investment is now less than depreciation and capital dilution, $(\delta + n)k_t$, so $\Delta k_t < 0$. The capital-labor ratio falls, eventually moving to k_2^*. Although the growth rate of output and capital have risen from n_1 to n_2, output per worker falls because $y_2^* = Ak_2^{*0.3}$ is below $y_1^* = Ak_1^{*0.3}$.

Panel (b) of Figure 6.10 shows how the capital-labor ratio and output per worker change over time as population growth rises. At time 0, capital per worker is at k_1^* and output per worker is at $Ak_1^{*0.3}$. With the rise in the population growth rate to n_2, the capital-accumulation equation tells us that $\Delta k_t = sAk_t^{0.3} - (\delta + n_2)k_t$ is negative because, as shown in panel (a), at this level of capital per worker, the investment function, $sAk_t^{0.3}$, is below the $(\delta + n_2)k_t$ line. Hence, as we see in panel (b), both k_t and y_t begin to fall. However, as k_t falls, panel (a) shows that the distance between the investment function, $s_2Ak_t^{0.3}$, and the $(\delta + n_2)k_t$ line shrinks, and so Δk_t becomes less negative, with the result that k_t and y_t fall at a slower rate, as can be seen in panel (b). Finally, when k_t declines to k_2^*, the investment function, $sAk_t^{0.3}$, and the $(\delta + n_2)k_t$ line intersect, as shown in panel (a). Thus Δk_t goes to zero and k_t no longer falls. Hence, in panel (b), k_t stays at k_2^* and y_t stays at $Ak_2^{*0.3}$ because they are at their steady states.

As long as labor force and total population grow at the same rate, the Solow model indicates that in the steady state **_higher population growth lowers the level of output per person._**

Population Growth and Real GDP Per Capita

Does the evidence support the Solow result that higher population growth makes the average person in a country poorer? The scatterplot in Figure 6.11 of real GDP per capita versus population growth rates in nearly one hundred countries provides support for the Solow proposition. Countries with low rates of population growth, like Italy and Japan, have higher income per person than countries with high population growth rates, such as the Ivory Coast and Sudan.

This view has led some policy makers to propose policies to limit population growth, as the next Policy and Practice case indicates. The interpretation is highly controversial. Many economists believe that causation does not run from lower population growth to higher per capita income, but rather the opposite way. As people get richer, they prefer to have fewer children and gain access to birth control, and so fertility rates decline. Other models of economic growth, which we will consider in the next chapter, yield a different view than that proposed by the Solow model: they imply that higher population growth could actually produce higher income per capita because it stimulates technological advances.

MyEconLab Mini-lecture

FIGURE 6.10

Response to a Rise in the Population Growth Rate

When the population growth rate rises from n_1 to n_2, the depreciation and capital dilution $(\delta + n)k_t$ line swings up from $(\delta + n_1)k_t$ to $(\delta + n_2)k_t$ in panel (a). At k_1^*, investment is less than depreciation and capital dilution, $(\delta + n)k_t$, and so the capital-labor ratio falls, eventually moving it to k_2^*. Panel (b) shows the corresponding movements of the capital-labor ratio and output per worker over time. At time 0, both k_t and y_t begin to fall, but as they decline, they fall at a slower rate. Finally, when $k_t = k_2^*$ and $y_t = sAk_2^{*0.3}$, both the capital-labor ratio and output per worker stop falling because they have reached their steady state.

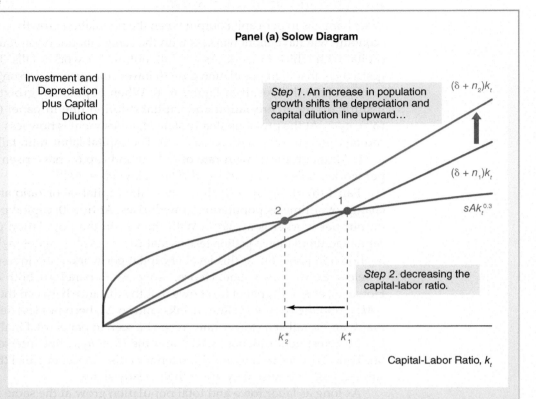

Panel (a) Solow Diagram

Investment and Depreciation plus Capital Dilution

Step 1. An increase in population growth shifts the depreciation and capital dilution line upward…

$(\delta + n_2)k_t$

$(\delta + n_1)k_t$

$sAk_t^{0.3}$

Step 2. decreasing the capital-labor ratio.

k_2^* k_1^*

Capital-Labor Ratio, k_t

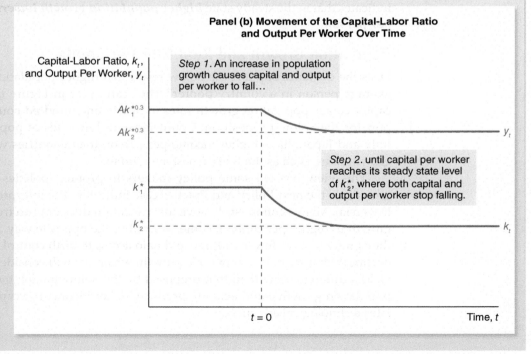

Panel (b) Movement of the Capital-Labor Ratio and Output Per Worker Over Time

Capital-Labor Ratio, k_t, and Output Per Worker, y_t

Step 1. An increase in population growth causes capital and output per worker to fall…

$Ak_1^{*0.3}$

$Ak_2^{*0.3}$

y_t

Step 2. until capital per worker reaches its steady state level of k_2^*, where both capital and output per worker stop falling.

k_1^*

k_2^*

k_t

$t = 0$

Time, t

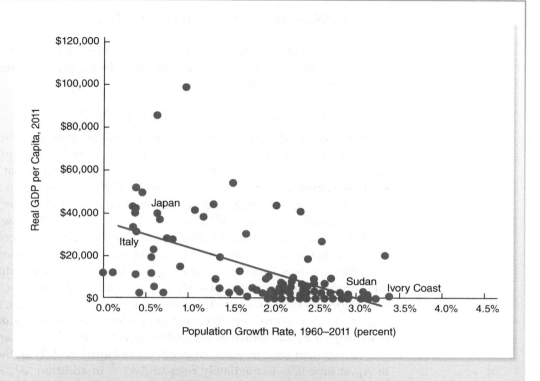

Source: The World Bank. World Development Indicators. http://data.worldbank.org/data-catalog

FIGURE 6.11

International Evidence on the Relationship of Population Growth and Income per Capita

The scatterplot of income per person versus population growth rates in nearly one hundred countries provides some support for the Solow proposition that higher population growth leads to lower per capita income. Countries with low rates of population growth, like Italy and Japan, have higher income per person than countries with high population growth rates, such as the Ivory Coast and Sudan.

Policy and Practice

China's One-Child Policy and Other Policies to Limit Population Growth

Many countries, particularly poor ones, have implemented policies to limit population growth. Some have taken the policy to an extreme through forced sterilizations. Others take a more benign approach, providing citizens with birth control and running campaigns to encourage smaller families. But the most famous (or infamous, depending on your point of view) is the Chinese government's "one-child" policy. Starting in 1979, couples with more than one child were ostracized, charged penalties, and denied access to preferential housing and wage hikes. The policy lowered fertility rates by over 70%, but has sparked controversy. Many people view the one-child policy as interfering with the basic human right to make decisions about reproduction.

Productivity Growth in the Solow Model

Our discussion of the Solow model has yet to explain why economies display sustained increases in the standard of living over time. To get there, we need to add growth in productivity, A, to the Solow model.

Technology Growth and the Steady State

Adding productivity growth into the Solow model is quite straightforward. Equation 10 for capital accumulation still holds true, and so the Solow diagram does not change at all. Now let's look at what happens if the discovery of a superfast memory chip creates a leap in computer technology so that productivity increases from A_1 to A_2. With higher productivity and therefore higher output at each level of k_t, the investment function shifts up from $sA_1k_t^{0.3}$ to $sA_2k_t^{0.3}$ in panel (a) of Figure 6.12. The rise in investment at any level of k_t means that at the old steady-state level of the capital-labor ratio, k_1^*, investment is greater than depreciation plus capital dilution, and so $\Delta k_t > 0$ and k_t rises. Only when k_t reaches the new steady state of k_2^*, where investment equals depreciation plus capital dilution, does $\Delta k_t = 0$ and k_t stop rising. Output per worker, $y_2^* = A_2k_2^{*0.3}$, is now higher for two reasons. First, A_2 is higher, as Figure 6.12 indicates, and second, k_2^* is also higher. In other words, **the direct effect of higher productivity on output per person is amplified by the additional positive effect from a higher capital-labor ratio.**

We can also see this result in panel (b) of Figure 6.12. With the rise in productivity to A_2, at time 0, y_t immediately rises to $A_2k_1^{*0.3}$. In addition, $\Delta k_t = sA_2k_t^{0.3} - (\delta + n)k_t$ is positive because, as shown in panel (a), at this level of capital per worker the investment function, $sA_2k_t^{0.3}$, is above the $(\delta + n)k_t$ line. Hence, as we see in panel (b), both k_t and y_t begin to rise. However, as k_t rises, panel (a) shows that the distance between the investment function and the $(\delta + n)k_t$ line shrinks, and so Δk_t declines, with the result that k_t and y_t rise at a slower rate, as can be seen in panel (b). Finally, when k_t gets to k_2^*, the investment function, $sA_2k_t^{0.3}$, and the $(\delta + n)k_t$ line intersect, as shown in panel (a). Thus Δk_t declines to zero and k_t no longer rises. Hence, in panel (b), k_t stays at k_2^* and y_t stays at $A_2k_2^{*0.3}$ because they are at their steady states.

The Solow model does not explain *why* productivity A grows over time. That said, given a constant growth rate of productivity, say, at g, output and capital per worker will grow at a sustained rate faster than g. In the appendix at the end of this chapter, we solve the Solow model algebraically and find that the Cobb-Douglas production function implies that output and capital per worker grow at a rate of 1.43 g. That is, a productivity growth rate of 1% leads to a growth rate in living standard of 1.43%, meaning there is an amplification effect of 43%.

Summing Up the Solow Model

The Solow model has proved to be one of the most durable and useful models in macroeconomics. We will now step back and summarize the results of the Solow model and discuss its limitations.

Solow Model: The Results

The Solow model describes a steady state of the variables k^*, c^*, and y^* toward which the economy moves in the long run. There are four basic conclusions from this analysis:

MyEconLab Mini-lecture

FIGURE 6.12

Response to a Rise in Productivity

When productivity increases from A_1 to A_2, the investment function shifts up from $sA_1k_t^{0.3}$ to $sA_2k_t^{0.3}$ in panel (a). At the old steady-state level of the capital-labor ratio, k_1^*, investment is greater than depreciation plus capital dilution, and so k_t rises until it reaches the new steady state of k_2^*, where investment equals depreciation plus capital dilution. Panel (b) shows the corresponding movements of the capital-labor ratio and output per worker over time. At time 0, y immediately rises to $A_2k_1^{*0.3}$. In addition, both k_t and y_t begin to rise, but as they increase, they grow at a slower rate. Finally, when $k_t = k_2^*$ and $y_t = A_2k_2^{0.3}$, both the capital-labor ratio and output per worker stop growing because they have reached their steady state. Because the capital-labor ratio rises as the production function rises, steady state output increases by more than a factor of one-to-one with the increase in A.

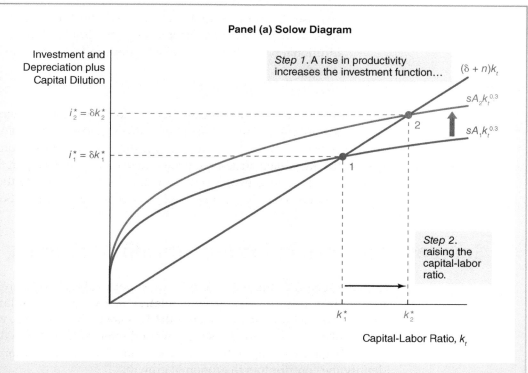

Panel (a) Solow Diagram

Investment and Depreciation plus Capital Dilution

$(\delta + n)k_t$

Step 1. A rise in productivity increases the investment function...

$sA_2k_t^{0.3}$

$sA_1k_t^{0.3}$

$i_2^* = \delta k_2^*$

$i_1^* = \delta k_1^*$

Step 2. raising the capital-labor ratio.

k_1^* k_2^*

Capital-Labor Ratio, k_t

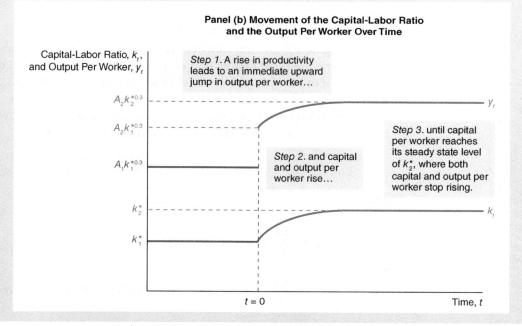

Panel (b) Movement of the Capital-Labor Ratio and the Output Per Worker Over Time

Capital-Labor Ratio, k_t, and Output Per Worker, y_t

Step 1. A rise in productivity leads to an immediate upward jump in output per worker...

$A_2k_2^{*0.3}$

$A_2k_1^{*0.3}$

$A_1k_1^{*0.3}$

Step 2. and capital and output per worker rise...

Step 3. until capital per worker reaches its steady state level of k_2^*, where both capital and output per worker stop rising.

y_t

k_2^*

k_1^*

k_t

$t = 0$

Time, t

1. Economies with similar production functions and saving rates that have low initial per capita income will have higher growth rates, while those with high initial per capita income will have lower growth rates.

2. A higher rate of saving, and hence a higher level of investment relative to income, leads to higher levels of capital and output per worker, but does not affect the long-run growth rates of these variables.

3. Higher population growth lowers the level of output per person.

4. Increases in productivity have amplified effects on per capita income because there is a direct effect through the production function and an additional positive effect from a higher capital-labor ratio.

Solow Model: Limitations

The results of our analysis indicate that the Solow model can help us understand why some countries are rich and others poor. However, *it does a poor job of explaining sustained increases in the standard of living*, a central feature of modern economies. Only productivity growth can explain sustained growth in standards of living in the Solow model. But productivity growth is exogenous, that is, determined outside the model. Put plainly, productivity growth in the Solow model is not addressed in the Solow model.

Sources of Economic Growth: Growth Accounting

We have seen that the Solow model does not explain productivity growth, but how important is productivity growth relative to capital accumulation and labor force growth in explaining economic growth? To answer this question, we need to look at the sources of economic growth using a method referred to as "growth accounting."

We begin by manipulating the production function into a format that allows us to identify the contributors to economic growth.

Growth Accounting Equation

The aggregate production function in Equation 1 at the beginning of this chapter tells us that there are three factors that determine the level of output: the level of capital, K; the amount of labor, L; and the level of technology (productivity), A. But what happens when any of these variables—A, K, or L—grows? With some basic math, we can modify the production function to show the relationship between the growth rate of output and the growth rate of the variables in the production function:

$$g_Y = g_A + 0.3\,g_K + 0.7g_L \qquad (11)$$

where

$$g_Y = \frac{\Delta Y}{Y} = \text{growth rate of output}$$

$$g_A = \frac{\Delta A}{A} = \text{growth rate of technology (total factor productivity)}$$

$$g_K = \frac{\Delta K}{K} = \text{growth rate of capital}$$

$$g_L = \frac{\Delta L}{L} = \text{growth rate of labor}$$

Equation 11 is the **growth accounting equation** (the growth version of the production function), which states that the growth rate of output equals the growth rate of total factor productivity plus the contributions from the growth of both capital and labor.[9]

The growth accounting equation retains the useful property of diminishing marginal product of capital and labor. If capital grows by 5%, output grows by only $0.3 \times 5\% = 1.5\%$. If the labor force grows by 5%, then output increases by only $3.5\% (= 0.7 \times 5\%)$. Productivity, as we saw in our study of the production function, does not suffer from diminishing marginal product. If new inventions boost total factor productivity by 5%, output grows by 5%, too.

Growth Accounting in Practice

Three terms in the growth accounting equation contribute to growth in output:

- Contribution from productivity growth[10] $= \Delta A / A$
- Contribution from capital growth $= 0.3 \, \Delta K / K$
- Contribution from labor growth $= 0.7 \, \Delta L / L$

Because it is difficult to directly measure total factor productivity, we must calculate it from measures of Y, K, and L. We do this with Equation 12, derived by solving Equation 1 for A at time t:

$$A_t = \frac{Y_t}{K_t^{0.3} L_t^{0.7}} \tag{12}$$

We also refer to the term A_t as the **Solow residual** because it shows the unexplained (*residual*) part of the production function and was first used in growth accounting by Robert Solow.

With the values of A, K, and L in hand, we can compare their levels over time and calculate growth rates for each. For example, let's say that after calculating the Solow

---

[9]To derive the growth accounting equation, we begin by writing the change in Y as follows:

$$\Delta Y = \frac{\partial Y}{\partial A} \times \Delta A + \frac{\partial Y}{\partial K} \times \Delta K + \frac{\partial Y}{\partial L} \times \Delta L$$

Because

$$\partial Y / \partial A = K^{0.3} L^{0.7} = A K^{0.3} L^{0.7} / A = Y / A$$

we can write the preceding equation as follows:

$$\Delta Y = (Y/A) \times \Delta A + MPK \times \Delta K + MPL \times \Delta L$$

Substituting in the calculations for MPK and MPL from Chapter 3 and dividing through by Y yields the following:

$$\frac{\Delta Y}{Y} = \frac{\Delta A}{A} + 0.3 \frac{\Delta K}{K} + 0.7 \frac{\Delta L}{L}$$

which, using the definitions in the text, is

$$g_Y = g_A + 0.3 \, g_K + 0.7 g_L$$

We also could have derived this equation by using the mathematical fact we discussed in Chapter 2 that the growth rate of a variable that is the product of several variables is the sum of the growth rates of the variables, along with the additional mathematical fact that the growth rate of a variable raised to some power is that power times the growth rate of that variable.

[10]Recall from Chapter 3 that when we talk about productivity, we are always referring to the general concept of total factor productivity, rather than labor productivity, which is the definition of productivity more commonly referred to in the media.

residual, over one year the growth rate of productivity, $\Delta A/A$, is 1.5%; the growth rate of the capital stock, $\Delta K/K$, is 2.0%; and the growth rate of the labor input, $\Delta L/L$, is 1.0%.

Using Equation 11, we know that productivity growth contributed 1.5% to output growth over the period. The contribution from capital growth is $0.3 \times \Delta K/K = 0.3 \times 2.0\% = 0.6\%$, and the contribution from labor growth is $0.7 \times \Delta L/L = 0.7 \times 1.0\% = 0.7\%$. Thus, output growth equals $1.5\% + 0.6\% + 0.7\% = 2.8\%$. Notice that productivity growth contributed more than half of the total increase in output (because 1.5% is more than half of 2.8%), while capital and labor growth contributed the remainder.

Application

U.S. Growth Rates in the Postwar Period

Let's apply growth accounting methodology to identifying the sources of U.S. economic growth since World War II. Figure 6.13 divides the years 1948–2011 into three periods: 1948–1973, 1974–1995, and 1996–2011. The leftmost (blue) bars in each sub-period represent output growth. The next three bars for each sub-period represent the contribution to output growth from productivity (purple), capital (red), and labor inputs (green).

The U.S. economy grew rapidly at close to a 4.0% growth rate until 1973, but then slowed considerably to a 2.9% growth rate until 1995. What explains this slowdown? It couldn't be capital growth, whose contribution to growth dropped only slightly, from 1.2% to 1.0%. Nor could it be labor growth, whose contribution to output growth also dropped slightly from 1.1% to 1.0%. The decline in the output growth rate was primarily caused by a slowdown of productivity growth. Indeed, annual productivity growth rates fell from 1.5% before 1973 to 0.9% in the 1974–1995 period.

Economists still hotly debate the causes of this productivity slowdown. Some note that oil prices began rising in 1973, and that the country began spending a lower proportion of its GDP on research and development. Still others point to the economy's transition from primarily manufacturing to service production, as well as increases in environmental and other government regulations. One unconventional argument is that the advance of information technology prompted a painful period of industrial restructuring, temporarily suppressing productivity growth.

The average economic growth rate fell even further from the 1974–1995 period to the 1996–2011 period (2.9% to 2.2%). Growth in the capital stock actually rose from 1.0% to 1.3% from the earlier to the later period, while productivity growth fell slightly, from 0.9% to 0.6%, so together they did not contribute much to the fall in the overall rate. The major source of the decline in the economic growth rate over the two periods was due to the sharp fall in the growth rate of labor, which declined from 1.0% in the 1974–1995 period to 0.3% in the 1996–2011 period. A key factor in this decline has been the large decline over the second period in the percentage of men that are employed, while the employment rate for women, which had risen dramatically up until the late 1990s, stopped rising and even fell in the aftermath of the Great Recession that started in 2007. These developments in the labor market are discussed in Chapter 20.

FIGURE 6.13

Sources of U.S. Economic Growth

The first bar, in blue, for each period shows the annual average growth rate for output, while the next three bars show the contribution to output growth from the growth in capital (red), the growth in labor inputs (green) and productivity growth (purple), respectively. Comparing sub-periods, the growth rate of output varies considerably, mostly due to swings in productivity growth rates.

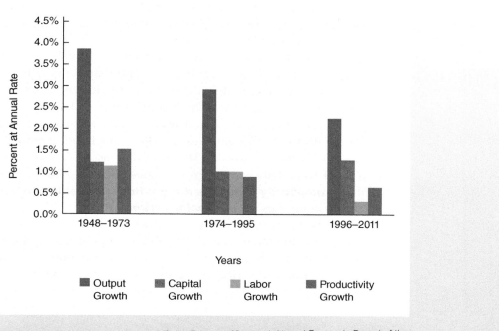

Sources: Bureau of Economic Analysis. www.bea.gov/national/nipaweb/SelectTable.asp?Selected=N; and Economic Report of the President. www.gpoaccess.gov/eop/tables10.html. Productivity growth is computed as Solow residual using capital share of 30%.

Cross-Country Differences in Growth Accounting Rates

Growth accounting indicates that different economies often have very different reasons for high output growth. To illustrate, consider the cases of Hong Kong, Singapore, South Korea, and Taiwan, known as the Asian Tigers because of their rapid rates of economic growth after 1960. These economic "tigers" followed very different paths to prosperity. In Singapore, where per capita GDP grew at 7% per year from 1960 to 1990, very high growth rates of capital accounted for virtually all of its output growth. In contrast, Hong Kong's 6% per capita GDP growth over the same period was driven by very high productivity growth, which averaged over 2% per year.[11] The citizens of Hong Kong and Singapore are now among the richest people in the world.

[11]For an analysis of why the sources of growth were so different in these two cities, see Alwyn Young, "A Tale of Two Cities: Factor Accumulation and Technical Change in Hong Kong and Singapore," NBER Macroeconomics Annual 7 (1992): 13–54. Note that Young's results are controversial. See Chang-Tai Hsieh, "What Explains the Industrial Revolution in East Asia? Evidence from the Factor Markets," American Economic Review 92, no. 3 (June 2002): 502–526, who argues that capital accumulation may have been overstated in Singapore, so that productivity growth may have been much higher in Singapore than Young suggests.

Research in economic growth seeks to explain such differences in growth rates among countries. For example, David Weil of Brown University divided nations into five categories, from the slowest-growing to the fastest-growing.[12] Then, using the growth accounting formula in Equation 11, he estimated the contribution to economic growth in these countries from productivity growth and from **factor accumulation**, or growth in labor and capital. He found that the growth of capital and labor added 0.74% per year to growth in the slowest-growing countries, versus 2.18% per year in the fastest-growing countries. That's a difference of 1.44%. Productivity actually declined for the slowest-growing countries, reducing economic growth by 1.31% per year. For the highest-growth countries, on the other hand, productivity growth contributed 1.22% to economic growth. That's a difference of 2.53%—much higher than the difference of 1.44% between the growth rates of factor accumulation. This analysis indicates that ***productivity growth is a more important source of variation in growth rates across countries than is factor accumulation.***

In the next chapter, we will explore additional theories of economic growth that try to explain both the level and growth rate of productivity. Our ability to do so is crucial, as we have just seen that productivity growth is more important than factor accumulation as a source of variation in growth rates across countries.

---

[12]See Chapter 7 of David N. Weil, *Economic Growth*, 2nd edition (Boston: Addison-Wesley, 2009).

SUMMARY

1. A tour of economic growth around the world indicates that almost all countries have experienced positive economic growth from 1960 to 2010, with France, the United Kingdom, Japan, South Korea, and India displaying convergence to the U.S. level of real GDP per capita. Other countries have not experienced convergence, with some, such as Kenya, Nigeria, and particularly Haiti, experiencing growth disasters in which their real income per capita has fallen relative to that of the United States.

2. The Solow growth model focuses on explaining how capital accumulation occurs and the role that it plays in producing economic growth. It shows that an economy reaches a steady state in the long run at the level of the capital-labor ratio at which investment equals depreciation plus capital dilution, that is, where $\Delta k_t = 0 = sAk_t^{0.3} - (\delta + n)k_t$. An important implication of the Solow model is that there is convergence: countries with different levels of per capita income will gravitate to a similar level. Economies that have low initial per capita income will have higher growth rates, while those with high initial per capita income will have lower growth rates.

3. In the Solow model, a higher saving rate, and hence a higher level of investment relative to income, leads to higher steady-state levels of capital and output per worker, but does not affect the long-run growth rates of these variables.

4. In the Solow model, population growth can explain why economies have sustained growth in output, but it does not explain why output per person grows at a sustained pace. Higher population growth lowers the level of output per person.

5. Increases in productivity raise output by more than the increase in productivity, directly by raising output per worker and indirectly by raising the capital-labor ratio.

6. Growth accounting is based on the growth version of the production function. It indicates that there are three contributions that add up to growth in GDP: the contribution from productivity growth, $\Delta A/A$; the contribution from capital growth, $0.3\Delta K/K$; and the contribution from labor growth, $0.7\Delta L/L$. The growth accounting equation is $g_Y = g_A + 0.3g_K + 0.7g_L$, where $g_Y = \Delta Y/Y$, $g_A = \Delta A/A$, $g_K = \Delta K/K$, and $g_L = \Delta L/L$.

7. Growth accounting demonstrates that productivity growth is a more important source of variation in growth rates across countries than factor accumulation.

KEY TERMS

capital-accumulation equation, p. 151
capital dilution, p. 159
capital-labor ratio, p. 149
convergence, p. 147
depreciation, p. 150

depreciation rate, p. 150
factor accumulation, p. 170
growth accounting equation, p. 167
investment, p. 150
investment function, p. 150

saving rate, p. 149
Solow diagram, p. 152
Solow growth model, p. 148
Solow residual, p. 167
steady state, p. 151

REVIEW QUESTIONS

All Questions are available in MyEconLab *for practice or instructor assignment.*

The Solow Growth Model

1. In the per-worker production function, what factors determine the level of output per worker? Which one of these factors does the Solow growth model consider to be exogenous?

2. Why does the per-worker production function have its particular shape and slope?
3. What determines the amount of investment per worker and capital accumulation in the Solow growth model?

4. What are the two determinants of the steady-state level of capital per worker? Why does capital per worker move to this steady-state level?

Saving Rate Changes in the Solow Model

5. Beginning from a steady state in the Solow growth model, explain how an increase in the saving rate will affect the levels and growth rates of capital and output per worker.

Population Growth in the Solow Model

6. How does population growth affect the steady-state levels of capital and output per worker?

7. In the Solow growth model, which variables are exogenous and which are endogenous?

Productivity Growth in the Solow Model

8. How does an increase in total factor productivity affect output per worker?

Summing Up the Solow Model

9. What are the four basic results of the Solow growth model? What is the model's chief weakness?

Sources of Economic Growth: Growth Accounting

10. According to the growth accounting equation, what are the three sources that contribute to economic growth?

PROBLEMS

All Problems are available in MyEconLab *for practice or instructor assignment.*

The Solow Growth Model

1. Assume that the per-worker production function is $y_t = 2k_t^{0.5}$. The saving and depreciation rates are estimated at 0.2 and 0.04, respectively.

a) Calculate the capital-labor ratio steady state for this economy.
b) Calculate consumption per worker at the steady state.

2. The tsunami that hit Japan in April of 2011 was the costliest national disaster in history. The following graph describes Japan's economy before the tsunami. Assume Japan was at its steady-state capital-labor ratio before the tsunami hit.

a) On the same graph, identify the new capital-labor ratio immediately after this event.

b) Describe how the capital-labor ratio will change in the aftermath of Japan's tsunami.

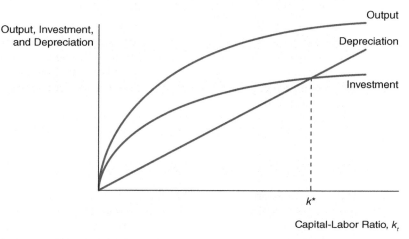

Saving Rate Changes in the Solow Model

3. Consider the effects of an increase in the saving rate on the United States capital-labor ratio, according to the Solow model.
   a) What would be the immediate effect of a saving rate increase on the capital-labor ratio? What would be the long-run effect?

b) Do you think it is beneficial to increase the saving rate? If so, by how much? (Would you save 95% of your income?)

Population Growth in the Solow Model

4. Assume that low standards of living (i.e., low capital-labor ratios, in the Solow model's terms) are the reason that some countries exhibit high fertility rates. Comment on the effect of population control policies to reduce fertility rates. Explain why you think such policies will or will not be effective.

5. One of the most well-known population control policies is the one-child policy implemented by China since the late 1970s.

Comment on the side effects of such a policy. This policy has been dubbed a success, since fertility rates dropped by a considerable amount. Do you agree with this type of population control?

6. Based on the Solow model's conclusions about population growth, comment on the effects of immigration on a country's
   a) aggregate output level.
   b) capital-labor ratio.

Productivity Growth in the Solow Model

7. Start by graphing the U.S. steady-state capital-labor ratio and labeling it k^*_{1900} (draw only the investment and the depreciation and capital dilution curves).
   a) On the same graph, show the effects of the following:

   ▪ The massive immigration wave of the early 1900s
   ▪ The increase in productivity derived from new technologies that occurred at the same time

b) Find the new steady-state capital-labor ratio considering that output per worker

in the United States grew at a positive rate between 1900 and 1910, and label it k^{ss}_{1910}.

Summing up the Solow Model

8. Start by drawing a given country's steady state, using only the investment and the depreciation and capital dilution curves. On the same graph, do the following:
   a) Consider the effects of an immigration wave of individuals who exhibit both

   higher saving and fertility rates than the current population. Draw the new curves.
   b) Identify the new steady-state capital-labor ratio level. Is it necessarily higher or lower than the previous steady state?

Sources of Economic Growth: Growth Accounting

9. Suppose the economy of India can be represented by the following production function: $Y = AK^{1/3}L^{2/3}$. Assume that during 2014, India's technological growth (Solow residual) is 4%, and the growth rates of both the capital and labor input stocks are 3%.
   a) Calculate India's output growth for 2014.
   b) What is the contribution of productivity growth to total output growth (in percentage terms)?

10. Suppose two countries have the same growth rates of capital and labor inputs. These factors contribute two percentage points to their respective countries' total output growth rates. Output growth rates are 2.5% for country 1 and 4.5% for country 2.
   a) Explain the difference in total output growth between these two countries.
   b) Calculate productivity growth for both countries.

DATA ANALYSIS PROBLEMS

The Problems update with real-time data in MyEconLab *and are available for practice or instructor assignment.*

1. Go to the St. Louis Federal Reserve FRED database, and find data on population and

GDP per capita for the following countries, with data codes provided in the table below.

Country	Population	GDP Per Capita
Brazil	POPTOTBRA647NWDB	PCAGDPBRA646NWDB
Canada	POPTOTCAA647NWDB	PCAGDPCAA646NWDB
China	POPTOTCNA647NWDB	PCAGDPCNA646NWDB
Egypt	POPTOTEGA647NWDB	PCAGDPEGA646NWDB
India	POPTOTINA647NWDB	PCAGDPINA646NWDB
Indonesia	POPTOTIDA647NWDB	PCAGDPIDA646NWDB
Japan	POPTOTJPA647NWDB	PCAGDPJPA646NWDB
Mexico	POPTOTMXA647NWDB	PCAGDPMXA646NWDB
Philippines	POPTOTPHA647NWDB	PCAGDPPHA646NWDB
United States	POPTOTUSA647NWDB	PCAGDPUSA646NWDB

a) For each country, calculate the average population growth rate per year by calculating the total percentage increase in population and dividing by the number of years in the sample, up to the most recent data available.

b) For each country, compare the average population growth rate per year to the level of GDP per capita reported for the most recent data available. Create a table to report these values, organizing the table with countries ordered from lowest population growth to highest. Choose the three countries with the lowest population growth and the three with the highest, and calculate their average population growth rates and average GDP per capita as groups. Are the results what you would expect? From the list of countries, are there any that don't follow the expected pattern? Briefly explain.

c) Create a scatterplot of the data (and insert a fitted line if possible). Comment on the relationship between population growth and GDP per capita.

2. Go to the St. Louis Federal Reserve FRED database, and find data on real GDP (GDPCA), the labor force (CLF16OV), and a measure of the capital stock, real consumption of fixed capital (A262RX1A020NBEA). Download all of the data onto a spreadsheet; for (CLF16OV), change the *frequency* setting to "annual" before downloading. In the spreadsheet, convert the data into real GDP per worker and capital per worker by dividing (GDPCA) and (A262RX1A020NBEA) by (CLF16OV) for each year. Note that this conversion will be represented as $ millions of output and capital per worker.

a) For each year from 1960 to the most current year available, calculate $k^{0.3}$ and use this value, along with the trans-

formed real GDP per worker series, to calculate a measure of total factor productivity.

b) For each decade (1960–1969, 1970–1979, 1980–1989, 1990–1999, 2000–2009, 2010 on), calculate the average growth rate per year from the beginning of the decade to the end of the decade for total factor productivity calculated in part (a), and capital per worker. To do this, take the value at the end of the time period and subtract it from the value at the beginning of the time period, and then divide by the value at the beginning of the time period. Then divide by the number of years in the period (10 for each full decade).

c) Use the growth accounting equation to calculate the average growth in output per worker for each decade, and then calculate the average across all decades for g_k, g_A, $0.3g_k$, and g_y. Which source of growth seems to be more important, total factor productivity or capital per worker? Briefly explain.

3. Go to the St. Louis Federal Reserve FRED database and find data on the net saving rate as a percentage of national income (W207RC1A156NBEA).

a) Calculate the average net saving rate over the period from 1960 to 1980, and again for the period from 1980 to the most current available data.

b) Based on your answer to part (a), what do you expect will happen to real GDP per capita in the United States?

c) Compare the average net saving rate for the 1960–1980 period and the post-1980 period with real GDP per capita (USARGDPC) in 1980 and in the most current available year, respectively. Do your results match the results predicted by the Solow model? Why or why not?

An online appendix, "The Golden Rule Level of the Capital-Labor Ratio," is available at the Companion Website, www.pearsonhighered.com/mishkin

Chapter 6
Appendix

The Algebra of the Solow Growth Model

An algebraic analysis of the Solow model allows us to directly obtain all the results found in the body of the chapter.

 ## Solving for the Steady State

The capital-accumulation equation when population growth is included is as follows:

$$\Delta k_t = sAk_t^{0.3} - \delta k_t - nk_t = sAk_t^{0.3} - (\delta + n)k_t \tag{1}$$

And the condition for the steady state when $\Delta k_t = 0$ is as follows:

$$sAk^{*0.3} = (\delta + n)k^* \tag{2}$$

Solving for k^*,

$$k^{*0.7} = k^{*(1 - 0.3)} = \frac{sA}{\delta + n}$$

$$k^* = \left(\frac{sA}{\delta + n}\right)^{(1/0.7)} = \left(\frac{sA}{\delta + n}\right)^{1.43} \tag{3}$$

Substituting Equation 3 into the per-worker production function to get output per worker, y^*:

$$y^* = A\left[\left(\frac{sA}{\delta + n}\right)^{1.43}\right]^{0.3} = A^{[1 + (1.43 \times 0.3)]}\left(\frac{s}{\delta + n}\right)^{(1.43 \times 0.3)} = A^{1.43}\left(\frac{s}{\delta + n}\right)^{0.43} \tag{4}$$

SUMMARY AND RESULTS

The following two results that we derived graphically now come directly from Equations 3 and 4:

1. Because the saving rate s is in the numerator in Equations 3 and 4, a rise in s indicates that both k^* and y^* rise—that is, a higher saving rate leads to a higher capital-labor ratio and a higher output per worker.

2. Because the rate of population growth, n, is in the denominator in Equations 3 and 4, a rise in n indicates that both k^* and y^* fall—that is, higher population growth leads to a lower capital-labor ratio and a lower level of output per worker.

A third result that is mentioned in the chapter also comes directly from Equations 3 and 4:

3. Because the productivity term A is raised to the 1.43 power in Equations 3 and 4, a rise in productivity growth of 1% leads to a rise in the capital-labor ratio and output per worker by 1.43%, an amplification effect of 43%.

REVIEW QUESTIONS AND PROBLEMS

All Questions and Problems are available in MyEconLab *for practice or instructor assignment.*

1. Use the following table to find the steady-state values of the capital-labor ratio and output per worker (i.e., complete the table) if the per-worker production function is $y_t = 2k_t^{0.3}$:

s	Saving rate	0.3
δ	Depreciation rate	0.05
n	Population growth rate	0.02
A	Technology	2
k^*	Steady state capital-labor ratio	
y^*	Steady state output	

2. Refer to Problem 1 for data and assume now that the saving rate increases to 50%. Calculate the new steady-state values of the capital-labor ratio and output. Explain your answer graphically.

3. Refer to Problem 1 for data and assume now that the population growth rate increases to 5%. Calculate the new steady-state values of the capital-labor ratio and output. Explain your answer graphically, and compare the new values of the capital-labor ratio and output per worker to those obtained in Problem 1.

4. Use the graphical representation of the Solow growth model to explain why an increase in the technology factor A leads to a more-than-proportional increase in both the capital-labor ratio and output per worker.

7

Drivers of Growth: Technology, Policy, and Institutions

Preview

In the last chapter, we used the Solow model to examine the role of capital accumulation in determining why some countries have experienced high economic growth, while others have not grown at all, leaving their citizens mired in abject poverty. A deeper question remains: Why do capital and productivity grow at rapid rates in some countries but not in others?

To answer this question, we start the chapter by discussing how technology differs from the conventional production inputs of capital and labor, which we discussed in the previous chapter. We will then explore policies to promote productivity growth, such as building physical infrastructure (roads and ports), increasing the knowledge and skills of workers, and providing incentives to stimulate research and development. We will also explore why the right set of basic *institutions*—including *property rights* and an effective legal system—is key to attaining high growth in capital and productivity, and hence economic growth. Rich countries like Japan, the United States, and those in Western Europe feature strong institutions that promote economic growth, while poor nations in parts of Africa, the Middle East and elsewhere have weak institutional frameworks, leaving large fractions of their populations unnecessarily stuck at low levels of income.

Finally, to understand more deeply why policies to promote institutional development and productivity growth are so crucial to improving living standards (economic growth), we develop a theory of economic growth that analyzes productivity changes *endogenously* through technological advancement.

Technology as a Production Input

An important conclusion from both growth accounting and the Solow growth model is that increases in total factor productivity, *A*, are a key driver of economic growth. Up until now, we have treated capital and labor as the only inputs of production and the productivity term, *A*, as *exogenous*, or given. We now put aside that assumption and look closely at *A*, which we can also think of as technology. Because technology is what increases the efficiency of capital and labor, we can think of it as an input of production, similar to capital and labor.

Technology Versus Conventional Production Inputs

To explain what causes *A* to grow over time, we first need to understand that technology differs from the conventional production inputs, capital and labor, in an important way. Capital and labor are physical things, or *objects*, while technology is a set of instructions, designs, or *ideas*. Objects are **rival** in their use, because when they are used in one activity, they cannot be used in another. Ideas, on the other hand, can be used by multiple people in more than one activity simultaneously, so we call them **nonrival.** For example, you and your roommate cannot both use the same computer to write a term paper at the same time, nor can you simultaneously write a term paper and wait tables in a restaurant. Your capital and labor are *objects*. A suggestion for a term paper topic posted on the Web might be used by many students across the country: it is an *idea*. Technology is a set of ideas, making it a special form of capital that is nonphysical, nonrivalrous, and endlessly reusable.

Technology and Excludability

A big idea—say, using bed nets to repel mosquitoes and thus prevent malaria—can sweep the world and improve standards of living everywhere. The flip side of the non-rivalry of ideas is their low *excludability*. That is, a technology cannot be padlocked like a factory and kept from unauthorized use. More formally, **excludability** is the ability of the owner of a piece of property to deny its use to others unless they pay for it. Owners of capital earn a rate of return by renting out excludable items, so investments in them can have high payoffs. On the other hand, it is hard to keep unauthorized users from using a technology, reducing the potential benefits you can reap from producing it. This nonexcludability may discourage investment in technology, which has important implications for policy, as we shall see next.

 # Policies to Promote Productivity

Our analysis of the Solow model indicates that policies that promote saving and productivity can lead to higher standards of living. We have already discussed policies to stimulate saving in Chapter 4; we now focus on government policies that stimulate the accumulation of capital and productivity.

Building Infrastructure

The responsibilities of laying roads and building ports and bridges often fall to governments, since such costly projects wouldn't be economical for any individual firm. Investments in public infrastructure have generated high economic returns and have raised living standards.[1]

But just how much should governments spend on physical infrastructure? In 2009, the Obama administration cited the sad state of many U.S. roads and bridges as a rationale for its 2009 stimulus package. It argued that government spending on infrastructure had fallen too low, leading to some devastating bridge collapses over recent years. Critics, however, dispute evidence that infrastructure investments boost productivity

---

[1]For example, see David A. Aschauer, "Is Public Expenditure Productive?" *Journal of Monetary Economics* (March 1989) and John Fernald, "Roads to Prosperity? Assessing the Link Between Public Capital and Productivity," *American Economic Review* 89 (3): 619–636.

and income. It may be instead that governments spend more on infrastructure in periods of rapid economic growth. Also, the government may overspend on infrastructure projects. It is tempting for businesses to contribute to political campaigns, or even pay bribes, to win contracts for infrastructure building, creating a recipe for wasteful spending.

The U.S. Interstate Highway System is one successful example of government spending on infrastructure. The Interstate Highway System, formally named the Dwight D. Eisenhower National System of Interstate and Defense Highways, is the largest highway system in the world, with nearly 50,000 miles of roads. It is also the largest public works program in history, costing several hundred billion in today's dollars. The Eisenhower administration sought legislation to create this system, which was started in 1956 and was largely completed by 1990. The Interstate Highway System has promoted tourism (almost all of us have taken family vacations using the system) and has substantially reduced the cost of shipping goods from one part of the country to another. Without the Interstate Highway System, U.S. productivity would likely be much lower and the U.S. way of life would be substantially different.

Increasing Human Capital

So far we have focused on two factors of production in discussing economic growth, physical capital and labor. However, another kind of capital, **human capital,** the knowledge and skills that workers have built up through education and training programs, has a very large effect on productivity. For example, scientists require many years of education and experience in the lab before they can produce new technology. Research finds that human capital is at least as important as physical capital in explaining differences in per-capita GDP across countries.[2]

With higher education and training, workers are much more productive and therefore earn much higher wages. You will be glad to know that your college education leads to a **college premium,** a higher wage over their lifetime for college graduates relative to high-school graduates. The return to education has risen substantially since 1980, with the college premium rising from 50% in 1980 to 80% today—so it is well worth your while to study hard and stay in school. (We will discuss why this college premium has increased in Chapter 20.)

Policy and Practice

Government Measures to Increase Human Capital

For most of the twentieth century, the United States set the global gold standard for educating its populace. Building on its global lead in providing free elementary education, the United States in the early part of the century invested heavily in universal high school education. By mid-century, its colleges and universities had become the world's best. The rest of the world lagged badly behind for much of the century. Fewer than 40% of older European teenagers attended secondary schools in the 1950s, compared with over 70% of older U.S. teenagers.

---

[2]For a discussion of research on the effect of human capital on productivity and economic growth, see David N. Weil, *Economic Growth* (Boston; Addison-Wesley, 2008).

As our productivity model would predict, investments in human capital through education spending made a sizable impact on economic growth. Between 1915 and 2005, educational improvements in the U.S. labor force accounted for about 15% of real per-capita GDP growth, or about 0.34 percentage point of growth a year. Data strongly suggest that without an educated population, countries will struggle to become productive members of the global economy. In a study of 114 nations, economists Claudia Goldin and Lawrence Katz of Harvard University identified a positive correlation between enrollment levels in secondary school and real GDP.[3] They noted, however, that educational improvements alone were not guaranteed to make a poor country wealthy.

The rest of the world has learned its lesson from U.S. successes. Today, even poor nations invest large sums in education, and wealthy regions like Europe have largely caught up to U.S. educational achievements. In a 2006 study of twenty-six wealthy nations, eighteen nations graduated a greater proportion of citizens from high school than did the United States. U.S. educational achievements began to stagnate in the 1970s, sparking a debate about whether the country had hit some natural limit on educational achievement, or whether a new educational strategy—perhaps focusing more on quality, and less on quantity, of schooling—was required.

Nevertheless, the United States continues to allocate large sums to finance education. With a budget of around $7 billion, the federally-funded Head Start Program supports local schools and other organizations that provide comprehensive child development services for poor pre-school children, giving them a leg up that will help them succeed when they go to elementary school. State and local governments spend on the order of $500 billion annually to provide fifty million children free public school education up through twelfth grade. Also, the government funds many colleges and universities and subsidizes loans to students who cannot afford college.

While not a direct investment in human capital, government spending on public health has the effect of keeping workers healthier and more productive. For example, in 2009, the U.S. government spent $1 billion on a new swine flu vaccine to contain the outbreak of the swine flu pandemic. Government spending on health care has become one of the largest items in the federal budget and is now close to $1 trillion per year.

Encouraging Research and Development

The importance of technology to economic growth suggests that countries can improve their standards of living by devoting increased resources to research and development (R&D). Private companies recognize the value of investing in research and spend a great deal on R&D. For instance, in 2009, Google invested $2.8 billion, or more than 12% of its revenue, in R&D. But because technology has the downside that it may be nonexcludable—that is, others can make use of it without paying for it—many economists believe that the private sector naturally underspends on R&D. Government encouragement of R&D is therefore less controversial among economists than is government spending on infrastructure.

There are three basic ways that governments can encourage R&D: government spending on R&D, government tax incentives, and *patents*.

[3]Claudia Goldin and Lawrence F. Katz, *The Race Between Education and Technology* (Cambridge, Mass: Belknap Press of Harvard University Press, 2008).

GOVERNMENT SPENDING ON R&D. Governments can directly increase R&D by engaging in research and development at government facilities. For example, many technological innovations have come from government labs, including nuclear power, jet planes, and the electronic computer. Governments also provide grants to universities and private researchers for basic research through agencies such as the National Science Foundation and the National Institutes of Health. Governments recognize that research universities can be an important source of economic growth for particular regions. For example, Boston has gained tremendously from having top research universities in its local area, such as Harvard University, MIT, Tufts, Boston University, and Brandeis. Similarly, Silicon Valley grew up around Stanford University. And India's own high-tech hub, Bangalore, flourished around the highly prestigious Indian Institute of Science. State and local governments, as well as the U.S. federal government, give direct subsidies to research universities. In recent years, Europeans have increased their support for research universities, recognizing the benefits that have accrued in the United States.

TAX INCENTIVES FOR R&D. Because private businesses are likely to be more efficient than the government at producing practical R&D that can be utilized immediately in developing new products and technology, governments also encourage R&D by giving private businesses tax breaks for research. U.S. tax credits for R&D were first implemented with the Economic Recovery Act of 1981. Congress has renewed these credits several times over the intervening years. Companies that qualify for the credit can deduct 20% of their research expenses above a base amount that is determined by historical expenses over a base period.

Almost all advanced economies offer some form of tax incentive for R&D. These incentives go beyond the form of tax credits by allowing firms to deduct 100% and sometimes more of their research expenses from their income in calculating their taxes. Other incentives allow firms to depreciate machinery and equipment that are involved in R&D at a higher rate than normal, thereby reducing their tax bills.

PATENTS. Another approach to managing the nonexcludability of technology is to grant intellectual property rights to inventors through a system of **patents** that give inventors the sole right to use, make, or sell licensing rights to others for a set period of time, typically around twenty years. For example, a drug company that earns a patent on a cholesterol-lowering medicine can sue anyone who tries to produce that drug without permission for decades. These property rights help businesses earn higher profits and recoup the investments they make in research and development, and encourage others to invest in R&D.

Patents are not a new idea. Indeed, at the very founding of the United States, the Constitution authorized Congress to enact laws to "promote the progress of science and useful arts, by securing for limited times to authors and inventors the exclusive right to their respective writings and discoveries." For example, firms in the drug industry have spent billions on research to develop drugs such as Lipitor or Tamiflu because their sole right to produce them for a number of years has provided them with enormous profits.

Effective design of a patent system is crucial. If patents are given too freely or for too long a period, technological growth may slow, since patent owners might refuse to share their knowledge or charge prohibitively high prices to license its use. Particularly worrisome in recent years has been the rise of colorfully named "patent trolls," who buy up patents and then try to extract large payments from companies that try to develop or use similar technologies. On the other hand, if the patent right is difficult to enforce, or if patents are not given for certain types of inventions, then there might not be enough investment in R&D. Alternatively, the inventor may be unwilling to share ideas with others in publicly available patent applications, thereby hindering technological advance. For example, the Coca-Cola Company has chosen to keep its soda formula a secret, rather than disclose it in a patent application, because it does not believe its patent rights would be enough to keep competitors from copying the recipe. Patents that do not give sufficient rights to the inventor may therefore leave technology nonexcludable, and so weaken the incentives for R&D and technological progress.

Institutions and Property Rights

We now go on to analyze the role of *institutions* in economic growth. **Institutions** are sets of rules, organizations, and customs that govern the behavior of individuals and firms. The most basic and fundamental set of institutions that affect economic growth are **property rights,** the protection of property from expropriation by the government or other parties. Property rights are necessary if people are to have incentives to make investments. Otherwise, the fruits of their investments (the profits) could be easily taken away. A farmer who does not have clear-cut ownership of his land, or who worries that armed marauders may take away his crops or farm equipment, is unlikely to buy enough seeds, fertilizer, and tractors to boost his farm's production. Weak property rights thus lead to low investment and low accumulation of capital.

In this section, we outline the key characteristics of legal systems that enforce property rights and examine the key obstacles faced by these legal systems.

The Legal System and Property Rights

Residents of advanced nations like the United States often take property rights for granted. The founding fathers and their British forbearers understood the importance of property rights to the success of an economy, and a vast body of U.S. law protects private property. The government cannot take your property when it wants to; people who steal property are jailed; and people who make use of our property (either physical or intellectual, that is, property based on ideas) without our permission can be sued in courts of law.

Property rights are established by the writing and enforcement of legal contracts. Strong property rights, needed to provide incentives to invest and accumulate capital, therefore require a legal system that operates quickly and at low cost. Douglass North, recipient of a Nobel Prize for his work on the role of institutions in economic development, has emphasized the importance of the legal system to economic growth: "The inability of societies to develop effective, low-cost enforcement of contracts is the most important source of both historical stagnation and contemporary underdevelopment in the Third World."[4]

There are several elements that make up an effective legal system: the ability to enforce contracts, adequate resources, and lawyers.

---

[4]Douglass North, *Institutions, Institutional Change, and Economic Development* (Cambridge: Cambridge University Press, 1990), 54.

ABILITY TO ENFORCE CONTRACTS. Enacting a good system of laws is the first step in creating strong property rights. Not all legal systems are alike in this regard. A legal system based on **common law,** in which the law is continually reinterpreted by judges, originated in England. The common-law legal system is in use in the United Kingdom and its former colonies, including the United States, Canada, Australia, and New Zealand, as well as in India and many countries in Africa. Alternative legal systems based on the Napoleonic Code, which was first developed in France, determine the law primarily by statutes. The Napoleonic legal system spread to much of continental Europe during the Napoleonic Wars at the beginning of the nineteenth century. The German and Swedish legal systems have elements of both the Napoleonic and the English common law systems, with laws determined by statutes that are subject to substantial modification by judges.

The English common law system is particularly effective at enforcing contracts because it is able to evolve with changing economic circumstances. Countries with legal systems derived from English common law outperform those with systems based on the Napoleonic Code in terms of financial development and economic growth, with the performance of the German and Swedish systems somewhere in between.[5] (See Table 7.1 for a list of countries and their style of legal system.) It also matters how the legal system was imposed on a country to begin with, a subject explored in the box, "Geography, the Legal System, and Economic Growth."

ADEQUATE RESOURCES. A well-functioning legal system requires sufficient funding for courts and qualified judges. India's legal system, for example, is based on the English common-law system, which suggests it should strongly protect property rights. However, India's legal system is starved for resources and is incredibly overburdened.

TABLE 7.1	LEGAL SYSTEM ORIGINS	
English Common Law	**Napoleonic Law**	**German/Swedish**
Australia	Argentina	Austria
Botswana	Brazil	Switzerland
Canada	Chile	Germany
U.K.	Cote d'Ivoire	Denmark
Hong Kong	Egypt	Japan
India	Spain	Korea
Ireland	France	Finland
Jamaica	Greece	Iceland
Singapore	Haiti	Taiwan
United States	Italy	Norway
South Africa	Turkey	Sweden

Source: Thorsten Beck, Asli Demirguc-Kunt, and Ross Levine. 2003. Law, endowments, and finance. *Journal of Financial Economics* 70, no. 2 (November): 137–181.

[5]See Rafael La Porta, Florencio Lopez-d-Silanes, Andrei Shleifer, and Robert W. Vishny, "Legal Determinants of External Finance," *Journal of Finance* 52 (1997): 1131–50; Rafael La Porta, Florencio Lopez-d-Silanes, Andrei Shleifer, and Robert W. Vishny, "Law and Finance," *Journal of Political Economy* 106 (1998): 1113–55; and Thorsten Beck and Ross Levine, "Legal Institutions and Financial Development," in *Handbook for New Institutional Economics*, eds. Claude Menard and Mary M. Shirley (Norwell MA: Kluwer Academic Publishers, 2005).

Geography, the Legal System, and Economic Growth

Geography plays an important role in economic growth. Countries closer to the equator with tropical climates have slower economic growth than countries farther from the equator with temperate climates.[*]

Colonies with tropical climates—for example, colonies in the Caribbean, in Africa, and on the Indian subcontinent—could not be settled by large numbers of Europeans because the death rates from native diseases were so high. The legal systems in these colonies were modified to benefit the small numbers of Europeans that ran the countries and enable them to exploit the countries' resources and local populations. As a result, legal systems in these countries were relatively ineffective at protecting the property rights of the average person, and became a serious handicap to growth as colonies became independent. On the other hand, in temperate climates, larger numbers of Europeans were able to settle in a colony, as in North America, and they were better able to resist exploitation by the home country. (The American Revolution is a dramatic manifestation of this point.) After these countries became independent, their legal systems effectively protected property rights and promoted high rates of economic growth. Indeed, differences in the quality of legal systems resulting from different patterns of European settlement can explain three-quarters of the differences in income per person among former colonies.

The variations in how colonies were settled explain why even countries whose legal systems were originally based on the British system, with its emphasis on protection of property rights, have shown such different economic performance. The United States, Canada, Australia, and New Zealand, with predominantly European populations that could resist exploitation, ended up with highly effective legal systems and prospered. On the other hand, former British colonies such as Jamaica, India, Pakistan, and Nigeria, where Europeans made up only a small fraction of the population, ended up with much less effective legal systems and have remained poor.

[*]See Daron Acemoglu, Simon Johnson, and James A. Robinson, "The Colonial Origins of Comparative Development: An Empirical Investigation," *American Economic Review* 91 (2001): 1369–1401; and William Easterly and Ross Levine, "Tropics, Germs and Crops: How Endowments Influence Economic Development," *Journal of Monetary Economics* 50 (2003).

In India, it takes many years to settle lawsuits. There are millions of backlogged cases in higher courts, many of which are ten years old or older. In Brazil, the airline Lufthansa was still in court almost a quarter of a century after the filing of an infamous wrongful-termination lawsuit.

ACCESS TO LAWYERS. Love them or hate them, lawyers are needed to promote property rights. When someone encroaches on your land or makes use of your property without your permission, you turn to a lawyer to stop them. Lawyers are necessary to protect your investments, and knowing you can hire one encourages you to invest in property in the first place. Without lawyers, there would be little to no investment, and thus little economic growth.

Obstacles to Effective Property Rights

Countries with strong property rights laws on the books still must enforce them to ensure a flow of investment in the economy. We will now look at obstacles to property rights systems, including corruption, costly legal processes, and greedy government officials.

CORRUPTION. Corruption, which is endemic in many less-developed countries, is a key obstacle to a well-functioning property rights system. If judges can be bribed, then property rights can be expropriated by the highest bidder for the judge's "services." An entrepreneur with a good idea or investment cannot protect it from the rich and powerful, those who can use the courts as a weapon to take it away and reap any rewards for themselves. If a government official has to be bribed to allow you to conduct your business, then he or she has in effect appropriated part of the value of your property. Corruption is like a cancer in the body of an economy: it weakens and sickens the economy by reducing the incentives for entrepreneurs to make investments and work hard to make profits. Corruption creates much uncertainty for entrepreneurs, who are left wondering if the bribe money is sufficient and if there will be future demands. Research finds that both lower investment relative to GDP and lower economic growth are associated with increases in corruption.[6]

THE HIGH COST OF ESTABLISHING LEGAL BUSINESSES. The high cost of setting up a legal business is another barrier to establishing clear property rights in many developing countries. In countries like the United States, opening a legal business is a simple procedure that requires filling out a form and paying a nominal licensing fee. But, as Peruvian economist Hernando De Soto documented in his fascinating book *The Mystery of Capital*, setting up a business in a less-developed country can be a nightmare.[7] To legally register a small garment workshop with one worker in Peru required 289 days, working six hours a day, at a total cost of $1,231—a figure thirty-one times the monthly minimum wage. In contrast, setting up a similar U.S. business takes only a few days at a small fraction of the cost. Peru may be an extreme example, but this problem is endemic in less-developed countries. These barriers to legally registering businesses allow only the rich to operate legal businesses and are a serious impediment to economic growth.

THE GRABBING HAND. Simply enacting property laws on the books does not guarantee their enforcement. Government officials in many less-developed countries can

Policy and Practice

The World Bank's *Doing Business*

Stimulated by Hernando De Soto's pioneering work on the barriers to setting up a legal business in a less-developed country, the World Bank in 2003 began to publish an annual report entitled *Doing Business*. The latest report covers ten types of indicators in over 180 countries drawn from two types of data: 1) reading of laws and regulations, and 2) time and motion studies, which take into consideration official fees, that estimate the cost in terms of time and money of achieving a goal such as setting up a legal business.

[6]See, for example, Paolo Mauro, "Corruption and Economic Growth," *Quarterly Journal of Economics* 110 (1995): 681–712; and Jakob Svensson, "Eight Questions about Corruption," *Journal of Economic Perspectives* 19, no. 5 (2005): 19–42.

[7]Hernando De Soto, *The Mystery of Capital: Why Capitalism Triumphs in the West and Fails Everywhere Else* (New York: Basic Books, 2000).

The *Doing Business* reports provide useful indicators of how easy or difficult it is to conduct business throughout the world, and they have spawned a massive amount of research on how barriers to conducting business affect economic growth. Even more importantly, the *Doing Business* reports have encouraged governments to strengthen property rights and make it easier for businesses to operate. Low *Doing Business* rankings have led many governments to pursue reforms of their regulations in order to streamline the process of setting up legal businesses and make it easier to enforce contracts, thereby improving their country's ranking. For example, countries such as Colombia and Egypt have moved up sharply in the *Doing Business* rankings by adopting an extensive reform agenda. Many economists consider the *Doing Business* initiative at the World Bank to be one of its most effective policies for promoting economic growth and eradicating poverty in poor countries.

arbitrarily expropriate an idea, a business, or an investment for personal gain. Robert Mugabe, the president of Zimbabwe, has impoverished his country by expropriating land and giving it to his cronies. When land can be taken away from a landowner without adequate compensation, landowners will stop investing in their land, and farm production will fall. Zimbabwe, once a highly successful producer of farm products that exported over 700,000 tons of corn in 1990, now exports less than one-twentieth of that amount. Andrei Schleifer of Harvard University and Robert Vishny of the University of Chicago have coined the term "the grabbing hand" to describe the often rapacious behavior of such governments, which have been given the name *kleptocracies* because they steal from their citizens in a variety of ways.[8]

Kleptocracies have been particularly common in Africa since former European colonies gained independence in the 1960s. Kleptocratic behavior by African governments explains, in large part, why Africa has failed to keep up with other regions in its economic growth, and has even seen a decline in income per person and an increase in poverty in many countries. Haiti, the poorest country in the Americas, has suffered a similar fate. The Duvaliers, Papa Doc and Baby Doc, dictators from 1957 to 1986, were notorious for stealing on a grand scale. Years of strife and misrule in Haiti prevented investment in strong building materials. As a result, the poor infrastructure became a death sentence for the hundreds of thousands of Haitians who died in the 2010 earthquake. Meanwhile, a much more powerful earthquake in Chile a few months later killed only a tiny fraction of the number killed in Haiti, in no small part because Chile had invested in quake-resistant buildings.

Property rights cannot exist if the rule of the gun supersedes the rule of law. Continual wars and rebellions diminish property rights because the threat of force allows aggressors to take property. We usually think of the cost of war in terms of the number of dead and wounded, but the economic cost is horrendous as well. Because the threat of war or rebellion makes it hard to retain the profits from productive investment, investment will not occur. A continual state of warfare and years of kleptocratic rule go a long way toward explaining the awful growth experience of many of the countries of sub-Saharan Africa since they gained independence in the 1960s.

---

[8]Andrei Shleifer and Robert W. Vishny, *The Grabbing Hand: Government Pathologies and Their Cures* (Cambridge, Mass.: Harvard University Press, 1998).

Policy and Practice

Does Foreign Aid Work?

One of the most hotly-debated policy issues today is whether rich countries should increase the amount of aid they direct to poorer countries. The percentage of GDP that rich countries currently give to foreign countries as aid for economic development is paltry: foreign aid as a percentage of gross national income in rich countries is below 0.2%, and it is below 0.05% in the United States. Prominent economists like Jeffrey Sachs of Columbia University and his colleagues at the United Nations Millennium Project have argued that a "big push" in public investments funded by a doubling of foreign aid would enable African countries to escape their poverty trap. In his book *The End of Poverty*, Sachs even argues that, if rich countries would increase their foreign aid budgets to between $135 and $195 billion over the next decade, they could eliminate extreme global poverty (defined as income of less than $1 per day).[9] Is increased foreign aid the answer to lifting nations out of poverty?

Many economists are skeptical as to whether foreign aid helps countries that receive it, because they worry that such aid might encourage governments to act as grabbing hands, or alternatively remove incentives to develop policies that promote economic growth. Since 1960, over $500 billion of aid has poured into Africa, with little to show for it. In his two books, *The Elusive Quest for Growth* and *The White Man's Burden*, William Easterly of New York University argues that foreign aid usually doesn't work because it does not provide the right incentives.[10] The aid that poor countries receive almost always goes to their governments, and the political elites that run these governments often use the funds to line their own or their friends' pockets, or to cement their power. Indeed, aid to poor countries may even make matters worse. A particularly notorious case is Zaire (Congo) under the rule of President Mobutu Sese Seko. For twenty-five years Zaire received one loan after another from several international institutions, including eleven (totaling nearly $2 billion) from the International Monetary Fund alone. Zaire received $20 billion in foreign aid during Mobutu's rule while he looted the country, leaving a resource-rich nation one of the poorest in the world. With access to increased resources, bad governments are even more likely to stay in power. Empirical evidence finds that kleptocratic policies are more likely to thrive when foreign aid and natural resources provide rulers with the means to buy off their opponents and reward their allies.[11]

[9]Jeffrey D. Sachs, *The End of Poverty: Economic Possibilities of Our Time* (London: Penguin Press, 2005). Sachs, along with rock stars like Bono, has also successfully campaigned for aid in the form of debt relief for the poorest countries, arguing that only when they escape from their debt burden will these countries be able to put resources into areas that will stimulate development.

[10]William Easterly, *The Elusive Quest for Growth: Economists' Adventures and Misadventures in the Tropics* (Cambridge: Cambridge University Press, 2001); and *The White Man's Burden: Why the West's Efforts to Aid the Rest Have Done So Much Ill and So Little Good* (New York: Penguin, 2006).

[11]Daron Acemoglu, James Robinson, and Thierry Verdier, "Kleptocracy and Divide-and-Rule: A Model of Personal Rule," *Journal of the European Economic Association Papers and Proceedings* 2 (April–May 2004): 162–192.

On the other hand, some foreign aid has been highly productive. Public health measures funded by foreign aid have led to dramatic improvements in health and life expectancy in developing countries.[12] One of the most successful instances of foreign aid cited by proponents of foreign aid is the Marshall Plan, which helped achieve the reconstruction of Europe after World War II. However, deeper analysis of the Marshall Plan suggests that it worked not because it handed over large amounts of money, but because it created incentives for European countries to eliminate price controls, pursue fiscal consolidation, improve the functioning of markets, and liberalize trade.[13]

Endogenous Growth Theory

To more deeply understand what promotes economic growth, we need to study a theory of what causes technological advancement, that is, what causes growth in A. This theory, which we outline here, is referred to as **endogenous growth theory,** because it explains why advances in technology *endogenously* (from within the system) fuel sustained economic growth. Because Paul Romer was so instrumental in developing this theory, endogenous growth models are often referred to as **Romer models.**[14]

Here we outline a simple version of a Romer model that highlights many of the important implications of endogenous growth theory. We extend the Solow model of the last chapter, using many of the same building blocks, but add a key feature—the production of ideas.

Allocation of Labor

The Solow model assumes that all labor, L, is allocated to the production of goods and services. The Romer model changes that assumption and states that some labor, L_P, is devoted to producing goods and services, while the rest, L_A, is devoted to producing new technology, which we will refer to as research and development (R&D). The total amount of labor is fixed at the total amount of the population, $\overline{N}$.

We can then write total labor, which we assume is the same as the population, $\overline{N}$, as follows:

$$\overline{N} = L_P + L_A \tag{1}$$

[12]There is quite a bit of controversy over whether foreign aid helps alleviate poverty, even when a country has good governance. For example, see Craig Burnside and David Dollar, "Aid, Policies, and Growth," *American Economic Review* 90, no. 4 (2000): 847– 868. However, William Easterly, Ross Levine, and David Rodman, "New Data, New Doubts: A Comment on Burnside and Dollar's 'Aid, Policies, and Growth' (2000)," National Bureau of Economic Research Working Paper 9846 (July 2003) and Raghuram G. Rajan and Arvind Subramanian, "Aid and Growth: What Does the Cross-Country Evidence Really Show?" National Bureau of Economic Research Paper 11513 (July 2005) contest Burnside's and Dollar's results because they find that they are not robust.

[13]Barry Eichengreen and Marc Uzan, "The Marshall Plan: Economic Effects and Implications for Eastern Europe and the Former USSR," *Economic Policy* 14 (1992): 13–77 and R. Glenn Hubbard and William Duggan, *The Aid Trap* (New York: Columbia Business School Press, 2009).

[14]Two of Paul Romer's most important contributions are Paul M. Romer, "Increasing Returns and Long-Run Growth," *Journal of Political Economy* 94 (October 1986): 1002–1037 and "Endogenous Technical Change," *Journal of Political Economy* 98, Part 2 (October 1990): S71–S102.

We will assume that a constant fraction, α, of the population is devoted to R&D, so that

$$L_A = \alpha \overline{N} \tag{2}$$

which from Equation 1 implies that the amount of labor devoted to producing goods and services is:

$$L_P = (1 - \alpha)\overline{N} \tag{3}$$

Production Function

The production of goods and services in the Romer model is described with largely the same Cobb-Douglas production function as in the previous chapter. Also, we add time subscripts, t, to reflect variables that can change over time.

$$Y_t = A_t K_t^{0.3} L_t^{0.7} \tag{4}$$

Because labor in Equation 4 is only that subset of labor devoted to producing goods and services, we replace L_t with L_p to yield the following:

$$Y_t = A_t K_t^{0.3} L_P^{0.7} \tag{5}$$

Next, we rewrite Equation 5 in terms of output per worker, just as we did in Equation 2 in the previous chapter, but recognize that the workers are only the ones engaged in the production of goods and services:

$$y_{Pt} = A_t k_{Pt}^{0.3} \tag{6}$$

Notice that output and capital per worker now have two subscripts, one to indicate that they can change over time, and the other to indicate that they are now defined in terms of workers that are devoted to the production of goods and services:

$$y_{Pt} = \frac{Y_t}{L_P}$$

$$k_{Pt} = \frac{K_t}{L_P}$$

The production function in Equation 6 has the same form as that used in the Solow model, so that all the analysis we applied in the previous chapter applies equally here.

Production of Technology

We now assume a very simple form of a production function for technology. Technology is produced by building on old ideas to create new ones, along the lines suggested by the famous quote from Sir Isaac Newton: "If I have seen farther than others, it is because I have stood on the shoulders of giants." In addition, we assume the increase in technology is proportional to the number of workers that are engaged in research and development, L_A. The production function for technology is thus as follows:

$$A_{t+1} - A_t = \Delta A_t = \chi A_t L_A \tag{7}$$

where the χ term indicates how productive labor is in producing ideas. When χ rises, a unit of labor engaged in research and development produces more knowledge than it did before.

Notice that technology, A_t, is used in producing more technology, ΔA_t, in Equation 7, and also in producing goods and services in Equations 5 and 6. How is this possible? Technology is nonrivalrous because it is a set of ideas that can be used over and over again to produce both new technology and also goods and services. This nonrivalry of ideas and technology in the Romer model gives technology a one-two punch in terms of economic growth. **With rivalry, as in the Solow model, diminishing returns to capital eventually lead output per capita to come to rest at a steady state without growth. Incorporating nonrivalry into our economic model allows us to explain sustained growth in per capita income.**

Dividing both sides of Equation 7 by A_t and replacing L_A by $\alpha\overline{N}$ from Equation 2, we can write the production function in terms of the growth rate of technology, g_A, as follows:

$$\frac{\Delta A_t}{A_t} = g_A = \chi\alpha\overline{N} \tag{8}$$

This technology production function tells us that the growth rate of technology is positively correlated to the productivity of research and development (χ), the fraction of the population that is devoted to R&D (α), and the total population of the economy ($\overline{N}$).

Sustained Growth in the Romer Model

With these building blocks in place, we can see how sustained growth in per capita income is an implication of the Romer model. From the Solow model, the production function in Equation 6 has a steady state k_P^*:

$$y_{Pt}^* = A_t k_P^{*0.3} \tag{9}$$

Equation 9 tells us that although there is a steady state at k_P^*, y_{Pt}^* will have a time subscript and changes over time because A_t changes over time. We can write this production function in terms of output per worker, which is the same as output per person, $y_t = Y_t/\overline{N}$, which can be written as $y_t = y_{Pt} \times (L_P/\overline{N})$.[15] Since $L_P/\overline{N} = (1 - \alpha)$ from Equation 3, we can get an expression for y_t by multiplying Equation 9 by $(1 - \alpha)$:

$$y_t^* = (1 - \alpha)A_t k_P^{*0.3} \tag{10}$$

From the production function for technology, we see that the A_t term is growing at a constant rate of g_A, and therefore output per person grows as well. Indeed, from our analysis of the Solow model in the previous chapter, this growth rate in A_t is amplified by a direct effect from the production function and an additional positive effect from a growing capital-labor ratio. The size of this amplification effect, with the Cobb-Douglas production function used here, was derived to be 1.43 in an appendix in Chapter 6, so with a growth rate of technology of g_A, the per-worker growth rate of output is $1.43 \times g_A$.

---

[15]You can see this by recognizing that $y_t = Y_t/\overline{N} = (Y_t/L_P) \times (L_P/\overline{N}) = y_{Pt} \times (L_P/\overline{N})$.

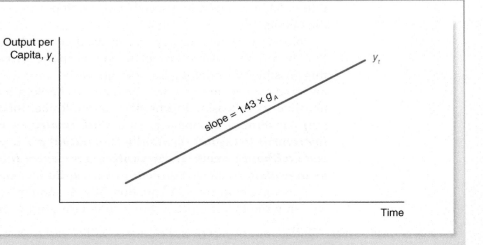

FIGURE 7.1

Balanced Growth Path in the Romer Model

When plotted against time with a logarithmic scale, output per capita grows at a steady rate of $1.43 \times g_A$, which is represented by a straight line with a slope of $1.43 \times g_A$.

In the Romer model, output per person keeps growing, but grows at a *steady rate*. Economists refer to growth at a constant rate as a **balanced growth path.** This constant growth rate contrasts with the Solow model, in which output per person eventually reaches a *steady state* from which it grows no further. We show the Romer model's balanced growth path in Figure 7.1. The vertical axis is a **ratio scale** (also called a **logarithmic scale**) in which equal distances reflect the same percentage change. When we plot a variable in a ratio scale against time, if it is growing at a constant rate per year, then it will appear as a straight line, with the slope representing the rate of growth. We show output per capita, y_t, in the Romer model as a straight line in Figure 7.1, with a slope of $1.43 \times g_A$, indicating that output per capita is growing at that rate.

Factors That Affect Endogenous Growth

Three factors in the Romer model can change the economy's growth rate: 1) the fraction of the population that is engaged in R&D, α; 2) the productiveness of R&D, χ; and 3) the total population in the economy, $\overline{N}$. Let's look at how growth responds to changes in each of these factors in turn.

Effects of an Increase in the Fraction of the Population Engaged in R&D, α

Suppose that at time 0, a country decides to devote more resources to developing technology. The fraction of the population engaged in R&D rises from α_1 to α_2 in Figure 7.2. From Equation 8, we see that the growth rate of technology rises from g_{A1} to g_{A2}. As in Figure 7.2, this increasing growth rate eventually will lead to balanced growth, where the growth rate of output per capita will rise from $1.43g_{A1}$ to $1.43g_{A2}$. However, there are two additional effects on the production function that must be considered.

FIGURE 7.2

Response to an Increase in the Fraction of the Population Engaged in R&D

At time 0, the fraction of the population engaged in R&D rises from α_1 to α_2, increasing the growth rate of technology from g_{A1} to g_{A2}. At time 0, there is an immediate decline in output per capita. Because workers move from the production of goods and services to the production of R&D, the capital-labor ratio k_{Pt} at first rises. However, it will fall back down toward the steady-state value of k_P^*, so that the growth rate will for a time be below the long-run growth rate of $1.43g_{A2}$. Over time, as the capital-labor ratio approaches the steady state, the growth rate of the economy will rise toward $1.43g_{A2}$, and the economy will be on a new, higher balanced growth path.

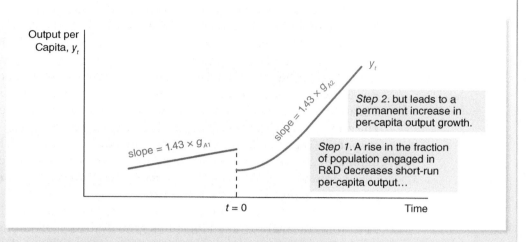

Output per Capita, y_t

slope = $1.43 \times g_{A1}$

slope = $1.43 \times g_{A2}$

y_t

Step 2. but leads to a permanent increase in per-capita output growth.

Step 1. A rise in the fraction of population engaged in R&D decreases short-run per-capita output…

$t = 0$

Time

1. As more labor is devoted to R&D production, less labor is devoted to the production of goods and services. Equation 10 indicates that there is an immediate decline in output per capita, as shown in Figure 7.2.

2. The decline in L_P pushes up the capital-labor ratio k_{Pt}. We know from the Solow analysis that, over time, k_{Pt} will decline toward the steady state value of k_P^*, so that the growth rate will for a time be below the long-run growth rate of $1.43g_{A2}$. As the capital-labor ratio approaches the steady state over time, the growth rate of the economy will rise toward the long-run growth rate of $1.43g_{A2}$, and the economy will be on a new, higher balanced growth path.

We show the resulting path of per capita income in Figure 7.2. The reasoning behind the path is a bit complicated. However, the basic conclusion from the analysis is fairly straightforward: *when more resources are devoted to research and development, the level of per-capita output at first falls, but the growth rate of per-capita output will rise permanently.* The analysis in the Romer model therefore suggests a trade-off to increasing the resources devoted to research and development: short-run living standards decline, while long-run living standards improve as per-capita output grows at a higher, sustained rate.

Endogenous growth theory provides an important rationale for why governments should spend money on R&D. With increased government expenditures on R&D, the resources going to production of technology increase, that is, α rises. As we see from the preceding analysis, this leads to a permanently higher growth rate of per-capita output.

Effect of Changes in the Productiveness of R&D, χ

Inventors have become particularly productive at certain times in history, causing productivity of R&D to suddenly rise. Let's see how the resulting increase in χ, the productivity of R&D, affects growth in income per capita using the Romer model. Suppose that at time 0, marked in Figure 7.3, χ rises from χ_1 to χ_2. The production function for technology in Equation 8 tells us that the growth rate of technology rises from g_{A1} to g_{A2}. Since there are no changes in the other elements of the production function in Equation 10, the steady state $k_\flat^*$ is unchanged and only the A_t term changes over time. The growth rate of output per capita rises from $1.43g_{A1}$ to $1.43g_{A2}$. The line showing how output per capita is growing over time immediately achieves a higher slope, as shown in Figure 7.3, indicating that the economy has immediately moved to a new, higher balanced growth path. The conclusion: ***when R&D becomes more productive, output per capita grows at a more rapid rate.***

Government policies aimed at making R&D more productive receive strong support from the analysis in endogenous growth theory. Spending on education, which results in an increase in human capital, can make workers in the R&D sector more productive, thus raising χ. As we see in Figure 7.3, this will lead to a higher growth rate of output per capita, making the nation's citizens richer over time.

Because the private sector is often more efficient than the government in developing new technology, government tax incentives to encourage private spending on R&D, rather than direct government spending on R&D, can help improve the efficiency of technology production, thereby increasing χ and economic growth. In addition, tax incentives to spur private spending on R&D can lead to increased resources going into R&D, which raises α and also promotes higher growth in per-capita output.

MyEconLab Mini-lecture

FIGURE 7.3

Response to a Rise in the Productiveness of R&D

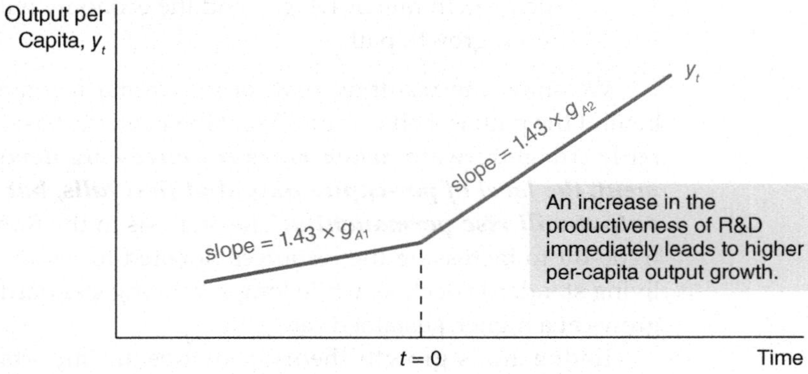

At time 0, the productiveness of R&D rises from χ_1 to χ_2, raising the growth rate of technology from g_{A1} to g_{A2}. Since there are no changes in the other elements of the production function, the steady state $k_\flat^*$ is unchanged and the growth rate of output per capita rises from $1.43g_{A1}$ to $1.43g_{A2}$. Y_t now has a higher slope, indicating that the economy has immediately moved to a new, higher balanced growth path.

An increase in the productiveness of R&D immediately leads to higher per-capita output growth.

MyEconLab Mini-lecture

FIGURE 7.4

Response to an Increase in the Total Population

At time 0, there is an increase in population from $\overline{N}_1$ to $\overline{N}_2$. The growth rate of technology rises from g_{A1} to g_{A2}. The rise in population leads to an immediate decline in the capital-labor ratio k_{Pt} and a fall in per-capita output. Because k_{Pt} has fallen below the steady-state value of

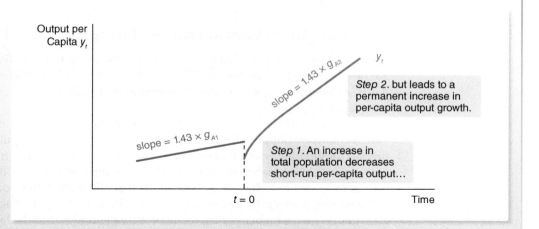

k_P^*, it will begin to rise, so that the growth rate will for a time be above the long-run growth rate of $1.43g_{A2}$. Over time, as the capital-labor ratio approaches the steady state, the growth rate of the economy will fall toward the long-run growth rate of $1.43g_{A2}$ on the balanced growth path.

Response to an Increase in the Total Population, $\overline{N}$

In the Solow model in the previous chapter, we saw that an increase in population lowers the standard of living because it leads to capital dilution. The Romer model, to the contrary, finds that there can be improvements in the standard of living from population increases.

To illustrate, suppose that at time 0 there is a surge in immigration that leads to an increase in population from $\overline{N}_1$ to $\overline{N}_2$ in Figure 7.4. As in the previous examples, we again see from Equation 8 that the growth rate of technology rises from g_{A1} to g_{A2}. More labor is engaged in producing new technology and, as before, there eventually will be balanced growth, in which the growth rate of output per capita will rise from $1.43g_{A1}$ to $1.43g_{A2}$. However, the rise in population will lead to an immediate decline in the capital-labor ratio k_{Pt}, so the production function in Equation 10 tells us that output per capita will at first fall. Because k_{Pt} has fallen below the steady state value of k_P^*, it will begin to rise, so that the growth rate will for a time be above the long-run growth rate of $1.43g_{A2}$. Over time, as the capital-labor ratio approaches the steady state, the growth rate of the economy will fall toward the long-run growth rate of $1.43g_{A2}$.

We show the resulting path of per capita income in Figure 7.4—and once again the reasoning is a little complicated. However, the basic conclusion holds: *a rise in population at first leads to a decline in per-capita output, but the growth rate of per-capita output will rise permanently.* The Romer model therefore suggests that an increase in population improves living standards in the long run. This result is a very different result from that given by the Solow model, although there is a decline in living standards in the short run.

Application

Does Population Growth Improve Living Standards?

When a country's population grows, does capital dilution lower living standards, as the Solow model predicts, or does the higher rate of technological progress increase living standards, as the Romer model predicts? As strange as it sounds, the conclusions of both models may be correct.

The Romer model's optimistic view of population growth may not apply well to individual countries. Suppose India, a country with a fast-growing population, develops a new process for growing wheat that helps farmers produce more wheat in less time. The process will improve living standards in India. However, the nonrivalry of ideas will lead the technology to spread to India's neighbors and eventually around the world. This phenomenon of **technological spillover** might explain why countries with high rates of population growth don't have higher per-capita income (see Figure 6.11 in the last chapter). If the productivity frontier A_t is similar across countries, then the Solow result still holds and rising population will be associated with lower per-capita income.

However, there is evidence that the Romer model's approach to population growth applies better to the world as a whole than the Solow model's approach. As Figure 7.5 shows, the world population has steadily grown from a little over 200 million people at the

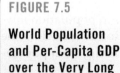

FIGURE 7.5

World Population and Per-Capita GDP over the Very Long Run

World population has steadily grown from a little over 200 million people at the beginning of the Christian era to over seven billion today, while per-capita GDP has risen dramatically, from under $500 to over $7,000 currently. Higher population appears to be positively associated with higher living standards, as endogenous growth theory predicts.

Source: Maddison, Angus. *Historical statistics*, population and per capita GDP levels, 1-2006. www.ggdc.net/maddison/

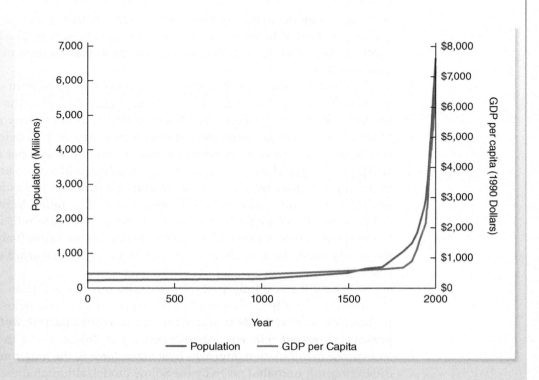

dawn of the Christian era to over seven billion today. Over this very long-run period, annual per-capita GDP rose dramatically, from under $500 to over $7,000 currently. This evidence suggests that higher populations are positively associated with higher living standards, as endogenous growth theory predicts.[16]

Indeed, Michael Kremer of Harvard University has produced some tantalizing evidence that suggests that higher populations stimulate technological progress and raise living standards.[17] The melting of the polar ice caps around 10,000 BC separated regions of the world and isolated their populations for thousands of years. Kremer found that the region that began with the highest population, the Eurasian-African land mass, developed more advanced technology and higher per capita income than the next most populated, the Americas. In turn, the Americas had a higher initial population than Australia, and developed better technology and a higher standard of living. A small island between Australia and Tasmania named Flinders Island had the lowest population at the time of separation and ended up with the fewest technological advances. Indeed, Flinders' population died off by 3,000 BC. Since the separation was exogenous—that is, caused by events outside of human control—the results indicate that population growth causes higher living standards, as endogenous growth theory predicts.

The Romer Model and Saving

A central feature of the Solow model is that an increase in saving leads to a higher level of per capita income and a temporary increase in economic growth, but does not lead to a sustained rise in economic growth. The Romer model comes to the same conclusion—that saving does not drive endogenous growth—as Figure 7.6 illustrates.

When the saving rate rises at time 0, the growth rate of technology remains unchanged at g_A, since none of the variables in the technology production function in Equation 8 change. Over time, though, greater saving generates investment in capital, lifting the capital-labor ratio k_{Pt}. The production function in Equation 10 tells us that output per capita will rise, so the growth rate will for a time be above the long-run growth rate of $1.43g_A$. As the capital-labor ratio comes to rest at a higher steady-state value, the economy will return to a balanced growth path in which per-capita output is growing at the same rate of $1.43g_A$. We show the path of per-capita output resulting from the rise in the saving rate at time 0 in Figure 7.6. This path shows that *a higher saving rate results in a higher level of output per capita, but not a higher sustained growth rate.*

More sophisticated models of technology production come to a more optimistic conclusion on the effects of saving. In these models, higher saving lifts the steady state capital-labor ratio and also generates investment in productivity-enhancing capital like computers and communications equipment. (In the simple model we have built,

---

[16]On the other hand, it's also possible that causality runs in the other direction, from higher per capita income to higher population; that is, as humans have grown wealthier, our populations have increased in size. (Economists are renowned for being able to argue both sides.)

[17]Michael Kremer, "Population Growth and Technological Change: One Million B.C. to 1990," *Quarterly Journal of Economics* 108 (August 1993): 681–716.

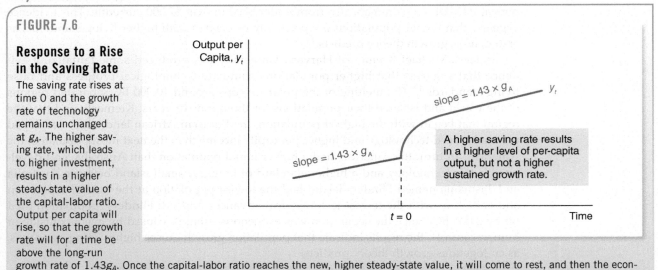

FIGURE 7.6

Response to a Rise in the Saving Rate

The saving rate rises at time 0 and the growth rate of technology remains unchanged at g_A. The higher saving rate, which leads to higher investment, results in a higher steady-state value of the capital-labor ratio. Output per capita will rise, so that the growth rate will for a time be above the long-run growth rate of $1.43g_A$. Once the capital-labor ratio reaches the new, higher steady-state value, it will come to rest, and then the economy will be back on the balanced growth path in which per-capita output grows at the same rate of $1.43g_A$.

technology is a function of labor, not capital.) As saving increases and the capital stock grows, more technology is produced, leading to a more rapid rate of growth for both A_t and per capita income.[18]

[18]For a discussion of this research and its implications for growth theory, see David Weil, *Economic Growth*, 2nd edition (Boston: Pearson, Addison-Wesley, 2008); and Charles Jones, *Introduction to Economic Growth* (New York: Norton, 2002).

SUMMARY

1. Technological ideas are an input into production and are nonrivalrous, that is, they can be used over and over again without limit. However, they often have a low level of excludability because it is hard to keep others from using them without permission. As a result, there may not be sufficient incentives to invest in technology.

2. Policies to stimulate productivity include building infrastructure, increasing human capital, government spending on R&D, tax incentives for R&D, and patents.

3. Property rights are the most fundamental institution required for economic growth and require 1) an effective legal system that can enforce contracts with adequate resources and plenty of lawyers; 2) an absence of corruption; 3) a low cost of establishing legal businesses; and 4) an absence of the "grabbing hand" by the government.

4. Endogenous growth theory using the Romer model explains endogenously how technology advances and leads economies to sustained economic growth. Its key equations are the fraction of the population devoted to R&D, $L_A = \alpha \overline{N}$; the production function for the growth of technology, $\Delta A_t / A_t = g_A = \chi \alpha \overline{N}$; and the production function in terms of output per person, $y_t^* = (1 - \alpha) A_t k_p^{*0.3}$. The Romer model produces a balanced growth path in which output per person grows at a steady rate.

5. Applying the Romer model yields the following results: When R&D becomes more productive, output per capita grows at a more rapid rate. When more resources are devoted to R&D, the level of per-capita output at first falls, but the growth rate of per-capita output will rise permanently. A rise in population at first leads to a decline in per-capita output, but the growth rate of per-capita output will rise permanently. A higher saving rate results in a higher level of output per capita, but not in a higher sustained growth rate.

KEY TERMS

balanced growth path, p. 192
college premium, p. 180
common law, p. 184
endogenous growth theory, p. 189
excludability, p. 179

human capital, p. 180
institutions, p. 183
logarithmic scale, p. 192
nonrival, p. 179
patents, p. 182

property rights, p. 183
ratio scale, p. 192
rival, p. 179
Romer models, p. 189
technological spillover, p. 196

REVIEW QUESTIONS

All Questions are available in MyEconLab *for practice or instructor assignment.*

Technology as a Production Input

1. As an input to production, how does technology differ from labor and capital inputs?

Policies to Promote Productivity

2. What government policies can be used to promote productivity growth?

3. Why may private R&D expenditures be too low?
4. What is a patent? Why do governments grant them?

Institutions and Property Rights

5. What are property rights and how do they influence economic growth?

6. What role does the legal system play in promoting property rights?

Endogenous Growth Theory

7. What shortcoming of the Solow growth model does the Romer model attempt to remedy?

8. Why is sustained per-capita growth possible in the Romer model but not in the Solow model?

Factors That Affect Endogenous Growth

9. In the Romer model, what three factors determine an economy's growth rate?

10. In the Romer model, how does an increase in the fraction of the population engaged in R&D affect the growth rate of per-capita output over time?

11. In the Romer model, how does an increase in total population affect the growth rate of per-capita output over time?

12. What is the impact of an increase in saving in the Romer model?

PROBLEMS

All Problems are available in MyEconLab *for practice or instructor assignment.*

Technology as a Production Input

1. Compare the following factors of production in terms of their rivalry and excludability:
   a) A robot that welds car frames and the idea of building a car in an assembly line

   b) A recipe to make pancakes and the recipe to manufacture a soda drink

Policies to Promote Productivity

2. The U.S. government has provided billions of dollars for broadband Internet access nationwide, including grants for rural broadband access, expansion of computer center capacity, and sustainable broadband adoption initiatives. Is there a good rationale for such a policy? Discuss.

3. Uruguay has implemented the One Laptop per Child (OLPC) initiative in which one laptop is given to every child and teacher in a public primary school. Comment on the effects of this program on the following:
   a) Uruguay's human capital stock
   b) Uruguay's output per capita growth rate

4. How might the effects of government spending on proper sewage infrastructure, which results in improved sanitation for crowded cities in poor countries, promote economic growth?

5. The International Property Rights Index (IPRI) ranks countries according to the significance and protection of both intellectual and physical property rights. What correlation between income per capita growth and the IPRI ranking might you expect? Why?

Institutions and Property Rights

6. Transparency International constructs the Corruption Perception Index (CPI), meant to measure "the perceived level of public-sector corruption in 180 countries and territories around the world." The CPI ranges from 0 (most corrupt) to 100 (least corrupt). Plot the CPI values for these selected countries and their per capita Gross National Income (GNI). Can you explain the trend you observe in the graph?

Country	GNI per capita (2008)	CPI value (2009)
United States	$50,610	73
France	$36,720	71
Sudan	$2,030	13
India	$3,840	36
Mexico	$16,680	34

7. Do you think corruption affects the enforcement of property rights, or is it that badly designed institutions create opportunities for corruption? In other words, does corruption determine the enforcement and design of property rights, or is it the other way around, with causality running from the design of property rights to corruption? Explain your arguments.

8. Do you tend to agree more with Sachs (foreign aid should be increased) or with Easterly (foreign aid can do more harm than good) in the foreign aid debate? Explain your arguments.

Endogenous Growth Theory

9. Suppose total population is 100 million and 25% is devoted to the production of research and development. Using the simplified version of the Romer model outlined in the chapter, calculate the following:

   a) The change in technology (ΔA_t), if $\chi = 0.0005$ and $A_t = 20$
   b) The growth rate of technology
   c) The per-person output growth rate

Factors That Affect Endogenous Growth

10. Consider the world economy and comment on the effect of the Industrial Revolution on the world growth rate of output per person, according to the assumptions of the Romer model.

11. During the late 1960s, Chinese authorities imposed the precepts of the "Cultural Revolution" on their people. As a result, almost all scholars and researchers were sent to the fields to perform manual agricultural tasks. Comment on the effect this had on the per-person output growth rate, according to the Romer model.

12. Michael Kremer's research suggests that higher population might stimulate technological progress. How can higher population stimulate technological change?

13. Discuss the validity of the following statement: "Unlike Solow's model, Romer's model concludes that changes in the saving rate do not affect the sustained per-capita output growth rate."

DATA ANALYSIS PROBLEMS

The Problems update with real-time data in MyEconLab *and are available for practice or instructor assignment.*

1. Go to the St. Louis Federal Reserve FRED database, and find data on the labor force, capital stock, GDP, and the price level for Turkey and South Korea, with data codes provided in the table below. Download each country's data on a separate spreadsheet by using the *add data series* feature.

   a) Convert GDP and the capital measure to real GDP and real capital, respectively, by dividing each by the price index measure for each year, then multiplying by 100. Do this for each country.

   b) Now convert real GDP and real capital to per-worker measures by dividing each by the labor measure for each year, and calculate $k^{0.3}$ for each year. Do this for each country.

   c) Use the data on output per person and $k^{0.3}$ to calculate a measure of total factor productivity (A) for each year. Do this for each country.

Country	GDP	Capital	Labor	Price Index
South Korea	MKTGDPKRA646NWDB	KORGFCFADSMEI	KORLFTOTADSMEI	KORGDPDEFAISMEI
Turkey	MKTGDPTRA646NWDB	TURGFCFADSMEI	TURLFTOTADSMEI	TURGDPDEFAISMEI

d) For each country, for both A and k, cal-culate the average growth rate per year from the year 2000 to the most current data available by calculating the total percentage change in the variable and dividing by the number of years in the sample, up to the most recent data available. Based on growth in total fac-tor productivity in the two countries, what do you expect should happen to real GDP per capita in each country?

e) Based on your answer to part (d) above, use the growth accounting equation to determine the average growth rate per year of real GDP per capita from 2000 to the most recent data available.

Country	2000	2013	2000–2013 Change
Singapore	87.7	88.0	0.3
Switzerland	76.8	81.0	4.2
United States	76.4	76.0	−0.4
Georgia	54.3	72.2	17.9
Mexico	59.3	67.0	7.7
Brazil	61.1	57.7	−3.4
Russia	51.8	51.1	−0.7
Argentina	70.0	46.7	−23.3

2. The Heritage Index, published yearly by the Heritage Foundation, provides a com-prehensive numerical measure of overall economic freedom for countries and reflects the strength or weakness of institutions, political freedom, ease of doing business, and rule of law, among other factors (for more information, see heritage.org/index). The table below reports these scores for the years 2000 and 2013. Scores closer to 100 represent "free" countries; countries with scores below 50 are considered "repressed." Go to the St. Louis Federal Reserve FRED database and find data on real GDP per capita for each country listed in the first table, using the data series shown below the first table. For the United States and Singapore, the data are available as a single series; for the other countries, the data must be constructed from nominal GDP per capita and a measure of the price level. In this case, for each year, take nominal GDP per capita, divide by the price level, then multiply by 100 to get real GDP per capita for the country.

FRED Data Codes:

	RGDP Per Capita	GDP Per Capita	Price Index
Singapore	SGPRGDPC		
Switzerland		PCAGDPCHA646NWDB	DDOE01CHA086NWDB
United States	USARGDPC		
Georgia		PCAGDPGEA646NWDB	DDOE01GEA086NWDB
Mexico		PCAGDPMXA646NWDB	DDOE01MXA086NWDB
Brazil		PCAGDPBRA646NWDB	DDOE02BRA086NWDB
Russia		PCAGDPRUA646NWDB	DDOE02RUA086NWDB
Argentina		PCAGDPARA646NWDB	DDOE01ARA086NWDB

a) From the table, choose the three countries with the highest economic freedom scores in 2013 and the three countries with the lowest scores in 2013. Calculate the average real per-capita GDP growth rate per year for each of these six countries, from 1980 to the most recent data available.

Calculate the average among the three countries with the highest scores, and the average among the three countries with the lowest scores. Comment on the relationship between the level of the scores and the average growth of real per-capita GDP.

b) Choose the three countries from the table with the largest magnitude change in score from 2000 to 2013, and the three countries with the smallest magnitude change in score from 2000 to 2013. Calculate the average real per-capita GDP growth rates per year for each of these six countries, from 1995 to 2004 (or from earliest year available to 2004) and from 2005 to the most recent data available. For each of the six countries, calculate the change in the average growth rate of real GDP per capita between the two time periods. Comment on the relationship between the magnitude and direction of the score changes and the average growth of real per-capita GDP. Are there any countries that do not conform to what you would expect?

c) How do your results from parts (a) and (b) help explain cross-country variation in total factor productivity?

3. The production function for technology in Equation 8 can be expressed as $A_{t+1} - A_t = \chi A_t \alpha_t \overline{N}_t$. Assume that $\chi = 1$, that both $\overline{N}$ and α can vary over time, and that $\overline{N}$ is interpreted as the labor force rather than population. Go to the St. Louis Federal Reserve FRED database, and find data on real GDP (GDPCA), the labor force (CLF16OV), and a measure of the capital stock, real consumption of fixed capital (A262RX1A020NBEA). Download all of the data onto a spreadsheet; for (CLF16OV), change the *frequency* setting to "annual" before downloading. In the spreadsheet, convert the labor force series so that it is "indexed" to 1 in 1980. To do this, for each year of (CLF16OV), divide the labor force number by the labor force number in 1980. Then convert the data into real GDP per worker and capital per worker by dividing (GDPCA) and (A262RX1A020NBEA) by the indexed labor force data for each year. Note that this conversion will be represented as $ millions of output and capital per worker.

a) Use the "production function for technology" expression given above to solve for α_t, the proportion of labor devoted to R&D, as a function of all other variables.

b) For each year from 1980 up to the most current year available, calculate $k^{0.3}$. Use this value, along with the transformed real GDP per worker series, to calculate a measure of total factor productivity.

c) Use your answers to parts (a) and (b) to construct a measure of α (the proportion of the labor force dedicated to R&D) for each year from 1980 to the most current data available. (Note: this will be one year less than your data availability spans, since you will need to use one year ahead TFP to determine the current year's α. Do not worry if some values of α are negative.)

d) Calculate the average value of α for the period from 1980 to 1999, and for the period from 2000 to the most current period available. Comment on the averages over the two periods. Based on the endogenous growth model, what do you expect, for the two periods, for growth rates in terms of real GDP per person?

e) Now, calculate the average yearly growth rate of real GDP per capita from 1980 to 1999, and from 2000 to the most current period available. To do this, take the value of real GDP per capita at the end of the time period, subtract it from the value at the beginning of the time period, and divide by the value at the beginning of the time period. Then divide by the number of years in the period. Report the average constructed values for α and g_y over the two periods, and comment on the results as they relate to your expectations in part (d).

Part 4

Business Cycles: The Short Run

Part 4 Business Cycles: The Short Run

In this part of the book, we move from analyzing long-run economic changes to explaining short-run economic fluctuations in aggregate output, unemployment, and inflation. Chapter 8 provides an introduction to the study of short-run economic fluctuations by describing the characteristics of the business cycle. Chapters 9–12 then develop the basic model used throughout this book to explain business cycle fluctuations, the *aggregate demand and supply model*. Chapter 13 uses this model to discuss macroeconomic policy.

Chapter 9 develops the first building block of the aggregate demand and supply model, the *IS* curve, which describes the interaction between real interest rates and aggregate output when the goods market is in equilibrium. Chapter 10 and its appendix describe how monetary policy makers set real interest rates with the *monetary policy (MP) curve*, which describes the relationship between inflation and real interest rates. The chapter then uses the *MP* curve and the *IS* curve to derive the *aggregate demand curve*, a key element in the aggregate demand and supply model that describes the relationship between inflation and aggregate output. Chapter 11 uses the *Phillips curve*, a relationship between the unemployment rate and inflation, to derive the *aggregate supply curve*, the relationship between aggregate output and inflation, the last building block of the aggregate demand and supply model.

Chapter 12 and its appendices then put all of the building blocks together to develop the aggregate demand and supply model, which we then use to explain business cycle fluctuations in the United States and abroad. The final chapter in this part of the book, Chapter 13, brings policy makers into the picture by examining their policy options for stabilizing inflation and output fluctuations.

We will examine applications in each chapter to make the critical connection between theory and real-world practice:

- "The Vietnam War Buildup, 1964–1969"
- "The Volcker Disinflation, 1980–1986"
- "Negative Demand Shocks, 2001–2004"
- "Negative Supply Shocks, 1973–1975 and 1978–1980"
- "Positive Supply Shocks, 1995–1999"
- "Negative Supply and Demand Shocks and the 2007–2009 Financial Crisis"
- "The United Kingdom and the 2007–2009 Financial Crisis"

- "China and the 2007–2009 Financial Crisis"
- "The Great Inflation"
- "Nonconventional Monetary Policy and Quantitative Easing"

In keeping with our focus on key policy issues and the techniques policy makers use in practice, we will also analyze the following specific examples in Policy and Practice cases:

- "The Fiscal Stimulus Package of 2009"
- "Movements Along the *MP* Curve: The Rise in the Federal Funds Rate Target, 2004–2006"
- "Shifts in the *MP* Curve: Autonomous Monetary Easing at the Onset of the 2007–2009 Financial Crisis"
- "The Phillips Curve Tradeoff and Macroeconomic Policy in the 1960s"
- "The Federal Reserve's Use of the Equilibrium Real Interest Rate, r^*"
- "The Activist/Nonactivist Debate over the Obama Fiscal Stimulus Package"
- "The Fed's Use of the Taylor Rule"
- "Abenomics and the Shift in Japanese Monetary Policy in 2013"

Business Cycles: An Introduction

8

Preview

Before the Great Recession of 2007, commentators marveled at the persistent strength of the U.S. economy. Except for a single, mild downturn between March and November of 2001, the United States enjoyed sixteen years of economic growth, leading some economists to declare the *business cycle*, the up-and-down fluctuations of the aggregate economy, dead and buried. Might the population be spared the lengthy periods of economic trauma experienced by virtually every prior generation?

The collapse of the subprime mortgage market in 2007 dashed these hopes. The economy fell into a slump in December 2007. Nine months later, the disruption to the U.S. financial system became especially severe with the bankruptcy of Lehman Brothers, and the decline in the economy accelerated.

U.S. GDP fell substantially in the fourth quarter of 2008, and by the fourth quarter of 2009, over 10% of those who wanted a job couldn't find one. (By comparison, unemployment rates in the 1990–1991 and 2001 recessions peaked at 7.8% and 5.8%, respectively.) No one talks anymore about the end of the business cycle; like death and taxes, it will always be with us.

This chapter introduces the characteristics of business cycles and the country's experiences with them over the past 150 years. We will explore the economic data that underlie the business cycle, such as gross domestic product and the unemployment rate. Finally, we introduce two schools of economic thought, *Keynesian* and *classical economics*, which take sharply different views on how governments should respond to business cycles. In later chapters, we will develop a theory of business cycles and an economic model to explain these fluctuations.

Business Cycle Basics

In their classic book *Measuring Business Cycles*,[1] Arthur Burns and Wesley Mitchell defined **business cycles** as fluctuations in aggregate economic activity in which many economic activities expand and contract together in a recurring, but not a periodic, fashion. In this section, we take a close look at the Burns and Mitchell definition of the business cycle to inform our look at U.S. business cycles over time.

---

[1]Arthur Burns and Wesley Mitchell, *Measuring Business Cycles* (New York: National Bureau of Economic Research, 1946).

Business Cycle Illustration

We illustrate the business cycle with a stylized view of economic activity over time in Figure 8.1. We mark the points on the horizontal axis where economic activity reaches a **trough,** or low point, with a T. Points marked with a P are the **peaks,** or the high points of economic activity. The period from a trough T to a peak P is a **business cycle expansion** (also called a **boom**), while the period from a peak P to a trough T is a **business cycle contraction.** Economists often refer to business cycle contractions as recessions, which we define in Chapter ... ods when economic activity declines ... ss cycle contraction is called a depres...

As Burns and ... is, they happen over and over again—... ntervals of the same length. The variab... to forecast.

An Alternative ...

Another way to lo ... ut into two compo- nents: the long-run ...

LONG-RUN TREN... ... nich occurs when all prices fully adjust ... **potential output,** and is denoted by ... -run level of output is determined by th... e economy, and the amount of labor su... generally viewed as growing steadily ... upward trend like that shown by the grey line in Figure 8.1. (Understanding why potential output grows

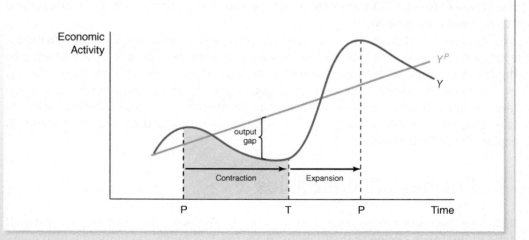

FIGURE 8.1

The Business Cycle

The grey line shows the (potential) level of output, while the blue line shows actual aggregate economic activity. The difference between the blue and the grey lines is the output gap. The peaks of the cycle are denoted by a *P* on the horizontal axis, and the troughs by a *T*. The period from a trough *T* to a peak *P* is marked as a business cycle expansion, while the period from a peak *P* to a trough *T* is marked as a contraction and is shaded.

Economic Activity

Y^P

Y

output gap

Contraction

Expansion

P   T   P   Time

over time involves the study of economic growth, which is covered in Chapters 6 and 7. However, business cycle analysis just takes potential output as given.)

SHORT-RUN DEVIATIONS FROM TREND. Shocks to the economy, such as bursts in consumer and business optimism, surges in government spending, and oil price shocks can cause aggregate economic activity to deviate from its potential level in the short run. This deviation, shown in Figure 8.1 as $Y - Y^P$, is referred to as the **output gap.** Business cycles can also be characterized as upward and downward swings of the output gap and, as you will see in coming chapters, the output gap plays a prominent role in our models of business cycles.

One challenge policy makers face is that output gaps can be hard to measure, because it is not easy to decide when resources have been fully utilized. Thus estimates of potential output may be inaccurate. Indeed, as we will see in Chapter 13, the high inflation of the 1970s can be attributed to mistakes made by monetary policy makers in measuring the output gap.

Co-Movement and Timing of Economic Variables

Many economic activities expand and contract together over time. This coincident movement, or co-movement, of individual economic variables is central to the Burns and Mitchell definition of a business cycle.

Dating Business Cycles

Ask a mechanic in the Bronx about the economy, and he will tell you straight away whether it is good or bad, no charts or graphs necessary. Economists too identify the onset of a recession by relying on judgment, as well as economic analysis.

The general economic downturn that characterizes all recessions can surface in a variety of forms, from slipping industrial production to weak consumer spending. Recessions usually begin with lengthy periods of falling real GDP, but not always. During the 2001 recession, GDP never declined for more than one quarter in a row. In the most recent recession, the economy deteriorated for at least a year before GDP first fell in the final three months of 2008. As a result, the official arbiter of defining the peaks and troughs of the business cycle, the National Bureau of Economic Research (NBER), dates the recession's onset as December 2007.

You may be surprised that the NBER is not a government agency—it is actually a private, not-for-profit organization. Burns and Mitchell wrote their book on business cycles as NBER employees. In their tradition, the bureau's Business Cycle Dating Committee examines data taken from a variety of economic activities.[2] Table 8.1, which we will refer to again later in the chapter, shows the official NBER business cycle dates, starting in 1854.

[2]See the NBER website at www.nber.org/cycles/recessions.html for a member listing of the NBER Business Cycle Dating Committee and the criteria it uses for deciding on business cycle peaks and troughs. The NBER puts particular emphasis on the following data series in dating business cycles: 1) personal income in real terms, 2) employment, 3) industrial production, 4) retail and manufacturing sales, and 5) real GDP.

TABLE 8.1	NBER BUSINESS CYCLE DATES

Source: NBER website. www.nber.org/cycles/main.html

Trough	Expansion (months from trough to peak)	Peak	Contraction (months from peak to trough)
Dec. 1854	30	June 1857	18
Dec. 1858	22	Oct. 1860	8
June 1861	46 (Civil War)	Apr. 1865	32
Dec. 1867	18	June 1869	18
Dec. 1870	34	Oct. 1873	65
Mar. 1879	36	Mar. 1882	38
May 1885	22	Mar. 1887	13
Apr. 1888	27	July 1890	10
May 1891	20	Jan. 1893	17
June 1894	18	Dec. 1895	18
June 1897	24	June 1899	18
Dec. 1900	21	Sept. 1902	23
Aug. 1904	33	May 1907	13
June 1908	19	Jan. 1910	24
Jan. 1912	12	Jan. 1913	23
Dec. 1914	44 (WWI)	Aug. 1918	7
Mar. 1919	10	Jan. 1920	18
July 1921	22	May 1923	14
July 1924	27	Oct. 1926	13
Nov. 1927	21	Aug. 1929	43 (Depression)
Mar. 1933	50	May 1937	13 (Depression)
June 1938	80 (WWII)	Feb. 1945	8
Oct. 1945	37	Nov. 1948	11
Oct. 1949	45 (Korean War)	July 1953	10
May 1954	39	Aug. 1957	8
Apr. 1958	24	Apr. 1960	10
Feb. 1961	106 (Vietnam War)	Dec. 1969	11
Nov. 1970	36	Nov. 1973	16
Mar. 1975	58	Jan. 1980	6
July 1980	12	July 1981	16
Nov. 1982	92	July 1990	8
Mar. 1991	120	Mar. 2001	8
Nov. 2001	73	Dec. 2007	18
June 2009	—		—

CO-MOVEMENT OF ECONOMIC VARIABLES. Economists use specific terms to describe the movement of variables over the business cycle. A **procyclical** economic variable moves up during expansions and down during contractions—that is, in the same direction as aggregate economic activity. In contrast, **countercyclical** economic variables move opposite to aggregate economic activity—that is, down during expansions and up during contractions. A variable is **acyclical** when its ups and downs do not consistently coincide with those of the business cycle.

TIMING OF VARIABLES. Economists also characterize macroeconomic variables by their timing relative to the business cycle. A **leading variable** reaches a peak or trough before the turning points of a business cycle. The turning points of a **lagging variable** occur after the business cycle changes course. A **coincident variable** reaches its peaks and troughs at the same time the business cycle reaches its peaks and troughs.

LEADING ECONOMIC INDICATORS. The timing and cyclicality of some economic variables make them useful gauges of the aggregate economy. A private economic research organization, the Conference Board, combines ten variables into an **index of leading indicators** that some economists use to forecast changes in the economy (see the Macroeconomics in the News box, "Leading Economic Indicators").

Macroeconomic Variables and the Business Cycle

We now look in detail at how the more prominent macroeconomic variables move over the course of the business cycle. In later chapters, we will explore the sources of the cyclical fluctuations in these variables to construct a theory of business cycles.

Real GDP and Its Components

Real gross domestic product is such a broad measure of aggregate economic activity that it is sometimes viewed as a proxy for the business cycle itself. Figure 8.2 plots

MACROECONOMICS IN THE NEWS

Leading Economic Indicators

The Conference Board's monthly index of leading indicators has taken a downward turn before almost every recession, boosting its credibility as a forecasting tool for the business cycle. But there are some good reasons to question the index's predictive power.

For one, the Conference Board regularly revises the index when more accurate data becomes available, sometimes many months after the fact. The initial readings of the data that underlie the index do not predict recessions nearly as well as the revised data. Second, Conference Board economists change components of the index over time, improving the index's historical record. A true test of the index's performance would use only *real-time* data available at the time—and such research shows that the index is far less accurate than the revised data would suggest at predicting recessions.*

*Francis Diebold and Glenn Rudebusch, "Forecasting Output with the Composite Leading Index: A Real-Time Analysis," *Journal of the American Statistical Association* (September 1991): 603–610.

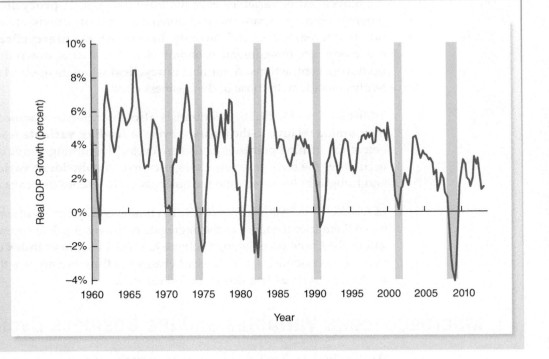

FIGURE 8.2

Real GDP Growth, 1960–2013

This figure shows the growth rate of GDP from four quarters earlier, with the recession periods (peak to trough) shaded. The recessions of 1973–1975, 1981–1982, and 2007–2009 are the most severe of the post–World War II period, with the recessions of 1960–1961, 1969–1970, 1990–1991, and 2001 much milder.

Source: Federal Reserve Bank of St. Louis, FRED Database. http://research .stlouisfed.org/fred2/

real GDP growth rates, annualized over four quarters, with shading indicating recession periods (peak to trough). Notice that the recessions of 1973–1975, 1981–1982, and, most recently, 2007–2009 were the most severe of the post–World War II period. None of these rivals the Great Depression of 1929–1933 or the recession of 1937–1938 in severity.

As you can see from Figure 8.3, two components of real GDP, real consumer spending and investment, are procyclical and coincident. Investment spending is far more volatile than consumer spending. Investment has always declined during recessions, sometimes by as much as 25%. Meanwhile, consumer spending still grew during the 1969–1970 and 2001 recessions, though it fell sharply in the 2007–2009 recession.

Unemployment

During recessions, firms hire fewer workers and lay off some of those they already employ. Not surprisingly, the unemployment rate is highly countercyclical, as Figure 8.4 demonstrates. Since it is not completely clear whether the unemployment rate leads or lags the business cycle, the Conference Board is unwilling to classify its timing.

Inflation

The rate of increase in the price level usually rises during expansions and falls during recessions, making inflation a procyclical variable, as we see in Figure 8.5. However, the inflation rate is lagging—it keeps rising for a time after the peak of the business cycle and falls for a time after the recession is over.

FIGURE 8.3

Consumer Spending and Investment Growth, 1960–2013

This figure shows the four-quarter growth rates of real consumer spending and investment. (Shaded areas denote recessions.) Both consumer spending in panel (a) and investment in panel (b) are highly procyclical and coincident variables, but investment is much more volatile than consumer spending.

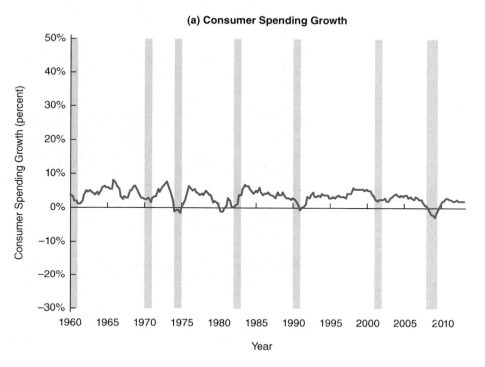

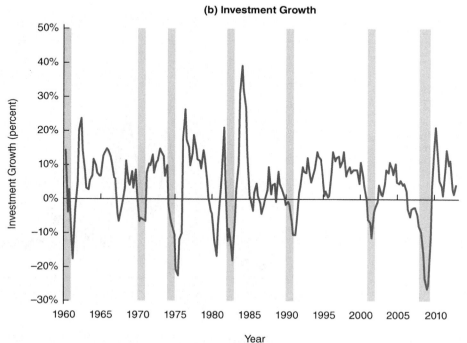

Source: Federal Reserve Bank of St. Louis, FRED Database. http://research .stlouisfed.org/fred2/

FIGURE 8.4

Unemployment Rate, 1960–2013

The shaded areas showing recessions indicate that the unemployment rate is highly counter-cyclical.

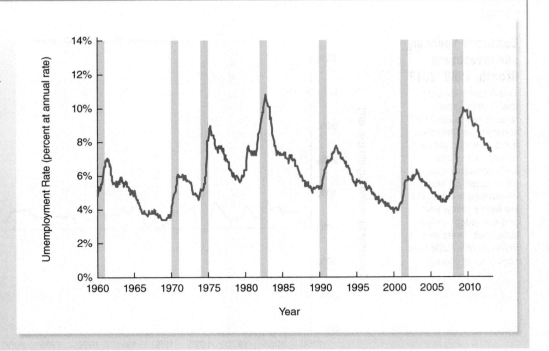

Source: Federal Reserve Bank of St. Louis, FRED Database. http://research .stlouisfed.org/fred2/

FIGURE 8.5

Inflation, 1960–2013

The shaded areas showing recessions indicate that inflation is a pro-cyclical and lagging variable.

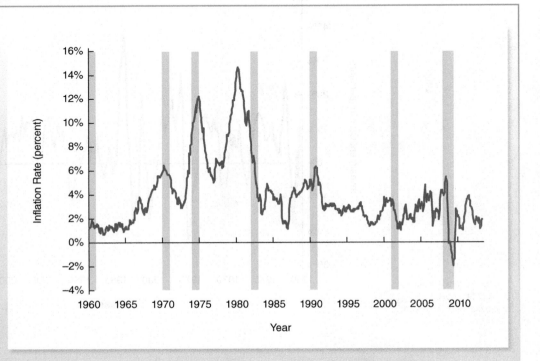

Source: Federal Reserve Bank of St. Louis, FRED Database. http://research .stlouisfed.org/fred2/

Financial Variables

Financial assets like stocks and bonds also tend to move with the business cycle. Perhaps the best-known financial variable is the stock market (Figure 8.6), which tends to top out before the business cycle's peak and begin to rise before the economy emerges from a recession. Of course, falling stock values don't always mean that a recession is on its way. As Nobel Prize-winning economist Paul Samuelson famously quipped, "Wall Street indexes predicted nine of the last five recessions."[3]

The rate of interest paid on short-term U.S. government bonds, known as Treasury bills, is both countercyclical and leading, as shown in Figure 8.7. Economists also look at spreads, or the difference between two interest rates, for clues to the business cycle. In panel (a) of Figure 8.8, the spread between long-term and short-term government bonds is leading and countercyclical, and a good predictor of recessions. Panel (b) shows the spread between interest rates on corporate bonds and government bonds. Since companies sometimes run out of money and stop paying interest, investors usually demand higher interest rates on corporate bonds than on government-issued bonds. When the economy is weaker and companies are more likely to run out of money, the spread between the rates paid on corporate bonds and government bonds rises dramatically. This is why we see a rise in this spread during recessions (see panel (b)).

MyEconLab Real-time data

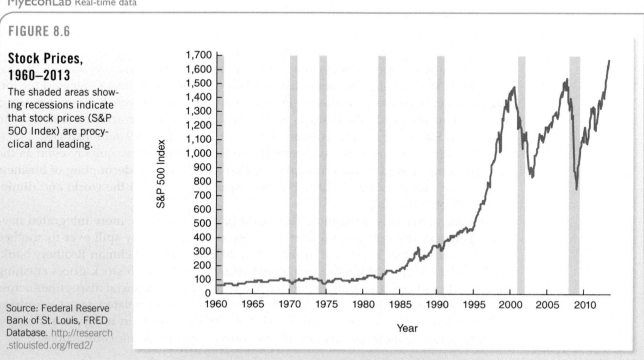

FIGURE 8.6

Stock Prices, 1960–2013

The shaded areas showing recessions indicate that stock prices (S&P 500 Index) are procyclical and leading.

Source: Federal Reserve Bank of St. Louis, FRED Database. http://research.stlouisfed.org/fred2/

[3]*Newsweek*, September 19, 1966.

MyEconLab Real-time data

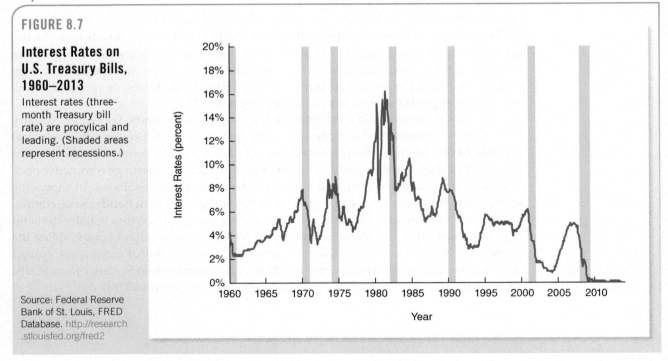

FIGURE 8.7

Interest Rates on U.S. Treasury Bills, 1960–2013

Interest rates (three-month Treasury bill rate) are procyclical and leading. (Shaded areas represent recessions.)

Source: Federal Reserve Bank of St. Louis, FRED Database. http://research .stlouisfed.org/fred2

International Business Cycles

In a heavily globalized economy, the fate of one economy is often intertwined with that of another. When a large economy like the United States is booming, demand for foreign products increases, causing foreign economies to boom as well. It is not surprising, then, that business cycle fluctuations in the rest of the world are correlated with those in the United States, the largest economy in the world, as Figure 8.9 demonstrates.

For a time, however, some economies, notably China, grew quickly even as the U.S. economy slowed. Some economists started to talk about a decoupling of business cycles. The recession of 2007–2009, however, spread throughout the world and diminished talk of decoupling.

Financial markets throughout the world have also become more integrated over time. Financial disruptions that start in one economy frequently spill over to another. This is exactly what happened in the fall of 2008, when the Lehman Brothers bankruptcy in the United States led to a global financial crisis, with stock prices crashing worldwide and credit spreads rising sharply. The spread of financial disruptions across borders provides another reason why business cycles are correlated across countries. When financial market conditions deteriorate simultaneously in many countries, the negative shock to their economies leads to simultaneous economic contractions.

FIGURE 8.8

Credit Spreads and Spreads Between Long- and Short-Term Bonds, 1960–2013

The spread between long- and short-term government bonds in panel (a) is a counter-cyclical and leading variable, while the credit spread (the spread between interest rates on corporate bonds and government bonds) in panel (b) is countercyclical and coincident. The shaded areas in both graphs represent recessions.

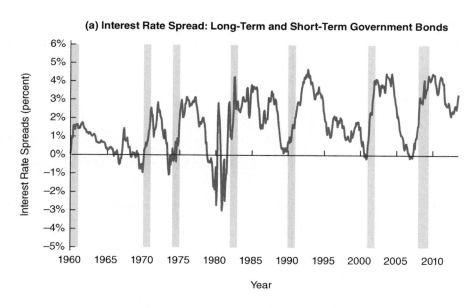

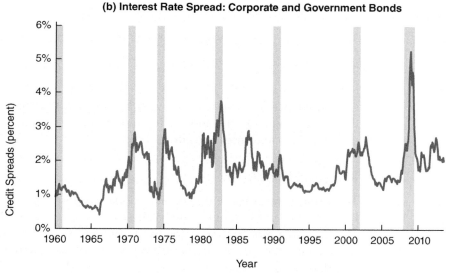

Source: Federal Reserve Bank of St. Louis, FRED Database. http://research .stlouisfed.org/fred2/

A Brief History of U.S. Business Cycles

The severity of the 2007–2009 recession jarred the U.S. psyche and raised questions about the status of the United States as a role model for the world. The "American Century," in which the U.S. economy dominated the globe, may be over.

To put the current business cycle episode in perspective, let's take a tour of U.S. business cycles over the past 150 years. We will refer to the high-level view of the

FIGURE 8.9

International Business Cycles, 1960–2013

The graph shows four-quarter real GDP growth rates. Business cycles in different countries generally move together.

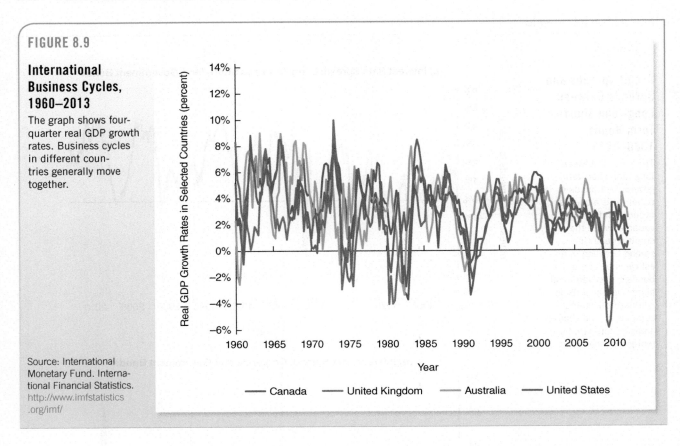

Source: International Monetary Fund. International Financial Statistics. http://www.imfstatistics.org/imf/

economy since 1890, shown in Figure 8.10, which illustrates annual real GDP growth, the unemployment rate, and the inflation rate. We will also refer to the NBER's record of expansions and recessions in Table 8.1.

Pre–World War I

The United States had emerged as a global economic power by the start of World War I in 1914, but not without some battle scars from numerous business cycle downturns. The sixty-five-month contraction from October 1873 to March 1879 is the longest in U.S. history (see Table 8.1). The downturn, which many business cycle historians classify as a depression, began with the failure of a widely respected financial firm, Jay Cooke & Co. Asset prices collapsed and many banks and nonfinancial institutions went out of business. Price levels began falling and a period of deflation, with zero or negative inflation rates, persisted for the remainder of the century.[4] In 1893, a string of bank failures prompted a severe, seventeen-month recession that pushed unemployment rates above 15%. In 1907, a severe recession followed the failure of the Knickerbocker Trust Company, one of the largest financial institutions in New York. Congress responded to the 1907–1908 recession by creating the Federal Reserve System.

[4]The association of severe economic contractions with financial crises, which are large-scale disruptions in financial markets characterized by sharp declines in asset prices and business failures, recurs throughout U.S. history. We will explore this subject further in Chapter 15.

FIGURE 8.10

Business Cycles in the United States: A Long-Term Perspective, 1890–2012

Panel (a) shows annual growth rates of real GDP, panel (b) shows the unemployment rate, and panel (c) shows the annual inflation rate.

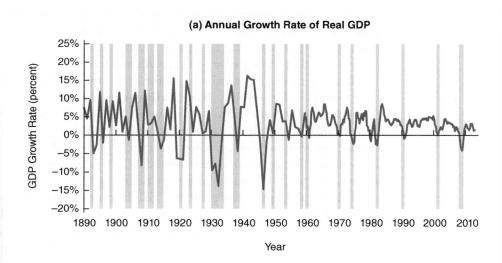

(a) Annual Growth Rate of Real GDP

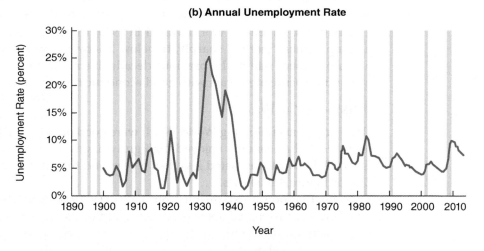

(b) Annual Unemployment Rate

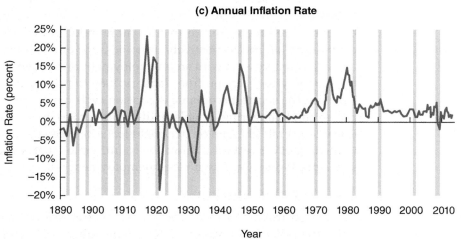

(c) Annual Inflation Rate

Source: Balke, Nathan and Robert J. Gordon. 1986. Appendix B historical data. In *The American business cycle: Continuity and change*, 781–850. National Bureau of Economic Research, Inc (1890–1983 period); and Bureau of Economic Analysis. National Income and Product Accounts. http://www.bea.gov/national/nipaweb/SelectTable.asp?Selected=N, U.S. Census Bureau, at http://www2.census.gov/prod2/statcomp/documents/CT1970p1-05.pdf and Bureau of Labor Statistics, at http://data.bls.gov/cgi-bin/surveymost?ln

The Interwar Period and the Great Depression

A sharp, short recession after World War I, caused by the Federal Reserve's monetary policy actions intended to halt inflation, lasted from 1920 to 1921 and pushed the unemployment rate above 10%. This period was followed by the "roaring 20s," which were characterized by strong economic growth and very low inflation.

The end of the 1920s ushered in the most severe economic contraction in U.S. history, the Great Depression. **Bank failures,** which occur when banks cannot pay off depositors and other creditors and thus go out of business, led to a sharp contraction of the U.S. money supply as deposits were converted into currency and businesses found themselves without their accustomed sources of credit. In the end, GDP contracted over 25% and the unemployment rate surged to 25% (see Figure 8.10). An insidious deflation set in, sending the price level down by nearly 30%.

The Great Depression provides evidence of how quickly the unemployment rate dec[...] 1937, real GDP growth averaged a r[...] ered just shy of 15%. Another eco-nor[...] nemployment rate back over 20%. Bec[...] red during the decade, some eco-non[...] Great Depression.

[...].S. economy began to boom. The unen[...] mid-1940s. Considering the 25% unen[...] nystery why many people of that gene[...]s.

Pos[...]

The e[...] for the U.S. economy. From 1945 until [...]ly low inflation, and mild reces-sions. [...] nemployment rate never pierced 7%, as [...]

Th[...]ntil December 1969, driven by wartime [...] led some economists to declare the end of the business cycle. The expansion produced inflationary pressures that lifted the inflation rate through the early 1980s, peaking at over 14%, leading economists to call this period in the 1970s the **Great Inflation.** Growth slowed and the unemployment rate nudged higher. Recessions became more severe, and recoveries more mild. In the 1973–1975 recession, the quadrupling of oil prices effectively imposed a tax on the economy, sending the economy into a severe recession with an unemployment rate above 8%. New oil shocks returned the economy to recession from January 1980 to July 1980. After just twelve months of recovery, the shortest economic expansion cycle on record, the Federal Reserve tried to put an end to lingering, double-digit inflation rates by boosting the **federal funds rate** (the interest rate charged on overnight loans between banks) to double-digit levels. The tightening of interest rates drove the country into what was then the most severe recession since World War II, with the unemployment rate rising above 10%.

The "Great Moderation"

The period from 1984 to 2007 saw only two recessions: one from July 1990 to March 1991, the other from March 2001 to November 2001. Both were only eight months in duration, among the shortest on record (refer back to Table 8.1). Furthermore, the 120-month expansion from March 1991 to March 2001 was the longest in U.S. history.

The volatility of real GDP and its components, as well as inflation, declined both in the United States and abroad, and the period became known as the **Great Moderation.** James Stock of Harvard University and Mark Watson of Princeton University observed that volatility (measured by the standard deviation) fell by 20–40% for many U.S. variables, with a decline of 33% for real GDP and 50% for inflation.[5] Economists and media commentators alike declared a new era of stability.

The Great Recession of 2007–2009

The Great Moderation period came to an abrupt halt when a financial crisis sparked by defaults on subprime mortgage loans, which are mortgage loans made to borrowers with poor credit records, struck in August 2007, leading to a record decline of over $11 trillion in U.S. household wealth in 2008. The unemployment rate climbed by more than five percentage points, from 4.5% in the first quarter of 2007 to 10% in the fourth quarter of 2009. (During the 1981–1982 recession, the unemployment rate increased by a little over three percentage points from 7.4% to 10.7%.) The 2007–2009 recession, the most severe since World War II, pales in comparison with the Great Depression—but it made clear that the business cycle will remain a front-burner concern for economists and policy makers.

We will examine the causes of the Great Recession of 2007–2009 and the effects of policy makers' responses later in this book.

 # Time Horizons in Macroeconomics

The study of business cycles focuses on short-run economic fluctuations like the ones we have just been describing. What happens to the economy in the long run, that is, over much longer time horizons, further informs our study of business cycles. We now preview the differences between the short and long runs and the models that economists use based on the weight they place on each period in impacting the economy's overall performance.

Keynesian and Classical Views on Economic Fluctuations

John Maynard Keynes was a great economist who carved out macroeconomics as a distinct field in the 1930s. He questioned the prevailing (*classical*) view that economies move quickly to their long-run equilibriums when conditions change. Short-run economic fluctuations, he argued, should be the primary focus of macroeconomists, since it takes a long time to get to the long run. Keynes summed up this idea brilliantly in a widely quoted (and often misunderstood) line: "In the long run, we are all dead."

Keynes and his followers, who are known as **Keynesians,** argue that the government should pursue active policies to stabilize economic fluctuations. Other economists, often referred to as *classicals*, maintain that the economy moves to the long run quite quickly. For example, as we saw in Chapter 5, classicals believe that a rise in the quantity of money leads to an immediate rise in the price level, but not to an expansion in economic activity. They therefore believe that the government should focus on policies that promote high long-run economic growth, such as keeping inflation low. Keynesians have also come to realize that what happens in the long run is still very

---

[5]James Stock and Mark Watson, "Has the Business Cycle Changed and Why?" *NBER Macroeconomics Annual* (Cambridge, Mass.: MIT Press, 2002), 159–218.

important: even if the long run takes a fairly long time to happen, over many years, the average rate of economic growth has an enormous effect on the well-being of citizens of a nation.

The Short Run Versus the Long Run

How does the short run differ from the long run? Economists make this distinction by focusing on the difference in the behavior of prices in response to changing economic conditions over the short and long runs. In the long run, prices of goods and services, as well as the price of labor (wages), adjust all the way to their long-run equilibrium, where supply equals demand, so supply equals demand, so *flexible*. Economists who believe that ria prefer to analyze macroeconomic i 2 and 3 of the book, which make use e framework exhibits the *classical di* is a total separation between real and such as inflation and the money supply e output (real GDP), real interest rates, display the classical dichotomy determ unction, with given amounts of capita by the interaction of saving and investi

Keynesian eco hat prices respond slowly to changes address the role of **sticky prices,** whi ibrium. In the short run, when prices h the classical dichotomy is no longer t variables, including

[Handwritten note: Economists who view the adjustment and flexibility of prices as quick are Classical model. Keynesian model allows for sticky prices & thus a longer period of time to adjust to long run]

TABLE 8.2	LONG-RUN VERSUS SHORT-RUN MODELS	
	Long-Run Models	**Short-Run Models**
Prices	Flexible, adjust quickly to long-run equilibrium	Sticky, adjust slowly to long-run equilibrium
Model Type	Classical	Keynesian
Relation of Real and Nominal Variables	Total separation with classical dichotomy	Classical dichotomy does not hold
Model Elements	Production function with a given amount of capital and labor determines aggregate output; interest rate determined by the interaction of saving and investment	Monetary policy affects real variables (aggregate output, the real interest rate, saving, and investment)
Policy Focus	Economic growth	Stabilizing fluctuations in real GDP and unemployment rates
Core Chapters in This Book	3–7	9–13

aggregate output, the real interest rate, saving, and investment. We typically refer to models with slowly adjusting (sticky) prices as **Keynesian models,** because it was John Maynard Keynes who first developed macroeconomic models in which the classical dichotomy did not hold. As a point of reference, Table 8.2 compares the key distinguishing features of the economic models that focus on the long run versus those that focus on the short run.

Price Stickiness

To understand why price stickiness occurs, we first need to look at market structure and contrast two views of how markets operate: *perfect competition* and *monopolistic competition*. We will then examine sources of price stickiness and empirical evidence on their impact.

Perfect Competition Versus Monopolistic Competition

In classical models, which include the traditional supply and demand analysis you have seen in other economics courses, we assume that economic actors are price takers whose only decision is how much to buy or sell. Furthermore, we assume that they are purchasing standardized products such as a commonly traded type of soybean or a financial instrument like a U.S. Treasury bond. Suppose a seller tries to charge a little more than a competitor for his soybeans, or a buyer seeks a Treasury bill for less than the market price. Both are likely to be shut out of the marketplace because the equilibrium price prevails. There is **perfect competition** in markets in which buyers and sellers are price takers.

Most goods and services are, however, not standardized. Firms typically have some *market (monopoly) power* in either buying or selling. A market is characterized by **monopolistic competition** when firms set prices, even if there is substantial competition within their market. Many economists, especially Keynesians, focus on the importance of monopoly power. For example, the market for laptop computers is highly competitive, but computer manufacturers still have substantial market power. If Dell raises the price of its laptops above those of Hewlett-Packard, you might decide to switch to an HP, but many other consumers will stick with Dell because they like some particular features of Dell laptops.

Sources of Price Stickiness

Why does a company like Dell in a monopolistically competitive market keep its prices fixed for a period of time even when market conditions change? To answer this question, we will now address the sources of price stickiness.

MENU COSTS. **Menu costs,** the costs a firm bears when it changes the prices of its goods, are one source of price stickiness. This cost of adjusting prices received its name because of the cost a restaurant incurs when it changes prices and has to print a new menu. Menu costs, however, are far more general: managers must draw up new guidelines for sales people, advertise the new prices to customers, and re-mark prices of goods on shelves and shelf labels. Menu costs are an important source of price stickiness for several reasons:

1. Changing prices is a complex process that involves many hidden costs.

2. Collecting information is costly, so firms and households may engage in **rational inattention** by making decisions about prices only at infrequent

intervals. This behavior is considered rational because time and effort are required to make pricing decisions. Firms ma… nly review pricing conditions a few times a ye… t immediately notice a … ices in the first place.

3. C… rs. If your grocer's fluc- t… enses for the week, for i…

> Price stickiness
> a factor of:
> (1) monopolistic over perfect competition
> (2) Menu costs: cost of changing prices. Menu cost take into account that prices have a many hidden cost in changing, rational inattention, changing prices alienates consumers
> (3) Staggered price

At firs… er all, with modern computers, printi… a fascinating study of menu costs in se… omplexity and magnitude of menu co… stantial: $105,000 per year, which was … ts net profits.

Even sm… ness. If Dell sets the price of its laptops a… e market, it will eventually lose market … ll hardly change, and any benefits gain… ven minimal menu costs. Contrast this … or example, a farmer sets a price for his … a bushel too high, the farmer will immediately find th… no one will buy them, and he or she will be forced to store the soybeans at a high cost. The soybean farmer will have to adjust his or her prices immediately when market conditions change, so soybean prices will be completely flexible.

Also, small menu costs may lead to price stickiness in the face of macroeconomic shocks, even if there is little price stickiness when the shocks come from changes in individual product markets. Dell might respond very quickly to changes in the computer market—say, the introduction of a sleeker computer from Apple—but it will not alter its prices quickly when there is a shift in monetary policy. The impact of monetary policy on the demand for Dell products is subtle and won't be nearly as important as what is happening in Dell's own market.

STAGGERED PRICE SETTING. Another source of price stickiness is the phenomenon of **staggered price setting,** when competitors adjust prices at different time intervals. Even if demand for new computers suddenly rises, Dell won't raise prices on January 1 if it knows that HP doesn't update its prices until January 15. Then, on January 15, HP might hesitate to raise prices if it knows Dell won't raise its prices until February 1. Prices of computers adjust more slowly with staggered pricing than with synchronized pricing decisions. Staggered pricing thus slows down price adjustment and increases the stickiness of prices.

Empirical Evidence for Price Stickiness

Empirical evidence tends to indicate substantial price stickiness in markets. A study by Alan Blinder of Princeton University, for example, asked firms how often they set prices. Blinder found that only 10% of firms changed their prices as often as once a week, while close to 40% changed prices once a year, and 10% changed prices less than

[6]Daniel Levy, Mark Bergen, Shantanu Dutta, and Robert Venable, "The Magnitude of Menu Costs: Direct Evidence from Large Supermarket Chains," *Quarterly Journal of Economics* 112 (August 1997): 791–825.

once a year.[7] Other approaches study actual price changes. Stephen Cecchetti, now of the Bank for International Settlements, found that magazine prices change very infrequently in response to inflation: with 4% inflation, magazines on average changed their prices every six years.[8] Even more remarkable is the fact that the price of Coca-Cola remained five cents a bottle for over seventy years.[9]

However, not all research indicates that prices are sticky. Mark Bils of the University of Rochester and Peter Klenow of Stanford University found that the average time between price changes of 350 categories of goods was just 4.3 months, a far shorter period than the research by Alan Blinder and Stephen Cecchetti indicated.[10] However, even these more frequent price changes do not rule out price stickiness with regard to macroeconomic shocks. Jean Boivin of the Bank of Canada, Marc Giannoni of Columbia University, and Ilian Mihov of INSEAD, for example, found that prices of goods are very sticky in response to monetary policy shocks, while these prices, in contrast, respond quickly to supply and demand shocks in individual markets that affect their prices relative to those of other goods.[11]

Road Map for Our Study of Business Cycles

In the next four chapters, Chapters 9 to 12, we carefully build a basic model, the *aggregate demand-aggregate supply (AD/AS) model*, in which prices are sticky. We will use this basic model throughout the rest of the book to discuss business cycle fluctuations and answer many of the questions posed in this chapter.

The initial discussion of the *AD/AS* model leaves out one important group of economic agents that play a prominent role in business cycle fluctuations: policy makers. We will bring policy makers into the *AD/AS* framework in Chapter 13 by discussing their objectives and policies and practices that can stabilize economic fluctuations. In Chapter 15, we will use the aggregate demand-aggregate supply model to examine how financial crises affect the business cycle. We will further extend the aggregate demand-aggregate supply model in Chapters 21 and 22 to incorporate the role of expectations in macroeconomic policy and to discuss modern business cycle theories, some of which are Keynesian (because they assume prices are sticky) and others more classical (because they assume that prices adjust rapidly). Finally, the Epilogue wraps up our analysis by examining state-of-the-art thinking on business cycles and identifying topics on which macroeconomists agree and disagree.

---

[7]Alan S. Blinder, "On Sticky Prices: Academic Theories Meet the Real World," in *Monetary Policy*, ed. N.G. Mankiw (Chicago: University of Chicago Press, 1994), 117–154.

[8]Stephen G. Cecchetti, "The Frequency of Price Adjustment: A Study of the Newsstand Prices of Magazines," *Journal of Econometrics* 31 (1986): 255–274. Anil Kashyap, "Sticky Prices: New Evidence from Retail Catalogs," *Quarterly Journal of Economics* (February 1995): 245–274, finds similar evidence on the infrequency of price adjustments for individual items in retail catalogs.

[9]Daniel Levy and Andrew Young, "The Real Thing: Nominal Price Rigidity of the Nickel Coke, 1886–1959," *Journal of Money, Credit and Banking* 36 (2004): 765–799.

[10]Mark Bils and Peter Klenow, "Some Evidence on the Importance of Sticky Prices," *Journal of Political Economy* (October 2004): 947–985.

[11]Jean Boivin, Marc Giannoni, and Ilian Mihov, "Sticky Prices and Monetary Policy: Evidence from Disaggregated U.S. Data," *American Economic Review* 99, no. 1 (2009): 350–384.

SUMMARY

1. Business cycles are fluctuations in aggregate economic activity in which many economic activities expand and contract together. One characterization of the business cycle is in terms of fluctuations of the output gap, the difference between actual output and its long-run potential level, $Y - Y^P$.

2. Over the course of the business cycle, macroeconomic variables are procyclical, countercyclical, or acyclical. They also are leading, lagging, or coincident. During the period from 1984 to 2007, economic activity became less volatile, and this period has become known as the Great Moderation.

3. Business cycles have been a fact of life in the United States for the last 150 years. Although the recent recession from 2007 to 2009 is the most severe that has been experienced in the post–World War II period, there have been much larger and longer-lived economic contractions in 1873–1879, 1929–1933, and 1937–1938.

4. In the long run, prices in the economy are able to adjust all the way to equilibrium levels and are completely flexible. The short run differs from the long run because in the short run, at least some prices are sticky, that is, they do not adjust immediately. Classical economists believe that the economy goes to the long run quickly and therefore advise that the government should focus on policies to promote economic growth, such as keeping inflation low. Keynesian economists believe that it takes a long time to get to the long run and so advocate active government policies to stabilize economic fluctuations.

5. Prices are sticky because there is monopolistic competition, in which firms have some market (monopoly) power in either buying or selling that enables them to set prices, even if there is substantial competition in their market. Prices are slow to adjust because of either menu costs or staggered price setting.

KEY TERMS

acyclical, p. 211
bank failures, p. 220
boom, p. 208
business cycle
   contraction, p. 208
business cycle expansion, p. 208
business cycles, p. 207
classical models, p. 222
coincident variable, p. 211
countercyclical, p. 211

federal funds rate, p. 220
Great Inflation, p. 220
Great Moderation, p. 221
index of leading
   indicators, p. 211
Keynesian models, p. 222
Keynesians, p. 221
lagging variable, p. 211
leading variable, p. 211
menu costs, p. 223

monopolistic competition, p. 223
output gap, p. 209
peaks, p. 208
perfect competition, p. 223
potential output, p. 208
procyclical, p. 211
rational inattention, p. 223
staggered price setting, p. 224
sticky prices, p. 222
troughs, p. 208

REVIEW QUESTIONS

All Questions are available in MyEconLab *for practice or instructor assignment.*

Business Cycle Basics

1. What are business cycles?

Macroeconomic Variables and the Business Cycle

2. Distinguish between procyclical and counter-cyclical economic variables.
3. Distinguish among leading, lagging, and coincident economic variables.
4. Classify the following economic variables as procyclical or countercyclical and as leading, lagging, or coincident: real consumer spending, real investment spending, unemployment, inflation, S&P 500 Index, spread between long- and short-term interest rates on U.S. government bonds, and spread between interest rates on corporate bonds and government bonds.

A Brief History of U.S. Business Cycles

5. What were the "Great Inflation" and the "Great Moderation"?

Time Horizons in Macroeconomics

6. How do macroeconomists distinguish between flexible and sticky prices and wages?
7. What is the difference between the short run and the long run in macroeconomic analysis? Why do macroeconomists differentiate between the two time horizons?

8. How do Keynesian views on macroeconomic fluctuations differ from those of classical macroeconomists?

Price Stickiness

9. How do conflicting views of market structure influence the ideas of classical and Keynesian macroeconomists regarding price and wage flexibility and how quickly the economy adjusts to long-run equilibrium?

10. How do menu costs contribute to sticky prices?

PROBLEMS

All Problems are available in MyEconLab *for practice or instructor assignment.*

Business Cycle Basics

1. Using the accompanying graph, measure the following:
    a) Expansions (in months from trough to peak)
    b) Contractions (in months from peak to trough)

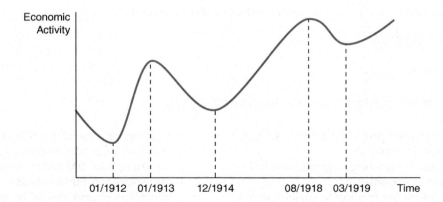

2. Discuss the following statement: "Real GDP has decreased for two quarters in a row; we definitively are living through a contraction."

3. The NBER Business Cycle Dating Committee stated that the U.S. economy entered a recession in December 2007. The S&P/Case-Shiller Home Price Index (a widely used measure of home prices) shows an increase in home prices from January 2000 to April 2006. From that date until May 2009, the index fell by over 30%, then stayed pretty level, and finally started rising at the beginning of 2012. According to this information,
   a) are home prices a countercyclical, acyclical, or procyclical variable?
   b) are home prices a leading, lagging, or coincident indicator?

4. Use the information given in the following table to answer the following questions.

Assume the business cycle is entirely determined by changes in real GDP.
   a) Identify the peak and trough during this period.
   b) Comment on the timing of the inflation rate and the stock prices index.

5. Refer to the data provided in Problem 4 to answer the following questions.
   a) Plot real GDP and the stock prices index on the same graph.
   b) Plot the unemployment and inflation rates on the same graph.
   c) Considering real GDP and the unemployment rate, when would you say that the economy reached its trough? Explain why.
   d) Considering these four indicators, would you agree that it is possible to determine the business cycle by measuring changes in only one indicator?

Date	Real GDP (billions of $)	Unemployment (%)	Inflation (%)	Stock Prices Index
January	10,100	4.5	3.4	8,800
February	10,500	4.7	3.6	8,400
March	9,850	5.2	3.8	8,000
April	9,250	5.9	4	8,600
May	9,950	6.3	3.7	9,300
June	11,200	6.1	3.5	10,100

Macroeconomic Variables and the Business Cycle

6. Consider the following variables: real GDP, consumer spending, investment, unemployment, inflation, stock prices, interest rates, and credit spreads. Classify each as procyclical, countercyclical, or acyclical, and as leading, lagging, or coincident.

A Brief History of U.S. Business Cycles

7. Using Table 8.1 (NBER business cycles), identify the longest and shortest expansion and contraction in the United States from December 1854 to November 2001. What are your thoughts about the periodicity and persistence of U.S. business cycles?

Time Horizons in Macroeconomics

8. Discuss the following statement: "When Keynes stated that 'in the long run, we are all dead' he meant that we should focus only on the short run and not pay attention to any long-run consequences of our actions, since we will be dead by then and we therefore should not care."

Price Stickiness

9. For each of the following products, state whether they are sold in a perfectly competitive market or in a monopolistically competitive market:
   a) Dairy products (e.g., milk, cheese, etc.)
   b) Cars
10. Suppose that in a given economy all goods and services produced are sold in perfectly competitive markets. Would you represent this economy using the classical or Keynesian approach? Explain why.
11. Do you think that the hourly wage (i.e., the price of labor) is a relatively flexible or a relatively sticky price? Explain why.

DATA ANALYSIS PROBLEMS

The Problems update with real-time data in MyEconLab *and are available for practice or instructor assignment.*

1. Go to the St. Louis Federal Reserve FRED database, and find data on recession dating (USRECQ) and real GDP (GDPC1), real consumption (PCECC96), and real private domestic investment (GPDIC1).
   a) Using the recession dating series (USRECQ), when did the most recent recession begin and end? (Use the "quarterly" setting for *frequency*, and report the recession dates by year and quarter.)
   b) For the data series above, calculate the quarter-to-quarter annualized growth rate of real GDP, real consumption, and real private domestic investment during the quarters of the recession in part (a), and do the same for the quarter after the recession ends through the most recent data available. To calculate quarter-to-quarter annualized growth rates, calculate the percentage change from the previous quarter's data, and then multiply by 4 to "annualize" the result. Now, calculate the average growth rates of these data during the recession and post-recession periods.
   c) Based on your answers to part (b), classify real GDP, real consumption, and real private domestic investment as procyclical, countercyclical, or acyclical.

2. Go to the St. Louis Federal Reserve FRED database, and find data on recession dating (USREC), the unemployment rate (UNRATE), nonfarm payroll employment (PAYEMS), and the mean duration of unemployment (UEMPMEAN).

a) Using the recession dating series (USREC), when did the most recent recession begin and end? (Use the "monthly" setting for *frequency*, and report the recession dates by year and month.)

b) Calculate the total percentage point change in the unemployment rate from the first month of the recession until the last month of the recession, and the total percentage point change in the unemployment rate from the first month after the end of the recession until the most recent month available. Is the unemployment rate a procyclical, countercyclical, or acyclical variable?

c) Using (PAYEMS), calculate the total net gain or loss in jobs for the recessionary period and for the period after the recession until the most recent data available. Is nonfarm payroll employment a procyclical, countercyclical, or acyclical variable?

d) Based on the dates of the most recent recession, determine the value and date near the beginning of the recession when (UEMPMEAN) began rising, and determine the value and date after the end of the recession when it was at its highest level. Based on your results, is the average duration of unemployment (average length, in weeks, of unemployment) procyclical, countercyclical, or acyclical? Is it a leading, lagging, or coincident variable?

3. Go to the St. Louis Federal Reserve FRED database, and find data on recession dating (USREC), consumer sentiment (UMCSENT), industrial production (INDPRO), and real retail and food service sales (RRSFS).

a) Using the recession dating series (USREC), when did the most recent recession begin and end?

b) Using the consumer sentiment index (UMCSENT), calculate the average of the index during the recessionary period, and also the average of the index from the month after the end of the recession to the most recent data available. Is consumer sentiment procyclical, countercyclical, or acyclical?

c) For industrial production (INDPRO), calculate the percentage change in the index during the recessionary period, and also the percentage change in the index from the month after the end of the recession to the most recent data available. Is industrial production procyclical, countercyclical, or acyclical?

d) For real retail and food sales (RRSFS), calculate the percentage change for the data during the recessionary period, and also the percentage change for the data from the month after the end of the recession to the most recent data available. Is real retail and food sales procyclical, countercyclical, or acyclical?

e) Classify (UMCSENT), (INDPRO), and (RRSFS) as leading, coincident, or lagging variables based on the entire data series.

4. Go to the St. Louis Federal Reserve FRED database, and find data on real GDP (GDPC1) and the GDP deflator price index (GDPDEF). Using the *units* setting, choose "Percent Change from Year Ago" to convert each measure into real GDP growth and the inflation rate, respectively. Download both series onto a spreadsheet.

a) For each measure of real GDP growth and the inflation rate, calculate the average and the standard deviation over the following periods: 1970–1982 (the Great Inflation), 1983–2007 (the Great Moderation), and 2008 to the most recent data available. In Excel, these values are easily computed by using the "=average()" and "=stdev()" cell commands.

b) Which period had the highest and lowest average real GDP growth rates? Which had the most volatile swings in real GDP growth?

c) Which period had the highest and lowest average inflation rates? Which had the most volatile swings in the inflation rate?

9

The *IS* Curve

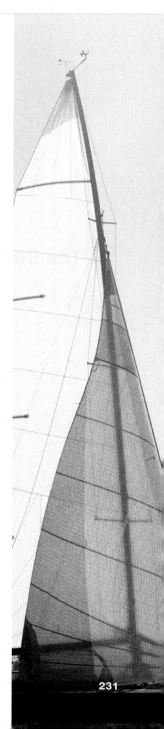

Preview

Before the Great Depression, most economists believed in the classical models we discussed in Parts 2 and 3 of this book in which aggregate output, even in the short run, is determined by how much an economy can produce with a given amount of capital and labor. The Great Depression challenged the validity of these classical models: the amount of capital and labor did not change very much, yet aggregate output fell precipitously, by 30%, with the unemployment rate rising to 25%. To explain why output fell so dramatically during the Great Depression, John Maynard Keynes—in his revolutionary book, *The General Theory of Employment, Interest, and Money*, published in 1936—presented a new concept: *aggregate demand*, the total amount of output demanded in the economy. He argued that short-run changes in aggregate output, such as the decline during the Great Depression, were determined by changes in aggregate demand. The concept of aggregate demand is a central element in the *aggregate demand-aggregate supply (AD/AS) model*, the basic macroeconomic model for explaining short-run fluctuations in aggregate output. We will build this model in Chapters 9–12.

In this chapter, we develop the first building block to understanding aggregate demand, the *IS curve*, which describes the relationship between real interest rates and aggregate output when the market for goods and services (more simply referred to as the *goods market*) is in equilibrium. We begin by deriving the *IS* curve and then go on to explain what factors cause the *IS* curve to shift. With our understanding of the *IS* curve, we can examine why the economic contraction during the Great Depression was so deep and how the fiscal stimulus package of 2009 affected the economy. Then, in later chapters, we make use of the *IS* curve to understand the role of monetary and fiscal policy in economic fluctuations.

Planned Expenditure

We start our analysis by discussing the concept of **planned expenditure**, the total amount that households, businesses, the government, and foreigners want to spend on domestically produced goods and services. In contrast, *actual expenditure* is the amount that they actually do spend, which equals the total amount of output produced in the economy. Keynes viewed **aggregate demand**, the total amount of output demanded in the economy, as being the same as planned expenditure. As we shall see shortly, planned expenditure explains the level of aggregate output when the goods market is in equilibrium, that is, when the planned expenditure on goods and services is equal to the actual amount of goods and services produced.

The total amount of planned expenditure (aggregate demand) is the sum of four types of spending:

1. **Consumption expenditure** (C), the total demand for consumer goods and services (e.g., hamburgers, iPods, rock concerts, visits to the doctor, etc.)

2. **Planned investment spending** (I), the total planned spending by businesses on new physical capital (e.g., machines, computers, factories) plus planned spending on new homes

3. **Government purchases** (G), the spending by all levels of government on goods and services (e.g., aircraft carriers, government workers, red tape), not including transfer payments

4. **Net exports** (NX), the net foreign spending on domestic goods and services, equal to exports minus imports

We represent the total planned expenditure (Y^{pe}) with the following equation:

$$Y^{pe} = C + I + G + NX \tag{1}$$

The Components of Expenditure

To understand what determines total planned expenditure in an economy, let's look at each of its components in detail.

Consumption Expenditure

What determines how much you spend on consumer goods and services? Your income is likely the most important factor; if your income rises, you will be willing to spend more. Keynes reasoned similarly that consumption expenditure is related to **disposable income**, the total income available for spending, equal to aggregate inc_____ saw in Chapter 2, is equivalent to aggregate output Y) minus tax___

cc_____ ionship between disposable income
Y_l _____ **on function** and expressed it as fol-
lc___

$Y_D \tag{2}$

(government payments to households and busi-
____ rnment transfers are Social Security payments or

[Handwritten note overlay:]

Planned expenditure as aggregate demand.
$Y^{pe} = C + I + G + NX$

Consumption a factor of
$\overline{C}$, as autonomous consumption
not able to be accounted for by Y_D
& Y_D (disposable income)
$= (Y-T)$ & MPC &
GDP, interest rates

The term $\overline{C}$ stands for **autonomous consumption expenditure**, the amount of consumption expenditure that is exogenous (independent of variables in the model, such as disposable income or interest rates). Autonomous consumption is related to consumers' optimism about their future income and household wealth, which induce consumers to increase spending (a topic we will discuss in detail in Chapter 18).

The term *mpc*, the **marginal propensity to consume**, reflects the change in consumption expenditure that results from an additional dollar of disposable income. Keynes assumed that *mpc* was a constant between the values of 0 and 1. If, for example, a $1.00 increase in disposable income leads to an increase in consumption expenditure of $0.60, then *mpc* = 0.6.

CONSUMPTION EXPENDITURE AND REAL INTEREST RATES. Keynes assumed that consumption expenditure is linearly related to income only. However, as we discuss in more detail in Chapter 18, consumption expenditure should also be negatively related to real interest rates: when the real interest rate is higher, the real return to saving is also higher, and so consumers will spend less.

We describe the resulting negative relationship between consumption expenditure and the real interest rate, *r*, by amending the consumption function as follows:

$$C = \overline{C} + mpc \times (Y - T) - cr \tag{3}$$

with *c* being a parameter that reflects how responsive consumption expenditure is to the real interest rate. Equation 3 states that consumption expenditure is made up of three components: autonomous consumption, the marginal propensity to consume times disposable income, and a term that indicates that how much consumption decreases in response to a rise in the real interest rate.

Planned Investment Spending

Investment spending is another key component of total expenditure. There are two types of investment: *fixed* and *inventory*.

FIXED INVESTMENT. **Fixed investment** is planned spending by firms on equipment (machines, computers, airplanes) and structures (factories, office buildings, shopping centers), and planned spending on new residential housing.

INVENTORY INVESTMENT. **Inventory investment** is spending by firms on additional holdings of raw materials, parts, and finished goods, calculated as the change in holdings of these items in a given time period—say, a year.

Inventory investment is a much smaller component of investment than fixed investment. We discuss it in detail at this juncture because it plays an important role in the determination of aggregate output. To illustrate, consider the following scenarios:

1. Suppose that Ford Motor Company has 100,000 cars sitting in its factory lots on December 31, 2015, ready to be shipped to dealers. If each car has a wholesale price of $20,000, Ford has an inventory worth $2 billion. If by December 31, 2016, its inventory of cars has risen to 150,000 with a value of $3 billion, its inventory investment in 2016 is $1 billion, the *change* in the level of its inventory over the course of the year ($3 billion minus $2 billion).

2. Now suppose that by December 31, 2016, Ford's inventory of cars has dropped to 50,000 with a value of $1 billion. Its inventory investment in 2016 is now negative $1 billion, the *change* in the level of its inventory over the course of the year ($1 billion minus $2 billion).

3. Ford may have additional inventory investment if the level of raw materials and parts that it is holding to produce these cars increases over the course of the year. If on December 31, 2015, it holds $50 million of steel used to produce its cars and on December 31, 2016, it holds $100 million, it has an additional $50 million of inventory investment in 2016.

An important feature of inventory investment is that some inventory investment can be unplanned (in contrast, fixed investment is always planned). Suppose the reason Ford finds itself with an additional $1 billion of cars on December 31, 2016, is that $1 billion less of its cars were sold in 2016 than expected. This $1 billion of inventory investment in 2016 was unplanned. In this situation, Ford is producing more cars than it can sell, and it will cut production in order to keep from accumulating unsold goods. Adjusting production to eliminate unplanned inventory investment plays a key role in the determination of aggregate output, as we shall see.

PLANNED INVESTMENT SPENDING AND REAL INTEREST RATES. Planned investment spending, a component of planned expenditure, Y^{pe}, is equal to planned fixed investment plus the amount of inventory investment *planned* by firms. Keynes considered the level of the real interest rate for investments a key determinant of planned investment spending.

To understand Keynes's reasoning, we need to recognize that businesses make investments in physical capital (machines and factories) as long as they expect to earn more from the physical capital than the interest cost of a loan to finance the investment. When the real interest rate for investments is high, say, at 10%, fewer investments in physical capital will earn more than the 10% cost of borrowed funds, and so planned investment spending will be low. When the real interest rate for investments is low, say, 1%, many investments in physical capital will earn more than the 1% interest cost of borrowed funds. Therefore, when real interest rates and hence the cost of borrowing are low, business firms are more likely to undertake an investment in physical capital, and planned investment spending will increase.[2]

Even if a company has surplus funds and does not need to borrow to undertake an investment in physical capital, its planned investment spending still will be affected by the real interest rate for investments. Instead of investing in physical capital, it could purchase a security, such as a corporate bond. If the real interest rate on this security is high, say, 10%, the opportunity cost (forgone interest earnings) of an investment is high. Planned investment spending will then be low, because the firm will probably prefer to purchase the security and earn the high 10% return than to invest in physical capital. As the real interest rate for investments and the opportunity cost of investing fall to, say, 1%, planned investment spending will increase because investments in physical capital are likely to earn greater income for the firm than the measly 1% the security will earn.

---

[2]We will examine models of investment in Chapter 19, and discuss in detail the link between real interest rates and investment.

PLANNED INVESTMENT AND BUSINESS EXPECTATIONS. Keynes also believed that planned investment spending is heavily influenced by business expectations about the future. Businesses that are optimistic about future profit opportunities are willing to spend more, while pessimistic businesses cut back their spending. Thus Keynes posited that there is a component of planned investment spending, which he called **autonomous investment**, $\bar{I}$, that is completely exogenous (unexplained by variables in his model such as output or interest rates).

Keynes believed that changes in autonomous spending are dominated by these unstable exogenous fluctuations in planned investment spending, which are influenced by emotional waves of optimism and pessimism—factors he labeled "**animal spirits**." His view was color͏ the collapse in investment spending during the Great Depression, which he saw ͏son for the economic contraction.

INVESTMEN ͏factors that drive investment leads to an investme ͏nt spending is related to the real inte ͏nt. We write it as follows:

(4)

where d ͏nt is to the real interest rate for inve ͏

H ͏ not only the real interest rate on sh ͏d by the central bank, but also **finar** ͏he real cost of borrowing caused by ͏. (We will discuss in more detail wh ͏Financial frictions make it harder for ͏er. Lenders need to charge a higher interest rate t ͏lity that the borrower may not pay back the loan, which lea ͏ference between the interest rate on loans to businesses and the interest ͏ely safe assets that are guaranteed to be paid back. Hence, financial frictions add to the ͏al interest rate for investments, so that:

$$r_i = r + \bar{f}$$

(5)

Substituting into Equation 4 the real interest rate for investments from Equation 5 yields:

$$I = \bar{I} - d(r + \bar{f})$$

(6)

Equation 6 states that investment is positively related to business optimism, as represented by autonomous investment, and is negatively related to the real interest rate and financial frictions.

Net Exports

As with planned investment spending, we can think of net exports as being made up of two components, *autonomous net exports* and the part of net exports that is affected by changes in real interest rates.

REAL INTEREST RATES AND NET EXPORTS. Real interest rates influence the amount of net exports through the **exchange rate**, the price of one currency, say, the dollar, in terms of another currency, say, the euro.[3] We will examine a model that explains the link between the exchange rate and real interest rates in Chapter 17, but here we will outline the intuition. When U.S. real interest rates rise, U.S. dollar assets earn higher returns relative to foreign assets. People then want to hold more dollars, so they bid up the value of dollars and thereby increase their value relative to that of other currencies. Thus a rise in U.S. real interest rates leads to a higher value of the dollar.

A rise in the value of the dollar makes U.S. exports more expensive in foreign currencies, so foreigners will buy less of them, thereby driving down net exports. It also makes foreign goods less expensive in terms of dollars, so U.S. imports will rise, also causing a decline in net exports. We see therefore that a rise in the real interest rate, which leads to a rise in the value of the dollar, leads to a decline in net exports.

AUTONOMOUS NET EXPORTS. The amount of exports is also affected by the demand by foreigners for domestic goods, while the amount of imports is affected by the demand by domestic residents for foreign goods. For example, if the Chinese have a poor harvest and want to buy more U.S. wheat, U.S. exports will rise. If the Brazilian economy is booming, then Brazilians will have more to spend on U.S. goods, and U.S. exports will rise. On the other hand, if U.S. consumers discover how good Chilean wine is and want to buy more, then U.S. imports will rise. Thus we can think of net exports as being determined by real interest rates as well as by a component called **autonomous net exports**, $\overline{NX}$, which is the level of net exports that is treated as exogenous (outside the model).[4]

NET EXPORT FUNCTION. Putting these two components of net exports together leads to a net export function:

$$NX = \overline{NX} - xr \tag{7}$$

where x is a parameter that indicates how net exports respond to the real interest rate. This equation tells us that net exports are positively related to autonomous net exports and negatively related to the level of real interest rates.

Government Purchases and Taxes

Now we bring the government into the picture. The government affects planned expenditure in two ways: through its purchases and through taxes.

FIXED LEVEL OF GOVERNMENT PURCHASES. As we saw in the planned expenditure Equation 1, government purchases add directly to planned expenditure. Here we

---

[3]If the government pegs the exchange rate to another currency so that it is fixed, in what is called a *fixed exchange rate regime* (see Chapter 17), then real interest rates do not directly affect net exports, as in Equation 7, and $NX = \overline{NX}$.

[4]Foreign aggregate output is outside the model, and so its effect on net exports is exogenous and hence is a factor that affects autonomous net exports. U.S. domestic output, Y, can also affect net exports because more domestic disposable income increases spending on imports and thus lowers net exports. To build this factor into the *IS* curve, we could modify the net export function given in Equation 7 as follows:

$$NX = \overline{NX} - xr - iY$$

where i is the marginal propensity to spend on imports. Using this equation instead of Equation 7 in the derivation of Equation 12 later in the chapter would lead to the *mpc* term being replaced by *mpc* − *i*.

assume that government purchases are also exogenous and so just write government purchases as follows:

$$G = \overline{G} \tag{8}$$

which says that government purchases are set at a fixed amount $\overline{G}$.

TAXES. The government affects spending through taxes because, as we discussed earlier, disposable income is equal to income minus taxes, $Y - T$, and disposable income affects consumption expenditure. Higher taxes T reduce disposable income for a given level of income and hence cause consumption expenditure to fall. The tax laws in a country like the United States are very complicated, so to keep the model simple, we assume that government taxes are exogenous and are set at a fixed amount $\overline{T}$:[5]

$$T = \overline{T} \tag{9}$$

 # Goods Market Equilibrium

Keynes recognized that equilibrium will occur in an economy when the total quantity of output produced in the economy equals the total amount of planned expenditure (aggregate demand). That is,

$$Y = Y^{pe} \tag{10}$$

When this equilibrium condition is satisfied, planned spending for goods and services is equal to the amount of goods and services produced. Producers are able to sell all their output and have no reason to change their production because there is no unplanned inventory investment. This analysis explains why aggregate output goes to a certain level by examining the factors that affect each component of planned spending.

Solving for Goods Market Equilibrium

With our understanding of what drives the components of planned expenditure, we can see how aggregate output is determined by using the planned expenditure Equation 1 to rewrite the equilibrium condition in Equation 10 as follows:

$$Y = C + I + G + NX \tag{11}$$

This equilibrium condition says that aggregate output will be the sum of consumption expenditure, planned investment spending, government purchases, and net exports.

   Now we can use our consumption, investment, and net export functions in Equations 3, 6, and 7, along with Equations 8 and 9, to determine aggregate

---

[5]For simplicity, we assume here that taxes are unrelated to income. However, because taxes increase with income, we can describe taxes with the following more realistic tax function:

$$T = \overline{T} + tY$$

Using this equation instead of Equation 9 in the derivation of Equation 12 later in the chapter would lead to *mpc* being replaced by *mpc* $(1 - t)$ in Equation 12.

output. Substituting all of these equations into the equilibrium condition yields the following:

$$Y = \overline{C} + mpc \times (Y - \overline{T}) - cr + \overline{I} - d(r + \overline{f}) + \overline{G} + \overline{NX} - xr$$

Collecting terms, we can rewrite this equation as follows:

$$Y = \overline{C} + \overline{I} - d\overline{f} + \overline{G} + \overline{NX} - mpc \times \overline{T} + mpc \times Y - (c + d + x)r$$

Subtracting $mpc \times Y$ from both sides of the equation gives

$$Y - mpc \times Y = Y(1 - mpc) = \overline{C} + \overline{I} - d\overline{f} + \overline{G} + \overline{NX} - mpc \times \overline{T} - (c + d + x)r$$

Then, dividing both sides of the equation by $1 - mpc$, we obtain an equation explaining how to determine aggregate output when the goods market is in equilibrium:[6]

$$Y = [\overline{C} + \overline{I} - d\overline{f} + \overline{G} + \overline{NX} - mpc \times \overline{T}] \times \frac{1}{1 - mpc} - \frac{c + d + x}{1 - mpc} \times r \quad (12)$$

Deriving the *IS* Curve

We refer to Equation 12 as the **IS curve**. The *IS* curve shows the relationship between aggregate output and the real interest rate when the goods market is in equilibrium. Equation 12 is made up of two terms. Since mpc is between zero and one, $1/(1 - mpc)$ is positive, so the first term tells us that increases in autonomous consumption, investment, government purchases, or net exports, or decreases in taxes or financial frictions, lead to an increase in output at any given real interest rate. In other words, the first term tells us about shifts in the *IS* curve. The second term tells us that an increase in real interest rates results in a decline in output, which is a movement along the *IS* curve.

 ## Understanding the *IS* Curve

To get a deeper understanding of the *IS* curve, we will proceed in several steps. In this section we begin by looking at the intuition behind the *IS* curve and then discuss a numerical example. We will also see how the *IS* curve relates to the saving-investment diagram of Chapter 4. Then, in the following section, we will outline the factors that shift the *IS* curve.

What the *IS* Curve Tells Us: Intuition

The *IS* curve traces out the points at which the goods market is in equilibrium. For each given level of the real interest rate, the *IS* curve tells us what aggregate output must be for the goods market to be in equilibrium. As the real interest rate rises, consumption expenditure, planned investment spending, and net exports fall, which in

---

[6]Note in Equation 12 that the term $1/(1 - mpc)$ that multiplies $\overline{G}$ is known as the *expenditure multiplier*, while the term $-mpc/(1 - mpc)$ that multiplies $\overline{T}$ is called the *tax multiplier* and is smaller in absolute value than the expenditure multiplier because $mpc < 1$. We discuss both of these multipliers in Chapter 16.

turn lowers planned expenditure; as a result, aggregate output must be lower for it to equal planned expenditure and satisfy the goods market equilibrium. Hence the *IS* curve is downward-sloping.

What the *IS* Curve Tells Us: Numerical Example

We can also better understand the *IS* curve with the following numerical example, in which we substitute specific values for the exogenous variables and for the parameters in Equation 12.

$$\overline{C} = \$1.3 \text{ trillion}$$
$$\overline{I} = \$1.2 \text{ trillion}$$
$$\overline{G} = \$3.0 \text{ trillion}$$
$$\overline{T} = \$3.0 \text{ trillion}$$
$$\overline{NX} = \$1.3 \text{ trillion}$$
$$\overline{f} = 1$$
$$mpc = 0.6$$
$$c = 0.1$$
$$d = 0.2$$
$$x = 0.1$$

With these values, we can rewrite Equation 12 as follows:

$$Y = [\,1.3 + 1.2 - 0.2 + 3.0 + 1.3 - 0.6 \times 3.0\,] \times \frac{1}{1 - 0.6} - \frac{0.1 + 0.2 + 0.1}{1 - 0.6} \times r$$

Simplifying Equation 12 yields the *IS* curve in Figure 9.1:

$$Y = \frac{4.8}{0.4} - \frac{0.4}{0.4} \times r = 12 - r \tag{13}$$

At a real interest rate $r = 3\%$, equilibrium output $Y = 12 - 3 = \$9$ trillion. We plot this combination of the real interest rate at equilibrium output as point A in Figure 9.1. At a real interest rate of $r = 1\%$, equilibrium output $Y = 12 - 1 = \$11$ trillion, which we plot as point B. The line connecting these points is the *IS* curve and, as you can see, it is downward-sloping.

Why the Economy Heads Toward Equilibrium

The concept of equilibrium is useful only if there is a tendency for the economy to settle there. Let's first consider what happens if the economy is located to the right of the *IS* curve (the orange shaded area), where there is an excess supply of goods. At point G in Figure 9.1 actual output of $10 trillion is above planned expenditure of $9 trillion, and so firms are saddled with unsold inventory. To keep from accumulating unsold goods, firms will cut production. As long as production is above the equilibrium level, output will exceed planned expenditure. Firms will continue cutting production, sending aggregate output toward the equilibrium level, as is indicated by the leftward arrow from point G to point A. Only when the economy moves to point A on the *IS* curve will there be no further tendency for output to change.

What happens if aggregate output is below the equilibrium level of output, where there is an excess demand for goods (the blue shaded area to the left of the *IS* curve)?

MyEconLab Mini-lecture

FIGURE 9.1

The *IS* Curve

The downward-sloping *IS* curve represents points at which the goods market is in equilibrium—in this case, points A and B. Notice that output changes as necessary to return to equilibrium. For example, at point G in the orange shaded area there is an excess supply of goods and so firms will cut production, decreasing aggregate output to the equilibrium level at point A. At point H in the blue shaded area there is an excess demand for goods, so firms will increase production and aggregate output will increase toward the equilibrium level at point B.

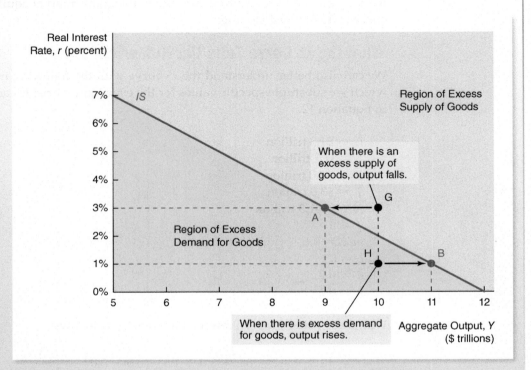

At point H in Figure 9.1, actual output is below planned expenditure, so firms will want to increase production because inventories are declining more than they desire, and aggregate output will increase, as shown by the rightward arrow. When the economy has moved to point B on the IS curve, there will again be no further tendency for output to change.

Why the *IS* Curve Has Its Name and Its Relationship with the Saving-Investment Diagram

To understand the *IS* curve's name, we need to recognize that the goods market equilibrium of the *IS* curve is equivalent to the equilibrium at which desired investment, *I*, equals desired saving, *S*, as in Chapter 4.[7] (Another way of saying this is that the goods market equilibrium that we discuss in this chapter is the same as the goods market equilibrium we discussed with the saving-investment diagram in Chapter 4.)

To illustrate, we look at the situation in which government purchases and net exports are both zero ($G = 0$ and $NX = 0$). Then goods market equilibrium occurs when

$$Y = C + I$$

Subtracting C from both sides of the preceding equation yields the following:

$$Y - C = I$$

---

[7]The name was given to the *IS* (an abbreviation for Investment-Saving) curve by Sir John Hicks in his famous paper, "Mr. Keynes and the Classics: A Suggested Interpretation," *Econometrica* (1937): 147–159.

FIGURE 9.2

A Saving-Investment Derivation of the *IS* Curve

Panels (a) and (b) demonstrate the relationship between saving and investment, and show the response of the *IS* curve to an increase in output. The rightward shift from S_1 to S_2 in the savings curve in panel (a) lowers the real interest rate, which leads to an increase in aggregate output in panel (b) that causes movement along the *IS* curve to a new equilibrium level at point 2.

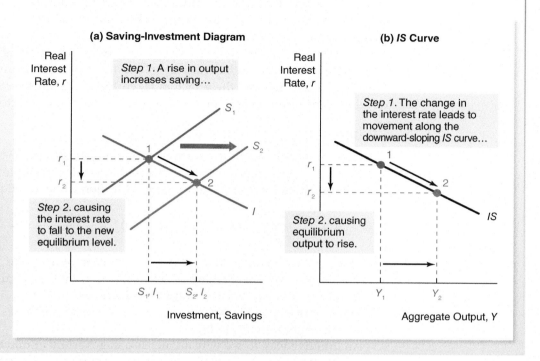

And since saving, S, is equal to $Y - C$, we can substitute to get

$$S = I$$

Hence goods market equilibrium occurs when $I = S$, and this is why the *IS* curve has its name.

Recognizing that the *IS* curve is the equilibrium level at which desired investment equals desired saving provides another way of deriving the *IS* curve: by using the saving and investment diagram we developed in Chapter 4. Consider the saving-investment diagram in panel (a) of Figure 9.2. The saving curves are upward-sloping because as the real interest rate rises, consumption expenditure falls, and saving, $S = Y - C$, rises. The investment curve is downward-sloping because as the interest rate rises, planned investment falls.

At any given level of the real interest rate r, when there is an increase in aggregate output Y, consumption increases by less than Y because the marginal propensity to consume is less than one. Thus, at any given level of r, an increase in Y will lead to an increase in $Y - C = S$. As we see in panel (a), when output rises, the saving curve shifts to the right from S_1 to S_2. Panel (a) demonstrates that as equilibrium output rises from Y_1 to Y_2, the real interest rate falls from r_1 to r_2. Panel (b) then plots the combinations of r and Y derived from equilibrium points 1 and 2 in panel (a), which leads to the movement along the downward-sloping IS curve that we saw in Figure 9.1.

Factors That Shift the *IS* Curve

You have now learned that the *IS* curve describes equilibrium points in the goods market—the combinations of the real interest rate and aggregate output that produce equilibrium. The *IS* curve shifts whenever there is a change in autonomous factors (factors independent of aggregate output and the real interest rate). Note that a change in the real interest rate that affects equilibrium aggregate output causes only a *movement along* the *IS* curve. A *shift* in the *IS* curve, by contrast, occurs when equilibrium output changes *at each given real interest rate*.

In Equation 12, we identified six candidates as autonomous factors that can shift planned expenditure and hence affect the level of equilibrium output. Although Equation 12 tells us how these factors taken together shift the *IS* curve, we will now develop some intuition as to how each separate autonomous factor does so.

Changes in Government Purchases

Let's look at what happens if government purchases rise from $3 trillion to $4 trillion in Figure 9.3. IS_1 represents the same *IS* curve that we developed in Figure 9.1. We determine the equation for IS_2 by inputting the $4 trillion value into Equation 12:

$$Y = [1.4 + 1.2 - 0.3 + 4.0 + 1.3 - 0.6 \times 3.0] \times \frac{1}{1 - 0.6} - r = \frac{5.8}{0.4} - r = 14.5 - r$$

Based on these results, at a real interest rate of $r = 3\%$, equilibrium output $Y = 14.5 - 3 = \$11.5$ trillion, which we mark as point C in Figure 9.3. At a real interest rate of $r = 1\%$, equilibrium output has increased to $Y = 14.5 - 1 = \$13.5$ trillion, which we mark as point D. The increase in government purchases therefore shifts the *IS* curve to the right from IS_1 to IS_2.

An intuitive way to see why an increase in government purchases leads to a rightward shift of the *IS* curve is to recognize that an increase in government purchases causes planned expenditure to increase at any given real interest rate. Since aggregate output

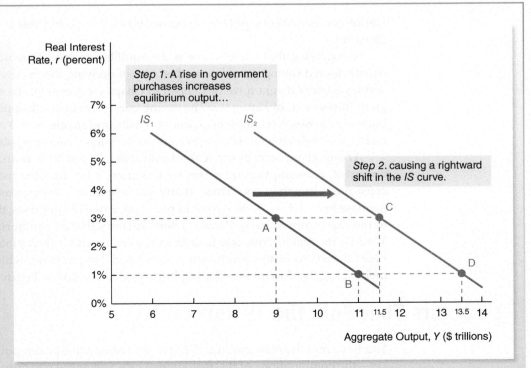

FIGURE 9.3

Shift in the *IS* Curve from an Increase in Government Purchases

IS_1 represents the *IS* curve we derived in Figure 9.1. IS_2 reflects a $1.0 trillion increase in government purchases. The increase in government purchases causes aggregate output to rise, shifting the *IS* curve to the right by $2.5 trillion from IS_1 to IS_2.

Real Interest Rate, *r* (percent)

Step 1. A rise in government purchases increases equilibrium output…

Step 2. causing a rightward shift in the *IS* curve.

Aggregate Output, *Y* ($ trillions)

equals planned expenditure when the goods market is in equilibrium, *an increase in government purchases that causes planned expenditure to rise also causes equilibrium output to rise, thereby shifting the IS curve to the right. Conversely, a decline in government purchases causes planned expenditure to fall at any given real interest rate, leading to a leftward shift of the IS curve.*

Application

The Vietnam War Buildup, 1964–1969

The United States' involvement in Vietnam began to escalate in the early 1960s. After 1964, the United States was fighting a full-scale war. Beginning in 1965, the resulting increases in military expenditure raised government purchases. How did policy makers make use of *IS* curve analysis to inform policy?

The rise in government purchases shifted the *IS* curve to the right, from IS_{1964} to IS_{1969} in Figure 9.4. Because the Federal Reserve decided to keep real interest rates constant at 2% during this period, equilibrium output rose from $3.0 trillion (in 2000 dollars) in 1964 to $3.8 trillion in 1969, with the unemployment rate falling steadily from 5% in 1964 to 3.4% in 1969. However, all was not well for the economy: the combination of an increase in government purchases and a constant real interest rate led to an overheating of the economy that eventually resulted in high inflation. (We will discuss the link between an overheating economy and inflation in the coming chapters.)

MyEconLab Mini-lecture

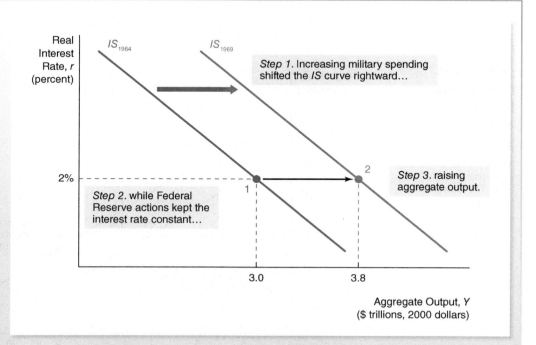

FIGURE 9.4

Vietnam War Buildup

Beginning in 1965, increases in military spending caused the *IS* curve to shift from IS_{1964} to IS_{1969}. Because the Federal Reserve decided to keep real interest rates constant at 2% during this period, equilibrium output rose from $3.0 trillion (in 2000 dollars) in 1964 to $3.8 trillion in 1969, setting the stage for an increase in inflation.

Step 1. Increasing military spending shifted the *IS* curve rightward...

Step 2. while Federal Reserve actions kept the interest rate constant...

Step 3. raising aggregate output.

Changes in Taxes

Now let's look at what happens in Figure 9.5 if the government raises taxes from $3 trillion to $4 trillion. IS_1 represents the same IS curve that we developed in Figure 9.1. We determine the equation for IS_2 by inputting the $4 trillion value in Equation 12:

$$Y = [1.3 + 1.2 - 0.2 + 3.0 + 1.3 - 0.6 \times 4.0] \times \frac{1}{1 - 0.6} - r = = \frac{4.2}{0.4} - r = 10.5 - r$$

At a real interest rate of $r = 3\%$, equilibrium output $Y = 10.5 - 3 = \$7.5$ trillion, which we mark as point E in Figure 9.5. At this real interest rate, equilibrium output has decreased from point A to point E, as shown by the leftward arrow. Similarly, at a real interest rate of $r = 1\%$, equilibrium output has decreased to $Y = 10.5 - 1 = \$9.5$ trillion, causing a leftward shift from point B to point F. The IS curve shifts to the left from IS_1 to IS_2 as a result of the increase in taxes.

We then have the following result: ***at any given real interest rate, a rise in taxes causes planned expenditure and hence equilibrium output to fall, thereby shifting the IS curve to the left. Conversely, a cut in taxes at any given real interest rate increases disposable income and causes planned expenditure and equilibrium output to rise, shifting the IS curve to the right***.

Policy makers use both tax and government purchases policies to stimulate the economy when it enters a recession, as the following Policy and Practice case illustrates.

MyEconLab Mini-lecture

FIGURE 9.5

Shift in the *IS* Curve from an Increase in Taxes

IS_1 represents the IS curve we derived in Figure 9.1. IS_2 reflects a $1.0 trillion increase in government tax revenue. The increase in taxes decreases aggregate output levels by $1.5 trillion, shifting the IS curve to the left from IS_1 to IS_2.

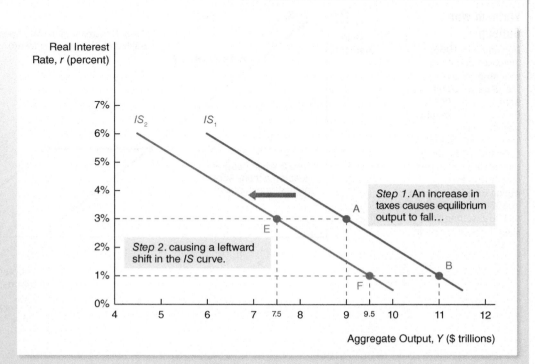

Changes in Autonomous Spending

As you can see in Equation 12, autonomous consumption, investment, and net exports—$\overline{C}$, $\overline{I}$, and $\overline{NX}$, respectively—all are multiplied by the term $1/(1 - mpc)$ in the same way the $\overline{G}$ term is. Thus an increase in any of these variables has the same impact on the *IS* curve as an increase in government purchases. For this reason, we can lump these variables together as **autonomous spending**, exogenous spending that is unrelated to variables in the model such as output or real interest rates. We look intuitively at how changes in each these variables affects the *IS* curve.

AUTONOMOUS CONSUMPTION. Earlier in the chapter, we learned that changes in the real interest rate affect consumption expenditure and hence the equilibrium level of output. This change in consumption expenditure merely causes a movement along the *IS* curve and not a shift. Suppose consumers find that their wealth has increased when there is a stock market boom, or they become increasingly optimistic about their future income prospects because there has been a positive productivity shock to the economy. Both of these events are autonomous, that is, they are not affected by the level of the real interest rate. *The resulting rise in autonomous consumption will raise planned expenditure and equilibrium output at any given interest rate, shifting the* **IS** *curve to the right. Conversely, a decline in autonomous consumption expenditure causes planned expenditure and equilibrium output to fall, shifting the* **IS** *curve to the left*.

Policy and Practice

The Fiscal Stimulus Package of 2009

In the fall of 2008, the U.S. economy was in crisis. By the time the new Obama administration had taken office, the unemployment rate had risen from 4.7% just before the recession began in December 2007 to 7.6% in January 2009. To stimulate the economy, the Obama administration proposed a fiscal stimulus package that, when passed by Congress, included $288 billion in tax cuts for households and businesses, and $499 billion in increased federal spending, including transfer payments. As our analysis indicates, these tax cuts and spending increases were intended to increase planned expenditure, thereby raising the equilibrium level of aggregate output at any given real interest rate and so shifting the *IS* curve to the right. Unfortunately, things didn't work out as the Obama administration had planned. Most of the government purchases did not kick in until after 2010, while the decline in autonomous consumption and investment were much larger than anticipated. The fiscal stimulus was more than offset by weak consumption and investment arising from an increase in financial frictions and worries about the economy, with the result that planned expenditure ended up contracting rather than expanding, and the *IS* curve did not shift to the right as hoped. Despite the good intentions of the fiscal stimulus package, the unemployment rate ended up rising to over 10% in 2009. Without the fiscal stimulus, however, the *IS* curve would likely have shifted further to the left, resulting in even more unemployment.

AUTONOMOUS INVESTMENT SPENDING. As with consumption expenditure, changes in planned investment spending resulting from a change in the real interest rate cause a movement along the *IS* curve rather than a shift. An autonomous rise in planned investment spending unrelated to the real interest rate—say, because companies become more confident about investment profitability after the stock market rises—increases planned expenditure. *An increase in autonomous investment spending therefore increases equilibrium output at any given interest rate, shifting the* **IS** *curve to the right. On the other hand, a decrease in autonomous investment spending causes planned expenditure and equilibrium output to fall, shifting the* **IS** *curve to the left*.

AUTONOMOUS NET EXPORTS. An autonomous rise in net exports unrelated to the real interest rate—say, because American-made handbags become more chic than French-made handbags, or because foreign countries have a boom and thus buy more U.S. goods—causes planned expenditure to rise. *An autonomous increase in net exports thus leads to an increase in equilibrium output at any given interest rate and shifts the* **IS** *curve to the right. Conversely, an autonomous fall in net exports causes planned expenditure and equilibrium output to decline, shifting the* **IS** *curve to the left*.

Changes in Financial Frictions

An increase in financial frictions, as occurred during the financial crisis of 2007–2009, raises the real interest rate for investments, r_i, at any given real interest rate on short-term, safe debt, r and hence causes investment spending and aggregate demand to fall. *An increase in financial frictions leads to a decline in equilibrium output at any given real interest rate and shifts the* **IS** *curve to the left. Conversely, a decline in financial frictions causes aggregate demand and equilibrium output to rise, shifting the* **IS** *curve to the right*.

Summary of Factors That Shift the *IS* Curve

As a study aid, Table 9.1 shows how each factor shifts the *IS* curve and the reason the shift occurs. Now that we have a full understanding of the *IS* curve, we can use this building block to examine the relationship between monetary policy and the aggregate demand curve in the following chapter.

| TABLE 9.1 | SHIFTS IN THE *IS* CURVE FROM AUTONOMOUS CHANGES IN $\overline{C}$, $\overline{I}$, $\overline{G}$, $\overline{T}$, $\overline{NX}$, AND $\overline{f}$ |

Variable	Change in Variable	Shift in *IS* Curve	Reason
Autonomous consumption expenditure, $\overline{C}$	↑	→	$C{\uparrow}\ Y{\uparrow}$
Autonomous investment, $\overline{I}$	↑	→	$I{\uparrow}\ Y{\uparrow}$
Government spending, $\overline{G}$	↑	→	$G{\uparrow}\ Y{\uparrow}$
Taxes, $\overline{T}$	↑	←	$T{\uparrow} \Rightarrow C{\downarrow}\ Y{\downarrow}$
Autonomous net exports, $\overline{NX}$	↑	→	$NX{\uparrow}\ Y{\uparrow}$
Financial frictions, $\overline{f}$	↑	←	$I{\downarrow}\ Y{\downarrow}$

Note: Only increases (↑) in the variables are shown; the effects of decreases in the variables on planned expenditure and aggregate output would be the opposite of those indicated in the last two columns.

SUMMARY

1. Aggregate demand, the total amount of goods demanded in an economy, is the same as planned expenditure, which is the sum of four types of spending: consumption expenditure, planned investment spending, government purchases, and net exports. We represent the total planned expenditure (Y^{pe}) with Equation 1: $Y^{pe} = C + I + G + NX$.

2. Consumption expenditure is described by the consumption function, which indicates that consumption expenditure will rise as disposable income increases. Consumption expenditure, planned investment spending, and net exports are all negatively related to real interest rates and positively related to their autonomous components. An increase in financial frictions raises the real interest rate for investments and hence lowers investment spending and aggregate demand. The government also affects planned expenditure by increased spending, which directly raises

planned expenditure, or by taxes, which indirectly affect planned expenditure by affecting disposable income and hence consumption expenditure.

3. The goods market is in equilibrium when aggregate output equals planned expenditure.

4. The *IS* curve traces out the combinations of the real interest rate and aggregate output at which the goods market is in equilibrium. The *IS* curve slopes downward because higher real interest rates lower consumption expenditure, planned investment spending, and net exports, and so lower equilibrium output.

5. The *IS* curve shifts to the right when there is a rise in autonomous consumption, a rise in autonomous investment, a rise in government purchases, a fall in taxes, a decline in financial frictions, or a rise in autonomous net exports. Movements of these six factors in the opposite directions will shift the *IS* curve to the left.

KEY TERMS

aggregate demand, p. 231
"animal spirits," p. 235
autonomous consumption expenditure, p. 233
autonomous investment, p. 235
autonomous net exports, p. 236
autonomous spending, p. 245
consumption expenditure, p. 232

consumption function, p. 232
disposable income, p. 232
exchange rate, p. 235
financial frictions, p. 235
fixed investment, p. 233
government purchases, p. 232
inventory investment, p. 233
IS curve, p. 238

marginal propensity to consume, p. 233
net exports, p. 232
planned expenditure, p. 231
planned investment spending, p. 232

REVIEW QUESTIONS

All Questions are available in MyEconLab for practice or instructor assignment.

Planned Expenditure

1. What are the four components of planned expenditure, and why did Keynesian analysis emphasize this concept?

The Components of Expenditure

2. According to the consumption function, what variables determine aggregate spending on consumer goods and services? How is consumption related to each of these variables?

3. What are the two types of planned investment spending?

4. How and why do changes in the real interest rate affect planned investment spending?

5. How does an increase in financial frictions affect planned investment spending?

6. How and why do changes in the real interest rate affect net exports?

Goods Market Equilibrium

7. What condition is required for equilibrium in the goods market?

8. What happens to aggregate output if unplanned inventory investment is either positive or negative?

Understanding the *IS* Curve

9. What does the *IS* curve show? Why does it slope downward?

Factors That Shift the *IS* Curve

10. What causes the *IS* curve to shift?

PROBLEMS

All Problems are available in MyEconLab *for practice or instructor assignment.*

Planned Expenditure

1. The Bureau of Economic Analysis valued nominal U.S. gross domestic product (i.e., actual expenditure) at $16,420 billion at the end of 2012. Suppose that consumption expenditure was $12,210 billion, planned investment spending was $1,680 billion, and government spending was $2,970 billion.

a) Assuming goods market is in equilibrium, calculate spending on net exports.

b) If U.S. imports are valued at $2,100 billion, calculate spending on U.S. exports.

The Components of Expenditure

2. Assume the following estimates:

Autonomous consumption: $1,625 billion
Disposable income: $11,500 billion

Using the consumption function in Equation 2, calculate consumption expenditure if an increase of $1,000 in disposable income leads to an increase of $750 in consumption expenditure.

3. Calculate consumption expenditure using the consumption function (as described by Equation 2) and the following estimates:

Autonomous consumption: $1,450 billion
Income: $14,000 billion
Taxes: $3,000 billion
Marginal propensity to consume: 0.8

4. Suppose that Dell Corporation has 20,000 computers in its warehouses on December 31, 2016, ready to be shipped to merchants (each computer is valued at $500). By December 31, 2017, Dell Corporation has 25,000 computers ready to be shipped, each valued at $450.

   a) Calculate Dell's inventory on December 31, 2016.
   b) Calculate Dell's inventory investment in 2017.
   c) What happens to inventory spending during the early stages of an economic recession?

Factors That Shift the *IS* Curve

5. Suppose the U.S. Congress declares China to be a "currency manipulator" and therefore legislates a tariff on Chinese goods. Considering only the decrease in imports,
   a) comment on the effect of such a measure on the *IS* curve.
   b) show your answer graphically.
6. Part of the 2009 stimulus package ($93 billion) was paid out in the form of tax credits. However, even though interest rates did not change significantly during that year, aggregate output did not increase. Using the parameters from the numerical example on page 239,
   a) calculate the decrease in autonomous consumption expenditure necessary to offset the effect of the $93 billion tax cut.
   b) show your answer graphically (show the effects of the tax cut and the decrease in autonomous consumption expenditure).
7. After the press conference that followed the Federal Open Market Committee meeting on June 19, 2013, there were reports in the media that Chairman Bernanke's comments were a signal that the Fed would raise interest rates sooner than expected. As a result, the yield on 10-year U.S. Treasury notes rose to almost 2.6%, the highest level since August 2011.
   a) Comment on how this would affect the *IS* curve.
   b) Show your answer graphically.
8. Suppose you read in the newspaper that prospects for stronger future economic growth will lead the dollar to strengthen and stock prices to increase.
   a) Comment only on the effect of the strengthened dollar on the *IS* curve.
   b) Comment only on the effect of the increase in stock prices on the *IS* curve.
9. Referring to Problem 8, what is the combined effect of these two events on the *IS* curve?

DATA ANALYSIS PROBLEMS

The Problems update with real-time data in MyEconLab *and are available for practice or instructor assignment.*

1. Go to the St. Louis Federal Reserve FRED database, and find data on Personal Consumption Expenditures (PCEC), Personal Consumption Expenditures: Durable Goods (PCDG), Personal Consumption Expenditures: Nondurable Goods (PCND), and Personal Consumption Expenditures: Services (PCESV).
   a) What percentage of total household expenditures is devoted to the consumption of goods (both durable and nondurable)?
   b) Given these data, which specific component of household expenditures would be most impacted by a reduction in overall household spending? Explain.
2. Go to the St. Louis Federal Reserve FRED database, and find data on the most recent values for Personal Income (PINCOME), Disposable Personal Income (DPI), and Personal Consumption Expenditures (PCEC).
   a) For the most recent quarter available, compute the difference between personal income and disposable personal income. What does the value of the difference between personal income and disposable personal income represent?
   b) Find personal consumption and disposable income, and calculate the average

of both of these over the last four quarters of data available, and over the four quarters prior to that. Calculate the changes in personal consumption and disposable income over the two periods, and the ratio of the changes. What is this ratio? Given the fact that disposable income increases dollar-for-dollar with a tax reduction, what can you conclude about the effect of a tax cut on spending by households?

3. Go to the St. Louis Federal Reserve FRED database, and find data on Real Private Domestic Investment (GPDIC1); a measure of the real interest rate, the 10-year Treasury Inflation-Indexed Security, *TIIS* (FII10); and a measure of financial frictions, the St. Louis Fed Financial Stress Index (STLFSI). For (FII10) and (STLFSI), convert the *frequency* setting to "quarterly" and download the data into a spreadsheet. For each quarter, add the (FII10) and (STLFSI) series to create r_i, the real interest rate for investments for that quarter. Then, calculate the change in both investment and r_i as the change in each variable from the previous quarter.

a) For the four most recent quarters available, calculate the average change in investment.

b) Assume that there is a one-quarter lag between movements in r_i and changes in investment; in other words, if r_i changes in the current quarter, it will affect investment in the next quarter. For the most recent quarters available, calculate the one-quarter lagged average change in r_i.

c) Take the ratio of your answer from part (a) divided by your answer from part (b). What does this value represent? Briefly explain.

d) Repeat parts (a) through (c) for the period 2008:Q3 to 2009:Q2. How do financial frictions help explain the behavior of investment during the financial crisis? How does the coefficient on investment compare between the current period and the financial crisis period? Briefly explain.

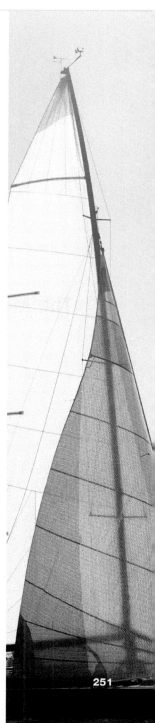

Monetary Policy and Aggregate Demand

10

Preview

At the height of the financial crisis in December 2008, the Federal Open Market Committee of the Federal Reserve announced a surprisingly bold policy decision that sent markets into a frenzy. The committee lowered the federal funds rate, the interest rate charged on overnight loans between banks, by seventy-five basis points (0.75 percentage point), moving the federal funds rate almost all the way to zero. The whole world wondered if this bold move would jolt the economy out of recession. Would it boost stock market values? Would it trigger higher inflation?

The short-run model of the aggregate economy that we are building step by step will allow us to analyze how a central bank's policy decisions affect the economy. We start this chapter by explaining why monetary policy makers set interest rates to rise when inflation increases, leading to a positive relationship between real interest rates and inflation, which is called the *monetary policy (MP) curve*. Then, using the *MP* curve with the *IS* curve we developed in the preceding chapter, we derive the *aggregate demand curve*, a key element in the aggregate demand-aggregate supply model framework used in the rest of this book to discuss short-run economic fluctuations.

The Federal Reserve and Monetary Policy

Central banks throughout the world use a very short-term interest rate on safe debt as their primary policy tool. In the United States, the Federal Reserve conducts monetary policy via its setting of the federal funds rate, the interest rate at which banks lend to each other overnight. For example, after the FOMC meeting of September 1–18, 2013, the Federal Reserve issued a statement that read, "[the] Committee decided to keep the target range for the federal funds rate at 0 to ¼ percent."

The Federal Reserve controls the federal funds rate by varying the liquidity it provides to the banking system. When the Fed provides more liquidity, banks have more money to lend to each other, and this excess liquidity causes the federal funds rate to fall. When the Fed drains liquidity from the banking system, banks have less to lend, and the shortage of liquidity leads to a rise in the federal funds rate. How the Federal Reserve sets the federal funds rate is discussed in more detail at the end of this chapter, but for now it is enough to know that the Federal Reserve has the ability to set the federal funds rate at whatever level it chooses.

The federal funds rate is a *nominal* interest rate, but as we learned in the previous chapter, it is the *real* interest rate that affects household and business spending, thereby determining the level of equilibrium output. How does the Federal Reserve's control of the federal funds rate enable it to control the real interest rate, through which monetary policy impacts the economy?

Recall from Chapter 2 that the real interest rate, r, is the nominal interest rate, i, minus expected inflation, π^e.

$$r = i - \pi^e$$

Changes in nominal interest rates can change the real interest rate only if actual and expected inflation remain unchanged in the short run. Here is where sticky prices, which we discussed in Chapter 8, enter the picture. When prices are sticky, changes in monetary policy will not have an immediate effect on inflation and expected inflation. As a result, **when the Federal Reserve lowers the federal funds rate, real interest rates fall; and when the Federal Reserve raises the federal funds rate, real interest rates rise**.

It is important to note that although the Federal Reserve can determine the real interest rate in the short run, it is not able to control the real interest rate in the long run. In the long run, prices are flexible. Recall from Chapter 4 that the real interest rate in the long run is determined by the interaction of saving and investment and *not* by the central bank. Indeed, we will see that the aggregate demand-aggregate supply model comes to exactly the same conclusion when analyzing the economy in the long run.

The Monetary Policy Curve

We have now seen how the Federal Reserve can control real interest rates in the short run. The next step in our analysis is to examine how monetary policy reacts to inflation. The **monetary policy (MP) curve** indicates the relationship between the real interest rate set by the central bank and the inflation rate. We can write this relationship as follows:

$$r = \bar{r} + \lambda\pi \tag{1}$$

where $\bar{r}$ is the autonomous (exogenous) component of the real interest rate set by the monetary policy authorities, which is unrelated to the current level of the inflation rate or to any other variable in the model, and where λ is the responsiveness of the real interest rate to the inflation rate.

To make our discussion of the monetary policy curve more concrete, Figure 10.1 shows an example of a monetary policy curve MP in which $\bar{r} = 1.0$ and $\lambda = 0.5$:

$$r = 1.0 + 0.5\,\pi \tag{2}$$

At point A, where inflation is at 1%, the Federal Reserve sets the real interest rate at 1.5%; at point B, where inflation is at 2%, the Fed sets the real interest rate at 2%; and at point C, where inflation is at 3%, the Fed sets the real interest rate at 2.5%. The line going through points A, B, and C is the monetary policy curve MP, and it is upward-sloping, indicating that monetary policy raises real interest rates when the inflation rate rises.

FIGURE 10.1

The Monetary Policy Curve

The upward slope of the *MP* curve indicates that the central bank raises real interest rates when inflation rises because monetary policy follows the Taylor principle.

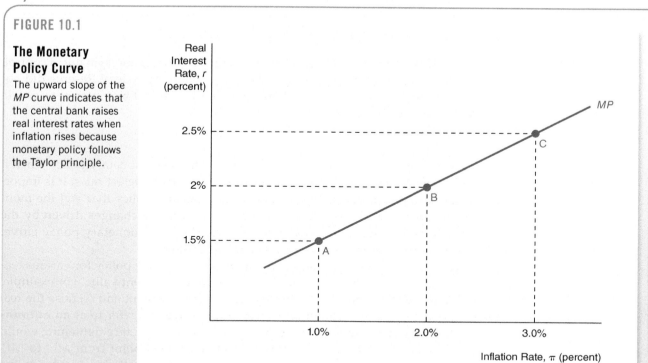

The Taylor Principle: Why the Monetary Policy Curve Has an Upward Slope

To see why the *MP* curve has an upward slope, we need to recognize that central banks seek to keep inflation stable. In order to stabilize inflation, monetary policy makers follow the **Taylor principle,** named after John Taylor of Stanford University, in which they raise *nominal* rates by more than any expected rise in inflation, so that *real* interest rates rise when there is a rise in inflation, as the *MP* curve suggests.[1] John Taylor and many other researchers have found that monetary policy makers tend to follow the Taylor principle in practice.

To see why monetary policy makers follow the Taylor principle, in which higher inflation results in higher real interest rates, consider what would happen if monetary policy makers instead allowed the real interest rate to fall when inflation rose. In this case, an increase in inflation would lead to a decline in the real interest rate, which would increase aggregate output, which would in turn cause inflation to rise further, which would cause the real interest rate to fall further, increasing aggregate output further.

[1]Note that the Taylor principle differs from the Taylor rule, which we will describe in Chapter 13, in that it does not provide a precise rule for how monetary policy should react to conditions in the economy, whereas the Taylor rule does.

Schematically, we can write this as follows:

$$\pi\uparrow \Rightarrow r\downarrow \Rightarrow Y\uparrow \Rightarrow \pi\uparrow \Rightarrow r\downarrow \Rightarrow Y\uparrow \Rightarrow \pi\uparrow$$

The result would be that inflation would continually keep rising and spin out of control. Indeed, this is exactly what happened in the 1970s, when the Federal Reserve did not raise nominal interest rates by as much as inflation rose, so that real interest rates fell. Inflation accelerated to over 10%.[2]

Shifts in the *MP* Curve

In common parlance, the Federal Reserve is said to "tighten" monetary policy when it raises real interest rates, and to "ease" it when it lowers real interest rates. It is important, however, to distinguish between changes in monetary policy that *shift* the monetary policy curve, which we call autonomous changes, and changes driven by the Taylor principle, which are reflected as *movements along* the monetary policy curve. Such changes are called *automatic* adjustments to interest rates.

Central banks may make autonomous changes to monetary policy for various reasons. They may wish to change the inflation rate from its current value. For example, to lower inflation, they could increase $\bar{r}$ by one percentage point and so raise the real interest rate at any given inflation rate, an action that we will refer to as an **autonomous tightening of monetary policy.** This autonomous monetary tightening would shift the monetary policy curve upward by one percentage point from MP_1 to MP_2 in Figure 10.2, thereby causing the economy to contract and inflation to fall. Or, the banks may have information unrelated to inflation that suggests interest rates must be adjusted to achieve good economic outcomes. For example, if the economy is going into a recession, monetary policy makers will want to lower real interest rates at any given inflation rate, an **autonomous easing of monetary policy,** in order to stimulate the economy and prevent inflation from falling. This autonomous easing of monetary policy would result in a downward shift of the monetary policy curve, say by one percentage point, from MP_1 to MP_3 in Figure 10.2.

Movements Along the *MP* Curve Versus Shifts in the Curve

A stumbling block for many students in understanding the aggregate demand-aggregate supply (*AD/AS*) framework that we will be studying in coming chapters is the distinction between shifts in the *MP* curve versus movements along the *MP* curve. Movements along the *MP* curve—that is, movements from point A to B to C in Figure 10.1—should be viewed as a central bank's normal response (also known as an endogenous response) of raising interest rates when inflation is rising. Thus we can think of a movement along the *MP* curve as a rise in the interest rate as inflation rises, which is an automatic response of the central bank to a change in inflation. Such a response does not involve a shift in the *MP* curve.

On the other hand, when the central bank raises interest rates *at a given level of the inflation rate,* that is, $\bar{r}$ rises in Equation 1, this is not an automatic response to higher inflation, but is rather an autonomous tightening of monetary policy that shifts the *MP* curve up, from MP_1 to MP_2 in Figure 10.2.

---

[2]In an appendix to Chapter 12, we formally demonstrate the instability of inflation when central banks do not follow the Taylor principle.

FIGURE 10.2

Shifts in the Monetary Policy Curve

Autonomous changes in monetary policy, such as when a central bank changes the real interest rate at any given inflation rate, shift the MP curve. An autonomous tightening of monetary policy that increases the real interest rate shifts the MP curve up to MP_2, while an autonomous easing of monetary policy that lowers the real interest rate shifts the MP curve down to MP_3.

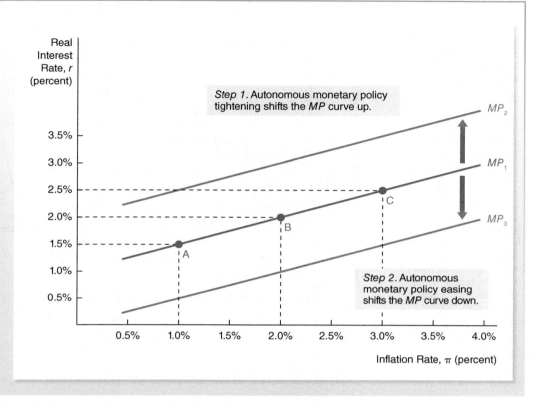

Step 1. Autonomous monetary policy tightening shifts the MP curve up.

Step 2. Autonomous monetary policy easing shifts the MP curve down.

The distinction between autonomous monetary policy changes and movements along the monetary policy curve is illustrated by the following two Policy and Practice cases, which outline the monetary policy actions taken by the Federal Reserve during the period from 2004 to 2006, and the actions taken in the fall of 2007, at the onset of the 2007–2009 financial crisis.

Policy and Practice

Movements Along the MP curve: The Rise in the Federal Funds Rate Target, 2004–2006

Fears of deflation—i.e., fears that inflation could turn negative—led the Federal Reserve to commit to keeping the federal funds rate at the very low level of 1% from June of 2003 to June of 2004. However, with the economy growing rapidly, inflationary pressures began to rise, and the FOMC decided at its June 2004 meeting to increase the federal funds rate by ¼ of a percentage point. Furthermore, the FOMC made this process an automatic one, raising the federal funds rate by exactly the same amount at every subsequent FOMC meeting through June of 2006 (see Figure 10.3). These monetary policy actions were clearly movements along the MP curve, similar to the movements from point A to B to C in Figure 10.1.

FIGURE 10.3

The Inflation Rate and the Federal Funds Rate, 2003–2013

From June of 2004 through June of 2006, because of pressures from rising inflation, the Fed increased the federal funds rate by ¼ of a percentage point at every FOMC meeting. The Fed began an aggressive autonomous easing of monetary policy in September 2007, bringing down its policy rate, the federal funds rate, despite the continuing high inflation.

Source: Federal Reserve Bank of St. Louis. FRED database. http://research .stlouisfed.org/fred2/ categories/118

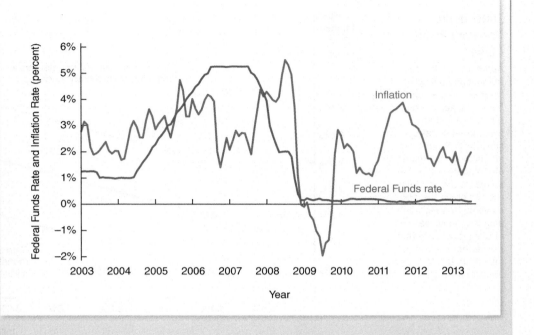

Policy and Practice

Shifts in the *MP* Curve: Autonomous Monetary Easing at the Onset of the 2007–2009 Financial Crisis

When the financial crisis started in August 2007, inflation was rising and economic growth was quite strong. A movement along the *MP* curve should have suggested that the Fed continue to raise interest rates, but instead the Fed did the opposite: it began an aggressive lowering of the federal funds rate, despite the rising inflation rate, as shown in Figure 10.3. The Fed thus shifted the monetary policy curve downward, from MP_1 to MP_3, as shown in Figure 10.2. The Fed pursued this autonomous monetary policy easing because the negative shock to the economy caused by the disruption to financial markets (more about this in Chapter 15) indicated that, despite the currently high inflation rates, the economy was likely to weaken in the near future, and the inflation rate would fall. Indeed, this is exactly what came to pass, with the economy going into recession in December 2007, and the inflation rate falling sharply after July 2008.

The Aggregate Demand Curve

We are now ready to derive the relationship between the inflation rate and aggregate output when the goods market is in equilibrium. This relationship is shown graphically by the **aggregate demand curve.** The *MP* curve we developed earlier in the chapter demonstrates how central banks respond to changes in inflation with changes in interest rates, in line with the Taylor principle. The *IS* curve we developed in Chapter 9 showed that changes in interest rates, in turn, affect equilibrium output. With these two curves, we can now link the quantity of aggregate output demanded with the inflation rate, given the public's expectations of inflation and the stance of monetary policy. The aggregate demand curve is central to the aggregate demand and supply analysis we develop further in the next two chapters, which allows us to explain short-run fluctuations in both aggregate output and inflation.

Deriving the Aggregate Demand Curve Graphically

Using the hypothetical *MP* curve from ... we know that when the inflation rate rises from 1% to 2% to 3%, r ... m 1.5% to 2% to 2.5%. We plot these points in panel (a) of F ... form the *MP* curve. In panel (b), we graph the *IS* curv ... 9 ($Y = 12 - r$). As the real interest rate rises ... moves from point 1 to point 2 to point 3 ... 10 trillion to $9.5 trillion. In ot ... vestment, and net exports c ... nel (c) demonstrates that as ir ... es from point 1 to point 2 to ... $10 trillion to $9.5 trillion.

The line that ... ate demand curve, *AD*, and i ... ing to each of the three real interest ... market for any given inflation rate. The a ... d slope, because a higher inflation rate leads th ... rest rates, thereby lowering planned spending and hen ... uilibrium aggregate output.

By using some algebra (see the box, "Der ... gregate Demand Curve Algebraically"), the *AD* curve in Figure 10.4 can be w ... umerically as follows:

$$Y = 11 - 0.5\,\pi \tag{3}$$

Factors That Shift the Aggregate Demand Curve

Movements along the aggregate demand curve describe how the equilibrium level of aggregate output changes as the inflation rate changes. When factors other than the inflation rate change, however, the aggregate demand curve can shift. We first review the factors that shift the *IS* curve, and then consider the factors that shift the *AD* curve.

MyEconLab Mini-lecture

FIGURE 10.4

Deriving the AD Curve

The *MP* curve in panel (a) shows that as inflation rises from 1.0% to 2.0% to 3.0%, the real interest rate rises from 1.5% to 2.0% to 2.5%. The *IS* curve in panel (b) then shows that higher real interest rates lead to lower planned investment spending, and hence aggregate output falls from $10.5 trillion to $10.0 trillion to $9.5 trillion. Finally, panel (c) plots the level of equilibrium output corresponding to each of the three real interest rates: the line that connects these points is the *AD* curve, and it is downward-sloping.

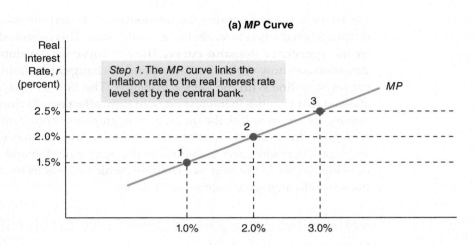

(a) MP Curve

Step 1. The *MP* curve links the inflation rate to the real interest rate level set by the central bank.

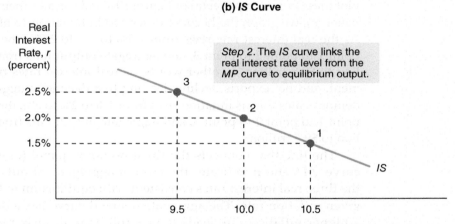

(b) IS Curve

Step 2. The *IS* curve links the real interest rate level from the *MP* curve to equilibrium output.

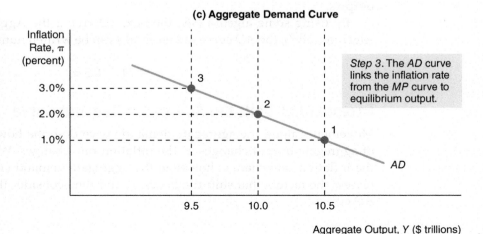

(c) Aggregate Demand Curve

Step 3. The *AD* curve links the inflation rate from the *MP* curve to equilibrium output.

Deriving the Aggregate Demand Curve Algebraically

To derive the numerical *AD* curve, we start by taking the numerical *IS* curve, Equation 13 from the preceding chapter:

$$Y = 12 - r$$

We then substitute in for *r* from the numerical *MP* curve in Equation 2, $r = 1.0 + 0.5\,\pi$, to yield

$$Y = 12 - (1.0 + 0.5\,\pi) = (12 - 1) - 0.5\,\pi = 11 - 0.5\,\pi$$

as in the text.

Similarly, we can derive a more general version of the *AD* curve using the algebraic version of the *IS* curve from Equation 12 in Chapter 9,

$$Y = [\overline{C} + \overline{I} - d\overline{f} + \overline{G} + \overline{NX} - mpc \times \overline{T}] \times \frac{1}{1 - mpc} - \frac{c + d + x}{1 - mpc} \times r$$

and then substitute in for *r* from the algebraic *MP* curve in Equation 1, $r = \overline{r} + \lambda\pi$, to yield the more general *AD* curve:

$$Y = [\overline{C} + \overline{I} - d\overline{f} + \overline{G} + \overline{NX} - mpc \times \overline{T}] \times \frac{1}{1 - mpc} - \frac{c + d + x}{1 - mpc} \times (\overline{r} + \lambda\pi) \qquad (4)$$

SHIFTS IN THE *IS* CURVE. We saw in Chapter 9 that six factors cause the *IS* curve to shift. It turns out that these same factors cause the aggregate demand curve to shift as well:

1. Autonomous consumption expenditure

2. Autonomous investment spending

3. Government purchases

4. Taxes

5. Autonomous net exports

6. Financial frictions

We examine how changes in these factors lead to a shift in the aggregate demand curve in Figure 10.5.

Suppose that inflation is at 2.0% and so the *MP* curve shows that the real interest rate is at 2.0% in Figure 10.5 panel (a). The IS_1 curve in panel (b) then shows that the equilibrium level of output is at $10 trillion at point A_1, which corresponds to an equilibrium level of output of $10 trillion at point A_1 on the AD_1 curve in panel (c).

MyEconLab Mini-lecture

FIGURE 10.5

Shift in the *AD* Curve From Shifts in the *IS* Curve

At a 2% inflation rate in panel (a), the monetary policy curve indicates that the real interest rate is 2%. An increase in government purchases shifts the *IS* curve to the right in panel (b). At a given inflation rate and real interest rate of 2.0%, equilibrium output rises from $10 trillion to $12.5 trillion, which is shown as a movement from point A_1 to point A_2 in panel (c), shifting the aggregate demand curve to the right from AD_1 to AD_2. Any factor that shifts the *IS* curve shifts the *AD* curve in the same direction.

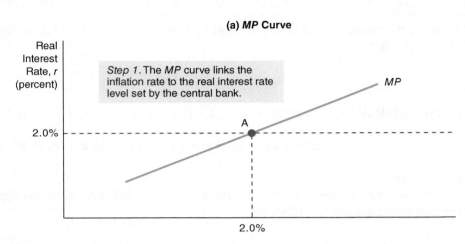

(a) *MP* Curve

Step 1. The *MP* curve links the inflation rate to the real interest rate level set by the central bank.

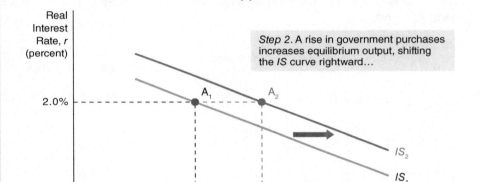

(b) *IS* Curve

Step 2. A rise in government purchases increases equilibrium output, shifting the *IS* curve rightward…

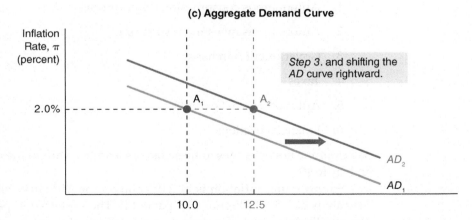

(c) Aggregate Demand Curve

Step 3. and shifting the *AD* curve rightward.

Now suppose there is rise in, for example, government purchases by $1 trillion. Panel (b) shows that with the inflation rate and real interest both held constant at 2.0%, the equilibrium moves from point A_1 to point A_2, with output rising to $12.5 trillion,[3] so the IS curve shifts to the right from IS_1 to IS_2. The rise in output to $12.5 trillion means that, holding inflation and the real interest rate constant, the equilibrium in panel (c) also moves from point A_1 to point A_2, and so the AD curve also shifts to the right from AD_1 to AD_2.

Figure 10.5 shows that *any factor that shifts the IS curve shifts the aggregate demand curve in the same direction*. Therefore, "animal spirits" that encourage a rise in autonomous consumption spending or planned investment spending, a rise in government purchases, a fall in taxes, a fall in financial frictions, or an autonomous rise in net exports—all of which shift the IS curve to the right—will also shift the aggregate demand curve to the right. Conversely, a fall in autonomous consumption spending, a fall in planned investment spending, a fall in government purchases, a rise in taxes, a rise in financial frictions, or an autonomous fall in net exports will cause the aggregate demand curve to shift to the left.

SHIFTS IN THE *MP* CURVE. We now examine what happens to the aggregate demand curve when the MP curve shifts. Suppose the Federal Reserve decides to autonomously tighten monetary policy by raising the real interest rate by one percentage point at any given level of the inflation rate because it is worried about the economy overheating. At an inflation rate of 2.0%, the real interest rate rises from 2.0% to 3.0% in Figure 10.6. The MP curve shifts up from MP_1 to MP_2 in panel (a). Panel (b) shows that when the inflation rate is at 2.0%, the higher interest rate results in the equilibrium moving from point A_1 to point A_2 on the IS curve, with output falling from $10 trillion to $9 trillion. The lower output of $9 trillion occurs because the higher real interest rate leads to a decline in consumption, investment, and net exports, which lowers aggregate demand. The lower output of $9 trillion then decreases the equilibrium output level from point A_1 to point A_2 in panel (c), and so the AD curve shifts to the left from AD_1 to AD_2.

Our conclusion from Figure 10.6 is that *an autonomous tightening of monetary policy—that is, a rise in the real interest rate at any given inflation rate—shifts the aggregate demand curve to the left. Similarly, an autonomous easing of monetary policy shifts the aggregate demand curve to the right*.

We have now derived and analyzed the aggregate demand curve—an essential element in the aggregate demand and supply framework that we examine in the next two chapters. We will use the aggregate demand curve in this framework to determine both aggregate output and inflation, as well as to examine events that cause these variables to change.

---

[3]As we saw in the numerical example in Chapter 9, a rise in government purchases by $1 trillion leads to a $2.5 trillion increase in equilibrium output at any given real interest rate, and this is why output rises from $10 trillion to $12.5 trillion when the real interest rate is 2.0%.

MyEconLab Mini-lecture

FIGURE 10.6

Shift in the *AD* Curve from Autonomous Monetary Policy Tightening

Autonomous monetary tightening that raises real interest rates by one percentage point at any given inflation rate shifts the *MP* curve up from MP_1 to MP_2 in panel (a). With the inflation rate at 2.0%, the higher 3% interest rate results in a movement from point A_1 to point A_2 on the *IS* curve, with output falling from $10 trillion to $9 trillion. This change in equilibrium output leads to movement from point A_1 to point A_2 in panel (c), shifting the aggregate demand curve to the left from AD_1 to AD_2.

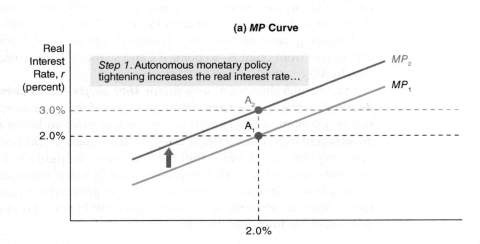

(a) *MP* Curve

Step 1. Autonomous monetary policy tightening increases the real interest rate...

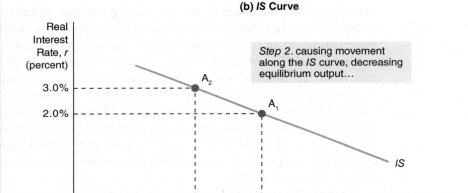

(b) *IS* Curve

Step 2. causing movement along the *IS* curve, decreasing equilibrium output...

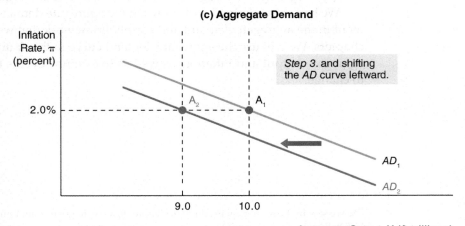

(c) Aggregate Demand

Step 3. and shifting the *AD* curve leftward.

The Money Market and Interest Rates

Earlier in the chapter, we gave only a very brief description of how the Federal Reserve sets the federal funds rate. At this point we will go into more detail, to describe how the Federal Reserve sets this nominal interest rate by analyzing the market for money using the **liquidity preference framework,** which determines the equilibrium nominal interest rate by equating the supply and demand for money.

Liquidity Preference and the Demand for Money

John Maynard Keynes developed a theory of money demand that he described as *liquidity preference theory*—hence the name of the framework—that carefully distinguishes between nominal quantities and real quantities. The nominal quantity of money is in terms of units of currency, like $50 billion. Liquidity preference theory, however, examines the demand for money in terms of the real goods and services it can buy. So, for example, if the price level doubled, the same $50 billion would buy only half as many goods. Keynes reasoned that when people decide how much money they want to hold (demand), they consider **real money balances,** the quantity of money in real terms.

In this model, demand for real money balances depends on real income, Y, and the nominal interest rate, i. We present Keynes' liquidity preference theory in equation form as follows:

$$M^d/P = L(\underset{-}{i}, \ \underset{+}{Y})$$

(5)

We refer to Equation 5 as the **liquidity preference function.** The minus sign below i means that as the nominal interest rate, i, rises, the demand for real money balances falls; the plus sign below Y means that as income, Y, rises, the demand for real money balances also rises. (See the chapter appendix for further discussion of Keynesian and other theories of money demand, as well as the empirical evidence on money demand.)

Why would the demand for real money balances have a negative relationship with the nominal interest rate i? The intuition for this relationship is provided by the concept of **opportunity cost** that you learned about in your principles of economics course. Recall that opportunity cost is the amount of income forgone (sacrificed) by holding money rather than alternative assets such as bonds. In Keynes's analysis, money earns little, if any, interest, since it is held as currency or in checking accounts. The opportunity cost of holding money is i, the nominal interest paid on bonds. As the interest rate i rises, it becomes more costly to hold money instead of bonds—that is, the opportunity cost rises—and the quantity of money demanded falls. Note that the demand for real money balances is related to the *nominal* interest rate i, while spending decisions are related to the *real* interest rate.

Real money balances are positively related to income for two reasons:

1. As income rises, households and firms conduct more transactions and so keep more money on hand to make purchases.

2. Higher incomes make households and firms wealthier, and the wealthy tend to hold larger quantities of all financial assets, including money.

Demand Curve for Money

The first step in our analysis is to use the liquidity preference function to obtain a demand curve that shows the relationship between the quantity demanded of real money balances and the interest rate when we hold all other economic variables, such as income, constant by treating their values as given. Because our analysis is for the short run, we will assume that prices are sticky and so the price level is fixed in the short run at $\overline{P}$. Referring to Figure 10.7, suppose that for a given level of income, at an interest rate of i_1, the quantity of real money balances that people want to hold is $M_1/\overline{P}$, which we mark as point A. As the liquidity preference function shows, lower interest rates encourage firms and households to desire higher quantities of real money balances, since the opportunity cost of holding money falls. When the interest rate falls to i^*, the quantity of real money balances demanded rises to $\overline{M}/\overline{P}$, marked as point E. As the rate falls to i_2 and the opportunity cost of money declines further, the quantity of real money balances demanded rises again to $M_2/\overline{P}$, at point D. Connecting these points— A, E, and D—creates the demand curve for real money balances, MD, in Figure 10.7. It slopes downward, since lower interest rates increase the quantity of real money balances demanded, all else being equal.

MyEconLab Mini-lecture

FIGURE 10.7

Equilibrium in the Money Market

The demand curve for real money balances, *MD*, slopes downward because as the interest rate and the opportunity cost of holding money fall, the quantity of money demanded rises. The supply curve for real money balances, *MS*, is vertical because the central bank sets the money supply at $\overline{M}$ and the price level is given at $\overline{P}$ in the short run, so the quantity supplied of real money balances is fixed at $\overline{M}/\overline{P}$ at any given interest rate. Equilibrium in the money market occurs at the intersection of the *MD* and *MS* curves at point E and an equilibrium nominal interest rate of i^*.

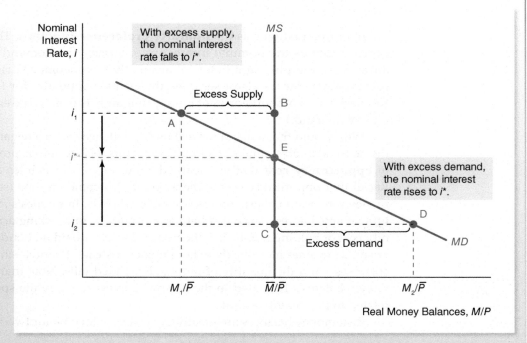

Supply Curve for Money

A central bank, such the Federal Reserve in the United States, can fix the money supply close to any level it desires by buying or selling government securities in open market operations, which we described in Chapter 5. Imagine that the Fed buys $1 billion of government securities (bonds) from banks. The Fed pays for the bonds by depositing $1 billion into accounts that banks must maintain at the central bank. These deposits, which we refer to as **reserves,** represent increased liquidity in the banking system. Flush with additional liquidity from higher reserves, banks loan out more money to their customers, increasing bank deposits. Since these deposits are included in the money supply, as we saw in Chapter 5, the ***open market purchase leads to an increase in liquidity and the money supply***. Similar reasoning leads to the conclusion that an ***open market sale of government securities leads to a decrease in liquidity and a decrease in the money supply***.

If the Fed can fix the money supply at the level $\overline{M}$, and the price level is also fixed in the short run at $\overline{P}$, then the quantity of real money balances supplied, M^s/P, is fixed at $\overline{M}/\overline{P}$ regardless of the interest rate. Thus the supply curve showing the quantity of real money balances supplied at each level of the nominal interest rate is a vertical line, shown in Figure 10.7 as the line *MS*.

Equilibrium in the Money Market

As the supply and demand analysis you learned in your principles course tells us, market equilibrium occurs when the amount people are willing to buy (quantity demanded) at a given price equals the amount supplied (quantity supplied) at a given price. In the money market, equilibrium occurs when the quantity of real money balances demanded equals the quantity of real money balances supplied:

$$\frac{M^d}{P} = \frac{M^s}{P} \tag{6}$$

In Figure 10.7, equilibrium occurs at point E (for "equilibrium"), where the demand and supply curves, *MD* and *MS*, intersect at an interest rate of *i**. Figure 10.7 demonstrates the tendency of interest rates to return to the equilibrium rate *i** when rates are too high or too low.

RESPONSE TO EXCESS SUPPLY. Once people have satisfied their demand for real money balances, they want to put any additional money into alternative assets like bonds or interest-bearing bank accounts. This condition of *excess supply* of money occurs when the interest rate is higher than the equilibrium level. At the rate i_1 in Figure 10.7, the quantity of real money balances supplied (point B) is greater than the quantity demanded (point A). As excess money pours into alternative assets, banks and bond issuers will realize they can pay lower rates of interest and still attract the same number of customers. As the downward arrow shows, the issuers of these assets will continue lowering interest rates to the equilibrium level *i**, at which point the excess supply of real money balances is eliminated.

RESPONSE TO EXCESS DEMAND. When people want to hold more money than is available, they will sell alternative assets like bonds and withdraw from interest-bearing bank accounts until they replenish their desired level of real money balances. This scenario of excess demand for money occurs when the interest rate is below the equilibrium interest rate i^*. In Figure 10.7, when the rate is at i_2, the quantity demanded at point D exceeds the quantity supplied at point C. People will pull money from bonds and bank accounts, inducing banks and bond issuers to raise the interest rates they offer to acquire new sources of funds. Rates will keep rising until they reach the equilibrium level i^*, at which point the excess demand for money is eliminated.

Changes in the Equilibrium Interest Rate

We can now use the supply and demand framework for the money market to analyze why interest rates change. To avoid confusion, remember the distinction between *movements along* a demand (or supply) curve and *shifts in* a demand (or supply) curve. When the quantity demanded changes as a result of a change in the interest rate, there is a *movement along* the demand curve, such as the change in the quantity demanded when we move from point A to E to D in Figure 10.7. A *shift in* the demand (or supply) curve, by contrast, occurs when the quantity demanded (or supplied) changes *at each given interest rate* in response to a change in some other factor besides the interest rate. When a change to one of these factors shifts the supply or demand curve, there will be a new equilibrium value for the interest rate.

FACTORS THAT SHIFT THE DEMAND CURVE. The liquidity preference function in Equation 5 states that the nominal interest rate i and real income Y determine demand for real money balances. As we've just seen in Figure 10.7, changes in i do not shift the demand curve; they instead lead to movement along the demand curve. A change in Y does shift the demand curve, since the quantity of real money balances demanded changes at any given interest rate. Figure 10.8 illustrates this effect. When income rises, demand for money increases from point A_1 on the initial demand curve to point A_2 at the same level of interest rates. At another level of interest rates, demand for money increases from point B_1 on the initial demand curve to point B_2. Continuing this reasoning for every point on the initial demand curve MD_1, we can see that the demand curve shifts to the right from MD_1 to MD_2.

With the supply of money balances set at $\overline{M}/\overline{P}$ and the supply curve stable at MS, the rightward shift of the demand curve moves the new equilibrium to point 2 at the intersection of the MD_2 curve with the supply curve MS. As you can see, the equilibrium interest rate rises from i_1 to i_2. ***Thus, when income rises (holding other variables, such as the price level and the quantity of money, constant), interest rates will rise***.

FACTORS THAT SHIFT THE SUPPLY CURVE. The quantity supplied of real money balances, M^s/P, can change, shifting the supply curve, for either of two reasons: 1) the quantity of money supplied by the Federal Reserve, M^s, changes, or 2) the price level, P, changes.

If the Federal Reserve increases the money supply from $\overline{M}_1$ to $\overline{M}_2$, with the price level fixed at $\overline{P}$, the quantity of real money balances supplied rises at any given interest rate. The supply curve then shifts to the right from MS_1 to MS_2 in panel (a) of Figure 10.9. The equilibrium moves from point 1 down to point 2, where the MS_2 supply curve intersects with the demand curve MD, and the equilibrium interest rate falls from i_1 to i_2. ***When the money supply increases (holding other economic variables constant), interest rates will decline***.

FIGURE 10.8

Response to Shift in the Demand Curve from a Rise in Income

If income rises, the demand curve shifts to the right from MD_1 to MD_2 as a result of the change in quantity demanded at all interest rates. Equilibrium moves from point 1 to point 2 and the interest rate rises from i_1 to i_2.

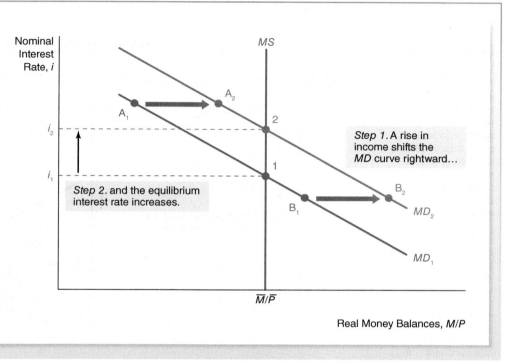

If, holding the money supply constant, the price level rises from $\overline{P}_1$ to $\overline{P}_2$, the quantity supplied of real money balances, M^s/P, falls at any given interest rate. The supply curve then shifts to the left from MS_1 to MS_2 in panel (b) of Figure 10.9, and the equilibrium moves from point 1 up to point 2, with the equilibrium interest rate rising from i_1 to i_2. **When the price level rises (holding the supply of money and other variables constant), interest rates will rise.**[4]

---

[4]The liquidity preference analysis given here provides another rationale for the Taylor principle when the path of the money supply and inflation expectations are unchanged. A rise in inflation means that the price level will be higher than it otherwise would be, and so we are in the situation depicted in panel (b) of Figure 10.9. With the same level of the money supply, the supply of real money balances falls, the MS curve shifts to the left, and both nominal and real interest rates rise (because inflation expectations are unchanged). Schematically, this can be written as follows:

$$\pi\uparrow \Rightarrow \frac{M}{P}\downarrow \Rightarrow i\uparrow \Rightarrow r\uparrow$$

MyEconLab Mini-lecture

FIGURE 10.9

Response to Shifts in the Supply Curve

In panel (a), when the money supply rises, the supply curve shifts to the right from MS_1 to MS_2 as a result of the change in quantity supplied at all interest rates. Equilibrium moves from point 1 to point 2 and the interest rate falls from i_1 to i_2. In panel (b), when the price level rises, the supply curve shifts to the left from MS_1 to MS_2 as a result of the change in quantity supplied at all interest rates. Equilibrium moves from point 1 to point 2 and the interest rate rises from i_1 to i_2.

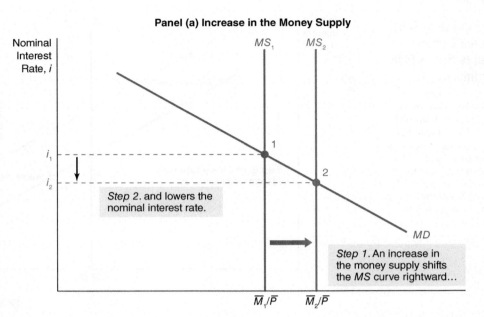

Panel (a) Increase in the Money Supply

Step 2. and lowers the nominal interest rate.

Step 1. An increase in the money supply shifts the *MS* curve rightward…

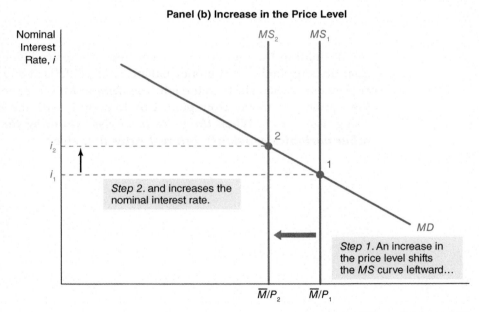

Panel (b) Increase in the Price Level

Step 2. and increases the nominal interest rate.

Step 1. An increase in the price level shifts the *MS* curve leftward…

SUMMARY

1. When the Federal Reserve lowers the federal funds rate by providing more liquidity to the banking system, real interest rates fall in the short run; and when the Federal Reserve raises rates by reducing the liquidity in the banking system, real interest rates rise in the short run.

2. The monetary policy (*MP*) curve shows the relationship between inflation and the real interest rate arising from monetary authorities' actions. Monetary policy follows the Taylor principle, in which higher inflation results in higher real interest rates, as represented by a movement upward along the monetary policy curve. An autonomous tightening of monetary policy occurs when monetary policy makers raise the real interest rate at any given inflation rate, resulting in an upward shift in the monetary policy curve. An autonomous easing of monetary policy and a downward shift in the monetary policy curve occur when monetary policy makers lower the real interest rate at any given inflation rate.

3. The aggregate demand curve tells us the level of equilibrium aggregate output (which equals the total quantity of output demanded) for any given inflation rate. It slopes downward because a higher inflation rate leads the central bank to raise real interest rates, which leads to a lower level of equilibrium output. The aggregate demand curve shifts in the same direction as the *IS* curve; hence it shifts to the right when government purchases increase, taxes decrease, "animal spirits" encourage consumer and business spending, financial frictions decrease, or autonomous net exports increase. An autonomous tightening of monetary policy—that is, an increase in real interest rates at any given inflation rate—leads to a decline in aggregate demand, and the aggregate demand curve shifts to the left.

4. The liquidity preference framework, which analyzes how nominal interest rates are determined as a result of the interaction between the demand and supply of real money balances in the money market, indicates that nominal interest rates rise when income or the price level rises, and fall when the money supply is increased.

KEY TERMS

aggregate demand curve, p. 257

autonomous easing of monetary policy, p. 254

autonomous tightening of monetary policy, p. 254

liquidity preference framework, p. 263

liquidity preference function, p. 263

monetary policy (*MP*) curve, p. 252

opportunity cost, p. 263

real money balances, p. 263

reserves, p. 265

Taylor principle, p. 253

REVIEW QUESTIONS

All Questions are available in MyEconLab *for practice or instructor assignment.*

The Federal Reserve and Monetary Policy

1. What is the real interest rate? Why can the Fed control the real interest rate in the short run but not in the long run?

The Monetary Policy Curve

2. What is the monetary policy curve? Why does it slope upward?

3. How does an autonomous tightening or easing of monetary policy by the Fed affect the *MP* curve?

The Aggregate Demand Curve

4. What is the aggregate demand curve? Why does it slope downward?
5. How do changes in planned expenditures affect the aggregate demand curve?

6. How does an autonomous tightening or easing of monetary policy by the Fed affect the aggregate demand curve?

The Money Market and Interest Rates

7. In Keynes's liquidity preference theory, what variables determine the demand for real money balances? How does the demand for real money balances respond to changes in each of these variables?
8. What are open market operations? How does the Fed use these operations to increase or decrease the money supply?

9. What condition is required for equilibrium in the money market? Why does the money market move toward equilibrium?
10. What can increase the equilibrium interest rate in the liquidity preference framework?

PROBLEMS

All Problems are available in MyEconLab *for practice or instructor assignment.*

The Monetary Policy Curve

1. Assume the monetary policy curve is given by $r = 1.5 + 0.75\,\pi$.
   a) Calculate the real interest rate when the inflation rate is at 2%, 3%, and 4%.
   b) Plot the monetary policy curve and identify the points from part (a).
2. Refer to the monetary policy curve described in Problem 1. Assume now that the monetary policy curve is given by $r = 2.5 + 0.75\,\pi$.

   a) Does the new monetary policy curve represent an autonomous tightening or loosening of monetary policy?
   b) Plot the new monetary policy curve on the graph you created in Problem 1.

The Aggregate Demand Curve

3. Suppose the monetary policy curve is given by $r = 1.5 + 0.75\,\pi$, and the *IS* curve is given by $Y = 13 - r$.
   a) Find the expression for the aggregate demand curve.
   b) Calculate aggregate output when the inflation rate is at 2%, 3%, and 4%.
   c) Plot the aggregate demand curve and identify the three points from part (b).
4. What would be the effect on the aggregate demand curve of an increase in U.S. net exports? Would an increase in net exports affect the monetary policy curve? Explain why or why not.

5. Suppose U.S. aggregate output is still below potential by 2018, when a new Fed chair is appointed. Suppose his or her approach to monetary policy can be summarized by the following statement: "I care only about increasing employment; inflation has been at very low levels for quite some time; my priority is to ease monetary policy to promote employment."
   a) Would you expect the monetary policy curve to shift upward or downward?
   b) What would be the effect on the aggregate demand curve?

The Money Market and Interest Rates

6. Assume the demand for real money balances is given by $\dfrac{M^d}{P} = \dfrac{Y}{6} - 150i$ (an interest rate of 2% is entered into this formula as 2). Suppose $Y = 12{,}900$ billion, so that $\dfrac{M^d}{P} = \dfrac{12{,}900}{6}$
   $- 150i$ (in billions of $).
   a) Calculate the demand for real money balances at interest rates of 4%, 3%, and 1%.
   b) Plot the points from part (a) on a graph with the nominal interest rate on the vertical axis and the quantity of real money balances on the horizontal axis.

7. Suppose the economy experiences a contraction in aggregate output. How would this event affect the demand curve for real money balances? On the graph from part (b) of Problem 6, draw the original and the new demand curve, if necessary.

8. Assume the demand for real money balances is given by $\dfrac{M^d}{P} = \dfrac{Y}{6} - 150i$.
   a) Find the equilibrium interest rate if the money supply is $1,700 billion and output equals $12,900 billion.
   b) Find the new equilibrium interest rate if the money supply is $1,700 billion and output increases to $13,800 billion.
   c) Plot both interest rates and demand curves on the same graph.

9. Consider the money market. Suppose the U.S. economy begins to boom and aggregate output increases. Describe the effect on the interest rate if the Federal Reserve decides to increase the money supply at the same time that aggregate output increases.

DATA ANALYSIS PROBLEMS

The Problems update with real-time data in MyEconLab *and are available for practice or instructor assignment.*

1. A measure of real interest rates can be approximated by the Treasury Inflation-Indexed Security, or TIIS. Go to the St. Louis Federal Reserve FRED database, and find data on the five year TIIS (FII5) and a measure of the price index, the personal consumption expenditure price index (PCECTPI). For the *frequency* setting for the TIIS, choose "quarterly," and download both data series. Convert the price index values to annualized inflation rates by taking the quarter-to-quarter percent change in the price index and multiplying by four. Be sure to multiply by 100 so that the rate is in percentage terms.
   a) Calculate the average inflation rate and the average real interest rate over the most recent four quarters available, and over the four quarters prior to that.
   b) Calculate the change in the average inflation rate between the most recent annual period and the period prior to that. Do the same for the change in the

average real interest rate for the two periods.
   c) Using your answers to part (b), compute the ratio of the change in average real interest rate to the change in average inflation. What does this ratio represent? Comment on how it relates to the Taylor principle.

2. A measure of real interest rates can be approximated by the Treasury Inflation-Indexed Security, or TIIS. Go to the St. Louis Federal Reserve FRED database, and find data on the five year TIIS (FII5) and a measure of the price index, the personal consumption expenditure price index (PCECTPI). For the *frequency* setting for the TIIS, choose "quarterly," and for the *units* setting on (PCECTPI), choose "Percent Change From Year Ago." Plot both series on the same graph, showing data from 2007 to the most current data available. Use the graph to identify periods of autonomous monetary policy changes. Briefly explain your reasoning.

3. Go to the St. Louis Federal Reserve FRED database, and find data on the Bank Prime Loan Rate (MPRIME), the Effective Fed Funds Rate (FEDFUNDS), and the 3-Month Treasury Bill: Secondary Market Rate (TB3MS). Use data from the most recent month available and data from the same month one year ago, five years ago, and ten years ago.

   a) Calculate the change in interest rates on money market instruments over these periods.

b) Now, find data on the M1 money stock (M1SL) and a measure of the price level, (PCEPI). Calculate the real money supply using the two data series, and then calculate the total percent change in the real money stock from one, five, and ten years earlier.

c) Compare the movements in interest rates to the growth rate in the real money supply over the two horizons. Are the results consistent with liquidity preference theory? Briefly explain.

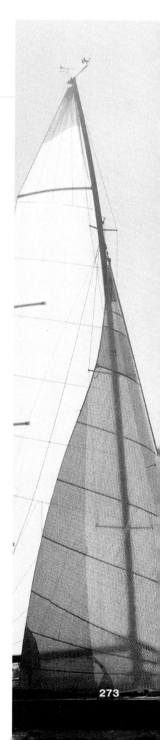

Chapter 10 Appendix

The Demand for Money

In this appendix, we go into more detail on Keynesian and other theories of the demand for money. In addition, we examine the empirical evidence on the demand for money.

 ## Keynesian Theories of Money Demand

In his famous 1936 book *The General Theory of Employment, Interest and Money*, John Maynard Keynes abandoned the quantity theory view we developed in Chapter 5 that velocity is a constant and developed a theory of money demand that emphasized the importance of interest rates. In his liquidity preference theory, Keynes presented three motives behind the demand for money: the transactions motive, the precautionary motive, and the speculative motive.

Transactions Motive

In the quantity theory approach, individuals are assumed to hold money because it is a medium of exchange that can be used to carry out everyday transactions. Keynes initially accepted the quantity theory view that the transactions component is proportional to income. Later, he and other economists recognized that new methods for payment, referred to as **payment technology,** could also affect the demand for money. For example, credit cards enable consumers to make even very small purchases without needing to hold money. Electronic payments that can be made from investors' brokerage accounts can also reduce money demand. As payment technology advances, the demand for money will be likely to decline relative to income.

Indeed, economists have been predicting a "cashless society" for decades, which would drive money demand to zero. However, the movement to a cashless society has been much slower than many have predicted.

Precautionary Motive

Keynes also recognized that people hold money as a cushion against unexpected needs. Suppose you have been thinking about buying a new Wii entertainment system and now see that it is on sale at 25% off. If you are holding money as a precaution for just such an occurrence, you can immediately buy it. Keynes argued that the precautionary money balances people want to hold would also be proportional to income.

Speculative Motive

Keynes also believed people choose to hold money as a store of wealth, which he called the *speculative motive*. Because the definition of money in Keynes's analysis includes currency (which earns no interest) and checking account deposits (which typically earn little interest), he assumed that money earns no interest and hence its opportunity cost relative to holding other assets, such as bonds, is the nominal interest rate on bonds, *i*. As the interest rate *i* rises, the opportunity cost of money rises (it is more costly to hold money relative to bonds) and the quantity of money demanded falls.

Putting the Three Motives Together

Combining the three motives for holding money balances into a demand for real money balances led to what Keynes called the liquidity preference function, which we presented as Equation 5 in this chapter:

$$\frac{M^d}{P} = L(i, Y) \tag{1}$$
$$\phantom{\frac{M^d}{P} = L(i,} {-} \ {+}$$

Equation 1 states that the demand for real money balances is negatively related to the nominal interest rate and is positively correlated to real income.

Later Keynesian economists, such as Nobel Prize winner James Tobin, expanded the analysis and showed that interest rates play a more important role in money demand than even Keynes supposed. They demonstrated that the transactions and precautionary demands for money would also be negatively related to the interest rate.[1]

An important implication of Keynesian theories of money demand is that velocity is not a constant and will fluctuate with changes in interest rates. To illustrate, we write the liquidity preference function as follows:

$$\frac{P}{M^d} = \frac{1}{L(i, Y)}$$

Multiplying both sides of this equation by Y and recognizing that we can replace M^d by M (because they must be equal in money market equilibrium), we solve for velocity:

$$V = \frac{PY}{M} = \frac{Y}{L(i, Y)} \tag{2}$$

---

[1]Three famous papers that elaborated on Keynes' approach to the demand for money are as follows: William J. Baumol, "The Transactions Demand for Cash: An Inventory Theoretic Approach," *Quarterly Journal of Economics* 66 (1952): 545–556; James Tobin, "The Interest Elasticity of the Transactions Demand for Cash," *Review of Economics and Statistics* 38 (1956): 241–247; and James Tobin, "Liquidity Preference as Behavior Towards Risk," *Review of Economic Studies* 25 (1958): 65–86. For further discussion of theories of the demand for money, see David Laidler, *The Demand for Money: Theories, Evidence and Problems*, 4th edition (New York: Harper Collins, 1993).

We know that the demand for money is negatively correlated to interest rates; when i goes up, $L(i,Y)$ declines, and therefore velocity rises. Because interest rates have substantial fluctuations, Keynesian theories of the demand for money indicate that velocity has substantial fluctuations as well. Thus Keynesian theories cast doubt on the classical quantity theory view that nominal income is determined primarily by movements in the quantity of money.

Portfolio Theories of Money Demand

Related to Keynes's analysis of the demand for money are so-called **portfolio theories** of money demand, in which people decide how much of an asset, such as money, they want to hold as part of their overall portfolio of assets.[2]

Portfolio Theory

Portfolio theory presents four main determinants of the demand for an asset:

1. *Wealth*, the total resources owned by individuals, including all assets

2. **Expected return,** the return expected on an asset relative to other assets

3. **Risk,** the degree of uncertainty associated with the return on an asset relative to other assets

4. **Liquidity,** the ease and speed with which an asset can be turned into cash relative to other assets

The demand for an asset should be positively correlated to wealth: as wealth increases, investors have more resources available to purchase assets. The demand for an asset should be positively related to the expected return on the asset relative to other assets, because as the expected return on an asset rises relative to other assets, that asset becomes more desirable. The demand for an asset is negatively correlated to risk. Most people do not like risk and are thus said to be **risk averse,** and so find riskier assets less desirable. The demand for an asset is positively correlated to liquidity, because being able to turn an asset into cash easily and quickly makes the asset more desirable.

Portfolio Theory and Keynesian Liquidity Preference

Portfolio theory can justify the conclusion from the Keynesian liquidity preference function that the demand for real money balances is positively related to income and negatively related to the nominal interest rate. Income and wealth tend to move together: when income is higher, wealth is likely to be higher as well, and the demand for real money balances will be higher.

Also, as interest rates rise, the expected return on money does not change. However, the return on bonds, an alternative asset, goes up. Thus, while the expected *absolute* return on money did not change, money's expected return *relative to bonds* went down. In other words, higher interest rates make money less desirable, and the demand for real money balances falls.

---

[2]This is the approach taken by Milton Friedman in his famous paper, "The Quantity Theory of Money: A Restatement," in *Studies in the Quantity Theory of Money*, ed. Milton Friedman (Chicago: University of Chicago Press, 1956), 3–21.

Other Factors That Affect the Demand for Money

Portfolio theory indicates that other factors besides income and the nominal interest rate can affect the demand for money. We look at each of these in turn.

WEALTH. Portfolio theory posits that as wealth increases, investors have more resources with which to purchase assets, increasing the demand for money. However, when income is held constant, greater wealth has only a small effect on the demand for money. In general, investors will hold only a small amount of money in their investment portfolios, preferring interest-bearing assets with similar risk and liquidity profiles, such as money market mutual funds, that are not included in measures of money such as M1. Currency and checkable deposits are sometimes said to be **dominated assets,** because investors can hold other assets that pay higher returns and yet are perceived to be just as safe.

RISK. It's hard to imagine an asset less risky than money. Currency will always be accepted, unless there's a revolution and the new government does not accept the old government's currency. And bank deposits are safe as long as there is deposit insurance. In portfolio theory, however, risk is always measured relative to another asset. Thus, if the stock market becomes more volatile, money can become less risky relative to stocks, and demand for it will increase. In addition, while money is extremely safe on a nominal basis, its real return (the nominal return minus expected inflation) can become highly variable when inflation becomes very variable. Higher variability in the real return on money lowers the demand for money, as people shift to alternative assets known as **inflation hedges,** whose real returns are less affected than that of money when inflation varies. Popular inflation hedges include TIPS (Treasury Inflation Protected Securities), gold, and real estate.

LIQUIDITY OF OTHER ASSETS. In recent years, financial innovation has led to the development of new liquid assets, such as money market mutual funds and home equity lines of credit, that allow households to write checks that are backed by their homes. As these alternative assets become more liquid, the relative liquidity of money falls, and so the demand for money falls as well.

Summary

Our analysis of the demand for money using Keynesian theories and portfolio theories indicates that there are seven factors that affect the demand for money: interest rates, income, payment technology, wealth, riskiness of other assets, inflation risk, and liquidity of other assets. As a study aid, Table 10A1.1 indicates the response of money demand to changes in each of these factors and gives a brief synopsis of the reasoning behind them.

Empirical Evidence on the Demand for Money

Here we examine the empirical evidence on the two key issues that distinguish different theories of money demand and their conclusions as to whether quantity of money is the primary determinant of aggregate spending: Is the demand for money sensitive to changes in interest rates, and is the demand for money function stable over time?

| TABLE 10A1.1 | **FACTORS THAT DETERMINE THE DEMAND FOR MONEY** |

Variable	Change in Variable	Money Demand Response	Reason
Interest rates	↑	↓	Opportunity cost of money rises
Income	↑	↑	Higher transactions
Payment technology	↑	↓	Less need for money in transactions
Wealth	↑	↑	More resources to put into money
Risk of other assets	↑	↑	Money relatively less risky and so more desirable
Inflation risk	↑	↓	Money relatively more risky and so less desirable
Liquidity of other assets	↑	↓	Money relatively less liquid and so less desirable

Interest Rates and Money Demand

We have established that if interest rates do not affect the demand for money, velocity is more likely to be constant—or at least predictable—and so the quantity theory view that aggregate spending is determined by the quantity of money is more likely to be true. However, the more sensitive the demand for money is to interest rates, the more unpredictable velocity will be, and the less clear the link between the money supply and aggregate spending will be. Indeed, there is an extreme case of ultrasensitivity of the demand for money to interest rates, called the **liquidity trap,** in which conventional monetary policy has no direct effect on aggregate spending because a change in the money supply has no effect on interest rates.[3]

The evidence on the interest sensitivity of the demand for money is remarkably consistent. Neither extreme case is supported by the data: in situations in which nominal interest rates have not hit a floor of zero, the demand for money is sensitive to interest rates, and there is little evidence that a liquidity trap has ever existed. However, when nominal interest rates fall to zero, they can go no lower. In this situation, a liquidity trap has occurred because the demand for money is now completely flat. Indeed, exactly this situation has occurred in the United States in recent years, which is why the Federal Reserve has had to resort to nonconventional monetary policy, as discussed in Chapter 13.

[3]If the demand for money is ultrasensitive to interest rates, a tiny change in interest rates produces a very large change in the quantity of money demanded. In this case, the demand for money is completely flat in the supply and demand diagrams of Chapter 10. Therefore, a change in the money supply that shifts the money supply curve to the right or left results in it intersecting the flat money demand curve at the same unchanged interest rate.

Stability of Money Demand

If the money demand function, like the one in Equation 1, is unstable and undergoes substantial, unpredictable shifts as Keynes believed, then velocity is unpredictable, and the quantity of money may not be tightly linked to aggregate spending, as it is in the quantity theory. The stability of the money demand function is also crucial to whether the Federal Reserve should target interest rates or the money supply. If the money demand function is unstable and so the money supply is not closely linked to aggregate spending, then the level of interest rates set by the Fed will provide more information about the stance of monetary policy than will the money supply.

Until the early 1970s, evidence strongly supported the stability of the money demand function. However, after 1973, the rapid pace of financial innovation, which changed the items that could be used as money, led to substantial instability in estimated money demand functions. The instability of the money demand function calls into question the adequacy of our theories and empirical analyses. It also has important implications for the conduct of monetary policy, because it casts doubt on the usefulness of the money demand function as a tool for providing guidance to policy makers. In particular, because the money demand function has become unstable, velocity is now harder to predict. Monetary policy makers have found that the money supply does not provide reliable information on the future course of the economy, leading them to think of monetary policy in terms of the setting of interest rates, as reflected by the monetary policy curve. The instability of money demand has thus led to a downgrading of the focus on money supply in the conduct of monetary policy.

SUMMARY

1. John Maynard Keynes suggested three motives for holding money: the transactions motive, the precautionary motive, and the speculative motive. His resulting liquidity preference theory views the transactions and precautionary components of money demand as proportional to income. However, the speculative component of money demand is viewed as sensitive to interest rates as well as to expectations about the future movements of interest rates. This theory, then, implies that velocity is unstable and cannot be treated as a constant.

2. Portfolio theory indicates that not only is the demand for money determined by interest rates, income, and payment technology, as in the Keynesian analysis, but also by wealth, riskiness of other assets, inflation risk, and liquidity of other assets.

3. There are two main conclusions drawn from the research on the demand for money: The demand for money is sensitive to interest rates, but there is little evidence that it is or has been ultrasensitive (liquidity trap) except when nominal interest rates have fallen to zero. Since 1973, money demand has been found to be unstable, with the most likely source of instability being the rapid pace of financial innovation. Because the money demand function is found to be both unstable and sensitive to interest rates, velocity cannot be viewed as constant and is not easily predictable. This has led to a downgrading of the focus on money supply in the conduct of monetary policy.

KEY TERMS

dominated assets, p. 276

expected return, p. 275

inflation hedges, p. 276

liquidity, p. 275

liquidity trap, p. 277

payment technology, p. 273

portfolio theories, p. 275

risk, p. 275

risk averse, p. 275

REVIEW QUESTIONS AND PROBLEMS

All Questions and Problems are available in MyEconLab *for practice or instructor assignment.*

1. What three motives for holding money did Keynes consider in his liquidity preference theory of the demand for real money balances? Based on these motives, what variables did he think determined the demand for money?

2. According to the portfolio theory of money demand, what are the four factors that determine money demand? What changes in these factors can increase the demand for money?

3. What evidence is used to assess the stability of the money demand function? What does the evidence suggest about the stability of money demand, and how has this evidence affected monetary policy making?

4. Suppose a new payment technology allows individuals to make payments using U.S. Treasury bonds (i.e., U.S. Treasury bonds are immediately cashed when needed to make a payment, and that balance is transferred to the payee). How do you think this payment technology would affect the transaction component of the demand for money?

5. Some payment technologies require infrastructure (e.g., merchants need to have access to credit card swiping machines). In most developing countries, this infrastructure is either nonexistent or very costly. Everything else being the same, would you expect the transaction component of the demand for money to be larger or smaller in a developing country than in a rich country?

6. In many countries, people hold money as a cushion against unexpected needs arising from a variety of potential scenarios (e.g., banking crises, natural disasters, health

problems, unemployment, etc.) that are usually not covered by insurance markets. Explain the effect of such behavior on the precautionary component of the demand for money.

7. Suppose the liquidity preference function is given by $L(i, Y) = \dfrac{Y}{8} - 1{,}000i$.

   For the data given in the table below, calculate velocity using Equation 2.

8. Plot the values of velocity you found in Problem 7, and comment on the volatility (i.e., fluctuations) of velocity.

9. Explain how the following events will affect the demand for money according to the portfolio theory approach to money demand:
   a) The economy experiences a business cycle contraction.
   b) Brokerage fees decline, making bond transactions cheaper.

10. Suppose a given country experienced low, stable inflation rates for quite some time, but then inflation picked up and has been relatively high and quite unpredictable over the past decade. Explain how this new inflationary environment would affect the demand for money according to the portfolio theory of money demand. What would happen if the government decided to issue inflation protected securities?

11. Consider the portfolio theory of money demand. How do you think the demand for money would be affected by a hyperinflation (i.e., monthly inflation rates in excess of 50%)?

12. According to the portfolio theory approach to money demand, what would be the effect of a stock market crash on the demand for money? (Hint: Consider both the increase in stock price volatility following a market crash and the decrease in the wealth of stockholders.)

13. Suppose a plot of the values of M2 and nominal GDP for a given country over forty years shows that these two variables are very closely related. In particular, a plot of their ratio (nominal GDP/M2) yields very stable and easy-to-predict values. Based on this evidence, would you recommend that the monetary authorities of this country conduct monetary policy by focusing mainly on the money supply, or by focusing on interest rates? Explain.

	Period 1	Period 2	Period 3	Period 4	Period 5	Period 6	Period 7
Y (in $ billions)	12,000	12,500	12,250	12,500	12,800	13,000	13,200
Interest rate	0.05	0.07	0.03	0.05	0.07	0.04	0.06

Aggregate Supply and the Phillips Curve

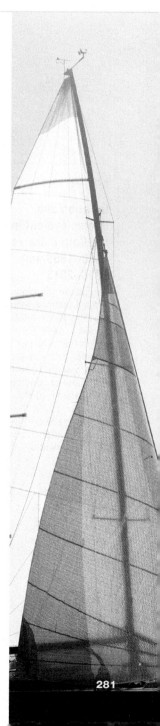

11

Preview

In the 1960s, the Kennedy and Johnson administrations followed the advice of Nobel Prize winners Paul Samuelson and Robert Solow and pursued expansionary macroeconomic policies to raise inflation a little bit, with the expectation that unemployment would be permanently lower. They were disappointed when, in the late 1960s and the 1970s, inflation accelerated and yet the unemployment rate stayed uncomfortably high. To understand why they were wrong, we turn to a concept called the *Phillips curve*, which describes the relationship between unemployment and inflation.

In the preceding chapter, we derived the aggregate demand curve, which shows the relationship between the inflation rate and the level of aggregate output when the goods market is in equilibrium. But how do we determine aggregate output and inflation? The aggregate demand curve provides half of the story; we also need to factor in the relationship between these two variables that is provided by the *aggregate supply curve*, which we develop in this chapter.

The Phillips curve provides the intuition for the aggregate supply curve. First, we will see how the economic profession's views on the Phillips curve have evolved over time and how this evolution has affected thinking about macroeconomic policy. Then we can use the Phillips curve to derive the aggregate supply curve, which will allow us to complete our basic aggregate demand-aggregate supply framework for analyzing short-run economic fluctuations in the next chapter.

The Phillips Curve

In 1958, New Zealand economist A.W. Phillips published a famous empirical paper that examined the relationship between unemployment and wage growth in the United Kingdom.[1] For the years 1861 to 1957, he found that periods of low unemployment were associated with rapid rises in wages, while periods of high unemployment were characterized by low growth in wages. Other economists soon extended his work to many other countries. Because inflation is more central to macroeconomic issues than wage growth, they estimated the relationship between unemployment and inflation. The negative relationship between unemployment and inflation that they found in many countries became known, naturally enough, as the **Phillips curve.**

[1]A.W. Phillips, "The Relationship Between Unemployment and the Rate of Change of Money Wages in the United Kingdom, 1861–1957," *Economica* 25 (November 1958): 283–299.

The idea behind the Phillips curve is quite intuitive. When labor markets are *tight*—that is, the unemployment rate is low—firms may have difficulty hiring qualified workers and may even have a hard time keeping their present employees. Because of the shortage of workers in the labor market, firms will raise wages to attract needed workers and raise their prices at a more rapid rate.

Phillips Curve Analysis in the 1960s

Because wage inflation feeds directly into overall inflation, in the 1960s, the Phillips curve became extremely popular as an explanation for inflation fluctuations because it seemed to fit the data so well. As shown in panel (a) of Figure 11.1's plot of the U.S. inflation rate against the unemployment rate from 1950 to 1969, there is a very clear negative relationship between unemployment and inflation. The Phillips curve for that period seemed to imply that there is a long-run trade-off between unemployment and inflation—that is, policy makers can choose policies that lead to a higher rate of inflation

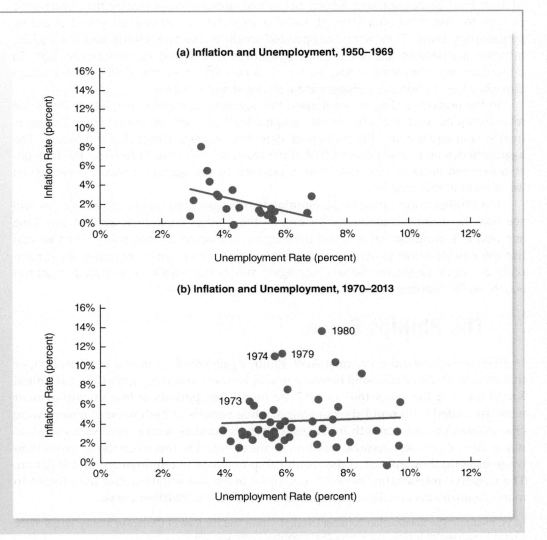

FIGURE 11.1

Inflation and Unemployment in the United States, 1950–1969 and 1970–2013

The plot of inflation against unemployment over the 1950–1969 period in panel (a) shows that a higher inflation rate was generally associated with a lower rate of unemployment. Panel (b) shows that after 1970, the negative relationship between inflation and unemployment disappeared.

Source: Economic Report of the President. www.gpoaccess.gov/eop/

Policy and Practice

The Phillips Curve Tradeoff and Macroeconomic Policy in the 1960s

In 1960, Paul Samuelson and Robert Solow published a paper outlining how policy makers could exploit the Phillips curve trade-off. The policy maker could choose between two competing goals—inflation and unemployment—and decide how high an inflation rate he or she would be willing to accept to attain a lower unemployment rate.[2] Indeed, Samuelson and Solow even said that policy makers could achieve a "nonperfectionist" goal of a 3% unemployment rate at what they considered to be a tolerable inflation rate of 4–5% per year. This thinking was influential during the Kennedy and then Johnson administrations, and contributed to the adoption of policies in the mid-1960s to stimulate the economy and bring the unemployment rate down to low levels. At first these policies seemed to be successful because the subsequent higher inflation rates were accompanied by a fall in the unemployment rate. However, the good times were not to last: from the late 1960s through the 1970s, inflation accelerated, yet the unemployment rate remained stubbornly high.

and end up with a lower unemployment rate on a sustained basis. This apparent trade-off was very influential in policy circles in the 1960s, as we can see in the Policy and Practice case.

The Friedman-Phelps Phillips Curve Analysis

In 1967 and 1968, Milton Friedman and Edmund Phelps pointed out a severe theoretical flaw in the Phillips curve analysis:[3] it was inconsistent with the view that workers and firms care about *real* wages, the amount of real goods and services that wages can purchase, and not *nominal* wages. Thus when workers and firms expect the price level to rise, they will adjust nominal wages upward so that the real wage rate does not decrease. In other words, wages and overall inflation will rise one-to-one with increases in expected inflation, as well as respond to tightness in the labor market. In addition, the Friedman-Phelps analysis suggested that in the long run the economy would reach the level of unemployment that would occur if all wages and prices were flexible, which they called the *natural rate of unemployment*.[4] The **natural rate of unemployment** is the full-employment level of unemployment, because there will still be some unemployment even when wages and prices are flexible, as we will show in Chapter 20.

[2]Paul A. Samuelson and Robert M. Solow, "Analytical Aspects of Anti-Inflation Policy," *American Economic Review* 50 (May 1960, Papers and Proceedings): 177–194.

[3]Milton Friedman outlined his criticism of the Phillips curve in his 1967 presidential address to the American Economic Association: Milton Friedman, "The Role of Monetary Policy," *American Economic Review* 58 (1968): 1–17. Phelps's reformulation of the Phillips curve analysis is given in Edmund Phelps, "Money-Wage Dynamics and Labor-Market Equilibrium," *Journal of Political Economy* 76 (July/August 1968, Part 2): 687–711.

[4]As we will discuss in Chapter 20, there will always be some unemployment that is either *frictional unemployment*, unemployment that occurs because workers are searching for jobs, or *structural unemployment*, unemployment that arises from a mismatch of skills with available jobs and is a structural feature of the labor markets. Thus even when wages and prices are fully flexible, the natural rate of unemployment is above zero.

The Friedman-Phelps reasoning suggested a Phillips curve that we can write as follows:

$$\pi = \pi^e - \omega(U - U_n) \qquad (1)$$

where π represents inflation, π^e expected inflation, U the unemployment rate, U_n the natural rate of unemployment, and ω the sensitivity of inflation to $U - U_n$. The presence of the π^e term explains why Equation 1 is also referred to as the **expectations-augmented Phillips curve:** it indicates that inflation is negatively related to the difference between the unemployment rate and the natural rate of unemployment $(U - U_n)$, a measure of tightness in the labor markets called the **unemployment gap.**

The expectations-augmented Phillips curve implies that long-run unemployment will be at the natural rate level, as Friedman and Phelps theorized. Recognize that in the long run, expected inflation must gravitate to actual inflation, and Equation 1 therefore indicates that U must be equal to U_n.

The Friedman-Phelps expectations-augmented version of the Phillips curve displays no long-run trade-off between unemployment and inflation and is thus consistent with the classical dichotomy that indicates that changes in the price level should not affect the real economy. To show this, Figure 11.2 presents the expectations-augmented Phillips curve, marked as PC_1, for a given expected inflation rate of 2% and a natural rate of unemployment of 5%. (PC_1 goes through point 1 because Equation 1 indicates that when $\pi = \pi^e = 2\%$, $U = U_n = 5\%$, and its slope is $-\omega$.) Suppose the economy

MyEconLab Mini-lecture

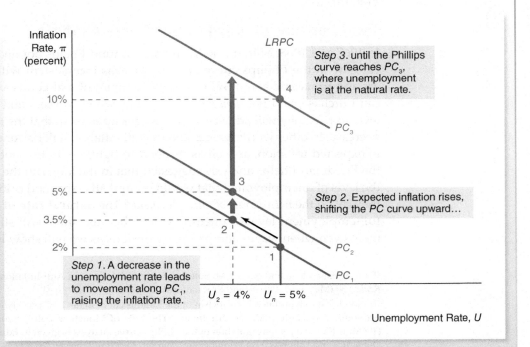

FIGURE 11.2

The Short- and Long-Run Phillips Curves

The expectations-augmented Phillips curve is downward-sloping because a lower unemployment rate results in a higher inflation rate for any given level of expected inflation. If the economy moves, due to a decline in the unemployment rate, from point 1 to point 2 on PC_1, the inflation rate rises. If unemployment remains at 4%, inflation rises further, shifting the short-run expectations-augmented Phillips curve upward to PC_2 and to point 3. Eventually, when the economy reaches point 4, at which $\pi^e = \pi = 10\%$, the expectations-augmented Philips curve, PC_3, will stop shifting because unemployment is at the natural rate of unemployment. The line connecting points 1 and 4 is the long-run Phillips curve, $LRPC$, and shows that long-run unemployment is at the natural rate of unemployment for any inflation rate.

Step 3. until the Phillips curve reaches PC_3, where unemployment is at the natural rate.

Step 2. Expected inflation rises, shifting the PC curve upward…

Step 1. A decrease in the unemployment rate leads to movement along PC_1, raising the inflation rate.

is initially at point 1, where the unemployment rate is at the natural rate level of 5%, but then government policies to stimulate the economy cause the unemployment rate to fall to 4%, a level below the natural rate level. The economy then moves along PC_1 to point 2, with inflation rising above 2%, say to 3.5%. Expected inflation will then rise as well, so the expectations-augmented Phillips curve will shift upward from PC_1 to PC_2. Continued efforts to stimulate the economy and keep the unemployment rate at 4%, below the natural rate level, will cause further increases in the actual and expected inflation rates, causing the expectations-augmented Phillips curve to shift upward to PC_2 and to point 3, where inflation is now 5%.

When will the expectations-augmented Phillips curve stop rising? Only when unemployment is back at the natural rate level, that is, when $U = U_n = 5\%$. Suppose this happens when inflation is at 10%; then expected inflation will also be at 10% because inflation has settled down to that level, with the expectations-augmented Phillips curve at PC_3 in Figure 11.2. The economy will now move to point 4, where $\pi = \pi^e = 10\%$, and unemployment is at the natural rate, $U = U_n = 5\%$. We thus see that in the long run, when the expectations-augmented Phillips curve is no longer shifting, the economy will be at points like 1 and 4. The line connecting these points is thus the **long-run Phillips curve,** which we mark as $LRPC$ in Figure 11.2.

Figure 11.2 leads us to three important conclusions:

1. ***There is no long-run trade-off between unemployment and inflation*** because, as the vertical long-run Phillips curve shows, a higher long-run inflation rate is not associated with a lower level of unemployment.

2. ***There is a short-run trade-off between unemployment and inflation*** because with a given expected inflation rate, policy makers can attain a lower unemployment rate at the expense of a somewhat higher than the expected inflation rate, as at point 2 in Figure 11.2.

3. ***There are two types of Phillips curves, long-run and short-run.*** The expectations-augmented Phillips curves—PC_1, PC_2, and PC_3—are actually short-run Phillips curves: they are drawn for given values of expected inflation and will shift if deviations of unemployment from the natural rate cause inflation and expected inflation to change.

The Phillips Curve After the 1960s

As Figure 11.2 indicates, the expectations-augmented Phillips curve shows that the negative relationship between unemployment and inflation breaks down when the unemployment rate remains below the natural rate of unemployment for any extended period of time. This prediction of the Friedman and Phelps analysis turned out to be exactly right. Starting in the 1970s, after a period of very low unemployment rates, the negative relationship between unemployment and inflation, which was so visible in the 1950s and 1960s, disappeared, as we can see in panel (b) of Figure 11.1. Not surprisingly, given the brilliance of Friedman and Phelps's work, they were both awarded Nobel Prizes.

The Modern Phillips Curve

With the sharp rise in oil prices in 1973 and 1979, inflation jumped up sharply (see panel (b) of Figure 11.1) and Phillips-curve theorists realized that they had to add one more feature to the expectations-augmented Phillips curve. Recall from Chapter 3 that supply shocks are shocks to supply that change the amount of output an economy can produce from the same amount of capital and labor. These supply shocks translate into **price shocks,** that is, shifts in inflation that are independent of tightness in labor markets or expected inflation. For example, when the supply of oil was restricted following the war between the Arab states and Israel in 1973, the price of oil more than quadrupled and firms had to raise prices to reflect their increased costs of production, thus driving up inflation. Price shocks also could come from a rise in import prices or from **cost-push shocks,** in which workers push for wages higher than productivity gains, thereby driving up costs and inflation. Adding price shocks (ρ) to the expectations-augmented Phillips curve leads to the modern form of the short-run Phillips curve:

$$\pi = \pi^e - \omega\,(U - U_n) + \rho \tag{2}$$

The modern, short-run Phillips curve implies that wages and prices are sticky. The more flexible wages and prices are, the more they, and inflation, respond to deviations of unemployment from the natural rate; that is, more flexible wages and prices imply that the absolute value of ω is higher, which implies that the short-run Phillips curve is steeper. If wages and prices are completely flexible, then ω becomes so large that the short-run Phillips curve is vertical, and it becomes identical to the long-run Phillips curve. In this case, there is no long-run or short-run trade-off between unemployment and inflation.

The Modern Phillips Curve with Adaptive (Backward-Looking) Expectations

To complete our analysis of the Phillips curve, we need to understand how firms and households form expectations about inflation. One simple way of thinking about how firms and households form their expectations about inflation is to assume that they do so by looking at past inflation. The simplest assumption is:

$$\pi^e = \pi_{-1}$$

where π_{-1} is the inflation rate in the previous period. This form of expectations is known as **adaptive expectations** or **backward-looking expectations** because expectations are formed by looking at the past and therefore change only slowly over time.[5] Substituting π_{-1} in for π^e in Equation 2 yields the following short-run Phillips curve:

$$\pi \quad = \quad \pi_{-1} \quad - \quad \omega\,(U - U_n) \quad + \quad \rho \tag{3}$$

Inflation = Expected − ω × Unemployment + Price
Inflation   Gap   Shock

This form of the Phillips curve has two advantages over the more general formulation in Equation 2. First, it takes on a very simple mathematical form that is convenient to use. Second, it provides two additional, realistic reasons why prices might be sticky.

---

[5]An alternative, modern form of expectations makes use of the concept of *rational expectations*, where expectations are formed using all available information, and so may react more quickly to new information. We discuss rational expectations and their role in macroeconomic analysis in Chapter 21.

One reason comes from the view that inflation expectations adjust only slowly as inflation trends change: inflation expectations are therefore sticky, which results in some inflation stickiness. Another reason is that the presence of past inflation in the Phillips curve formulation can reflect the fact that some wage and price contracts might be backward-looking, that is, tied to past inflation trends, and so inflation might not fully adjust to changes in inflation expectations in the short run.

There is, however, one important disadvantage of the adaptive-expectations form of the Phillips curve in Equation 3: it takes a very mechanical view of how inflation expectations are formed. More sophisticated analysis of expectations formation has important implications for the conduct of macroeconomic policy, as we will see in Chapter 21. For the time being, we will make use of the simple form of the Phillips curve with adaptive expectations, keeping in mind that the π_{-1} term represents expected inflation.

There is another convenient way of looking at the adaptive-expectations form of the Phillips curve. By subtracting π_{-1} from both sides of Equation 3, we can rewrite it as follows:

$$\Delta \pi = \pi - \pi_{-1} = -\omega (U - U_n) + \rho \qquad (4)$$

Written in this form, the Phillips curve indicates that a negative unemployment gap (tight labor market) causes the inflation rate to rise, that is, accelerate. This relationship is why the Equation 4 version of the Phillips curve is often referred to as an **accelerationist Phillips curve.** With this formulation, the term U_n has another interpretation. Since inflation stops accelerating (changing) when the unemployment rate is at U_n, we also refer to this term as the **non-accelerating inflation rate of unemployment** or, more commonly, **NAIRU.**

The Aggregate Supply Curve

To complete our aggregate demand and supply model, we need to use our analysis of the Phillips curve to derive an **aggregate supply curve,** which represents the relationship between the total quantity of output that firms are willing to produce and the inflation rate. In the typical supply and demand analysis, we have only one supply curve, but this is not the case in the aggregate demand and supply framework. We can translate the short- and long-run Phillips curves into short- and long-run aggregate supply curves. We begin by examining the long-run aggregate supply curve. We then derive the short-run aggregate supply curve and see how it shifts over time as the economy moves from the short run to the long run.

Long-Run Aggregate Supply Curve

What determines the amount of output an economy can produce in the long run? As we saw in Chapter 3, the key factors that determine long-run output are available technology, the amount of capital in the economy, and the amount of labor supplied in the long run, all of which are unrelated to the inflation rate. The level of aggregate output supplied at the natural rate of unemployment is often referred to as the **natural rate of output.** However, the natural rate of output is more commonly referred to as *potential output*, a term we encountered in Chapter 8, because it is the level of production that an economy can sustain in the long run.

MyEconLab Mini-lecture

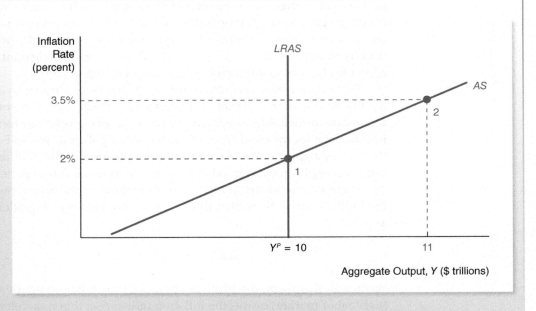

FIGURE 11.3

Long- and Short-Run Aggregate Supply Curves

The amount of aggregate output supplied at any given inflation rate is at potential output in the long run, so that the long-run aggregate supply curve *LRAS* is a vertical line at Y^P. The short-run aggregate supply curve, *SRAS*, is upward sloping because as *Y* rises relative to Y^P, labor markets get tighter and inflation rises. *SRAS* intersects *LRAS* at point 1, where current inflation equals the expected inflation.

The preceding reasoning indicates that because the long-run Phillips curve is vertical, the long-run aggregate supply curve is vertical as well.[6] Indeed, the long-run aggregate supply curve (*LRAS*) is vertical at potential output, denoted by Y^P, say, at a quantity of $10 trillion, as drawn in Figure 11.3. Another way to think about the vertical long-run aggregate supply curve is that when wages and prices fully adjust, there is a decoupling of the relationship between unemployment and inflation. The classical dichotomy that we discussed in Chapters 5 and 8 indicates that what happens to the price level is divorced from what is happening in the real economy.

Short-Run Aggregate Supply Curve

We can translate the modern Phillips curve into a short-run aggregate supply curve by replacing the unemployment gap $(U - U_n)$ with the *output gap* we discussed in Chapter 8, the difference between output and potential output $(Y - Y^P)$. To do this, we need to make use of a relationship between unemployment and aggregate output that was discovered by the economist Arthur Okun, once the chairman of the Council of Economic Advisors and later an economist with the Brookings Institution.[7] **Okun's law** describes the negative relationship between the unemployment gap and the output gap.

---

[6]Higher inflation can make for a less efficient economy and thus lead to a decline in the quantity of output actually produced. In this case, the long-run aggregate supply curve might have a downward slope. This insight does not change the basic lessons from aggregate demand and supply analysis in any significant way, so for simplicity we will assume that the long-run aggregate supply curve is vertical.

[7]Arthur M. Okun, "Potential GNP: Its Measurement and Significance," in *Proceeding of the Business and Economics Section: American Statistical Association* (Washington, D.C.: American Statistical Association, 1962), pp. 98–103; reprinted in Arthur M. Okun, *The Political Economy of Prosperity* (Washington, D.C.: Brookings Institution, 1970), pp. 132–145.

OKUN'S LAW. Okun's law states that for each percentage point that output is above potential, the unemployment rate is one-half of a percentage point below the natural rate of unemployment. Algebraically, it can be written as follows:[8]

$$U - U_n = -0.5 \times (Y - Y^P) \tag{5}$$

Another way of thinking about Okun's law is that a one percentage point increase in output leads to a one-half percentage point decline in unemployment.[9] Figure 11.4 shows that the evidence for Okun's law is quite strong because there is a tight negative relationship between the percentage change in unemployment and real GDP growth.

FIGURE 11.4

Okun's Law, 1960–2013

The plot of the percentage point change in the unemployment rate versus the GDP growth rate reveals a linear relationship, represented by the solid line with a slope of $-\frac{1}{2}$.

Source: Unemployment, quarterly, 1960–2013 and real GDP growth, quarterly, 1960–2013. Bureau of Labor Statistics and Bureau of Economic Analysis.

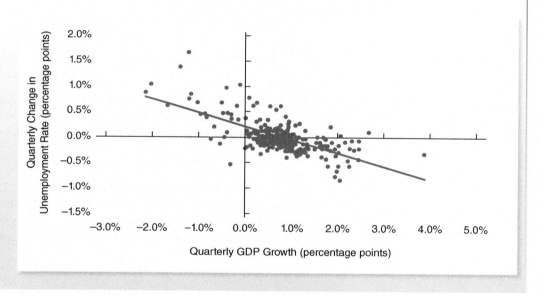

[8]The output gap, $Y - Y^P$, in Okun's law is most accurately expressed in percentage terms, so the units of Y and Y^P would normally be in logs. However, to keep the algebra simple in this and later chapters, we will treat Y and Y^P as levels and not logs both in the Okun's law equation and in the short-run aggregate supply curve developed here.

[9]To see this algebraically, take the differences of Equation 5 and assume that U_n remains constant (a reasonable assumption because the natural rate of unemployment changes very slowly over time). Then,

$$\%\Delta U = -0.5 \times (\%\Delta Y - \%\Delta Y^P)$$

where $\%\Delta$ indicates a percentage point change. Since potential output grows at a fairly steady rate of around three percent a year, $\%\Delta Y^P = 3\%$, we can also write Okun's law as follows:

$$\%\Delta U = -0.5 \times (\%\Delta Y - 3)$$

or

$$\%\Delta Y = 3 - 2.0 \times \%\Delta U$$

Hence we can state Okun's law in the following way: for every percentage point rise in output (real GDP), unemployment falls by one-half of a percentage point. Alternatively, for every percentage point rise in unemployment, real GDP falls by two percentage points.

Why is the rate of decline in unemployment only half the rate of increase in output? When output rises, firms do not increase employment commensurately with the increase in output, a phenomenon that is known as *labor hoarding*. Rather, they work employees harder, increasing their hours. Furthermore, when the economy is expanding, more people enter the labor force because job prospects are better, and so the unemployment rate does not fall by as much as employment increases.

DERIVING THE SHORT-RUN AGGREGATE SUPPLY CURVE. Using the Okun's law Equation 5 to substitute for $U - U_n$ in the short-run Phillips curve Equation 2 yields the following:

$$\pi = \pi^e + 0.5\,\omega\,(Y - Y^P) + \rho$$

Replacing $0.5\,\omega$ by γ, which describes the sensitivity of inflation to the output gap, produces the short-run aggregate supply curve:

$$\pi \quad = \quad \pi^e \quad + \quad \gamma\,(Y - Y^P) \quad + \quad \rho \tag{6}$$

$$\text{Inflation} = \text{Expected} + \gamma \times \text{Output} + \text{Price}$$
$$\text{Inflation} \qquad\qquad \text{Gap} \qquad \text{Shock}$$

As we did in the Phillips curve analysis, we need to make an assumption about how expectations of inflation are formed, and again we will assume that they are adaptive so that $\pi^e = \pi_{-1}$. The short-run aggregate supply curve then becomes

$$\pi = \pi_{-1} + \gamma(Y - Y^P) + \rho \tag{7}$$

Let's assume that inflation last year was at 2%, so that $\pi_{-1} = 2\%$, and that there was no supply shock, so $\rho = 0$, and potential output $Y^P = \$10$ trillion. Let's also assume that the parameter γ, which describes how inflation responds to the output gap, equals 1.5. Then we can write the short-run aggregate supply curve as follows:

$$\pi = 2 + 1.5\,(Y - 10) \tag{8}$$

If Y is at potential output, $Y^P = \$10$ trillion, then the output gap, $Y - 10$, is zero. Equation 8 then shows that at a level of output of $10 trillion, at which the output gap is zero, $\pi = 2\%$. We mark this level as point 1 on the short-run aggregate supply curve, *AS*, in Figure 11.3 on page 288. Note that the short-run supply curve intersects the long-run supply curve at the point at which the 2% current inflation rate equals 2% expected inflation.

Now suppose that aggregate output rises to $11 trillion. Because there is a positive output gap ($Y = \$11$ trillion $> Y^P = \$10$ trillion), Equation 8 indicates that inflation will rise above 2% to 3.5%, marked as point 2. The curve connecting points 1 and 2 is the short-run aggregate supply curve, *AS*, and it is upward sloping. The intuition behind this upward slope comes directly from Okun's law and Phillips curve analysis. When Y rises relative to Y^P and $Y > Y^P$, Okun's law indicates that the unemployment rate falls. With the labor market tighter, the short-run Phillips curve tells us that firms will raise their wages at a more rapid rate. Firms will therefore also raise their prices at a more rapid rate, causing inflation to rise.

Our discussion of how the short-run aggregate supply curve works indicates that there is a close relationship between the Phillips curve and the short-run aggregate supply curve, as is discussed in the box, "The Relationship of the Phillips Curve and the Short-Run Aggregate Supply Curve."

The Relationship of the Phillips Curve and the Short-Run Aggregate Supply Curve

The derivation of Equation 6 illustrates that the short-run aggregate supply curve is in reality just a Phillips curve, but with the unemployment gap replaced by an output gap. Indeed, whenever we talk about the short-run aggregate supply curve, we can think of it as a Phillips curve. However, because output gaps and unemployment gaps are inversely related through Okun's law, the negative relationship between inflation and the unemployment gap implies a positive relationship between inflation and the output gap.

STICKY WAGES AND PRICES IN THE SHORT-RUN AGGREGATE SUPPLY CURVE. As we saw earlier, the short-run Phillips curve implies that wages and prices are sticky. Since we derived the short-run aggregate supply curve from the Phillips curve, sticky wages and prices are embodied in the short-run aggregate supply curve as well. In the short-run aggregate supply curve, the more flexible wages and prices are, the more inflation responds to the output gap. The value of γ would then be higher, which implies that the short-run aggregate supply curve is steeper. When wages and prices are completely flexible, γ becomes so large that the short-run aggregate supply curve becomes vertical and is identical to the long-run supply curve. Completely flexible wages and prices put us back in a classical framework in which aggregate output is always at its potential level.

Shifts in Aggregate Supply Curves

Now that we have derived the long-run and short-run aggregate supply curves, we can look at why each of these curves shifts.

Shifts in the Long-Run Aggregate Supply Curve

The quantity of output supplied in the long run is determined by the production function we examined in Chapter 3. The production function suggests three factors that cause potential output to change, producing a shift in the long-run aggregate supply curve: 1) the total amount of capital in the economy, 2) the total amount of labor supplied in the economy, and 3) the available technology that puts labor and capital together to produce goods and services. When any one of these three factors increases, potential output rises and the long-run aggregate supply curve shifts to the right from $LRAS_1$ to $LRAS_2$, as in Figure 11.5.

Because all three of these factors typically grow fairly steadily over time, Y^P and the long-run aggregate supply curve will keep on shifting to the right at a steady pace. To keep things simple in diagrams in this and later chapters, when Y^P is growing at a steady rate, we represent Y^P and the long-run aggregate supply curve as fixed.

Another source of shifts in the long-run aggregate supply curve is changes in the natural rate of unemployment. If the natural rate of unemployment declines, labor is being more heavily utilized, and so potential output will increase. A decline in the natural

MyEconLab Mini-lecture

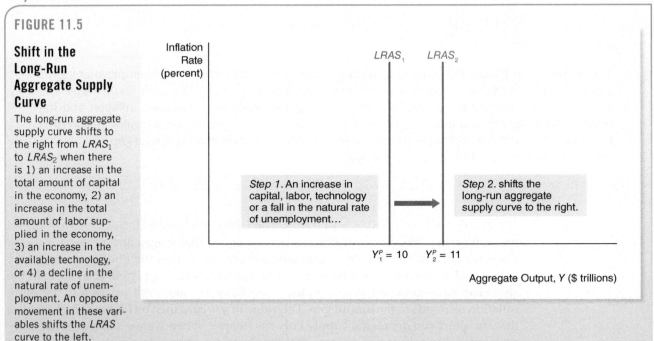

FIGURE 11.5

Shift in the Long-Run Aggregate Supply Curve

The long-run aggregate supply curve shifts to the right from $LRAS_1$ to $LRAS_2$ when there is 1) an increase in the total amount of capital in the economy, 2) an increase in the total amount of labor supplied in the economy, 3) an increase in the available technology, or 4) a decline in the natural rate of unemployment. An opposite movement in these variables shifts the $LRAS$ curve to the left.

rate of unemployment thus shifts the long-run aggregate supply curve to the right from $LRAS_1$ to $LRAS_2$, as in Figure 11.5. A rise in the natural rate of unemployment would have the opposite effect, shifting the long-run aggregate supply curve to the left. In Chapter 20, we discuss factors that cause the natural rate of unemployment to change.

Shifts in the Short-Run Aggregate Supply Curve

The three terms on the right-hand side of Equation 6 for the short-run aggregate supply curve suggest that there are three factors that can shift the short-run aggregate supply curve: 1) expected inflation, 2) price shocks, and 3) a persistent output gap.

EXPECTED INFLATION. Even though we have written expected inflation as π_{-1} in Equation 6, it is important to recognize that expected inflation might change for reasons that are unrelated to the past level of inflation. For example, what if a newly appointed chairman of the Federal Reserve does not think that inflation is costly and so is willing to tolerate an inflation rate that is two percentage points higher? Households and firms will then expect that the Fed will pursue policies that will let inflation rise by two percentage points in the future. In such a situation, expected inflation will jump by two percentage points and the short-run aggregate supply curve will shift upward and to the left, from AS_1 to AS_2 in Figure 11.6.

PRICE SHOCKS. Suppose that energy prices suddenly shoot up because terrorists destroy a number of oil fields. This supply restriction causes the price shock term in Equation 6 to jump up, and so the short-run aggregate supply curve will shift up and to the left, from AS_1 to AS_2 in Figure 11.6.

MyEconLab Mini-lecture

FIGURE 11.6

Shift in the Short-Run Aggregate Supply Curve from Changes in Expected Inflation and Price Shocks

A rise in expected inflation or a positive price shock of two percentage points shifts the short-run aggregate supply curve upward from AS_1 to AS_2. (A decrease in expected inflation or a negative price shock would lead to a downward shift of the AS curve.)

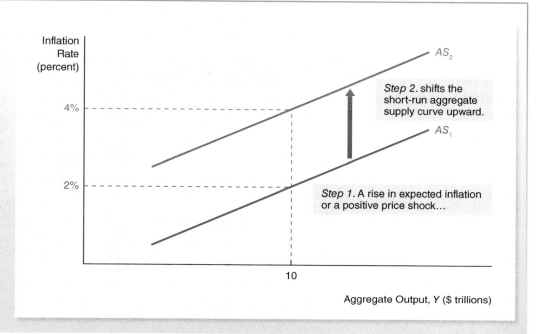

PERSISTENT OUTPUT GAP. We have already seen that a higher output gap leads to higher inflation, causing a movement along the short-run aggregate supply curve. We represent this change by the movement from point 1 to point 2 on the initial short-run aggregate supply curve AS_1 in Figure 11.7. A persistent output gap, however, will cause the short-run aggregate supply curve to shift by affecting expected inflation. To see this, consider what happens if the economy stays at $11 trillion $> Y^P =$ $10 trillion, so that the output gap remains persistently positive. At point 2 on the initial short-run aggregate supply curve AS_1, output has risen to $11 trillion and inflation has risen from 2% to 3.5%. Expected inflation in the next period will rise to 3.5%, and so the short-run aggregate supply curve in the next period, AS_2, will shift upward to

$$\pi = 3.5 + 1.5\,(Y - 10) \tag{9}$$

If output remains at $11 trillion at point 3, then Equation 9 tells us that inflation will rise to 5% $[=\ 3.5\% + 1.5\,(11 - 10)\%]$. As the vertical arrow indicates, the short-run aggregate supply curve will then shift upward to AS_3 in the next period:

$$\pi = 5.0 + 1.5\,(Y - 10) \tag{10}$$

We see that as long as output remains above potential, the short-run aggregate supply curve will keep shifting up and to the left.

When will the short-run aggregate supply curve stop rising? Only when output returns to its potential level and the output gap disappears. Suppose this happens when inflation is at 10% and aggregate output at point 4 is at $Y^P =$ $10 trillion. Now expected inflation is at 10% and the output gap is zero, so the aggregate supply curve drawn through point 4, AS_4, has no further reason to shift.

FIGURE 11.7

Shift in the Short-Run Aggregate Supply Curve from a Persistent Positive Output Gap

When output is at $11 trillion, the economy moves along the AS_1 curve from point 1 to point 2, and inflation rises to 3.5%. If output continues to remain at $11 trillion, where the output gap is positive, the short-run aggregate supply curve shifts up to AS_2 and then to AS_3. The short-run aggregate supply curve stops shifting up when the economy reaches point 4 on the short-run aggregate supply curve, AS_4, where $\pi^e = 10\%$ and the output gap is zero.

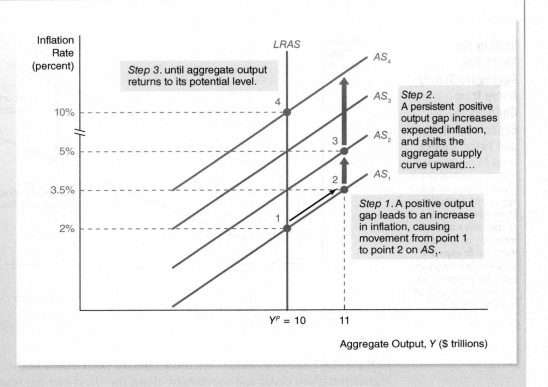

The same reasoning indicates that if aggregate output is kept below potential, $Y < Y^P$, for a sufficiently long period of time, then the short-run aggregate supply curve will shift downward and to the right. This downward shift of the aggregate supply curve will stop only when output returns to its potential level and the economy is back on the long-run aggregate supply curve.

Now that we have a full understanding of aggregate supply curves and why they shift, we have all the building blocks necessary to develop the aggregate demand and supply analysis in the next chapter.

SUMMARY

1. The modern Phillips curve, $\pi = \pi^e - \omega(U - U_n) + \rho$, indicates that inflation is negatively correlated to the unemployment gap and is positively correlated to expected inflation and price shocks. Although the long-run Phillips curve is vertical—that is, unemployment is at the natural rate of unemployment for any inflation rate—the short-run Phillips curve, which is determined for a given level of expected inflation, is downward-sloping (a lower level of the unemployment gap leads to higher inflation). In other words, there is no long-run trade-off between unemployment and inflation, but there is a short-run trade-off.

2. The long-run aggregate supply curve is vertical at potential output, Y^P. The short-run aggregate supply curve, $\pi = \pi^e + \gamma(Y - Y^P) + \rho$, slopes upward because as output rises relative to potential output and labor markets tighten, inflation rises. Assuming that expectations of inflation are adaptive so that $\pi^e = \pi_{-1}$, the short-run aggregate supply curve can be written as $\pi = \pi_{-1} + \gamma(Y - Y^P) + \rho$.

3. Four factors cause the long-run aggregate supply curve to shift to the right: 1) a rise in the total amount of capital in the economy, 2) a rise in the total amount of labor supplied in the economy, 3) better technology that generates more output from the same amount of capital and labor, and 4) a fall in the natural rate of unemployment. Three factors cause the short-run aggregate supply curve to shift upward: 1) a rise in expected inflation, 2) a price shock that leads to higher inflation, and 3) a positive output gap.

KEY TERMS

accelerationist Phillips
  curve, p. 287
adaptive expectations, p. 286
aggregate supply curve, p. 287
backward-looking
  expectations, p. 286
cost-push shocks, p. 286

expectations-augmented Phillips
  curve, p. 284
long-run Phillips curve, p. 285
natural rate of output, p. 287
natural rate of
  unemployment, p. 283

non-accelerating inflation
  rate of unemployment
  (NAIRU), p. 287
Okun's law, p. 288
Phillips curve, p. 281
price shocks, p. 286
unemployment gap, p. 284

REVIEW QUESTIONS

All Questions are available in MyEconLab *for practice or instructor assignment.*

The Phillips Curve

1. What basic relationship does the short-run Phillips curve describe? What trade-offs does this relationship seem to offer policy makers?
2. What basic relationship does the long-run Phillips curve describe? How does this relationship differ from that described by the short-run Phillips curve?
3. According to the expectations-augmented Phillips curve, what factors determine the rate of inflation? How do changes in each factor affect the short-run Phillips curve?
4. What are adaptive expectations? What justifies the assumption of adaptive expectations in Phillips curve analysis?
5. According to modern Phillips curve analysis, what factors determine the rate of inflation? How do changes in each factor affect the short-run Phillips curve?

The Aggregate Supply Curve

6. What relationship does the aggregate supply curve describe? How is this relationship depicted with the long-run aggregate supply curve?
7. What is Okun's law? How do we combine it with Phillips curve analysis to derive the short-run aggregate supply curve?

8. Why does the short-run aggregate supply curve slope upward?

Shifts in Aggregate Supply Curves

9. What causes the long-run aggregate supply curve to shift?

10. What causes the short-run aggregate supply curve to shift?

PROBLEMS

All Problems are available in MyEconLab *for practice or instructor assignment.*

The Phillips Curve

1. Plot the Phillips curve for Canada using the following data. Do you find evidence in favor of the Phillips curve in your plot? Explain.

	1960	1961	1962	1963	1964	1965	1966	1967	1968	1969
Inflation Rate (%)	1.4	1	1.1	1.6	1.9	2.3	3.8	3.6	4.1	4.6
Unemployment Rate (%)	7	7.2	6	5.6	4.7	4	3.4	3.8	4.5	4.4

2. The following graph shows inflation and unemployment rates for Canada for the period between 1970 and 2012. Does this graph show evidence in favor of the Phillips curve?

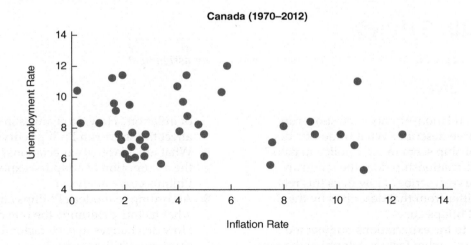

3. Suppose that the expectations-augmented Phillips curve is given by $\pi = \pi^e - 0.5(U - U_n)$. If expected inflation is 3% and the natural rate of unemployment is 5%, complete the following:

   a) Calculate the inflation rate according to the Phillips curve if unemployment is at 4%, 5%, and 6%.

   b) Plot the points from part (a) on a graph, and label the Phillips curve.

c) If wages were to become more rigid, what would happen to the slope of this Phillips curve?

4. During 2007, the U.S. economy was hit by a price shock when the price of oil increased from around $60 per barrel to around $130 per barrel by June 2008. While inflation increased during the fall of 2007 (from around 2.5% to 4.0%), unemployment did not change significantly (it even increased slightly). Explain the relationship between inflation and unemployment in 2007 using the modern Phillips curve concept.

The Aggregate Supply Curve

5. Suppose Okun's law can be expressed according to the following formula:
$U - U_n = -0.75 \times (Y - Y^P)$. Assuming that potential output grows at a steady rate of 2.5% and that the natural rate of unemployment remains unchanged,
   a) Calculate by how much unemployment increases when real GDP decreases by one percentage point.
   b) Calculate by how much real GDP increases when unemployment decreases by two percentage points.

6. Assuming that Okun's law is given by
$U - U_n = -0.75 \times (Y - Y^P)$ and that the Phillips curve is given by $\pi = \pi^e - 0.6 \times (U - U_n) + \rho$,
   a) Obtain the short-run aggregate supply curve if expectations are adaptive, inflation was 3% last year, and potential output is $10 trillion (assume $\rho = 0$).

   b) Calculate inflation when output is $8, $10, and $12 trillion, and plot the short-run aggregate supply curve.

7. Using the expression for the short-run aggregate supply curve obtained in Problem 6, draw a new short-run aggregate supply curve on the same graph if there is a price shock such that $\rho = 2$. Calculate inflation when output is $8, $10, and $12 trillion, respectively.

8. Although Okun's law holds for different countries, those with more flexible labor markets experience a higher response of unemployment to changes in GDP. During the recent financial crisis, real GDP decreased in the United States, Germany, and France. Considering that the U.S. labor market is more flexible than European labor markets, would you expect the same increase in unemployment in these three countries?

Shifts in Aggregate Supply Curves

9. Internet sites that allow people to post their resumes online reduce the costs of job searches and create opportunities for individuals looking for jobs to be matched with potential employers more quickly. Assume that these advantages of Internet job hunting reduce the average amount of time people are unemployed.
   a) How do you think the Internet has affected the natural rate of unemployment?

   b) Show graphically how use of the Internet by job searchers and employers affects long-run aggregate supply.

10. Some Federal Reserve officials have discussed the possibility of increasing interest rates as a way of fighting potential increases in expected inflation. If the public came to expect higher inflation rates in the future, what would be the effect on the short-run aggregate supply curve? Show your answer graphically.

DATA ANALYSIS PROBLEMS

The Problems update with real-time data in MyEconLab *and are available for practice or instructor assignment.*

🌐 1. Go to the St. Louis Federal Reserve FRED database, and find data on the unemployment rate (UNRATE) and a measure of the price level, the personal consumption expenditure price index (PCECTPI). For both series, choose the *frequency* as "quarterly," and for the price index series, choose the *units* as "Percent Change From Year Ago." Download both series onto a spreadsheet.

a) Create a scatter plot of the quarterly unemployment and inflation data, from 2000 to the most recent available data. Identify the point that represents the most recent data on inflation and unemployment. Do the data support a Phillips curve–like inverse relationship between inflation and unemployment?

b) (Advanced) Using the unemployment and inflation data above, create a fitted (or regression) line of the data on the scatter plot, using the unemployment rate as the independent variable. (Excel has scatter plot layouts that you can use to do this automatically, or you can use Data Analysis with the ToolPak for Excel.) Report the equation for the fitted line.

 i. Based on the fitted line, how much would inflation have to change, on average, in order to lower the unemployment rate by one percentage point? What would be the most recent readings of inflation and the unemployment rate if that happened?

 ii. How much predictive power does your estimated Phillips curve have? Why might the Friedman-Phelps or modern Phillips curves perform better? Briefly explain.

2. Go to the St. Louis Federal Reserve FRED database, and find data on potential output (GDPPOT), real GDP (GDPC1), and a measure of the price level, the personal consumption expenditure price index (PCECTPI). For the price index series, choose the *units* as "Percent Change From Year Ago." Download the series onto a spreadsheet. Create a measure of the output gap, defined as the percentage difference between (actual) real GDP and potential GDP, for each quarter.

a) Identify the periods, from 2000 to the most recent data available, in which output is consistently either above or below potential (ignore an isolated quarter that switches or is transitory).

b) For each of the periods identified in part (a), calculate the average output gap and the percentage point change in the inflation rate from the beginning to the end of the period.

c) Are your results in part (b) consistent with an accelerationist view of the Phillips curve? Why or why not? Briefly explain.

3. (Advanced) Go to the St. Louis Federal Reserve FRED database, and find data on potential output (GDPPOT), real GDP (GDPC1), a measure of the price level, the personal consumption expenditure price index (PCECTPI), and the University of Michigan inflation expectations measure, (MICH). For the price index series, choose the *units* as "Percent Change From Year Ago," and for the inflation expectations measure, choose the *frequency* as "Quarterly." Download all of the series onto a spreadsheet. Create a measure of the output gap, defined as the percentage difference between (actual) real GDP and potential GDP, for each quarter.

a) Estimate a version of the short-run aggregate supply curve using inflation as the dependent (Y) variable and the inflation expectations and output gap measures as independent variables (X variables). Use the transformed data above, from 2000 to the most recent data available, and run a linear regression of these variables. (You can do this in Excel by using the Data Analysis ToolPak.)

b) Are the regression results consistent with a short-run aggregate supply curve model? Are the coefficient values sensible? Interpret the coefficients and briefly explain.

c) How much predictive power does your estimated short-run aggregate supply curve have? Compare your results with those you obtained in Problem 1(b) above (if applicable). Explain the difference in predictive power between the simple Phillips curve estimation and the short-run aggregate supply curve estimation you just created.

d) Based on the most current data available and your regression results, by how much would inflation change if policy makers were to close the output gap?

The Aggregate Demand and Supply Model

12

Preview

In 2007 and 2008, the U.S. economy encountered a perfect storm. Oil prices more than doubled, climbing to a record high of over $140 per barrel by July 2008 and sending gasoline prices to over $4 per gallon. At the same time, defaults by borrowers with weak credit records in the subprime mortgage market seized up the financial markets and caused consumer and business spending to decline. The result was a severe economic contraction at the same time that the inflation rate spiked.

To understand how developments in 2007–2008 had such negative effects on the economy, we now put together the aggregate demand and aggregate supply concepts from the previous three chapters to develop a basic tool, aggregate demand and supply analysis. As with the supply and demand analysis from your earlier economics courses, equilibrium occurs at the intersection of the aggregate demand and aggregate supply curves.

Aggregate demand and supply analysis is a powerful tool for studying short-run fluctuations in the macroeconomy and analyzing how aggregate output and the inflation rate are determined. The analysis will help us interpret episodes in the business cycle such as the recent severe recession in 2007–2009. In addition, in later chapters it will also enable us to evaluate the debates on how economic policy should be conducted.

Recap of the Aggregate Demand and Supply Curves

As a starting point, let's take stock of the building blocks for the aggregate demand and aggregate supply model that we developed across Chapters 9–11 by revisiting the aggregate demand and aggregate supply curves.

The Aggregate Demand Curve

Recall that the aggregate demand curve indicates the relationship between the inflation rate and the level of aggregate output when the goods market is in equilibrium, that is, when aggregate output equals the total quantity of output demanded. We saw in Chapter 10 that the aggregate demand curve is downward sloping because a rise in inflation leads the monetary policy authorities to raise real interest rates to keep inflation from spiraling out of control, which lowers planned expenditure (aggregate demand) and hence the equilibrium level of aggregate output. The negative relationship between inflation and equilibrium output reflected in the downward sloping aggregate demand curve can be illustrated by the following schematic.

$$\pi \uparrow \Rightarrow r \uparrow \Rightarrow I \downarrow, C \downarrow, NX \downarrow \Rightarrow Y \downarrow$$

Factors That Shift the Aggregate Demand Curve

As we saw in Chapter 10, seven basic factors that are exogenous to the model can shift the aggregate demand curve to a new position: 1) autonomous monetary policy, 2) government purchases, 3) taxes, 4) autonomous net exports, 5) autonomous consumption expenditure, 6) autonomous investment, and 7) financial frictions. (The use of the term *autonomous* in the factors above sometimes confuses students, and so it is discussed in the box "What Does *Autonomous* Mean?") As we examine each case, we ask what happens when each of these factors changes holding the inflation rate constant. As a study aid, Table 12.1 summarizes the shifts in the aggregate demand curve from each of these seven factors.

1. *Autonomous monetary policy.* When the Federal Reserve autonomously tightens monetary policy, it raises the autonomous component of the real interest rate, $\bar{r}$, that is unrelated to the current level of the inflation rate. The higher real interest rate at any given inflation rate leads to a higher real interest rate for financing investment projects, which leads to a decline in investment spending and planned expenditure. Higher real interest rates also lead to lower consumption spending and net exports. Therefore the equilibrium level of aggregate output falls at any given inflation rate, as the following schematic demonstrates.

$$\bar{r} \uparrow \Rightarrow I \downarrow, C \downarrow, NX \downarrow \Rightarrow Y \downarrow$$

The aggregate demand curve therefore shifts to the left.

TABLE 12.1 **FACTORS THAT SHIFT THE AGGREGATE DEMAND CURVE**

Note: Only increases (↑) in the factors are shown. The effect of decreases in the factors would be the opposite of those indicated in the "Shift" column.

Factor	Change	Shift in Demand Curve
Autonomous monetary policy, $\bar{r}$	↑	←
Government purchases, $\bar{G}$	↑	→
Taxes, $\bar{T}$	↑	←
Autonomous net exports, $\overline{NX}$	↑	→
Consumer optimism, $\bar{C}$	↑	→
Business optimism, $\bar{I}$	↑	→
Financial frictions, $\bar{f}$	↑	←

What Does *Autonomous* Mean?

When economists use the word *autonomous*, they are referring to the component of the variable that is exogenous (independent of other variables in the model). For example, autonomous monetary policy is the component of the real interest rate set by the central bank that is unrelated to inflation or to any other variable in the model. Changes in autonomous components therefore are never associated with movements along a curve, but always with shifts in the curves. Hence a change in autonomous monetary policy shifts the *MP* and *AD* curves but is never a movement along those curves.

2. *Government purchases.* An increase in government purchases at any given inflation rate adds directly to planned expenditure and hence the equilibrium level of aggregate output rises:

$$\overline{G}\uparrow \Rightarrow Y\uparrow$$

As a result, the aggregate demand curve shifts to the right.

3. *Taxes.* At any given inflation rate, an increase in taxes lowers disposable income, which will lead to lower consumption expenditure and planned expenditure, so that the equilibrium level of aggregate output falls:

$$\overline{T}\uparrow \Rightarrow C\downarrow \Rightarrow Y\downarrow$$

At any given inflation rate, the aggregate demand curve shifts to the left.

4. *Autonomous net exports.* An autonomous increase in net exports at any given inflation rate adds directly to planned expenditure and so raises the equilibrium level of aggregate output:

$$\overline{NX}\uparrow \Rightarrow Y\uparrow$$

Thus the aggregate demand curve shifts to the right.

5. *Autonomous consumption expenditure.* When consumers become more optimistic, autonomous consumption expenditure rises, and so they spend more at any given inflation rate. Planned expenditure therefore rises, as does the equilibrium level of aggregate output:

$$\overline{C}\uparrow \Rightarrow Y\uparrow$$

The aggregate demand curve shifts to the right.

6. *Autonomous investment.* When businesses become more optimistic, autonomous investment rises, and they spend more at any given inflation rate. Planned investment increases and the equilibrium level of aggregate output rises.

$$\overline{I}\uparrow \Rightarrow Y\uparrow$$

The aggregate demand curve shifts to the right.

7. *Financial frictions.* The real interest rate for investments reflects not only the real short-term interest rate on default-free debt instruments, r, that central banks set, but also financial frictions, denoted by $\bar{f}$, which are the extra costs of borrowing caused by barriers to efficient functioning of financial markets. When financial frictions increase, the real interest rate for investments increases, so that planned investment spending falls at any given inflation rate and the equilibrium level of aggregate output falls.

$$\bar{f}\uparrow \Rightarrow r_i\uparrow \Rightarrow I\downarrow \Rightarrow Y\downarrow$$

The aggregate demand curve shifts to the left.

Short- and Long-Run Aggregate Supply Curves

As we saw in the preceding chapter, the aggregate supply curve, which indicates the relationship between the total quantity of output supplied and the inflation rate, comes in short- and long-run varieties.

Because in the long run wages and prices are fully flexible, the long-run aggregate supply curve is determined by the factors of production—labor and capital—and the technology that is available at the time, as well as the natural rate of unemployment. We typically assume that technology, the factors of production, and the natural rate of unemployment are independent of the level of inflation. As a result, the long-run supply curve is vertical at the level of potential output, Y^P: output higher or lower than this level would cause inflation to adjust until output returned to its potential level.

Because wages and prices take time to adjust to economic conditions—as they are sticky—wages and prices will not fully adjust in the short run to keep output at its potential level. Instead, output above potential, which means that labor and product markets are tight, will cause inflation to rise above its current level. However, the rise will be limited in the short run, in contrast to the long run. As a result, the short-run aggregate supply curve is upward sloping, but not vertical: as output rises relative to potential, inflation rises from its current level.

Factors that Shift the Long-Run Aggregate Supply Curve

The long-run aggregate supply curve shifts when there are shocks to the natural rate of unemployment and technology or long-run changes in the amounts of labor or capital that affect the amount of output that the economy can produce. Because technology improves over time and factors of production accumulate too, Y^P steadily but gradually moves to the right (for simplicity, we ignore this gradual drift in our analysis).

Factors that Shift the Short-Run Aggregate Supply Curve

Three factors can shift the short-run aggregate supply curve: 1) expected inflation, 2) price shocks, and 3) a persistent output gap. As a study aid, Table 12.2 summarizes the shifts in the short-run aggregate supply curve from each of these three factors.

1. *Expected inflation.* When expected inflation rises, workers and firms will want to raise wages and prices more, causing inflation to rise. Higher expected inflation thus leads to an upward and leftward shift in the short-run aggregate supply curve.

TABLE 12.2	FACTORS THAT SHIFT THE SHORT-RUN AGGREGATE SUPPLY CURVE

Note: Only increases (↑) in the factors are shown. The effect of decreases in the factors would be the opposite of those indicated in the "Shift" column.

Factor	Change	Shift in Supply Curve
Expected inflation, π^e	↑	↑
Price shocks, ρ	↑	↑
Output gap, $(Y - Y^P)$	↑	↑

2. *Price shocks.* Negative supply shocks or workers pushing for higher wages can cause firms to raise prices, which causes inflation to rise and shifts the short-run aggregate supply curve upward and to the left.

3. *Persistent output gap.* When output remains high relative to potential output, the output gap is persistently positive $(Y > Y^P)$. Labor and product markets remain tight, which raises the current level of inflation from its initial level. As long as the output gap persists, inflation will continue to rise next period, as will expected inflation. The positive output gap leads to an upward and leftward shift in the short-run aggregate supply curve.

Equilibrium in Aggregate Demand and Supply Analysis

We can now put the aggregate demand and supply curves together to describe **general equilibrium** in the economy, when all markets are simultaneously in equilibrium at the point where the quantity of aggregate output demanded equals the quantity of aggregate output supplied. We represent general equilibrium graphically as the point where the aggregate demand curve intersects with the aggregate supply curve. However, recall that we have two aggregate supply curves: one for the short run and one for the long run. Consequently, in the context of aggregate supply and demand analysis, there are short-run and long-run equilibriums. In this section, we illustrate equilibrium in the short and long runs. In following sections we examine aggregate demand and aggregate supply shocks that lead to changes in equilibrium.

Short-Run Equilibrium

Figure 12.1 illustrates a short-run equilibrium in which the quantity of aggregate output demanded equals the quantity of output supplied. In Figure 12.1, the short-run aggregate demand curve *AD* and the short-run aggregate supply curve *AS* intersect at point E with an equilibrium level of aggregate output $Y^* = \$10$ trillion and an equilibrium inflation rate $\pi^* = 2\%$. (We derive the equilibrium output and inflation rate algebraically in the box "Algebraic Determination of the Equilibrium Output and Inflation Rate.")[1]

---

[1]A Web appendix to this chapter, found at www.pearsonhighered.com/mishkin, outlines a more general algebraic analysis of the *AD/AS* model.

FIGURE 12.1

Short-Run Equilibrium

Short-run equilibrium occurs at point E at the intersection of the aggregate demand curve *AD* and the short-run aggregate supply curve *AS*.

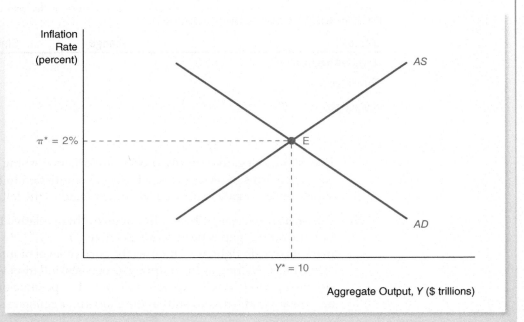

Algebraic Determination of the Equilibrium Output and Inflation Rate

The *AD* curve in Figure 12.1 is the aggregate demand curve we discussed in Chapter 10,

$$Y = 11 - 0.5\pi \qquad (1)$$

The *AS* curve is the short-run aggregate supply curve described in Chapter 11, where the inflation rate last period is 2%:

$$\pi = 2 + 1.5\,(Y - 10) \qquad (2)$$

To show algebraically that equilibrium occurs where $Y = \$10$ trillion and $\pi = 2\%$, we substitute the expression for π from Equation 2 into Equation 1 to get,

$$Y = 11 - 0.5[\,2 + 1.5(Y - 10)\,]$$
$$= 11 - 1 - .75Y + 7.5$$

Collecting terms in Y,

$$Y[\,1 + .75\,] = 17.5$$

Dividing both sides by 1.75 shows that equilibrium $Y = \$10$ trillion. Then substituting this value of equilibrium output into the short-run aggregate supply Equation 2 yields the following:

$$\pi = 2 + 1.5\,(10 - 10) = 2$$

So the equilibrium inflation rate is 2%.

Long-Run Equilibrium

In supply and demand analysis, once we find the equilibrium at which the quantity demanded equals the quantity supplied, there is typically no need for additional analysis. In *aggregate* supply and demand analysis, however, that is not the case. Even when the quantity of aggregate output demanded equals the quantity supplied at the intersection of the aggregate demand curve and the short-run aggregate supply curve, if output differs from its potential level ($Y^* \neq Y^P$), the equilibrium will move over time. To understand why, recall that if the current level of inflation changes from its initial level, the short-run aggregate supply curve will shift as wages and prices adjust to a new expected rate of inflation.

Short-Run Equilibrium over Time

We look at how the short-run equilibrium changes over time in response to two situations: when short-run equilibrium output is initially above potential output (the natural rate of output) and when it is initially below potential output. We will once again assume that potential output equals $10 trillion.

In panel (a) of Figure 12.2, the initial equilibrium occurs at point 1, the intersection of the aggregate demand curve AD and the initial short-run aggregate supply curve AS_1. The level of equilibrium output, $Y_1 = \$11$ trillion, is greater than potential output $Y^P = \$10$ trillion. Unemployment is therefore less than its natural rate, and there is excessive tightness in the labor market. As the Phillips curve analysis in Chapter 11 indicates, tightness at $Y_1 = \$11$ trillion drives wages up and causes firms to raise their prices at a more rapid rate. Inflation will then rise above the initial inflation rate, π_1. Hence, next period, firms and households adjust their expectations and expected inflation is higher. Wages and prices will then rise more rapidly, and the aggregate supply curve shifts up and to the left from AS_1 to AS_2.

The new short-run equilibrium at point 2 is a movement up the aggregate demand curve and output falls to Y_2. However, because aggregate output Y_2 is still above potential output Y^P, wages and prices increase at an even higher rate, so inflation again rises above its value last period. Expected inflation rises further, eventually shifting the aggregate supply curve up and to the left to AS_3. The economy reaches long-run equilibrium at point 3 on the vertical long-run aggregate supply curve ($LRAS$) at Y^P. Because output is at potential, there is no further pressure on inflation to rise and thus no further tendency for the aggregate supply curve to shift.

The movements in panel (a) indicate that the economy will not remain at a level of output higher than potential output of $10 trillion over time. Specifically, the short-run aggregate supply curve will shift to the left, raise the inflation rate, and cause the economy (equilibrium) to move upward along the aggregate demand curve until it comes to rest at a point on the long-run aggregate supply curve at potential output $Y^P = \$10$ trillion.

In panel (b), at the initial equilibrium at point 1, output $Y_1 = \$9$ trillion is below the level of potential output. Because unemployment is now above its natural rate, there is excess slack in the labor markets. This slack at $Y_1 = \$9$ trillion decreases inflation, shifting the short-run aggregate supply curve in the next period down and to the right to AS_2.

The equilibrium will now move to point 2 and output rises to Y_2. However, because aggregate output Y_2 is still below potential, Y^P, inflation again declines from its value last

MyEconLab Mini-lecture

FIGURE 12.2

Adjustment to Long-Run Equilibrium in Aggregate Supply and Demand Analysis

In both panels, the initial short-run equilibrium is at point 1 at the intersection of *AD* and *AS*₁. In panel (a), initial short-run equilibrium is above potential output, the long-run equilibrium, so the short-run aggregate supply curve shifts upward until it reaches *AS*₃, where output returns to Y^P. In panel (b), initial short-run equilibrium is below potential output, so the short-run aggregate supply curve shifts downward until output again returns to Y^P. In both panels, the economy's self-correcting mechanism returns it to the level of potential output.

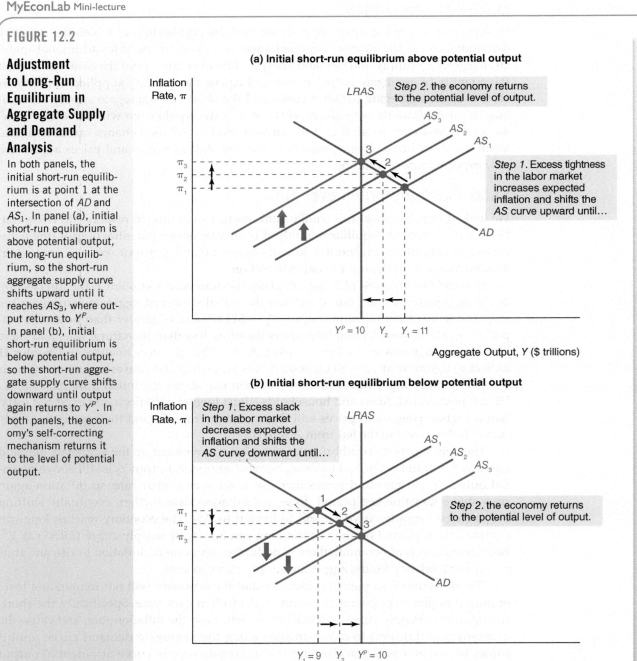

period, shifting the aggregate supply curve down until it comes to rest at *AS*₃. The economy (equilibrium) moves downward along the aggregate demand curve until it reaches the long-run equilibrium point 3, the intersection of the aggregate demand curve (*AD*) and the long-run aggregate supply curve (*LRAS*) at $Y^P = \$10$ trillion. Here, as in panel (a), the economy comes to rest when output has again returned to its potential level.

Self-Correcting Mechanism

Notice that in both panels of Figure 12.2, regardless of where output is initially, it returns eventually to potential output, a feature we call the **self-correcting mechanism**. The self-correcting mechanism occurs because the short-run aggregate supply curve shifts up or down to restore the economy to full employment (aggregate output at potential) over time.

Changes in Equilibrium: Aggregate Demand Shocks

With an understanding of the distinction between the short-run and long-run equilibria, you are now ready to analyze what happens when there are **demand shocks**, shocks that cause the aggregate demand curve to shift. Figure 12.3 depicts the effect of a rightward shift in the aggregate demand curve due to positive demand shocks caused by one or more of the following:

- An autonomous easing of monetary policy ($\bar{r}\downarrow$, a lowering of the real interest rate at any given inflation rate)
- An increase in government purchases ($\overline{G}\uparrow$)
- A decrease in taxes ($\overline{T}\downarrow$)
- An increase in net exports ($\overline{NX}\uparrow$)
- An increase in the willingness of consumers and businesses to spend because they become more optimistic ($\overline{C}\uparrow$, $\overline{I}\uparrow$)
- A decrease in financial frictions ($\bar{f}\downarrow$)

Figure 12.3 shows the economy initially in long-run equilibrium at point 1, where the initial aggregate demand curve AD_1 intersects the short-run aggregate supply

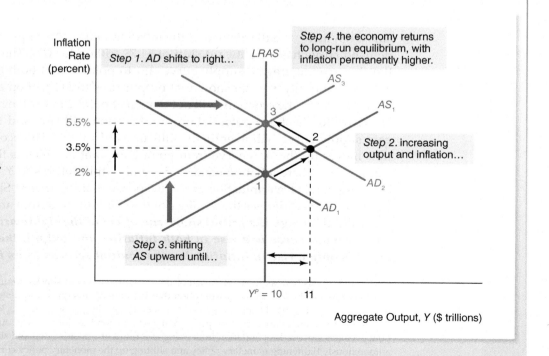

FIGURE 12.3

Positive Demand Shock

A positive demand shock shifts the aggregate demand curve upward from AD_1 to AD_2 and moves the economy from point 1 to point 2, resulting in higher inflation at 3.5% and higher output of $11 trillion. Because output is greater than potential output, the short-run aggregate supply curve begins to shift up, eventually reaching AS_3. At point 3, the economy returns to long-run equilibrium, with output at $Y^P = $10 trillion and the inflation level rising to 5.5%.

Algebraic Determination of the Response to a Rightward Shift of the Aggregate Demand Curve

We begin our algebraic look at the increase in aggregate demand the same way we did our graphical analysis: suppose that the aggregate demand curve shifts rightward by $1.75 trillion to AD_2, which we represent in equation form as $Y = 12.75 - 0.5\pi$. Substituting in for $\pi = 2 + 1.5(Y - 10)$ from the AS_1 curve yields the following:

$$Y = 12.75 - 0.5[2 + 1.5(Y - 10)]$$

$$= 12.75 - 1 - 0.75Y + 7.5$$

$$= 19.25 - 0.75Y$$

Collecting the terms in Y

$$Y(1 + 0.75) = 19.25$$

and dividing both sides of the equation by 1.75 shows that the equilibrium output at point 2 is 19.25/1.75 = $11 trillion. Substituting this value of equilibrium output into the short-run aggregate supply equation, $\pi = 2 + 1.5(Y - 10)$, yields the following:

$$\pi = 2 + 1.5(11 - 10) = 3.5$$

so the equilibrium inflation rate is 3.5%.

Long-run output goes to the potential level of output, so $Y = Y^P = $10 trillion. Substituting this value of output into the aggregate demand curve AD_2, $Y = 12.75 - 0.5\pi$,

$$10 = 12.75 - 0.5\pi$$

which we can rewrite as

$$0.5\pi = 12.75 - 10 = 2.75$$

Dividing both sides of the equation by 0.5 indicates that $\pi = 5.5$. Thus at the long-run equilibrium at point 3, the inflation rate is 5.5% as in Figure 12.3.

curve AS_1 at $Y^P = $10 trillion and the inflation rate = 2%. Suppose that the aggregate demand curve has a rightward shift of $1.75 trillion to AD_2. The economy moves up the short-run aggregate supply curve AS_1 to point 2, and both output and inflation rise. Algebraically, we can show that output rises to $11 trillion and inflation rises to 3.5%. However, the economy will not remain at point 2 in the long run, because output at $11 trillion is above potential output. Inflation will rise, and the short-run aggregate supply curve will eventually shift upward to AS_3. The economy (equilibrium) thus moves up the AD_2 curve from point 2 to point 3, which is the point of long-run equilibrium where inflation equals 5.5% and output returns to $Y^P = $10 trillion. (The box, "Algebraic Determination of the Response to a Rightward Shift of the Aggregate Demand Curve," derives these values of the equilibrium output and inflation rate algebraically.) ***Although the initial short-run effect of the rightward shift in the aggregate demand curve is a rise in both inflation and output, the ultimate long-run effect is only a rise in inflation because output returns to its initial level at Y^P.***[2]

[2]Note the analysis here assumes that each of these positive demand shocks occurs holding everything else constant, the usual *ceteris paribus* assumption that is standard in supply and demand analysis. Specifically this means that the central bank is assumed to not be responding to demand shocks. In Chapter 13, we relax this assumption and allow monetary policy makers to respond to these shocks. As we will see, if monetary policy makers want to keep inflation from rising as a result of a positive demand shock, they will respond by autonomously tightening monetary policy and shifting up the monetary policy curve.

We now turn to applying the aggregate demand and supply model to demand shocks, as a payoff for our hard work constructing the model. Throughout the remainder of this chapter, we will apply aggregate supply and demand analysis to a number of business cycle episodes, both in the United States and in foreign countries, over the last forty years. To simplify our analysis, we always assume in all examples that aggregate output is initially at the level of potential output.

Application

The Volcker Disinflation, 1980–1986

When Paul Volcker became the chairman of the Federal Reserve in August 1979, inflation had spun out of control and the inflation rate exceeded 10%. Volcker was determined to get inflation down. By early 1981, the Federal Reserve had raised the federal funds rate to over

MyEconLab Mini-lecture

FIGURE 12.4

The Volcker Disinflation

Panel (a) shows that Fed Chairman Volcker's actions to decrease inflation were successful but costly: the autonomous monetary policy tightening caused a negative demand shock that decreased aggregate demand and in turn inflation, resulting in soaring unemployment rates. The data in panel (b) supports this analysis: note the decline in the inflation rate from 13.5% in 1980 to 1.9% in 1986, while the unemployment rate increased as high as 9.7% in 1982.

Source: Economic Report of the President.

(a) Aggregate Demand and Aggregate Supply Analysis

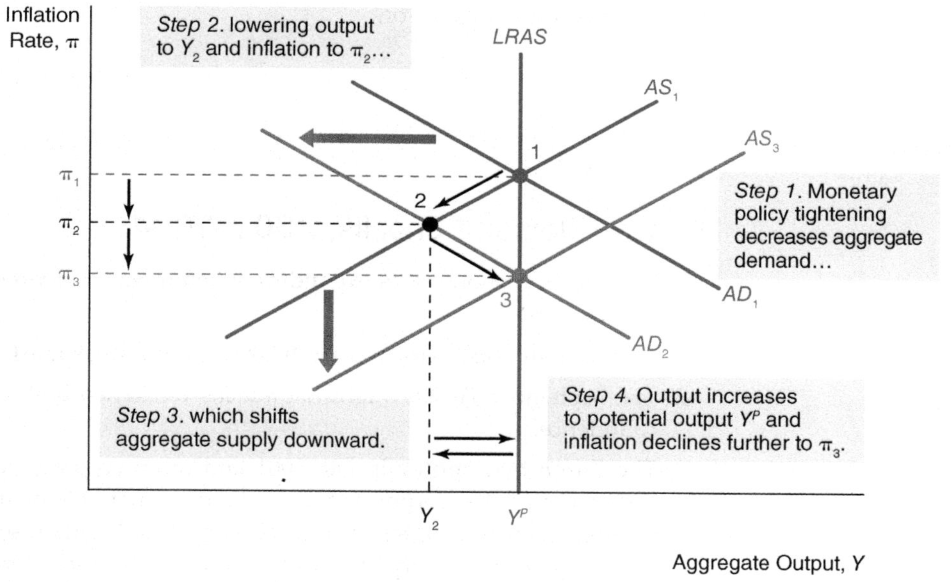

Step 2. lowering output to Y_2 and inflation to π_2...

Step 1. Monetary policy tightening decreases aggregate demand...

Step 3. which shifts aggregate supply downward.

Step 4. Output increases to potential output Y^p and inflation declines further to π_3.

(b) Unemployment and Inflation, 1980–1986

Year	Unemployment Rate (%)	Inflation (Year to Year) (%)
1980	7.1	13.5
1981	7.6	10.3
1982	9.7	6.2
1983	9.6	3.2
1984	7.5	4.3
1985	7.2	3.6
1986	7.0	1.9

20%, which led to a sharp increase in real interest rates. Volcker was indeed successful in bringing inflation down, as panel (b) of Figure 12.4 indicates, with the inflation rate falling from 13.5% in 1980 to 1.9% in 1986. The decline in inflation came at a high cost: the economy experienced the worst recession up to that time since World War II, with the unemployment rate soaring to 9.7% in 1982.

This outcome is exactly what our aggregate demand and supply analysis predicts. The autonomous tightening of monetary policy decreased aggregate demand and shifted the aggregate demand curve to the left from AD_1 to AD_2, as we show in panel (a) of Figure 12.4. The economy moved to point 2, indicating that unemployment would rise and inflation would fall. With unemployment above the natural rate and output below potential, the short-run aggregate supply curve shifted downward and to the right to AS_3. The economy moved toward long-run equilibrium at point 3, with inflation continuing to fall, output rising back to potential output, and the unemployment rate moving toward its natural rate level. Figure 12.4 panel (b) shows that by 1986, the unemployment rate had fallen to 7% and the inflation rate was 1.9%, just as our aggregate demand and supply analysis predicts.

The next period we will examine, 2001–2004, again illustrates negative demand shocks—this time, three at once.

Application

Negative Demand Shocks, 2001–2004

In 2000, the U.S. economy was expanding when it was hit by a series of negative shocks to aggregate demand.

1. The "tech bubble" burst in March 2000 and the stock market fell sharply.

2. The September 11, 2001, terrorist attacks weakened both consumer and business confidence.

3. The Enron bankruptcy in late 2001 and other corporate accounting scandals in 2002 revealed that corporate financial data were not to be trusted, and so financial frictions increased. Interest rates on corporate bonds rose as a result, making it more expensive for corporations to finance their investments.

All these negative demand shocks led to a decline in household and business spending, decreasing aggregate demand and shifting the aggregate demand curve to the left from AD_1 to AD_2 in panel (a) of Figure 12.5. At point 2, as our aggregate demand and supply analysis predicts, unemployment rose and inflation fell. Panel (b) of Figure 12.5 shows that the unemployment rate, which had been at 4% in 2000, rose to 6% in 2003, while the annual rate of inflation fell from 3.4% in 2000 to 1.6% in 2002. With unemployment above the natural rate (estimated to be around 5%) and output below potential, the short-run aggregate supply curve shifted downward to AS_3, as we show in panel (a) of Figure 12.5. The economy moved to point 3, with inflation falling, output rising back to potential output, and the unemployment rate returning to its natural rate level. By 2004, the self-correcting mechanism feature of aggregate demand and supply analysis began to come into play, with the unemployment rate dropping back to 5.5% (see Figure 12.5 panel (b)).

MyEconLab Mini-lecture

FIGURE 12.5

Negative Demand Shocks, 2001–2004

Panel (a) shows that the negative demand shocks from 2001–2004 decreased consumption expenditure and investment, shifting the aggregate demand curve to the left from AD_1 to AD_2. The economy moved to point 2, where output fell, unemployment rose, and inflation declined. The large negative output gap when output was less than potential caused the short-run aggregate supply curve to begin falling to AS_3. The economy moved toward point 3, where output would return to potential: inflation declines further to π_3 and unemployment falls back again to its natural rate level of around 5%. The data in panel (b) supports this analysis, with inflation declining to around 2% and the unemployment rate dropping back to 5.5% by 2004.

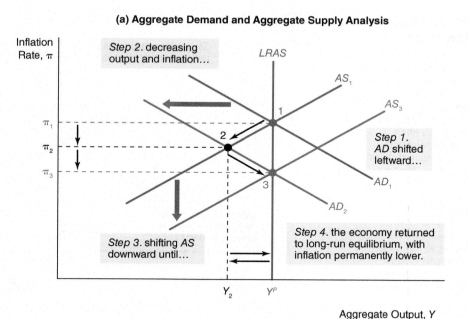

(a) Aggregate Demand and Aggregate Supply Analysis

Step 2. decreasing output and inflation…

Step 1. AD shifted leftward…

Step 3. shifting AS downward until…

Step 4. the economy returned to long-run equilibrium, with inflation permanently lower.

(b) Unemployment and Inflation, 2000–2004

Year	Unemployment Rate (%)	Inflation (Year to Year) (%)
2000	4.0	3.4
2001	4.7	2.8
2002	5.8	1.6
2003	6.0	2.3
2004	5.5	2.7

Source: Economic Report of the President.

Changes in Equilibrium: Aggregate Supply (Price) Shocks

The aggregate supply curve can shift from temporary supply (price) shocks in which the long-run aggregate supply curve does not shift, or from permanent supply shocks in which the long-run aggregate supply curve does shift. We look at these two types of supply shocks in turn.

Temporary Supply Shocks

In our discussion of the Phillips curve in Chapter 11, we showed that inflation will change independent of tightness in the labor markets or of expected inflation

FIGURE 12.6

Temporary Negative Supply Shock

A temporary negative supply shock shifts the short-run aggregate supply curve from AS_1 to AS_2 and the economy moves from point 1 to point 2, where inflation increases to 3% and output declines to $9 trillion. Because output is less than potential, the short-run aggregate supply curve begins to shift back down, eventually returning to AS_1, where the economy is again at the initial long-run equilibrium at point 1.

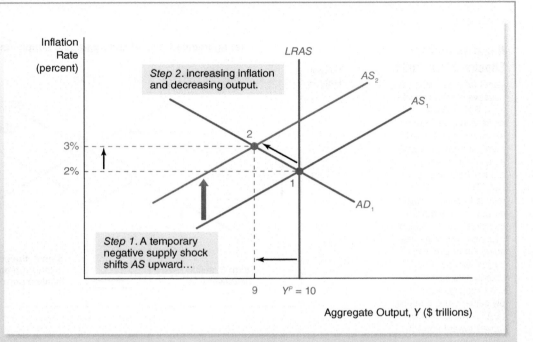

To see how a temporary supply shock affects the economy using our aggregate supply and demand analysis, we start by assuming that the economy has output at its potential level of $10 trillion and inflation at 2% at point 1. Suppose that there is a temporary negative supply shock because of a war in the Middle East. When the negative supply shock hits the economy and oil prices rise, the price shock term ρ causes inflation to rise above 2%, and the short-run aggregate supply curve shifts up and to the left from AS_1 to AS_2 in Figure 12.6.

The economy will move up the aggregate demand curve from point 1 to point 2, where inflation rises above 2% but aggregate output *falls* below $10 trillion. We call a situation of rising inflation but a falling level of aggregate output, as pictured in Figure 12.6, **stagflation** (a combination of the words *stagnation* and *inflation*). Because the supply shock is temporary, productive capacity in the economy does not change, and

when there is a temporary supply shock, such as a change in the supply of oil, that causes prices either to rise or to fall. When the temporary shock involves a restriction in supply, we refer to this type of supply shock as a *negative (or unfavorable) supply shock*, and it results in a rise in commodity prices (recall our discussion of negative supply shocks related to technology, the natural environment, and energy in Chapter 3). Examples of temporary negative supply shocks are a disruption in oil supplies, a rise in import prices when a currency declines in value, or a cost-push shock from workers pushing for higher wages that outpace productivity growth, driving up costs and inflation. When the supply shock involves an increase in supply, it is called a *positive (or favorable) supply shock*. Temporary positive supply shocks can come from, for example, a particularly good harvest or a fall in import prices.

so Y^P and the long-run aggregate supply curve $LRAS$ remain stationary at $10 trillion. At point 2, output is therefore below its potential level (say at $9 trillion), so inflation falls and shifts the short-run aggregate supply curve back down to where it was initially at AS_1. The economy (equilibrium) slides down the aggregate demand curve AD_1 (assuming the aggregate demand curve remains in the same position) and returns to the long-run equilibrium at point 1, where output is again at $10 trillion and inflation is at 2%.

Although a temporary negative supply shock leads to an upward and leftward shift in the short-run aggregate supply curve, which raises inflation and lowers output initially, the ultimate long-run effect is that output and inflation are unchanged.

A favorable (positive) supply shock—say an excellent harvest of wheat in the Midwest—moves all the curves in Figure 12.6 in the opposite direction and so has the opposite effects. *A temporary positive supply shock shifts the short-run aggregate supply curve downward and to the right, leading initially to a fall in inflation and a rise in output. In the long run, however, output and inflation will be unchanged (holding the aggregate demand curve constant).*

We now will once again apply the aggregate demand and supply model, this time to temporary supply shocks. We begin with negative supply shocks in 1973–1975 and 1978–1980. (Recall that we assume aggregate output is initially at the natural rate level.)

Application

Negative Supply Shocks, 1973–1975 and 1978–1980

In 1973, the U.S. economy was hit by a series of negative supply shocks:

1. As a result of the oil embargo stemming from the Arab–Israeli war of 1973, the Organization of Petroleum Exporting Countries (OPEC) engineered a quadrupling of oil prices by restricting oil production.

2. A series of crop failures throughout the world led to a sharp increase in food prices.

3. The termination of U.S. wage and price controls in 1973 and 1974 led to a push by workers to obtain wage increases that had been prevented by the controls.

The triple thrust of these events shifted the short-run aggregate supply curve sharply upward and to the left from AS_1 to AS_2 (as shown in panel (a) of Figure 12.7), and the economy moved to point 2. As the aggregate demand and supply diagram in Figure 12.7 predicts, both inflation and unemployment rose (inflation by 2.9 percentage points and unemployment by 3.5 percentage points, as per panel (b) of Figure 12.7).

The 1978–1980 period was almost an exact replay of the 1973–1975 period. By 1978, the economy had just about fully recovered from the 1973–1975 supply shocks when poor harvests and a doubling of oil prices (a result of the overthrow of the Shah of Iran) led to another sharp upward and leftward shift of the short-run aggregate supply curve in 1979. The pattern predicted by Figure 12.7 played itself out again—inflation and unemployment both shot upward.

MyEconLab Mini-lecture

FIGURE 12.7

Negative Supply Shocks, 1973–1975 and 1978–1980

Panel (a) shows that the temporary negative supply shocks in 1973 and 1979 led to an upward shift in the short-run aggregate supply curve from AS_1 to AS_2. The economy moved to point 2, where output fell, and both unemployment and inflation rose. The data in panel (b) support this analysis: note the increase in the inflation rate from 6.2% in 1973 to 9.1% in 1975 and the increase in the unemployment rate from 4.8% in 1973 to 8.3% in 1975. In the 1978–1980 shock, inflation increased from 7.6% in 1978 to 13.5% in 1980, while the unemployment rate increased from 6.0% in 1978 to 7.1% in 1980.

Source: Economic Report of the President.

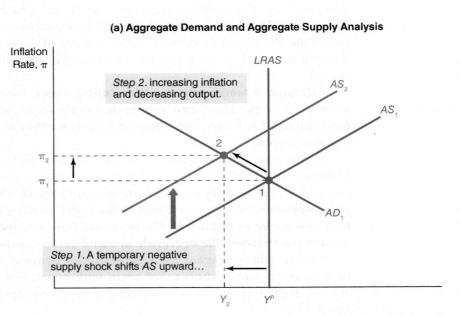

(a) Aggregate Demand and Aggregate Supply Analysis

Step 2. increasing inflation and decreasing output.

Step 1. A temporary negative supply shock shifts *AS* upward…

(b) Unemployment and Inflation, 1973–1975 and 1978–1980

Year	Unemployment Rate (%)	Inflation (Year to Year) (%)
1973	4.8	6.2
1974	5.5	11.0
1975	8.3	9.1
1978	6.0	7.6
1979	5.8	11.3
1980	7.1	13.5

Permanent Supply Shocks

But what if the supply shock is not temporary? A permanent negative supply shock—such as an increase in ill-advised regulations that causes the economy to be less efficient, thereby reducing supply—would decrease potential output from, say, $Y_1^P = \$10$ trillion to $Y_2^P = \$8$ trillion and shift the long-run aggregate supply curve to the left from $LRAS_1$ to $LRAS_2$, as shown in Figure 12.8.

Because the permanent supply shock will result in higher prices, there will be an immediate rise in inflation—say to 3%—from its previous level of 2%, and so the short-run aggregate supply curve will shift up and to the left from AS_1 to AS_2. Although output at point 2 has fallen to $9 trillion, it is still above $Y_2^P = \$8$ trillion: the positive

MyEconLab Mini-lecture

FIGURE 12.8

Permanent Negative Supply Shock

A permanent negative supply shock leads initially to a decline in output and a rise in inflation. In the long run, it leads to a permanent decline in output and a permanent rise in inflation, as indicated by point 3, where inflation has risen to 4% and output has fallen to $8 trillion.

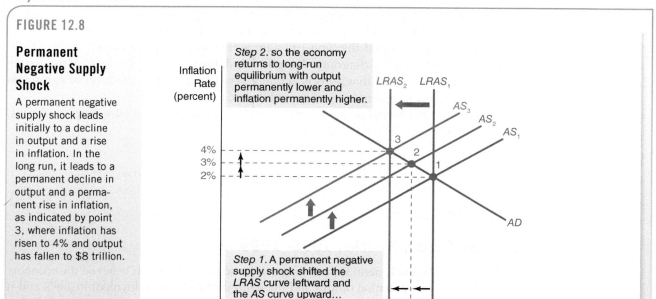

Step 2. so the economy returns to long-run equilibrium with output permanently lower and inflation permanently higher.

Step 1. A permanent negative supply shock shifted the *LRAS* curve leftward and the *AS* curve upward…

output gap means that the aggregate supply curve will again shift up and to the left. It continues to do so until it reaches AS_3 at the intersection of the aggregate demand curve AD and the long-run aggregate supply curve $LRAS_2$. Now, because output is at $Y_2^P = \$8$ trillion at point 3, the output gap is zero and, at an inflation rate of 4%, there is no further upward pressure on inflation.

Figure 12.8 generates the following result when we hold the aggregate demand curve constant: *a permanent negative supply shock leads initially to both a decline in output and a rise in inflation. However, in contrast to a temporary negative supply shock, in the long run a permanent negative supply shock, which results in a fall in potential output, leads to a permanent decline in output and a permanent rise in inflation.*[3]

The opposite conclusion follows from a positive supply shock, for example, one caused by the development of new technology that raises productivity or an increase in the supply of labor. *A permanent positive supply shock lowers inflation and raises output both in the short run and the long run.*

To this point, we have assumed that potential output Y^P and hence the long-run aggregate supply curve are given. However, over time, the potential level of output increases as a result of economic growth (which is the topic of Chapters 6 and 7). If

---

[3]The discussion of the effects of permanent supply shocks assumes that monetary policy is not changing, so that the monetary policy (*MP*) curve and the aggregate demand curve remain unchanged. Monetary policy makers, however, might shift the *MP* curve if they want to shift the aggregate demand curve to keep inflation at the same level. See Chapter 13.

the productive capacity of the economy is growing at a steady rate of 3% per year, for example, every year Y^P will grow by 3% and the long-run aggregate supply curve at Y^P will shift to the right by 3%. To simplify the analysis, when Y^P grows at a steady rate, we represent Y^P and the long-run aggregate supply curve as fixed in the aggregate demand and supply diagrams. Keep in mind, however, that the level of aggregate output pictured in these diagrams is actually best thought of as the level of aggregate output relative to its normal rate of growth (trend).

The 1995–1999 period serves as an illustration of permanent positive supply shocks, as the following application indicates.

Application

Positive Supply Shocks, 1995–1999

In February 1994, the Federal Reserve began to raise interest rates. It believed the economy would be reaching potential output and the natural rate of unemployment in 1995, and it might become overheated thereafter, with output climbing above potential and inflation rising. As we can see in panel (b) of Figure 12.9, however, the economy continued to grow rapidly, with the unemployment rate falling to below 5% in 1997. Yet inflation continued to fall, declining to around 1.6% in 1998.

Can aggregate demand and supply analysis explain what happened? Two permanent positive supply shocks hit the economy in the late 1990s.

1. Changes in the health care industry, such as the emergence of health maintenance organizations (HMOs), reduced medical care costs substantially relative to other goods and services.

2. The computer revolution finally began to impact productivity favorably, raising the potential growth rate of the economy (which journalists dubbed the "new economy").

In addition, demographic factors, which we will discuss in Chapter 20, led to a fall in the natural rate of unemployment. These factors led to a rightward shift in the long-run aggregate supply curve to $LRAS_2$ and a downward and rightward shift in the short-run aggregate supply curve from AS_1 to AS_2, as shown in panel (a) of Figure 12.9. Aggregate output rose and unemployment fell, while inflation also declined.

Conclusions

Aggregate demand and supply analysis yields the following important conclusions.

1. The economy has a self-correcting mechanism that returns it to potential output and the natural rate of unemployment over time.

2. A shift in the aggregate demand curve—caused by changes in autonomous monetary policy (changes in the real interest rate at any given inflation rate), government purchases, taxes, autonomous net exports,

autonomous consumption expenditure, autonomous investment, or financial frictions—affects output only in the short run and has no effect in the long run. Furthermore, the initial change in inflation is lower than the long-run change in inflation when the short-run aggregate supply curve has fully adjusted.

3. A temporary supply shock affects output and inflation only in the short run and has no effect in the long run (holding the aggregate demand curve constant).

4. A permanent supply shock affects output and inflation both in the short and the long run.

We close the section with one final application—this time with both supply and demand shocks at play—featuring the 2007–2009 financial crisis.

MyEconLab Mini-lecture

FIGURE 12.9

Positive Supply Shocks, 1995–1999

Panel (a) shows that the positive supply shocks from lower health care costs and the rise in productivity from the computer revolution led to a rightward shift in the long-run aggregate supply curve from $LRAS_1$ to $LRAS_2$ and a downward shift in the short-run aggregate supply curve from AS_1 to AS_2. The economy moved to point 2, where aggregate output rose, and unemployment and inflation fell. The data in panel (b) support this analysis: note that the unemployment rate fell from 5.6% in 1995 to 4.2% in 1999, while the inflation rate fell from 2.8% in 1995 to 2.2% in 1999.

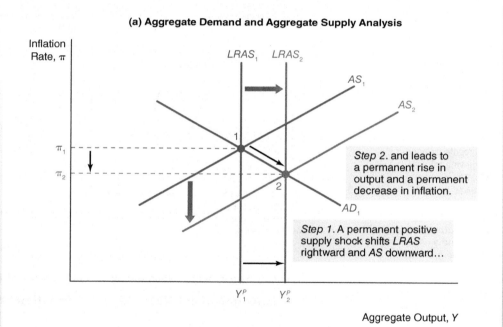

(a) Aggregate Demand and Aggregate Supply Analysis

Step 2. and leads to a permanent rise in output and a permanent decrease in inflation.

Step 1. A permanent positive supply shock shifts *LRAS* rightward and *AS* downward…

(b) Unemployment and Inflation, 1995–1999

Year	Unemployment Rate (%)	Inflation (Year to Year) (%)
1995	5.6	2.8
1996	5.4	3.0
1997	4.9	2.3
1998	4.5	1.6
1999	4.2	2.2

Source: Economic Report of the President.

Application

Negative Supply and Demand Shocks and the 2007–2009 Financial Crisis

We described the perfect storm of 2007–2009 in the chapter opener. At the beginning of 2007, higher demand for oil from rapidly growing developing countries like China and India and the slowing of production in places like Mexico, Russia, and Nigeria drove up oil prices sharply from around the $60 per barrel level. By the end of 2007, oil prices had

MyEconLab Mini-lecture

FIGURE 12.10

Negative Supply and Demand Shocks and the 2007–2009 Crisis

Panel (a) shows that the negative price shock from the rise in the price of oil shifted the short-run aggregate supply curve up from AS_1 to AS_2, while a negative demand shock from the financial crisis led to a sharp contraction in spending, resulting in the aggregate demand curve moving from AD_1 to AD_2. The economy thus moved to point 2, where there was a sharp contraction in aggregate output, which fell to Y_2, and a rise in unemployment, while inflation rose to π_2. The fall in oil prices shifted the short-run aggregate supply curve back down to AS_1, while the deepening financial crisis shifted the aggregate demand curve to AD_3. As a result, the economy moved to point 3, where inflation fell to π_3 and output to Y_3. The data in panel (b) support this analysis: note that the unemployment rate rose from 4.6% in 2006 to 5.5% in June of 2008, while inflation rose from 2.5% to 5.0%.

(a) Aggregate Demand and Aggregate Supply Analysis

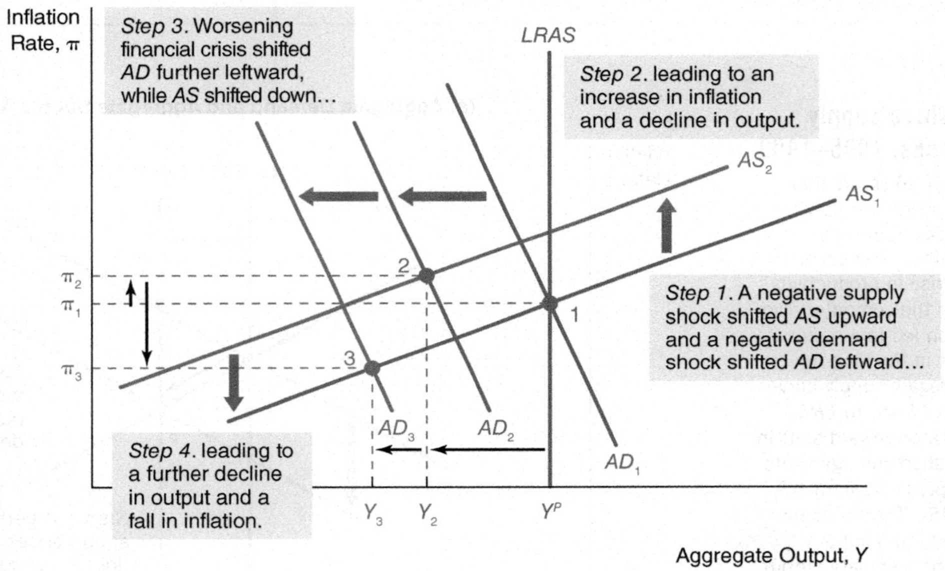

Step 3. Worsening financial crisis shifted AD further leftward, while AS shifted down…

Step 2. leading to an increase in inflation and a decline in output.

Step 1. A negative supply shock shifted AS upward and a negative demand shock shifted AD leftward…

Step 4. leading to a further decline in output and a fall in inflation.

Aggregate Output, Y

(b) Unemployment and Inflation During the Perfect Storm of 2007–2009

Year	Unemployment Rate (%)	Inflation (Year to Year) (%)
2006	4.6	2.5
2007	4.6	4.1
2008, June	5.5	5.0
2008, Dec.	7.2	0.1
2009, June	9.5	−1.2
2009, Dec.	10.0	2.8

Source: Economic Report of the President.

risen to $100 per barrel, and they reached a peak of over $140 per barrel in July 2008. The run up of oil prices, along with increases in other commodity prices, led to a negative supply shock that shifted the short-run aggregate supply curve (shown in panel (a) of Figure 12.10) sharply upward from AS_1 to AS_2. To make matters worse, a financial crisis hit the economy starting in August 2007, causing a sharp increase in financial frictions, which led to contraction in both household and business spending (more on this in Chapter 15). This negative demand shock shifted the aggregate demand curve to the left from AD_1 to AD_2 (see panel (a) of Figure 12.10) and moved the economy to point 2. These shocks led to a rise in the unemployment rate, a rise in the inflation rate, and a decline in output, as point 2 indicates. As our aggregate demand and supply analysis predicts, this perfect storm of negative shocks led to a recession starting in December 2007, with the unemployment rate rising from the 4.6% level in 2006 and 2007 to 5.5% by June 2008, and with the inflation rate rising from 2.5% in 2006 to 5% in June 2008 (see panel (b) of Figure 12.10).

After July 2008, oil prices fell sharply, shifting short-run aggregate supply downward. However, in the fall of 2008, the financial crisis entered a particularly virulent phase following the bankruptcy of Lehman Brothers, decreasing aggregate demand sharply. As a result, the economy suffered from increasing unemployment, with the unemployment rate rising to 10.0% by the end of 2009, while the inflation rate fell to 2.8% (see panel (b) of Figure 12.10).

AD/AS Analysis of Foreign Business Cycle Episodes

Our aggregate demand and supply analysis also can help us understand business cycle episodes in foreign countries. Here we look at two: the business cycle experience of the United Kingdom during the 2007–2009 financial crisis and the quite different experience of China during the same period.

Application

The United Kingdom and the 2007–2009 Financial Crisis

As in the United States, the rise in the price of oil in 2007 led to a negative supply shock. In Figure 12.11 panel (a), the short-run aggregate supply curve shifted up from AS_1 to AS_2 in the United Kingdom. The financial crisis did not at first have a large impact on spending, so the aggregate demand curve did not shift and equilibrium instead moved from point 1 to point 2 on AD_1. The aggregate demand and supply framework indicates that inflation would rise, which is what occurred (see the increase in the inflation rate from 2.3% in 2007 to 3.9% in December 2008 in Figure 12.11 panel (b)). With output below potential and oil prices falling after July of 2008, the short-run aggregate supply curve shifted down to AS_1. At the same time, the financial crisis after the Lehman Brothers bankruptcy impacted spending worldwide, causing a negative demand shock that shifted the aggregate demand curve to the left to AD_2. The economy now moved to point 3, with a further fall in output, a rise in unemployment, and a fall in inflation. As the aggregate demand and supply analysis predicts, the UK unemployment rate rose to 7.8% by the end of 2009, with the inflation rate falling to 2.1%.

MyEconLab Mini-lecture

FIGURE 12.11

UK Financial Crisis, 2007–2009

Panel (a) shows that a supply shock in 2007 from rising oil prices shifted the short-run aggregate supply curve up and to the left from AS_1 to AS_2 in the United Kingdom. The economy moved to point 2. With output below potential and oil prices falling after July of 2008, the short-run aggregate supply curve began to shift down to AS_1. A negative demand shock following the escalating financial crisis after the Lehman Brothers bankruptcy shifted the aggregate demand curve to the left to AD_2. The economy now moved to point 3, where output fell to Y_3, unemployment rose, and inflation decreased to π_3. The data in panel (b) support this analysis: note that the unemployment rate increased from 5.4% in 2006 to 7.8% in December 2009, while the inflation rate rose from 2.3% to 3.9% and then fell to 2.1% over this same time period.

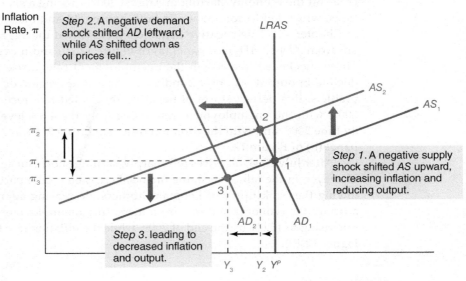

(a) Aggregate Demand and Aggregate Supply Analysis

Step 2. A negative demand shock shifted AD leftward, while AS shifted down as oil prices fell…

Step 1. A negative supply shock shifted AS upward, increasing inflation and reducing output.

Step 3. leading to decreased inflation and output.

(b) Unemployment and Inflation, 2006–2009

Year	Unemployment Rate (%)	Inflation (Year to Year) (%)
2006	5.4	2.3
2007	5.3	2.3
2008, June	5.3	3.4
2008, Dec.	6.4	3.9
2009, June	7.8	2.1
2009, Dec.	7.8	2.1

Source: Office of National Statistics, UK. www.statistics.gov.uk/statbase/tsdtimezone.asp

Application

China and the 2007–2009 Financial Crisis

The financial crisis that began in August 2007 at first had very little impact on China. When the financial crisis escalated in the United States in the fall of 2008 with the collapse of Lehman Brothers, all this changed. China's economy had been driven by extremely strong export growth, which up until September of 2008 had been growing at over a 20% annual rate.

MyEconLab Mini-lecture

FIGURE 12.12

China and the Financial Crisis, 2007–2009

Panel (a) shows that the collapse of Chinese exports starting in 2008 led to a negative demand shock that shifted the aggregate demand curve to AD_2, moving the economy to point 2, where output growth fell below potential and inflation declined. A massive fiscal stimulus package and autonomous easing of monetary policy shifted the aggregate demand curve back to AD_1, and the economy very quickly moved back to long-run equilibrium at point 1. The data in panel (b) supports this analysis; note that output growth slowed but then bounced back again, while inflation dropped sharply.

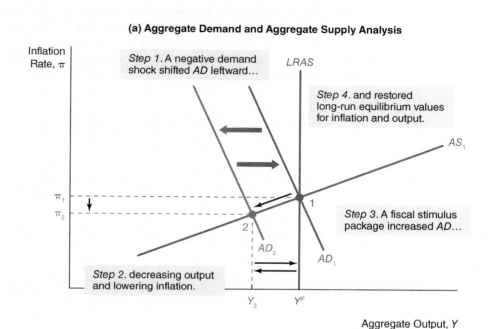

(a) Aggregate Demand and Aggregate Supply Analysis

Step 1. A negative demand shock shifted AD leftward…

Step 4. and restored long-run equilibrium values for inflation and output.

Step 3. A fiscal stimulus package increased AD…

Step 2. decreasing output and lowering inflation.

(b) Chinese Output Growth and Inflation, 2006–2009

Year	Output Growth (%)	Inflation (Year to Year) (%)
2006	11.8	1.5
2007	12.4	4.8
2008, June	11.2	7.9
2008, Dec.	4.4	3.9
2009, June	11.1	−1.1
2009, Dec.	10.4	−0.3

Source: International Monetary Fund. International Financial Statistics. Country Tables.
http://www.imf.org/external/data.htm

Starting in October 2008, Chinese exports collapsed, falling at around a 20% annual rate through August 2009.

The negative demand shock from the collapse of exports led to a decline in aggregate demand, shifting the aggregate demand curve to AD_2 and moving the economy from point 1 to point 2 in Figure 12.12 panel (a). As aggregate demand and supply analysis indicates, China's economic growth slowed from over 11% in the first half of 2008 to under 5% in the second half, while inflation declined from 7.9% to 3.9%, and then became negative thereafter (see Figure 12.12 panel (b)).

Instead of relying solely on the economy's self-correcting mechanism, the Chinese government proposed a massive fiscal stimulus package of $580 billion in 2008, which at 12.5%

of GDP was three times larger than the U.S. fiscal stimulus package relative to GDP. (We discuss the U.S. fiscal stimulus package in Chapter 13.) In addition, the People's Bank of China, the central bank, began taking measures to autonomously ease monetary policy. These decisive actions shifted the aggregate demand curve back to AD_1, and the Chinese economy very quickly moved back to point 1. The Chinese economy thus weathered the financial crisis remarkably well, with output growth rising rapidly in 2009 and inflation becoming positive thereafter.

SUMMARY

1. The aggregate demand curve indicates the quantity of aggregate output demanded at each inflation rate, and it is downward sloping. The primary sources of shifts in the aggregate demand curve are 1) autonomous monetary policy, 2) government purchases, 3) taxes, 4) net exports, 5) autonomous consumption expenditure, 6) autonomous investment, and 7) financial frictions.

   The long-run aggregate supply curve is vertical at potential output. The long-run aggregate supply curve shifts when technology changes, when there are long-run changes to the amount of labor or capital, or when the natural rate of unemployment changes. The short-run aggregate supply curve slopes upward because inflation rises as output rises relative to potential output. The short-run supply curve shifts when there are price shocks, changes in expected inflation, or persistent output gaps.

2. Equilibrium in the short run occurs at the point where the aggregate demand curve intersects the short-run aggregate supply curve. Although this is where the economy heads temporarily, the self-correcting mechanism leads the economy to settle permanently at the long-run equilibrium, where aggregate output

   is at its potential. Shifts in either the aggregate demand curve or the short-run aggregate supply curve can produce changes in aggregate output and inflation.

3. A positive demand shock shifts the aggregate demand curve to the right and initially leads to a rise in both inflation and output. However, in the long run, it only leads to a rise in inflation, because output returns to its initial level at Y^P.

4. A temporary positive supply shock leads to a downward and rightward shift in the short-run aggregate supply curve, which lowers inflation and raises output initially. However, in the long run, output and inflation are unchanged. A permanent positive supply shock leads initially to both a rise in output and a decline in inflation. However, in contrast to a temporary positive supply shock, in the long run a permanent positive supply shock, which results in a rise in potential output, leads to a permanent rise in output and a permanent decline in inflation.

5. Aggregate supply and demand analysis is just as useful for analyzing foreign business cycle episodes as it is for analyzing domestic business cycle episodes.

KEY TERMS

demand shocks, p. 307
general equilibrium, p. 303

self-correcting mechanism, p. 307
stagflation, p. 312

REVIEW QUESTIONS

All Questions are available in MyEconLab *for practice or instructor assignment.*

Recap of Aggregate Demand and Supply Curves

1. Explain why the aggregate demand curve slopes downward and the short-run aggregate supply curve slopes upward.
2. Identify changes in three factors that will shift the aggregate demand curve to the right and changes in three different factors that will shift the aggregate demand curve to the left.

3. What factors shift the short-run aggregate supply curve? Do any of these factors shift the long-run aggregate supply curve? Why?

Equilibrium in Aggregate Demand and Supply Analysis

4. How does the condition for short-run equilibrium differ from that for long-run equilibrium?
5. Describe the adjustment to long-run equilibrium if an economy's short-run equilibrium output is above potential output.

Changes in Equilibrium: Aggregate Demand Shocks

6. What are demand shocks? Distinguish between positive and negative demand shocks.
7. Starting from a situation of long-run equilibrium, what are the short- and long-run effects of a positive demand shock?

Changes in Equilibrium: Aggregate Supply (Price) Shocks

8. What are supply shocks? Distinguish between positive and negative supply shocks and between temporary and permanent ones.
9. Starting from a situation of long-run equilibrium, what are the short- and long-run effects of a temporary negative supply shock?

10. Starting from a situation of long-run equilibrium, what are the short- and long-run effects of a permanent negative supply shock?

PROBLEMS

All Problems are available in MyEconLab *for practice or instructor assignment.*

Recap of the Aggregate Demand and Supply Curves

1. Suppose that Congress passes legislation that establishes a tax credit for small businesses and tax incentives for all businesses that invest in new plant and equipment.
   a) What is the anticipated effect of these proposals on aggregate demand, if any?
   b) Show your answer graphically.
2. Evaluate the accuracy of the following statement: "The recent depreciation of the U.S. dollar had a positive effect on the U.S. aggregate demand curve."
3. Suppose that the White House decides to sharply reduce military spending without

   increasing government spending in other areas.
   a) Comment on the effect of this measure on aggregate demand.
   b) Show your answer graphically.
4. Oil prices declined in the summer of 2008, following months of increases since the winter of 2007. Considering only this fall in oil prices, explain the effect on short-run aggregate supply and long-run aggregate supply, if any.

Changes in Equilibrium: Aggregate Demand Shocks

5. Suppose that in an effort to reduce the current federal government budget deficit, the White House decides to sharply decrease government spending. Assuming the economy is at its long-run equilibrium, carefully explain the short- and long-run consequences of this policy.
6. According to aggregate demand and supply analysis, what would be the effect of

   appointing a Federal Reserve System chairman known to have no interest in fighting inflation?
7. An article in the *Wall Street Journal* reported that inflation-adjusted wages have slumped in recent years. Is this statement consistent with the aggregate demand and supply analysis of the recent U.S. economic crisis? Explain.

Changes in Equilibrium: Aggregate Supply (Price) Shocks

8. The consequences of climate change on the economy is a popular topic in the media. Suppose that a series of wildfires destroys crops in the western states at the same time a hurricane destroys refineries on the Gulf Coast.
   a) Using aggregate demand and supply analysis, explain how output and the inflation rate would be affected in the short and long runs.
   b) Show your answer graphically.

9. Suppose that the President gets legislation passed that encourages investment in research and development of new technologies. Assuming this policy results in positive technological change for the U.S. economy, what does aggregate demand and supply analysis predict in terms of inflation and output?

DATA ANALYSIS PROBLEMS

The Problems update with real-time data in MyEconLab *and are available for practice or instructor assignment.*

1. Go to the St. Louis Federal Reserve FRED database, and find data on real government spending (GCEC1), real GDP (GDPC1), taxes (W006RC1Q027SBEA), and a measure of the price level, the personal consumption expenditure price index (PCECTPI). Download all the data onto a spreadsheet, and convert the tax data series into real taxes. To do this, for each quarter, take taxes and divide by the price index, then multiply by 100.
   a) Calculate the level change in real GDP over the most recent four quarters of data available and over the previous four quarters before that.
   b) Calculate the level change in real government spending and real taxes over the most recent four quarters of data available and over the previous four quarters before that.
   c) Are these results consistent with what you would expect? How do your answers to part (b) above help explain, if at all, the answers to part (a)? Explain as it relates to the *IS* and *AD* curves.

2. Go to the St. Louis Federal Reserve FRED database, and find data on real personal disposable income (DPIC96), a measure of household net worth (TNWBSHNO), a measure of the price level, the personal consumption expenditure price index (PCECTPI), the University of Michigan consumer sentiment index (UMCSENT), personal consumption expenditures (PCEC), and real GDP (GDPC1). Convert the (UMCSENT) data to "Quarterly"

using the *frequency* setting. Download all the data onto a spreadsheet, and convert the household net worth series to real household net worth. To do this, for each quarter, take household net worth and divide by the price index, then multiply by 100. (Note that you may have to adjust the rows of the net worth data series to align with the appropriate quarters of the other data.)
   a) Calculate the level change in real GDP over the most recent four quarters of data available and over the previous four quarters before that.
   b) Calculate the level change in real personal disposable income, the change in real household net worth, the change in consumer confidence, and the change in personal consumption expenditures over the most recent four quarters of data available and over the previous four quarters before that.
   c) Are these results consistent with what you would expect? How do your answers to part (b) above help explain, if at all, the answers to part (a)? Explain as it relates to the *IS* and *AD* curves.

3. Go to the St. Louis Federal Reserve FRED database, and find data on real GDP (GDPC1), real private domestic investment (GPDI), corporate profits (CP), a measure of the price level (PCECTPI), a measure of economic uncertainty (USEPUINDXM), and a measure of real interest rates (FII5). Convert the real interest rate and uncertainty data

series to "Quarterly" under the *frequency* setting. Download all the data onto a spreadsheet, and convert the corporate profits series to real corporate profits. To do this, for each quarter, take corporate profit and divide by the price index, then multiply by 100.

a) Calculate the level change in real GDP over the most recent four quarters of data available and over the previous four quarters before that.

b) Calculate the level change in real corporate profits, the uncertainty index, the change in the real interest rate, and the change in investment over the most recent four quarters of data available and over the previous four quarters before that.

c) Are these results consistent with what you would expect? How do your answers to part (b) above help explain, if at all, the answers to part (a)? Explain as it relates to the *IS* and *AD* curves.

4. Go to the St. Louis Federal Reserve FRED database, and find data on a measure of the price level (PCECTPI), real compensation per hour (COMPRNFB), a measure of worker productivity (OPHNFB), the price of a barrel of oil (OILPRICE), and the University of Michigan survey of inflation expectations (MICH). Convert the oil price and inflation expectations data series to "Quarterly" under the *frequency* setting, and use the *units* setting to convert the price index to "Percent Change From Year Ago." Download all the data onto a spreadsheet, and convert the compensation and productivity measures to a single indicator. To do this, for each quarter, take the compensation number and subtract the productivity number; call this "Net Wages Above Productivity."

a) Calculate the change in the inflation rate over the most recent four quarters of data available and over the previous four quarters before that.

b) Calculate the change in net wages above productivity, the price of oil, and inflation expectations over the most recent four quarters of data available and over the previous four quarters before that.

c) Are these results consistent with what you would expect? How do your answers to part (b) above help explain, if at all, the answers to part (a)? Explain as it relates to the short-run aggregate supply curve.

5. Go to the St. Louis Federal Reserve FRED database, and find data on real GDP (GDPC1) and a measure of the price level, the personal consumption expenditure price index (PCECTPI). Convert the price index to inflation rate by setting the *units* to "Percent Change From Year Ago." Download the data into a spreadsheet.

a) Calculate the level change in real GDP and the change in the inflation rate over the most recent four quarters of data available, and over the previous four quarters before that.

b) Based on your answers to part (a) and to Questions 1 through 4 above (if assigned), explain, using a basic aggregate demand and supply analysis, how the economy could end up with the output and inflation outcomes from the data in part (a).

Online appendices "The Taylor Principle and Inflation Stability," "The Effects of Macroeconomic Shocks on Asset Prices" and "The Algebra of the Aggregate Demand and Supply Model" are available at the Companion Website, www.pearsonhighered.com/mishkin

Macroeconomic Policy and Aggregate Demand and Supply Analysis

 13

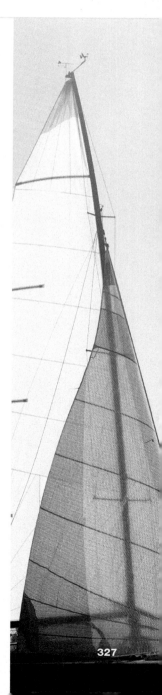

Preview

Between September 2007 and December 2008, the Federal Reserve lowered the target for its policy interest rate, the federal funds rate, from $5\frac{1}{4}\%$ all the way down to zero. Why did the Fed lower interest rates this aggressively? Did lower rates mitigate the effects of the recession that began in December 2007? Did they spark undesirable inflation?

Our aggregate demand–aggregate supply (AD/AS) framework developed in the previous chapters provides insights into these questions. But to apply it we need to include an important set of actors who play a prominent role in business cycle fluctuations: policy makers. In this chapter, we bring policy makers into the analysis by exploring their use of macroeconomic policy to stabilize both inflation and output fluctuations. Although the chapter discusses fiscal policy, our primary focus is on monetary policy, policy makers' most commonly used tool to stabilize the economy. After outlining the objectives of macroeconomic policy, we apply the aggregate demand and supply (AD/AS) framework to four big questions: What are the roots of inflation? Does stabilizing inflation stabilize output? Should policy be *activist*—by responding aggressively to fluctuations in economic activity—or passive and *nonactivist*? How can monetary policy work when interest rates hit a floor of zero?

The Objectives of Macroeconomic Policy

Monetary policy, and macroeconomic policy in general, has two primary objectives: stabilizing economic activity and stabilizing inflation around a low level.[1]

---

[1]Chapter 15 will show that financial instability can lead to sharp contractions in economic activity. Hence the objective of stabilizing economic activity also implies that policy makers should have an objective of financial stability, and so financial stability is a subset of the stabilizing economic activity objective. Pursuing financial stability not only involves macroeconomic policy actions to prop up aggregate demand in the face of financial shocks, but also financial regulation. For discussion of financial regulation and the financial stability objective, see Frederic S. Mishkin, *The Economics of Money, Banking, and Financial Markets*, 10th edition (Boston: Pearson Addison-Wesley, 2013).

Stabilizing Economic Activity

The unemployment rate, a key gauge of economic activity that we introduced in Chapter 2, is central to monetary policy for two primary reasons: (1) high unemployment causes much human misery, and (2) high unemployment leaves workers, factories, and other resources idle, reducing output.

NATURAL RATE OF UNEMPLOYMENT. If unemployment is such a negative force in the economy, should policy makers target a zero rate of unemployment, when no worker is out of a job? In fact, the economy is better off with a small level of **frictional unemployment,** which occurs because workers and firms need time to make suitable matchups. A young paralegal in Kansas City trying to find higher-paid work as a legal consultant may need to quit his or her current position for a time to find that work. Similarly, a police officer in California who returns to the work force after two years at home caring for his or her children will probably need at least a few weeks, or months, to find suitable work. One undesirable but perpetual source of unemployment is **structural unemployment,** a mismatch between job requirements and the skills or availability of local workers. Monetary policy has limited impact on both frictional and structural unemployment.

Policy makers target an unemployment rate above zero that is consistent with the maximum sustainable level of employment at which there is no tendency for inflation to increase or decrease. This level is called the *natural rate of unemployment*, a concept we first encountered in our discussion of the Phillips curve in Chapter 11. (We will discuss the sources of frictional and structural unemployment more extensively in Chapter 20 on the labor markets.)

UNEMPLOYMENT RATES IN PRACTICE. Identifying the natural rate of unemployment is not as straightforward as it might seem. Clearly, an unemployment rate of more than 20%, like that seen during the Great Depression, is too high. But is 4% too low? In the 1960s, policy makers achieved a 4% unemployment rate but also set off accelerating inflation. Currently, most economists believe the natural rate of unemployment is between 5% and 6%, but this estimate is subject to much uncertainty and disagreement. Also, the natural rate can change over time. A government program that spreads information about job vacancies and training programs, for example, might reduce structural unemployment, lowering the natural unemployment rate.

In general terms, achieving the natural rate of unemployment is equivalent to stabilizing the economy. At the natural rate of unemployment, the economy moves to its natural rate of output, which we refer to more commonly as potential output. To achieve maximum sustainable employment, output (Y) must move closer to potential output (Y^P), so that the output gap ($Y - Y^P$) stabilizes around zero. Monetary policy that stabilizes unemployment around the natural rate of unemployment will also stabilize output around potential output, which is what we refer to as stabilizing economic activity.[2]

---

[2]Note that stabilizing economic activity and achieving maximum sustainable employment still allow economic output to fluctuate when permanent supply shocks lead to fluctuations in potential output.

Stabilizing Inflation: Price Stability

A growing body of evidence suggests that high inflation, which is always accompanied by high variability of inflation, reduces economic growth and strains society. Consumers, businesses, and governments struggle to interpret the information conveyed by rapidly changing prices of goods and services.[3] Parents find it more difficult to plan for the cost of a child's education. Public opinion toward inflation turns hostile, and society splinters as segments of the population strain to keep up with the rising level of prices.

Over the past few decades, greater awareness of these costs has increased the number of central banks that pursue a policy of **price stability**—defined as low and stable inflation—as the central monetary policy goal. Central banks must set inflation objectives with great care: aiming for zero inflation increases the risk of negative inflation, or deflation, which introduces pernicious problems of its own. (We will discuss deflation further in Chapter 15.) Even when inflation is above zero, it can still be too low. An excessively low inflation rate might lead to more instances in which nominal interest rates hit a floor of zero percent and so can go no lower, as happened from 2008 to 2013, in the United States, handicapping a central bank's ability to autonomously ease monetary policy and lower the real interest rate.

Central banks pursue a price stability objective with a goal of maintaining inflation, π, close to a target level (π^T), referred to as an **inflation target**, that is slightly above zero. Most central banks set π^T between 1% and 3%. An alternative way to think about the price stability objective is that monetary policy should try to minimize the difference between inflation and the inflation target ($\pi - \pi^T$), which we refer to as the **inflation gap**.[4]

Establishing Hierarchical Versus Dual Mandates

Should price stability be the chief goal of economic policy, or just one goal among many? Central banks differ in their stances. The Maastricht Treaty that established the European Central Bank states that the central bank's "primary objective ... shall be to maintain price stability." The treaty also says that the bank "shall support the general economic policies in the Community"—including a high level of employment and sustainable and noninflationary growth—but only "without prejudice to the objective of price stability." **Hierarchical mandates** require stable inflation as a condition of pursuing other goals. Beyond the European Central Bank, hierarchical mandates govern the behavior of the Bank of England, the Bank of Canada, and the Reserve Bank of New Zealand.

In contrast, the legislation defining the mission of the Federal Reserve states that it should "promote effectively the goals of maximum employment, stable prices, and

---

[3]For example, see the survey in Stanley Fischer, "The Role of Macroeconomic Factors in Growth," *Journal of Monetary Economics* 32 (1993): 485–512.

[4]Academic articles describe mathematically the two objectives of monetary policy, stabilizing economic activity and price stability, by stating that the monetary authority tries over the current and all future periods to minimize the loss function, L:

$$L = \alpha(\pi - \pi^T)^2 + (1 - \alpha)(Y - Y^P)^2$$

where α describes how much weight policy makers put on inflation stabilization as opposed to output stabilization. $\alpha = 1$ is the case in which the monetary authorities care only about stabilizing inflation and not at all about stabilizing output. $\alpha = 0$ is the case in which the monetary authorities care only about stabilizing output and not at all about stabilizing inflation.

moderate interest rates." Because long-term interest rates will be very high only if there is high inflation, and employment cannot be above its maximum sustainable rate in the long run, this statement, in practice, indicates two co-equal objectives: stable inflation and maximum sustainable employment. These co-equal objectives of price stability and maximum sustainable employment are referred to as the **dual mandate**. Is it better for an economy to operate under a hierarchical or a dual mandate? To answer this question, we need to examine how policy seeks to stabilize both economic activity and inflation.

The Relationship Between Stabilizing Inflation and Stabilizing Economic Activity

In our analysis of aggregate demand and supply in Chapter 12, we examined three categories of economic shocks—demand shocks, temporary supply shocks, and permanent supply shocks—and the consequences of each on inflation and output. In this section, we describe a central bank's appropriate policy responses to each of these shocks. In the case of both demand shocks and permanent supply shocks, central banks can simultaneously pursue price stability and stability in economic activity. Following a temporary supply shock, however, policy makers can achieve either price stability or economic activity stability, but not both. This tradeoff poses a thorny dilemma for central banks with dual mandates. Before considering policy responses, we delve a bit more into the relationship between inflation and the real interest rate as context.

Monetary Policy and the Equilibrium Real Interest Rate

At long-run equilibrium, when the economy is producing at its potential and the inflation rate is consistent with price stability, we call the prevailing real interest rate the **equilibrium real interest rate** (also referred to as the **natural real interest rate**), which we represent as r^*. The equilibrium real interest rate maintains the quantity of aggregate output demanded equal to potential output, and thus reduces the output gap to zero. Because, as we saw in the previous chapter, aggregate output goes to potential output in the long run, the equilibrium real interest rate is also the long-run real interest rate for the economy.

We illustrate the equilibrium real interest rate in Figure 13.1. The aggregate supply and demand diagram in panel (b) shows an economy at point 1, where aggregate output is at potential output Y^P—making the output gap zero—and inflation is at π^T, the level consistent with price stability. Panel (a) of Figure 13.1 shows the initial monetary policy curve MP_1 that generates the downward-sloping aggregate demand curve at AD_1 in panel (b). Note in panel (a) that at point 1, where inflation is at the inflation target π^T, the real interest rate is r^*, or the equilibrium real interest rate.

Central bankers make heavy use of the equilibrium real interest rate, as described in the Policy and Practice case, "The Federal Reserve's Use of the Equilibrium Real Interest Rate, r^*."

Recall that our monetary policy curve indicates the relationship between the real interest rate set by the Fed and the inflation rate. With autonomous tightening of monetary policy, the Fed raises the federal funds rate at any given inflation rate, increasing r and

FIGURE 13.1

The Monetary Policy Curve and the Equilibrium Real Interest Rate, *r**

At point 1 in panel (a), the inflation rate is at π^T and the real interest rate on the monetary policy curve is at the equilibrium real interest rate *r**. This level of the interest rate results in the economy being at point 1 in panel (b), where the output gap is zero and the economy is at long-run equilibrium.

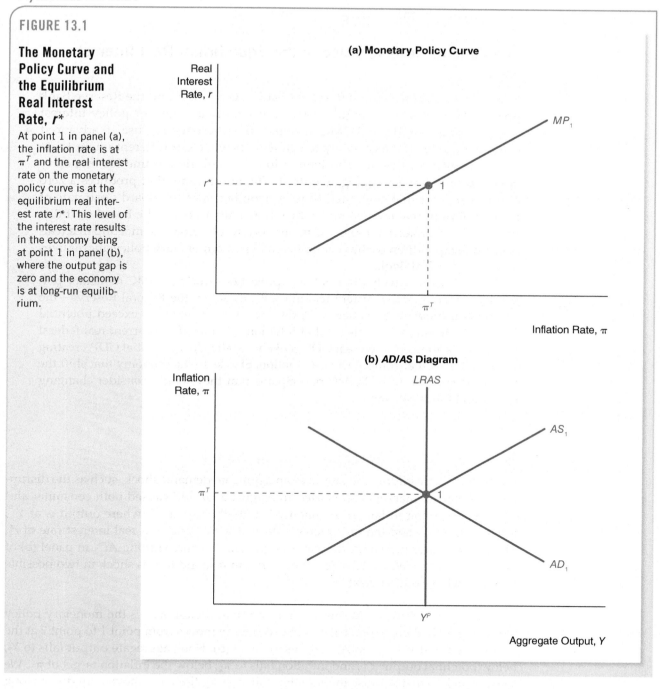

leading to a decrease in aggregate demand. With autonomous easing of monetary policy, the Fed lowers the federal funds rate at any given inflation rate, decreasing *r* and leading to an increase in aggregate demand. With our monetary policy curve analysis in place, we are now prepared to analyze monetary policy responses to various kinds of shocks using aggregate demand and supply analysis.

Policy and Practice

The Federal Reserve's Use of the Equilibrium Real Interest Rate, r^*

Every six weeks, the Federal Reserve Board of Governors and the Reserve Bank presidents meet in Washington, DC, to formulate a target for policy interest rates. In advance of these FOMC meetings, Board economists use an advanced computer model of the economy to simulate the effects of different interest rate decisions over a three-year horizon, a long enough time frame for monetary policy to fully impact aggregate output. The interest rate that produces a zero output gap over that simulated time horizon becomes the Board's estimate of the equilibrium real interest rate, which it actually calls r^*. The Board staff distributes the r^* projection to FOMC members a week before the meeting in a teal-covered compendium of the economic forecast and monetary policy alternatives known as the Teal Book.[5]

Policy makers actively discuss the r^* projections during FOMC monetary policy deliberations. If the current real interest rate set by the Federal Reserve—the real federal funds rate—is below r^*, then real GDP is likely to exceed potential GDP in the future, which means that inflation will rise. If the current real federal funds rate is above r^*, then real GDP is likely to fall below potential GDP, creating economic slack that could decrease inflation. Shocks to the economy that shift the level of r^* suggest to the FOMC participants that they should consider changing the federal funds rate target.

Response to an Aggregate Demand Shock

We begin by considering the effects of an aggregate demand shock, such as the disruption to financial markets that started in August 2007 and caused both consumer and business spending to fall. The economy is initially at point 1, where output is at Y^P, inflation is at π^T, and the real interest rate is at the equilibrium real interest rate of r_1^*. The negative demand shock decreases aggregate demand, shifting AD_1 in panel (b) of Figure 13.2 to the left to AD_2. Policy makers can respond to this shock in two possible ways, which we outline next.

NO POLICY RESPONSE. At this stage, if the central bank leaves the monetary policy curve in panel (a) unchanged at MP_1, the economy moves from point 1 to point 2 at the intersection of the AD_2 and AS_1 curves in panel (b). Here, aggregate output falls to Y_2, below potential output Y^P, and inflation falls to π_2, below the inflation target of π^T. We see in panel (a) that because inflation has fallen to π_2, there is a movement down along

---

[5]Up until 2010, the Board's economic forecast and monetary policy alternatives were in two separate documents, one covered in green and the other covered in blue. In 2010, these two documents were combined into one document with a teal cover (the color teal is a combination of green and blue), and so is referred to as the Teal Book. All of these FOMC documents are made public after five years, and their content can be found at www.federalreserve.gov/monetarypolicy/fomc_historical.htm

FIGURE 13.2

Aggregate Demand Shock: No Policy Response

An aggregate demand shock shifts the aggregate demand curve leftward from AD_1 to AD_2 in panel (b) and moves the economy from point 1 to point 2, where aggregate output falls to Y_2 while inflation falls to π_2. With output below potential, the short-run aggregate supply curve shifts down to AS_3, and the economy moves to point 3, where output is back at Y^P but inflation has fallen to π_3. Panel (a) shows that there has been movement along the MP curve, with the real interest rate falling from r_1^* to r_2 to r_3^*, the new equilibrium real interest rate.

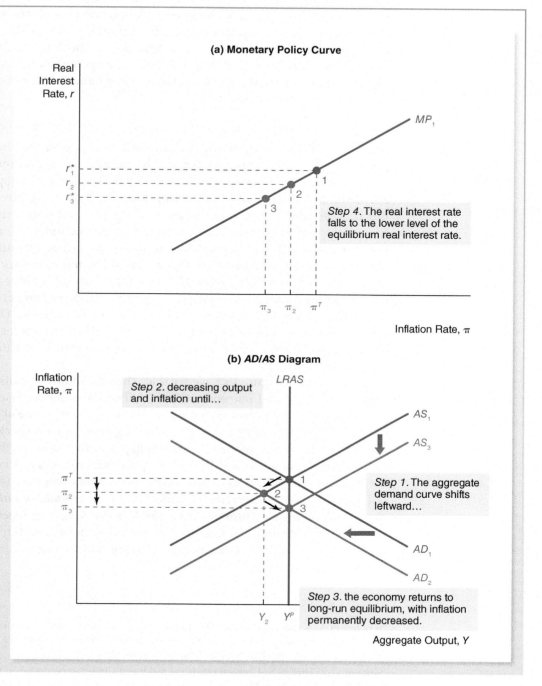

(a) **Monetary Policy Curve**

Real Interest Rate, r

MP_1

r_1^*
r_2
r_3^*

1
2
3

Step 4. The real interest rate falls to the lower level of the equilibrium real interest rate.

π_3 π_2 π^T

Inflation Rate, π

(b) **AD/AS Diagram**

Inflation Rate, π

LRAS

Step 2. decreasing output and inflation until...

AS_1

AS_3

π^T
π_2
π_3

1
2
3

Step 1. The aggregate demand curve shifts leftward...

AD_1

AD_2

Step 3. the economy returns to long-run equilibrium, with inflation permanently decreased.

Y_2 Y^P

Aggregate Output, Y

the MP curve and the real interest rate falls to r_2. (Note that there is no asterisk on r_2: it is not an equilibrium real interest rate because, at point 2, output is at Y_2 and not at Y^P.) With output below potential, slack begins to develop in the labor and product markets, reducing inflation. Again referring to panel (b) of Figure 13.2, the short-run aggregate supply curve will shift down and to the right to AS_3, and the economy will move to point 3. Output will again be back at its potential level, while inflation will fall to a lower level of π_3. At the lower inflation rate of π_3, there is a further movement along the *MP* curve in panel (a), with the real interest rate falling to the lower level of the equilibrium interest rate at r_3^*. At first glance, this long-run outcome looks favorable—inflation is lower and output is back at its potential. But aggregate output may remain below potential for some time, and if inflation was initially at its target level, the fall in inflation is undesirable.

POLICY STABILIZES ECONOMIC ACTIVITY IN THE SHORT RUN. Policy makers can eliminate both the output gap and the inflation gap in the short run by pursuing policies to increase aggregate demand to its initial level and return the economy to its preshock state. One approach, which we discussed in Chapter 12, is to pursue expansionary fiscal policy by cutting taxes or increasing government spending.[6] But it takes time to put fiscal measures in place, and policy makers use them less frequently than monetary policy to stabilize the economy. So, more often than not, policy makers will autonomously ease monetary policy by cutting the real interest rate at any given inflation rate. This action shifts the monetary policy curve downward from MP_1 to MP_3 in Figure 13.3 panel (a), stimulating investment spending and increasing the quantity of aggregate output demanded at any given inflation rate. As a result, the aggregate demand curve shifts to the right from AD_2 to AD_1 in panel (b), and the economy returns to point 1. (The Federal Reserve took exactly these steps by lowering the federal funds rate from 5% to $\frac{1}{4}$% to zero over fifteen months, starting in September 2007.)

In panel (a) of Figure 13.3, we see that when the monetary policy curve shifts downward, the real interest rate ends up at r_3^*. When the economy is at point 1 in panel (b), with output back at potential, the equilibrium real interest rate at point 3 in panel (a) is now at a lower level of r_3^* as a result of the negative demand shock. In other words, it is now r_3^*, not r_1^*, that maintains the output gap at zero and keeps the inflation rate equal to the target level π^T. This is the same equilibrium real interest rate that resulted from the negative demand shock when there was no policy response (as we saw in panel (a) of Figure 13.2). This illustrates an important point: *__monetary policy has no effect on the equilibrium real interest rate, which is the long-run level of the real interest rate.__* The equilibrium real interest rate is instead determined by fundamentals in the economy, such as the balance between saving and investment, and not by monetary policy.[7]

---

[6]If policy makers use expansionary fiscal policy (a cut in taxes or a rise in government purchases) to shift the aggregate demand curve back to AD_1, the monetary policy curve in Figure 13.2 panel (a) will remain unchanged and the equilibrium interest rate will remain at r_1^*.

[7]Since this equilibrium real interest rate is the real interest rate that occurs when the economy is in long-run equilibrium, it is the same long-run equilibrium real interest rate that comes out of the analysis in Chapter 4, in which we equated saving to investment at potential output. The real interest rate that results in the quantity of aggregate output demanded being equal to potential output is also the real interest rate that results in the equilibrium level of aggregate output on the *IS* curve equal to potential output. As we demonstrated in Chapter 9, the goods market equilibrium given by the *IS* curve is the same as the goods market equilibrium given by equating saving and investment: when either framework examines goods market equilibrium when output is at its potential, it gives the same answer for the level of the equilibrium real interest rate. Note that because an autonomous shift in monetary policy does not affect the *IS* curve, the equilibrium real interest rates at point 3 in panel (a) of both Figures 13.2 and 13.3 must be the same.

FIGURE 13.3

Aggregate Demand Shock: Policy Stabilizes Output in the Short Run

An aggregate demand shock shifts the aggregate demand curve leftward from AD_1 to AD_2 in panel (b) and moves the economy from point 1 to point 2, where aggregate output falls to Y_2 while inflation falls to π_2. An autonomous easing of monetary policy lowers the real interest rate at any given inflation rate and shifts the monetary policy curve from MP_1 to MP_3 in panel (a). In panel (b), the AD curve shifts back to AD_1 and aggregate output returns to potential at point 1. The monetary response stabilizes inflation at π^T by lowering the real interest rate to the equilibrium real interest rate r_3^* at point 3 in panel (a).

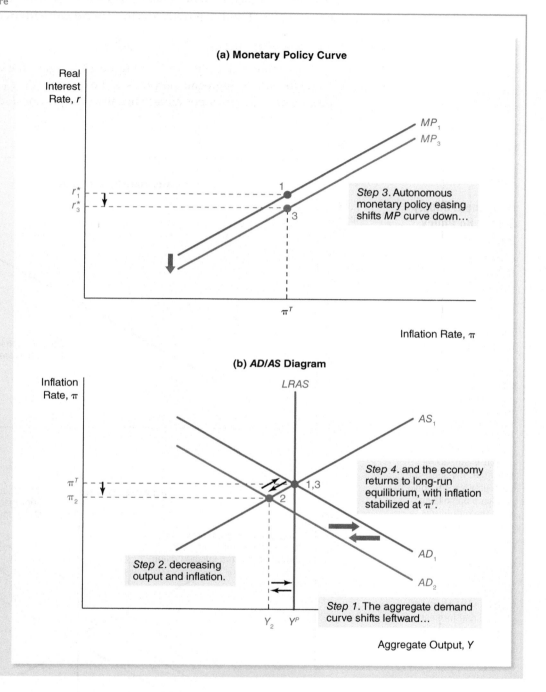

(a) **Monetary Policy Curve**

Real Interest Rate, r

Step 3. Autonomous monetary policy easing shifts *MP* curve down...

π^T

Inflation Rate, π

(b) *AD/AS* Diagram

Inflation Rate, π

Step 4. and the economy returns to long-run equilibrium, with inflation stabilized at π^T.

Step 2. decreasing output and inflation.

Step 1. The aggregate demand curve shifts leftward...

Y_2 Y^P

Aggregate Output, Y

Our analysis of this monetary policy response also shows that *in the case of aggregate demand shocks, there is no tradeoff between the pursuit of price stability and the pursuit of economic activity stability.* A focus on stabilizing inflation leads to exactly the same monetary policy response as a focus on stabilizing economic activity. There is no conflict between the dual objectives of stabilizing inflation and stabilizing economic activity, an outcome that Olivier Blanchard (formerly of MIT, but now at the International Monetary Fund) referred to as the **divine coincidence.**

Response to a Permanent Supply Shock

We illustrate a permanent supply shock in Figure 13.4. Again the economy starts out at point 1 in panel (b), where aggregate output is at the natural rate Y_1^P and inflation is at π^T. Suppose the economy suffers a permanent negative supply shock caused by an increase

MyEconLab Mini-lecture

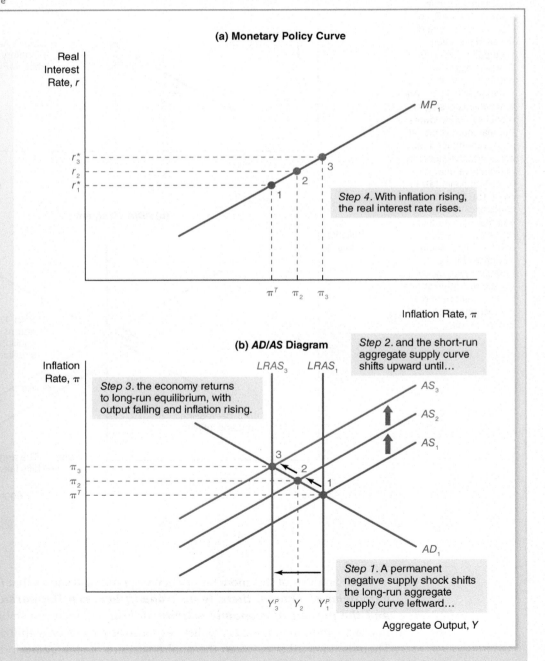

FIGURE 13.4

Permanent Supply Shock: No Policy Response

A permanent negative supply shock decreases potential output from Y_1^P to Y_3^P, and the long-run aggregate supply curve shifts to the left from $LRAS_1$ to $LRAS_3$ in panel (b) while the short-run aggregate supply curve shifts upward from AS_1 to AS_2. The economy moves to point 2, with inflation rising to π_2 and output falling to Y_2. Because aggregate output is still above potential, the short-run aggregate supply curve will keep on shifting until the output gap is zero when it reaches AS_3. The economy moves to point 3, where inflation rises to π_3 while output falls to Y_3^P. With the rise in inflation from π_1 to π_2 to π_3, the real interest rate rises from r_1^* to r_2 to r_3^* in panel (a).

(a) Monetary Policy Curve

Real Interest Rate, r

MP_1

r_3^* ... r_2 ... r_1^*

Step 4. With inflation rising, the real interest rate rises.

π^T π_2 π_3

Inflation Rate, π

(b) AD/AS Diagram

Inflation Rate, π

$LRAS_3$ $LRAS_1$

Step 2. and the short-run aggregate supply curve shifts upward until...

Step 3. the economy returns to long-run equilibrium, with output falling and inflation rising.

AS_3

AS_2

AS_1

π_3 π_2 π^T

AD_1

Step 1. A permanent negative supply shock shifts the long-run aggregate supply curve leftward...

Y_3^P Y_2 Y_1^P

Aggregate Output, Y

in regulations that permanently reduce the level of potential output. Potential output falls from Y_1^P to Y_3^P, and the long-run aggregate supply curve shifts leftward from $LRAS_1$ to $LRAS_3$. The permanent supply shock triggers a price shock that shifts the short-run aggregate supply curve upward from AS_1 to AS_2. There are two possible policy responses to this permanent supply shock, discussed next.

NO POLICY RESPONSE. If policy makers leave the monetary policy curve unchanged at MP_1 in panel (a) of Figure 13.4, the economy will move to point 2 in panel (b), with inflation rising to π_2 and output falling to Y_2. Because this level of output is still higher than potential output, Y_3^P, the short-run aggregate supply curve keeps shifting up and to the left until it reaches AS_3, where it intersects AD_1 on $LRAS_3$. The economy moves to point 3, eliminating the output gap but leaving inflation higher at π_3 and output lower at Y_3^P. In panel (a), we see that the rise in inflation from π^T to π_2 to π_3 results in a movement along the MP curve, with the real interest rate rising from r_1^* to r_2 to r_3^*.

POLICY STABILIZES INFLATION. Referring to panel (b) of Figure 13.5, monetary authorities can keep inflation at the target inflation rate and stabilize inflation by decreasing aggregate demand. The goal is to shift the aggregate demand curve leftward to AD_3, where it intersects the long-run aggregate supply curve $LRAS_3$ at the target inflation rate of π^T. Because the equilibrium interest rate that would keep the output gap at zero has risen from r_1^* to r_3^*, monetary authorities will autonomously tighten monetary policy and shift the monetary policy curve up from MP_1 to MP_3 in panel (a). The rise in the real interest rate at any given inflation rate shifts the aggregate demand curve leftward to AD_3 in panel (b). At point 3 in panel (b), the output gap is zero and inflation is at the target level of π^T. Panel (a) shows that at point 3, the real interest rate has risen to the higher equilibrium real interest rate of r_3^*.

Here again, keeping the inflation gap at zero leads to a zero output gap, so stabilizing inflation has stabilized economic activity.[8] ***The divine coincidence still remains true when there is a permanent supply shock: there is no tradeoff between the dual objectives of stabilizing inflation and stabilizing economic activity.***

Response to a Temporary Supply Shock

When a supply shock is temporary, such as when the price of oil surges because of political unrest in the Middle East, the divine coincidence does not always hold. Policy makers face a short-run tradeoff between stabilizing inflation and stabilizing economic activity. To illustrate, we start with the economy at point 1 in panel (b) of Figure 13.6, where aggregate output is at the natural rate Y^P and inflation is at π^T. The negative

---

[8]The movement to point 3 in panel (b) of Figure 13.5 might be immediate if expected inflation remains at π^T when the permanent supply shock occurs and the aggregate demand curve is immediately shifted to AD_3. As we noted in Chapter 12, the short-run aggregate supply curve intersects the long-run aggregate supply curve at a point where current inflation and expected inflation are equal. If firms and households expect monetary policy to stabilize inflation at π^T, then the short-run supply curve must shift the same amount to the left as the long-run aggregate supply curve, as represented by the way the AS_2 curve is drawn in panel (b) of Figure 13.5. Then, when the monetary authorities autonomously tighten monetary policy and shift the aggregate demand curve to AD_3, the economy will immediately move to point 3, where both the output gap and the inflation gap are zero.

MyEconLab Mini-lecture

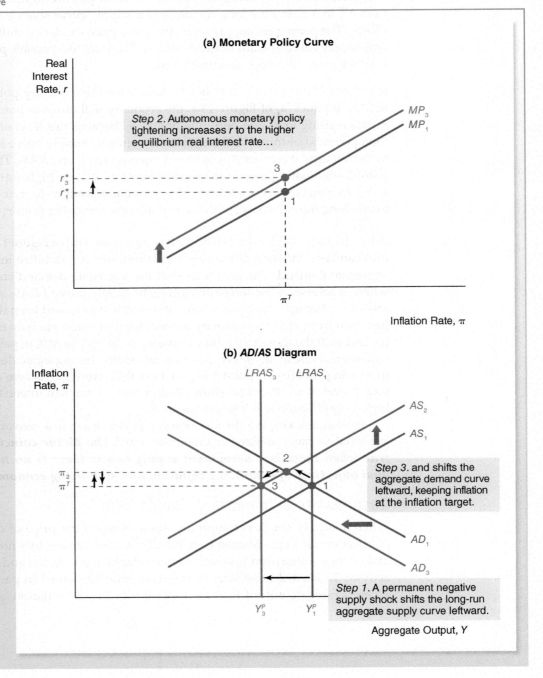

FIGURE 13.5

Permanent Supply Shock: Policy Stabilizes Inflation

A permanent negative supply shock decreases potential output from Y_1^P to Y_3^P, and the long-run aggregate supply curve shifts to the left from $LRAS_1$ to $LRAS_3$ in panel (b) while the short-run aggregate supply curve shifts upward from AS_1 to AS_2. An autonomous tightening of monetary policy that shifts the monetary policy curve from MP_1 to MP_3 in panel (a) shifts the aggregate demand curve to the left to AD_3 in panel (b), thereby keeping the inflation rate at π^T at point 3. At point 3 in panel (a), the real interest rate goes to the higher level of the equilibrium real interest rate of r_3^*.

(a) Monetary Policy Curve

Real Interest Rate, r

Step 2. Autonomous monetary policy tightening increases r to the higher equilibrium real interest rate...

MP_3
MP_1

3

r_3^*
r_1^*

1

π^T

Inflation Rate, π

(b) AD/AS Diagram

Inflation Rate, π

$LRAS_3$ $LRAS_1$

AS_2
AS_1

2

π_2
π^T

3   1

Step 3. and shifts the aggregate demand curve leftward, keeping inflation at the inflation target.

AD_1

AD_3

Step 1. A permanent negative supply shock shifts the long-run aggregate supply curve leftward.

Y_3^P Y_1^P

Aggregate Output, Y

supply shock shifts the short-run aggregate supply curve up and to the left from AS_1 to AS_2 but leaves the long-run aggregate supply curve unchanged because the shock is temporary. The economy moves to point 2, with inflation rising to π_2 and output falling to Y_2. Policy makers can respond to the temporary supply shock in three possible ways.

FIGURE 13.6

Response to a Temporary Aggregate Supply Shock: No Policy Response

A temporary negative supply shock shifts the short-run aggregate supply curve upward from AS_1 to AS_2 in panel (b), moving the economy to point 2, with inflation rising to π_2 and output falling to Y_2. If the monetary policy curve remains at MP_1 in panel (a), the short-run aggregate supply curve will shift back down and to the right in panel (b) in the long run, eventually returning to AS_1, and the economy will move back to point 1.

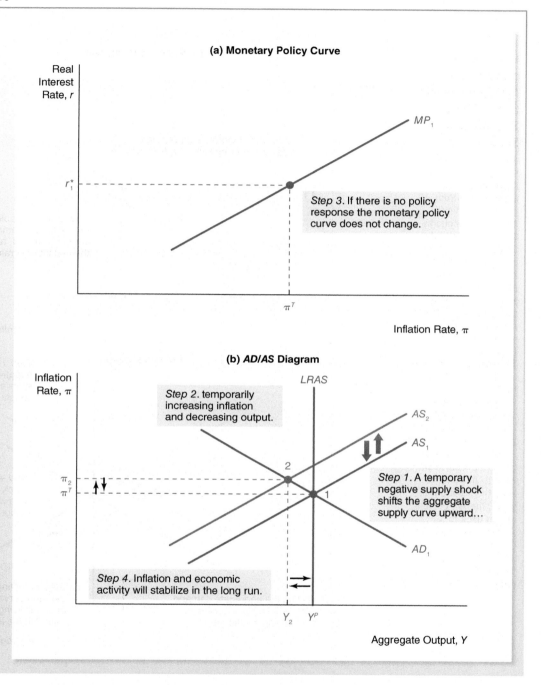

(a) Monetary Policy Curve

Real Interest Rate, r

MP_1

r_1^*

Step 3. If there is no policy response the monetary policy curve does not change.

π^T

Inflation Rate, π

(b) AD/AS Diagram

Inflation Rate, π

LRAS

Step 2. temporarily increasing inflation and decreasing output.

AS_2

AS_1

2

π_2

π^T

Step 1. A temporary negative supply shock shifts the aggregate supply curve upward...

1

AD_1

Step 4. Inflation and economic activity will stabilize in the long run.

Y_2 Y^P

Aggregate Output, Y

NO POLICY RESPONSE. One policy choice is to refrain from making an autonomous change in monetary policy, so that the monetary policy curve remains unchanged at MP_1 in panel (a) of Figure 13.6. Since aggregate output is less than potential output Y^P, the short-run aggregate supply curve eventually will shift back down to the right, returning to AS_1. The economy will return to point 1, and both the output and inflation gaps will close as output and inflation return to the initial levels of Y^P and π^T. In the

MyEconLab Mini-lecture

FIGURE 13.7

Response to a Temporary Aggregate Supply Shock: Short-Run Inflation Stabilization

A temporary negative supply shock shifts the short-run aggregate supply curve from AS_1 to AS_2 in panel (b), moving the economy to point 2, with inflation rising to π_2 and output falling to Y_2. Autonomous tightening of monetary policy shifts the monetary policy curve up to MP_3 in panel (a), with the real interest rate rising to r_3 at point 3. The aggregate demand curve in panel (b) shifts to the left to AD_3 and the economy moves to point 3, where inflation is at π^T. With output below potential at point 3, the short-run aggregate supply curve shifts back to AS_1 and, to keep the inflation rate at π^T, the MP curve is moved back to MP_1, shifting the aggregate demand curve back to AD_1 and the economy back to point 1 in both panels (a) and (b).

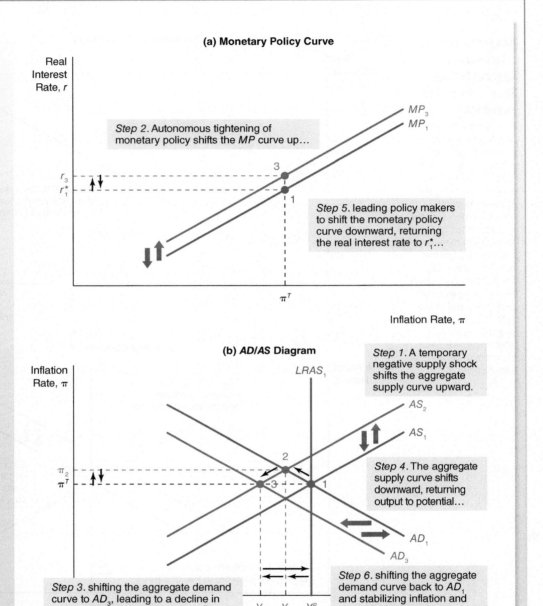

(a) Monetary Policy Curve

Real Interest Rate, r

Step 2. Autonomous tightening of monetary policy shifts the MP curve up…

MP_3
MP_1

r_3
r_1^*

3

1

Step 5. leading policy makers to shift the monetary policy curve downward, returning the real interest rate to r_1^*…

π^T

Inflation Rate, π

(b) AD/AS Diagram

Inflation Rate, π

$LRAS_1$

Step 1. A temporary negative supply shock shifts the aggregate supply curve upward.

AS_2
AS_1

2

π_2
π^T

3

1

Step 4. The aggregate supply curve shifts downward, returning output to potential…

AD_1
AD_3

Step 3. shifting the aggregate demand curve to AD_3, leading to a decline in output, but keeping inflation at π^T.

Y_3 Y_2 Y^P

Step 6. shifting the aggregate demand curve back to AD_1 and stabilizing inflation and output in the long run.

Aggregate Output, Y

long run, both inflation and economic activity stabilize. While we wait for the long run, however, the economy will undergo a painful period of reduced output and higher inflation rates. This opens the door for monetary policy makers to try to stabilize economic activity or inflation in the short run.

POLICY STABILIZES INFLATION IN THE SHORT RUN. A second policy option for monetary authorities is to keep inflation at the target level of π^T in the short run by autonomously tightening monetary policy by raising the real interest rate at any given inflation rate. Doing so would shift the monetary policy curve upward to MP_3, as shown in Figure 13.7 panel (a), moving inflation back to π^T and the real interest rate up to r_3 at point 3. Higher interest rates at any given inflation rate discourage investment spending, reducing aggregate output at any given inflation rate. The aggregate demand curve shifts leftward to AD_3 in Figure 13.7 panel (b), where it intersects the short-run aggregate supply curve AS_2 at an inflation rate of π^T at point 3. Because output is below potential at point 3 in panel (b), the slack in the economy shifts the short-run aggregate supply curve back down to AS_1. In order to keep the inflation rate at π^T, the monetary authorities will need to move the short-run aggregate demand curve back to AD_1 by reversing the autonomous tightening and returning the monetary policy curve back to MP_1. Eventually, the economy will return to point 1 in panel (b), with the real interest rate at r_1^* at point 1 in panel (a).

As Figure 13.7 illustrates, stabilizing inflation reduces aggregate output to Y_3 in the short run, and only over time will output return to potential output at Y^P. ***Stabilizing inflation in response to a temporary supply shock leads to a larger deviation of aggregate output from potential, and so this action does not stabilize economic activity.***

POLICY STABILIZES ECONOMIC ACTIVITY IN THE SHORT RUN. A third policy option is for monetary policy makers to stabilize economic activity rather than inflation in the short run by increasing aggregate demand. Referring to Figure 13.8, they now would shift the aggregate demand curve to the right to AD_3 in panel (b), where it intersects the short-run aggregate supply curve AS_2 and the long-run aggregate supply at point 3. To do this, they would have to autonomously ease monetary policy by lowering the real interest rate at any given inflation rate, and thus shift the monetary policy curve down to MP_3 in Figure 13.8 panel (a). At point 3 in panel (b), the output gap returns to zero, so monetary policy has stabilized economic activity. However, inflation has risen to π_3, which is greater than π^T, so inflation has not been stabilized. ***Stabilizing economic activity in response to a temporary supply shock results in a rise in inflation, so inflation has not been stabilized.***

The Bottom Line: The Relationship Between Stabilizing Inflation and Stabilizing Economic Activity

We can draw the following conclusions from this analysis:

1. ***If most shocks to the macroeconomy are aggregate demand shocks or permanent aggregate supply shocks, then policy that stabilizes inflation will also stabilize economic activity, even in the short run.***

2. ***If temporary supply shocks are more common, then a central bank must choose between the two stabilization objectives in the short run.***

MyEconLab Mini-lecture

FIGURE 13.8

Response to a Temporary Aggregate Supply Shock: Short-Run Output Stabilization

A temporary negative supply shock shifts the short-run aggregate supply curve from AS_1 to AS_2 in panel (b), moving the economy to point 2, with inflation rising to π_2 and output falling to Y_2. To stabilize output, autonomous monetary policy easing shifts the monetary policy curve in panel (a) down from MP_1 to MP_3, and this shifts the aggregate demand curve rightward to AD_3. At point 3, the monetary policy action has stabilized economic activity, but inflation at π_3 is greater than π^T.

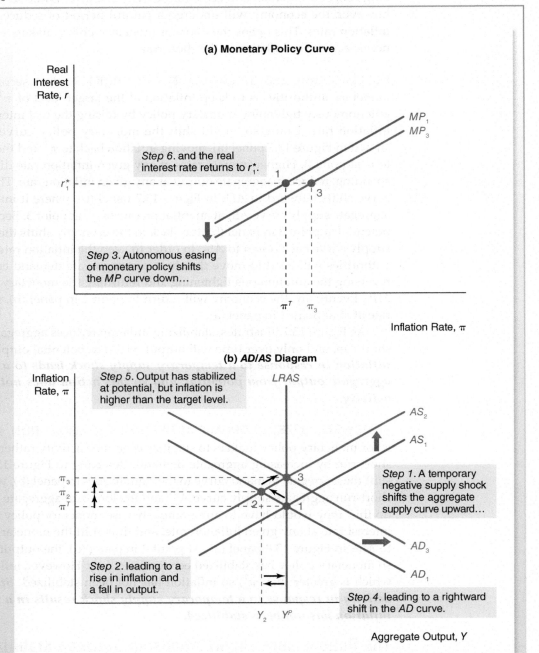

(a) Monetary Policy Curve

Real Interest Rate, r

MP_1
MP_3

Step 6. and the real interest rate returns to r_1^*.

r_1^* ——— 1
3

Step 3. Autonomous easing of monetary policy shifts the *MP* curve down...

π^T π_3

Inflation Rate, π

(b) AD/AS Diagram

Inflation Rate, π

Step 5. Output has stabilized at potential, but inflation is higher than the target level.

LRAS

AS_2
AS_1

π_3
π_2
π^T

3

2
1

Step 1. A temporary negative supply shock shifts the aggregate supply curve upward...

AD_3

AD_1

Step 2. leading to a rise in inflation and a fall in output.

Step 4. leading to a rightward shift in the AD curve.

Y_2 Y^P

Aggregate Output, Y

How Actively Should Policy Makers Try to Stabilize Economic Activity?

All economists have similar policy goals (to promote both high employment and price stability), yet they often disagree on the best approach to achieving those goals. Suppose policy makers confront an economy that has high unemployment resulting from a negative demand or supply shock that has reduced aggregate output. **Nonactivists** believe that wages and prices are very flexible and so the self-correcting mechanism will be very rapid. They argue that the short-run aggregate supply curve will shift down, returning the economy to full employment very quickly. They thus fall into the classical camp and believe that government action is not necessary to eliminate unemployment. **Activists**, many of whom are followers of Keynes and are thus referred to as Keynesians, regard the self-correcting mechanism, which works through wage and price adjustment, as very slow because wages and prices are sticky. As a result, they believe it takes a very long time to reach the long run, agreeing with Keynes's famous adage that "In the long run, we are all dead." They therefore see the need for the government to actively pursue policies to eliminate high unemployment when it develops.

Lags and Policy Implementation

If policy makers could shift the aggregate demand curve instantaneously, activist policies could be used to immediately move the economy to the full-employment level, as we saw in the previous section. However, several types of lags prevent this immediate shift from occurring, and there are differences in the lengths of these lags for monetary versus fiscal policy.

1. The **data lag** is the time it takes for policy makers to obtain data that indicate what is happening in the economy. Accurate data on GDP, for example, are not available until several months after a given quarter is over.

2. The **recognition lag** is the time it takes for policy makers to be sure of what the data are signaling about the future course of the economy. For example, to minimize errors, the National Bureau of Economic Research (the private organization that officially dates business cycles) will not officially declare the economy to be in a recession until at least six months after it has determined that a recession has begun.

3. The **legislative lag** represents the time it takes to pass legislation to implement a particular policy. The legislative lag does not exist for most monetary policy actions, such as lowering interest rates. It is, however, important for the implementation of fiscal policy, since it can sometimes take six months to a year to pass legislation to change taxes or government purchases.

4. The **implementation lag** is the time it takes for policy makers to change policy instruments once they have decided on a new policy. Again, this lag is less important for the conduct of monetary policy than it is for fiscal policy, because the Federal Reserve can immediately change its policy interest rate. Actually implementing fiscal policy may take substantial

time, however; for example, getting government agencies to change their spending habits takes time, as does changing tax tables.

5. The **effectiveness lag** is the time it takes for the policy to have an actual impact on the economy. The effectiveness lag is both long (often a year or longer) and variable (that is, there is substantial uncertainty about how long this lag will be).

The existence of these lags makes the policy makers' job far more difficult and therefore weakens the case for activism. When there is high unemployment, activist policy intended to shift the aggregate demand curve rightward to restore the economy to full employment may not produce desirable outcomes. Indeed, if the policy lags described above are very long, then by the time the aggregate demand curve shifts to the right, the self-correcting mechanism may have already returned the economy to full employment. Thus, when the activist policy kicks in, it may lead output to rise above potential, leading to a rise in inflation. In situations in which policy lags are longer than the time required for the self-correcting mechanism to work, a policy of nonactivism may produce better outcomes.

The activist/nonactivist debate came to the fore when the Obama administration advocated a fiscal stimulus package when it first came to office in 2009, as indicated in the following Policy and Practice case. We will return to the issue of just how active policy should be in Chapter 21, when we look at the role expectations play in macroeconomic policy.

Policy and Practice

The Activist/Nonactivist Debate Over the Obama Fiscal Stimulus Package

When President Obama entered office in January 2009, he faced a very serious recession, with unemployment over 7% and rising rapidly. Although policy makers had been using monetary policy aggressively to stabilize the economy (see Chapter 10), many activists argued that the government needed to do more, namely by implementing a massive fiscal stimulus package. They argued that monetary policy, which had already lowered the federal funds rate to close to zero and so could not lower nominal interest rates further, would be unable to increase aggregate demand to the full-employment level. On the other hand, nonactivists opposed the fiscal stimulus package, arguing that fiscal stimulus would take too long to work because of long implementation lags. They cautioned that if the fiscal stimulus kicked in after the economy had already recovered, this could lead to increased volatility in inflation and economic activity.

The economics profession split over the desirability of fiscal stimulus. Approximately 200 economists who supported fiscal stimulus signed a petition that was published in the *Wall Street Journal* and the *New York Times* on January 28, 2009. An opposing petition, also signed by around 200 economists, was published on February 8. The Obama administration came down squarely on the side of the activists and proposed the American Recovery and Reinvestment Act of 2009, a $787 billion fiscal stimulus package that Congress passed on February 13, 2009 (see Chapter 9). In the House, the vote was 246 to 183, with 176 Republicans and 7 Democrats opposing the bill, while in the Senate the vote was 60 to 38, with all Democrats and 3 Republicans supporting the bill. Even after the fact, the desirability of the 2009 stimulus package is still hotly debated, with some believing it helped stabilize the economy and others believing it was not effective.

The Taylor Rule

Our stabilization policy analysis based on the monetary policy curve shows how central banks like the Federal Reserve shift the monetary policy curve to respond to economic shocks. We now describe another monetary policy approach, proposed by John Taylor of Stanford University, that has become known as the *Taylor rule*.[9]

The Taylor Rule Equation

The **Taylor rule** proposes that the Federal Reserve set the real federal funds rate, its policy instrument, at its historical average of 2% plus a weighted average of the inflation gap and the output gap. (The Taylor rule is distinct from the Taylor principle introduced in Chapter 10, and this is clarified in the box, "The Difference Between the Taylor Rule and the Taylor Principle.") The weights on the inflation gap and the output gap, both expressed as percentages, are chosen to be equal to 1/2 for both terms. We write the Taylor rule as follows, denoting the real federal funds rate by r and the output gap, as a percent, by $Y - Y^P$:

$$r = 2.0 + \frac{1}{2}(\pi - \pi^T) + \frac{1}{2}(Y - Y^P) \tag{1}$$

The Taylor rule is usually stated in terms of the nominal interest rate rather than the real interest rate. Recognizing that the nominal federal funds rate, i, is equal to the real federal funds rate, r, plus inflation ($i = r + \pi$), and adding π to both sides of Equation 1, we can rewrite the Taylor rule in terms of the nominal federal funds rate, or simply the federal funds rate, as follows:

$$\text{Federal funds rate} = \pi + 2.0 + \frac{1}{2}(\pi - \pi^T) + \frac{1}{2}(Y - Y^P) \tag{2}$$

or, in words,

Federal funds rate = inflation rate + historical average of the real federal funds rate

$$+ \frac{1}{2}(\text{inflation gap}) + \frac{1}{2}(\text{output gap})$$

---

[9]John Taylor, "Discretion Versus Policy Rules in Practice," *Carnegie-Rochester Conference Series on Public Policy* (1993): 195–214.

The Difference Between the Taylor Rule and the Taylor Principle

It is easy to confuse the Taylor rule discussed here with the Taylor principle discussed in earlier chapters. The Taylor rule describes how the monetary policy authorities should set the real interest rate in response to the *level of output* as well as to inflation, and provides a *complete* description of how the monetary authorities should conduct monetary policy in any situation. In contrast, the Taylor principle describes only how the real interest rate is set in response to the level of inflation (ignoring the level of output) and provides only a *partial* description of how monetary policy is conducted. In the earlier analysis in this chapter, which relies only on the Taylor principle, the monetary authorities have a choice about how to react to shocks, which is a more realistic description of central bank behavior. In contrast, if the monetary authorities operate under the Taylor rule, their decisions are completely automatic, with no discretion allowed.

To illustrate the use of the Taylor rule, suppose the inflation rate target is 2%, while the current inflation rate is 3%. Suppose also that the positive inflation gap of 1% [= 3% − 2%] pushes real GDP to 1% above its potential, resulting in a positive output gap of 1%. The Taylor rule suggests that the Federal Reserve should set the federal funds rate at 6% [= 3% + 2% + 2 (1%) + 2 (1%)].

The Taylor Rule Versus the Monetary Policy Curve

By incorporating the inflation gap and the output gap, the Taylor rule suggests similar policy actions to those described in this chapter. The inflation term of the Taylor rule indicates that the Fed should raise real interest rates as inflation rises. The same conclusion follows from the upward-sloping monetary policy curve, since real interest rates rise with an increase in the inflation gap (a movement along the MP curve). Also, our analysis of stabilization policy in Figure 13.3 argues that in response to aggregate demand shocks, the Fed should adjust monetary policy by using the federal funds rate policy tool, shifting the MP curve upward (autonomous tightening) or downward (autonomous easing) in response to changes in the output gap, to stabilize inflation. Thus even if a central bank cares only about stabilizing inflation, there should also be a positive relationship between output gaps and the real federal funds rate, as the Taylor rule suggests.

The analysis in Figure 13.8 suggests an additional reason for the positive relationship between the real federal funds rate and the output gap. If there is a negative temporary aggregate supply shock and the central bank wishes to stabilize economic activity by increasing aggregate demand, it will autonomously ease monetary policy and lower the real interest rate to eliminate the negative output gap, $Y < Y^P$, at the expense of higher inflation. Because the Federal Reserve's dual mandate requires it to focus on economic activity in addition to inflation, the presence of aggregate supply shocks argues for a positive relationship between the real federal funds rate and output gaps, as in the Taylor rule.

FIGURE 13.9

The Taylor Rule and the Federal Funds Rate, 1960–2013

The Taylor rule roughly describes the actual federal funds rate under chairmen Greenspan and Bernanke from 1987 to 2013, but there have been substantial deviations.

Source: Author's calculations and Federal Reserve. www .federalreserve.gov/ releases

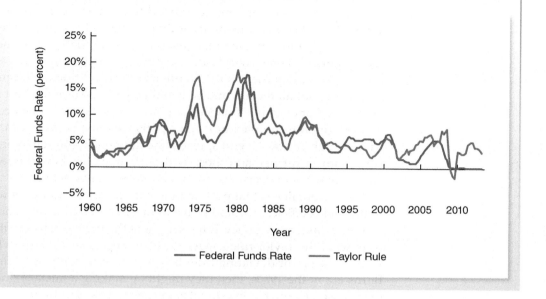

The Taylor Rule in Practice

As Figure 13.9 shows, the Taylor rule roughly describes the Fed's control of the federal funds rate after 1987 under its two most recent chairmen, Alan Greenspan and Ben Bernanke. However, there are some substantial deviations, such as from 1995 to 1999, from 2003 to 2006, and from 2011 to 2013. (In the 1970s, the Fed did not raise the real interest rate as inflation rose, diverging even more for the Taylor rule, and the outcomes, as we know, were very poor.) We discuss the Federal Reserve's use of the Taylor rule in the following Policy and Practice case.

Policy and Practice

The Fed's Use of the Taylor Rule

Why hasn't the Fed put the federal funds rate on Taylor rule autopilot, guided by a computer? There are several reasons why the Fed hasn't taken this drastic action. First and foremost, there is no perfect model of the economy, and even the best and brightest economists do not know the current inflation rate and output gaps with certainty at any given moment. In addition, the economy is changing all the time, so the Taylor rule coefficients are unlikely to stay constant.

Even if we could determine these gaps with certainty, monetary policy is by necessity a forward-looking activity, because it takes a long time for monetary policy to affect the economy. Good monetary policy requires that the Fed forecast inflation rates and economic activity with a certain degree of accuracy, and then adjust the policy instrument accordingly. The Fed will therefore look at a much wider range of information than just the current inflation rate and output gaps in setting policy. In other words, the conduct of monetary policy is as much an art as it is a science, requiring both careful analytics and human judgment. The Taylor rule leaves out all the art, and so is unlikely to produce the best monetary policy outcomes. For example, financial crises, such as the crisis that occurred from 2007 to 2009, require complex monetary policy actions because changes in financial frictions, which affect credit spreads (the difference between interest rates on securities with credit risk and those without), may alter how the federal funds rate affects investment decisions, and therefore economic activity.

The bottom line is that putting monetary policy on autopilot with a Taylor rule with fixed coefficients would be a bad idea. The Taylor rule is, however, useful as a guide to monetary policy. If the setting of the policy instrument is very different from what the Taylor rule suggests, policy makers should ask whether they have a good reason for deviating from this rule. If they don't, as during the Chairman Burns era in the 1970s, then they might be making a mistake. Indeed, the FOMC makes use of Taylor rule estimates in exactly this way by referring to Taylor rule estimates to inform their decisions about the federal funds rate target.[10]

Inflation: Always and Everywhere a Monetary Phenomenon

In Chapter 5, we discussed Milton Friedman's famous adage that in the long run, "Inflation is always and everywhere a monetary phenomenon." This conclusion is also borne out by aggregate demand and supply analysis because it shows that monetary policy makers can target any inflation rate in the long run by shifting the monetary policy curve with autonomous monetary policy. To illustrate, look at Figure 13.10, where the economy is at point 1 with the real interest rate at r_1^* in panel (a), aggregate output is at potential output Y^P in panel (b), and inflation is at an initial inflation target of π_1^T in both panels.

Suppose the central bank believes this inflation target is too low and chooses to raise it to π_3^T. It eases monetary policy autonomously by lowering the real interest rate at any given inflation rate, shifting the monetary policy curve in panel (a) from MP_1 to MP_3. The lower real interest rate at any given inflation rate means that investment spending and the quantity of aggregate output demanded are higher, thereby increasing aggregate demand. In Figure 13.10, the aggregate demand curve shifts to AD_3 in panel (b). The economy then moves to point 2 at the intersection of AD_3 and AS_1 in panel (b), with inflation rising to π_2 and the real interest rate to r_2 in panel (a). Because aggregate output is above potential output ($Y_2 > Y^P$), the short-run aggregate supply

[10]For an in-depth discussion of the FOMC's actual use of the Taylor rule in its policy deliberations, see Pier Francesco Asso, George A. Kahn, and Robert Leeson, "The Taylor Rule and the Practice of Central Banking," Federal Reserve Bank of Kansas City Working Paper RWP 10-05 (February 2010).

MyEconLab Mini-lecture

FIGURE 13.10

A Rise in the Inflation Target

To raise the inflation target to π_3^T, the central bank undertakes an autonomous monetary policy easing, shifting MP_1 to MP_3 in panel (a) and shifting the aggregate demand curve rightward to AD_3 in panel (b). The economy then moves to point 2, and the short-run aggregate supply curve shifts up and to the left, eventually stopping at AS_3, moving the economy to point 3 with the output gap at zero and inflation at π_3^T, while the real interest rate is at r_1^* at point 3 in panel (a).

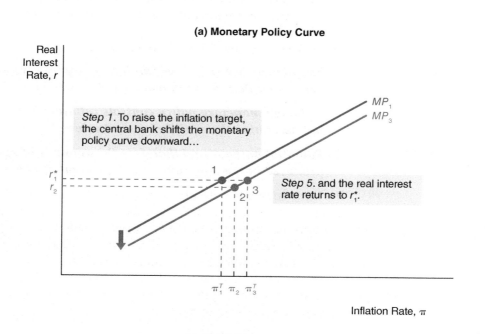

(a) Monetary Policy Curve

Step 1. To raise the inflation target, the central bank shifts the monetary policy curve downward…

Step 5. and the real interest rate returns to r_1^*.

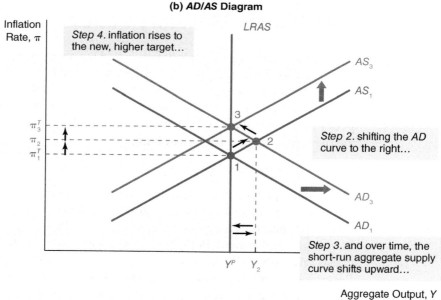

(b) *AD/AS* Diagram

Step 4. inflation rises to the new, higher target…

Step 2. shifting the *AD* curve to the right…

Step 3. and over time, the short-run aggregate supply curve shifts upward…

Aggregate Output, *Y*

curve in panel (b) shifts up and to the left, eventually stopping at AS_3, with inflation now at the higher target level of π_3^T and the output gap back at zero. With the output gap at zero at π_3^T, the real interest rate rises again to r_1^*, indicated by point 3 in panel (a) of Figure 13.10.[11]

The analysis in Figure 13.10 demonstrates several key points.

1. ***The monetary authorities can target any inflation rate in the long run with autonomous monetary policy adjustments.***

2. ***Although monetary policy controls inflation in the long run, it does not determine the equilibrium real interest rate.***

3. ***Potential output—and therefore the quantity of aggregate output produced in the long run—is independent of monetary policy.***

The last two points reflect the concepts of the *classical dichotomy* and *monetary neutrality* described in Chapter 5. Both of these concepts are correct in the long run, even when we derive them from the sticky price framework using aggregate demand and supply. Recall that the *classical dichotomy* indicates that with prices completely flexible, real variables are not affected by nominal variables, and so real variables are unaffected by monetary policy (*monetary neutrality*). This is exactly what the second and third points tell us by indicating that monetary policy has no effect on the equilibrium interest rate or output in the long run.

Causes of Inflationary Monetary Policy

If everyone agrees that high inflation is bad for an economy, why do we see so much of it? Do governments pursue inflationary monetary policies intentionally? We have seen that monetary authorities can set the inflation rate in the long run, so it must be that in trying to achieve other goals, governments end up with overly expansionary monetary policy and high inflation. In this section, we will examine the government policies that are the most common sources of inflation.

High Employment Targets and Inflation

The primary goal of most governments is high employment, and the pursuit of this goal can bring high inflation. The U.S. government is committed by law (the Employment Act of 1946 and the Humphrey-Hawkins Act of 1978) to engage in activist policy to promote high employment. Both laws require a commitment to a high level of employment consistent with stable inflation—yet in practice the U.S. government and the Federal Reserve have often pursued a high employment target with little concern about the inflationary consequences of policies. This tendency was especially true in the mid-1960s and 1970s, when the government and the Fed began to take an active role in attempting to stabilize unemployment.

---

[11]To see that the real interest rate is at r_1^* when the inflation rate reaches the higher target of π_3^T and the output gap is zero, recognize that there is no reason for the IS curve to shift and that the equilibrium interest rate r_1^* is at the point on the IS curve at which aggregate output is at Y^P. Hence, after the initial decline in the real interest rate when the monetary policy curve shifts down to MP_3, there is a rise in inflation that leads to a rise in the real interest rate (movement along the MP_3 curve). The rise in the real interest rate stops only when the real interest rate is back at r_1^*, where the IS curve indicates that aggregate output has fallen back to Y^P.

Two types of inflation can result from an activist stabilization policy to promote high employment:

1. **Cost-push inflation** results either from a temporary negative supply shock or a push by workers for wage hikes beyond what productivity gains can justify.

2. **Demand-pull inflation** results from policy makers pursuing policies that increase aggregate demand.

We will now use aggregate demand and supply analysis to examine the effect of a high employment target on both types of inflation.

COST-PUSH INFLATION. Consider the economy in Figure 13.11, which is initially at point 1, the intersection of the aggregate demand curve AD_1 and the short-run aggregate supply curve AS_1. Suppose workers succeed in pushing for higher wages, either because they want to increase their real wages (wages in terms of the goods and services they can buy) above what is justified by productivity gains, or because they expect inflation to be high and wish their wages to keep up with it. This cost push shock, which acts like a temporary negative supply shock, raises the inflation rate and shifts the short-run

MyEconLab Mini-lecture

FIGURE 13.11

Cost-Push Inflation

A cost-push shock (which acts like a temporary negative supply shock) shifts the short-run aggregate supply curve up and to the left to AS_2, and the economy moves to point 2'. To keep aggregate output at Y^P and lower the unemployment rate, policy makers shift the aggregate demand curve to AD_2 so that the economy will return quickly to potential output at point 2 and an inflation rate of π_2. Further upward and leftward shifts of the short-run aggregate supply curve to AS_3 and so on lead the policy makers to keep on increasing aggregate demand, leading to a continuing increase in inflation—a cost-push inflation.

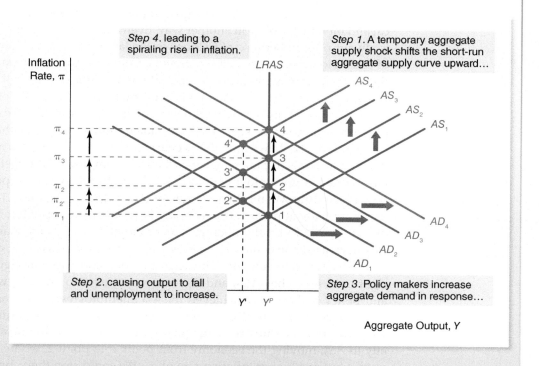

aggregate supply curve up and to the left to AS_2. If the central bank takes no action to change the equilibrium interest rate and the monetary policy curve remains unchanged, the economy moves to point 2′ at the intersection of the new short-run aggregate supply curve AS_2 and the aggregate demand curve AD_1. Output declines to Y', below potential output, and the inflation rate rises to $\pi_{2'}$, leading to an increase in unemployment.

In contrast, activist policy makers with a high employment target would implement policies, such as a cut in taxes, an increase in government purchases, or an autonomous easing of monetary policy, to increase aggregate demand. These policies would shift the aggregate demand curve in Figure 13.11 to AD_2, quickly returning the economy to potential output at point 2 and increasing the inflation rate to π_2. The workers fare quite well, gaining both higher wages and government policies that protect against excessive unemployment.

The workers' success might encourage them to seek even higher wages. In addition, other workers might now realize that their wages have fallen relative to those of their fellow workers, leading them to seek wage increases. As a result, there would be another temporary negative supply shock that would raise the price level, causing the short-run aggregate supply curve in Figure 13.11 to shift up and to the left again, to AS_3. Unemployment develops again when we move to point 3′, prompting activist policies to once again shift the aggregate demand curve rightward to AD_3 and return the economy to full employment at a higher inflation rate of π_3. If this process continues, the result will be a continuing increase in inflation—a cost-push inflation.

DEMAND-PULL INFLATION. The goal of high employment can lead to inflationary fiscal and monetary policy in another way. Even at full employment, some unemployment is always present because of frictions in the labor market that complicate the matching of unemployed workers with employers. Consequently, the unemployment rate when there is full employment (the natural rate of unemployment) will be greater than zero. When policy makers mistakenly underestimate the natural rate of unemployment and so set a target for unemployment that is too low (i.e., less than the natural rate of unemployment), they set the stage for expansionary monetary policy that produces inflation.

Figure 13.12 shows how this scenario might unfold using an aggregate supply and demand analysis. If policy makers set a 4% unemployment target that is below the 5% natural rate of unemployment, they are trying to achieve an output target greater than potential output. We mark this target level of output in Figure 13.12 as Y^T. Suppose that we are initially at point 1: the economy is at potential output but below the target level of output Y^T. To hit the unemployment target of 4%, policy makers must enact policies, such as expansionary fiscal policy or an autonomous easing of monetary policy, to increase aggregate demand. The aggregate demand curve in Figure 13.12 shifts to the right until it reaches AD_2, and the economy moves to point 2′, where output is at Y^T and policy makers have achieved the 4% unemployment rate goal—but there is more to the story. At Y^T, the 4% unemployment rate is below the natural rate level, causing wages to rise. The short-run aggregate supply curve will shift up and to the left, eventually to AS_2, moving the economy from point 2′ to point 2, where it is back at potential output but at a higher inflation rate of π_2. We could stop there, but because unemployment is again higher than the target level, policy makers will again shift the aggregate demand curve rightward to AD_3 to hit the output target at point 3′—and the whole process will continue to drive the economy to point 3 and beyond. The overall result is a steadily rising inflation rate.

FIGURE 13.12

Demand-Pull Inflation

Too low an unemploy-ment target (too high an output target of Y^T) causes the government to increase aggregate demand, shifting the AD curve rightward from AD_1 to AD_2 to AD_3 and so on. Because the unemployment rate is below the natural rate level, wages will rise and the short-run aggre-gate supply curve will shift up and leftward from AS_1 to AS_2 to AS_3 and so on. The result is a continuing rise in inflation known as a demand-pull inflation.

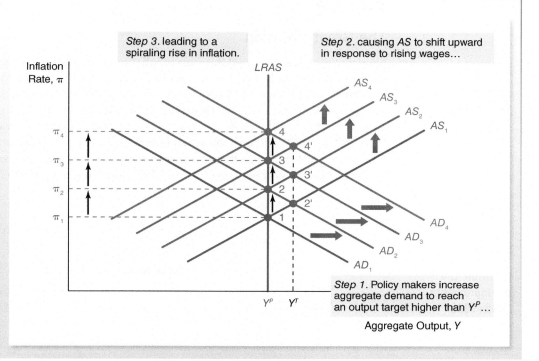

Step 3. leading to a spiraling rise in inflation.

Step 2. causing AS to shift upward in response to rising wages…

Step 1. Policy makers increase aggregate demand to reach an output target higher than Y^P…

Pursuing too low an unemployment rate target or, equivalently, too high an out-put target thus leads to inflationary monetary or fiscal policy. Policy makers fail on two counts: they have not achieved their unemployment target, and they have caused higher inflation. If, however, the target rate of unemployment is below the natural rate, the process we see in Figure 13.12 will be well under way before they realize their mistake.

COST-PUSH VERSUS DEMAND-PULL INFLATION. When inflation occurs, how do we know whether it is demand-pull inflation or cost-push inflation? We would nor-mally expect to see demand-pull inflation when unemployment is below the natural rate level and cost-push inflation when unemployment is above the natural rate level. Unfortunately, economists and policy makers still struggle with measuring the natural rate of unemployment. Complicating matters further, a cost-push inflation can be initi-ated by a demand-pull inflation, blurring the distinction. When a demand-pull inflation produces higher inflation rates, expected inflation will eventually rise and cause work-ers to demand higher wages (cost-push inflation) so that their real wages do not fall. Finally, expansionary monetary and fiscal policies produce both kinds of inflation, so we cannot distinguish between them on this basis.

In the United States, as we will see in the following application, the primary reason for inflationary policy has been policy makers' adherence to a high employment target. In Chapter 16, we will see that high inflation can also occur because of persistent gov-ernment budget deficits.

Application

The Great Inflation

Now that we have examined the roots of inflationary monetary policy, we can investigate the causes of the rise in U.S. inflation from 1965 to 1982, a period dubbed the "Great Inflation."

Panel (a) of Figure 13.13 documents the rise in inflation during those years. Just before the Great Inflation started, the annual inflation rate was below 2%; by the late 1970s, it averaged around 8%; and it peaked at nearly 14% in 1980, after the oil price shock of 1979. Panel (b) of Figure 13.13 compares the actual unemployment rate with estimates of the natural rate of unemployment. Notice that the economy experienced unemployment below the natural rate in all but one year between 1960 and 1973, as represented by the blue shaded areas. This

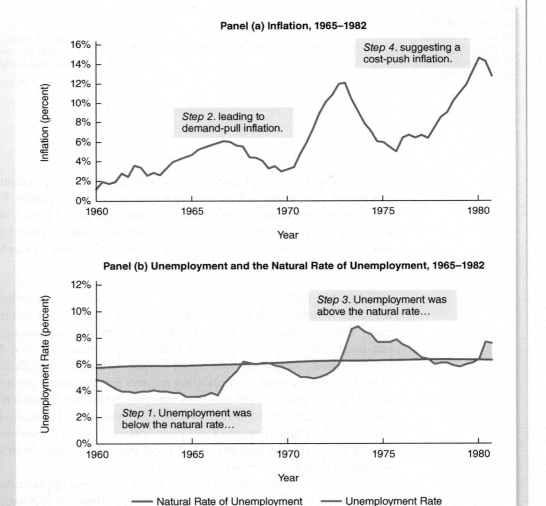

FIGURE 13.13

Inflation and Unemployment, 1965–1982

As shown in panel (a), the CPI annual inflation rate was below 2% in the early 1960s, but by the late 1970s it was averaging around 8%, and it peaked at over 14% in 1980 after the oil price shock of 1979. As shown in panel (b), the economy experienced unemployment below the natural rate in all but one year between 1960 and 1973, suggesting a demand-pull inflation as described in Figure 13.12. After 1974, the unemployment rate was regularly above the natural rate of unemployment, suggesting a cost-push inflation as described in Figure 13.11.

Source: Economic Report of the President.

insight suggests that from 1965 to 1973, the U.S. economy experienced the demand-pull inflation we described in Figure 13.12. That is, policy makers, in trying to achieve an output target that was too high, pursued a policy of autonomous monetary policy easing that shifted the aggregate demand curve to the right, thus increasing inflation. Policy makers, economists, and politicians were committed in the mid-1960s to a target unemployment rate of 4%, a level of unemployment they believed to be consistent with price stability. In hindsight, most economists today agree that the natural rate of unemployment was substantially higher in this period, between 5% and 6%, as shown in panel (b) of Figure 13.13. The inappropriate 4% unemployment target initiated the most sustained inflationary episode in U.S. history.

Panel (b) of Figure 13.13 shows that after 1974, the unemployment rate was usually above the natural rate of unemployment (see the red shaded area), with the exception of a brief period in 1978 and 1979. Yet inflation continued to rise, as per panel (a), indicating the phenomenon of a cost-push inflation, as we described in Figure 13.11 (the impetus for which was the earlier demand-pull inflation). The public's knowledge that government policy was aimed squarely at high employment explains the persistence of inflation. The higher rate of expected inflation from the demand-pull inflation shifted the short-run aggregate supply curve in Figure 13.11 upward and to the left, causing a rise in unemployment that policy makers tried to eliminate by autonomously easing monetary policy, shifting the aggregate demand curve to the right. The result was a continuing rise in inflation.

Only when the Federal Reserve committed to an anti-inflationary monetary policy under Chairman Paul Volcker, which involved hiking the federal funds rate to the 20% level, did inflation come down, ending the Great Inflation (see Chapter 12).

Monetary Policy at the Zero Lower Bound

So far we have assumed that a central bank can always keep lowering the real interest rate as inflation falls by lowering its policy rate, say the federal funds rate, so that the *MP* curve is always upward-sloping. However, because the federal funds rate is a nominal interest rate, it can never fall below a value of zero. A negative federal funds rate implies that financial institutions are willing to earn a lower return by lending in the federal funds market than they could earn by holding cash, with its zero rate of return. The zero floor on the policy rate is referred to as the **zero lower bound,** and as we shall see, it creates a particular problem for the conduct of monetary policy.

Deriving the Aggregate Demand Curve with the Zero Lower Bound

To see what problems the zero lower bound creates for the conduct of monetary policy, let's look at what happens to the aggregate demand curve when a central bank cannot lower its policy rate below zero. Panel (a) of Figure 13.14 shows an *MP* curve in which the zero lower bound occurs. For our purposes, let's assume that expected inflation moves closely with the actual inflation rate on the horizontal axis of panel (a), as it usually does. Let's start with point 3 on the *MP* curve, at which inflation is at 3% and the real interest rate is at 2%. Now let's see what happens as inflation falls from 3% to 2%, the point at which, following the Taylor principle, monetary authorities will want the real interest rate to be at point 2, say at –2%, a level which requires them to lower the policy rate to zero ($r = 0 - 2\% = -2\%$). At point 2 in panel (a), the zero lower bound

MyEconLab Mini-lecture

FIGURE 13.14

Derivation of the Aggregate Demand Curve with a Zero Lower Bound

In panel (a), the *MP* curve has the usual upward slope from point 2 to point 3, but has a downward slope in the segment including points 1 and 2 because, with the policy rate at zero, as inflation and expected inflation fall, the real interest rate rises. In panel (b), the *AD* curve has the usual downward slope from point 3 to point 2, but has an upward slope from point 1 to point 2 because, as inflation rises, the real interest rate falls and the level of equilibrium output rises.

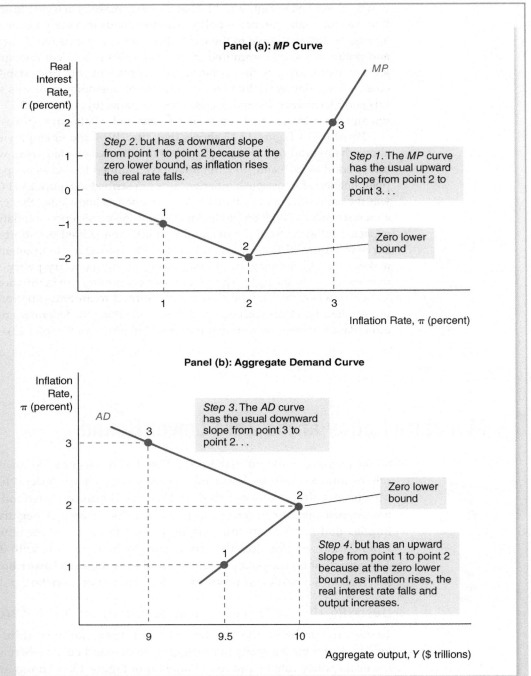

Panel (a): *MP* Curve

Real Interest Rate, *r* (percent)

MP

Step 1. The *MP* curve has the usual upward slope from point 2 to point 3...

Step 2. but has a downward slope from point 1 to point 2 because at the zero lower bound, as inflation rises the real rate falls.

Zero lower bound

Inflation Rate, π (percent)

Panel (b): Aggregate Demand Curve

Inflation Rate, π (percent)

AD

Step 3. The *AD* curve has the usual downward slope from point 3 to point 2...

Zero lower bound

Step 4. but has an upward slope from point 1 to point 2 because at the zero lower bound, as inflation rises, the real interest rate falls and output increases.

Aggregate output, *Y* ($ trillions)

has been reached on the *MP* curve. So far, our analysis is identical to our analysis in Chapter 10, with the *MP* curve having its usual upward slope.

Now, what if the inflation rate falls even further, say to 1%? The monetary authorities would like to lower the real interest rate by lowering the policy rate, but they can't do so because the policy rate has hit the floor of zero. Indeed, as point 1 on the *MP* curve shows, the real interest rate at an inflation rate of 1% has risen to -1% ($r = 0 - 1\% = -1\%$). Hence the segment of the *MP* curve that goes from point 2 to point 1 is downward sloping, the opposite of what we found in Chapter 10.

Now let's see what happens to the aggregate demand curve in panel (b). Suppose that at a 3% inflation rate and a real interest rate of 2%, at point 3 on the *MP* curve in panel (a), the equilibrium level of output is at $9 trillion, marked as point 3 on the aggregate demand curve in panel (b). Now, when inflation falls to 2% and the real interest rate is at -2%, as indicated by point 2 on the *MP* curve in panel (a), aggregate output rises to $10 trillion, because planned investment spending rises with the lower real interest rate. The inflation rate of 2% and level of output of $10 trillion is point 2 on the *AD* curve in panel (b), which is also marked as the zero lower bound point on the *AD* curve.

If inflation falls to 1%, point 1 on the *MP* curve in panel (a) indicates that the real interest rate has risen to -1%, and so planned investment spending falls, lowering the level of equilibrium output to, say, $9.5 trillion, at point 1 on the *AD* curve in panel (b). In panel (b), in going from point 1 to point 2, the aggregate demand curve slopes upward rather than downward. The presence of the zero lower bound thus can produce a kinked aggregate demand curve of the type seen in panel (b).

The Disappearance of the Self-Correcting Mechanism at the Zero Lower Bound

Now let's analyze what happens in the aggregate demand and supply diagram when the economy is hit by a large negative shock, such as occurred during the global financial crisis (which we will discuss in Chapter 15), so that the zero lower bound is binding. In this situation, the initial short-run aggregate supply curve intersects the upward-sloping part of the aggregate demand curve at point 1 in Figure 13.15, where aggregate output is below potential output. Because $Y_1 < Y^P$, there is slack in the economy, and so the short-run aggregate supply curve will fall to AS_2 and the economy will move to point 2 at the intersection of the AS_2 and the *AD* curves, at which point inflation and output will have declined to π_2 and Y_2, respectively. Now Y_2 is even lower relative to Y^P, and the short-run aggregate supply curve shifts down even further to AS_3. The economy will move to point 3, where inflation and output have fallen further, to π_3 and Y_3, respectively.

Figure 13.15 reveals two key results.

- First, the self-correcting mechanism is no longer operational. When the economy is in a situation in which equilibrium output is below potential and the zero lower bound on the policy rate has been reached, output is not restored to its potential level if policy makers do nothing. Indeed, the opposite occurs, with the economy going into a downward spiral.
- Second, in this situation, the economy goes into a deflationary spiral, with inflation continually falling.

The intuition behind these two results is fairly straightforward. When output is below its potential and the policy rate hits the floor of zero, the resulting fall in inflation leads to higher real interest rates, which depress output further, which causes inflation to fall further, and so on. Schematically, this can be expressed as:

$$Y < Y^P \Rightarrow \pi\downarrow \Rightarrow r\uparrow \Rightarrow Y\downarrow \Rightarrow Y \ll Y^P \Rightarrow \pi\downarrow \Rightarrow r\uparrow \Rightarrow Y\downarrow$$

As a result, both output and inflation go into downward spirals.

MyEconLab Mini-lecture

FIGURE 13.15

The Absence of the Self-Correcting Mechanism at the Zero Lower Bound

At the initial equilibrium level at point 1, $Y_1 < Y^P$, so the short-run aggregate supply curve shifts down to AS_2, with the economy moving to point 2, where output and inflation have fallen to Y_2 and π_2, respectively. Y_2 is even lower relative to Y^P than Y_1, so the short-run aggregate supply curve shifts down even further to AS_3, and the economy moves to point 3, where output and inflation have fallen even further to Y_3 and π_3, respectively. Both output and inflation therefore experience downward spirals.

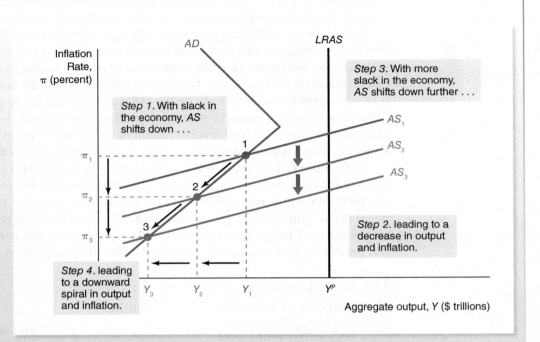

Step 1. With slack in the economy, AS shifts down . . .

Step 2. leading to a decrease in output and inflation.

Step 3. With more slack in the economy, AS shifts down further . . .

Step 4. leading to a downward spiral in output and inflation.

Application

Nonconventional Monetary Policy and Quantitative Easing

At the zero lower bound, conventional expansionary monetary policy is no longer an option because the monetary policy authorities are unable to lower the policy rate. Can monetary policy still be used to expand the economy and thereby avoid the downward spirals in output and inflation described in Figure 13.15?

   Using our analysis of the aggregate demand curve, we can see that the answer is yes, because the monetary authorities have other options for easing monetary policy that do not require lowering the policy rate. These options, which are referred to as **nonconventional monetary policy,** take three forms: liquidity provision, asset purchases, and management of expectations. To see how each of these measures works, recall from Chapter 9 that the real interest rate for investments reflects not only the short-term real interest rate set by the central bank, r, but an additional term, $\bar{f}$, which we referred to as financial frictions: i.e.,

$$r_i = r + \bar{f} \tag{3}$$

Each of these nonconventional monetary policy measures helps raise aggregate output and inflation by lowering $\bar{f}$ in the AD/AS model described in the preceding chapter. Let's look at each of these measures in turn. (How these nonconventional monetary policy measures were actually implemented by the Federal Reserve both during and after the global financial crisis will be discussed in more detail in Chapter 15.)

Liquidity Provision

The zero lower bound situation depicted in Figure 13.16 often arises when credit markets seize up, as during the recent financial crisis, and there is a sudden shortage of liquidity. The shortage of liquidity results in a sharp rise in financial frictions, which leaves the aggregate demand curve at AD_1, where it intersects the aggregate supply curve at point 1, a point at which the policy rate has hit a floor of zero and output is below potential. A direct way of bringing down financial frictions is for the central bank to increase its lending facilities in order to provide liquidity to impaired markets so that they can return to their normal functions, thereby bringing down the $\bar{f}$ term. As we saw in Chapter 12, this decline in financial friction lowers the real interest rate for investments, $r_i = r + \bar{f}$, and so increases equilibrium output at any given inflation rate and the corresponding real interest rate set by the central bank. The aggregate demand curve thus shifts to the right to AD_2 and the economy moves to point 2, where both output and inflation rise. Indeed, if the liquidity provision is sufficiently successful, the economy can move back to its full employment level, where output returns to potential, as at point 2 in Figure 13.16.

Asset Purchases

The monetary authorities can also lower the $\bar{f}$ term by lowering credit spreads through the purchase of private assets. When monetary authorities purchase a privately issued security,

MyEconLab Mini-lecture

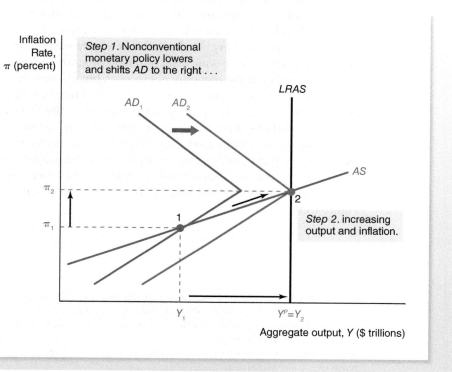

FIGURE 13.16

Response to Nonconventional Monetary Policy

Nonconventional monetary policy, whether it involves liquidity provision, asset purchases, or management of expectations, lowers $\bar{f}$, which in turn lowers the real interest rate for investments at any given inflation rate and shifts the aggregate demand curve to AD_2. The economy moves to point 2, where output and inflation have risen to Y_2 and π_2, respectively.

Step 1. Nonconventional monetary policy lowers and shifts *AD* to the right . . .

Step 2. increasing output and inflation.

Inflation Rate, π (percent)

Aggregate output, Y ($ trillions)

the purchase raises the security's price and therefore lowers its interest rate, thereby lowering the credit spread and hence $\bar{f}$ and the real interest rate for investments. The decline in the real interest rate for investments at any given inflation rate then causes the aggregate demand curve to shift to the right as in Figure 13.16, and both output and inflation rise.

Because investments are typically intended for long-term projects, the real interest rate for investments is likely to be a long-term interest rate and therefore differs from the short-term real interest rate r. Hence the $\bar{f}$ term in Equation 3 can be viewed as reflecting not only financial frictions and credit spreads, but also the spread between long- and short-term rates. This means that asset purchases of long-term government securities (rather than short-term securities, which is the norm) can lower the real interest rate for investments. When the Federal Reserve purchases long-term U.S. Treasury bonds, for example, this raises their price and lowers long-term interest rates, causing a decline in $\bar{f}$ and the real interest rate for investments at any given inflation rate. This action will also shift the aggregate demand curve to the right to AD_2 in Figure 13.16, thereby raising output and inflation.

Quantitative Easing Versus Credit Easing

When a central bank engages in liquidity provision or asset purchases, its balance sheet necessarily expands. Indeed, as we will see in Chapter 15, from before the financial crisis began in September 2007 to 2013, the amount of Federal Reserve assets rose from about $800 billion to over $3.8 trillion. This expansion of the balance sheet is referred to as **quantitative easing**, because it leads to a huge increase in liquidity in the economy, which can be a powerful force in stimulating the economy in the short term and possibly producing inflation down the road.

However, an expansion in the central bank balance sheet in and of itself may not stimulate the economy. As we have seen in the AD/AS analysis of the zero lower bound, unless quantitative easing is able to lower the real interest rate for investments, there is no impact on the aggregate demand curve and hence on output and inflation. If the asset purchase program consists only of buying short-term government securities, it is unlikely to affect credit spreads or the spread between long- and short-term interest rates, and so will leave $\bar{f}$ and the real interest rate for investments unchanged. The result will be a minimal impact on the aggregate economy.[12] Indeed, this is exactly what happened in Japan when the Bank of Japan pursued a large-scale asset purchase program, primarily in short-term government bonds. Not only did the economy not recover, but inflation turned negative as well.

The liquidity provision and asset purchase programs that led to the expansion in the Fed's balance sheet were not directed at expanding the Fed's balance sheet per se. Rather, the Fed's programs were aimed at altering the composition of the Fed's balance sheet in order to lower the real interest rates for investments. Indeed, Chairman Bernanke was adamant that the Fed's policies should not be characterized as quantitative easing, but instead should be referred to as "credit easing," and that they were highly effective in reducing the real interest rate for investments, thereby helping to stabilize the economy, as depicted in Figure 13.16.

---

[12]There are other reasons that quantitative easing, by itself, will not necessarily be stimulative. Large expansions in a central bank's balance sheet do not necessarily result in a large increase in the money supply. As the application in the appendix to Chapter 5 indicates, this is exactly what happened from 2007 to 2013 in the United States, when the huge expansion in the Fed's balance sheet and the monetary base did not result in a large increase in the money supply and bank lending, because most of it just flowed into holdings of excess reserves.

Management of Expectations

A commitment to keeping the policy rate low for a long period of time is another way of lowering long-term interest rates relative to short-term rates, and thereby lowering $\bar{f}$ and the real interest rate for investments. Because investors have the option of investing in a long-term bond or investing in a sequence of short-term bonds, the interest rate on long-term bonds is closely related to an average of the short-term-bond interest rates that markets expect to occur over the life of the long-term bond.[13] By committing to a future policy action of keeping the federal funds rate at zero for an extended period, a central bank can lower the market's expectations for future short-term interest rates, thereby causing the long-term interest rate to fall. The result will be a decline in $\bar{f}$ and the real interest rate for investments, which will shift the aggregate demand curve to the right as in Figure 13.16, raising both output and inflation. Michael Woodford of Columbia University has referred to such a strategy as **management of expectations**.

So far, the mechanisms for the efficacy of nonconventional monetary policies have operated through the $\bar{f}$ term and rightward shifts in the aggregate demand curve, as indicated in Figure 13.16. However, management of expectations can also operate by shifting the short-run aggregate supply curve by raising expectations of inflation, as is shown in Figure 13.17. As we saw in Chapter 12, a rise in inflation expectations, say because the central bank commits to doing whatever it takes to raise inflation in the future, shifts the short-run aggregate supply curve up to AS_2 in Figure 13.17, moving the economy to point 2, where output and inflation rise to Y_2 and π_2, respectively. The intuition behind this result is straightforward: the

MyEconLab Mini-lecture

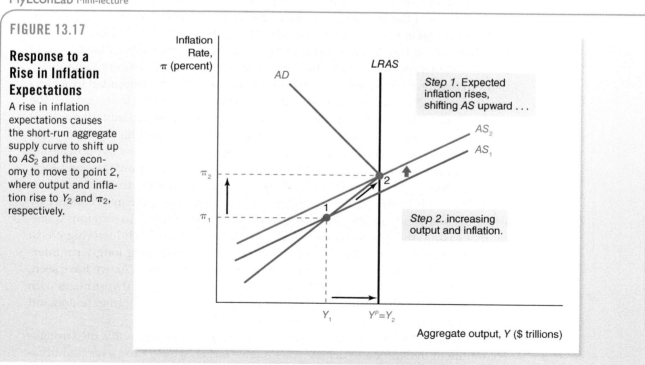

FIGURE 13.17

Response to a Rise in Inflation Expectations

A rise in inflation expectations causes the short-run aggregate supply curve to shift up to AS_2 and the economy to move to point 2, where output and inflation rise to Y_2 and π_2, respectively.

Step 1. Expected inflation rises, shifting *AS* upward . . .

Step 2. increasing output and inflation.

---

[13]For further discussion of the relationship between short- and long-term interest rates, see Chapter 6, "The Risk and Term Structure of Interest Rates," in Frederic S. Mishkin, *The Economics of Money, Banking, and Financial Markets*, 10th edition (Boston: Pearson Addison-Wesley, 2013).

rise in expected inflation with the policy rate set at zero leads to a decline in the real interest rate, which causes investment spending and aggregate output to rise as the economy slides up the aggregate demand curve, from point 1 to point 2 in Figure 13.17. One problem with this strategy, however, is that the public must believe that inflation will actually rise in the future. If the central bank's commitment to raising inflation is not credible, inflation expectations may not rise and this type of management of expectations will not work.

Policy and Practice

Abenomics and the Shift in Japanese Monetary Policy in 2013

By 2012, the Japanese economy had been in a funk for well over ten years, with very low growth, the policy rate at the zero lower bound, and the economy experiencing deflation. With this backdrop, Shinzo Abe won Japan's general election in December of 2012. After taking office, he promoted a major shift in economic policy to stimulate economic growth, which the media has dubbed "Abenomics." A key element of Abenomics was a sea change in monetary policy. First, Abe pressured the Bank of Japan to double its inflation target from 1% to 2% in January of 2013, over the objections of the former Governor of the Bank of Japan, who then resigned in March. After taking his position in March of 2013, the new Bank of Japan Governor, Haruhiko Kuroda, announced a major change in the way the Bank of Japan would conduct monetary policy. First, in contrast to the previous Governor, who never made a commitment to achieve the 1% inflation target, Kuroda committed to achieving the higher 2% inflation objective within two years. Second, he indicated that the Bank of Japan would now engage in a massive asset-purchase (quantitative easing) program that would not only double the size of the Bank of Japan's balance sheet but also purchase a very different set of assets. Specifically, rather than purchasing short-term government bonds, the Bank of Japan would now purchase long-term bonds, including private securities such as real-estate investment trusts.

We can see how this shift in monetary policy would affect Japan's economy by using the analysis from the preceding section. First, in contrast to previous quantitative easing, the Abenomics program would lower $\bar{f}$ by both lowering credit spreads through the purchase of private securities and lowering long-term interest rates through the purchase of long-term government bonds. As we have seen, both of these effects on $\bar{f}$ would lower the real interest rate for investments with the policy rate at the zero lower bound, thereby shifting the aggregate demand curve to the right to AD_2 as shown in Figure 13.18.

Second, the rise in the inflation target, and even more importantly, the stronger commitment by Kuroda to achieve this higher target, would raise expected inflation and hence shift the short-run aggregate supply curve to AS_2. As we can see in Figure 13.18, the economy would move to point 2, where both output and inflation would rise.

In other words, the two-pronged attack would both lower the real interest rate for investments directly through the asset purchase program and also directly raise inflation expectations, providing another factor for driving down the real interest rate. These mechanisms would then operate in tandem to promote economic expansion and an exit from the deflationary environment that the Japanese had been experiencing for fifteen years. How well this strategy will work is unknown at the time of this writing, but the monetary component of Abenomics is an important attempt to change the dynamic in the Japanese economy.

MyEconLab Mini-lecture

FIGURE 13.18

Response to the Shift in Japanese Monetary Policy in 2013

The Bank of Japan's asset purchase program lowers $\bar{f}$, which lowers the real interest rate for investments at any given inflation rate and shifts the aggregate demand curve to AD_2. The rise in inflation expectations causes the short-run aggregate supply curve to shift up to AS_2. The economy then moves to point 2, where output and inflation rise to Y_2 and π_2, respectively.

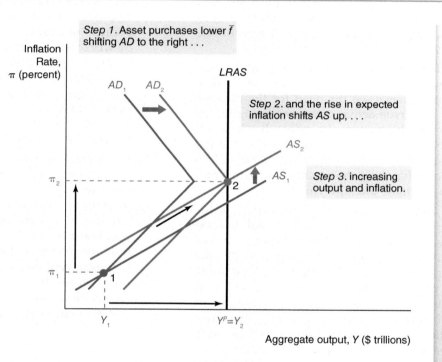

Step 1. Asset purchases lower $\bar{f}$ shifting AD to the right . . .

Step 2. and the rise in expected inflation shifts AS up, . . .

Step 3. increasing output and inflation.

SUMMARY

1. Monetary policy, and macroeconomic policy in general, has two primary objectives: stabilizing inflation around a low level (price stability) and stabilizing economic activity.

2. For most shocks—that is, aggregate demand shocks or permanent supply shocks—the price stability and economic activity stability objectives are consistent: stabilizing inflation stabilizes economic activity, even in the short run. For temporary supply shocks, however, there is a tradeoff between stabilizing inflation and stabilizing economic activity in the short run. In the long run, there is no conflict between stabilizing inflation and stabilizing economic activity.

3. Activists regard the self-correcting mechanism through wage and price adjustment as very slow and hence see the need for the government to pursue active, accommodating policy to decrease high unemployment when it develops. Nonactivists, by contrast, believe that the self-correcting mechanism is fast and therefore advocate that the government avoid active policy to eliminate unemployment.

4. The Taylor rule, $r = 2.0 + \frac{1}{2}(\pi - \pi^T) + \frac{1}{2}(Y - Y^P)$, indicates that the real federal funds rate, the Federal Reserve's policy instrument, should be set at a rate equal to 2% (the historical average level of the real federal funds rate) plus a weighted average of the inflation gap and the output gap, with each having an equal weight of $\frac{1}{2}$. The Taylor rule characterizes the Fed's setting of the federal funds rate under chairmen Greenspan and Bernanke.

5. Milton Friedman's view that, in the long-run, inflation is always and everywhere a monetary phenomenon is borne out by aggregate demand and supply analysis: it shows that monetary policy makers can target any inflation rate in the long run throughout autonomous monetary policy, which adjusts the equilibrium real interest rate by using the federal funds rate policy tool to change the level of aggregate demand.

6. Two types of inflation can result from an activist stabilization policy to promote high employment: cost-push inflation, which occurs because of negative supply shocks or a push by workers for higher wages than are justified by productivity gains; and demand-pull inflation, which results when policy makers pursue high output and employment targets through policies that increase aggregate demand. Both demand-pull and cost-push inflation led to the Great Inflation from 1965 to 1982.

7. When the policy rate hits the zero lower bound, the aggregate demand curve becomes upward sloping, which means the self-correcting mechanism that returns the economy to full employment is no longer operational. At the zero lower bound, in order to boost output and inflation, the monetary authorities must turn to nonconventional policies, which are of three types: liquidity provision, asset purchases (typically referred to as quantitative easing), and the management of expectations.

KEY TERMS

activists, p. 343

cost-push inflation, p. 351

data lag, p. 343

demand-pull inflation, p. 351

divine coincidence, p. 336

dual mandates, p. 330

effectiveness lag, p. 344

equilibrium real
   interest rate, p. 330

frictional unemployment, p. 328

hierarchical mandates, p. 329

implementation lag, p. 343

inflation gap, p. 329

inflation target, p. 329

legislative lag, p. 343

management of
   expectations, p. 361

natural real interest rate, p. 330

nonactivists, p. 343

nonconventional monetary policy,
   p. 358

price stability, p. 329

quantitative easing, p. 360

recognition lag, p. 343

structural unemployment, p. 328

Taylor rule, p. 345

zero lower bound, p. 355

REVIEW QUESTIONS

All Questions are available in MyEconLab *for practice or instructor assignment.*

The Objectives of Monetary Policy

1. Describe the two primary objectives of macro-economic stabilization policy.
2. Should policy makers strive to achieve zero rates of unemployment and inflation? Why or why not?

3. Distinguish between hierarchical and dual mandates. Which best describes the policy making environment in the United States?

The Relationship Between Stabilizing Inflation and Stabilizing Economic Activity

4. What is the equilibrium real interest rate? How does it influence the interest rate decisions of Federal Reserve policy makers?
5. Is stabilization policy more likely to be conducted with monetary policy or fiscal policy? Why?

6. Why does the divine coincidence simplify the job of policy making? In what situations will it prevail? Why?

How Actively Should Policy Makers Try to Stabilize Economic Activity?

7. Summarize the main points of disagreement in the debate between activists and nonactivists.
8. Why do activists believe the economy's self-correcting mechanism is slow?

9. Describe the five time lags involved in implementing stabilization policy.

The Taylor Rule

10. How does the Taylor rule relate to the monetary policy curve?

11. Would it be a good idea for monetary policy makers to set the federal funds rate solely using the Taylor rule?

Inflation: Always and Everywhere a Monetary Phenomenon

12. How can the monetary authorities target any inflation rate they want?

Causes of Inflationary Monetary Policy

13. Explain the processes of cost-push and demand-pull inflation. How do macroeconomists distinguish between the two?

Monetary Policy at the Zero Lower Bound

14. How does the policy rate hitting a floor of zero lead to an upward-sloping aggregate demand curve?

15. Why does the self-correcting mechanism stop working when the policy rate hits the zero lower bound?

16. What nonconventional monetary policies shift the aggregate demand curve, and how do they work?

PROBLEMS

All Problems are available in MyEconLab *for practice or instructor assignment.*

The Objectives of Macroeconomic Policy

1. According to the Reserve Bank of New Zealand Act of 1989 (section 8): "The primary function of the Bank is to formulate and implement monetary policy directed to the economic objective of achieving and maintaining stability in the general level of prices."

   a) Do you think that this statement constitutes a hierarchical or dual mandate for the conduct of monetary policy?
   b) Is this mandate consistent with a positive inflation rate target?

The Relationship Between Stabilizing Inflation and Stabilizing Economic Activity

2. Suppose the current administration decides to decrease government expenditures as a means of cutting the existing government budget deficit.
   a) According to the aggregate demand and supply analysis, what will be the effect of such a measure in the short run? Describe changes in the inflation rate and output level.
   b) What will be the effect on the real interest rate, inflation rate, and output level if the Federal Reserve decides to stabilize the inflation rate?

3. The recent debate about healthcare reform in the United States included arguments about how the proposed reform might affect the efficiency of the U.S. economy. Based on the aggregate demand and supply analysis, do you think that a more or less efficient economy is an important issue in this debate? (Hint: consider the long-run effect of a less efficient economy on the output level.)

4. The following table shows the inflation rate and output level for four consecutive periods in a given economy. In period 1, the economy is at its long-run equilibrium (i.e., the inflation rate equals its target and output equals potential output). In period 2, there is a temporary supply shock (e.g., an increase in energy prices).

Period	Inflation rate (%)	Output ($ trillions)
1	2.5	8
2	4.5	7
3	2.5	6
4	2.5	8

   a) Based on the table, determine which type of response was implemented by policy makers (e.g., no response versus stabilizing inflation or economic activity).
   b) Show your argument using a graph (draw the *MP* curve and the *AD/AS* diagram consistent with the table data).

How Actively Should Policy Makers Try to Stabilize Economic Activity?

5. Suppose one could measure the welfare gains derived from eliminating output (and unemployment) fluctuations in the economy. Assuming these gains are relatively small for the average individual, how do you think this conclusion would affect the activist/nonactivist debate?

6. The following panels describe two different short-run aggregate supply curves. In which situation is the case for nonactivist policy stronger? Explain why.

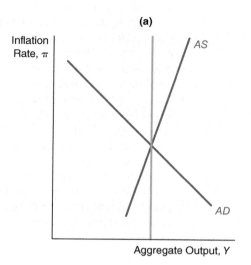

(a)

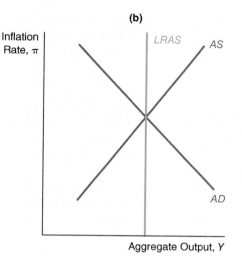

(b)

The Taylor Rule

7. Assume that policy makers are using the Taylor rule as a basis for policy changes, as specified in Equation 1. Under each of the following scenarios, show how the real interest rate, output, and inflation behave in both the short and long run. Use an *IS* graph and the *AD/AS* graph, and show the Taylor rule in an *MP* curve graph.

   a) In 1973, the United States experienced an unexpected slowdown in productivity, which reduced potential output.

   b) The U.S. economy was experiencing high inflation in the late 1970s. To combat this high inflation, the Fed under Chairman Paul Volcker significantly reduced the target inflation rate.

Causes of Inflationary Monetary Policy

8. The following table shows unemployment and inflation rates for Canada during the 1972–1982 period:

	1972	1973	1974	1975	1976	1977	1978	1979	1980	1981	1982
Unemployment Rate	6.2	5.6	5.3	6.9	7.1	8.1	8.4	7.6	7.6	7.6	11
Inflation Rate	4.98	7.48	10.99	10.67	7.54	7.97	8.97	9.14	10.12	12.47	10.76

Source: OECD Statistics.

   a) Plot Canada's unemployment rates during this period. On the same graph, draw a horizontal line at 7.3%, representing Canada's estimated natural rate of unemployment.

   b) Considering the graph, how would you describe Canada's inflationary policy during the 1972–1982 period?

9. The Taylor rule suggests that the policy rate target should be increased when the output gap is positive. Do you think the Taylor rule encourages or discourages demand-pull inflation? Which might be a limitation of the Taylor rule with respect to demand-pull inflation?

Monetary Policy at the Zero Lower Bound

10. In 2003, as the economy finally seemed poised to exit its ongoing recession, the Fed began worrying about a "soft patch" in the economy; in particular, it worried about the possibility of deflation. As a result, the Fed proactively lowered the federal funds rate from 1.75% in late 2002 to 1% by mid-2003, at the time the lowest historical federal funds rate. In addition, the Fed committed to keeping the federal funds rate at this level for a considerable period of time. This policy was considered highly expansionary and was seen by some as potentially inflationary and unnecessary.
    a) How might fears of a zero lower bound justify such a policy, even if the economy was not actually in a recession?

    b) Show the impact of these policies on an *MP* curve graph and an *AD/AS* graph, specifying the initial condition in 2003 and the impact of the Fed's policy to eliminate the deflation threat.

11. Suppose that $\bar{f}$ is determined by two factors: financial panic and asset purchases.
    a) Using an *MP* curve and an *AS/AD* graph, show how a sufficiently large financial panic can pull the economy below the zero lower bound and into a destabilizing deflationary spiral.
    b) Using an *MP* curve and an *AS/AD* graph, show how a sufficient amount of asset purchases can reverse the effects of the financial panic depicted in part (a).

DATA ANALYSIS PROBLEMS

The Problems update with real-time data in MyEconLab and are available for practice or instructor assignment.

1. On January 29, 2013, the Federal Reserve released a special statement that clarified its goals of "price stability" and "maximum employment." Specifically, it stated that "the Committee judges that inflation at the rate of 2 percent, as measured by the annual change in the price index for personal consumption expenditures, is most consistent over the longer run with the Federal Reserve's statutory mandate" and that "FOMC participants' estimates of the longer-run normal rate of unemployment had a central tendency of 5.2 percent to 6.0 percent." Assume this statement implies that the natural rate of unemployment is believed to be 5.6%. Go to the St. Louis Federal Reserve FRED database, and find data on the personal consumption expenditure price index (PCECTPI), the unemployment rate (UNRATE), real GDP (GDPC1), and an estimate of potential GDP (GDPPOT). For

the price index, adjust the *units* setting to "Percent Change From Year Ago"; then download the data into a spreadsheet.
    a) For the most recent four quarters of data available, calculate the average inflation gap using the 2% target referenced by the Fed. Calculate this as the average of the inflation gaps over the four quarters.
    b) For the most recent four quarters of data available, calculate the average output gap using the GDP measure and the potential GDP estimate. Calculate the gap as the percentage deviation of output from the potential level of output. Calculate the average over the most recent four quarters of data available.
    c) For the most recent 12 months of data available, calculate the average unemployment gap, using 5.6% as

the presumed natural rate of unemployment. Calculate the average unemployment gap over the most recent 12 months of data available.

d) Based on your answers to parts (a) through (c), does the divine coincidence apply to the current economic situation? Why or why not? What does this say about the sources of shocks that have impacted the current economy? Briefly explain.

2. Go to the St. Louis Federal Reserve FRED database, and find data on the personal consumption expenditure price index (PCECTPI), the unemployment rate (UNRATE), and an estimate of the natural rate of unemployment (NROU). For the price index, adjust the *units* setting to "Percent Change From Year Ago." Select the data from 2000 to the most current data available, download the data, and plot all three variables on the same graph. Using the graph, identify periods of demand-pull or cost-push movements in the inflation rate. Briefly explain your reasoning.

3. Go to the St. Louis Federal Reserve FRED database, and find data on the personal consumption expenditure price index (PCECTPI), real GDP (GDPC1), an estimate of potential GDP (GDPPOT), and the federal funds rate (DFF). For the price index, adjust the *units* setting to "Percent Change From Year Ago" to convert the data to the inflation rate. For the federal funds rate, change the *frequency* setting to "Quarterly" and download the data into a spreadsheet. Assuming the inflation target is 2%, calculate the inflation gap and the output gap for each quarter, from 2000 until the most recent data available. Calculate the output gap as the percentage deviation of output from the potential level of output.

a) Use the output and inflation gaps to calculate, for each quarter, the Taylor rule prediction for the federal funds rate. Assume that the weights on inflation stabilization and output stabilization are both ½ (see the formula in the chapter). Compare the current (quarterly average) federal funds rate to the federal funds rate prescribed by the Taylor rule. Does the Taylor rule accurately predict the current rate? Briefly comment.

b) Create a graph that compares the predicted Taylor rule values with the actual quarterly federal funds rate averages. How well, in general, does the Taylor rule prediction fit the average federal funds rate? Briefly explain.

c) Based on the results from the 2008–2009 period, explain the limitations of the Taylor rule as a formal policy tool. How do these limitations help to explain the use of nonconventional monetary policy during that time?

d) Suppose Congress changes the Fed's mandate to a hierarchical one, in which inflation stabilization takes priority over output stabilization. In this context, recalculate the predicted Taylor rule for each quarter since 2000, assuming that the weight on inflation stabilization is ¾ and the weight on output stabilization is ¼. Create a graph showing the Taylor rule from part (a), the new "hierarchical" Taylor rule, and the fed funds rate. How, if at all, does changing the mandate change the predicted policy paths? How would the fed funds rate be affected? Briefly explain.

Part 5

Finance and the Macroeconomy

Part 5 — Finance and the Macroeconomy

Now that we have developed frameworks in Parts 2, 3, and 4 to analyze what happens in the long run and the short run, we can turn to the important role that finance plays in macroeconomics in both the long and the short runs. Chapter 14 focuses on the long run and shows how a well-functioning financial system promotes economic growth. It develops tools that are then used in Chapter 15 to examine how finance can affect the economy in the short run. When the financial system suddenly stops working well—that is, it experiences a *financial crisis*—it leads to sharp contractions in economic activity. Chapter 15 develops a framework for analyzing the dynamics of financial crises and then applies this analysis to explaining the most recent worldwide financial crisis as well as earlier crisis episodes in our history. In a Web chapter available at the Companion Website, www.pearsonhighered.com/mishkin, this analysis is extended to financial crises in *emerging market economies*, economies in an early stage of market development that have recently opened up to the flow of goods, services, and capital from the rest of the world.

We will examine applications in each chapter to make the critical connection between theory and real-world practice:

- "The Tyranny of Collateral"
- "Is China a Counter-Example to the Importance of Financial Development to Economic Growth?"
- "The Mother of All Financial Crises: The Great Depression"
- "The Global Financial Crisis of 2007–2009"

In keeping with our focus on key policy issues and the techniques policy makers use in practice, we will also analyze the following specific examples in Policy and Practice cases:

- "Was the Fed to Blame for the Housing Price Bubble?"
- "The Federal Reserve's Nonconventional Monetary Policies and Quantitative Easing During the Global Financial Crisis"
- "Japan's Lost Decade, 1992–2002"
- "Debate Over Central Bank Response to Bubbles"

14 The Financial System and Economic Growth

Preview

Quite understandably, ordinary people (and many economists) underestimate the importance of the financial system. What, after all, do investment bankers and other finance workers produce to deserve such towering salaries and bonuses, sometimes in the millions of dollars? Why did the government rescue financial firms during the 2007–2009 financial crisis at great expense, while leaving businesses in other industries to fail?

We examine the role that the financial system plays in the economy in this and the following chapter. This chapter focuses on the long run, that is, on the role the financial system plays in promoting economic growth. It discusses why a well-functioning financial system is a key condition for high economic growth. The following chapter focuses on the short run, that is, it looks at what happens when the financial system suddenly stops working well, which can cause a sharp contraction in economic activity.

We start this chapter by first outlining the financial system's role in channeling funds within the economy. Then, we describe the two kinds of information problems that can interfere with the flow of funds in the financial system, and the roles of banks and governments in resolving those problems. The tools that we develop to conduct this analysis will also be building blocks for the discussion of financial crises in the following chapter. Finally, we review the empirical evidence for a link between a well-functioning financial system and a healthy economy.

The Role of the Financial System

Households and firms with surplus funds to invest require access to productive investment opportunities in new businesses, products, and ideas. How does society match up those with surplus funds to those with viable investment opportunities who need funds? And how does society ensure that funds are channeled to worthwhile investment opportunities, so as to not squander its resources?

Enter the financial system, which can act as the brain of the economy by performing the essential coordinating function of channeling funds from households and firms with surplus funds to those individuals and firms with both a shortage of funds *and* productive investment opportunities. A well-functioning financial system directs funds to where they can do the most good, promoting economic stability and growth.

Channeling funds efficiently through the financial system is a complex task, as illustrated by the schematic diagram in Figure 14.1. Lender-savers—those with excess funds to invest—are at the left, and borrower-spenders with productive investment opportunities are at the right: funds move between these two parties via two main conduits.

Direct Finance

One way that funds move directly from lender-savers (investors) to borrower-spenders via financial markets is through the *direct finance* route shown at the bottom of Figure 14.1. With direct finance, borrowers borrow funds directly from savers via financial markets by selling them **securities** (also called **financial instruments**), which are claims on the borrowers' future income or assets in the form of common stock or bonds. Securities are assets for the firm or person who buys them, but they are **liabilities** (IOUs or debts) for the individual or firm that sells (issues) them. For example, if a textile company in Malaysia needs to borrow funds to pay for a new factory to produce shirts, it might seek funds from U.S. investors by selling them **equities,** like common stock that represents a share of ownership of a corporation, or **bonds,** debt securities that offer a stream of payments for a fixed period of time. Financial institutions engaged in direct finance facilitate transactions in financial markets. These include **exchanges,** where buyers and sellers of securities (or their agents or brokers) meet in one central location to conduct trades, or **investment banks** that both trade securities and help corporations issue securities by guaranteeing a price for the securities and then selling them.

FIGURE 14.1

Flow of Funds Through the Financial System

Direct finance, the route shown at the bottom, involves borrowers borrowing funds directly from savers. Indirect finance, in which financial intermediaries stand between savers and borrowers, is more circuitous and operates through two different routes: 1) financial intermediaries obtain funds from savers and then use them to make loans to borrowers (the arrows at the top of the figure), and 2) financial intermediaries use the funds from savers to purchase securities issued by borrowers (shown by the arrow from financial intermediaries to financial markets).

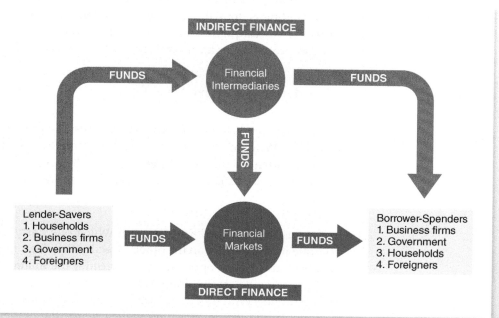

Indirect Finance

Most funds are channeled to borrowers through the circuitous *indirect finance* route shown at the top of Figure 14.1. With indirect finance, a **financial intermediary**—a type of financial institution such as a bank, insurance company, finance company, mutual fund, or pension fund—stands between lender-savers and borrower-spenders, as the top part of Figure 14.1 indicates. (Descriptions of the types of financial intermediaries can be found in the box, "Financial Intermediaries.") In other words, a financial intermediary acts as an *intermediary* between lender-savers and borrower-spenders. For example, a bank obtains funds from savers by issuing deposits and then uses these funds to make loans, say for a young couple to buy a house. Another example is an insurance company that obtains funds by issuing insurance policies and collecting premiums, and then makes loans to a corporation to build a hotel.

A second way in which financial intermediaries can stand between lender-savers and borrower-spenders is depicted in Figure 14.1 by the arrow that shows funds flowing from financial intermediaries to financial markets, and then from financial markets to borrower-spenders. For example, a mutual fund obtains funds from investors and then uses these funds to purchase securities, such as common stocks, in the financial markets. Another example is a pension fund that receives funds from employees and their employer, and then buys securities such as bonds in the financial markets. This process of linking borrower-spenders and lender-savers through financial intermediaries is called **financial intermediation.**

Most borrowers in advanced countries obtain credit through financial intermediation. Financial intermediaries are a more important source of financing for businesses than securities markets, supplying close to 60% of the funds flowing to nonfinancial businesses. Most bonds and about half of all stocks are purchased by financial intermediaries in financial markets (the downward arrow in Figure 14.1).

In developing countries, where stock and bond markets are often tiny or nonexistent, almost all lending is done through financial intermediation. In these places, households and firms borrow through rural moneylenders, savings and credit associations, family networks, or programs for **microcredit,** which offer very small loans, often less than $100.

Information Challenges and the Financial System

Why don't more funds move directly to those who need them, without passing through a middleman? Why do we need financial intermediaries at all? To answer these questions, we first identify the impediments to a well-functioning financial system, which are referred to as *financial frictions*, and then discuss ways to overcome them.

Asymmetric Information

Asymmetric information, a situation in which one party in a transaction has much less accurate information than the other, impedes the direct movement of funds to those with the best investment opportunities. Consider the managers of a Russian company and its investors, the stockholders who own the company and the bondholders who have lent it money. Who is better placed to know if the managers are honest people, and whether the company is performing well? Clearly, the managers themselves are. This imbalance is particularly severe if the stockholders and bondholders are foreigners and do not know the ins and outs of doing business in Russia. Similarly, a person seeking

Financial Intermediaries

There are six basic types of financial intermediaries.

1. **Banks,** also known as *depository institutions*, are financial institutions that acquire funds by issuing deposits and using the proceeds to make loans. Banks include commercial banks, savings and loan associations, mutual savings banks, and credit unions.

2. **Insurance companies,** which include life insurance companies and fire and casualty insurance companies, acquire funds from premiums paid by policyholders and in turn insure policyholders against financial hazards like death or against loss from theft, fire, or accidents.

3. **Pension funds,** which include private and government pension funds, acquire funds through contributions from employees and their employers, and provide retirement income to the employees covered by the pension plan.

4. **Finance companies** raise funds by selling commercial paper (a short-term debt instrument) and by issuing stocks and bonds. They then use the funds to lend to consumers and businesses.

5. **Mutual funds** acquire funds by selling shares to individuals and use the proceeds to buy securities such as stocks and bonds.

6. **Hedge funds** are a special type of mutual fund that also acquires funds by selling shares, but only to very wealthy people, so they are less regulated than mutual funds. Hedge funds then use the proceeds to purchase securities and engage in complex financial transactions.

To understand these financial intermediaries better, we can look at their **balance sheet,** a list of the institution's assets and liabilities. As the name implies, the list balances; that is, it has the characteristic that

$$\text{Total assets} = \text{Total liabilities} + \text{Capital}$$

In other words, **capital** (also referred to as **net worth**) equals the value of the institution's assets minus the value of its liabilities. If the value of the assets falls, holding the value of liabilities constant, then the net worth or capital of the institution falls. Table 14.1 provides a guide to these financial intermediaries by describing their primary assets (uses of funds) and their primary liabilities (sources of funds).

TABLE 14.1	**PRIMARY ASSETS AND LIABILITIES OF FINANCIAL INTERMEDIARIES**	
Type of Financial Intermediary	**Primary Assets (Uses of Funds)**	**Primary Liabilities (Sources of Funds)**
Banks	Business and consumer loans, mortgages, government securities	Deposits
Insurance companies	Corporate bonds, mortgages, business loans, government securities	Premiums from policies
Pension funds	Corporate bonds, mortgages, business loans, government securities	Employer and employee contributions
Finance companies	Consumer and business loans	Commercial paper, stocks, and bonds
Mutual funds	Stocks and bonds	Shares
Hedge funds	Numerous types of securities and financial derivatives	Shares

a loan to buy a car knows his or her ability to make monthly payments, but a potential lender like a bank may not. A parent gives a child money to buy a healthy lunch—but he could be buying candy instead.

In a financial system, asymmetric information creates two types of problems that make it hard to channel funds to their most productive use, both before the transaction is entered into and after.

ADVERSE SELECTION. **Adverse selection** is the problem that arises when the party who is most eager to engage in a transaction is the one most likely to produce an undesirable (adverse) outcome for the other party. It occurs before a transaction is completed, and makes it more likely that loans will be made to bad credit risks. As a result, lenders may decide not to make any loans at all, even though there are good credit risks in the marketplace.

To illustrate, suppose you have two businesses that want to borrow from you. The first business, Rock Solid Company, is very conservative and only borrows when it has an investment that will almost surely pay off. The other business, Risky Ventures Corporation, likes to take big risks that have high payoffs. Which business is more likely to contact you to seek out a loan? Risky Ventures, of course, because it has so much to gain if the investment pays off. You, however, would not want to make a loan to Risky Ventures: there is a high probability that its investment will turn sour and it will be unable to pay you back. If you knew both companies very well—that is, if your information were symmetric so that you had the same information as the companies' managers—you would identify Risky Ventures as a bad risk and would not lend to it. Suppose, though, that you don't know these businesses well. You are more likely to lend to Risky Ventures rather than to Rock Solid because Risky Ventures is more likely to apply for the loan. The possibility of adverse selection might lead you to decide not to lend to either of the companies, even though there are times when Rock Solid, an excellent credit risk, might need a loan for a worthwhile investment.

MORAL HAZARD. **Moral hazard,** the second problem created by asymmetric information, is the risk (*hazard*) that the other party will engage in activities that are undesirable (*immoral*) from your point of view. It arises after a transaction occurs.

As an example, suppose that you loan $10,000 to Rock Solid to computerize its billing operations. Once you have made the loan, however, Rock Solid may decide to use the money to fund a high-risk operation, say, speculating in the stock market. If the speculation works, and Rock Solid makes $100,000 with your money, it will be able to pay you back your $10,000 and enjoy the remaining $90,000. But if the speculation doesn't pan out, as is likely, Rock Solid won't pay you back. Rock Solid only loses its reputation as a conservative company: it has incentives to take risk at your expense. If you knew what Rock Solid was up to, you might be able to stop it from speculating in the stock market and prevent moral hazard. However, it is hard for you to keep informed about Rock Solid's activities because information is asymmetric. The risk of moral hazard might therefore discourage you from making the $10,000 loan to Rock Solid, even if you were sure that it would pay you back if it used the funds to buy computers.

Free-Rider Problem

How do lenders and investors avoid the adverse selection and moral hazard problems that result from asymmetric information? The answer is clear—they need to collect information to eliminate the information asymmetry—but its implementation is not.

An important impediment to information collection is the **free-rider problem**: private investors who do not spend their resources on collecting information can take advantage of (get a *free ride* on) the information that other investors collect. To understand the free-rider problem, imagine you are Warren Buffett and have spent a lot of time and money gathering information that tells you which firms are good investments and which are bad. You believe the resources you have spent are worthwhile because you can make up the cost of acquiring this information, and then some, by purchasing the securities of good firms that you identify as undervalued. The moment you begin to buy shares, however, other savvy free-riding investors, knowing you have produced good information—after all, you *are* Warren Buffett—will buy right along with you, even though they have not paid for any of the information you have gathered. The increased demand for the undervalued good securities will cause their low prices to be bid up immediately to reflect their true value, before you have been able to buy all you might want.

Because of these free riders, you will not be able to capture most of the profits from your information production, so you will cut back on the amount of resources you spend on producing it. (Of course this doesn't mean that you won't get rich; just that you won't get as rich as you would otherwise.) Other investors who might think about spending resources on gathering information will come to the same realization, and they will also cut back on information collection. The inability to fully profit from information collection limits the amount of information available in the marketplace, and so asymmetric information problems will remain severe.

Financial Intermediaries Address Asymmetric Information Problems

Well-functioning financial intermediaries play a key role in solving asymmetric information problems and reducing financial frictions. Financial intermediaries make it their business to collect information to overcome adverse selection and moral hazard problems.

ROLE OF PRIVATE LOANS. Financial intermediaries can avoid the free-rider problem primarily by making private loans. Because private loans are not traded in financial markets, it is hard for anyone else to free ride on the financial intermediary's information-collection activities. The intermediary making private loans thus benefits from its information collection and will therefore find it profitable to continue the activity. The ability to profit from information collection makes indirect finance involving financial intermediaries the most prevalent source of funds for households and businesses.

ADVANTAGES OF BANKS. Of all the types of financial intermediaries, banks are the most important. Their basic business is taking in deposits and using these funds to make loans. In the United States, banking institutions (which include commercial banks, savings and loan associations, mutual savings banks, and credit unions) are the most significant category of financial intermediaries. Figure 14.2 shows that banking institutions held $19.4 trillion in assets at the end of 2012, compared to the next largest category, mutual funds, with $13.0 trillion. Figure 14.3 shows that the dominance of banks is even more striking in other countries. While banks supply only 18% of total

FIGURE 14.2

Assets of Different U.S. Financial Intermediaries, 2012

Banking institutions are the most important financial intermediary, with total assets of $19.4 trillion in 2012.

Source: Federal Reserve Flow of Funds Accounts. www.federalreserve.gov/releases/z1

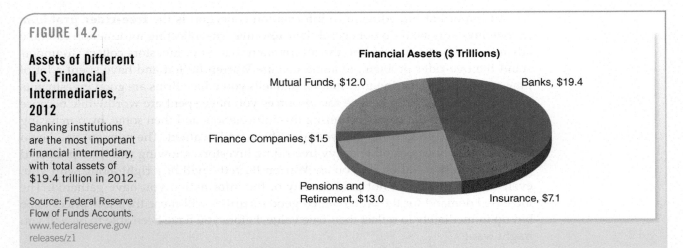

Financial Assets ($ Trillions)

Mutual Funds, $12.0

Banks, $19.4

Finance Companies, $1.5

Pensions and Retirement, $13.0

Insurance, $7.1

credit to U.S. nonfinancial businesses, they supply 56% in Canada, 76% in Germany, and 78% in Japan.[1]

Banks are particularly critical in the financial system because they have unique advantages over other financial intermediaries in that they use several practices to solve asymmetric information problems and reduce financial frictions.

1. *Screening:* Collecting information about potential borrowers before a transaction occurs in order to avoid adverse selection problems is called **screening.** A bank that is considering giving you a mortgage loan asks you about your income, your employment record, your bank accounts, the value of your house, and so on. Banks are particularly good at screening because they develop long-term relationships with potential borrowers.[2] These relationships enable them to know their customers well, making it cheaper for them to screen out bad borrowers.

2. *Monitoring:* Collecting information after a transaction occurs in order to prevent moral hazard is called *monitoring*. After a financial institution makes a loan, the loan officer checks on how the borrower is using the funds lent to him or her and will follow up on any signs of risky behavior. Banks have a natural advantage in monitoring a borrowing firm's behavior because they observe a firm's checking account, which yields a great deal of information about the borrower's financial condition. For example, a sustained drop in the borrower's checking account balance may signal that the borrower is having financial trouble. Unusual account activity may suggest that the borrower is engaging in risky activities. A change in

[1]For a discussion of the relative sizes of different financial intermediaries and how much credit they supply in different economies, see Chapter 2, "An Overview of the Financial System," and Chapter 8, "An Economic Analysis of Financial Structure," in Frederic S. Mishkin, *The Economics of Money, Banking, and Financial Markets*, 10th edition (Boston: Pearson Addison-Wesley, 2013).

[2]For a discussion of how banks screen and develop long-term relationships, see Chapter 10, "Banking and the Management of Financial Institutions," in Frederic S. Mishkin, *The Economics of Money, Banking, and Financial Markets*, 10th edition (Boston: Pearson Addison-Wesley, 2013).

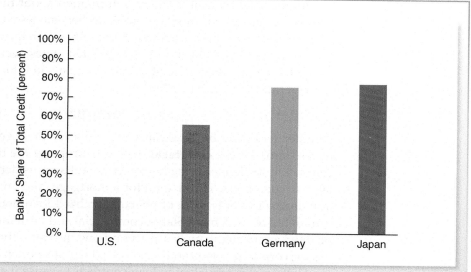

FIGURE 14.3

Banks' Share of Total Credit to Nonfinancial Businesses in United States, Canada, Germany, and Japan

Banks are even more dominant in financial systems of other countries than they are in the United States. Banks supply 18% of total credit to U.S. nonfinancial businesses, 56% in Canada, 76% in Germany, and 78% in Japan.

Source: Andreas Hackethal and Reinhard H. Schmidt. 2004. Financing patterns: Measurement concepts and empirical results. Johann Wolfgang Goethe-Universitat Working Paper No. 125, January. The data are from 1970 to 2000 and are gross flows as percentage of the total, not including trade and other credit data, which are not available.

suppliers, as indicated by the payees on the firms' checks, may suggest that the borrower is pursuing a new line of business. Banks' long-term relationships with their customers also give them an advantage in monitoring borrowers. If the borrower has borrowed from the bank before, the bank has already established procedures for monitoring that customer, reducing the cost of monitoring the new loan.

3. *Restrictive Covenants.* Banks also try to prevent moral hazard by writing provisions into debt contracts, called **restrictive covenants**, that restrict borrowers' activities. For example, banks often rely on legal professionals to write provisions into their loan contracts that forbid borrowers from going into risky businesses, promote desirable behavior, or require borrowers to provide periodic accounting statement reports. For example, a loan contract might require the firm to keep a certain percentage of its assets in cash so that it is more likely to be able to pay off the loan. But what if a bank does not think through every contingency when it writes the restrictive covenants into the loan contract? The bank's ability to cut off future lending gives the borrower an incentive to behave well.

BANKS' ROLE AS ECONOMIES DEVELOP. Developing countries face particularly difficult challenges from asymmetric information. Information about private firms is hard for investors to get because these countries' accounting standards and information technology are generally weak. Securities markets in developing countries are therefore typically underdeveloped, and banks, which are particularly well-suited to avoiding free-rider problems, play an even more dominant role in the financial system.

As financial systems develop, information about firms becomes easier to acquire, and so asymmetric information problems become less severe and it becomes easier for firms to issue securities. The importance of banks in the financial system then begins to diminish. We can see this trend in the United States over the past twenty years, during which there have been incredible improvements in information technology and banks' share of total lending has fallen.

Collateral and Asymmetric Information Problems

Another tool used by financial intermediaries to solve adverse selection and moral hazard problems is **collateral**, which is property the borrower promises in the loan contract to the lender if the borrower defaults on its debt. Most household debt is collateralized: a house is collateral for a mortgage, and an automobile is collateral for an auto loan. (The only form of noncollateralized loan households tend to have is credit card debt.) In the United States, commercial and farm mortgages, for which property is pledged as collateral, make up around one-quarter of borrowing by nonfinancial businesses; corporate bonds and other bank loans also often require pledges of collateral.

Collateral is prevalent in loan contracts because it ameliorates both adverse selection and moral hazard problems. Adverse selection interferes with the functioning of financial markets only if a lender suffers a loss when a borrower defaults on its loan payments. Collateral reduces the consequences of adverse selection because, if a borrower defaults on a loan, the lender can sell the collateral and use the proceeds to make up for its losses on the loan. For example, if you fail to make your mortgage payments, the lender can take the title to your house, auction it off, and use the receipts to pay off the loan. Borrowers are willing to supply collateral because the reduced risk for the lender makes it more likely that they will get the loan, and perhaps at a lower interest rate.

Collateral also reduces moral hazard by decreasing the incentives for borrowers to take on too much risk. When borrowers pledge collateral on their loans, they have more to lose (sometimes referred to as "skin in the game") if they can't pay the lender back, and so they are naturally more reluctant to engage in risky activities. Lawyers play a critical role in collecting collateral from borrowers.

Application

The Tyranny of Collateral

To use property, such as land or capital, as collateral, a person must legally own it. Unfortunately, as Hernando De Soto documented in *The Mystery of Capital*, it is extremely expensive and time consuming for the poor in developing countries to make their ownership of property legal. Obtaining legal title to a dwelling on urban land in the Philippines, for example, involved 168 bureaucratic steps and fifty-three public and private agencies, and the process took thirteen to twenty-five years. For desert land in Egypt, obtaining legal title took seventy-seven steps, thirty-one public and private agencies, and five to fourteen years. To legally buy government land in Haiti, an ordinary citizen had to go through 176 steps over nineteen years. These barriers do not mean the poor do not invest; they still build houses and buy equipment even if they don't have legal title to these assets. By De Soto's calculations, the "total value of the real estate held but not legally owned by the poor of the Third World and former communist nations is at least $9.3 trillion."[3]

Without legal title, however, none of this property can be used as collateral to borrow funds, a requirement for most lenders. Even when people have legal title to their property, the legal system in most developing countries is so inefficient that collateral does not mean much. Typically creditors must first sue the defaulting debtor for payment, which takes several years, and then, once obtaining a favorable judgment, the creditor has to sue again to obtain title to the collateral. This process often takes in excess of five years. By the time the lender acquires the collateral, it is likely to have been neglected or stolen and thus has little value. In addition, governments often block lenders from foreclosing on borrowers in politically powerful sectors of a society, such as agriculture.

When the financial system is unable to use collateral effectively, the adverse selection problem will be worse, because the lender will need even more information about the quality of the borrower to distinguish a good loan from a bad one. Little lending will take place, especially in transactions that involve collateral, such as mortgages. In Peru, for example, the value of mortgage loans relative to the size of the economy is less than 1/20 that in the United States.

The poor have an even harder time obtaining loans because it is too costly for them to get title to their property, and they therefore have no collateral to offer, resulting in what Raghuram Rajan and Luigi Zingales, both of the University of Chicago, refer to as the "tyranny of collateral."[4] Even when poor people have a good idea for a business and are willing to work hard, they cannot get the funds to finance their business, making it difficult for them to escape poverty.

Government Regulation and Supervision of the Financial Sector

We have seen that when more information is collected, there is less information asymmetry and the financial system works more smoothly. However, we have also seen that the free-rider problem creates a serious impediment to information production. Can government intervention in the financial system help? In this section, we will discuss the three main government-based approaches for improving the quality of information in financial markets. (The government can also intervene in credit markets by directing credit, as discussed in the box, "Government-Directed Credit.")

Government Regulation to Promote Transparency

Governments can decrease information asymmetry by directly promoting transparency. Specifically, the government can regulate financial markets to require that firms distribute full and accurate information to enable investors to evaluate their true performance. The U.S. Securities and Exchange Commission (SEC) requires firms selling their securities in public markets to disclose information about their sales, assets, and earnings. Governments also have laws that force firms to adhere to standard accounting

---

[3]Hernando De Soto, *The Mystery of Capital: Why Capitalism Triumphs in the West and Fails Everywhere Else* (New York: Basic Books, 2000), 35.

[4]Raghuram Rajan and Luigi Zingales, *Saving Capitalism from the Capitalists: Unleashing the Power of Financial Markets to Create Wealth and Spread Opportunity* (New York: Crown Business, 2003).

Government-Directed Credit

Many governments, particularly those in poor, developing countries, have programs that direct credit to particular sectors of the economy. Governments direct credit by creating development financial institutions to make specific types of loans at artificially low rates, or by directing existing institutions to lend to certain entities or sectors of the economy. Governments can also effectively direct credit by owning banks; state-owned banks are very common in many developing countries.

Government-directed credit helps get funds to sectors of the economy, such as manufacturing or high tech, that are key drivers of economic growth. Yet, in contrast to governments, private institutions have incentives to solve adverse selection and moral hazard problems and to lend to those borrowers with the most productive investment opportunities. If private institutions do not make wise loans, they will not earn any profits. Governments, on the other hand, lack this profit incentive. Government-directed programs are unlikely to channel funds to sectors that will produce high growth for the economy; instead, these programs typically result in less efficient investment that hampers growth.

Research has associated large programs to direct credit and wide-scale state ownership of banks with less financial development and low growth rates.* The negative features of state-owned banks led a major World Bank study to conclude that "whatever its original objectives, state ownership of banks tends to stunt financial sector development, thereby contributing to slower growth."**

*For example, see Edward Kane, "Good Intentions and Unintended Evil: The Case against Selective Credit Allocation," *Journal of Money, Credit and Banking* 9 (1977): 55–69; World Bank, *Finance for Growth: Policy Choices in a Volatile World* (Oxford: World Bank and Oxford University Press, 2001); Rafael La Porta et al., "Government Ownership of Banks," *Journal of Finance* 57 (2002): 265–301; and James R. Barth, Gerard Caprio, Jr., and Ross Levine, "Banking Systems Around the Globe: Do Regulation and Ownership Affect Performance and Stability?" in *Prudential Regulation and Supervision: What Works and What Doesn't*, ed. Frederic S. Mishkin (Chicago: University of Chicago Press, 2001), 31–97.

**World Bank, *Finance for Growth: Policy Choices in a Volatile World* (Oxford: World Bank and Oxford University Press, 2001), 123.

principles that allow for profit verification and impose stiff criminal and civil penalties on individuals who commit fraud by hiding and stealing profits.

Although government regulation to increase transparency is crucial to reducing adverse selection and moral hazard problems, poorly performing firms and executives have strong incentives to falsify reports. Strong-looking firms fetch a high price for their securities. When firms misrepresent their financials to boost performance, executives receive higher compensation. Not surprisingly, government regulation does not always solve the problem, as illustrated by the collapse of Enron in 2001 (discussed in the box, "The Enron Implosion") and the accounting scandals shortly afterward at other corporations, like WorldCom in the United States and Parmalat and Royal Dutch Shell in Europe.

Government Safety Net

We have already seen that banks are particularly well-suited to solving adverse selection and moral hazard problems because they make private loans that help avoid the free-rider problem. However, this solution gives rise to two additional problems in the banking system. First, depositors might be reluctant to put their money into

The Enron Implosion

Until 2001, Enron Corporation, a firm that specialized in trading in the energy market, appeared to be spectacularly successful. It controlled a quarter of the energy-trading market and was valued as high as $77 billion in August 2000 (just a little over a year before its collapse), making it the seventh-largest corporation in the United States at that time. However, toward the end of 2001, Enron came crashing down. In October 2001, Enron announced a third-quarter loss of $618 million and disclosed accounting "mistakes." The SEC then engaged in a formal investigation of Enron's financial dealings with partnerships led by its former finance chief. It became clear that Enron was engaged in a complex set of transactions by which it was keeping substantial amounts of debt and financial contracts off of its balance sheet. These transactions enabled Enron to hide its financial difficulties. Despite securing as much as $1.5 billion of new financing from J.P. Morgan Chase and Citigroup, the company was forced to declare bankruptcy in December 2001, up to then the largest bankruptcy in U.S. history.

The Enron collapse illustrates that government regulation can lessen asymmetric information problems but cannot eliminate them. Managers have tremendous incentives to hide their companies' problems, making it hard for investors to know the true value of the firm. The Enron bankruptcy not only increased concerns in financial markets about the quality of accounting information supplied by corporations, but also led to hardship for many of the firm's former employees, who found that their pensions had become worthless. Outrage against the duplicity of executives at Enron has been high, and several executives have been indicted, with some convicted and sent to jail.

a bank if they cannot easily tell whether bank managers themselves are engaging in moral hazard and taking on too much risk or are outright crooks. Second, depositors' lack of information about the quality of a bank's assets can lead to the wholesale collapse of many banks at the same time, which we will see in Chapter 15 is a central element of financial crises. Without banks to solve adverse selection and moral hazard problems, lending and investment will decline, and the economy will experience a sharp economic downturn, such as occurred in the United States during the Great Depression of the 1930s.

The government can intervene in the financial system by encouraging depositors to put their money in banks and by preventing multiple, simultaneous bank failures by creating a safety net for depositors. The government may either provide deposit insurance (such as that from the Federal Deposit Insurance Corporation in the United States) or else make funds available directly to troubled financial institutions. This safety net can accomplish two goals. If depositors are protected and are sure they won't suffer any losses when a bank fails, they will be more willing to provide the bank with funds. Depositor protection also means that depositors no longer have reasons to pull their money out of a bank at the first sign of trouble, even if they are unsure about its ultimate financial health. Depositor protection therefore greatly reduces contagion caused by one bank failure potentially leading to another.

The government safety net of deposit insurance can have negative consequences. It increases the moral hazard problem because, with a safety net, depositors have less incentive to withdraw their funds if they suspect the bank is taking on too much risk. The presence of a government safety net increases the incentive for banks to take on greater risk than they otherwise would, with taxpayers often paying the bill if the bank subsequently fails.

Role of Prudential Regulation and Supervision

Given the moral hazard incentives created by a government safety net, there is a need for **prudential regulation**, rules set by the government to prevent banks from taking on too much risk. Governments can limit banks' risk level by adopting regulations to promote disclosure of banks' activities. With this information, the market is more likely to pull funds out of a bank that is engaging in risky activities. The government can also establish regulations to restrict those activities and asset categories it considers too risky for banks, encourage banks to diversify, promote accurate disclosure of banks' financial condition to the markets, and require that banks hold minimum levels of capital as a cushion against bad loans.

To make sure that these regulations are enforced, the government must also engage in **prudential supervision**, in which it monitors banks by examining them on a regular basis. Effective prudential regulation and supervision are needed to make the financial system work well. But what if government officials do not do their jobs well? When government regulation and supervision are inadequate, the financial system will be unable to channel funds to those with productive investment opportunities, negatively impacting the financial system, as we will discuss in Chapter 15.

Financial Development and Economic Growth: The Evidence

Developing all the fundamental institutions to support a sound financial system that promotes economic growth is a daunting task.[5] Is it worth all the effort? Let's turn to the evidence.

The evidence that financial development, often called **financial deepening**, and economic growth are linked is quite strong.[6] A pioneering study by Robert King and Ross Levine using a sample of eighty countries found that those with large financial sectors back in 1960 experienced greater economic growth over the subsequent thirty years than countries with small financial sectors.[7] Later studies using more sophisticated techniques have confirmed this finding, associating a doubling of the size of private credit in an average developing country with a two-percentage-point annual increase in economic growth.[8] Through the magic of compound interest, a two-percentage-point

---

[5]A Web appendix to this chapter found at the Companion Website, www.pearsonhighered.com/mishkin, discusses how free trade and financial globalization help promote financial development and economic growth.

[6]For an excellent recent survey of the link between finance and economic growth, see Asli Demirguc-Kunt, "Finance and Economic Development: The Role of Government," in *The Oxford Handbook of Banking*, eds. Alan N. Berger, Philip Molyneux, and John Wilson (Oxford: Oxford University Press, 2010), 641–662.

[7]Robert King and Ross Levine, "Finance and Growth: Schumpeter Might Be Right," *Quarterly Journal of Economics* 108 (1993): 717–737.

[8]For example, see Ross Levine et al., "Financial Intermediation and Growth: Causality and Causes," *Journal of Monetary Economics* 46 (2000): 31–77; Ross Levine and Sara Zervos, "Stock Markets, Banks, and Economic Growth," *American Economic Review* 88 (1998): 537–558; and Thorsten Beck et al., "Finance and the Sources of Growth," *Journal of Financial Economics* 58 (2000): 261–300.

annual increase results in a doubling of national income in thirty-five years.[9] Research has established several key insights:

1. Industries and firms that are highly dependent on external sources of funds will benefit greatly from financial deepening and will grow faster in countries that are better developed financially.[10]

2. More new firms are created in countries with better-developed financial systems than in countries with weak financial systems.

3. Financial development stimulates growth more through its improvements in the allocation of capital (which raises overall productivity) than through its encouragement of higher levels of investment.[11]

These findings have led former World Bank researcher and now governor of the central bank of Ireland, Patrick Honohan, to state that, "The causal link between finance and growth is one of the most striking empirical macroeconomic relationships uncovered in the last decade."[12]

Although financial deepening improves an economy's rate of economic growth, it is theoretically possible that the degree of poverty could remain the same or even increase because the resulting growth could lead to greater income inequality. However, research finds no evidence of this effect. In countries with strong financial development, the income of the poorest fifth of the population actually grows faster than average GDP per person, indicating clearly that financial development is associated with reductions in poverty and even with reductions in the use of child labor.[13] This finding is in concert with the predictions of economic theory: financial development increases the access of the poor to credit, which previously was limited largely to the rich.

Although this chapter shows that financial development is a powerful force in promoting economic growth in the long run, it can have a dark side. We will explore this dark side in the next chapter and a chapter on this book's website, where we will see

---

[9]To see how compound interest works, recognize that after one year, a 2% growth rate means that national income would be 1.02 times the initial year's income; at year 2, it would be $(1.02) \times (1.02) = (1.02)^2 = 1.0404$ times the initial year's income; and at year 3, it would be $(1.02)^3 = 1.0612$ times the initial year's income. Hence, for year 35, national income would be $(1.02)^{35} = 2.0$ times the initial year's income.

[10]See Raghuram Rajan and Luigi Zingales, "Financial Dependence and Growth," *American Economic Review* 88 (1998): 559–586; and Asli Demirguc-Kunt and Vojislav Maksimovic, "Law, Finance and Firm Growth," *Journal of Finance* 53 (1998): 2107–2137.

[11]Evidence on the link between financial development and growth in overall productivity (total factor productivity) can be found in Thorsten Beck et al., "Finance and the Sources of Growth," *Journal of Financial Economics* 58 (2000); William Easterly and Ross Levine, "It's Not Factor Accumulation: Stylized Facts and Growth Models," *World Bank Economic Review* 15 (2001): 177–219; and Ross Levine, "Finance and Growth: Theory and Evidence," in *Handbook of Economic Growth*, eds. Philippe Aghion and Steven Durlauf (Amsterdam: Elsevier Science, 2005), 865–934.

[12]Patrick Honohan, "Financial Development, Growth and Poverty: How Close Are the Links?" World Bank Policy Working Paper 3203 (February 2004), 2.

[13]See Hongyi Li, "Explaining International and Intertemporal Variations in Income Inequality," *Economic Journal* 108 (2001): 26–43; Thorsten Beck, Asli Dmirguc-Kunt, and Ross Levine, "Finance, Inequality and Poverty: Cross-Country Evidence," World Bank, mimeo. (April 2004); Patrick Honohan, "Financial Development, Growth and Poverty: How Close Are the Links?" World Bank Policy Working Paper 3203 (February 2004); and Rajeev H. Dehejia and Roberta Gatti, "Child Labor: The Role of Income Variability and Access to Credit in a Cross Section of Countries," World Bank Policy Research Paper 2767 (January 2002).

that the financial development process can, at times, have negative short-run effects when it leads to financial crises that produce sharp economic contractions.[14]

Application

Is China a Counter-Example to the Importance of Financial Development to Economic Growth?

Although China appears to be on its way to becoming an economic powerhouse, its financial development remains in the early stages. The country's legal system is weak: financial contracts are difficult to enforce, while accounting standards are lax, making high-quality information about borrowers hard to find. Regulation of the banking system is still in its formative stages, and the banking sector is dominated by large, state-owned banks. Yet the Chinese economy has enjoyed one of the highest growth rates in the world over the last twenty years. How has China been able to grow so rapidly given its low level of financial development?

China's income per person is currently around $7,000, one-sixth of per capita income in the United States. With an extremely high saving rate, averaging around 40% over the past two decades, the country has nonetheless been able to rapidly build up its capital stock and shift a massive pool of underutilized labor from the subsistence-agriculture sector into higher-productivity activities that use capital. Even though the financial system has not allocated available savings to their most productive uses, the huge increase in capital, combined with the gains in productivity from moving labor out of low-productivity, subsistence agriculture, have been enough to produce high growth.

As China gets richer, however, this strategy is unlikely to continue to work. The former Soviet Union provides a graphic example of why this is so. In the 1950s and 1960s, the Soviet Union shared many characteristics with modern-day China: high growth fueled by a high saving rate, a massive buildup of capital, and a large pool of underutilized labor shifting from subsistence agriculture to manufacturing. During this high-growth phase, the Soviet Union was unable to develop the institutions needed for its financial system to allocate capital efficiently. Once the pool of subsistence laborers was used up, the Soviet Union's growth slowed dramatically, and it was unable to keep up with the Western economies. Today no one considers the Soviet Union an economic success story, and its inability to develop the institutions necessary for its financial system to sustain growth was an important reason for the demise of this superpower.

To move into the next stage of development, China will need to allocate its capital more efficiently, which requires improving its financial system. The Chinese leadership is well aware of this challenge: in 2003, the government announced plans to put state-owned banks on the path to privatization. In addition, the government is engaged in legal reform to strengthen financial contracts. For example, China has been developing new bankruptcy laws to enable lenders to take over the assets of firms that default on their loan contracts. Whether the Chinese government will succeed in developing a first-rate financial system, thereby enabling China to join the ranks of the developed countries, is a big question mark.

---

[14]The Web chapter "Financial Crises in Emerging Market Economies" can be found at the Companion Website, www.pearsonhighered.com/mishkin.

SUMMARY

1. The financial system is important to economic growth because it helps channel funds from lender-savers to borrower-spenders who have productive investment opportunities. In direct finance, borrower-spenders access funds directly from lender-savers via financial markets. However, most funds get to borrowers through indirect finance, in which a financial intermediary obtains funds from lender-savers and then uses them to make loans to borrowers or to buy securities in financial markets.

2. Achieving a well-functioning financial system requires solving asymmetric information (adverse selection and moral hazard) problems, thereby reducing financial frictions. Banks are particularly effective at solving asymmetric information problems because they can avoid the free-rider problem by making private loans, preventing others from taking advantage (free-riding) of the information they collect. Banks engage in screening, monitoring, and the use of collateral to overcome adverse selection and moral hazard problems.

3. The government can improve the functioning of the financial system through regulations that promote transparency and through prudential regulation and supervision, which reduce excessive risk taking.

4. There is strong evidence that financial development (also called financial deepening) stimulates economic growth.

KEY TERMS

adverse selection, p. 376
asymmetric information, p. 374
balance sheet, p. 375
banks, p. 375
bonds, p. 373
capital, p. 375
collateral, p. 380
equities, p. 373
exchanges, p. 373
finance companies, p. 375

financial deepening, p. 384
financial instruments, p. 373
financial intermediary, p. 374
financial intermediation, p. 374
free-rider problem, p. 377
hedge funds, p. 375
insurance companies, p. 375
investment banks, p. 373
liabilities, p. 373
microcredit, p. 374

moral hazard, p. 376
mutual funds, p. 375
net worth, p. 375
pension funds, p. 375
prudential regulation, p. 384
prudential supervision, p. 384
restrictive covenants, p. 379
screening, p. 378
securities, p. 373

REVIEW QUESTIONS

All Questions are available in MyEconLab *for practice or instructor assignment.*

The Role of the Financial System

1. What role does the financial system play in promoting economic growth?

2. How does direct finance differ from indirect finance? Which form of finance is more important?

Information Challenges and the Financial System

3. What is asymmetric information? What two asymmetric information problems hinder the operation of the financial system?

4. Why are financial intermediaries willing to engage in information collection activities when investors in financial instruments may be unwilling to do so?

5. What specific procedures do financial intermediaries use to reduce asymmetric information problems in lending?

6. Why are asymmetric information problems particularly challenging in developing countries? What does this imply about the importance of financial intermediation and the role of banks in these countries?

Government Regulation and Supervision of the Financial Sector

7. What steps can the government take to reduce asymmetric information problems and help the financial system function more smoothly and efficiently?

8. How can asymmetric information problems lead to a bank panic?

9. Why do governments provide safety nets for bank depositors, and what are their consequences?

Financial Development and Economic Growth: The Evidence

10. What are the benefits of financial deepening?

PROBLEMS

All Problems are available in MyEconLab *for practice or instructor assignment.*

The Role of the Financial System

1. Suppose a firm has a great idea: overnight shipping. This idea will decrease costs for many businesses and will therefore result in a more efficient economy. If the entrepreneurs who create this concept cannot get funds to put their idea to work, what do you think the consequences will be for the economy?

2. Suppose a given country encourages its citizens to save 20% of their income and then allocates these funds through government-owned financial intermediaries. As a result, many government officials get mortgages to buy expensive houses (and often default on their payments). Do you think funds were allocated to their most productive use? Comment on the efficiency of such a financial system.

Information Challenges and the Financial System

3. Identify the type of asymmetric information problem described in each of the following scenarios:
   a) A loan officer requests information about your work and credit history before approving your car loan application.
   b) The same loan officer explains that there will be a lien placed on your car title until you pay off the total amount of the loan.
   c) The owner of a football team signs a contract with a new football star. The contract clearly specifies that the player may not skydive.

4. Suppose you go to a bank intending to buy a certificate of deposit with your savings. Explain why you would not offer a loan to the next individual who applies for a car loan at the bank at a higher interest rate than the rate the bank pays on certificates of deposit (but lower than the rate the bank charges on car loans).

5. In December 2001, Argentina announced that it would not honor its sovereign

(government-issued) debt. Many investors were left holding Argentinean bonds that were now priced at a fraction of their recent value. A few years later, Argentina announced that it would pay back 25% of the face value of its debt. Comment on the effects of information asymmetries on government bonds markets. Do you think investors are currently willing to buy bonds issued by the government of Argentina?

6. Gustavo is a young doctor who lives in a country with a relatively inefficient legal system and (probably as a consequence) an inefficient financial system. When Gustavo applied for a mortgage, he found that banks (he visited many) usually required collateral for up to 300% of the amount of the loan. Explain why banks might require that much property as collateral in such a financial system. Comment on the consequences of such a system for economic growth.

Government Regulation and Supervision of the Financial Sector

7. Financial regulators have been working to improve transparency and reduce risk in the derivatives market. How do you think increased transparency will affect financial intermediaries that trade derivatives? How do you think it will affect the overall performance of the financial system?

8. Many policy makers in developing countries have proposed the implementation of systems of deposit insurance like the one that exists in the United States. Explain why this might create more problems than solutions in the financial system of a developing country.

Financial Development and Economic Growth: The Evidence

9. One of the main characteristics of financial deepening is that more individuals participate in the financial system: more people open checking and saving accounts, and more firms rely on financial intermediaries as a source of funds. Comment on the effect of financial deepening on a central bank's ability to conduct monetary policy.

10. Microcredit programs (i.e., very small loans issued to the extremely poor) usually target a group of women and assign funds to them under the condition that decisions about the use of funds are made by all women in the group. How do you think this procedure will help solve asymmetric information problems?

DATA ANALYSIS PROBLEMS

The Problems update with real-time data in MyEconLab *and are available for practice or instructor assignment.*

1. Go to the St. Louis Federal Reserve FRED database, and find data on the three-month U.S. Treasury note (TB3MS), the three-month AA nonfinancial commercial paper rate (CPN3M), the three-month AA financial commercial rate (CPF3M), and the St. Louis Fed financial stress index (STLFSI). Use the *frequency* setting to convert the financial stress index to "Monthly." Download the data into a spreadsheet.
    a) Calculate the credit spread, or the difference between the commercial paper rate and the treasury rate, for both commercial paper series. What are the spreads for the most recent data available?

able? How do the financial and nonfinancial spreads differ, if at all?
    b) Report the current credit spreads for the most recent data available, along with the spreads for one year earlier and for October 2008. Comment on the differences in the spreads. How does asymmetric information help explain the differences in the spreads?
    c) Create a graph showing the financial stress index along with the credit spreads since 2000. How do the credit spreads behave compared to the financial stress index? Given that the financial stress index indicates asymmetric

information problems (or lack thereof), what can you conclude about the relationship between asymmetric information and credit spreads?

2. Go to the St. Louis Federal Reserve FRED database, and find data on the St. Louis Fed financial stress index (STLFSI), the percent value of loans collateralized for commercial and industrial loans (ESAXDBNQ), and the net percentage of loan officers reporting tighter credit standards (DRTSCILM). Use the *frequency* setting to convert the financial stress index to "Quarterly." Download the data into a spreadsheet.

   a) Calculate the average of the three series over the most recent four quarters of data available, and the average over the four quarters prior to that. How has the amount of collateralization, credit standards, and financial stress changed over these two periods?

   b) Repeat part (a) by calculating the averages for 2007 and 2008.

   c) Assuming the financial stress index reflects asymmetric information problems, comment on how collateral and credit standards change as asymmetric information problems change. Is this consistent with what you would expect? Why or why not?

3. The Heritage Index, published yearly by the Heritage Foundation, provides a comprehensive numerical measure of overall economic freedom for countries, with specific indicators reflecting the overall quality of financial markets through two indicators: financial freedom and investment freedom (for more information, see heritage.org/index). The table in the next column reports the average of both scores for the years 1995, 2005, and 2013. Scores closer to 100 represent "free" countries; countries with scores below 50 are considered "repressed" with regard to that particular indicator. Use the investment and financial freedom data in the table, and go to the St. Louis Federal Reserve FRED database and find data on

real GDP per capita for the United Kingdom (GBRRGDPC), Australia (AUSRGDPC), the Czech Republic (CZERGDPC), the United States (USARGDPC), France (FRARGDPC), and Italy (ITARGDPC). Download the data into a single spreadsheet.

Investment & Financial Freedom Average

	1995	2005	2013
United Kingdom	80	90	85
Australia	80	80	85
Czech Republic	80	80	75
United States	70	80	70
Italy	60	70	70
France	50	60	67.5

   a) For each country, calculate the average yearly growth rate from 1995 to 2005, and from 2005 to the most current period available. To do this, take the value at the beginning of the period, subtract it from the value at the end of the period, and divide by the beginning period value. Multiply by 100 to change the result to a percent, and then divide by the number of years in the period. Report the growth rates for each country across each period.

   b) Calculate the average of the per capita real GDP growth rates for the 1995 to 2005 and 2005 to current periods for the top three countries listed in 2013, and also for the bottom three countries listed. Do you see any relationship between financial market freedom and economic growth? Briefly explain.

   c) The United States, Italy, France, and the United Kingdom all increased their scores by 10 between 1995 and 2005, while the scores of Australia and the Czech Republic remained constant during this period. Comment on the effect of increases in a country's score over time versus the overall level of the score as it relates to economic growth.

The online appendix "Free Trade, Financial Globalization, and Growth" is available at the Companion Website, www.pearsonhighered.com/mishkin

Financial Crises and the Economy

15

Preview

Recall from Chapter 1 that financial crises are major disruptions in financial markets characterized by sharp declines in asset prices and firm failures. Beginning in August 2007, defaults in the mortgage market by subprime borrowers (borrowers with weak credit records) sent a shudder through the financial markets, leading to the worst U.S. financial crisis since the Great Depression. Alan Greenspan, former chairman of the Fed, described the 2007–2009 financial crisis as a "once-in-a-century credit tsunami." Wall Street firms and commercial banks suffered losses amounting to hundreds of billions of dollars. Households and businesses found that they had to pay higher rates on their borrowings and that it was much harder to obtain credit. World stock markets crashed, with U.S. shares falling by as much as half from their peak in October 2007. Many financial firms, including commercial banks, investment banks, and insurance companies, went belly-up. The recession that began in December 2007 worsened by the fall of 2008, leading to steep declines in economic activity.

Financial crises are a major source of economic fluctuations. Indeed, all deep recessions and depressions are linked to major financial crises. Why did the 2007–2009 financial crisis occur? Why have financial crises been so prevalent throughout U.S. and world history, and why are they almost always followed by severe contractions in economic activity?

In this chapter we will use the aggregate demand and supply analysis developed in Chapter 12, along with our understanding of the financial system and information issues from Chapter 14, as a backdrop for examining the dynamics of financial crises in advanced countries like the United States. We apply the analysis to the two worst U.S. financial crises in the last one hundred years—the Great Depression of 1930–1933 and the 2007–2009 financial crisis—to explain how these crises evolved and how they affected the economy.[1]

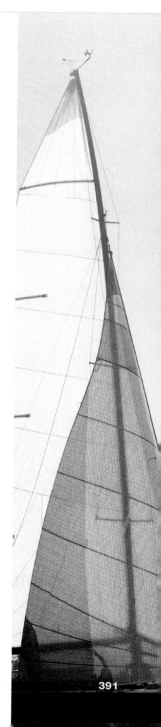

[1]In a Web chapter available at the Companion Website, www.pearsonhighered.com/mishkin, we extend the analysis to *emerging market economies*, economies in an early stage of market development that have recently opened up to the flow of goods, services, and capital from the rest of the world.

Asymmetric Information and Financial Crises

We established in Chapter 14 that a fully functioning financial system is critical to a robust economy. The financial system performs the essential function of channeling funds to individuals or businesses with productive investment opportunities. If capital goes to the wrong uses or does not flow at all, the economy will operate inefficiently or go into an economic downturn.

Asymmetric Information Problems

In Chapter 14, we saw how the smooth functioning of financial markets is impeded when one party in a financial transaction does not know enough about the other party or its investments to make accurate decisions. Recall that this lack of information, known as *asymmetric information*, creates two basic types of problems in the financial system:

1. *Adverse selection*, in which lenders must select from a pool of bad (*adverse*) credit risks, because the most undesirable potential borrowers are the most active in seeking out a loan

2. *Moral hazard*, when there is the risk (*hazard*) that the borrower has better information than the lender about whether the borrower will engage in activities that are undesirable (*immoral*) from the point of view of the lender

Because the adverse selection and moral hazard problems make it less likely that a borrower will pay back a loan, lenders may decide they would rather not make a loan, even though there are good credit risks in the marketplace. In other words, barriers to the efficient functioning of financial markets rise and so financial frictions increase.

What Is a Financial Crisis?

Academic finance literature calls the analysis of how asymmetric information problems can generate adverse selection and moral hazard problems **agency theory.** Agency theory provides the basis for our definition of a financial crisis. When asymmetric information problems worsen and so financial frictions increase, it is harder for lenders to ascertain the creditworthiness of borrowers. They need to charge a higher interest rate to protect themselves against the possibility that the borrower may not pay back the loan, which leads to a higher **credit spread,** the difference between the interest rate on loans to businesses and the interest rate on completely safe assets that are sure to be paid back.

A **financial crisis** occurs when information flows in financial markets experience a particularly large disruption, with the result that financial frictions and credit spreads increase sharply, and financial markets stop functioning. Economic activity then collapses.

Dynamics of Financial Crises

As earth-shaking and headline-grabbing as the most recent financial crisis was, it was only one of a number of financial crises that have hit industrialized countries like the United States over the years. These experiences have helped economists uncover insights into present-day economic turmoil.

Financial crises in advanced economies have progressed in two and sometimes three stages. To understand how these crises have unfolded, refer to Figure 15.1, which traces the stages of financial crises in industrialized economies.

Stage One: Initiation of Financial Crisis

Financial crises can begin in several ways: credit and asset-price booms and busts, or a general increase in uncertainty caused by failures of major financial institutions.

CREDIT BOOM AND BUST. The seeds of a financial crisis are often sown when an economy introduces new types of loans or other financial products, known as **financial innovation,** or when countries engage in **financial liberalization,** the elimination of restrictions on financial markets and institutions. (Recall from Chapter 14 that financial institutions are of two types: financial intermediaries, such as banks, that act as intermediaries between savers and borrowers, and other financial institutions, such as investment banks, that facilitate transactions in financial markets.) In the long run, financial liberalization promotes financial development and encourages a well-run financial system that allocates capital efficiently. However, financial liberalization has a dark side: in the short run, it can prompt financial institutions to go on a lending spree, called a **credit boom.** Unfortunately, lenders may not have the expertise, or the incentives, to manage risk appropriately in these new lines of business. Even with proper management, credit booms eventually outstrip the ability of institutions—and government regulators—to screen and monitor credit risks, leading to overly risky lending.

Government safety nets such as deposit insurance weaken market discipline and increase the moral hazard incentive for banks to take on greater risk than they otherwise would. Since lender-savers know that government-guaranteed insurance protects them from losses, they will supply even undisciplined banks with funds. Banks and other financial institutions can make risky, high-interest loans to borrower-spenders. They will walk away with nice profits if the loans are repaid, and rely on government deposit insurance, funded by taxpayers, if borrower-spenders default. Without proper monitoring, risk-taking grows unchecked.

Eventually, losses on loans begin to mount and the value of the loans (on the asset side of the balance sheet) falls relative to liabilities, thereby driving down the net worth (capital) of banks and other financial institutions. With less capital, these financial institutions cut back on their lending to borrower-spenders, a process called **deleveraging.** Furthermore, with less capital, banks and other financial institutions become riskier, causing lender-savers and other potential lenders to these institutions to pull out their funds. Fewer funds mean fewer loans to fund productive investments and a credit freeze: the lending boom turns into a lending crash, producing what is often referred to as a **leverage cycle.**

When financial institutions stop collecting information and making loans, they limit the financial system's ability to address the asymmetric information problems of adverse selection and moral hazard, and so financial frictions increase (as shown by the arrow pointing from the first factor, "Deterioration in Financial Institutions' Balance Sheets," in the top row of Figure 15.1). The rise in financial frictions raises the real interest rate on investments, which leads to a decline in investment spending at any given

FIGURE 15.1

Sequence of Events in Financial Crises in Advanced Economies

The solid arrows trace the sequence of events during a typical financial crisis; the dotted arrows show the additional set of events that occur if the crisis develops into a debt deflation. The sections separated by the dashed horizontal lines show the different stages of a financial crisis.

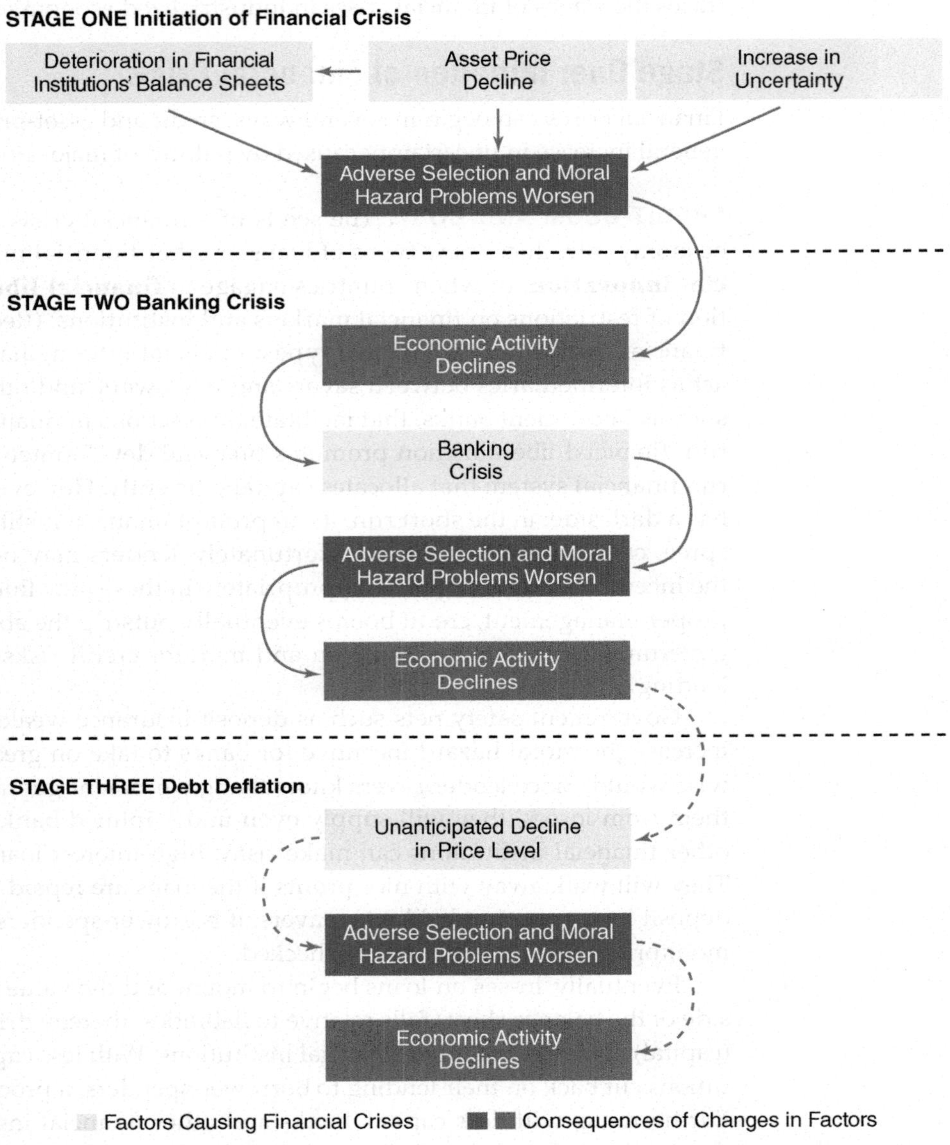

STAGE ONE Initiation of Financial Crisis

Deterioration in Financial Institutions' Balance Sheets ← Asset Price Decline Increase in Uncertainty

Adverse Selection and Moral Hazard Problems Worsen

STAGE TWO Banking Crisis

Economic Activity Declines

Banking Crisis

Adverse Selection and Moral Hazard Problems Worsen

Economic Activity Declines

STAGE THREE Debt Deflation

Unanticipated Decline in Price Level

Adverse Selection and Moral Hazard Problems Worsen

Economic Activity Declines

▨ Factors Causing Financial Crises   ■ Consequences of Changes in Factors

inflation rate, and so the aggregate demand curve in Figure 15.2 shifts to the left to AD_2 and the economy moves from point 1 to point 2, where both output and inflation fall.

ASSET-PRICE BOOM AND BUST. Prices of assets such as equity shares and real estate can be driven by investor psychology well above their **fundamental economic values,** that is, their values based on realistic expectations of the assets' future income streams.

FIGURE 15.2

Aggregate Demand and Supply Analysis of Financial Crises

In the first stage, deterioration in financial institutions' balance sheets, asset-price declines, and increases in uncertainty increase financial frictions, shifting the aggregate demand curve from AD_1 to AD_2 and moving the economy from point 1 to point 2, with output and inflation falling. In the second stage, bank panics raise financial frictions further, shifting the aggregate demand curve from AD_2 to AD_3. The slack in the economy shifts the short-run aggregate supply curve from AS_1 to AS_3, moving the economy from point 2 to point 3, with an even greater fall in output and inflation. If the fall in inflation is substantial enough, it can turn into a deflation, which leads to the debt-deflation phenomenon that shifts the aggregate demand curve even further to the left, from AD_3 to AD_4, and shifts the short-run aggregate supply curve to AS_4. If this occurs, the economy moves from point 3 to point 4, leading to a prolonged economic contraction.

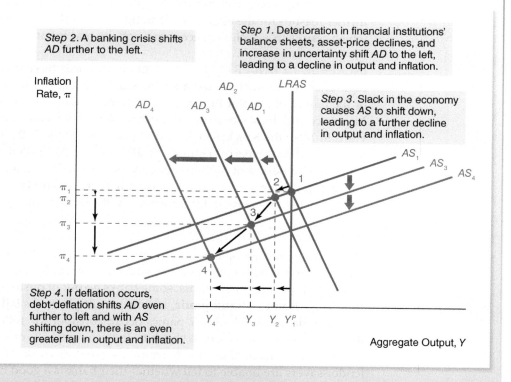

Step 2. A banking crisis shifts *AD* further to the left.

Step 1. Deterioration in financial institutions' balance sheets, asset-price declines, and increase in uncertainty shift *AD* to the left, leading to a decline in output and inflation.

Step 3. Slack in the economy causes *AS* to shift down, leading to a further decline in output and inflation.

Step 4. If deflation occurs, debt-deflation shifts *AD* even further to left and with *AS* shifting down, there is an even greater fall in output and inflation.

The rise of asset prices above their fundamental economic values is an **asset-price bubble.** Examples of asset-price bubbles are the tech stock market bubble of the late 1990s and the recent housing price bubble that we will discuss later in this chapter. Asset-price bubbles are often also driven by credit booms, in which the large increase in credit is used to fund purchases of assets, thereby driving up their price.

When the bubble bursts and asset prices realign with fundamental economic values, stock and real estate prices tumble, companies see their net worth (the difference between their assets and their liabilities) decline, and the value of collateral they can pledge drops. Now these companies have less at stake because they have less "skin in the game," and so they are more likely to make risky investments because they have less to lose, the problem of moral hazard. As a result, financial frictions increase and financial institutions tighten lending standards for borrower-spenders and lending contracts (as shown by the downward arrow pointing from the second factor, "Asset Price Decline," in the top row of Figure 15.1).

The asset-price bust also causes a decline in the value of financial institutions' assets, thereby causing a decline in their net worth and hence a deterioration in their balance sheets (shown by the arrow from the second factor to the first factor in the top row of Figure 15.1), which causes them to deleverage. The deleveraging and tightening of lending standards and the resulting increase in financial frictions then provides further reasons for the aggregate demand curve to shift to the left to AD_2 in Figure 15.2, which results in a decline in economic activity and inflation.

INCREASE IN UNCERTAINTY. U.S. financial crises have usually begun in periods of high uncertainty, such as just after the start of a recession, a crash in the stock market, or the failure of a major financial institution. Crises began after the failure of Ohio Life Insurance and Trust Company in 1857; the Jay Cooke and Company in 1873; Grant and Ward in 1884; the Knickerbocker Trust Company in 1907; the Bank of the United States in 1930; and Bear Stearns, Lehman Brothers, and AIG in 2008. With information hard to come by in a period of high uncertainty, adverse selection and moral hazard problems increase, reducing lending and economic activity (as shown by the arrow pointing from the last factor, "Increase in Uncertainty," in the top row of Figure 15.1).

Stage Two: Banking Crisis

Deteriorating balance sheets and tougher business conditions lead some financial institutions into insolvency, the point at which net worth becomes negative. Unable to pay off depositors or other creditors, some banks go out of business. If severe enough, these factors can lead to a **bank panic,** in which multiple banks fail simultaneously.

To understand why bank panics occur, consider the following situation. Suppose that as a result of an adverse shock to the economy, 5% of the banks have such large losses on their loans that they become insolvent. Because of asymmetric information, lender-savers are unable to tell whether their bank is a good bank or one of the 5% that are insolvent. Depositors (lender-savers) at bad *and* good banks recognize that they may not get back 100 cents on the dollar for their deposits (because there is either no deposit insurance or limited amounts of it) and will want to withdraw them. Banks operate on a first-come-first-served basis, so depositors have a very strong incentive to be the first to show up at the bank ("run to the bank"): if they are later in line, the bank may not have enough funds left to pay them anything. Uncertainty about the health of the banking system in general can lead to runs on banks, both good and bad, which will force banks to sell off assets quickly to raise the necessary funds. These **fire sales** of assets may cause their prices to decline so much that the bank becomes insolvent, and the resulting contagion can then lead to multiple bank failures and a full-fledged bank panic.

With fewer banks operating, information about the creditworthiness of borrower-spenders disappears. Increasingly severe adverse selection and moral hazard problems in financial markets deepen the financial crisis, causing declines in asset prices and the failure of firms throughout the economy that lack funds for productive investment opportunities. Figure 15.1 represents this progression in the Stage Two portion. Bank panics were a feature of all U.S. financial crises during the nineteenth and twentieth centuries, occurring every twenty years or so until World War II—1819, 1837, 1857, 1873, 1884, 1893, 1907, and 1930–1933.[2]

---

[2]For a discussion of U.S. banking and financial crises in the nineteenth and twentieth centuries, see Frederic S. Mishkin, "Asymmetric Information and Financial Crises: A Historical Perspective," in *Financial Markets and Financial Crises,* ed. R. Glenn Hubbard (Chicago: University of Chicago Press 1991), 69–108.

Stage Two of financial crises leads to a further sharp decrease in the efficient functioning of financial markets, and the resulting rise in financial frictions causes investment spending to decline at any given inflation rate, shifting the aggregate demand curve to the left to AD_3 in Figure 15.2. In addition, the slack in the economy shifts the short-run aggregate supply curve from AS_1 to AS_3. The economy now deteriorates even further, moving from point 2 to point 3, with aggregate output and inflation falling further.

Eventually, public and private authorities shut down insolvent firms and sell them off or liquidate them. Uncertainty in financial markets declines, the stock market recovers, and balance sheets improve. Adverse selection and moral hazard problems diminish and the financial crisis subsides. With the financial markets able to operate well again, the stage is set for an economic recovery.

Stage Three: Debt Deflation

If, however, the economic downturn leads to a sufficiently sharp decline in inflation, then inflation turns negative and the price level falls, so the recovery process is short-circuited. In Stage Three of Figure 15.1, **debt deflation** occurs when a substantial unanticipated decline in the price level sets in, leading to a further deterioration in firms' net worth because of the increased burden of indebtedness.

In economies with moderate inflation, which characterizes most advanced countries, many debt contracts with fixed interest rates are typically of fairly long maturity, usually ten years or more. Because debt payments are contractually fixed in nominal terms, an unanticipated decline in the price level raises the value of borrowing firms' liabilities in real terms (increases the burden of the debt) but does not raise the real value of borrowing firms' assets. The borrowing firm's net worth in real terms (the difference between assets and liabilities in real terms) thus declines.

To better understand how this decline in net worth occurs, consider what happens if a firm in 2015 has assets of $100 million (in 2015 dollars) and $90 million of long-term liabilities, so that it has $10 million in net worth. If the price level falls by 10% in 2015, the real value of the liabilities would rise to $99 million in 2015 dollars, while the real value of the assets would remain unchanged at $100 million. The result would be that real net worth in 2015 dollars would fall from $10 million to $1 million ($100 million minus $99 million).

The substantial decline in real net worth of borrowers from a sharp drop in the price level causes an increase in the adverse selection and moral hazard problems facing lenders, and so causes a contraction of lending and an additional leftward shift of the aggregate demand curve in Figure 15.2, from AD_3 to AD_4. With the slack in the economy, the short-run aggregate supply curve shifts further downward from AS_3 to AS_4, moving the economy from point 3 to point 4, with even lower output and inflation. Hence, lending and economic activity decline for a long time. The most significant financial crisis that displayed debt deflation was the Great Depression, the worst economic contraction in U.S. history.

Application

The Mother of All Financial Crises: The Great Depression

With our framework for understanding financial crises in place, we are prepared to analyze how a financial crisis unfolded during the Great Depression and how it led to the worst economic downturn in U.S. history.

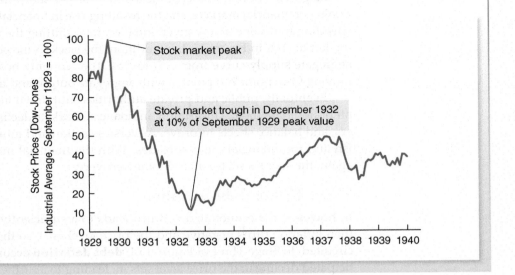

FIGURE 15.3

Stock Price Data During the Great Depression Period

Stock prices crashed in 1929, falling by 40% by the end of 1929, and then continued to fall to only 10% of their peak value by 1932.

Source: Dow-Jones Industrial Average (DJIA). Global Financial Data. www .globalfinancialdata.com/ index_tabs.php?action=det ailedinfo&id=1165

Stock Market Crash

In 1928 and 1929, prices doubled in the U.S. stock market. Federal Reserve officials viewed the stock market boom as excessive speculation. To curb it, they pursued an autonomous tightening of monetary policy to raise interest rates and decrease aggregate demand. The Fed got more than it bargained for when the stock market crashed in October 1929, falling by 40% by the end of 1929, as shown in Figure 15.3.

Bank Panics

By the middle of 1930, stocks recovered almost half of their losses and credit market conditions stabilized. What might have been a normal recession turned into something far worse, however, when severe droughts in the Midwest led to a sharp decline in agricultural production, with the result that farmers could not pay back their bank loans. The resulting defaults on farm mortgages led to large loan losses on bank balance sheets in agricultural regions. The general weakness of the economy, and the weakness of banks in agricultural regions in particular, prompted substantial withdrawals from banks, building to a full-fledged panic in November and December 1930, with the stock market falling sharply. For more than two years, the Fed sat by idly through one bank panic after another, the most severe spate of panics in U.S. history. After what would be the era's final panic in March 1933, President Franklin Delano Roosevelt declared a bank holiday, a temporary closing of all banks. "The only thing we have to fear is fear itself," Roosevelt told the nation.

The damage was done, however, and more than one-third of the U.S. commercial banks had failed.

Adverse Selection and Moral Hazard Worsen

Stock prices kept falling. By mid-1932, stocks had declined to 10% of their value at the 1929 peak, as shown in Figure 15.3—and the increase in uncertainty from the unsettled business conditions created by the economic contraction worsened adverse selection and moral

FIGURE 15.4

Credit Spreads During the Great Depression

Credit spreads (the difference between rates on Baa corporate bonds and U.S. Treasury bonds) rose sharply during the Great Depression.

Source: Federal Reserve Bank of St. Louis FRED database http://research.stlouisfed.org/fred2/

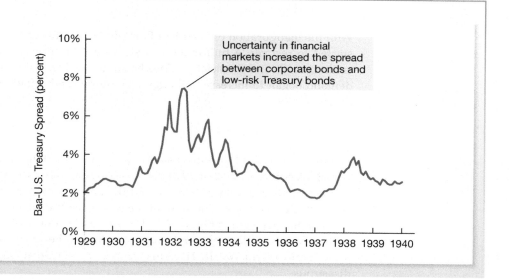

hazard problems in financial markets. With a greatly reduced number of financial inter-mediaries still in business, adverse selection and moral hazard problems intensified even further. Financial markets struggled to channel funds to borrower-spenders with productive investment opportunities.

Financial institutions began charging businesses much higher interest rates to protect themselves from credit losses. The resulting rise in the credit spread is shown in Figure 15.4, which displays the difference between interest rates on corporate bonds with a Baa (medium-quality) credit rating and rates on similar-maturity Treasury bonds. With the increase in financial frictions, the amount of outstanding commercial loans fell by half from 1929 to 1933, and investment spending collapsed, declining by 90% from its 1929 level. Our *AD/AS* analysis in the preceding section demonstrated how these increases in financial frictions would lead to a decline in both output and inflation. Indeed, the contraction of aggregate demand caused real GDP to fall at such a rapid rate that the price level now began to decline at a −10% annual rate.

Debt Deflation

The ongoing deflation that started in 1930 eventually led to a 25% decline in the price level. This deflation short-circuited the normal recovery process that occurs in most recessions. The huge decline in prices triggered a debt deflation in which net worth fell because of the increased burden of indebtedness borne by firms. The decline in net worth and the resulting increase in adverse selection and moral hazard problems led to a prolonged economic contraction along the lines of the contraction we discussed in the previous section, and unemployment rose to 25% of the labor force. The financial crisis of the Great Depression was the worst ever experienced in the United States.[3]

---

[3]For a discussion of the role of asymmetric information problems in the Great Depression period, see Ben Bernanke, "Nonmonetary Effects of the Financial Crisis in the Propagation of the Great Depression," *American Economic Review* 73 (1983): 257–276; and Charles Calomiris, "Financial Factors and the Great Depression," *Journal of Economic Perspectives* (Spring 1993): 61–85.

Recovery Begins

With the inauguration of President Franklin Delano Roosevelt, the financial markets finally started to recover. A bull market in stocks got underway, as shown in Figure 15.3, and credit spreads and financial frictions began to decline. With these developments, aggregate demand began to increase and aggregate output and inflation began to rise, while unemployment fell.

International Dimensions

Although the Great Depression started in the United States, it was not just a U.S. phenomenon. Bank panics in the United States also spread to the rest of the world, and the contraction of the U.S. economy sharply decreased the demand for foreign goods. Aggregate demand contracted in economies throughout the world, leading other countries to face a similar scenario to that depicted in Figure 15.2. The worldwide depression caused great hardship, with millions upon millions of people out of work, and the resulting discontent led to the rise of fascism and World War II. The consequences of the Great Depression financial crisis were disastrous.

Application

The Global Financial Crisis of 2007–2009

Most economists thought that financial crises of the type experienced during the Great Depression were a thing of the past for the United States. Unfortunately, the financial crisis that engulfed the world in 2007–2009 proved them wrong.

Causes of the 2007–2009 Financial Crisis

We begin our look at the 2007–2009 financial crisis by examining three central factors that led to a credit and asset-price boom: financial innovation in mortgage markets, agency problems in mortgage markets, and the role of asymmetric information in the credit rating process.

FINANCIAL INNOVATION IN THE MORTGAGE MARKETS. Before 2000, only the most credit-worthy (prime) borrowers could obtain residential mortgages. However, advances in computer technology and new statistical techniques, known as data mining, led to enhanced, quantitative evaluation of the credit risk for a new class of risky residential mortgages. Households with credit records could now be assigned a numerical credit score, known as a FICO score (named after the Fair Isaac Corporation that developed it), that would predict how likely they would be to default on their loan payments. In addition, by lowering transaction costs, computer technology enabled the bundling together of smaller loans (like mortgages) into standard debt securities, a process known as **securitization.** These factors made it possible for banks to offer **subprime mortgages** to borrowers with less-than-stellar credit records.

The ability to cheaply quantify the default risk of the underlying high-risk mortgages and bundle them into standardized debt securities called **mortgage-backed securities** provided a new source of financing for these mortgages. Financial innovation didn't stop there. **Financial engineering,** the development of new, sophisticated financial instruments, led to **structured credit products** that paid out income streams from a collection of underlying assets designed to have particular risk characteristics that appealed to investors with differing preferences. The most notorious of these products were collateralized debt obligations (CDOs), which are described in the accompanying box.

Collateralized Debt Obligations (CDOs)

The creation of a collateralized debt obligation involves a corporate entity called a *special purpose vehicle (SPV)* that buys a collection of assets such as corporate bonds and loans, commercial real estate bonds, and mortgage-backed securities. The SPV then separates the payment streams (cash flows) from these assets into a number of "buckets" that are referred to as *tranches*. The highest-rated tranches, referred to as *super senior tranches*, are the ones that are paid off first and so have the least risk. The super senior CDO is a bond that pays out these cash flows to investors and, because it has the least risk, it also has the lowest interest rate. The next bucket of cash flows, known as the *senior tranche*, is paid out next, and so the senior CDO has a little more risk and pays a higher interest rate. The next tranche of payment streams, the *mezzanine tranche* of the CDO, is paid out after the super senior and senior tranches, and so it bears more risk and has an even higher interest rate. The lowest tranche of the CDO is the *equity tranche*, and this is the first set of cash flows that are not paid out if the underlying assets go into

default and stop making payments. This tranche has the highest risk and is often not traded.

If all of this sounds complicated, it is. There were even CDO^2s and CDO^3s that sliced and diced risk even further, paying out the cash flows from CDOs to CDO^2s and from CDO^2s to CDO^3s. Although financial engineering has the potential benefit of creating products and services that match investors' risk appetites, it also has a dark side. The structured products like CDOs, CDO^2s, and CDO^3s can get so complicated that it can be hard to value the cash flows of the underlying assets for a security or to determine who actually owns these assets. Indeed, at a speech given in October 2007, Ben Bernanke, the chairman of the Federal Reserve, joked that he "would like to know what those damn things are worth." In other words, the increased complexity of structured products can actually reduce the amount of information in financial markets, thereby worsening asymmetric information in the financial system and increasing the severity of adverse selection and moral hazard problems.

AGENCY PROBLEMS IN THE MORTGAGE MARKETS. The mortgage brokers who originated the risky loans often did not make a strong effort to evaluate whether the borrower could pay off the loan, since they would quickly sell (distribute) the loans to investors in the form of mortgage-backed securities. This **originate-to-distribute** business model was exposed to **principal-agent problems** (also referred to more simply as **agency problems**), in which the mortgage brokers acted as agents for investors (the principals) but did not have the investors' best interests at heart. Once the mortgage broker earns his or her fee, why should the broker care if the borrower makes good on his or her payment? The more volume the broker originates, the more he or she makes.

Not surprisingly, adverse selection became a major problem. Risk-loving investors lined up to obtain loans to acquire houses that would be very profitable if housing prices went up, knowing they could "walk away" if housing prices went down. The principal-agent problem also created incentives for mortgage brokers to encourage households to take on mortgages they could not afford, or to commit fraud by falsifying information on borrowers' mortgage applications in order to qualify them for their mortgages. Compounding this problem was lax regulation of originators, who were not required to disclose information to borrowers that would have helped them assess whether they could afford the loans.

The agency problems went even deeper. Commercial and investment banks, which were earning large fees by underwriting mortgage-backed securities and structured credit products like CDOs, also had weak incentives to make sure that the ultimate holders of the securities would be paid off. Large fees from writing financial insurance contracts called **credit default swaps,** which provide payments to holders of bonds if they default, also drove units of insurance companies like AIG to write hundreds of billions of dollars' worth of these risky contracts.

ASYMMETRIC INFORMATION AND CREDIT RATING AGENCIES. Credit rating agencies, agencies that rate the quality of debt securities in terms of the probability of default, were another contributor to asymmetric information in financial markets. The rating agencies advised clients on how to structure complex financial instruments, like CDOs, at the same time they were rating these identical products. The rating agencies were thus subject to conflicts of interest, because the large fees they earned from advising clients on how to structure products that the agencies themselves were rating meant that they did not have sufficient incentives to make sure their ratings were accurate. The result was wildly inflated ratings that enabled the sale of complex financial products that were far riskier than investors recognized.

Effects of the 2007–2009 Financial Crisis

Consumers and businesses alike suffered as a result of the 2007–2009 financial crisis. The impact of the crisis was most evident in five key areas: the U.S. residential housing market, financial institutions' balance sheets, the shadow banking system, global financial markets, and the headline-grabbing failures of major firms in the financial industry.

Residential Housing Prices: Boom and Bust

Aided by liquidity from huge cash inflows into the United States from countries like China and India, and low interest rates on residential mortgages, the subprime mortgage market took off after the recession ended in 2001. By 2007, it had become over a trillion-dollar market. The development of the subprime mortgage market was actively encouraged by politicians because it led to a "democratization of credit" and helped raise U.S. homeownership rates to the highest levels in history.[4] The asset-price boom in housing (see Figure 15.5), which took off after the 2000–2001 recession ended, also helped stimulate the growth of the subprime mortgage market. High housing prices meant that subprime borrowers could refinance their houses with even larger loans when their homes appreciated in value. With housing prices rising, subprime borrowers were unlikely to default because they could always sell their house to pay off the loan, making investors happy because the securities backed by cash flows from subprime mortgages had high returns. The credit boom in the subprime mortgage market, in turn, increased the demand for houses and so fueled the boom in housing prices, resulting in a housing price bubble.

As housing prices rose and profitability for mortgage originators and lenders remained high, the underwriting standards for subprime mortgages fell to lower and lower standards. High-risk borrowers were able to obtain mortgages, and the amount of the mortgage relative

---

[4]For a discussion of the government's role in encouraging the boom which led to the bust in the housing market, see Thomas Sowell, *The Housing Boom and Bust*, Revised Edition (New York: Basic Books, 2010).

FIGURE 15.5

Housing Prices and the Financial Crisis of 2007–2009

Housing prices boomed from 2002 to 2006, fueling the market for subprime mortgages and forming an asset-price bubble. Housing prices began declining in 2006, falling by more than 30% subsequently, which led to defaults by subprime mortgage holders.

Source: Case-Shiller U.S. National Composite House Price Index. www.macromarkets.com/csi_housing/index.asp

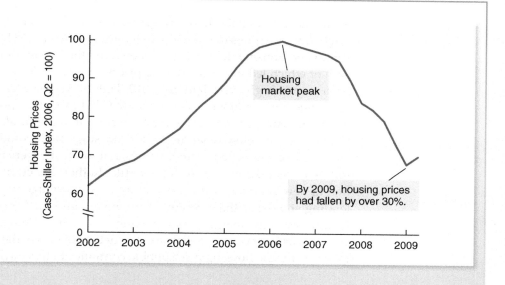

to the value of the house, the loan-to-value ratio (LTV), rose. Borrowers were often able to get piggyback, second, and third mortgages on top of their original 80% loan-to-value mortgage, so that they had to put almost no money down. When asset prices rise too far out of line with fundamentals—in the case of housing, how much housing costs if purchased relative to the cost of renting it, or the cost of houses relative to households' median income—they must come down. Eventually the housing price bubble burst, leading to a credit bust. With housing prices falling after their peak in 2006 (see Figure 15.5), the rot in the financial system began to be revealed. The decline in housing prices led to many subprime borrowers finding that their mortgages were "underwater"—that is, the value of the house fell below the amount of the mortgage. When this happened, struggling homeowners had tremendous incentives to walk away from their homes and just send the keys back to the lender. Defaults on mortgages shot up sharply, eventually leading to millions of mortgage foreclosures.

Policy and Practice

Was the Fed to Blame for the Housing Price Bubble?

Some economists—most prominently, John Taylor of Stanford University—have argued that the low rate interest policies of the Federal Reserve in the 2003–2006 period caused the housing price bubble.[5] During this period, the Federal Reserve relied on autonomous easing of monetary policy to set the federal funds rate well

[5]John Taylor, "Housing and Monetary Policy," in Federal Reserve Bank of Kansas City, *Housing, Housing Finance and Monetary Policy* (Kansas City: Federal Reserve Bank of Kansas City, 2007), 463–476.

below the level that the Taylor rule, discussed in Chapter 13, suggested was appropriate. Taylor argues that the low federal funds rate led to low mortgage rates that stimulated housing demand and encouraged the issuance of subprime mortgages, both of which led to rising housing prices and a bubble.

In a speech given in January 2010, Federal Reserve Chairman Ben Bernanke countered this argument.[6] He concluded that monetary policy was not to blame for the housing price bubble. First, he said, it is not at all clear that the federal funds rate was below what the Taylor rule suggested would be appropriate. Rates only seemed low when current values, not forecasts, were used in the output and inflation calculations for the Taylor rule. Rather, the culprits were the proliferation of new mortgage products that lowered mortgage payments, a relaxation of lending standards that brought more buyers into the housing market, and capital inflows from emerging-market countries such as China and India. Bernanke's speech was very controversial, and the debate over whether monetary policy was to blame for the housing price bubble continues to this day.

DETERIORATION OF FINANCIAL INSTITUTIONS' BALANCE SHEETS. The decline in U.S. housing prices led to rising defaults on mortgages. As a result, the value of mortgage-backed securities and CDOs collapsed, leading banks and other financial institutions to have a lower value of assets and thus a decline in net worth. With weakened balance sheets, these banks and other financial institutions began to deleverage, selling off assets and restricting the availability of credit to both households and businesses. With no one else able to step in to collect information and make loans, the reduction in bank lending meant that adverse selection and moral hazard problems increased in financial markets.

RUN ON THE SHADOW BANKING SYSTEM. The sharp decline in the value of mortgages and other financial assets triggered a run on the **shadow banking system,** comprised of hedge funds, investment banks, and other non-depository financial firms that are not as tightly regulated as banks. Funds from shadow banks flowed through the financial system and for many years supported the issuance of low-interest-rate mortgages and auto loans.

These securities were funded primarily by **repurchase agreements (repos),** or short-term borrowing agreements that, in effect, use assets such as mortgage-backed securities as collateral. Rising concern about the quality of a financial institution's balance sheet led lenders to require larger amounts of collateral, known as **haircuts.** For example, if a borrower took out a $100 million loan in a repo agreement, it might have to post $105 million of mortgage-backed securities as collateral, and the haircut is then 5%.

With rising defaults on mortgages, the value of mortgage-backed securities fell, which then led to a rise in haircuts. At the start of the crisis, haircuts were close to zero, but eventually rose to nearly 50%.[7] The result was that the same amount of collateral would only

---

[6]Ben S. Bernanke, "Monetary Policy and the Housing Bubble," speech given at the annual meeting of the American Economic Association, Atlanta, Georgia, January 3, 2010, www.federalreserve.gov/newsevents/speech/bernanke20100103a.htm

[7]See Gary Gorton and Andrew Metrick, "Securitized Banking and the Run on Repo," National Bureau of Economic Research Working Paper No. 15223 (August 2009).

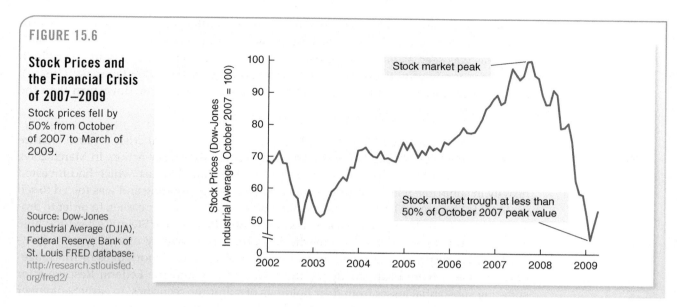

FIGURE 15.6

Stock Prices and the Financial Crisis of 2007–2009

Stock prices fell by 50% from October of 2007 to March of 2009.

Source: Dow-Jones Industrial Average (DJIA), Federal Reserve Bank of St. Louis FRED database; http://research.stlouisfed.org/fred2/

allow financial institutions to borrow half as much. Thus, in order to raise funds, financial institutions had to engage in fire sales and sell off their assets very quickly. Because selling assets quickly requires lowering their price, the fire sales led to a further decline in financial institutions' asset values. This lowered the value of collateral further, raising haircuts and thereby forcing financial institutions to scramble even more for liquidity. The result was similar to the run on the banking system that occurred during the Great Depression, causing a restriction of lending and a decline in economic activity.

The decline in asset prices in the stock market (which fell by over 50% from October 2007 to March 2009, as shown in Figure 15.6) and the more than 30% drop in residential house prices (shown in Figure 15.5), along with the fire sales resulting from the run on the shadow banking system, weakened both firms' and households' balance sheets. This worsening of asymmetric information problems manifested itself in widening credit spreads, causing higher costs of credit for households and businesses and tighter lending standards. The resulting decline in lending meant that both consumption expenditure and investment fell, causing aggregate demand to contract, leading to a decline in output and inflation along the lines we outlined in Figure 15.2.

GLOBAL FINANCIAL MARKETS. Although the problem originated in the United States, the wake-up call for the financial crisis came from Europe, a sign of how extensive the globalization of financial markets had become. After Fitch and Standard & Poor's announced ratings downgrades on mortgage-backed securities and CDOs totaling more than $10 billion, on August 7, 2007, a French investment house, BNP Paribas, suspended redemption of shares held in some of its money market funds that had sustained large losses. The run on the shadow banking system began, only to become worse and worse over time. Despite huge injections of liquidity into the financial system by the European Central Bank and the Federal Reserve, discussed later in this chapter, banks began to hoard cash and were unwilling to lend to each other. The drying up of credit led to the first major bank failure in the United Kingdom in over 100 years when Northern Rock, which had relied on short-term borrowing in the repo market rather than deposits for its funding, collapsed in September 2007. A string of other European financial institutions then failed as well. Particularly hard hit were countries like Ireland, which up until this crisis was seen as one of the most successful countries in Europe with a very high rate of economic growth (see the box, "Ireland and the 2007–2009 Financial Crisis"). European countries actually experienced a more severe economic downturn than the United States.

FAILURE OF HIGH-PROFILE FIRMS. The impact of the financial crisis on firm balance sheets forced major players in the financial markets to take drastic action. In March 2008, Bear Stearns, the fifth-largest investment bank in the United States, which had invested heavily in subprime related securities, had a run on its repo funding and was forced to sell itself to J.P. Morgan for less than 5% of what it was worth just a year earlier. In order to broker the deal, the Federal Reserve had to take over $30 billion of Bear Stearns's hard-to-value assets. In July, Fannie Mae and Freddie Mac, the two privately owned government-sponsored enterprises that together insured over $5 trillion of mortgages or mortgage-backed assets, were propped up by the U.S. Treasury and the Federal Reserve after suffering substantial losses from their holdings of subprime securities. In early September 2008, they were then put into conservatorship (in effect, run by the government).

Ireland and the 2007–2009 Financial Crisis

From 1995 to 2007, Ireland had one of the highest economic growth rates in the world, with real GDP growing at an average annual rate of 6.3%. As a result, Ireland earned the title the "Celtic Tiger," and it became one of Europe's wealthiest nations, with more Mercedes owners per capita than even Germany. But behind the scenes, soaring real estate prices and a boom in mortgage lending were laying the groundwork for a major financial crisis that hit in 2008, sending the Irish economy into a severe recession.

Irish banks eased loan standards, offering to cover a greater share of housing costs and at longer terms. As in the United States, there was a housing price bubble, with Irish home values rising even more rapidly, doubling once between 1995 and 2000, and then again from 2000 to 2007. By 2007, residential construction reached 13% of GDP, twice the average of other wealthy nations, with Irish banks increasing their mortgage loans by 25% a year.

With the onset of the financial crisis in late 2007, home prices collapsed—falling nearly 20%, among the steepest housing price declines in the world. Irish banks were particularly vulnerable because of their exposure to mortgage markets and because they had funded their balance sheet expansions through short-term borrowing in the repo market. The combination of tighter funding and falling asset prices led to large losses, and in October 2008, the Irish government guaranteed all deposits. By early 2009, the government had nationalized one of the three largest banks and injected capital into the other two. Banks remained weak, with the government announcing a plan to shift "toxic" bank assets into a government-funding vehicle.

The financial crisis in Ireland triggered a painful recession, among the worst in modern Irish history. Unemployment rose from 4.5% pre-crisis to over 12%, while GDP levels tumbled by more than 10%. Tax rolls thinned and losses in the banking sector continued to escalate, leading to an astronomical government budget deficit of over 30% of GDP in 2010. In dire straights, Ireland suffered the humiliation of having to be bailed out by the European Union and the International Monetary Fund.

On Monday, September 15, 2008, after suffering losses in the subprime market, Lehman Brothers, the fourth-largest investment bank by asset size with over $600 billion in assets and 25,000 employees, filed for bankruptcy, making it the largest bankruptcy filing in U.S. history. The day before, Merrill Lynch, the third-largest investment bank, which also suffered large losses on its holding of subprime securities, announced its sale to Bank of America for a price 60% below its value a year earlier. On Tuesday, September 16, AIG, an insurance giant with assets over $1 trillion, suffered an extreme liquidity crisis when its credit rating was downgraded. It had written over $400 billion of insurance contracts (credit default swaps) that had to make payouts on possible losses from subprime mortgage securities. The Federal Reserve then stepped in with an $85 billion loan to keep AIG afloat (with total government loans later increased to $173 billion).

Height of the 2007–2009 Financial Crisis

The financial crisis reached its peak in September 2008 after the House of Representatives, fearing the wrath of constituents who were angry about bailing out Wall Street, voted down a $700 billion dollar bailout package proposed by the Bush administration. The Emergency Economic Stabilization Act finally passed nearly a week later. The stock market crash accelerated, with the week beginning October 6, 2008, showing the worst weekly decline in U.S. history. Credit spreads went through the roof over the next three weeks, with the spread between Baa corporate bonds (just above investment grade) and U.S. Treasury bonds rising to over 5.5 percentage points (550 basis points), as illustrated by Figure 15.7.

The impaired financial markets and surging interest rates faced by borrower-spenders led to sharp declines in consumer spending and investment. As suggested by the aggregate demand and supply analysis we conducted in Figure 15.2, both output and inflation fell even further, with the economy moving from point 2 to point 3. Real GDP declined sharply, falling at a −1.3% annual rate in the third quarter of 2008 and then at a −5.4% and −6.4% annual rate in the next two quarters. The unemployment rate shot up,

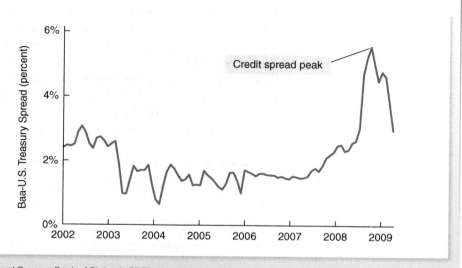

FIGURE 15.7

Credit Spreads and the 2007–2009 Financial Crisis

Credit spreads (the difference between rates on Baa corporate bonds and U.S. Treasury bonds) rose by more than four percentage points (400 basis points) during the crisis. Debate over the bailout package and the stock market crash caused credit spreads to peak in December 2008.

Source: Federal Reserve Bank of St. Louis FRED database. http://research.stlouisfed.org/fred2/

going over the 10% level in late 2009. The recession that started in December 2007 became the worst economic contraction in the United States since World War II. Given the resulting slack in the economy, inflation then fell, even going negative for a brief time in 2009.

Starting in March 2009, a bull market in stocks got underway (see Figure 15.6), and credit spreads began to fall (Figure 15.7).[8] With the recovery in financial markets, aggregate demand began to increase and aggregate output and inflation began to rise.

Why the 2007–2009 Financial Crisis Did Not Lead to a Depression

Although the recession produced by the financial crisis that started in August 2007 was very severe, the economy did not experience the extreme decreases in aggregate demand that occurred during the Great Depression period. Why was the economic contraction and decline in inflation so much less severe in the 2007–2009 crisis than in the Great Depression? The answer is that the U.S. government and the Federal Reserve did not sit idly by as they did during the Great Depression period. Massive government intervention in the financial markets, both in the United States and abroad, propped up financial markets and stimulated aggregate demand.

Aggressive Federal Reserve Actions

During the 2007–2009 financial crisis, the Federal Reserve took extraordinary actions, involving both monetary policy and liquidity provision, to contain the crisis.

CONVENTIONAL MONETARY POLICY. The Federal Reserve's proactive policies were central to containing the crisis. When the financial crisis hit in August 2007, the U.S. economy was growing strongly. Recognizing the contractionary effects of financial crises, the Federal Reserve and its chairman, Ben Bernanke, undertook autonomous easing of monetary policy by lowering the federal funds rate target by half a percentage point, from 5.25% to 4.75%, despite rising inflation, as shown in Figure 15.8. This downward shift in the monetary policy curve led to a decrease in real interest rates at any given inflation rate, which would increase aggregate demand and shift the aggregate demand curve to the right. This monetary policy action was highly unusual given the strong economy and rising inflation: in the past, the Federal Reserve had typically started an easing cycle only when economic growth slowed substantially or the economy had already entered a recession.

At the October and December FOMC meetings, the Federal Reserve cut the target federal funds rate by a quarter of a percentage point each time. When the financial crisis worsened, the Fed cut the federal funds rate even more aggressively, lowering it by one

---

[8]The financial market recovery was aided by the U.S. Treasury's requirement, announced in February 2009, that the nineteen largest banking institutions undergo what became known as the *bank stress tests* (the Supervisory Capital Assessment Program or SCAP). The stress tests were a supervisory assessment, led by the Federal Reserve in cooperation with the Office of the Comptroller of the Currency and the FDIC, of the balance sheet position of these banks to ensure that they had sufficient capital to withstand bad macroeconomic outcomes. The Treasury announced the results in early May and they were well received by market participants, allowing these banks to raise substantial amounts of capital from private capital markets. The stress tests were a key factor that helped increase the amount of information in the marketplace and strengthened financial institutions' balance sheets, thereby reducing asymmetric information and adverse selection and moral hazard problems.

MyEconLab Real-time data

FIGURE 15.8

Federal Reserve Policy Rate During the 2007–2009 Financial Crisis

The Federal Reserve started lowering its federal funds rate in response to the crisis in August 2007, with the federal funds rate eventually reaching zero in December 2008.

Source: Federal Reserve Board. www.federalreserve.gov/fomc/fundsrate.htm

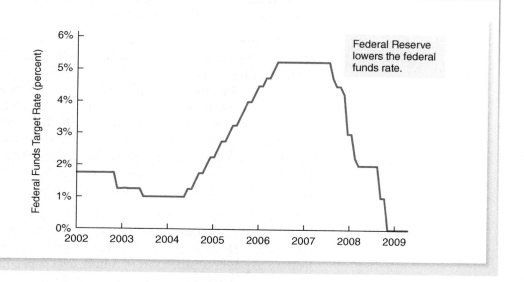

and a quarter percentage points in January alone. The Fed then kept lowering the federal funds rate target steadily, to the 2% level in April 2008. In the aftermath of the Lehman Brothers failure, the Fed became even more aggressive in lowering interest rates and finally, in December 2008, set a target range for the federal funds rate of 0 to 0.25%. Now the federal funds rate could go no lower because it had hit the *zero lower bound*.

NONCONVENTIONAL MONETARY POLICY. The contractionary effects of the financial crisis continued, requiring further stimulation of aggregate demand, but the federal funds policy rate had already hit the zero lower bound. Without being able to lower the federal funds rate further, the Fed had to resort to the nonconventional monetary policy tools we discussed in Chapter 13 to stimulate the economy. The details of the actual measures used by the Fed are described in the following Policy and Practice case.

Policy and Practice

The Federal Reserve's Nonconventional Monetary Policies and Quantitative Easing During the Global Financial Crisis

Liquidity Provision

During the crisis, the Federal Reserve implemented unprecedented increases in its lending facilities to provide liquidity to the financial markets.

1. *Discount Window Expansion*: At the outset of the crisis in mid-August 2007, the Fed lowered the discount rate (the interest rate on loans it makes to banks) from the normal 100 basis points to 50 basis points (0.50 percentage point) above the federal funds rate target. It then

lowered the discount rate further in March 2008, to only 25 basis points above the federal funds rate target.

2. *Term Auction Facility:* To encourage additional borrowing, the Fed set up a temporary Term Auction Facility (TAF) in which it made loans at a rate determined through competitive auctions. It was more widely used than the discount window facility because it enabled banks to borrow at a competitively determined rate less than the discount rate, rather than at a penalty rate. The TAF auctions started at amounts of $20 billion, but as the crisis worsened, the Fed raised the amounts dramatically, with a total outstanding of over $400 billion. (The European Central Bank conducted similar operations, with one auction in June of 2008 of over 400 billion euros.)

3. *New Lending Programs:* The Fed broadened its provision of liquidity to the financial system well outside of its traditional lending to banking institutions. These actions included lending to investment banks and lending to promote purchases of commercial paper, mortgage backed-securities, and other asset-backed securities. In addition, the Fed engaged in lending to AIG to prevent its failure. The enlargement of the Fed's lending programs during the 2007–2009 financial crisis was indeed remarkable, expanding the Fed's balance sheet by over one trillion dollars by the end of 2008, with the balance-sheet expansion continuing into 2009.

Asset Purchases (Quantitative Easing)

The Fed's open market operations normally involve only purchase of government securities, particularly those that are short-term. However, during the crisis, the Fed started two new asset-purchase programs to lower interest rates for particular types of credit.

1. In November 2008, the Fed set up a Government Sponsored Entities Purchase Program in which the Fed eventually purchased $1.25 trillion of mortgage-backed securities (MBS) guaranteed by Fannie Mae and Freddie Mac. Through these purchases, the Fed hoped to prop up the MBS market and to lower interest rates on residential mortgages to stimulate the housing market.

2. In November 2010, the Fed announced that it would purchase $600 billion of long-term Treasury securities at a rate of about $75 billion per month. This purchase program, which became known as *QE2* (which stands for Quantitative Easing 2, not the Cunard cruise ship), was intended to lower long-term interest rates. Although *short-term* interest rates on Treasury securities hit a floor of zero during the global financial crisis, *long-term* interest rates did not. Since investment projects have a long life, long-term interest rates are more

relevant than short-term ones to investment decisions. The Fed's purchase of long-term Treasuries to lower long-term interest rates could therefore help stimulate investment spending and the economy.

3. In September 2012, the Federal Reserve announced a third asset-purchase program, which has become known as QE3, which combined elements of QE1 and QE2 by conducting monthly purchases of $40 billion of mortgage-backed securities and $45 billion of long-term Treasuries. However, QE3 differed in one major way from the previous QE programs in that it was not for a fixed dollar amount but instead was open-ended, with the purchase plan continuing "if the outlook for the labor market does not improve substantially."

These programs of liquidity provision and asset purchases resulted in an unprecedented quadrupling of the Federal Reserve's balance sheet (shown in Figure 15.9).

Management of Expectations: Commitment to Future Policy Actions

Although short-term interest rates could not be driven below zero in the aftermath of the global financial crisis, the Federal Reserve could take another route: it

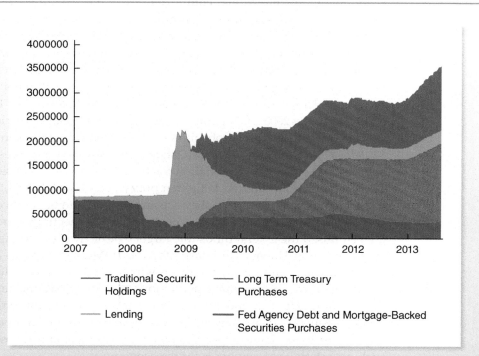

FIGURE 15.9

Expansion of the Federal Reserve's Balance Sheet During and After the Global Financial Crisis

Each shaded area shows the Federal Reserve's holdings of four different categories of assets: traditional security holdings, long-term Treasuries, lending, and agency debt and mortgage-backed securities. The Federal Reserve's lending and asset-purchase programs have resulted in a quadrupling of the Fed's balance sheet.

Traditional Security Holdings

Lending

Long Term Treasury Purchases

Fed Agency Debt and Mortgage-Backed Securities Purchases

Source: Federal Reserve Bank of Cleveland. www.clevelandfed.org/research/data/redit_easing/index.cfm

could lower long-term interest rates to stimulate the economy. This route involved a commitment by the Fed to keep the federal funds rate at zero for a long period of time in order to lower the market's expectations for future short-term interest rates, thereby causing the long-term interest rate to fall. As we saw in Chapter 13, this strategy is referred to as *management of expectations.*

The Fed pursued this strategy when it announced, after its FOMC meeting on December 16, 2008, that it would not only lower the federal funds rate target to between 0 and ¼%, but also that "the Committee anticipates that weak economic conditions are likely to warrant exceptionally low levels of the federal funds rate for some time." The Fed continued to use this language in its FOMC statements for several years afterward, and then moved to announcing specific dates, eventually stating that "the exceptionally low levels of the federal funds rate are likely to be warranted until mid-2015." Although long-term interest rates on Treasury securities did subsequently fall with these announcements, it is not clear how much of this decline was due to the Fed's attempt to manage expectations versus weakness in the economy.

There are two types of commitments to future policy actions: *conditional* and *unconditional*. The commitment to keep the federal funds rate at zero for an extended period starting in 2008 was *conditional* because the Fed mentioned that the decision was predicated on a weak economy going forward. The FOMC was indicating that it might abandon the commitment if economic circumstances changed. Alternatively, the Fed could have made an *unconditional* commitment by stating that it would keep the federal funds rate at zero for an extended period without indicating that this decision would be based on the future state of the economy. An unconditional commitment has the advantage of being stronger than a conditional commitment because it does not suggest that the commitment will be abandoned, and so it is likely to have a larger effect on long-term interest rates. Unfortunately, it has the disadvantage that even if circumstances change in such a way that it would be better to abandon the commitment, the Fed may feel that it cannot go back on its word, and so the rate will remain unchanged.

The problem of an unconditional commitment is illustrated by the Fed's experience during the 2003–2006 period. In 2003, the Fed became worried that inflation was too low and that the probability of a deflation was significant. At the August 12, 2003, FOMC meeting, the FOMC stated, "In these circumstances, the Committee believes that policy accommodation can be maintained for a considerable period." Then, when the Fed started to tighten policy at its June 30, 2004, FOMC meeting, it changed its statement to "policy accommodation can be removed at a pace that is likely to be measured." For the next ten FOMC meetings, through June 2006, the Fed raised the federal funds rate target by exactly ¼ percentage point at every single meeting. The market interpreted the FOMC's statements as indicating an unconditional commitment, and this is why the Fed may have felt constrained not to deviate from a ¼ percentage point move at every FOMC meeting. In retrospect, this commitment led to monetary policy that was too easy for too long, with inflation subsequently rising to well above desirable levels and, as discussed earlier in the chapter, it may have helped promote the housing bubble whose bursting led to such devastating consequences for the economy.

When the Fed announced a specific date for exiting from exceptionally low rates, many market participants viewed this announcement as an unconditional commitment, despite the Federal Reserve's objections. To avoid the problems associated with an unconditional commitment, in December of 2012 the Fed changed its statement to a more clearly conditional statement by indicating that "the exceptionally low range for the federal funds rate will be appropriate at least as long as the unemployment rate remains above 6-1/2 percent, inflation between one and two years ahead is projected to be no more than a half percentage point above the Committee's 2 percent longer-run goal." Although an improvement over the fixed-date commitment, this conditional approach based on thresholds is not without its problems. First, it may be viewed as a Federal Reserve commitment to achieve a specific unemployment rate regardless of the monetary stimulus required to reach it. As we saw in Chapter 13, it was exactly this kind of commitment that got the Fed into trouble in the 1970s and produced the escalation in inflation that became known as the "Great Inflation." Second, this approach could be viewed as an attempt to increase the inflation target from 2% to 2.5% or as a weakening of the Federal Reserve's credibility regarding its commitment to keeping inflation low and stable. As we will see in Chapter 21, this loss of credibility can result in poor outcomes when attempting to stabilize inflation and economic activity.

Worldwide Government Intervention Through Bailouts

The U.S. government's active role in providing liquidity to financial institutions was critical to the continued running of the financial system during the 2007–2009 financial crisis. The cross-country coordination of similar efforts was a key factor in containing the impact of the financial crisis on the global economy.

Congress passed the Bush administration's Economic Recovery Act of 2008 in October 2008. Its most important provision was the creation of the Treasury Asset Relief Plan (TARP), which authorized the Treasury to spend $700 billion purchasing subprime mortgage assets from troubled financial institutions or to inject capital into banking institutions. In addition, the Act raised the federal deposit insurance limit temporarily, from $100,000 to $250,000, in order to limit withdrawals from banks. Shortly thereafter, the FDIC put in place a guarantee for certain types of debt newly issued by banks, and the Treasury guaranteed for a year money market mutual fund shares at par value.

The spreading bank failures in Europe in the fall of 2008 led to bailouts of financial institutions, as we detail in Table 15.1. Both the scale of these bailout packages, which were in excess of $10 trillion and involved over twenty countries, and the degree of international coordination were unprecedented.

Aggressive Fiscal Policy

Fiscal stimulus to directly increase aggregate demand was another key piece of the U.S. government's response to the crisis. In February 2008, Congress passed the Bush administration's Economic Stimulus Act of 2008 to increase aggregate demand. The legislation gave out one-time tax rebates totaling $78 billion by sending individual taxpayers $600 checks in the second quarter of the year. However, as we will discuss in Chapter 16, the impact of this fiscal stimulus appears to have been quite small.

TABLE 15.1	**WORLDWIDE GOVERNMENT BAILOUTS DURING THE 2007–2009 FINANCIAL CRISIS**
Country	**Government Bailout Action**
France	Provided $400 billion to guarantee bank debt and inject capital into financial system
Germany	Provided $50 billion to Hypo Real Estate Holdings and $500 billion to guarantee bank debt and inject capital into financial system
Greece	Guaranteed all commercial banks and interbank lending
Iceland	Took over country's three largest banks
Ireland	Guaranteed all commercial banks and interbank lending
Netherlands, Belgium, Luxembourg	Provided $16 billion to European bank Fortis
Netherlands	Provided $13 billion to ING, banking and insurance giant
South Korea	Provided $100 billion to guarantee bank debt and inject capital into financial system
Spain	Provided $70 billion to banks
Sweden	Provided $200 billion to guarantee bank debt and inject capital into financial system
Switzerland	Provided $65 billion to UBS, a top-ten bank worldwide
UK	Provided $600 billion to guarantee bank liabilities, fund asset swaps with government bonds, and fund equity stakes in banks

The Obama administration proposed a much bigger $787 billion fiscal stimulus package, which resulted in the American Recovery and Reinvestment Act of 2009 (see Chapter 13). The plan featured $288 billion of tax cuts and $499 billion in government spending increases. The fiscal stimulus surely helped stimulate aggregate demand, but because most of the additional government spending did not go into effect until 2010, its overall impact during the financial crisis period was limited. Most economists believe that the actions of the Federal Reserve and the U.S. Treasury bailouts of the banking system were far more important than fiscal policy in preventing the financial crisis from sending the economy into a depression.

The following Policy and Practice case, which describes Japan's economy from 1992 to 2002, illustrates the consequences when government policy makers do not take aggressive actions to contain a financial crisis.

Policy and Practice

Japan's Lost Decade, 1992–2002

In the early 1990s, Japan seemed poised to overtake the United States as the world's richest country. The average Japanese earned 86% of the typical U.S. worker's income in 1991, up from 73% in 1981. But Japan's economic momentum was squandered over the rest of the 1990s, with GDP growing only 1% a year. The story of Japan's "lost decade" offers a timely lesson in the dangers of underestimating the magnitude of problems in the financial sector.

Japan experienced a major banking crisis in 1992 that slowed the economy and reduced inflation. Rather than shuttering insolvent banks and providing sufficient capital to surviving financial institutions, as our framework for analyzing financial crises suggests, the banking regulators in Japan's Ministry of Finance instead followed a path of *regulatory forbearance*. The government permitted insolvent banks to artificially inflate the value of their assets so as to appear sound, valuing holdings of stocks at levels that were much higher than historical levels. With regulators' acquiescence, banks acted as if loans to insolvent "zombie firms" would be repaid. The government also allocated too little money to properly recapitalizing the banking system.[9]

Not surprisingly, economic growth ground to a halt and inflation dropped. Deflation struck in 1995 and 1996, returning again in 1998 and lingering for several more years. The crisis subsided in 2003, when the Japanese government finally addressed its broken banking system. By then, the damage had been done: in 2003, per capita income in Japan had fallen back to 74% of U.S. levels.

Policy Response to Asset-Price Bubbles

Asset-price bubbles have been a feature of economies for hundreds of years.[10] One of the lessons we learned from our discussion of the 2007–2009 financial crisis is how costly asset-price bubbles can be. When the asset-price bubble in the housing market popped, it severely hampered the flow of funds in the financial system, leading to an economic downturn, a rise in unemployment, and personal hardship in communities and families who were forced to leave their homes after foreclosures. The high cost of asset-price bubbles raises the following question: what policy measures should policy makers use to address them in the future? To answer this question, we first need to identify the different kinds of bubbles and appropriate policy responses.

Types of Asset-Price Bubbles

There are two types of asset-price bubbles: ones that are driven by credit and others that are driven purely by overly optimistic expectations.

---

[9]Regulatory forbearance is a common phenomenon that was also practiced in the United States during the savings and loan crisis of the 1980s. For a discussion of why regulatory forbearance occurs and why it happened in the United States, see the Web appendix to Chapter 11, "The Savings and Loan Crisis and its Aftermath," in Frederic S. Mishkin, *The Economics of Money, Banking, and Financial Markets*, 10th edition (Boston: Pearson Addison-Wesley, 2013), which can be found on the Companion Website to that book at http://wps.aw.com/bp_mishkin_econmbfm_10/. For a discussion of the Japanese government's regulatory forbearance and the shift in its policies in 2003, see Takeo Hoshi and Anil Kashyap, "Will the U.S. Bank Recapitalization Succeed? Eight Lessons from Japan." NBER Working Paper No. 14401 (2009), *Journal of Financial Economics*, September 2010, vol. 97(3), pp. 398–417.

[10]For a classic history of asset-price bubbles and financial crises, see Charles P. Kindleberger, *Manias, Panics, and Crashes: A History of Financial Crises*, 5th edition (New York: Wiley, 2005).

CREDIT-DRIVEN BUBBLES. When a credit boom begins, it can lead to an asset-price bubble because individuals and firms can use the widely available credit to purchase particular assets and thereby raise their prices. The rise in asset values in turn encourages further lending to purchase these assets, both because it increases the value of collateral, making it easier to borrow, and because it raises the value of capital at financial institutions, which improves their balance sheet positions and gives them more capacity to lend. The lending available for these assets then can increase demand for them further and hence raise their prices even more. This feedback loop—wherein a credit boom drives up asset prices, which in turn further fuels the credit boom, driving asset prices higher, and so on—can generate a bubble in which asset prices rise well above their fundamental values.

Credit-driven bubbles are particularly dangerous, as the recent financial crisis demonstrated via the housing market. When the bubble bursts, the collapse in asset prices then leads to a reversal of the feedback loop: loans go sour, lenders cut back on credit supply, the demand for assets declines further, and asset prices drop even more.

OPTIMISTIC EXPECTATIONS ("IRRATIONAL EXUBERANCE")-DRIVEN BUBBLES. In contrast, bubbles that are driven solely by overly optimistic expectations, which Alan Greenspan dubbed "irrational exuberance," pose much less risk to the financial system than credit-driven bubbles. For example, the bubble in technology stocks in the late 1990s was not fueled by credit, and the bursting of the tech-stock bubble did not deteriorate financial institutions' balance sheets. The bursting of the tech-stock bubble thus did not have a very severe impact on the economy, and the recession that followed was quite mild.

Policy and Practice

Debate Over Central Bank Response to Bubbles

Under Alan Greenspan, the Federal Reserve Chairman until 2006, the Fed took a strong position indicating that it should not respond to asset-price bubbles that were driven by irrational exuberance, as is often the case with bubbles in the stock market. Greenspan argued that such bubbles are nearly impossible to identify. If central banks or government officials know that a bubble is in progress, why wouldn't market participants know as well? If they did know, then a bubble would be unlikely to fully develop, because market participants would know that asset prices were above their fundamental economic values and so they would not buy the assets. Unless central banks or government officials are more knowledgeable than market participants, which is unlikely given the especially high wages that market participants garner, they will be unlikely to identify bubbles of this type when they are occurring.

In the aftermath of the 2007–2009 financial crisis, both central bankers and academic economists challenged Greenspan's position, leading to an active debate on what central banks should do about asset-price bubbles. Those who disagree with Greenspan argue that when asset-price bubbles are rising rapidly at the same time that credit is booming, there is a greater likelihood that asset prices are deviating from their fundamental values. In this case, central bank or government officials have a greater likelihood than market participants of ascertaining that a bubble is in progress. This was indeed the case during the U.S. housing market bubble: government officials had information that financial institutions had weakened lending standards and that credit extension in the mortgage markets was rising at abnormally high rates. Credit-driven bubbles do seem possible to identify, and they are capable of doing serious damage to the economy if left unrestrained.

There is thus a strong case that central banks should respond to possible credit-driven bubbles—but what is the best policy response? There are three strong arguments against using autonomous tightening of monetary policy to pop credit-driven asset-price bubbles.

1. Higher real interest rates have highly uncertain effects on credit-driven asset-price bubbles. On the one hand, higher real interest rates can be ineffective in restraining the bubble when market participants continue to expect high rates of return from buying bubble-driven assets. On the other hand, if higher real interest rates succeed in bursting the bubble, it can unleash major damage on the economy, as occurred in 1929.

2. The blunt tool of monetary policy tends to push many asset prices lower, even when a bubble may be present in only a small fraction of assets.

3. To prick a bubble, real interest rates might need to rise to such a high level that the decline in aggregate demand and the resulting economic contraction would create much hardship, as jobs are lost and inflation falls below a desirable level.

Although the preceding reasoning suggests that monetary policy should not be used to prick bubbles, as has been argued by Ben Bernanke and other high officials at the Federal Reserve, there are contrary views in both academia and central banks.[11] If asset-price bubbles are so costly, and autonomous tightening of monetary policy can help restrain them, then a case can be made for a response by monetary policy to contain them.[12]

---

[11]For example, see the panel discussion in *Monetary Policy: A Journey from Theory to Practice* (Frankfurt; European Central Bank, March 16–17, 2006); William Dudley, "Asset Bubbles and the Implications for Central Bank Policy" (speech, Economic Club of New York, April, 7, 2010), http://www.newyorkfed.org/newsevents/speeches/2010/dud100407.html; and Tobias Adrian, Arturo Estrella, and Hyun Song Shin, "Monetary Cycles, Financial Cycles, and the Business Cycle," Federal Reserve Bank of New York, *Staff Reports*, No. 421 (2010).

[12]Note that even if it is unwise to use monetary policy to contain asset price bubbles, there is still a strong reason for monetary policy to respond to fluctuations in asset prices in order to stabilize the economy. The level of asset prices does affect aggregate demand (discussed in more detail in Chapters 18 and 19 on consumption and investment) and thus the evolution of the economy. Monetary policy should react to fluctuations in asset prices to the extent that they affect inflation and economic activity.

Regulatory Policy Responses to Asset Bubbles

Regulatory policy to affect what is happening in credit markets in the aggregate, referred to as **macroprudential regulation**, is a less controversial option than autonomous tightening of monetary policy for addressing asset-price bubbles.

Financial regulation and supervision on an ongoing basis, either by central banks or other government entities, can prevent the excessive risk-taking that can directly trigger a credit boom, which in turn leads to credit-driven asset-price bubbles. When a rapid rise in asset prices accompanied by a credit boom provides a signal that a bubble might be forming, central banks and other government regulators could then consider implementing policies to reign in credit growth directly or implementing measures to make sure credit standards are sufficiently high. Appropriate macroprudential regulation can then help limit credit-driven bubbles and improve the performance of both the financial system and the economy.[13]

---

[13]For a more extensive discussion of the types of regulatory and supervisory measures that can be used to restrain asset-price bubbles, see Chapters 11 and 16 of Frederic S. Mishkin, *The Economics of Money, Banking, and Financial Markets*, 10th Edition (Boston: Pearson Addison-Wesley, 2013).

SUMMARY

1. A financial crisis occurs when a disruption in the financial system causes an increase in asymmetric information that makes adverse selection and moral hazard problems far more severe, thereby rendering financial markets incapable of channeling funds to households and firms with productive investment opportunities, and causing a sharp contraction in economic activity.

2. There are several possible ways that financial crises can start in advanced countries like the United States: credit and asset-price booms and busts or a general increase in uncertainty when there are failures of major financial institutions. The result is a substantial increase in adverse selection and moral hazard problems that leads to a contraction of lending and a decline in economic activity. The worsening business conditions and deterioration in bank balance sheets then trigger the second stage of the crisis, the simultaneous failure of many banking institutions, a banking crisis. The resulting decline in the number of banks causes a loss of their information capital, leading to a further decline of lending and a spiraling down of the economy. In some instances, the resulting economic downturn leads to a sharp decline of prices, which increases the real liabilities of firms and households and there-fore lowers their net worth, leading to a debt deflation. The further decline in borrowers' net worth worsens adverse selection and moral hazard problems, so that lending, investment spending, and aggregate economic activity remain depressed for a long time.

3. The most significant financial crisis in U.S. history, that which led to the Great Depression, involved several stages: a stock market crash, bank panics, worsening of asymmetric information problems, and finally a debt deflation.

4. The financial crisis of 2007–2009 was triggered by mismanagement of financial innovations involving subprime residential mortgages and the bursting of a housing price bubble. The crisis spread globally with substantial deterioration in banks' and other financial institutions' balance sheets, a run on the shadow banking system, and the failure of many high-profile firms.

5. The 2007–2009 financial crisis did not lead to a depression because of aggressive Federal Reserve actions, worldwide government intervention through bailouts of financial institutions, and aggressive fiscal policy.

6. The role of the asset-price boom and bust in causing the crisis has led to an active debate about how central banks should respond to asset-price bubbles.

KEY TERMS

agency problem, p. 401
agency theory, p. 392
asset-price bubble, p. 395
bank panic, p. 396
credit boom, p. 393
credit default swaps, p. 401
credit spread, p. 392
debt deflation, p. 397
deleveraging, p. 393
financial crisis, p. 392

financial engineering, p. 400
financial innovation, p. 393
financial liberalization, p. 393
fire sales, p. 396
fundamental economic values, p. 394
haircuts, p. 404
leverage cycle, p. 393
macroprudential regulation, p. 418

mortgage-backed securities, p. 400
originate-to-distribute, p. 401
principal-agent problem, p. 401
repurchase agreements (repos), p. 404
securitization, p. 400
shadow banking system, p. 404
structured credit products, p. 400
subprime mortgages, p. 400

REVIEW QUESTIONS

All Questions are available in MyEconLab *for practice or instructor assignment.*

Asymmetric Information and Financial Crises

1. How does asymmetric information help us define a financial crisis?

Dynamics of Financial Crises

2. Why is a financial crisis likely to lead to a contraction in economic activity?
3. Describe the three factors that commonly initiate financial crises, and explain how each one contributes to a crisis.

4. What causes bank panics and why do they worsen financial crises?
5. Why does debt deflation make financial crises worse?

The Mother of All Financial Crises: The Great Depression

6. What is a credit spread? Why do credit spreads rise during financial crises?

The 2007–2009 Financial Crisis

7. How did financial innovations in mortgage markets contribute to the 2007–2009 financial crisis?

8. What principal-agent problems resulted from the originate-to-distribute mortgage lending model?

Why the 2007–2009 Financial Crisis Did Not Lead to a Depression

9. What prevented the financial crisis of 2007–2009 from becoming a depression?

Policy Response to Asset-Price Bubbles

10. What are the two types of asset-price bubbles? Which type poses a bigger threat to the financial system? Why?

11. How should central banks respond to asset-price bubbles?

PROBLEMS

All Problems are available in MyEconLab *for practice or instructor assignment.*

Asymmetric Information and Financial Crises

1. Suppose you are about to buy a car and ask to see a vehicle history report to check on previous accidents or problems reported for that car. When you are told that this information is not available, you decide not to buy the car.

a) Do you think this example illustrates an adverse selection or moral hazard problem?
b) What is the connection between the lack of information and the probability that a transaction will occur?

Dynamics of Financial Crises

2. The following figure, from the Federal Reserve Monetary Policy Report to the Congress (July 21, 2009), shows the gross issuance of mortgage-backed securities (MBS) in the United States from 2007 to the second quarter of 2009. Comment on the drastic changes in the gross issuance of MBS in the United States during this period.

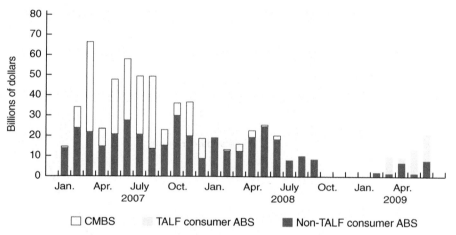

Source: Bajaj, Vikas. 2007. Home prices fall in more than half of nation's biggest markets. *New York Times*, February 16. www.nytimes.com/2007/02/16/business/16home.html

3. As the effects of the 2007–2009 financial crisis became more pervasive, legislators and policy makers debated about the role played by the Federal Reserve as a regulatory agency. While the Federal Reserve argued for more regulatory oversight of the financial system, some policy makers wanted to remove these powers from the Federal Reserve, claiming it had failed to act as a proper regulator. Using the concept of asymmetric information, explain why the debate was centered around financial system regulations. Do you think the Federal Reserve failed in its attempt to properly enforce regulations that were current at the time?

4. According to the FDIC, thirty banks failed or were assisted during 2008: six were based in California, two in Florida, and five in Nevada. The *New York Times* reported in 2007 that Nevada (-36.1%), Florida (-30.8%), and California (-21.3%) were among the top five states in which home sales dropped (percentage drops in sales are given in parentheses) the most between the fourth quarter of 2005 until the fourth quarter of 2006. Explain how real estate market conditions in these areas can explain almost 50% of bank failures in 2008.

5. The following figure, from the Federal Reserve Monetary Policy Report to the Congress (July 21, 2009), shows mortgage delinquency rates from 2001 to 2009 in the United States.

a) Explain why mortgage delinquency rates were higher for subprime mortgages.
b) Explain why adjustable rate mortgages experienced higher delinquency rates.

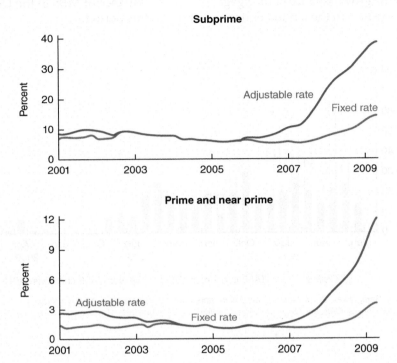

Source: Federal Reserve Monetary Policy Report to the Congress (July 21, 2009).
www.federalreserve.gov/monetarypolicy/mpr_20090721_part1.htm

Why the 2007–2009 Financial Crisis Did Not Lead to a Depression

6. According to the Federal Reserve Act of 1913 (Section 13.3), "In unusual and exigent circumstances, the Board of Governors of the Federal Reserve System, […] may authorize any Federal Reserve bank, during such periods as the said board may determine, […] to discount for any individual, partnership, or corporation, notes, drafts, and bills of exchange […]." During the 2007–2009 financial crisis, the Federal Reserve was highly criticized for providing liquidity to corporations and individual market participants (most notably in the commercial market paper). Do you think the Federal Reserve acted according to its mandate, or that it wrongfully used its ability to support the financial system?

7. Critics of the Federal Reserve in 2013 warned that the Federal Reserve's commitment to keeping the federal funds rate near zero for an extended period of time might increase expected inflation. Explain why low levels of interest rates might fuel inflation expectations and what the Federal Reserve should do to avoid such expectations.

Policy Response to Asset-Price Bubbles

8. Suppose a central bank identifies an increase in lending to the floral industry. In particular, many small businesses are borrowing aggressively to import tulips. As market participants observe a sharp increase in the price of tulips, the central bank considers its actions.

a) Which type of price bubble does this illustrate?

b) What do you think the central bank should do?

c) How would your answer to part (b) change if there was no increase in lending to the floral industry, but tulip prices were nonetheless increasing sharply?

9. Describe the effects on the economy if the Federal Reserve uses monetary policy to burst a wrongfully identified asset-price bubble.

10. One of the possible solutions to asset-price bubbles is the enforcement of macroprudential regulation. Financial intermediaries have an incentive to constantly look for profitable opportunities, which often implies the design of new financial instruments and even the circumvention of contemporaneous regulations. How do you think the process of financial innovation affects the effectiveness of macroprudential regulation?

11. Most legal systems assume that it is better not to incarcerate a guilty individual than to incarcerate an innocent person (i.e., if you are making a mistake, at least choose the lesser of the two). As central banks can potentially make a mistake when bursting asset-price bubbles, which mistake do you think is worse: bursting a bubble when it is not necessary, or not bursting a bubble when it is necessary?

DATA ANALYSIS PROBLEMS

The Problems update with real-time data in MyEconLab *and are available for practice or instructor assignment.*

1. Go to the St. Louis Federal Reserve FRED database, and find data on house prices (SPCS20RSA), stock prices (SP500), a measure of the net wealth of households (TNWBSHNO), and personal consumption expenditures (PCEC). For all four measures, be sure to convert the *frequency* setting to "Quarterly." Download the data into a spreadsheet, and make sure the data align correctly with the appropriate dates. For all four series, for each quarter, calculate the annualized growth rate from quarter to quarter. To do this, take the current period data minus the previous quarter data, and then divide by the previous quarter data. Multiply by 100 to change each result to a percent, and multiply by 4 to annualize the data.

   a) For the four series, calculate the average growth rates over the most recent four quarters of data available. Comment on the relationships among house prices, stock prices, net wealth of households, and consumption as they relate to your results.

   b) Repeat part (a) for the four quarters of 2005 and for the period from 2008:Q3 to 2009:Q2. Comment on the relationships among house prices, stock prices, net wealth of households, and consumption, before and during the crisis, as they relate to your results.

   c) How do the current household data compare to the data from the period prior to the financial crisis and during the crisis? Do you think the current data are indicative of a bubble?

2. Go to the St. Louis Federal Reserve FRED database, and find data on corporate net worth of nonfinancial businesses (TNWMVBSNNCB), private domestic investment (GPDIC1), and a measure of financial frictions, the St. Louis Fed financial stress index (STLFSI). For all three measures, be sure to convert the *frequency* setting to "Quarterly." Download the data into a spreadsheet, and make sure the data align correctly with the appropriate dates. For corporate net worth and private domestic investment, calculate the annualized growth rates from quarter to quarter. To do this, take the current period data minus the previous quarter data, and then divide by the previous quarter data. Multiply by 100 to change the results to percentage form, and then multiply by 4 to annualize the data.

   a) Calculate the average growth rates over the most recent four quarters of data available for the corporate net worth and private domestic investment variables. Calculate the difference between the value of the stress index during the most recent quarter and the value of the stress index one year earlier. Comment on the relationships among financial stress, net wealth of corporate businesses, and private domestic investment.

b) Repeat part (a) for the four quarters of 2005 and for the period from 2008:Q3 to 2009:Q2. Comment on the relationships among financial stress, net wealth of corporate businesses, and private domestic investment, before and during the crisis, as they relate to your results. Assuming the financial stress measure is indicative of heightened asymmetric information problems, comment on how the crisis-period data relate to the typical dynamics of a financial crisis.

c) How do the current investment data compare to the data for the period prior to the financial crisis and during the crisis? Do you think the current data are indicative of a bubble?

3. Go to the St. Louis Federal Reserve FRED database, and find data on the three-month U.S. Treasury note (TB3MS), the three-month AA nonfinancial commercial paper rate (CPN3M), the federal funds rate (FEDFUNDS), and the total volume of assets on the Federal Reserve's balance sheet (WALCL). Convert the balance sheet data *frequency* to "Monthly," and download all the data into a spreadsheet. For each month, calculate the credit spread as the difference between the commercial paper rate and the Treasury rate. Create a series showing the year-by-year growth rate in the Fed balance sheet by finding, for each month, the percentage change in the value from the same month one year earlier.

a) For the most recent data available, calculate the average growth rate in the Fed's balance sheet over the last year period, the level change in the federal funds rate from the same month one year earlier, and the average value of the credit spread over the last year period.

b) Repeat part (a) for the periods from January 2007 to January 2008 (pre-crisis) and September 2008 to September 2009 (crisis).

c) Compare the monetary policy responses of the most recent period, the pre-crisis period, and the crisis period.

Macroeconomic Policy

Part 6   Macroeconomic Policy

This part of the book delves deeper into macroeconomic policy. Chapter 16 and its appendix discuss fiscal policy: the chapter first examines the government budget and its relationship to government debt, and then examines the long- and short-run effects of budget deficits, tax cuts, and government spending. Chapter 17 and its appendices examine international economic policy by developing a supply and demand analysis of how exchange rates are determined, and then discusses the effects of exchange rate fluctuations on the economy.

We will examine applications in each chapter to make the critical connection between theory and real-world practice:

- "The Global Financial Crisis and the Dollar"
- "Why Are Exchange Rates So Volatile?"
- "How Did China Accumulate Over $3 Trillion of International Reserves?"

In keeping with our focus on key policy issues and the techniques policy makers use in practice, we will also analyze the following specific examples in Policy and Practice cases:

- "The Entitlements Debate: Social Security and Medicare/Medicaid"
- "The European Sovereign Debt Crisis"
- "Tax Smoothing"
- "The 2009 Debate Over Tax-Based Versus Spending-Based Fiscal Stimulus"
- "Two Expansionary Fiscal Contractions: Denmark and Ireland"
- "The Debate Over Fiscal Austerity in Europe"
- "The Bush Tax Cuts and Ricardian Equivalence"
- "Will the Euro Survive?"
- "The Collapse of the Argentine Currency Board"

Fiscal Policy and the Government Budget

16

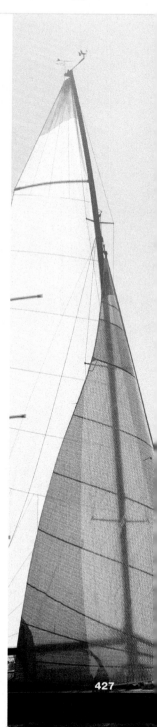

Preview

In the midst of a severe recession in early 2009, President Obama signed into law a $787 billion fiscal stimulus package in an effort to create several million new jobs and upgrade U.S. infrastructure to promote future economic growth. The Recovery Act, as the law came to be known, cut taxes and increased government spending, swelling the U.S. government's budget deficit in 2009 to $1.2 trillion, nearly 9% of U.S. GDP. Not since World War II had the deficit swelled so large relative to economic output.

Do fiscal stimulus programs like the Recovery Act actually create jobs and grow output? Can they bankrupt a government or produce other undesirable effects, such as higher inflation or lower economic output? These same questions apply to the largest ongoing government programs, Medicare and Social Security.

Taken broadly, fiscal policy involves decisions about government spending and taxation. In this chapter, we first examine the relationship between the government budget and the growth of government debt. Then we look at the long- and short-run economic effects of budget deficits, tax cuts, and increased government spending.

The Government Budget

Like any household or office budget, the government's budget reflects both outlays (in the form of government spending) and income (in the form of tax revenue). To better understand the causes of budget deficits, we explore in some detail these two components. (Recall from Chapter 1 that budget deficits are an excess of government spending relative to revenue; surpluses occur when government revenue exceeds spending.) We then examine budget deficits and how they are financed.

Government Spending

In 2012, total spending by all levels of government was $6101 billion (see Table 16.1), nearly $20,000 per person. The media typically focuses on federal spending, but Washington is responsible for only about three-fifths of all government spending, with state and local governments responsible for the rest. Government spending has four major components: government purchases, transfer payments, grants in aid, and net interest payments.

TABLE 16.1 — THE GOVERNMENT BUDGET, 2012

	Federal ($ Billions)	Percent	State and Local ($ Billions)	Percent	Total ($ Billions)	Percent
Current Expenditures						
Government purchases	993.9	26.2%	1,544.3	66.7%	2,538.2	41.6%
Transfers	1,910.6	50.4%	554.2	24.0%	2,464.8	40.4%
Grants in aid	448.4	11.8%	0.0	0.0%	448.4	7.3%
Net interest	434.7	11.5%	215.5	9.3%	650.2	10.7%
Total	3,787.5	100.0%	2,313.9	100.0%	6,101.4	100.0%
Current Receipts						
Personal taxes	1,194.0	44.1%	358.8	15.5%	1,552.8	32.6%
Contributions for social insurance	955.3	35.3%	17.3	0.7%	972.6	20.4%
Taxes on production and imports	118.0	4.4%	1,088.3	43.6%	1,126.3	23.6%
Corporate taxes	347.9	12.8%	51.3	2.2%	399.2	8.4%
Grants in aid	0.0	0.0%	448.4	19.4%	448.4	9.4%
Other	93.8	3.5%	175.6	7.6%	269.4	5.6%
Total	2,709.0	100.0%	2,059.7	100.0%	4,768.7	100.0%
Deficit	1,078.5		254.2		1,332.7	
% of GDP	6.6%		1.5%		8.1%	

Source: National Income and Product Accounts. Bureau of Economic Analysis, Tables 3.2 and 3.3 at www.bea.gov/national/nipaweb/SelectTable.asp?Selected=N#S3. Note that subsidies are included in transfers, while government investment, capital transfer payments, net purchases of nonproduced goods, and consumption of fixed capital are included in government purchases.

1. **Government purchases** (G) are expenditures on goods and services, and in 2012 amounted to 26% of federal spending and 67% of state and local government spending. Government purchases consist of two components: *government investment* (G_I), spending on capital goods like highways and schools, which add to the capital stock and promote economic growth, and *government consumption* (G_C). In other words,

$$G = G_C + G_I$$

   Around five-sixths of government purchases are government consumption, and one-sixth is government investment. Over two-thirds of federal government consumption is spending on national defense.

2. **Transfer payments** *(TRANSFERS)* are direct payments to individuals—such as unemployment insurance benefits, Social Security benefits, Medicare, or welfare payments—for which goods or services are not provided in return. Transfer payments have grown over time as a percentage of the government budget and in 2012 accounted for 50% of federal

spending and 24% of state and local government spending. They are commonly referred to as **entitlements** because they are not made on a discretionary basis, but are locked in by earlier legislation.

3. **Grants in aid** reflect federal assistance to state and local governments. Grants in aid account for 12% of federal spending.

4. **Net interest payments** *(INTEREST)* are interest payments made to holders of government debt such as U.S. Treasury bonds, less the interest paid to the government for debts such as student loans. The net interest payments are at 12% for the federal government and 9% for state and local governments.

Table 16.1 shows the share of the government spending for each of these components for federal, state, and local governments.

Given the media attention paid to critics of big government, you might think that the United States is a big spender. But in a comparison of thirty-three industrialized countries, U.S. government spending relative to GDP is lower than that of twenty-five of those countries, as shown in Figure 16.1.

FIGURE 16.1

Government Spending as a Percentage of GDP for Thirty-Three Advanced Countries, 2012

U.S. government spending relative to GDP is lower than twenty-five other industrialized countries.

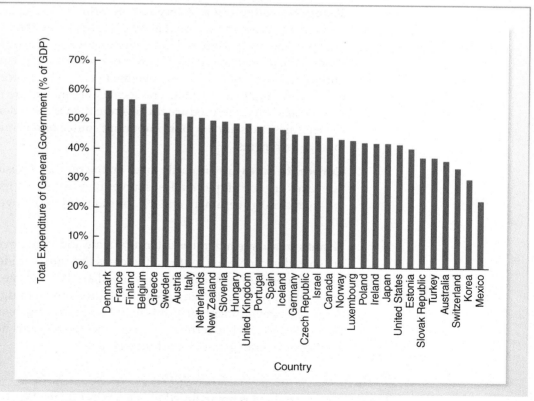

Source: Total expenditure of general government divided by GDP, 2011. National Accounts, OECD Stats, Organization of Economic Cooperation and Development at http://stats.oecd.org/

Revenue

Tax revenue fills in the other side of the government budget.[1] We describe the four major components of tax revenue (*TAXES*) here. Table 16.1 shows each component's contribution to total revenue for 2012.

1. **Personal taxes** are composed of income taxes and property taxes and are a major source of total government revenue, at 44% for the federal government and 16% for state and local governments in 2012. Federal income taxes were unconstitutional until the passage of the Sixteenth Amendment in 1913; they stayed very low until World War II but are now the primary source of federal tax revenue.

2. **Contributions for social insurance** are primarily Social Security taxes, which are assessed as a fixed percentage of a worker's wages, up to a fixed ceiling (or cap). These taxes began when the federal government established the Social Security system in 1935. For most workers, employers pay half of this tax and deduct the other half from the worker's paycheck. Total contributions accounted for 35% of federal revenue and only 1% of state and local government revenue in 2012.

3. **Taxes on production and imports** are primarily sales taxes, but they also include taxes on imported goods, known as **tariffs.** This category now provides only 4% of federal government revenue, but a much larger share, 44%, of state and local government revenue. Tariffs were the most important source of federal tax revenue in early U.S. history, but they are now a very small source. State and local governments are far more dependent on sales taxes to produce tax revenue than is the federal government. In fact, sales taxes are the most important source of revenue for state and local governments.

4. **Corporate taxes** are primarily taxes on the profits of businesses. Corporate taxes are one of the smallest sources of government revenue, at 13% for the federal government and 2% for state and local governments in 2012.

5. **Grants in aid** are federal assistance to state and local governments and are considered revenue for them (whereas they are considered spending for the federal government). Grants in aid are 19% of state and local government revenue. In looking at the total government budget, spending by the federal government on grants in aid is exactly matched by the revenue that state and local governments receive, so these grants do not change the size of the overall government budget balance.

Budget Deficits and Surpluses

The federal government is not required to balance its budget. When government revenue exceeds spending, the government runs a surplus. When government spending outstrips revenue, the government runs a deficit. Budget deficits for the federal government are the norm in the United States ($1,079 billion in 2012, as seen at the bottom of Table 16.1),

[1]We disregard revenue from fees, such as entrance charges to national parks, which account for a tiny proportion of revenue.

because the federal government usually spends more than it receives in taxes. One exception was during the late 1990s, when the government budget was in surplus.

The formula for the government budget deficit is as follows:[2]

$$\begin{aligned} \text{Deficit} &= \text{spending} - \text{tax revenues} \\ &= (\text{government purchases} + \text{transfers} + \text{net interest}) - \text{tax revenues} \quad (1) \\ &= (G + TRANSFERS + INTEREST) - TAXES \end{aligned}$$

Government Budget Constraint

Although the government can run a deficit, it still must pay its bills. To raise revenue to pay for the goods and services it buys, the government has the option to raise taxes. It can also finance a deficit by borrowing. Since governments borrow by selling (issuing) bonds (either to the public or to their central banks), thus adding to the amount of government bonds outstanding, the deficit equals the change in the stock of government bonds, ΔB.

$$\text{Deficit} = \Delta B \quad (2)$$

This equation is more formally referred to as the **government budget constraint.**

Size of the Government Debt

A good indicator of a country's indebtedness is the amount of debt relative to the available income to pay it back, and this is measured by the amount of debt in nominal terms relative to nominal GDP, that is, the **debt-to-GDP ratio**.

There are two sources of changes in the debt-to-GDP ratio. First, as the government budget constraint indicates, higher deficits lead to a larger amount of government debt outstanding, thereby increasing the debt-to-GDP ratio if nominal GDP is held constant. Second, if nominal GDP is growing, either because real GDP is growing or because inflation is high, then holding the amount of government debt constant results in a falling debt-to-GDP ratio.

We now look at how U.S. government debt has grown, fallen, and then grown again relative to GDP in the United States. We will see that both deficits and growth in nominal GDP have played a prominent role in these fluctuations in the debt-to-GDP ratio. We then compare the U.S. debt level to that of other key industrialized nations.

Growth of U.S. Government Debt over Time

Budget deficits are reflections of major events in history, mirroring the effects of wars, depressions, and changing political ideologies. We now begin a tour of recent U.S. history, told through the story of the budget deficit from 1940 to the present day, as pictured in Figure 16.2.

During World War II from 1939–1945, the U.S. federal government quadrupled its spending to defeat the Germans and the Japanese. Deficits reached a peak of 30% of GDP. The government covered some of the extra expense by raising taxes, but it did

---

[2]There are other measures of the government budget deficit, and they are described in a Web appendix to this chapter found at www.pearsonhighered.com/mishkin.

MyEconLab Real-time data

FIGURE 16.2

U.S. Federal Deficit and the Size of U.S. Government Debt Relative to GDP, 1940–2013

When budget deficits are very high, as during World War II and again more recently, the debt-to-GDP ratio rises. When deficits are small, high real GDP growth and inflation lead to a decline in the debt-to-GDP ratio.

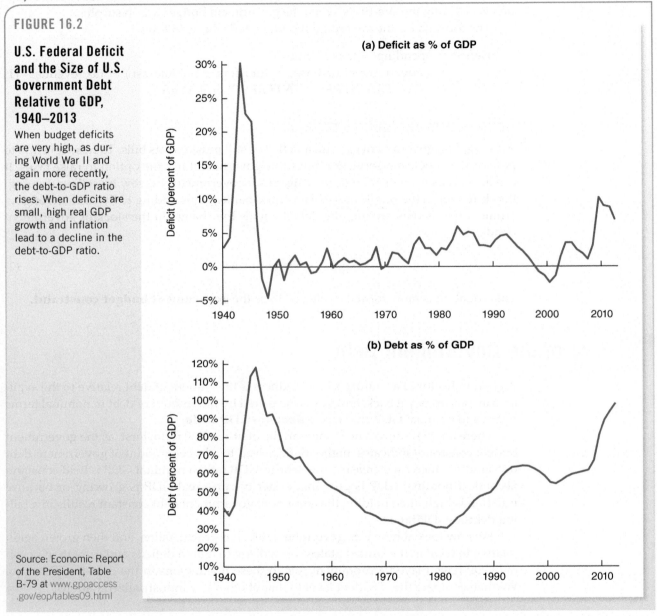

Source: Economic Report of the President, Table B-79 at www.gpoaccess .gov/eop/tables09.html

not want current taxpayers to bear the full cost of the war, so it borrowed to cover the remainder of the war expenses, thereby generating federal budget deficits of between 20% and 30% of GDP during the war years. As the government budget constraint indicates, the debt-to-GDP ratio skyrocketed to over 100% of GDP.

After the war ended in 1945, government spending moderated and the budget returned to balance, so that the stock of government debt essentially remained constant. But high rates of real GDP growth and inflation combined to produce rapid nominal GDP growth, which brought the debt-to-GDP ratio to a low near 30% of GDP in the mid-1970s.

In the 1980s, large deficits returned. Large income tax reductions during the Reagan administration brought the average deficit over the decade to nearly 4% of GDP. The debt-to-GDP ratio rose to over 60% by 1993. Large tax increases during the Clinton administration produced such substantial new revenue that the federal budget returned to surplus from 1997 to 2001. The debt-to-GDP ratio declined to 55%. When the second Iraq War began in 2002, government spending once again surged. Compounding the effect on the deficit, the administration of George W. Bush introduced tax cuts that brought the deficit to 10% of GDP by the end of Bush's term in 2009. The debt-to-GDP ratio once again began to climb, and it rose even further during the first years of the Obama administration, which passed a large fiscal stimulus package. The debt-to-GDP ratio reached 99% by 2012, with projections for future values expected to rise further. The prospects for the budget over the next fifty years are cause for concern, as the following Policy and Practice case suggests.

Policy and Practice

The Entitlements Debate: Social Security and Medicare/Medicaid

Public discussion of the federal budget tends to focus on the current deficit. Another consideration is government commitments to increases in pension and medical spending mandated by legislation for programs such as Social Security, Medicare, and Medicaid. These entitlement programs have grown to account for close to half of federal spending.

At its establishment in 1935, Social Security was intended to operate like a pension plan. Workers would contribute a portion of their paychecks to a trust fund, which would invest and protect the money until the workers reached retirement age. In fact, the Social Security Administration immediately transfers most workers' contributions to current-day retirees. This "pay-as-you-go" system works fine as long as there are enough workers contributing to pay Social Security benefits in full.

However, the demographic situation has changed dramatically since the early years of Social Security:

1. Today's retirees live far longer than retirees did in the 1930s and thus draw on Social Security's lifetime benefits for much longer.

2. There are far more retirees today, a result of the baby boom in the years after World War II.

3. U.S. birth rates have declined over the years, increasing the **dependency ratio,** which is the ratio of retirees to workers who make Social Security contributions.

For these reasons, the Congressional Budget Office projects that Social Security spending will rise from 4.9% of GDP in 2013 to 5.9% in 2050, an increase of over 20%, with even greater growth expected in Medicare and Medicaid spending. (See Figure 16.3 for more details.)

In recent years, policy makers and elected officials have debated how best to address these challenges and have proposed various reforms. Proposed reforms of the Social Security system come in three varieties: 1) invest Social Security trust

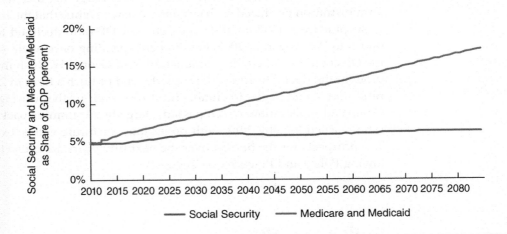

FIGURE 16.3

Social Security and Medicare/Medicaid Spending as a Percent of GDP, 2013–2050

Projected spending on Social Security is projected to rise from 4.9% in 2013 to 5.9% in 2050, while government spending on Medicaid and Medicare is projected to rise from 5% in 2013 to 12% by 2050.

Source: Long-Term Budget Outlook, Congressional Budget Office, 2011, at http://www.cbo.gov/publication/42465

funds in high-return (and thus high-risk) assets, 2) double Social Security taxes on workers, or 3) cut retirement benefits by one-third. All of these approaches come with painful tradeoffs. If the Social Security trust fund invests in private assets rather than in low-yielding U.S. Treasury securities, it will be exposed to crisis if asset prices suddenly fall. Social Security tax rate increases could eventually raise taxes to such high levels that people would have little incentive to work. If reform trims benefits too much or raises the minimum age at which one can receive benefits too high, the safety net of the Social Security system could fail many elderly. Yet, if policy makers take no action, budget deficits will almost certainly skyrocket.[3]

With such tough choices, it's easy to see why Social Security has often been described as a "third rail of politics": touch it and you are dead. The longer it takes to reform the Social Security system, the worse the problem becomes, and the more drastic the measures that will be needed to fix it.

Growing health care costs and increases in government medical benefits expose the health care entitlements of Medicare and Medicaid to similar issues, although the growth of these programs will impact the government budget far more in the future than Social Security will. Projected spending on these two health care programs is expected to rise from around 5% in 2013 to 12% by 2050, as Figure 16.3 shows. After a bruising year-long political debate, Congress passed a health care overhaul in early 2010 that extended medical insurance to thirty million more people while increasing payroll taxes and trimming subsidies to some health care providers. How this legislation will affect future government spending on health care is far from clear.

[3]See Martin Feldstein, "Structural Reform of Social Security," *Journal of Economic Perspectives* (Spring 2005): 33–55.

| TABLE 16.2 | INTERNATIONAL COMPARISON OF THE RELATIVE SIZES OF GOVERNMENT DEBT FOR THIRTY ADVANCED COUNTRIES, 2011 |

Country	Debt (% of GDP)	Country	Debt (% of GDP)
1 Japan	228	16 Netherlands	76
2 Iceland	134	17 Poland	64
3 Italy	120	18 Denmark	62
4 Canada	106	19 Finland	58
5 United Kingdom	104	20 New Zealand	49
6 Ireland	104	21 Sweden	49
7 Greece	104	22 Slovak Republic	48
8 United States	103	23 Czech Republic	48
9 Belgium	102	24 Australia	47
10 France	100	25 Switzerland*	44
11 Portugal	98	26 Turkey	40
12 Germany	86	27 Mexico*	38
13 Hungary	86	28 Korea	36
14 Austria	80	29 Norway	34
15 Spain	77	30 Luxembourg	26

Source: Finance, OECD Stats, Organization of Economic Cooperation and Development at http://stats.oecd.org/index.aspx. *Data corresponds to 2009.

International Comparison: The Size of Government Debt

The amount of U.S. government debt relative to the size of the economy is high and rising. How does U.S. government debt compare to that of other advanced countries? Government debt in various countries has been fluid since the global financial crisis of 2007–2009. Table 16.2 provides an international comparison of the amount of government debt as a percentage of GDP as of the year 2011, when the data was last updated. Notice that many countries—such as Japan and Italy—had much higher debt-to-GDP ratios than the United States. However, other countries—such as Norway and Luxembourg—had very little debt relative to GDP, with debt-to-GDP ratios of well less than 50%. The United States is in the top third of countries in terms of government indebtedness, with government debt relative to GDP at 103% as of 2011.

Sovereign Debt Crises

Sovereign debt crises, a collapse in the market for a country's government debt, have been with us for centuries, as documented by Carmen Reinhart and Kenneth Rogoff, both of Harvard University, in their classic book, *This Time It's Different: Eight Centuries of Financial Folly* (Princeton, NJ: Princeton University Press, 2009).

To understand how a sovereign debt crisis develops, we first make use of the analysis in the preceding section, which indicated that the debt-to-GDP ratio of a country will rise if budget deficits increase or nominal GDP growth falls. However, if the debt-to-GDP ratio of a sovereign government rises to the point where investors become concerned that the sovereign government will be unable to pay back its debt, then an adverse feedback loop can develop that produces a sovereign debt crisis. As the probability of default rises, investors pull out of the country's bonds, and the resulting decline in their price leads to a surge in interest rates on this debt. Government interest payments on newly issued debt then rise sharply as well, leading to a large increase in budget deficits, which in turn causes a rise in the debt-to-GDP ratio and makes it even more likely that the government will default on its debt. Schematically, this situation can be described as follows:

$$\text{Debt-to-GDP} \uparrow \Rightarrow \text{Probability of default} \uparrow \Rightarrow \text{Interest payments} \uparrow \Rightarrow \text{Deficit} \uparrow \Rightarrow$$

$$\text{Debt-to-GDP} \uparrow \Rightarrow \text{Probability of default} \uparrow \Rightarrow \text{Interest payments} \uparrow \Rightarrow \text{Deficit} \uparrow, \text{etc.}$$

With this dynamic, eventually the market for this sovereign debt collapses and the country defaults on its debt, with potentially disastrous effects on its economy. This scenario has recently been playing out in Europe, as the following Policy and Practice case indicates.

Policy and Practice

The European Sovereign Debt Crisis

The global financial crisis of 2007–2009 led not only to a worldwide recession but also to a sovereign debt crisis that currently threatens to destabilize Europe. Up until 2007, all of the countries that had adopted the euro found their interest rates converging to very low levels. However, with the global financial crisis, several of these countries were hit very hard by the contraction in economic activity, which reduced tax revenues at the same time that government bailouts of failed financial institutions required additional government outlays. The resulting surge in budget deficits and rapid rise in debt-to-GDP ratios then led to the adverse feedback loop described above.[4]

Greece was the first domino to fall in Europe. In September 2009, with a weakening economy suffering from reduced tax revenues and increased spending demands, the Greek government was projecting a budget deficit for the year of 6% and a debt-to-GDP ratio of nearly 100%. However, when a new government was elected in October, it revealed that the budget situation was far worse than anyone had imagined because the previous government had provided misleading numbers about both the budget deficit, which was at least double the 6% number,

---

[4]For a discussion of the dynamics of sovereign debt crises and case studies of the European debt crisis, see David Greenlaw, James D. Hamilton, Frederic S. Mishkin, and Peter Hooper, "Crunch Time: Fiscal Crises and the Role of Monetary Policy," *U.S. Monetary Policy Forum* (Chicago: Chicago Booth Initiative on Global Markets, 2013).

and the amount of government debt, which was ten percentage points higher relative to GDP than previously reported. Despite austerity measures intended to dramatically cut government spending and raise taxes, interest rates on Greek debt soared, eventually rising to nearly 40%, and the debt-to-GDP ratio climbed to 160% of GDP in 2012. Even with bailouts from other European countries and liquidity support from the European Central Bank, Greece was forced to write down the value of its debt held in private hands by more than half, and the country was subject to civil unrest, with massive strikes and the resignation of the prime minister.

The sovereign debt crisis spread from Greece to Ireland, Portugal, Spain, and Italy, with their governments forced to embrace austerity measures to shore up their public finances, while interest rates climbed to double-digit levels. Only after a speech in July 2012 by Mario Draghi, the president of the European Central Bank (ECB), in which he stated that the ECB was ready to do "whatever it takes" to save the euro, did the markets begin to calm down. Nonetheless, despite a sharp decline in interest rates, these countries experienced severe recessions, with unemployment rates rising to double-digit levels and with Spain's unemployment rate exceeding 25%. The stresses that the European sovereign debt crisis produced for the "euro zone" have raised doubts as to whether the euro will survive, a topic we will return to in Chapter 17.

 # Fiscal Policy and the Economy in the Long Run

The amount of U.S. government debt per person is over $50,000 and rising. Will paying back this debt strain the economy? We now consider two sides to the debate over the burden of long-run debt on future generations.

Why High Government Debt Is Not a Burden

One side in the debate maintains that the large amount of debt may be less of a problem than it first appears, based on how the government spent the money. For example, government debt issued to invest in **government capital,** composed of physical assets such as highways, broadband networks, and schools, will increase the economy's future productivity. And **human capital** investments such as education increase worker productivity and, in turn, wages, generating additional tax revenue that can go toward repaying the government debt. In addition, the government will eventually repay the debt held by American households and businesses, in the form of government bonds, by transferring future tax revenues to these bondholders. If the households and businesses paying taxes are the same ones that are holding the bonds, then the tax payment that goes out from one hand will just be paid back to the other hand.

Why High Government Debt Is a Burden

There are a number of compelling arguments on the other side of the debate, which points to the burden of rising government debt.

REDUCTIONS IN NATIONAL SAVING. We learned from the uses-of-saving identity in Chapter 4 that national saving, the sum of private and government saving, is equal to investment plus net exports:

$$S \qquad = (Y - T - C) + \qquad (T - G) \qquad = \qquad I \qquad + \qquad NX \quad (3)$$

National saving = Private saving + Government saving = Investment + Net exports

When government saving, $T - G$, is negative because budget deficits are large, then national saving will be lower and the sum of investment and net exports will be lower. Reductions in national saving that arise from budget deficits are therefore likely to reduce private investment, a phenomenon that is called **crowding out.** The lower capital stock from the reduction in private investment implies that the economy will produce fewer goods and services in the future, so that future generations will be worse off.

VALUE OF GOVERNMENT CAPITAL INVESTMENT. There is reason to be skeptical of the argument that the government takes on debt to make wise investments in physical and human capital. First, most government spending is for government consumption, which is current government spending that does not boost the capital stock, such as spending on medical care and military personnel, or for transfer payments such as unemployment insurance or Social Security payments. Second, government investment may be unproductive. Some critics deride government spending as loaded with "pork," or wasteful spending. A particularly flagrant example of pork was the infamous "bridge to nowhere" that legislators proposed to Congress in 2005, a bridge that was to connect Gravina Island's fifty residents to Ketchikan, Alaska, at a projected cost of $398 million. (That's $8 million per resident!) Congress eventually dropped the bridge from the bill. Nonetheless, the government has approved many pork-barrel investments, suggesting that a substantial fraction of government investment is not very productive.

INDEBTEDNESS TO FOREIGNERS. Even if much of the country's debt is owed to itself, Equation 3 suggests that a reduction in national saving can also lower net exports and thereby increase U.S. indebtedness to foreigners. As we saw in Chapter 4, negative net exports are financed by foreign purchases of U.S. assets, especially government bonds. Budget deficits that reduce national saving could, over time, increase U.S. foreign debt. The Chinese are already the largest holders of U.S. government debt, representing a substantial burden on future generations.

REDISTRIBUTION EFFECTS. The argument that deficits and rising government debt are not a burden because much of the debt is owed to the government itself does not take into account the fact that the people paying taxes may not be the same people who hold government bonds. People who do not own bonds have to pay higher taxes to pay off the principal and interest on government bonds, while those who hold bonds receive more in interest and principal payments relative to the amount they pay in taxes. Government budget deficits and rising government debt thus involve a transfer of wealth in the future to government bondholders. Since bondholders are likely to be richer than those who do not own bonds, rising government debt involves redistributing from relatively poor people to relatively rich people, which could widen income inequality.[5]

DEBT INTOLERANCE. At some point, when the amount of government debt relative to the size of the economy gets very large, investors may begin to fear the government will default on the debt and, by engaging in **debt repudiation**, fail to pay it all back. The point at which this may happen depends on the past history of a country's fiscal policy. Many countries, with Argentina a leading example, have defaulted on their debt repeatedly and are often referred to as "serial defaulters." These countries may then experience **debt intolerance** when they are unable to sell their debt, even at relatively low ratios of government debt to GDP, and so are far more likely to default on their government debt at much lower levels of debt relative to GDP.[6] Many emerging market countries are exposed to debt intolerance: a default on government debt can send these countries into a financial crisis, with disastrous effects on the economy.[7] Large budget deficits and rising government debt can then pose a very large threat to the health of emerging market economies.

NEGATIVE INCENTIVE EFFECTS. High budget deficits that generate large government debt increase the need for governments to raise future taxes to pay back the debt. Higher taxes come with a hidden cost to the economy if they create **distortions,** which are departures from the most efficient economic outcomes. To illustrate, consider a 40% income tax. For every dollar you earn, you would get only sixty cents, with the result that you might work less hard, and the economy would then produce less. Similarly, an investor who pays a 20% capital gains tax on the profits he or she earns from his or her investments may be less willing to make these investments, resulting in lower capital stock and economic growth. These so-called **tax wedges**—the difference between what people earn after taxes on their labor or investments and what they are paid before they make their tax payments—can therefore reduce the efficiency and growth of an economy over time.

The bottom line from the discussion in this section is that although there are reasons why rising government debt may not always be a burden, it does pose some very high costs for the economy.

Policy and Practice

Tax Smoothing

The distortions of high tax rates provide a rationale for **tax smoothing**, a policy of keeping tax rates fairly stable when government spending fluctuates. Consider the financing choices of a government that is planning five years of heavy investment in the highway system, followed by five years of normal spending. The

---

[5]This redistribution is currently even more problematic because income inequality has been rising for other reasons in recent years, as we will discuss in Chapter 20. Of course, other tax policies to raise taxes on the rich could counteract this rise in income inequality.

[6]Carmen Reinhart, Kenneth S. Rogoff, and Miguel A. Savastano, "Debt Intolerance," *Brookings Papers on Economic Activity* Vol 1 (Spring 2003): 1–74.

[7]This issue is discussed further in the Web chapter "Financial Crises in Emerging Market Economies," found at the Companion Website, www.pearsonhighered.com/mishkin.

government has two options for funding: (1) raise the tax rate from 20% to 30% over the next five years and then return the rate to 20% once the highway spending is complete, or (2) "smooth" the tax increase, setting a new rate of 25% for ten years. The government would balance the budget over the whole ten-year period, but there would be large deficits in the first five years and large surpluses in the following five years. Setting a constant rate would eliminate the distortion of raising the tax rate from 20% to 30% between the two five-year periods.

Tax smoothing can justify deficits when government spending is likely to be temporarily high. For example, during World War II, the U.S. government had budget deficits of 20–30% of GDP, exactly as tax smoothing predicts. The tax smoothing argument does not, however, justify large government deficits *if the rise in spending is expected to be permanent*. Expected permanent rises in government spending should be paid for with tax rate increases. Otherwise, the resulting budget deficits will not be matched by surpluses in future years, thereby leading to a permanent rise in government debt, which places a substantial burden on future generations. For this reason, many economists support raising taxes today to help pay for high future spending on entitlement programs such as Social Security and Medicare.

Fiscal Policy and the Economy in the Short Run

We have looked at how fiscal policy affects the economy in the long run. Fiscal policy also has important effects on the economy in the short run. We saw in Chapter 12 that expansionary fiscal policy, either a cut in taxes or an increase in government spending, leads to an increase in aggregate demand, thereby causing both aggregate output and inflation to rise in the short run. This may be only part of the story, however. Let's look more closely at the effects of fiscal policy, such as the Obama 2009 stimulus package, on the economy by using our aggregate demand and supply analysis.

Aggregate Demand and Fiscal Policy

Figure 16.4 shows the short-run effect of fiscal policy on the economy. Suppose, for example, that aggregate demand decreases and the economy is at point 1 in the figure, with the aggregate demand curve at AD_1 and aggregate output at Y_1, below potential output at Y^P. The government can pursue either of two policies to increase the quantity of aggregate output demanded at any given rate of inflation: it can cut taxes, or it can increase government spending. An income tax cut would increase households' disposable income, resulting in higher consumption spending. An increase in government spending adds directly to aggregate demand. As a result, the aggregate demand curve shifts to the right from AD_1 to AD_2 in Figure 16.4. Tax cuts and higher spending both move the economy from point 1 to point 2, where aggregate output rises back up to potential at Y^P and inflation rises π_2.

Expenditure and Tax Multipliers

In Chapter 9, we found that increases in government purchases of $1 trillion led to an increase in equilibrium output of $2.5 trillion, a multiple of 2.5, when we held the real

MyEconLab Mini-lecture

FIGURE 16.4

Fiscal Policy Expansion and the Economy in the Short Run

A cut in taxes or an increase in government spending increases aggregate demand, shifting the aggregate demand curve to the right from AD_1 to AD_2 and moving the economy from point 1 to point 2. Aggregate output rises from Y_1 to Y^P, and inflation rises from π_1 to π_2.

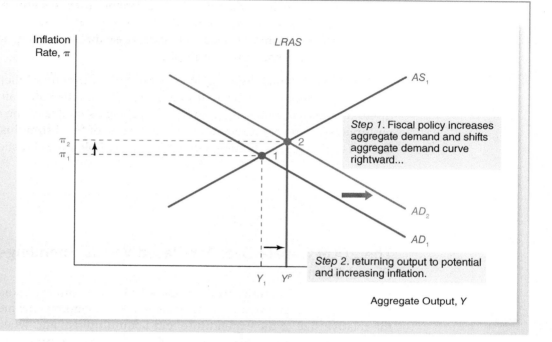

interest rate constant. Equation 12 in Chapter 9 represents this multiple generally as $1/(1 - mpc)$, so the value is always greater than 1 because the marginal propensity to consume is less than 1. We call the change in equilibrium output caused by a change in government purchases, $\Delta Y/\Delta G$, the **expenditure multiplier.**

In Chapter 9, we also found that an increase in taxes of $1 trillion decreases equilibrium output by $1.5 trillion, a smaller multiple than 2.5. The **tax multiplier** is the change in equilibrium output caused by a change in taxes, $\Delta Y/\Delta T$, and it is always less in absolute value than the expenditure multiplier because the initial change in spending occurs through consumption expenditure, which responds to the tax change by less than a one-to-one ratio (equal to the mpc).

Many Keynesian economists argue that the expenditure multiplier is greater than 1 and is larger in absolute value than the tax multiplier, but other economists disagree. There are two reasons the expenditure multiplier may be smaller than indicated by the analysis in Chapter 9:

1. The analysis in Chapter 9 assumes that real interest rates remain constant when either government purchases or taxes change. Our analysis in Chapters 10 to 12, however, indicates that this assumption is usually incorrect. When government purchases rise, inflation rises, and so real interest rates rise, leading to a cutback in private spending (referred to as crowding out) on investment, consumption expenditure, and net exports, producing an overall smaller increase in equilibrium output.[8]

---

[8]The Web appendix to Chapter 12, which outlines the algebra of the AD/AS model, shows in its Equation 6 that $\Delta Y/\Delta G = 1/[1 - mpc + (c + d + \chi)\lambda\gamma]$, which is less than $1/[1 - mpc]$. This reflects the additional term $1 - mpc + (c + d + \chi)\lambda\gamma$ in the denominator, which reflects that as output rises, inflation rises and hence the real interest rate rises.

2. The expenditure multiplier may be smaller because households and businesses anticipate that higher government purchases will lead to higher budget deficits that will require financing with higher taxes. As a result, households and businesses will decrease their spending, again leading to a smaller expenditure multiplier.

These two arguments suggest that the expenditure multiplier may be lower than Keynesian economists believe. It may be smaller in absolute value than the tax multiplier and may even be smaller than 1. Varying estimates of the expenditure and tax multipliers led to very different views on the role of fiscal stimulus during the financial crisis of 2007–2009, as discussed in the following Policy and Practice case.

Policy and Practice

The 2009 Debate Over Tax-Based Versus Spending-Based Fiscal Stimulus

When the Obama administration proposed a fiscal stimulus package to jump-start the economy when it first came to office in 2009, a vigorous debate followed over the relative size of the expenditure and tax multipliers and whether tax cuts or increased government spending should provide more stimulus to the economy.

Republicans favored tax cuts, which they argued would immediately boost disposable income and stimulate spending and reduce distortions in the economy, increasing potential output in the future. Democrats, on the other hand, argued that increases in government spending add directly to aggregate demand, and thus would be more effective at stimulating the economy than tax cuts. Democrats also argued that the recession was worsened by shortfalls in physical and human capital, prompting proposals to increase government investment in education, improve health care, and combat global warming.

These opposing views were supported by different sectors of the economics profession. Christina Romer, the Chairwoman of the Council of Economic Advisors and a member of the Obama administration, argued that the expenditure multiplier was well above 1, on the order of 1.5, and was larger in absolute value than the tax multiplier. Research of other economists who were not in the Obama administration led to a different conclusion—that the expenditure multiplier was less than 1, on the order of 0.5, and that the tax multiplier would be larger in absolute value than the expenditure multiplier.[9]

A compromise emerged from the vigorous debate on the size of expenditure and tax multipliers: the $787 billion fiscal stimulus package passed in February 2009, called the American Recovery and Reinvestment Act, offered a mix of tax cuts ($288 billion) and government spending increases ($499 billion).

---

[9]This debate and the research on the magnitude of expenditure and tax multipliers is discussed in Sylvain Leduc, "Fighting Downturns with Fiscal Policy," *Federal Reserve Bank of San Francisco Economic Letter*, 2009-20 (June 19, 2009), which can be found at www.frbsf.org/publications/economics/letter/2009/el2009-20.html.

Fiscal Multipliers at the Zero Lower Bound

In Chapter 13, we saw that when the policy interest rate hits the floor of the zero lower bound, as has occurred in recent years, monetary policy works very differently. This is also the case for fiscal policy. Here we examine how fiscal multipliers change when the zero lower bound on the policy rate is reached (see Figure 16.5).

Recall from Chapter 13 that when the zero lower bound is reached, the aggregate demand curve takes on an upward, rather than the usual downward, slope, producing a kinked aggregate demand curve like AD_1 in Figure 16.5. We now look at the effects of expansionary fiscal policy on aggregate output for two cases in which aggregate output is initially at the same level of Y_1:

1. Initially, the short-run aggregate supply curve AS_1 intersects the aggregate demand curve AD_1 at point 1, where the policy rate is above zero, and so the aggregate demand curve has the usual downward slope.

2. Initially, the short-run aggregate supply curve $AS_{1'}$ intersects the aggregate demand curve AD_1 at point 1', where the policy rate has hit the zero lower bound, and so the aggregate demand curve has an upward slope.

Let's see what happens in each of these cases.

An expansionary fiscal policy, say an increase in government spending, will shift the aggregate demand curve to the right to AD_2 in Figure 16.5. For case 1, the economy moves to point 2 at the intersection of AD_2 and AS_1, and aggregate output rises from Y_1 to Y_2. For case 2, in which the policy rate has hit the zero lower bound, the economy moves to point 2' at the intersection of AD_2 and $AS_{1'}$, and aggregate output rises to $Y_{2'}$.

You will immediately notice that $Y_{2'}$ is substantially greater than Y_2, which yields the following result: ***the fiscal multiplier is substantially larger when the policy rate has hit the zero lower bound than when it has not.*** What is the intuition behind this result? In case 1, when expansionary fiscal policy leads to a rise in the inflation rate from π_1 to π_2, in going from point 1 to point 2, the monetary authorities follow the Taylor principle and the real interest rate rises. This rise in the real interest rate deters investment, and so there is a smaller increase in aggregate output. Schematically, this can be described as follows:

$$G\uparrow \Rightarrow \pi\uparrow \Rightarrow r\uparrow \Rightarrow I\downarrow \Rightarrow Y\uparrow \text{ by a smaller amount}$$

On the other hand, when the policy rate is at the zero lower bound, the monetary authorities would prefer that the policy rate be below that level, and so when inflation rises, they keep the rate fixed at zero. Now, when the inflation rate rises from $\pi_{1'}$ to $\pi_{2'}$, the real interest rate falls, thereby stimulating investment, which gives an extra kick to the increase in aggregate output. Schematically,

$$G\uparrow \Rightarrow \pi\uparrow \Rightarrow \text{policy rate fixed at zero} \Rightarrow r\downarrow \Rightarrow I\uparrow \Rightarrow Y\uparrow \text{ by a larger amount}$$

The result that fiscal multipliers should be substantially higher when the policy rate has hit the zero lower bound can explain why economists have had different views on the size of fiscal multipliers in recent years. Those who have analyzed the impact of fiscal policy when the zero lower bound on the policy rate has been reached are more likely to argue that fiscal multipliers are above 1, whereas those who base their analysis on periods when the policy rate is above zero are more likely to believe that fiscal multipliers

FIGURE 16.5

Fiscal Expansion and the Zero Lower Bound

Expansionary fiscal policy shifts the aggregate demand curve from AD_1 to AD_2. In the case in which the economy is initially at point 1, where the policy rate is above the zero lower bound, the economy moves to point 2, where output rises to Y_2. In the case in which the economy is initially at point 1', where the policy rate has hit the zero lower bound, the economy moves to point 2', where output rises to $Y_{2'}$, which is higher than Y_2. This figure thus demonstrates that the fiscal multiplier is higher when the policy rate is at the zero lower bound.

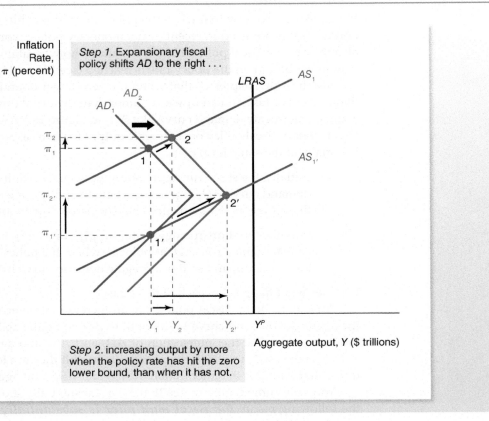

Step 1. Expansionary fiscal policy shifts AD to the right . . .

Step 2. increasing output by more when the policy rate has hit the zero lower bound, than when it has not.

are below 1. The analysis of fiscal multipliers at the zero lower bound thus has a bearing on the debate over the 2009 fiscal stimulus package, but is especially relevant to the debates over austerity in Europe that have occurred in the wake of its sovereign debt crisis in recent years, as discussed in the Policy and Practice case on page 448.

Aggregate Supply and Fiscal Policy

We will now show how fiscal policy can also affect aggregate supply. Specifically, tax cuts might affect both the short- and long-run aggregate supply curves. Consider the case in which the economy is at point 1 in Figure 16.6, where aggregate output at Y_1 is below potential output at Y^P. A temporary cut in the **payroll tax**, taxes on wages such as Social Security taxes, acts just like a temporary positive supply shock, which we introduced in Chapter 12: it lowers the wage cost of production and reduces inflation at each level of aggregate output, so that the short-run aggregate supply curve in Figure 16.6 shifts downward and to the right from AS_1 to AS_2.[10] Because a payroll tax increases disposable

[10]The analysis here is for a temporary cut in the payroll tax. If the payroll tax cut is permanent, we obtain the same conclusions that output rises and inflation may fall. However, a permanent payroll tax cut may have even more beneficial effects. In this case, the permanent decline in the cost of labor for firms might cause the long-run aggregate supply curve to shift to the right, and the higher future income that results may then induce households and businesses to spend more, thus boosting aggregate demand further. The result would be an even larger increase in output and an even lower inflation rate.

MyEconLab Mini-lecture

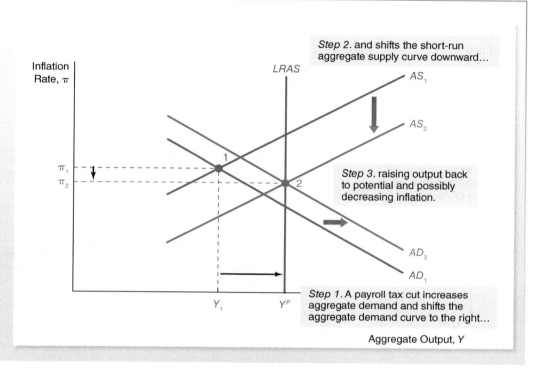

FIGURE 16.6

Effect of a Temporary Payroll Tax Cut

A cut in payroll taxes shifts the aggregate demand curve to the right from AD_1 to AD_2, and it also shifts the short-run aggregate supply curve downward and to the right from AS_1 to AS_2. The economy therefore moves from point 1 to point 2, where the downward and rightward shifts in the short-run aggregate supply curve might be sufficiently large to lead to an inflation rate of π_2 that is below the initial level of π_1.

Step 2. and shifts the short-run aggregate supply curve downward…

Step 3. raising output back to potential and possibly decreasing inflation.

Step 1. A payroll tax cut increases aggregate demand and shifts the aggregate demand curve to the right…

income and thereby consumption expenditure, it also increases aggregate demand, shifting the aggregate demand curve rightward from AD_1 to AD_2 in Figure 16.5. The economy therefore moves from point 1 to point 2, where aggregate output rises back to Y^P, but in contrast to Figure 16.4, inflation may not necessarily rise. It might even fall if the downward and rightward shifts in the aggregate supply curve are sufficiently large that the inflation rate of π_2 is below the initial level of π_1, as shown in Figure 16.6.

Supply-Side Economics and Fiscal Policy

Some economists, known as **supply-siders,** of whom Arthur Laffer is the most famous, believe the favorable effects of tax cuts on aggregate supply are amplified. Supply-siders believe that permanent cuts in tax rates, even ones that do not directly lower costs, such as income taxes, increase aggregate supply as well as demand. We present supply-side analysis of tax cuts in Figure 16.7. An income tax cut shifts the aggregate demand curve in the figure rightward from AD_1 to AD_2 and also induces more investment and greater work effort, so that there is a large, positive, permanent effect on aggregate supply. In Chapter 12, we analyzed the impact of a permanent aggregate supply shock. The cut in income tax rates increases long-run aggregate supply, shifting the long-run aggregate supply curve rightward from $LRAS_1$ to $LRAS_2$ in Figure 16.7. The lower inflation then decreases short-run aggregate supply, shifting the short-run aggregate supply curve down and to the right from AS_1 to AS_2. Cuts in tax rates that increase both aggregate demand and long-run aggregate supply are therefore highly expansionary. At point 2 in Figure 16.7, aggregate output rises to Y_2, while inflation at π_2 is possibly lower than its initial level of π_1.[11]

[11]The fall in inflation results from the assumption that the long-run aggregate supply curve shifts by more than the aggregate demand curve.

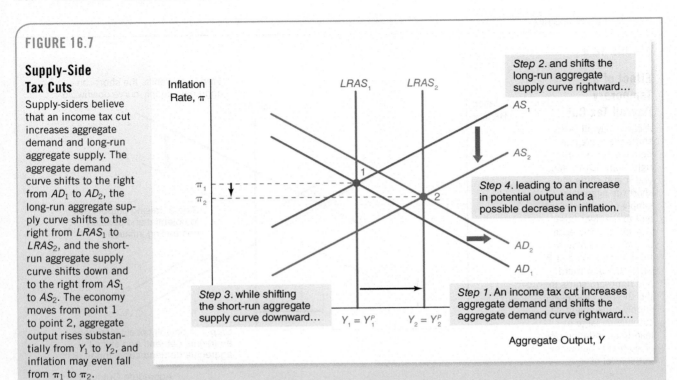

FIGURE 16.7

Supply-Side Tax Cuts

Supply-siders believe that an income tax cut increases aggregate demand and long-run aggregate supply. The aggregate demand curve shifts to the right from AD_1 to AD_2, the long-run aggregate supply curve shifts to the right from $LRAS_1$ to $LRAS_2$, and the short-run aggregate supply curve shifts down and to the right from AS_1 to AS_2. The economy moves from point 1 to point 2, aggregate output rises substantially from Y_1 to Y_2, and inflation may even fall from π_1 to π_2.

Step 2. and shifts the long-run aggregate supply curve rightward...

Step 4. leading to an increase in potential output and a possible decrease in inflation.

Step 3. while shifting the short-run aggregate supply curve downward...

Step 1. An income tax cut increases aggregate demand and shifts the aggregate demand curve rightward...

Some supply-siders, like Arthur Laffer, believe that the expansion in aggregate output from cuts in tax rates is so large that the tax base (the income on which taxes are levied) will rise enough that tax revenue will go up, despite the cut in tax rates. The cut in tax rates would then be self-financing: cutting taxes would not increase the budget deficit. This "you can have your cake and eat it, too" scenario is highly controversial. Although there may be some permanent effect on aggregate supply from cutting tax rates, most economists believe that the increase in the tax base is not sufficient to offset the lower tax rates and so tax revenue is likely to fall, not rise. Nonetheless, the supply-siders' line of reasoning indicates that there is likely to be some offset to the loss of revenue from lowering tax rates.

Balancing the Budget: Expansionary or Contractionary?

Our aggregate demand and supply analysis of the impact of fiscal policy suggests that higher budget deficits, arising from either a cut in taxes or an increase in government spending, are expansionary in the short run. We would then expect balancing the government budget to be contractionary because it would require that we decrease aggregate demand.

Is this view always true? Not necessarily: it does not take into account that balancing the budget may have beneficial future effects that will influence the behavior of households and businesses today, particularly if the policies employed to balance the budget are sustained. A sustained cut in the budget deficit means the government will not have to raise taxes to finance future deficits. A sustained cut in the budget deficit, from either a decrease in government spending or higher taxes, then implies that future taxes will be lower. Because, as we will see in Chapter 19, lower taxes will increase capital formation and decrease distortions in the economy, measures to balance the budget can act just like a permanent positive supply shock. Figure 16.7 shows that a permanent positive supply shock increases long-run aggregate supply and causes the short-run aggregate supply curve to shift down and to the right. However, when households and businesses see the permanent decrease in government spending, they may anticipate the higher level of aggregate output that will occur as a result of the increase in the long-run aggregate supply. The anticipation of higher future aggregate output may then offset the negative effects of cutting government spending or raising taxes on aggregate demand, and so households and businesses will therefore increase their spending sufficiently to increase aggregate demand. The analysis is then exactly the same as the analysis we saw in Figure 16.7, where the economy moves to point 2 and aggregate output increases to Y_2. This scenario is not just theoretical, as the following Policy and Practice case indicates.

Policy and Practice

Two Expansionary Fiscal Contractions: Denmark and Ireland

In 1982, a conservative government came into power in Denmark and began a major program of fiscal retrenchment, lowering the budget deficit by 15% of GDP over the next four years. Instead of causing a contraction in economic activity, as conventional analysis would indicate, real GDP averaged a high 3.6% growth rate from 1983 to 1986. Consumption spending rose rapidly despite a reduction in disposable income due to higher taxes, while investment also boomed.

Ireland had a similar experience a few years later. In 1987, the new prime minister, Charles Haughey, launched a tough austerity program that brought down the deficit by 7% of GDP. The Irish economy, which had previously been stagnant, began to boom. After this fiscal retrenchment, Ireland experienced what many have called the "Irish miracle," with Ireland characterized as the "Celtic Tiger" because its economy had such impressive growth rates.

Both of these episodes suggest that fiscal retrenchments can be expansionary because they lower future taxes and boost aggregate demand and long-run aggregate supply. Whether this is the full story behind the Danish and Irish experiences is debated, but it does show that a mechanism to make a fiscal contraction expansionary for economic activity is a real possibility.[12]

---

[12]For an analysis of these two episodes, see Francesco Giavazzi and Marco Pagano, "Can Severe Fiscal Contractions Be Expansionary? Tales of Two Small European Countries," *NBER Macroeconomics Annual*, (1990): 75–122.

Policy and Practice

The Debate Over Fiscal Austerity in Europe

As a condition for financial assistance, European countries such as Greece, Ireland, Italy, and Spain, which were experiencing the sovereign debt crises described earlier in the chapter, have been required to reduce their budget deficits immediately by cutting spending and raising taxes. These austerity measures have spawned a contentious debate in Europe among economists, the public, and the politicians.

Proponents of austerity see three important benefits to austerity. First, balanced budgets will ease concerns about defaults, thereby helping bring down interest rates, which will stimulate aggregate demand and help boost economic activity. Second, reduced deficits will lead to an end to the sovereign debt crises, thereby reducing uncertainty about possible disruptions to markets, which should help stimulate investment spending. Third, getting spending under control today means that future taxes will not have to pay for it, and expectations of lower future tax rates will then encourage households and businesses to spend more today. As discussed in the previous Policy and Practice case, some fiscal retrenchments in the past may well have been expansionary.

Critics of austerity argue that cutting spending and raising taxes to reduce budget deficits have been counterproductive because they have led to economic contractions that have produced much hardship. They see fiscal multipliers as being quite high, especially for countries in the euro zone in which the policy rate has been near the zero lower bound. The policy rate is set at a particular value for the entire euro zone and so is fixed for each individual country. The analysis of fiscal multipliers at the zero lower bound is then relevant, because tight fiscal policy in an individual country not only reduces spending directly but also causes real interest rates in that country to rise as inflation falls, thereby reducing spending and shifting the aggregate demand curve further to the left.

Critics of austerity also worry that too tight a fiscal policy may not lead to a successful fiscal consolidation, for two reasons. First, the decline in economic activity from the austerity measures may reduce tax revenue by so much that the budget deficit may not decline. Second, the decline in economic activity reduces nominal GDP and so results in a rising debt-to-GDP ratio, even if the budget deficit is reduced substantially.

The debate over austerity in Europe is waged not only in the hallowed halls of academia and in policy-making institutions, but also on the street. Strikes and demonstrations, sometimes violent, have been frequent in Europe, and once unknown political parties that oppose austerity measures have found surprising success at the ballot box.

Budget Deficits and Inflation

Expansionary fiscal policy that increases the budget deficit, either from a cut in taxes or an increase in government spending, leads to higher inflation in the short run. However, as we discussed in Chapter 13, inflation in the long run will not rise as long as monetary policy focuses on price stability and takes steps to keep inflation under control. Monetary authorities, however, are not able to control inflation in the long run when budget deficits are too large, as we will see in this section.

Government-Issued Money

To illustrate the challenge of inflation and budget deficits, let's go back to the government budget constraint in Equation 2 (Deficit $= \Delta B$), which we will modify to reflect that the bonds issued to finance the deficit (ΔB) can be sold to either private investors ($\Delta B_{investors}$) or to the central bank ($\Delta B_{central\ bank}$): that is,

$$\text{Deficit} = \Delta B = \Delta B_{investors} + \Delta B_{central\ bank} \tag{4}$$

If private investors are unwilling to purchase all the government bonds the government needs to issue to finance its deficit, and the central bank is either willing or is coerced into buying them, then $\Delta B_{central\ bank}$ will be positive and the central bank will pay for the bonds by issuing money, ΔM.[13] That is,

$$\Delta B_{central\ bank} = \Delta M$$

Substituting ΔM for $\Delta B_{central\ bank}$ in Equation 4 leads to a new characterization of the government budget constraint:

$$\text{Deficit} = \Delta B = \Delta B_{investors} + \Delta M \tag{5}$$

This version of the government budget constraint tells us that the government budget deficit has to be financed either by the sale of government bonds to private investors ($\Delta B_{investors}$) or by the issuance of money (ΔM), which we more commonly refer to as **printing money**. The use of the word *printing* is slightly misleading—it is not the actual printing of the money that is important, but rather that the central bank has issued money that enables the government to purchase goods and services. We call the revenue the government receives from this issuance of currency **seignorage**.[14] Because the central bank actually issues money by purchasing government debt and then paying for it with money, printing money is also referred to as **monetizing the debt**.

Now let's see what happens if the government wants to purchase $100 billion of medical care but does not want to raise taxes to pay for it, and the public is unwilling to purchase bonds. The government, via the central bank, will print money, issuing $100 billion of currency to pay for the medical care.

---

[13]Money here, *M*, is more accurately called *high-powered money*, which is currency in circulation plus the total reserves in the banking system. High-powered money is directly linked to the money supply through the money multiplier, which we described in an appendix to Chapter 5.

[14]The term comes from *seigneur*, the French word for feudal lord, who in the Middle Ages had the right to coin money.

As we saw in Chapter 5, printing money will impact inflation. In the long run, the inflation rate will move very closely with the growth rate of the money supply:

$$\pi = \Delta M/M \tag{6}$$

Hence large budget deficits financed by printing money lead to high inflation. Indeed, in Chapter 5, we cited the recent example of hyperinflation in Zimbabwe. In all cases of hyperinflation, the source of the inflation has been very high money growth that resulted from very large budget deficits.

Revenue from Seignorage

How much revenue in real terms can the government obtain from seignorage? To answer this question, we need to rearrange the terms in Equation 6. First, let's multiply both sides of Equation 6 by M, to get

$$\Delta M = \pi \times M \tag{7}$$

Then, dividing both sides by the price level, P, we have

$$\Delta M/P = \pi \times (M/P) \tag{8}$$

Equation 8 tells us that the revenue from printing money in real terms, $\Delta M/P$, is the inflation rate, π, multiplied by the amount of real money balances, M/P. This equation explains why economists also refer to seignorage as an **inflation tax,** because the resulting higher inflation leads to a tax on holders of money balances, which lose value in real terms. For any tax, revenue in real terms equals the tax rate multiplied by the tax base in real terms. We see this relationship in Equation 8, where the tax rate is the inflation rate and the real tax base is the amount of real money balances.

Intuitively, we can see that the government collects this inflation tax if we recognize that the value of money balances held by households and businesses declines every year by the inflation rate. In real terms, holders of money balances have lost in total the amount on the right-hand side of Equation 8, which is just like a tax on them. The amount of revenue the government has collected from the inflation tax is represented by the left-hand side of Equation 8, because the government has used new money it has printed in real terms, $\Delta M/P$, to purchase real goods and services.

Concern about a government's desire to exploit the inflation tax to raise revenue when it has high budget deficits has led to calls for measures aimed at preventing high government budget deficits.

Budget Deficits and Ricardian Equivalence

So far we have discussed the traditional view of how fiscal policy and budget deficits affect the economy in both the short and long run. Robert Barro of Harvard University, however, argues that some types of fiscal policy, particularly budget deficits resulting from tax cuts, may not have much impact on the economy. His argument—which he dubbed **Ricardian equivalence** after the great nineteenth century economist David Ricardo, who discussed this possibility—suggests that tax cuts have no effect on spending and national saving.

Ricardian equivalence is based on the view that consumers are very forward-looking in their behavior, and factor their current disposable income and future income into decisions about the amount they want to spend.[15] To see the rationale behind Ricardian equivalence, suppose the government cuts taxes today, without any changes in current or future government spending. Forward-looking consumers will recognize that the budget deficit of today will have to be paid for through higher future taxes. Knowing they will have to pay these taxes in the future, consumers understand that even though current disposable income, $Y - T$, rises, they will have lower disposable income in the future. As a result, they will not change their spending behavior and will save more today in order to pay those future taxes.

Implications of Ricardian Equivalence

The Ricardian equivalence view has important implications for the effects of tax changes on 1) aggregate demand, 2) national saving and the burden on future generations, and 3) inflation.

AGGREGATE DEMAND. Ricardian equivalence implies that tax cuts will have little impact on household spending and therefore will not lead to an increase in aggregate demand. Ricardian equivalence thus calls into question whether tax cuts will have the expansionary impact, through increased consumption spending, that our aggregate demand and supply analysis in Figure 16.4 indicates. Ricardian equivalence does not rule out supply-side effects on output and inflation from tax cuts with features that affect aggregate supply.

NATIONAL SAVING AND THE BURDEN ON FUTURE GENERATIONS. Ricardian equivalence also implies that since tax cuts do not affect national saving, the resulting budget deficits that arise (if government spending remains unchanged) are not a burden on future generations. That is, tax cuts have little impact on consumer spending and aggregate output: when taxes and therefore government saving $(T - G)$ fall, private saving $(Y - T - C)$ rises by exactly the same amount. National saving, the sum of government and private saving, thus remains unchanged. As we can see from Equation 3, since national saving stays constant, tax cuts do not crowd out private investment or lead to lower net exports that must be financed by greater indebtedness to foreigners.

INFLATION. The third implication is that budget deficits that result from tax cuts will only be inflationary if the government has trouble selling the bonds used to finance budget deficits. When a budget deficit arises from tax cuts, inflation will not rise: lower taxes today leave consumer spending unchanged and induce more saving. But where can households put their increased saving? They put them into the bond market. Cutting taxes today therefore leads households to purchase more government bonds, so that the government does not have to print money to finance the resulting budget deficit. Cutting taxes therefore does not lead to higher money supply growth and so does not produce inflation.

---

[15]We will explore this viewpoint in much greater detail in Chapter 18 on consumption.

Objections to Ricardian Equivalence

Although Ricardian equivalence is an elegant theory, several important objections support the traditional view that tax cuts raise consumer spending, lower national saving, and burden future generations.

MYOPIA. Ricardian equivalence requires that people recognize that lower taxes today will just mean higher taxes tomorrow, so in reality they are no better off, and therefore they do not alter their spending plans. But what if people are shortsighted, or just don't understand that lower taxes today will mean higher taxes tomorrow? Lower taxes will likely make most people feel better off, so they will spend more. Not only will tax cuts be expansionary, in contrast to the conclusion reached by Ricardian equivalence, but the rise in private saving will be lower than the decrease in government saving, leading to lower national saving. The tax cuts and the resulting budget deficit will burden future generations.

BORROWING CONSTRAINTS. Even if people are forward-looking and recognize that lower taxes today imply higher taxes tomorrow, they may still spend more when they have higher disposable income today, because of their lower tax payments. Increased spending will occur if these people are subject to **borrowing constraints** that prevent them from borrowing the full amount they would like to borrow. Suppose that Leroy, who is subject to borrowing constraints, has a future income that is considerably higher than his current income, a situation that many students face. He will not be able to spend more than his current income because he is unable to borrow to do so. A cut in taxes today would raise his current income, now making him both willing and able to spend more. If a significant percentage of the population is borrowing-constrained, as seems sensible, then tax cuts will stimulate spending and lower national saving.

CONCERN FOR FUTURE GENERATIONS. A cut in taxes today does not mean that governments will raise taxes in the near future. Indeed, by the time taxes are raised to pay for the budget shortfall, many of the people who today are the beneficiaries of the tax cut may no longer be alive. These individuals may be perfectly happy to spend more today. After all, the current generation is made better off by the tax cuts if it doesn't care about future generations. Therefore, a tax cut can benefit the current generation at the expense of future generations.

Robert Barro has countered this argument by pointing out that we do care about our children and our children's children. Indeed, many people leave large bequests (inheritances) to their children and grandchildren, suggesting that they may value future generations' welfare as much as their own. In this case, lower taxes today will induce them to save more and not increase their spending today. Many people, however, do not leave bequests, perhaps because they lack the financial resources or they don't have children, don't like their children, or expect their children to be richer than they are. When tax cuts give them more income today, they will not increase their saving and will instead spend more, placing a greater burden on future generations.

Bottom Line on Ricardian Equivalence

The debate over whether tax cuts are expansionary and lead to a reduction in national saving centers on how consumers behave. If they are forward-looking, not subject to borrowing constraints, and care a lot about their children and their children's children, then Ricardian equivalence will hold and tax cuts will not burden future generations. On the other hand, if households are myopic, borrowing-constrained, or don't care about future generations, then tax cuts will raise consumer spending, lower national saving, and put a burden on future generations. The empirical evidence on Ricardian equivalence is mixed, as the following Policy and Practice case suggests.

Policy and Practice

The Bush Tax Cuts and Ricardian Equivalence

In 2001 and 2003, Congress passed legislation put forth by the George W. Bush administration to permanently lower taxes. What does Ricardian equivalence predict should have happened to household saving?

According to Ricardian equivalence, household saving should have risen to pay for the future tax increases that the higher budget deficits would require. Instead, household saving, which was at an already-low 3.5% of personal disposable income in 2003, fell even further to an average of 2.2% from 2004 to 2007. At first glance, households did not behave as Ricardian equivalence suggests. Household behavior appears to have been in line with the traditional view of how fiscal policy and government deficits affect the economy.

However, as is often the case in economics, the evidence from this period is not definitive due to other factors. The boom in housing prices and the stock market raised wealth and may have induced households to reduce saving. Or, people may have expected that lower taxes would lead to lower future government spending, as President Bush had promised, and so felt that they would be better off as a result of the tax cuts because their future disposable income would be higher. The debate still continues on whether the traditional view or Ricardian equivalence view reigns supreme.

SUMMARY

1. The government deficit equals government spending minus tax revenues: Deficit = Spending − Tax Revenues = $(G + TRANSFERS + INTEREST) − TAXES$. The government budget constraint tells us that the government can finance the deficit either by selling bonds or by printing money, that is, Deficit = change in amount of debt (bonds) in the hands of the public and central bank = ΔB.

2. During World War II, federal government spending led to massive increases in budget deficits, increasing the debt-to-GDP ratio to over 100% of GDP. Subsequently, the debt-to-GDP ratio fell because of the rapid growth of GDP, with the stock of government debt changing relatively little. In recent years, large budget deficits have led to an increase in the debt-to-GDP ratio. This ratio could rise even further due to the entitlements of Social Security and Medicare/Medicaid. Although government debt relative to the size of the economy has risen in recent years, the U.S. debt-to-GDP ratio is still lower than that of many other countries.

3. Sovereign debt crises occur when a sufficiently high debt-to-GDP ratio raises the probability of default, leading to a surge in interest rates on this debt, which raises government interest payments and raises the deficit, which in turn causes a rise in the debt-to-GDP ratio, and so on, until the bond market for government debt collapses.

4. Although some government spending goes into capital formation and much of it is held by U.S. households, suggesting that government debt may not be a burden on future generations, there are other reasons that government debt is a burden. First, government budget deficits may crowd out private investment and so lower the future capital stock, resulting in fewer goods and services being produced in the future. Second, not all U.S. government debt is owned by U.S. households, and the large amount owed to foreigners is a burden on future generations. Third, rising government debt involves future payments to bondholders, who are likely to be richer than non-bondholders, and so it involves a redistribution from relatively poorer people to richer people. Fourth, governments may be subject to debt intolerance so that rising debt may lead to a default

that can trigger a financial crisis, with devastating effects on the economy. Fifth, high levels of government debt lead to higher future taxes, which can lead to a less efficient economy. The distortions due to high tax rates provide an argument for tax smoothing, that is, keeping tax rates relatively constant when there are temporary swings in government spending.

5. Fiscal policy has important effects on the economy in the short run. The conventional view is that expansionary fiscal policy, such as a cut in taxes or an increase in government spending, leads to an increase in aggregate demand that leads to higher output and inflation. Fiscal multipliers are likely to be even higher when the policy interest rate has hit the zero lower bound. Possible effects on aggregate supply from tax cuts may make them even more expansionary because they lead to an increase in long-run aggregate supply. Supply-siders argue that the expansionary effects of tax cuts are so large that they may not even lead to higher budget deficits. This view is highly controversial. Aggregate supply effects do suggest that balancing the budget can sometimes be expansionary.

6. Budget deficits can lead to inflation if they cannot be financed by the issuance of bonds and the government instead resorts to financing its deficits by printing money. Financing deficits by printing money is referred to as an inflation tax because the resulting higher inflation leads to a tax on holders of money balances, which lose value in real terms. The revenue from printing money in real terms is $\Delta M/P = \pi \times (M/P)$.

7. In contrast to the traditional view that tax cuts lead to higher spending, Ricardian equivalence suggests that tax cuts have no effect on spending. Ricardian equivalence is based on the view that consumers are very forward-looking, and so tax cuts today lead to expectations of higher taxes in the future. When consumers recognize that tax cuts make them no richer in the long run, they do not spend more. Ricardian equivalence implies that tax cuts do not affect aggregate demand and lead to a rise in private saving equal to the decline in government saving, so that national saving remains unchanged. Thus tax cuts do not create a burden on future generations. Ricardian equivalence also suggests

that tax cuts do not lead to higher inflation, because the resulting increase in private saving enables the government to finance the deficit by selling bonds without resorting to printing money. Objections to Ricardian equivalence include the following: consumers are subject to myopia, are borrowing-constrained, and do not care about future generations.

KEY TERMS

borrowing constraints, p. 452

contributions for social insurance, p. 430

corporate taxes, p. 430

crowding out, p. 438

debt intolerance, p. 439

debt repudiation, p. 439

debt-to-GDP ratio, p. 431

dependency ratio, p. 433

distortions, p. 439

entitlements, p. 429

expenditure multiplier, p. 441

government budget constraint, p. 431

government capital, p. 437

government purchases, p. 428

grants in aid, p. 429

human capital, p. 437

inflation tax, p. 450

monetizing the debt, p. 449

net interest payments, p. 429

payroll tax, p. 444

personal taxes, p. 430

printing money, p. 449

Ricardian equivalence, p. 450

seignorage, p. 449

sovereign debt crises, p. 435

supply-siders, p. 445

tariffs, p. 430

tax multiplier, p. 441

tax smoothing, p. 439

tax wedges, p. 439

taxes on production and imports, p. 430

transfer payments, p. 428

REVIEW QUESTIONS

All Questions are available in MyEconLab *for practice or instructor assignment.*

The Government Budget

1. Identify the four main categories of government spending and give an example of each. What are the government's four main revenue sources?

2. What is a budget deficit, and what are the two main ways in which the government can finance deficit spending? Which of these methods of financing deficits does the U.S. government most commonly use?

Size of the Government Debt

3. What factors have influenced the debt-to-GDP ratio in the United States since 1940?

Fiscal Policy and the Economy in the Long Run

4. What arguments should be considered in assessing the burden that government debt imposes on future generations?

Fiscal Policy and the Economy in the Short Run

5. How can government increase the quantity of aggregate output demanded by changing government spending and taxes? Why does the multiplier for spending changes differ from that for tax changes?

6. How does a supply-side analysis of the effects of a tax cut differ from one that focuses solely on aggregate demand?

7. Is balancing the budget a contractionary macroeconomic policy?

8. Why are fiscal multipliers higher when the policy rate has hit the floor of the zero lower bound?

Budget Deficits and Inflation

9. What determines whether budget deficits will result in inflation in the long run?

Budget Deficits and Ricardian Equivalence

10. How does the Ricardian equivalence view of the effects of tax cuts (and budget deficits) differ from the traditional view? What objections to the Ricardian equivalence view have been raised?

PROBLEMS

All Problems are available in MyEconLab *for practice or instructor assignment.*

The Government Budget

1. Suppose government purchases amount to $2.5 trillion, transfer payments amount to $1 trillion, net interest payments are $0.5 trillion, and tax revenue is valued at $3 trillion.
   a) Calculate the government deficit.
   b) Calculate the primary deficit.
2. Assume that Social Security tax rates remain constant but the number of employed people in the United States declines over time.
   a) Explain the effect of such a scenario on the size of contributions for social insurance and the government deficit in the United States.
   b) Assume now that employment remains constant but there is an increase in unemployment insurance benefits. How would your answer to part (a) change?
3. The definition of the government deficit is a matter of debate. What would be the effect on the measurement of the government deficit if one considered Social Security taxes a "forced loan to the government" and benefit payments (e.g., Medicare, Social Security benefits, etc.) a "repayment of principal plus interest"?

Size of the Government Debt

4. In recent years, the United States has experienced a sharp increase in obesity rates (in particular amongst teenagers), which is considered to increase the probability of chronic diseases like diabetes. Even if the dependency ratio is constant, what would be the effect of such a trend on the size of the government debt?

Fiscal Policy and the Economy in the Long Run

5. As announced by the Obama administration, part of the 2009 fiscal stimulus package was directed to making broadband Internet access available to most Americans.
   a) Should this plan be considered government consumption or government investment?
   b) Describe the effect of such expenditures on the government debt burden.
6. Concerns about the ability of the U.S. government to finance its own budget deficit might lead to higher interest rates on U.S Treasury securities.

a) Explain the effect of higher interest rates on Treasury securities on the government deficit.

b) What would be the long run effect of distrust in the U.S. government's ability to finance its own deficit?

Fiscal Policy and the Economy in the Short Run

7. Assume that the expenditure and tax multipliers can be estimated at 0.75 and 0.5, respectively.
   a) Would you recommend expansionary fiscal policy based on tax cuts or increased government expenditures?
   b) Suppose there is substantial evidence that supports the hypothesis of a crowding-out effect in this economy. How would your answer to part (a) change?

8. A government committed to long-run fiscal discipline (i.e., low or zero budget deficits) usually conducts contractionary fiscal policy at some point to reduce the government deficit. If that action is interpreted as a commitment to long-run fiscal discipline,
   a) describe the effects on autonomous consumption and investment expenditure.

b) describe the effects on the cost of borrowing by issuing bonds.

9. Use an *IS* graph, an *MP* graph, and an *AD/AS* graph to show the effects of a decrease in taxes on short-run output in the two cases described in parts (a) and (b). Assume that the tax decrease is the same size in both cases and that the economy starts out at the same level of output in each case.
   a) The economy starts out above the zero lower bound.
   b) The economy starts out below the zero lower bound.
   c) What do your answers to parts (a) and (b) say about the potential impact of the American Recovery and Reinvestment Act of 2009?

Budget Deficits and Inflation

10. What would happen to revenue from seignorage if the inflation rate was very high? Hint: check Equation 8 and assume a quickly rising price level.

Budget Deficits and Ricardian Equivalence

11. Consider the effect of a tax cut (if government spending remains the same) in a country with an underdeveloped financial system.
   a) Assuming individuals are forward-looking (i.e., the Ricardian equivalence argument holds), what do you think might happen to national saving in this case?
   b) How do you think forward-looking individuals might overcome the limitations of an underdeveloped financial system?

DATA ANALYSIS PROBLEMS

The Problems update with real-time data in MyEconLab *and are available for practice or instructor assignment.*

1. Go to the St. Louis Federal Reserve FRED database, and find data on the total government debt as a percentage of GDP (GFDEGDQ188S) and gross domestic product (GDP).

a) Report the most current available debt-to-GDP ratio, and the ratio one year prior and five years prior. Based on the entire available database for this series, when was the last time the debt-to-GDP ratio reached a peak? What was the peak value, and how does it compare to the most recent value?

b) What is the percentage point difference in the debt-to-GDP ratio between the most recent period and one year ago? Between the most recent period and five years ago?

c) Calculate the total percentage increase in GDP from one year prior to the most recent period available, and also from five years prior to the most recent period available.

d) Compare the change in the debt-to-GDP ratio and the growth rate of GDP over the periods mentioned in parts (b) and (c). What can you conclude about the behavior of debt and GDP over the last year? Over the last five years?

2. Go to the St. Louis Federal Reserve FRED database, and find data on the total public debt by the federal government (GFDEBTN) and the amount of debt held by foreign and international investors (FDHBFIN). Download the data into a spreadsheet, and make sure both data series are in the same units of measurement (either millions or billions of dollars). To do this, if a series is in millions and you are converting it to billions, divide the series by 1000.

a) Calculate the percentage of the debt held by foreigners and international investors for each quarter. What is the most recent value? Comment on the size of foreign bond holdings to total debt.

b) Create a graph showing the percentage of debt held by foreign and international investors, from 1980 to the most recent data available. How has this relationship changed over time? What, if anything, does it say about the burden of U.S. debt?

3. Go to the St. Louis Federal Reserve FRED database, and find data on the budget deficit (FYFSD), the amount of federal debt held by

the public (FYGFDPUN), and the amount of federal debt held by the Federal Reserve (FDHBFRBN). Convert the two "debt held" series to "Annual" using the *frequency* setting. Download all three series into a spreadsheet. Make sure that the rows of data align properly with the correct dates. Note that for the deficit series, a negative number indicates a deficit; multiply the series by –1 so that a deficit is indicated by a positive number. Convert the three series so that all data are given in terms of the same units (either millions or billions of dollars). To do this, if a series is in millions and you are converting it to billions, divide the series by 1000. Finally, for each year, convert the two "debt held" series into one "changes in debt holdings by the public and the Federal Reserve" series by taking, for each year, the difference in bond holdings from the preceding year.

a) Create a scatter plot showing the deficit on the horizontal axis and the change in bond holdings by the public on the vertical axis, using data from 1980 to the most recent period. Insert a fitted line into the scatter plot, and comment on the relationship between the deficit and the change in public bond holdings.

b) Create a scatter plot showing the deficit on the horizontal axis and the change in bond holdings by the Federal Reserve on the vertical axis, using data from 1980 to the most recent period. Insert a fitted line into the scatter plot, and comment on the relationship between the deficit and the change in Federal Reserve bond holdings.

c) Based on your results in parts (a) and (b), comment on how, if at all, the monetizing of the debt is exhibited in the data. Do you think the relationship between the deficit and the change in bond holdings of the Federal Reserve has changed since 2008? Why or why not?

An online appendix, "Other Measures of the Government Budget Deficit," is available at the Companion Website, *www.pearsonhighered.com/mishkin.*

Exchange Rates and International Economic Policy

17

Preview

From 2000 until July 2008, the value of the U.S. dollar relative to other currencies fell by over 17%. Over the course of a few particularly volatile months during the worldwide financial crisis from 2007–2009, the dollar underwent a dramatic recovery. It rose by 20% relative to the euro by the end of October 2008 and by 15% relative to a wider basket of currencies.

The price of one currency in terms of another is called the *exchange rate*. How do swings in the exchange rate affect economic activity? What drives fluctuations in the exchange rate? How do fluctuations in exchange rates affect macroeconomic policy?

We answer these questions in this chapter by examining the financial market that determines exchange rates in the long and short runs and then seeing why exchange rates are so important in our everyday lives. We then develop a supply and demand analysis to see how exchange rates are determined. Finally, we examine the impact of exchange rate fluctuations on the economy and explore their impact on macroeconomic policy.

Foreign Exchange Market and Exchange Rates

Most countries of the world have established currencies: the United States has its dollar; the member countries of the European Monetary Union, the euro; Brazil, the real; and China, the yuan. Trade between countries requires the mutual exchange of different currencies (or, more often, of bank deposits denominated in different currencies). When a U.S. firm buys foreign goods, services, or financial assets, for example, the firm must exchange U.S. dollars (typically, bank deposits denominated in U.S. dollars) for foreign currency (bank deposits denominated in the foreign currency).

The trading of currencies and bank deposits denominated in particular currencies to determine exchange rates takes place in the **foreign exchange market.** Transactions in the foreign exchange market determine the exchange rates at which individuals and firms exchange currencies, which in turn determine the costs of purchasing foreign goods and financial assets.

Foreign Exchange Rates

There are two kinds of exchange rate transactions. The predominant ones, called **spot transactions,** affect the immediate (two-day) exchange of bank deposits.

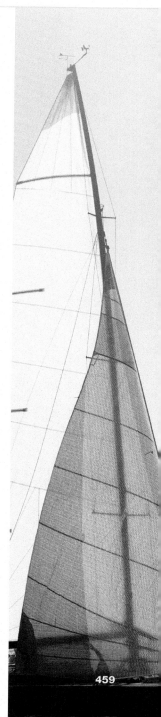

Forward transactions ensure the exchange of bank deposits at some specified future date. The **spot exchange rate** is the exchange rate for the spot transaction and the **forward exchange rate** is the exchange rate for the forward transaction.

Exchange rate quotes are stated as either units of foreign currency per domestic currency or units of domestic currency per foreign currency. For example, the media typically quotes Japanese yen as the amount of the currency per dollar (amount of yen per dollar). An exchange rate of 100 yen/$ means that for every dollar, you can get 100 yen. In other cases, such as the British pound or the euro, the currency quote is typically the amount of dollars per unit of the foreign currency (dollars per pound or euro). For example, an exchange rate of $1.50/euro means you can exchange a euro for $1.50.

When a currency increases in value relative to other currencies, it experiences **appreciation;** when it falls in value, it undergoes **depreciation.** At the beginning of 1999, when the euro first came into existence, it was valued at 1.18 dollars; on May 21, 2013, it was valued at 1.29 dollars, as indicated in the Macroeconomics in the News box, "Foreign Exchange Rates." The euro *appreciated* by 9%: $(1.29 - 1.18)/1.18 = 0.09 = 9\%$. That is, when you exchange euros for dollars, you get more dollars. Equivalently, we could say that the U.S. dollar, which went from a value of 0.85 euro per dollar at the beginning of 1999 to a value of 0.77 euro per dollar on May 21, 2013, *depreciated* by 9%: $(0.77 - 0.85)/0.85 = -0.09 = -9\%$. When you exchange dollars for euros, you now get fewer euros.

Throughout this chapter, we quote the exchange rate for a currency, denoted by E, using the convention that an appreciation of the currency corresponds to a rise in the exchange rate. That is, for the U.S. dollar, we will always present the exchange rate as units of foreign currency per dollar (say, yen per dollar).[1]

The Distinction Between Real and Nominal Exchange Rates

We can present exchange rates in *real* or *nominal* terms, which you will see is an important distinction.

NOMINAL EXCHANGE RATE. In precise terms, we refer to the exchange rate, which is the relative price of one currency in terms of another, as the **nominal exchange rate.** It is defined in nominal terms and not in terms of purchasing power: it does not tell you the amount of foreign goods and services the currency can buy. For example, if the nominal exchange rate between the U.S. dollar and the Japanese yen is 100 yen per dollar, you might think that you can get bargains in Japan because you get so many yen for each dollar. However, anyone who has visited Tokyo knows it is an expensive destination because it takes a lot of yen to buy goods and services there.

REAL EXCHANGE RATE. The **real exchange rate** is the relative price of goods in two countries, that is, the rate at which you can exchange domestic goods for foreign goods. Alternatively, think of it as the price of domestic goods denominated in foreign currency relative to the price of foreign goods in the foreign currency. It tells you how expensive one currency is in terms of another in real terms, that is, in terms of purchasing power. We also refer to the real exchange rate as the **terms of trade.**

---

[1]In professional writing, many economists quote exchange rates as units of domestic currency per foreign currency, so that an appreciation of the domestic currency is portrayed as a fall in the exchange rate. We use the opposite convention in this text, because it is more intuitive to think of an appreciation of the domestic currency as a rise in the exchange rate.

Foreign Exchange Rates

Foreign exchange rates are published daily in newspapers. The exchange rate is quoted in two ways: for example, on May 21, 2013, the spot exchange rate was quoted both as $1.2907 per euro and as 0.7748 euro per dollar. For many countries, there are typically three other entries, which give the rates for forward transactions (forward exchange rates) that will take place one month, three months, and six months in the future.

To illustrate the real exchange rate, suppose a sweatshirt in New York costs $20, while the cost of a sweatshirt in Tokyo is 4,000 yen. With the nominal exchange rate at 100 yen per dollar, the $20 sweatshirt in New York translates to a cost of 2,000 yen. Despite the large number of yen per dollar, sweatshirts in New York are quite a bit cheaper than in Tokyo: a sweatshirt in New York costs, in real terms, one-half as much as a sweatshirt in Tokyo. We can also say that a sweatshirt in New York trades for 0.5 sweatshirts in Tokyo. The real exchange rate of 0.5 is below 1.0, indicating that goods are cheaper in the United States than in Japan.

We can write the preceding calculation as follows:

$$\text{Real Exchange Rate} = \frac{(100\,\text{yen/dollar}) \times (20\,\text{dollars/U.S. sweatshirt})}{(4000\,\text{yen/Japanese sweatshirt})}$$

$$= 0.5 \, \frac{\text{Japanese sweatshirt}}{\text{U.S. sweatshirt}}$$

We can extend this calculation to a basket of goods. With P as the price level in the United States (measured in dollars) and P^* as the price level in Japan (measured in yen), the real exchange rate ε is as follows:

$$
\begin{array}{ccccc}
\varepsilon & = & E & \times & (P/P^*) \\[4pt]
\text{Real} & & \text{Nominal} & & \text{Relative} \\
\text{Exchange} & = & \text{Exchange} & \times & \text{Price} \\
\text{Rate} & & \text{Rate} & & \text{Levels}
\end{array}
\qquad (1)
$$

To summarize the preceding equation, ***the real exchange rate is the nominal exchange rate times the relative price levels. When the real exchange rate is low (below 1), domestic goods are cheap relative to foreign goods; when the real exchange rate is high (greater than 1), domestic goods are expensive relative to foreign goods.*** In other words, the real exchange rate indicates whether a country's goods are relatively cheap or relatively expensive compared with goods from other countries.

The Importance of Exchange Rates

As Equation 1 indicates, if prices are sticky—meaning price levels change slowly over time and can be taken as given in the short run—then changes in nominal exchange rates affect the relative price of domestic and foreign goods. Indeed, this is exactly what

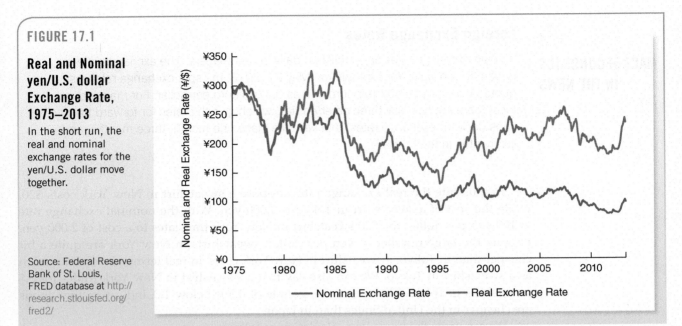

FIGURE 17.1

Real and Nominal yen/U.S. dollar Exchange Rate, 1975–2013

In the short run, the real and nominal exchange rates for the yen/U.S. dollar move together.

Source: Federal Reserve Bank of St. Louis, FRED database at http://research.stlouisfed.org/fred2/

we see in the data, as Figure 17.1 illustrates for the yen/U.S. dollar exchange rate: real and nominal exchange rates move together in the short run. The dollar price of Japanese goods to a U.S. consumer is determined by the interaction of two factors: the price of Japanese goods in yen and the yen/dollar exchange rate.

To illustrate, suppose Abe the American decides to buy the Japanese sweatshirt mentioned previously because he thinks the logo on it is cool. With the price of the sweatshirt in Japan at 4,000 yen and the yen exchange rate of $0.01 (100 yen per U.S. dollar), the sweatshirt will cost Abe $40. Now suppose that Abe delays his purchase by a year, at which time the yen has appreciated to $0.015 per yen. If the domestic price of the sweatshirt remains at 4,000 yen because prices are sticky, its dollar cost will have risen from $40 to $60.

The same currency appreciation, however, makes the price of foreign goods in the domestic country less expensive. At an exchange rate of $0.01 per yen, an Apple computer priced at $2,000 costs Taka the Technician 200,000 yen in Japan; if the exchange rate increases to $0.015 per yen, the computer will cost only 133,333 yen.

On the other hand, a depreciation of the yen lowers the cost of Japanese goods in the United States but raises the cost of U.S. goods in Japan. If the yen drops in value to $0.005, Abe's Japanese sweatshirt will cost him only $20 instead of $40, and the Apple computer will cost Taka 400,000 yen rather than 200,000 yen.

Such reasoning leads to the following conclusion: *when a country's currency appreciates (rises in value relative to other currencies) with sticky prices, the country's goods abroad become more expensive and foreign goods in that country become cheaper (holding domestic prices constant in the two countries). Conversely, when a country's currency depreciates, its goods abroad become cheaper and foreign goods in that country become more expensive.*

Depreciation of a currency makes it easier for domestic manufacturers to sell their goods abroad and makes foreign goods less competitive in domestic markets. From 2000 to 2008, the depreciating dollar helped U.S. industries sell more goods, but it hurt

U.S. consumers because foreign goods were more expensive. The price of Japanese sweatshirts and the cost of vacationing abroad all rose as a result of the weak dollar.

Foreign Exchange Trading

You cannot go to a physical location to watch exchange rate transactions; currencies are not traded on exchanges such as the New York Stock Exchange. Instead, the foreign exchange market is an over-the-counter market in which several hundred dealers (mostly banks) stand ready to buy and sell bank deposits denominated in foreign currencies. For example, dealers facilitate exchanges for a fixed amount of euro bank deposits for a given amount of dollar bank deposits. Because these dealers are in constant telephone and computer contact, the market is very competitive; in effect, it functions no differently than a physical market.

When banks, companies, and governments buy and sell currencies in foreign exchange markets, they do not take a fistful of dollar bills and sell them for British pound notes. Rather, most trades involve the buying and selling of bank deposits denominated in different currencies. When we say that a bank is buying dollars in the foreign exchange market, we actually mean that the bank is buying *deposits denominated in dollars*. The volume in this market is colossal, exceeding $4 trillion per day.

Individual trades in the foreign exchange market consist of transactions in excess of $1 million and determine the exchange rates we referenced in the Macroeconomics in the News box. To buy foreign currency for a trip abroad, you would go to the retail market, with dealers such as American Express, or to a bank. Because retail prices are higher than wholesale prices on the foreign exchange market, when we buy foreign exchange as individuals, we obtain fewer units of foreign currency per dollar than the foreign exchange rate quote indicates.

Exchange Rates in the Long Run

Like the price of any good or asset in a free market, exchange rates are determined by the interaction of supply and demand. To simplify our analysis of exchange rates in a free market, we divide it into two parts. First, we examine how exchange rates are determined in the long run; then, in the following section, we use our knowledge of the long-run determinants of the exchange rate to see how exchange rates are determined in the short run. The starting point for understanding long-run exchange rates is the *law of one price*.

Law of One Price

According to the **law of one price,** if two countries produce an identical good, and transportation costs and trade barriers are very low, the price of the good should be the same in both countries no matter which country produces it. As a result, we can determine the exchange rate necessary for the price of a good to be equal in two countries.

To illustrate, suppose U.S. steel costs $100 per ton and identical Japanese steel costs 10,000 yen per ton. For the law of one price to hold, the exchange rate between the yen and the dollar must be 100 yen per dollar ($0.01 per yen), so that one ton of U.S. steel sells for 10,000 yen in Japan (the price of Japanese steel) and one ton of Japanese steel sells for $100 in the United States (the price of U.S. steel). The real exchange rate is always equal to 1.0, so that we can exchange one ton of U.S. steel for exactly one ton of Japanese steel.

If the exchange rate were 200 yen to the dollar, Japanese steel would sell for $50 per ton in the United States, or half the price of U.S. steel, and U.S. steel would sell for 20,000 yen per ton in Japan, twice the price of Japanese steel. Because U.S. steel would be more expensive than Japanese steel in both countries, and because it is identical to Japanese steel, the demand for U.S. steel would go to zero. Given a fixed dollar price for U.S. steel, the resulting excess supply would be eliminated only if the exchange rate fell to 100 yen per dollar, making the price of U.S. steel and Japanese steel the same in both countries and the real exchange rate equal to 1.

Theory of Purchasing Power Parity

What is the relationship between this insight about the law of one price and exchange rate determination? The most prominent theory of how exchange rates are determined in the long run is the **theory of purchasing power parity (PPP),** which states that exchange rates between any two currencies will adjust to reflect changes in the price levels of the two countries. The theory of PPP is simply an application of the law of one price to national price levels rather than to individual prices. Suppose the yen price of Japanese steel rises 10% (to 11,000 yen) relative to the dollar price of U.S. steel (unchanged at $100). For the law of one price to hold and the real exchange rate to remain at 1.0, the exchange rate must rise to 110 yen to the dollar, a 10% appreciation of the dollar. Applying the law of one price to the price levels in the two countries produces the theory of purchasing power parity, which maintains that if the Japanese price level rises 10% relative to the U.S. price level, the dollar will appreciate by 10%.

Another way of understanding PPP is to recognize that if PPP holds, the real exchange rate is always equal to 1.0, so the purchasing power of the dollar is the same as the purchasing power of other currencies such as the yen or the euro. Then, using Equation 1, we can see that when P^* rises by 10%, causing the U.S. price level to fall by 10% relative to Japan's, E must rise by 10% to keep the real exchange rate at 1.0.

Although there is evidence that PPP holds in the very long run, it is questionable over short periods, as we discuss in the box entitled, "Big Macs and PPP." This limitation makes sense because countries do not produce identical goods: for example, Toyotas and Chevys are clearly quite different automobiles, so the law of one price will not hold. Furthermore, many goods and services (whose prices are included in a measure of a country's price level) are **nontradable,** that is, they are not traded across borders.

Big Macs and PPP

Twice a year, *The Economist* magazine publishes data on the cost of a Big Mac in different countries, in both local currency and U.S. dollars. We show the data from July 2013 in Table 17.1. The second column gives the Big Mac price in terms of local currency, while the third column uses the exchange rate for each currency to convert the Big Mac price into dollars. If PPP held exactly, then the real exchange rate would be 1.0 and all the prices in terms of dollars would be identical. Notice, however, that this is not the case, with the price of Big Macs in some countries (for example, Norway and Switzerland) well above the price in the United States, and the price in other countries (such as China, Indonesia, and Malaysia) well below.

TABLE 17.1   *THE ECONOMIST* MAGAZINE'S BIG MAC INDEX, JULY 2013

Country	Big Mac Price		Exchange Rate (local currency/$)	
	Local Currency	Dollars	Predicted	Actual
Norway	46.00	$7.51	10.10	6.13
Switzerland	6.50	$6.72	1.43	0.97
Canada	5.53	$5.26	1.21	1.05
Euro Area	3.62	$4.66	0.80	0.78
Australia	5.04	$4.62	1.10	1.09
United States	4.56	$4.56	1.00	1.00
Turkey	8.50	$4.34	1.87	1.96
Britain	2.69	$4.02	0.59	0.67
Hungary	860.00	$3.76	188.79	228.46
South Korea	3900.00	$3.43	855.89	1135.70
United Arab Emirates	12.00	$3.27	2.63	3.67
Japan	320.00	$3.20	70.23	100.11
Mexico	37.00	$2.86	8.12	12.94
Thailand	89.00	$2.85	19.53	31.28
Indonesia	27939.00	$2.80	6161.46	9965.00
Poland	9.20	$2.73	2.02	3.37
Saudi Arabia	10.00	$2.67	2.13	3.75
Russia	87.00	$2.64	19.09	32.94
Taiwan	79.00	$2.63	17.34	30.03
China	16.00	$2.61	3.51	6.13
Egypt	16.75	$2.39	3.68	7.01
Malaysia	7.30	$2.30	1.60	3.18
South Africa	18.33	$1.82	4.02	10.05

Although the Big Mac prices indicate that PPP does not hold exactly, PPP does help predict exchange rates for these countries. According to PPP, when the Big Mac has a high price in terms of local currency, then the units of local currency per U.S. dollar should be higher. We see this relationship in the fourth and fifth columns of Table 17.1. The predicted exchange rate in the fourth column is the exchange rate that would make the price of the Big Mac equal to the price in the United States (the real exchange rate would be 1.0). Notice that when the predicted exchange rate has a large number of units of local currency per U.S. dollar, this relationship is also true for the actual exchange rate in the fifth column. However, the predicted value of the exchange rate often departs quite substantially from the actual exchange rate. For example, Mexico's predicted rate is 8.12 pesos/$, versus the actual exchange rate of 12.94 pesos/$.

The evidence from Big Macs suggests that purchasing power parity provides some explanation for the value of exchange rates, but it does not give a complete explanation.

Source: The Economist, July 2013, at http://www.economist.com/content/big-mac-index

Housing, land, and services such as restaurant meals, haircuts, and golf lessons are non-tradable. Even though the prices of these items might rise, leading to a higher price level relative to another country's price level, there probably will be little direct effect on the exchange rate in the short run. As a result, we need a supply and demand framework to understand what determines exchange rates in the short run.

Exchange Rates in the Short Run

The key to understanding the short-run behavior of exchange rates is to recognize that an exchange rate is the price of domestic assets (bank deposits, bonds, equities, and so on denominated in the domestic currency) in terms of foreign assets (similar assets denominated in a foreign currency). Because the exchange rate is the price of one asset in terms of another, we investigate the short-run determination of exchange rates using an asset market approach that emphasizes the demand for the stock of domestic assets.[2]

A traditional approach to exchange rate determination emphasized the demand for flows of exports and imports over short periods. The asset market approach used here is more accurate because export and import transactions are small relative to the amount of domestic and foreign assets at any given time. For example, U.S. foreign exchange transactions each year are well over twenty-five times greater than the amount of U.S. exports and imports. Thus, over short periods, decisions on whether to hold domestic or foreign assets play a much greater role in exchange rate determination than the demand for exports and imports does.[3]

Supply Curve for Domestic Assets

We start by discussing the supply curve for domestic assets. We treat the United States as the home country, so we denominate domestic assets in dollars. For simplicity, we use euros to stand for any foreign country's currency, so we denominate foreign assets in euros.

The quantity of dollar assets supplied is primarily the quantity of bank deposits, bonds, and equities in the United States—for all practical purposes, we can take this amount as fixed with respect to the exchange rate. The quantity supplied at any exchange rate does not change, so the supply curve, S, is vertical, as shown in Figure 17.2.

Demand Curve for Domestic Assets

The demand curve traces out the quantity demanded at each current exchange rate by holding everything else constant, particularly the expected future value of the exchange rate. We write the current exchange rate (the spot exchange rate) as E_t and the expected exchange rate for the next period as E^e_{t+1}. If there is **capital mobility,** with assets traded freely between countries, the most important determinant of the quantity of domestic (dollar) assets demanded is expected return on domestic assets relative to foreign assets.

---

[2]We conduct the analysis here in terms of supply and demand for domestic assets. An alternative way to conduct the analysis is with a concept called *interest parity*, and this is described in an appendix to this chapter on the Companion Website at www.pearsonhighered.com/mishkin.

[3]For a further description of the modern asset market approach to exchange rate determination that we use here, see Frederic S. Mishkin, *The Economics of Money, Banking, and Financial Markets*, 10th edition (Boston: Pearson Addison-Wesley, 2013); and Paul Krugman and Maurice Obstfeld, *International Economics*, 9th edition (Boston: Pearson Addison-Wesley, 2012).

FIGURE 17.2

Equilibrium in the Foreign Exchange Market

Equilibrium in the foreign exchange market occurs at point B, the intersection of the demand curve *D* and the supply curve *S*. The equilibrium exchange rate is *E**, where the quantity demanded of dollar assets equals the quantity supplied.

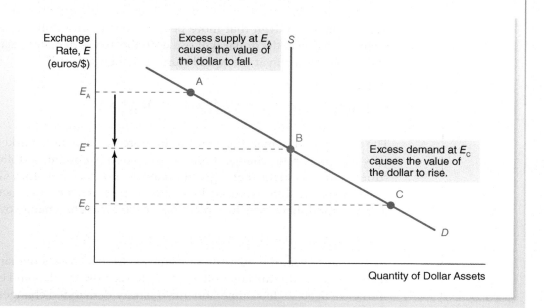

The **expected return** on an asset is any payments from the asset, such as interest, and any expected change in its value, as a fraction of its price.

To see why the demand curve has the conventional downward slope in Figure 17.2, we start at point A in the figure, where the current exchange rate is at E_A. If we hold the future expected value of the exchange rate constant at E_{t+1}^e, a lower value of the exchange rate at E^* implies that the dollar is more likely to rise in value (appreciate). The greater the expected rise (appreciation) of the dollar, the higher is the expected return on dollar (domestic) assets. Because dollar assets are now more desirable to hold, the quantity of dollar assets demanded will rise to point B in Figure 17.2. If the current exchange rate is even lower at E_C, there is an even higher expected appreciation of the dollar, a higher expected return, and therefore an even greater quantity of dollar assets demanded. Point C represents this scenario in the figure. The resulting demand curve, *D*, which connects these points, is downward sloping, indicating that at lower current values of the dollar (everything else being equal), the quantity demanded of dollar assets is higher.

Equilibrium in the Foreign Exchange Market

As in the usual supply and demand analysis, the market is in equilibrium when the quantity of dollar assets demanded equals the quantity supplied. In Figure 17.2, equilibrium occurs at point B, the intersection of the demand and supply curves. At point B, the exchange rate is E^*.

Suppose the exchange rate is at E_A, which is higher than the equilibrium exchange rate of E^*. Notice in Figure 17.2 that the quantity of dollar assets supplied is then greater than the quantity demanded, a condition of excess supply. Given that more people want to sell dollar assets than want to buy them, the value of the dollar will fall. As long as the exchange rate remains above the equilibrium exchange rate, an excess supply of dollar assets will continue to be available, and the dollar will fall in value until it reaches the equilibrium exchange rate of E^*.

Similarly, if the exchange rate is less than the equilibrium exchange rate at E_C, the quantity of dollar assets demanded will exceed the quantity supplied, a condition of excess demand. Given that more people want to buy dollar assets than want to sell them, the value of the dollar will rise until the excess demand disappears and the value of the dollar is again at the equilibrium exchange rate of E^*.

Analysis of Changes in Exchange Rates

The supply and demand analysis of the foreign exchange market illustrates how and why exchange rates change. Because we take the amount of dollar assets as fixed, the supply curve is vertical at a given quantity and does not shift. Given that the supply curve does not shift, we need look only at those factors that increase or decrease the demand for dollar assets to explain how exchange rates change over time.

Changes in the Demand for Domestic Assets

As we have seen, the quantity of domestic (dollar) assets demanded depends on the relative expected return on dollar assets. To see how the demand curve for dollar assets shifts, we need to determine how the quantity demanded changes, holding the current exchange rate, E_t, constant, when other factors change.

For insight into whether demand increases or decreases, suppose you are an investor who is considering putting funds into domestic (dollar) assets. When a factor changes, you must decide whether, at a given level of the current exchange rate and holding all other variables constant, you would earn a higher or lower expected return on dollar assets versus foreign assets. This decision tells you whether you want to hold more or fewer dollar assets and thus whether the quantity demanded increases or decreases at each level of the exchange rate. The direction of the change in the quantity demanded at each exchange rate indicates which way the demand curve shifts: if the relative expected return on dollar assets rises, holding the current exchange rate constant, the demand curve shifts to the right. If the relative expected return falls, the demand curve for dollar assets shifts to the left.

DOMESTIC REAL INTEREST RATE, r^D. When the domestic real interest rate on dollar assets r^D rises, holding the current exchange rate E_t and everything else constant, the return on dollar assets increases relative to foreign assets, so people will want to hold more dollar assets.[4] The quantity of dollar assets demanded increases at every value of the exchange rate, as shown by the rightward shift of the demand curve from D_1 to D_2 in panel (a) of Figure 17.3. At the new equilibrium point 2, at the intersection of D_2 and S, the equilibrium exchange rate rises from E_1 to E_2. *An increase in the domestic real interest rate shifts the demand curve for domestic assets, D, to the right and causes the domestic currency to appreciate ($E\uparrow$).*

[4]A rise in the domestic real interest rate is the same as a rise in the nominal interest rate when everything else is held constant, which includes the expected inflation rate. Thus the results described in the text about the effect of changes in real interest rates on the exchange rate are the same as for changes in the nominal interest rate. The reason for thinking about the response of the foreign exchange market in terms of changes in real interest rates rather than nominal interest rates is that nominal interest rates typically rise with expected inflation, so that many changes in nominal interest rates occur when it is inappropriate to assume that everything else is held constant.

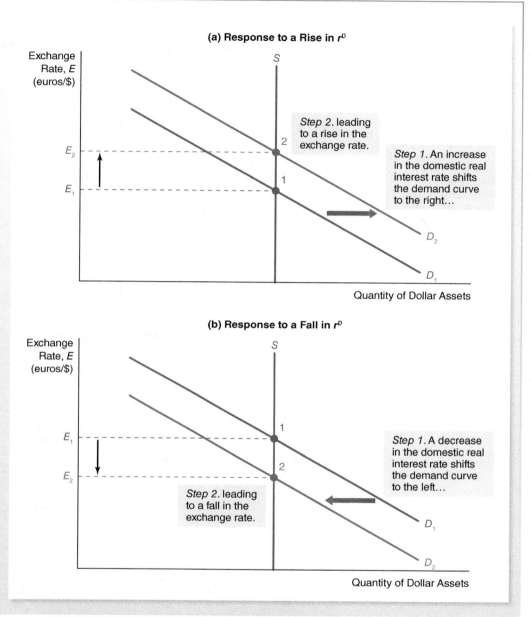

FIGURE 17.3

Response to a Change in Domestic Real Interest Rates, r^D

Panels (a) and (b) show the effect of changes in the domestic real interest rate, r^D. In panel (a), an increase in r^D raises the relative expected return on domestic (dollar) assets, shifting the demand curve to the right. The equilibrium exchange rate rises from E_1 to E_2. In panel (b), a decrease in r^D lowers the relative expected return on domestic (dollar) assets, shifting the demand curve to the left. The equilibrium exchange rate falls from E_1 to E_2.

Conversely, if r^D falls, the relative expected return on dollar assets falls, the demand curve shifts to the left from D_1 to D_2 in panel (b) of Figure 17.3, and the exchange rate falls from E_1 to E_2. **A decrease in the domestic real interest rate r^D shifts the demand curve for domestic assets, D, to the left and causes the domestic currency to depreciate ($E\downarrow$).**

FOREIGN REAL INTEREST RATE, r^F. When the foreign real interest rate rises, holding the current exchange rate E_t and everything else constant, the return on foreign assets rises relative to dollar assets. Thus the relative expected return on dollar assets falls. Now people want to hold fewer dollar assets and the quantity demanded decreases at

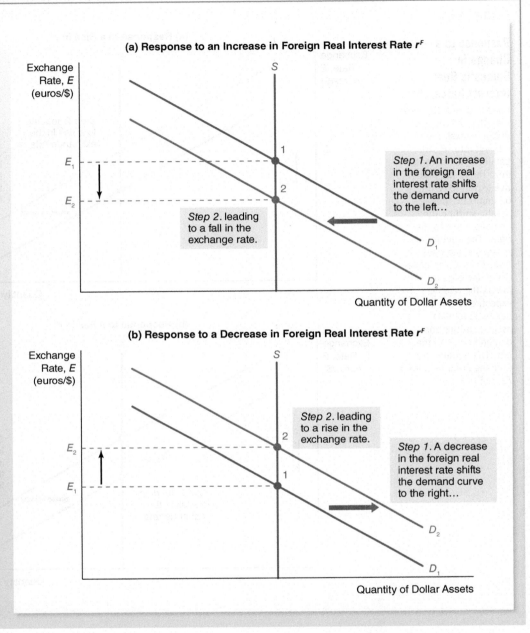

FIGURE 17.4

Response to a Change in Foreign Real Interest Rates, r^F

Panels (a) and (b) show the effect of changes in the foreign real interest rate, r^F. In panel (a), an increase in r^F lowers the relative expected return on domestic (dollar) assets, shifting the demand curve to the left. The equilibrium exchange rate falls from E_1 to E_2. In panel (b), a decrease in r^F raises the relative expected return on domestic (dollar) assets, shifting the demand curve to the right. The equilibrium exchange rate increases from E_1 to E_2.

every value of the exchange rate, as shown by the leftward shift of the demand curve from D_1 to D_2 in panel (a) of Figure 17.4. At the new equilibrium point 2, the exchange rate has decreased. Conversely, a decrease in r^F raises the relative expected return on dollar assets, shifts the demand curve to the right from D_1 to D_2 in panel (b), and raises the exchange rate. To summarize, *an increase in the foreign real interest rate r^F shifts the demand curve D to the left and causes the domestic currency to depreciate; a fall in the foreign real interest rate r^F shifts the demand curve D to the right and causes the domestic currency to appreciate.*

Application

The Global Financial Crisis and the Dollar

With the start of the global financial crisis in August 2007, the dollar began an accelerated decline in value, falling by 9% against the euro until mid-July 2008 and by 6% against a wider basket of currencies. After hitting an all-time low against the euro on July 11, 2008, the dollar suddenly shot upward by over 20% against the euro by the end of October 2008, and by 15% against a wider basket of currencies.

How did the global financial crisis lead to these large swings in the value of the dollar? In the first year of the crisis, its negative effects on economic activity were mostly confined to the United States. The Federal Reserve acted aggressively with autonomous easing of monetary policy to decrease interest rates to counter the contractionary effects, lowering the federal funds rate target by 325 basis points (3.25 percentage points) from September 2007 to April 2008. In contrast, other central banks, like the European Central Bank, did not see the need to lower interest rates, particularly because high energy prices had led to a surge in inflation. The relative expected return on dollar assets thus declined, shifting the demand curve for dollar assets to the left, as in panel (b) of Figure 17.3, leading to a decline in the equilibrium exchange rate. Our analysis of the foreign exchange market thus explains why the global crisis in its early phase led to a decline in the value of the dollar.

Our analysis also explains why the value of the dollar rose thereafter. Starting in the summer of 2008, the effects of the global crisis on economic activity began to spread more widely throughout the world. Foreign central banks started to cut interest rates via autonomous easing of monetary policy, with the expectation that they would do so even more in the future. The expected decline in foreign interest rates then increased the relative expected return on dollar assets, leading to a rightward shift in the demand curve and an increase in the equilibrium exchange rate, as shown in panel (b) of Figure 17.4.

Another factor driving the dollar upward was a "flight to quality" that occurred when the financial crisis reached a particularly virulent stage in September and October 2008. Both U.S. and foreign investors now wanted to put their money in the safest asset possible: U.S. Treasury securities. The resulting increase in the demand for dollar assets provided an additional reason for the demand curve for dollar assets to shift to the right, thereby helping to produce a sharp appreciation of the dollar.

CHANGES IN THE EXPECTED FUTURE EXCHANGE RATE, E^e_{t+1}. Expectations about the future value of the exchange rate play an important role in shifting the current demand curve, because the demand for domestic assets, like the demand for any financial asset or durable good, depends on the expected future resale price. Any factor that causes the expected future exchange rate, E^e_{t+1}, to rise increases the expected appreciation of the dollar. The result is a higher relative expected return on dollar assets, which increases the demand for dollar assets at every exchange rate, thereby shifting the demand curve to the right from D_1 to D_2 in panel (a) of Figure 17.5. The equilibrium exchange rate rises to E_2 at point 2. *A rise in the expected future exchange rate, E^e_{t+1}, shifts the demand curve to the right and causes an appreciation of the domestic currency.* Using the same reasoning, in panel (b), *a fall in the expected future exchange rate, E^e_{t+1}, shifts the demand curve to the left and causes a depreciation of the currency.*

FIGURE 17.5

Response to a Change in the Expected Future Exchange Rate, E_{t+1}^e

Panels (a) and (b) show the effect of changes in the expected future exchange rate, E_{t+1}^e. In panel (a), an increase in E_{t+1}^e raises the relative expected return on domestic (dollar) assets, shifting the demand curve to the right. The equilibrium exchange rate increases from E_1 to E_2. In panel (b), a decrease in E_{t+1}^e lowers the relative expected return on domestic (dollar) assets, shifting the demand curve to the left. The equilibrium exchange rate decreases from E_1 to E_2.

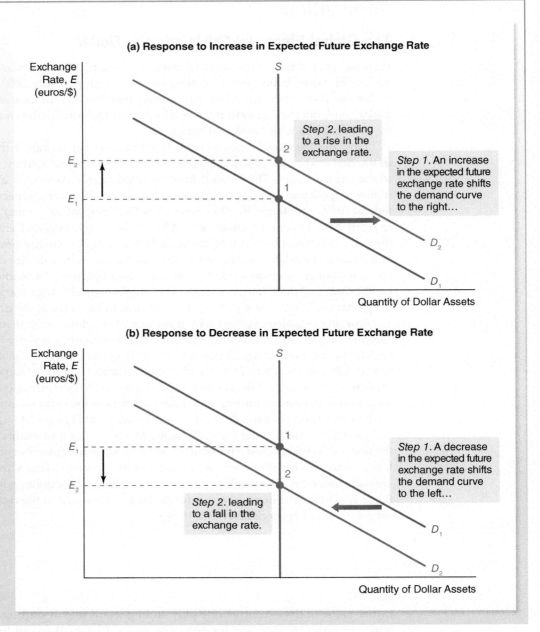

(a) Response to Increase in Expected Future Exchange Rate

Exchange Rate, E (euros/$)

Step 2. leading to a rise in the exchange rate.

Step 1. An increase in the expected future exchange rate shifts the demand curve to the right...

Quantity of Dollar Assets

(b) Response to Decrease in Expected Future Exchange Rate

Exchange Rate, E (euros/$)

Step 1. A decrease in the expected future exchange rate shifts the demand curve to the left...

Step 2. leading to a fall in the exchange rate.

Quantity of Dollar Assets

What are the possible events that might affect the expected future exchange rate? Any factor that increases the demand for domestically produced, traded goods relative to foreign traded goods, such as a rise in the demand for exports, will cause long-run appreciation of the domestic currency, because domestic goods will continue to sell well even when the value of the domestic currency is higher. As a result, the expected future exchange rate E_{t+1}^e will rise, leading to a higher expected return on dollar assets, shifting the demand curve to the right and increasing the current exchange rate, as in panel (a). Similarly, any factor that increases the demand for foreign tradable goods relative to domestic traded goods, such as a rise in the demand for imports, will lead to a long-run depreciation of the domestic currency and will cause E_{t+1}^e to fall, as in panel (b). The demand curve then shifts to the left and the exchange rate depreciates.

Let's analyze what happens if the Japanese price level rises relative to the U.S. price level. The higher Japanese price level increases the demand for U.S. goods because they are now relatively cheaper, with the result that the U.S. dollar exchange rate appreciates in the long run and the expected future exchange rate E_{t+1}^e therefore rises. The resulting increase in the relative expected return on dollar assets shifts the demand curve to the right, as in panel (a) of Figure 17.5, and the equilibrium exchange rate rises. Indeed, this is the same result that we obtained from the theory of purchasing power parity: an increase in the foreign price level relative to the domestic price level leads to an appreciation of the domestic currency.

Application

Why Are Exchange Rates So Volatile?

Forty or so years ago, economists generally believed that the determination of exchange rates in the free market would not lead to large fluctuations in their values. Recent experience has proved them wrong: exchange rates have been very volatile, often with swings of several percentage points in a single day.

The asset market approach to exchange rate determination that we have outlined in this chapter gives a straightforward explanation of why exchange rates are so volatile. Because expected appreciation of the domestic currency affects the relative expected return on domestic deposits, expectations about the future play an important role in determining the exchange rate. When these expectations change, our model implies that there will be an immediate effect on the expected return on domestic deposits and therefore on the exchange rate. The foreign exchange market is just like any other asset market in which expectations of the future matter. Thus, like other asset markets such as the stock market, the foreign exchange market displays substantial price volatility, and exchange rates are therefore notoriously hard to forecast.

The volatility of exchange rates presents a challenge to policy makers because it causes relative prices of domestic versus foreign goods to fluctuate. This uncertainty makes it hard for you to plan whether you will take your vacation in the United States or abroad and can dramatically change the competitiveness of a domestic industry, increasing the volatility of economic activity.

 # Exchange Rates and Aggregate Demand and Supply Analysis

Now that we understand how foreign exchange markets determine exchange rates, we can examine how they affect aggregate output and inflation using our aggregate demand and supply framework.

At the beginning of this chapter, we explained why a rise in the real exchange rate—that is, a real appreciation of the domestic currency—makes domestic goods more expensive relative to foreign goods. Because prices are sticky and change slowly over time, a rise in the nominal exchange rate implies a rise in the real exchange rate in the short run. Thus the demand for exports, which are now more expensive, will fall and the demand for imports, which are now cheaper, will rise. An exogenous rise in the exchange rate ($E \uparrow$) thus leads to a decline in net exports ($NX \downarrow$), which, because net exports are a component of aggregate demand, leads to a fall in the equilibrium level of output ($Y \downarrow$):

$$E \uparrow \Rightarrow NX \downarrow \Rightarrow Y \downarrow$$

At any given rate of inflation, an exogenous appreciation of the domestic currency therefore leads to a lower level of equilibrium output; as a result, the aggregate demand curve shifts to the left from AD_1 to AD_2 in Figure 17.6.

The appreciation of the dollar also acts as a temporary positive supply shock to the short-run aggregate supply curve because it makes imports less expensive and thus lowers the inflation rate. As a result, the short-run aggregate supply curve shifts down from AS_1 to AS_2. Because the shift in the short-run aggregate supply curve is typically small relative to the shift in the aggregate demand curve, as shown in Figure 17.6, the economy moves from point 1 to point 2 at the intersection of AD_2 and AS_2. Aggregate output falls to Y_2 and inflation falls to π_2.

How should the monetary authorities respond to the exchange rate appreciation if they want to stabilize both output and inflation? The central bank should autonomously ease monetary policy by lowering the real interest rate at any given inflation rate. As we saw in panel (b) of Figure 17.3, this lowering of the real interest rate would decrease

---

FIGURE 17.6

Response of Aggregate Output and Inflation to an Increase in the Exchange Rate

A rise in the nominal exchange rate leads to a rise in the real exchange rate, which causes net exports and therefore aggregate demand to fall. As a result, the aggregate demand curve shifts to the left to AD_2. The appreciation of the dollar acts as a beneficial supply shock, driving the short-run aggregate supply curve down to AS_2. The economy moves to point 2, where aggregate output and inflation have fallen to Y_2 and π_2.

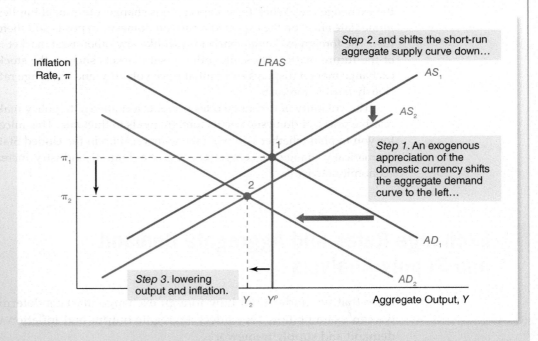

Step 2. and shifts the short-run aggregate supply curve down...

Step 1. An exogenous appreciation of the domestic currency shifts the aggregate demand curve to the left...

Step 3. lowering output and inflation.

the relative expected return for domestic assets, thereby shifting the demand curve for domestic assets to the left and causing the exchange rate to fall. The resulting higher price of imports would then raise prices, shifting the short-run aggregate supply curve upward, while the higher net exports would increase aggregate demand and shift the aggregate demand curve to the right. In addition, lower real interest rates would increase investment spending, providing a further reason for aggregate demand to increase. The monetary policy action would therefore return the economy to point 1 in Figure 17.6.

We can conclude the following points from our analysis: ***an exogenous appreciation of the exchange rate is contractionary and leads to a decline in both aggregate output and inflation. Autonomous monetary policy easing can, however, counteract the contractionary shock from an exchange rate appreciation.*** Similarly, ***an exogenous depreciation of the currency is expansionary, raising both output and inflation, but can be counteracted by autonomous monetary policy tightening.***[5] Our analysis therefore explains why central banks pay a lot of attention to exchange rate fluctuations in formulating monetary policy.

Intervention in the Foreign Exchange Market

So far, we have analyzed the foreign exchange market as if it were a completely free market that responds only to market pressures. Like many other markets, however, the foreign exchange market is subject to government intervention, particularly by central banks. Central banks regularly engage in international financial transactions called **foreign exchange interventions** to influence exchange rates. In our current international environment, exchange rates fluctuate from day to day, but central banks attempt to influence their countries' exchange rates by buying and selling currencies. For example, the Chinese government could decide to use yuan to buy U.S. dollars. We can use the supply and demand analysis of foreign exchange rates to analyze the impact of central bank intervention on the foreign exchange market.

Foreign Exchange Intervention

The first step in understanding how central bank intervention in the foreign exchange market affects exchange rates is to examine the impact on a central bank's balance sheet when it sells some of its foreign-currency denominated assets (say, euros), which are called **international reserves.** (The appendix to Chapter 5 examines central bank balance sheets in detail.) Suppose the Fed wants to boost the value of the dollar and decides to sell $1 billion of euro assets in exchange for $1 billion of assets denominated in U.S. currency. We describe this transaction by saying that the Fed has sold euros and bought dollars in the foreign exchange market. (This transaction is conducted at the foreign exchange desk at the Federal Reserve Bank of New York.) The Fed's purchase of dollar assets has two effects. First, it reduces the Fed's holding of international reserves by $1 billion. Second, it drains liquidity from the financial system because banks' deposits with the Fed, known as reserves, fall.

---

[5]However, for emerging market economies, which have much of their debt denominated in foreign currencies, an exchange rate depreciation, although inflationary, may lead to a sharp contraction in economic activity because the decline in the value of the currency destroys balance sheets and can precipitate a financial crisis. We discuss this mechanism more extensively in the Web chapter on emerging market economies available at the Companion Website, www.pearsonhighered.com/mishkin.

To see how a foreign exchange intervention works, we use a tool called a T-account, which is a simplified balance sheet with lines in the form of a T, that lists only the changes that occur in assets and liabilities starting from some initial balance sheet position. Just like a balance sheet, both sides of the T-account must balance.

Let's see what happens when the Fed sells the $1 billion of foreign assets (international reserves) in exchange for bank deposits denominated in dollars. The "foreign assets" item in the Fed's T-account drops by $1 billion. At the same time, the Fed subtracts the $1 billion of bank deposits it receives from the total holding of banks' deposits at the Federal Reserve. Reserves (deposits with the Fed) then fall by $1 billion, as we show in the following T-account.

Federal Reserve System

Assets		Liabilities	
Foreign assets (international reserves)	−$1 billion	Deposits with the Fed (reserves)	−$1 billion

The Fed's purchase of dollars and sale of euros leads to an equal decline in international reserves and reserves (deposits with the Fed) held by the banking system. The resulting decline in reserves held by banks reduces liquidity in the financial system, lowers the money supply, and causes interest rates to rise, as per our analysis in Chapter 10. We can state the results as follows: *a central bank's purchase of domestic currency and corresponding sale of foreign assets in the foreign exchange markets leads to an equal decline in international reserves held by the central bank and reserves held by the banking system. The decline in reserves in the banking system then leads to a rise in interest rates.*

Intervention and the Exchange Rate

Now that we understand the impact of a foreign exchange intervention on reserves and the interest rate, we can look at what happens when a central bank buys its currency in the foreign exchange market and sells foreign assets. As the preceding T-account indicates, the intervention whereby the Federal Reserve buys dollars and sells foreign assets in the foreign exchange market decreases liquidity in the financial system, causes the money supply to fall, and increases interest rates. Because prices are sticky, the rise in nominal interest rates leads to a rise in the real interest rate r^D, and so the relative expected return on dollar assets increases the demand for those assets, shifting the demand curve to the right from D_1 to D_2 in Figure 17.7. The equilibrium moves from point 1 to point 2, with the exchange rate rising from E_1 to E_2.

Our analysis leads us to the following conclusion about interventions in the foreign exchange market:[6] *an intervention in which the central bank buys domestic currency leads to a loss of international reserves and an appreciation of the domestic*

---

[6]The intervention we are describing here is referred to as an *unsterilized intervention* because it results in a change in reserves and hence in interest rates. However, a central bank can counter the effect of a foreign exchange rate intervention on reserves by conducting an offsetting open market operation in domestic bonds. In this case, reserves in the banking system will not change, and the intervention is referred to as a *sterilized intervention*. Chapter 18 of Frederic Mishkin, *The Economics of Money, Banking, and Financial Markets*, 10th edition (Boston: Pearson Addison-Wesley, 2013) shows that sterilized interventions are unlikely to have much of an impact on the exchange rate.

FIGURE 17.7

Effect of a Purchase of Dollar Assets

A Fed purchase of dollar assets and sale of foreign assets decreases liquidity in the financial system and raises the domestic real interest rate r^D. The resulting rise in the relative expected return for dollar assets shifts the demand curve to the right from D_1 to D_2, and the exchange rate rises from E_1 to E_2.

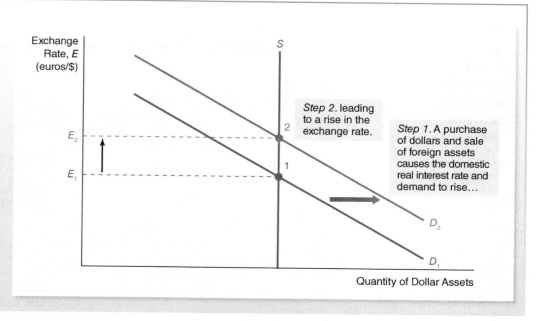

Step 2. leading to a rise in the exchange rate.

Step 1. A purchase of dollars and sale of foreign assets causes the domestic real interest rate and demand to rise…

currency. The result is the reverse for an intervention in which domestic currency is sold to purchase foreign assets. ***An intervention in which domestic currency is sold to purchase foreign assets leads to an increase in international reserves and a depreciation of the domestic currency.***

Fixed Exchange Rate Regimes

Exchange rate regimes in the international financial system fall into two basic types: *fixed* and *floating.* In a **fixed exchange rate regime,** the value of a currency is pegged relative to the value of another currency (called the **anchor currency**) so that the exchange rate is fixed. In some fixed exchange rate regimes, the government simply announces that it is committed to taking the steps necessary to keep the currency fixed relative to the anchor currency. A type of fixed exchange rate regime with an even stronger commitment is a **currency board,** in which the domestic currency is backed 100% by the anchor currency, and the government or central bank stands ready to exchange domestic currency for the anchor currency at a fixed rate whenever the public requests it.

In a **floating** (also called **flexible**) **exchange rate regime,** the value of a currency is determined by supply and demand in the foreign exchange market, without exchange rate interventions. When countries attempt to influence their exchange rates by buying and selling currencies, we refer to the regime as a **managed float regime** (or a **dirty float**).

We now focus on fixed exchange rate regimes, examining their workings and policy challenges.

Fixed Exchange Rate Regime Dynamics

Figure 17.8 shows how a fixed exchange rate regime works in practice. Panel (a) depicts a situation in which the domestic currency is fixed relative to an anchor currency.

FIGURE 17.8

Intervention in the Foreign Exchange Market Under a Fixed Exchange Rate Regime

In panel (a), the exchange rate at E_{par} is overvalued. To keep the exchange rate at E_{par} (point 2), the central bank must purchase domestic currency to shift the demand curve to D_2. In panel (b), the exchange rate at E_1 is undervalued, so the central bank must sell domestic currency to shift the demand curve to D_2 and keep the exchange rate at E_{par} (point 2).

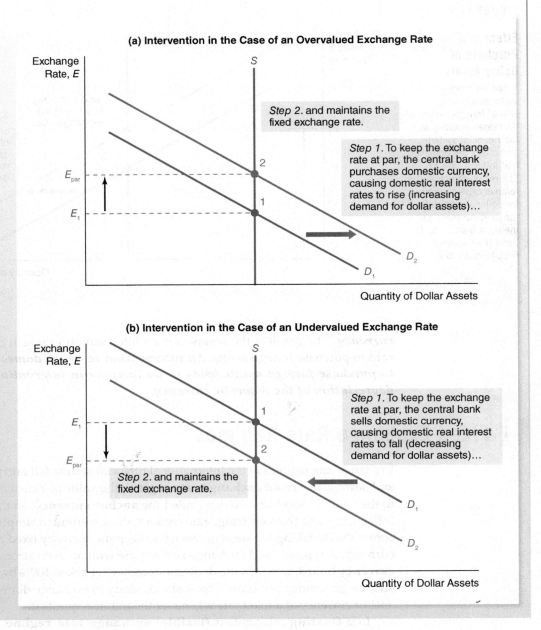

(a) Intervention in the Case of an Overvalued Exchange Rate

Exchange Rate, E

Step 2. and maintains the fixed exchange rate.

Step 1. To keep the exchange rate at par, the central bank purchases domestic currency, causing domestic real interest rates to rise (increasing demand for dollar assets)...

E_{par}

E_1

D_2

D_1

Quantity of Dollar Assets

(b) Intervention in the Case of an Undervalued Exchange Rate

Exchange Rate, E

Step 1. To keep the exchange rate at par, the central bank sells domestic currency, causing domestic real interest rates to fall (decreasing demand for dollar assets)...

E_1

E_{par}

Step 2. and maintains the fixed exchange rate.

D_1

D_2

Quantity of Dollar Assets

The demand curve D_1 intersects the supply curve at an exchange rate E_1, which is lower than the fixed (par) value of the exchange rate, E_{par}. In this case, the currency is *overvalued*. To keep the exchange rate at E_{par}, the central bank must intervene in the foreign exchange market and purchase domestic currency by selling foreign assets, thereby losing international reserves. As we have seen, this action decreases liquidity in the financial system, causes the money supply to fall, and therefore drives up real interest rates on domestic assets, r^D. This increase in the domestic real interest rate raises the relative expected return on domestic assets, shifting the demand curve to the right. The central bank will continue purchasing domestic currency until the demand curve reaches D_2 and the equilibrium exchange rate is at E_{par} (point 2 in panel (a)).

We have thus come to the conclusion that ***when the domestic currency is overvalued, the central bank must purchase domestic currency to keep the exchange rate fixed, but as a result it loses international reserves.***

Panel (b) in Figure 17.8 describes the situation in which the demand curve D_1 initially intersects the supply curve at exchange rate E_1, which is above E_{par}, so that the currency is *undervalued*. In this situation, the central bank must sell domestic currency and purchase foreign assets, thereby gaining international reserves. This action increases liquidity in the financial system, causes the money supply to rise, and therefore lowers the real interest rate on domestic assets. The central bank keeps selling domestic currency and lowers real interest rates until the demand curve shifts leftward all the way to D_2, where the equilibrium exchange rate is at E_{par}—point 2 in panel (b). Our analysis thus leads us to the following result: ***when the domestic currency is undervalued, the central bank must sell domestic currency to keep the exchange rate fixed, but as a result, it gains international reserves.***

DEVALUATION AND REVALUATION. As we have seen, if a country's currency is overvalued, its central bank's attempts to keep the currency from depreciating will result in a loss of international reserves. If the country's central bank eventually runs out of international reserves, it cannot keep its currency from depreciating, and a **devaluation** must occur in which it resets the par exchange rate at a lower level.

If, by contrast, a country's currency is undervalued, its central bank's intervention to keep the currency from appreciating leads to a gain of international reserves. The central bank might not want to acquire these international reserves, and so it might reset the par value of its exchange rate at a higher level—a **revaluation.**

PERFECT CAPITAL MOBILITY. If there is perfect capital mobility—that is, if there are no barriers to domestic residents purchasing foreign assets or foreigners purchasing domestic assets—and a country fixes its exchange rate to an anchor currency of a larger country, it then loses control of monetary policy. If the larger country pursues a tighter monetary policy and raises the real interest rate, there is an appreciation of the larger country's currency and a depreciation of the smaller country's currency. The smaller country, having locked in its exchange rate to the anchor currency, will now find its currency overvalued and will therefore have to sell the anchor currency and buy its own to keep its currency from depreciating. The foreign exchange intervention thus leads to a decline in the smaller country's international reserves, a decline in liquidity in the banking system, and a rise in real interest rates. Hence the real interest rate in the smaller country moves with the real interest rate in the larger country, and the smaller country no longer controls real interest rates or monetary policy.

The Policy Trilemma

Our preceding analysis indicates that a country (or a currency area like the Eurozone) can't pursue the following three policies at the same time: 1) free capital mobility, 2) a fixed exchange rate, and 3) an independent monetary policy. Economists call

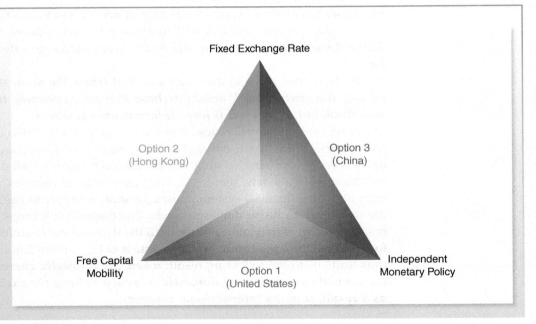

FIGURE 17.9

The Policy Trilemma

A country (or monetary union) cannot pursue the following three policies at the same time: 1) free capital mobility, 2) a fixed exchange rate, and 3) an independent monetary policy. Instead, it must choose two of the three policies on each side of the triangle.

this result the **policy trilemma** or, more graphically, the **impossible trinity.** Figure 17.9 illustrates the policy trilemma. A country can choose only two of the three options, which are denoted by each side of the triangle. In option 1, a country (or currency area) chooses to have capital mobility and an independent monetary policy, but not a fixed exchange rate. The Eurozone and the United States have made this choice. Hong Kong and Belize have chosen option 2, in which there is free capital mobility and the exchange rate is fixed, so the country or currency area does not have an independent monetary policy. Other countries, like China, have chosen option 3, in which they have a fixed exchange rate and pursue an independent monetary policy but do not have free capital mobility because they have **capital controls,** which are restrictions on the free movement of capital across their borders.

The policy trilemma thus leaves countries or currency areas with a difficult choice. Do they accept exchange rate volatility (option 1), give up independent monetary policy (option 2), or restrict capital flows (option 3)?

Monetary Unions

A variant of a fixed exchange rate regime is a **monetary** (or **currency**) **union,** in which a group of countries decides to adopt a common currency, thereby fixing their exchange rates relative to each other. One of the early examples of a monetary union occurred in 1787 when the thirteen colonies formed the United States and gave up their individual currencies for the U.S. dollar. The most recently formed monetary union is the European Monetary Union (EMU), in which eleven original member countries adopted a new currency, the euro, in January of 1999.

The key economic advantage of a monetary union is that it makes trade across borders easier, because goods and services in all of the member countries are now priced

Application

How Did China Accumulate Over $3 Trillion of International Reserves?

By 2013, China had accumulated more than $3 trillion of international reserves. How did the Chinese get their hands on this vast amount of foreign assets? After all, China is not yet a rich country.

The answer is that China pegged its exchange rate to the U.S. dollar at a fixed rate of 8.28 yuan (also called renminbi) to the dollar in 1994. Because of China's rapidly growing productivity, which led to increased demand for its exports, the long-run value of the yuan increased, leading to a higher relative expected return for yuan assets and an increase in the demand for yuan assets. As a result, despite some restrictions on capital flows, the Chinese found themselves in the situation depicted in panel (b) of Figure 17.8, in which the yuan is undervalued. To keep the yuan from appreciating above E_{par} to E_1 in the figure, the Chinese central bank has been engaging in massive purchases of U.S. dollar assets. Today, the Chinese government is one of the largest holders of U.S. government bonds in the world.

The pegging of the yuan to the U.S. dollar has created several problems for Chinese authorities. First, the Chinese now own a significant amount of U.S. assets, particularly U.S. Treasury securities, which have very low returns. Second, the undervaluation of the yuan has made Chinese goods so cheap abroad that many countries have threatened to erect trade barriers against these goods if the Chinese government does not allow an upward revaluation of the yuan. Third, as we learned earlier in the chapter, the Chinese purchase of dollar assets has resulted in a substantial increase in the Chinese money supply, which has the potential to produce high inflation in the future. In July 2005, China finally made its peg somewhat more flexible by letting the value of the yuan rise 2.1%, and subsequently allowed it to appreciate at a gradual pace. The central bank also indicated that it would no longer fix the yuan to the U.S. dollar, but would instead maintain its value relative to a basket of currencies.

Why have the Chinese authorities maintained this exchange rate peg for so long, despite the problems it has created? One answer is that they wanted to keep their export sector humming by keeping the prices of their export goods low. A second answer might be that they wanted to accumulate a large amount of international reserves as a "war chest" that could be sold to buy yuan, in order to keep the yuan from declining at some future date. Given the pressure on the Chinese government from government officials in the United States and Europe to further revalue its currency, further adjustments in China's exchange rate policy are likely in the future.

using the same currency. However, as we saw above, as with any fixed exchange rate regime and free capital mobility, a monetary union means that individual countries no longer have their own independent monetary policy with which to address shortfalls of aggregate demand. This disadvantage of a monetary union has raised questions about whether the Eurozone will break up, as we discuss in the following Policy and Practice case.

Policy and Practice

Will the Euro Survive?

The global financial crisis of 2007–2009 led to economic contractions throughout Europe, with the countries in the southern part of the Eurozone hit especially hard. Unemployment in the hard-hit countries climbed much faster than in the northern countries, with Germany in particular escaping severe economic contractions. Furthermore, with the contractions of their economies, many of the southern countries began to experience large government budget deficits and sovereign debt crises (described in Chapter 16) in which investors pulled back from purchasing these countries' bonds, sending interest rates to extremely high levels. The resulting collapse of the southern countries' economies implied that they would benefit greatly from easing of monetary policy to stimulate aggregate demand, but this option was unavailable because the European Central Bank was forced to conduct monetary policy for the entire Eurozone, which as a whole was not suffering as badly as the individual southern countries.

The "straight jacket" effect of the euro has resulted in a weakening of support for the euro in the southern countries, and there is increased talk of abandoning the euro. Support for the euro has also weakened in the stronger, northern countries because they have been called on to provide bailouts to the weaker member countries. Because the stronger countries might want to exit to limit their transfer of funds to the weaker countries, and the weaker countries might want to abandon the euro so they can pursue more expansionary monetary policy and depreciate of their currency in order to boost their economy, there are doubts that the European Monetary Union can survive. However, the euro is seen by many as an important step in the creation of a more united and powerful Europe, and this political consideration has created strong support for the monetary union.

To Peg or Not to Peg

Fixed exchange rate regimes have a long history. They can take the form of fixing the value of the domestic currency to a commodity such as gold, the key feature of the "gold standard" of the late nineteenth and early twentieth centuries. More recently, fixed exchange rate regimes have fixed the value of the domestic currency to that of a large, low-inflation country like the United States (the anchor country). Another alternative is to adopt a **crawling peg,** in which a currency is allowed to depreciate at a steady rate so that the inflation rate of the pegging country can be higher than that of the anchor country.

Advantages of Exchange-Rate Pegging

Pegging the exchange rate has several advantages. It contributes to keeping inflation under control by tying the inflation rate for internationally traded goods to that found in the anchor country. The foreign price of internationally traded goods is set by the world market, whereas the domestic price of these goods is fixed by the exchange-rate peg. For example, in Argentina until 2002, the exchange rate for the Argentine peso was exactly one peso to the dollar, so that a bushel of wheat that traded internationally at five dollars had its price set at five pesos. If the exchange-rate target is credible (i.e., expected to be adhered to), the exchange-rate peg has the added benefit of anchoring inflation expectations to the inflation rate in the anchor country.

An exchange-rate peg also means that the country has in effect adopted the monetary policy of the anchor country. If the anchor county has a monetary policy that is noninflationary, then monetary policy in the pegging country will be noninflationary as well.

Given its advantages, it is not surprising that industrialized countries have used exchange-rate pegging successfully to control inflation. Both France and the United Kingdom, for example, successfully used exchange-rate pegging to lower inflation by tying the values of their currencies to the German mark. In 1987, when France first pegged its exchange rate to the mark, its inflation rate was 3%, two percentage points above the German inflation rate. By 1992, its inflation rate had fallen to 2%, a level that can be argued is consistent with price stability and was even below the German rate. By 1996, the French and German inflation rates had converged to a number slightly below 2%. Similarly, after pegging to the German mark in 1990, the United Kingdom was able to lower its inflation rate from 10% to 3% by 1992, when it was forced to abandon the exchange-rate peg.

Exchange-rate pegging has also been an effective means of reducing inflation quickly in emerging market countries. For example, before the devaluation in Mexico in 1994, its exchange-rate peg to the dollar enabled it to bring inflation down from levels above 100% in 1988 to levels below 10% in 1994.

Disadvantages of Exchange-Rate Pegging

Despite the inherent advantages of exchange-rate pegging, several serious criticisms of this strategy can be made. As we saw earlier in the chapter, with capital mobility, the pegging country can no longer pursue its own independent monetary policy to respond to domestic shocks that are independent of those hitting the anchor country. Furthermore, an exchange-rate peg means that shocks to the anchor country are directly transmitted to the pegging country, because changes in interest rates in the anchor country lead to corresponding changes in interest rates in the pegging country.

A striking example of these problems occurred when Germany reunified in 1990. In response to concerns about inflationary pressures arising from reunification and the massive fiscal expansion required to rebuild East Germany, real long-term German interest rates rose until February 1991, and real short-term rates rose until December 1991. This rise in real interest rates in Germany, the anchor country, was transmitted directly to the other countries whose currencies were pegged to the mark, Germany's currency prior to the adoption of the euro, and their real interest rates rose in tandem with Germany's. Countries such as France that adhered to the exchange-rate peg experienced slowed economic growth and increased unemployment.

Exchange-rate pegs also leave countries open to **speculative attacks** on their currencies—massive sales of a weak currency that lead to a sharp decline in the country's exchange rate.[7] Indeed, one fallout of German reunification was the foreign exchange crisis of September 1992. The rise in real interest rates in Germany following reunification

---

[7]A more detailed discussion of the dynamics of speculative attacks can be found in the second Web appendix to this chapter, found at the Companion Website, www.pearsonhighered.com/mishkin.

meant that the countries pegged to the mark were subjected to a negative demand shock that led to a decline in economic growth and a rise in unemployment. It was certainly feasible in these circumstances for the governments of these countries to keep their exchange rates fixed relative to the mark and allow real interest rates in their countries to rise, but speculators began to question whether these countries' commitment to the exchange-rate peg would weaken. Speculators reasoned that these countries would not tolerate the rise in unemployment that resulted from keeping interest rates high enough to fend off attacks on their currencies. At this stage, speculators were, in effect, presented with a one-way bet, because the currencies of countries like France, Spain, Sweden, Italy, and the United Kingdom could go in only one direction and depreciate against the mark. Selling these currencies before the likely depreciation occurred gave speculators an attractive profit opportunity with potentially high expected returns. The result was a speculative attack in September 1992. Only in France was the commitment to the fixed exchange rate strong enough that France did not devalue. The governments of the other countries were unwilling to defend their currencies at all costs and eventually allowed their currencies to fall in value.

The different responses of France and the United Kingdom to the September 1992 exchange-rate crisis illustrates the potential cost of an exchange-rate peg. France, which continued to peg its currency to the mark and was thus unable to use monetary policy to respond to domestic conditions, found that economic growth remained slow after 1992, and unemployment increased. The United Kingdom, on the other hand, which dropped the exchange-rate peg, had much better economic performance: economic growth was higher, the unemployment rate fell, and yet its inflation was not much worse than France's.

In contrast to industrialized countries, emerging market countries (including the transition countries of Eastern Europe) may not lose much by giving up an independent monetary policy when they peg exchange rates. Because many emerging market countries have not developed the political or monetary institutions that allow the successful use of discretionary monetary policy, they may have little to gain from an independent monetary policy, but a lot to lose. Thus they are better off, in effect, by adopting the monetary policy of a country like the United States through pegging exchange rates than by pursuing their own independent policy. This is one of the reasons that so many emerging market countries have adopted exchange-rate pegging.

Nonetheless, exchange-rate pegging is highly dangerous for these countries, because it leaves them open to speculative attacks that can have far more serious consequences for their economies than for those of industrialized countries. This is the hard lesson that Argentina learned, which we discuss in the following Policy and Practice case, "The Collapse of the Argentine Currency Board."

Policy and Practice

The Collapse of the Argentine Currency Board

Argentina has had a long history of monetary instability, with inflation rates fluctuating dramatically and sometimes surging to beyond 1,000% per year. To end this cycle of inflationary surges, Argentina decided to adopt a currency board in April 1991. The Argentine currency board worked by fixing the peso/dollar exchange rate at one-to-one; a member of the public could go to the Argentine central bank and exchange a peso for a dollar, or vice versa, at any time.

The early years of Argentina's currency board looked stunningly successful. Inflation, which had been running at an 800% annual rate in 1990, fell to less than 5% by the end of 1994, and economic growth was rapid, averaging almost 8% per year from 1991 to 1994. In the aftermath of the Mexican peso crisis, however, concern about the health of the Argentine economy resulted in the public pulling money out of the banks (deposits fell by 18%) and exchanging Argentine pesos for dollars, thus causing a contraction of the Argentine money supply. A sharp drop in Argentine economic activity followed, with real GDP shrinking by more than 5% in 1995 and the unemployment rate jumping above 15%. Only in 1996 did the economy begin to recover.

Because the central bank of Argentina had no control over monetary policy under the currency board system, it was relatively helpless to counteract the contractionary monetary policy stemming from the public's behavior. Furthermore, because the currency board did not allow the central bank to create pesos and lend them to the banks, it had very little capability to act as a lender of last resort. With help from international agencies, such as the IMF, the World Bank, and the Inter-American Development Bank, which lent Argentina more than $5 billion in 1995 to help shore up its banking system, the currency board survived.

However, in 1998 Argentina entered another recession, which was both severe and very long lasting. By the end of 2001, unemployment reached nearly 20%, a level comparable to that experienced in the United States during the Great Depression of the 1930s. The result was civil unrest and the fall of the elected government, as well as a major banking crisis and a default on nearly $150 billion of government debt. Because the Central Bank of Argentina had no control over monetary policy under the currency board system, it was unable to use monetary policy to expand the economy and get out of its recession. In January 2002, the currency board finally collapsed and the peso depreciated by more than 70%. The result was a full-scale financial crisis, with inflation shooting up and an extremely severe depression. Clearly, the Argentine public is not as enamored of its currency board as it once was.[8]

---

[8]The Argentine financial crisis is discussed in the Web chapter, "Financial Crises in Emerging Market Economies," found at the Companion Website, www.pearsonhighered.com/mishkin.

SUMMARY

1. Foreign exchange rates (the price of one country's currency in terms of another's) are important because they affect the prices of domestically produced goods sold abroad and the cost of foreign goods bought domestically. The real exchange rate, which is the nominal exchange rate times the relative price levels, indicates whether a country's goods are relatively cheap or expensive.

2. The law of one price indicates that if two countries produce an identical good, and transportation costs and trade barriers are very low, the price of the good should be the same throughout the world no matter which country produces it. Applying the law of one price to national price levels produces the theory of purchasing power parity, which suggests that long-run changes in the exchange rate between two countries are affected by changes in the relative price levels in the two countries.

3. Equilibrium in the foreign exchange market occurs when the quantity of dollar assets demanded equals the quantity supplied.

4. In the short run, exchange rates are determined by changes in the relative expected return on domestic assets, which cause the demand curve to shift. Any factor that changes the relative expected return on domestic assets will lead to changes in the exchange rate. Such factors include changes in the real interest rate on domestic and foreign assets as well as changes in the expected future exchange rate.

5. An appreciation of the exchange rate is contractionary, leading to a decline in both aggregate output and inflation, while a depreciation has the opposite effect and is expansionary. Monetary policy can counteract the shocks caused by exchange rate changes.

6. A central bank intervention, in which a central bank sells the domestic currency to purchase foreign assets, leads to a gain in international reserves, an increase in liquidity, a rise in the money supply, a decline in domestic interest rates, and therefore a depreciation of the domestic currency.

7. In a fixed exchange rate regime, when the domestic currency is overvalued, the central bank must purchase domestic currency to keep the exchange rate fixed. If the domestic currency is undervalued, the central bank must sell domestic currency. The policy trilemma indicates that a country (or a currency area) cannot pursue the following three policies at the same time: 1) free capital mobility, 2) a fixed exchange rate, and 3) an independent monetary policy.

8. Exchange-rate pegging has the following advantages for the pegging country: (1) it directly keeps inflation under control by tying the inflation rate for internationally traded goods to that found in the anchor country to which its currency is pegged; and (2) it adopts the monetary policy of the anchor country, which if it is noninflationary implies that the monetary policy in the pegging country will be noninflationary as well. Exchange-rate pegging also has serious disadvantages: (1) It results in a loss of independent monetary policy; and (2) it leaves the pegging country open to speculative attacks.

KEY TERMS

anchor currency, p. 477

appreciation, p. 460

capital controls, p. 480

capital mobility, p. 466

crawling peg, p. 482

currency board, p. 477

depreciation, p. 460

devaluation, p. 479

expected return, p. 467

fixed exchange rate regime, p. 477

floating (flexible) exchange rate regime, p. 477

foreign exchange interventions, p. 475

foreign exchange market, p. 459

forward exchange rate, p. 460

forward transaction, p. 460

impossible trinity, p. 480

international reserves, p. 475

law of one price, p. 463

managed float regime (dirty float), p. 477

monetary (currency) union,
  p. 480
nominal exchange rate, p. 460
nontradable, p. 464
policy trilemma, p. 480

real exchange rate, p. 460
revaluation, p. 479
speculative attacks, p. 483
spot exchange rate, p. 460

spot transaction, p. 459
terms of trade, p. 460
theory of purchasing power parity
  (PPP), p. 464

REVIEW QUESTIONS

All Questions are available in MyEconLab *for practice or instructor assignment.*

Foreign Exchange Market and Exchange Rates

1. What is the foreign exchange market? Describe the two types of transactions that take place in this market.
2. Differentiate the nominal and real exchange rates between dollars and euros. Do the two exchange rates move together? Why is appreciation or depreciation of real exchange rates important?

Exchange Rates in the Long Run

3. How is the theory of purchasing power parity related to the law of one price? Why doesn't PPP hold in the short run?

Exchange Rates in the Short Run

4. Why does the foreign exchange market move toward equilibrium when the foreign exchange rate for the dollar is either above or below its equilibrium value?

Analysis of Changes in Exchange Rates

5. Identify three factors that might cause the exchange rate for a currency to rise.

Aggregate Demand and Supply Analysis of Exchange Rate Effects

6. What are the short-run effects on aggregate output and the inflation rate when the domestic currency appreciates or depreciates?

Intervention in the Foreign Exchange Market

7. Why do central banks intervene in foreign exchange markets? How do these interventions affect their international reserves and exchange rates?

Fixed Exchange Rate Regimes

8. How do fixed, floating, and managed (dirty) float exchange rate regimes differ?
9. What happens in a fixed exchange rate regime if a currency is overvalued? What problem can this create?

10. What is the policy trilemma?

To Peg or Not to Peg

11. What are the advantages and disadvantages of exchange-rate pegging?

PROBLEMS

All Problems are available in MyEconLab *for practice or instructor assignment.*

Foreign Exchange Market and Exchange Rates

1. Suppose a bottle of wine sells for $16 in California and for €10 in France. Assuming a nominal exchange rate of 0.75 euro per dollar,
   a) calculate the real exchange rate between U.S. wine and French wine.

   b) calculate the real exchange rate between U.S. wine and French wine if the domestic price of U.S. wine drops to $12 a bottle.

Exchange Rates in the Long Run

2. A Starbucks coffee sells for 10 yuan in Beijing, China, and for $2 in Chicago.
   a) Calculate the nominal exchange rate if the law of one price holds.
   b) Assume that the nominal exchange rate is currently 7 yuan per dollar. What would the purchasing power parity theory predict about the future value of the nominal exchange rate? (Hint: which nominal exchange rate makes the real exchange rate equal to 1?)
3. In each of the following examples, the law of one price does not hold (i.e., at current nominal

   exchange rates, the prices of these goods or services are not the same). For each case, explain what prevents the law of one price from holding.
   a) A ton of sugar in the United States and a ton of sugar in Brazil
   b) A three-bedroom apartment in Manhattan and a three-bedroom apartment in Mexico City
   c) A pound of the finest Swiss chocolate and a pound of Hershey's kisses

Analysis of Changes in Exchange Rates

4. On June 19, 2013, following the FOMC's regular policy meeting, the Chair of the FOMC made remarks during a press conference that were widely interpreted in financial markets to mean that the Fed might begin reducing

   the size of its $85 billion in monthly asset purchases sooner than expected.
   a) What effect, if any, should this statement have had on interest rates and dollar exchange rates?

b) In the days following the press conference, the Fed worried that markets had over-reacted, and several Fed officials, including the Chairman, strongly reiterated that reductions of asset purchases would begin only if economic conditions warranted, indicating that reductions in asset purchases might not happen sooner than expected. What effect, if any, should this statement have had on interest rates and dollar exchange rates?

5. The following table shows the nominal exchange rate between the U.S. dollar and the euro (U.S. dollars per euro) at different points in time.

November 2012	December 2012	January 2012	February 2012	March 2012
1.2953	1.3025	1.2983	1.3197	1.3059

Source: Federal Reserve Bank of St. Louis, FRED database at http://research.stlouisfed.org/fred2/.

a) Plot the nominal exchange rate, and determine whether the U.S. dollar has been appreciating or depreciating with respect to the euro during this period. Note that the exchange rate is quoted as dollars per euro.

b) Calculate the percentage change in the exchange rate from November 2012 to December 2012 and from January 2013 to February 2013. Comment on the size of these fluctuations.

6. Suppose the Federal Reserve cannot convince the public of its commitment to fighting inflation in the United States in the near future.
a) What would be the effect on the expected appreciation of the U.S. dollar?
b) What would be the effect on the spot exchange rate for the U.S. dollar? Explain your answer using a graph.

Aggregate Demand and Supply Analysis of the Effects of Exchange Rates

7. Brazil has announced the discovery of huge oil reserves that could potentially transform the country into a big exporter of oil.
a) What would be the effect of the increase in revenues from oil exports on Brazil's exchange rate?

b) How would this affect other Brazilian exports? Is this a desirable outcome for the country as a whole?

Intervention in the Foreign Exchange Market

8. The following T-account (in billions of dollars) depicts an intervention by the Federal Reserve in the foreign exchange market:

Assets		Liabilities	
Foreign Assets	+ $5	Reserves	+ $5

a) Did the Federal Reserve buy or sell U.S. dollars?
b) What is the effect of this intervention on the exchange rate?

Fixed Exchange Rate Regimes

9. Explain why a central bank might want to intervene in the foreign exchange market to prevent an excessive appreciation of its currency, even if it previously stated that it would allow its currency to respond to supply and demand conditions in the foreign exchange market.

To Peg or Not to Peg

10. Assume that a country has pegged the value of its currency to another country's currency and that the anchor country increases its interest rate. Describe the effects on the following:
    a) The export sector of the pegging country
    b) Households' net worth if the pegging country is forced to devalue its currency and most debts are denominated in the foreign (anchor) currency

DATA ANALYSIS PROBLEMS

The Problems update with real-time data in MyEconLab *and are available for practice or instructor assignment.*

1. Go to the St. Louis Federal Reserve FRED database, and find data on daily dollar exchange rates for the euro (DEXUSEU), British pound (DEXUSUK), Japanese yen (DEXJPUS), Chinese yuan (DEXCHUS), and Canadian dollar (DEXCAUS).
    a) Report the exchange rates for the most recent available day, and the day closest to one year prior to that.
    b) Which currencies appreciated against the U.S. dollar, and which depreciated? Based on these results, what do you expect happened to exports and imports from each of the countries, from the U.S. perspective?

2. Go to the St. Louis Federal Reserve FRED database and find data on the exchange rate of U.S. dollars per British pound (DEXUSUK). A Mini Cooper can be purchased in London, England, for £17,865 or in Boston, United States, for $23,495.
    a) Use the most recent exchange rate available to calculate the real exchange rate of London Mini per Boston Mini.
    b) Based on your answer to part (a), are Mini Coopers relatively more expensive in Boston or in London?
    c) What price, in British pounds, would make the Mini Cooper equally expensive in both locations, all else being equal?

3. Go to the St. Louis Federal Reserve FRED database, and find data on the daily dollar exchange rates for the euro (DEXUSEU), British pound (DEXUSUK), and Japanese yen (DEXJPUS). Also, find data on the daily three-month London Interbank Offer Rate (LIBOR) for the

United States dollar (USD3MTD156N), euro area (EUR3MTD156N), British pound (GBP3MTD156N), and Japanese yen (JPY3MTD156N). LIBOR is a measure of interest rates denominated in each country's respective currency.
    a) Calculate the difference between the LIBOR rate in the United States and the LIBOR rates in the three other countries for one year ago.
    b) Based on the interest rate differentials, would you have expected one year ago that the dollar would depreciate or appreciate with respect to the other currencies?
    c) Report the percentage change in the exchange rates over the past year. Are the results you predicted in part (b) consistent with the actual exchange rate behavior?

4. Go to the St. Louis Federal Reserve FRED database, and find data on the monthly U.S. dollar exchange rates to the Chinese yuan, Canadian dollar, and South Korean won. Download the data onto a spreadsheet.
    a) Over the most recent five-year period of data available, use the average, max, min, and stdev functions in Excel to calculate the average, highest, and lowest exchange rate values, as well as the standard deviation of the exchange rate to the dollar (this is an absolute measure of the volatility of the exchange rate), for each of the three exchange rates.
    b) Using the maximum and minimum values of each exchange rate over the last five years, calculate the ratio of the

difference between the maximum and minimum values to the average level of the exchange rate (expressed as a percentage by multiplying by 100). This value gives an indication of how tightly the exchange rate moves. Based on your results, which of the three currencies is most likely to peg its currency to the U.S. dollar? How does this currency compare with the other two?

c) Calculate the ratio of the standard deviation to the average exchange rate over the last five years (expressed as a percentage by multiplying by 100). This value gives an indication of how volatile the exchange rate is. Based on your results, which of the three currencies is mostly likely to be pegged to the U.S. dollar? How does this currency compare with the other two?

Online appendices "The Interest Parity Condition" and "Speculative Attacks and Foreign Exchange Crises" are available at the Companion Website, www.pearsonhighered.com/mishkin.

Part 7

Microeconomic Foundations of Macroeconomics

Part 7 Microeconomic Foundations of Macroeconomics

This part of the book develops microeconomic analysis of households' and firms' behavior to provide a deeper understanding of the macroeconomic relationships featured earlier in the book. Chapter 18 discusses the microeconomic foundations of consumption and saving. Chapter 19 develops microeconomic models of investment behavior and applies them to explain recent economic history and to explain the tools policy makers use to influence investment spending. Chapter 20 develops a supply and demand analysis of the labor market and uses it to explain increasing labor force participation by women, the increase in returns to education in recent years, the increase in income inequality, and the sources of unemployment.

We will examine applications in each chapter to make the critical connection between theory and real-world practice:

- "Consumer Confidence and the Business Cycle"
- "Housing, the Stock Market, and the Collapse of Consumption in 2008 and 2009"
- "Stock Market Crashes and Recessions"
- "Why Has Labor Force Participation of Women Increased?"
- "Why Are Income Inequality and Returns to Education Increasing?"
- "Why Are European Unemployment Rates Generally Much Higher Than U.S. Unemployment Rates?"

In keeping with our focus on key policy issues and the techniques policy makers use in practice, we will also analyze the following specific examples in Policy and Practice cases:

- "The 2008 Tax Rebate"
- "Behavioral Policies to Increase Saving"
- "U.S. Government Policies and the Housing Market"
- "Unemployment Insurance and Unemployment"
- "Minimum Wage Laws"

18

Consumption and Saving

Preview

From 2001 to 2007, buoyant households increased consumption expenditure at a rapid rate of 3% a year. In 2008 and 2009, when households began to save more, consumption expenditure fell, declining at a 0.25% rate in 2008 and a 0.6% rate in 2009. Because consumption expenditure is 70% of total spending in the economy, the collapse of consumer spending was a major factor in the contraction of economic activity in those two years, resulting in the worst recession in the postwar period.

Why did households suddenly decide to save more and cut back on their spending? To answer this question, we need to delve deeper into what affects consumers' decisions to spend and save. In this chapter, we do so by discussing the *microeconomic* foundations of consumption and saving behavior. We first discuss a basic theory of consumption developed by Irving Fisher that explains *intertemporal choice,* decisions about spending today versus spending tomorrow. Then we examine the three most common theories of consumption that are used today: one developed by John Maynard Keynes that we discussed in Chapter 9, known as the *Keynesian consumption function,* and two others, the *permanent income hypothesis* and the *life-cycle hypothesis,* developed by Milton Friedman and Franco Modigliani, respectively, both of whom won Nobel Prizes for their research. These theories, which have been refined further over time, provide us with an understanding of consumer behavior that is a basic building block for the macroeconomic analysis in the rest of this book.

The Relationship Between Consumption and Saving

What we consume today we can't save for tomorrow. Seen in this way, consumption and saving are really two sides of the same coin. **Saving,** S, is the difference between the amount of income a person has to spend and his or her current spending. The income available to spend, **disposable income,** is total (gross) income net of (minus) taxes. Here, for simplicity, we denote disposable income as Y.[1] For a household, current spending is consumer expenditure, so we define saving by the identity:

$$S = Y - C \tag{1}$$

Taking the level of disposable income, Y, as given, we can determine consumption expenditure, C, by developing a theory of saving, S. Conversely, if we have a theory of saving, S, then Equation 1 tells us that we also have a theory of consumption, C. Throughout this chapter, then, when we talk about how to determine consumption, we are also talking about how saving is determined, and vice versa.

Intertemporal Choice and Consumption

The great U.S. economist Irving Fisher developed the basic theory of consumption. Fisher used microeconomic analysis to explain intertemporal choice, the decisions about spending today versus spending tomorrow. His theory, published in 1930, is called the **theory of intertemporal choice.** It describes consumption decisions in terms of a simplified world with only two periods of time—today (period 1) and the future (period 2). In this world, the consumer takes his or her current and future disposable income, as well as his or her wealth, as given.[2] And this person intends to spend all of his or her money before the end of period 2, bequeathing nothing to a spouse or a child. The real interest rate at which the consumer can borrow or which is paid on savings is given as r.

Fisher's theory then proceeds in three steps. First, it defines an **intertemporal budget constraint,** laying out how much a person can consume today versus tomorrow, given a consumer's total resources. Second, it describes consumer preferences for spending today versus spending tomorrow. Third, it shows how consumers optimize (maximize their happiness) given the budget constraint and their preferences. We will now examine these three areas in detail.

Before we start, keep in mind that this model describes all dollar amounts and interest rates in *real* terms. That is, dollar amounts represent the real purchasing power of those dollars, and interest rates refer to the amount of extra real purchasing power a lender must be paid for the rental of his or her money.

The Intertemporal Budget Constraint

We begin by considering the consumption constraints of Carmencita the Consumer, who has an income today in constant dollars (Y_1) of $50,000, an expected income tomorrow (Y_2) of $52,000, and initial wealth (assets) (W) of $10,000. She faces a real interest rate (r) of 4% at which she can borrow and lend.[3]

---

[1]Note that in Chapters 2, 4, and 9, we distinguished between disposable income, which subtracts out taxes, and total income, which does not. Here we use the term Y to denote disposable income rather than total income as in those chapters to simplify the notation. In addition, in contrast to Chapters 2 and 4, S here refers to private saving and not national saving (which includes government saving).

[2]Irving Fisher, *The Theory of Interest* (New York: Macmillan, 1930).

[3]The second-period income, Y_2, does not include the interest income earned on savings because that is already included in the intertemporal budget constraint in Equation 2 via the $r(W + Y_1 - C_1)$ term. Another way of reaching this determination is to say that Y refers to labor income only.

If Carmencita plans to spend C_1 in the first period, we can determine her consumption in the second period, C_2. She'll have her initial wealth, W, plus whatever income she doesn't spend in the first period, $Y_1 - C_1$. At the start of the first period, Carmencita can put this amount, $(W + Y_1 - C_1)$, in her bank account and earn interest, leaving her with an amount of $(1 + r)(W + Y_1 - C_1)$ in the second period, plus whatever she earns in the second period, Y_2. (Remember, these are real variables adjusted for inflation.) Since Carmencita has no desire to leave a bequest (inheritance), she will spend everything she has in period 2. Her second-period consumption, C_2, is then as follows:

$$C_2 = (1 + r)(W + Y_1 - C_1) + Y_2 \tag{2}$$

Equation 2 is her budget constraint across the two periods, her *intertemporal budget constraint*. To make our analysis more concrete, let's consider three scenarios, using the preceding numbers, to show the combinations of Carmencita's spending in periods 1 and 2 that satisfy the intertemporal budget constraint (see Figure 18.1). First, let's say Carmencita lives only for the future and consumes nothing today, so that $C_1 = 0$. Plugging in all the numbers for r, Y_1, Y_2, and W, her consumption in period 2 will be as follows:

$$C_2 = (1 + .04)(\$10,000 + \$50,000 - 0) + \$52,000 = \$114,400$$

Plotting the resulting combination of $C_2 = \$114,400$ and $C_1 = 0$ in Figure 18.1, we get point A.

MyEconLab Mini-lecture

FIGURE 18.1

The Intertemporal Budget Line

The intertemporal budget line, marked as *IBL*, is a straight line that is downward sloping, with a slope of $-(1 + r)$. It shows that there is a trade-off between current consumption and future consumption: the more you spend today, the less you have available to spend tomorrow. Note that point B is the point at which there is no borrowing or lending, with lending occurring to the left of point B, and borrowing occurring to the right of point B.

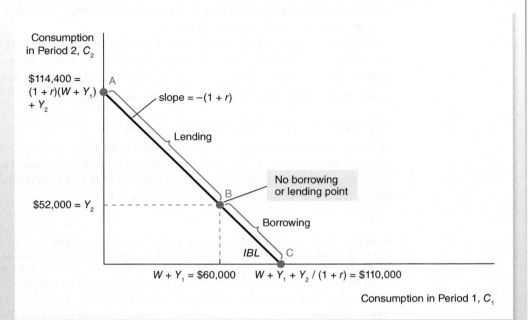

Suppose instead that Carmencita wants to spend everything she has without going into debt. She consumes everything she has in period 1, so $W + Y_1 - C_1 = 0$. She will then choose $C_1 = W + Y_1 = \$50,000 + \$10,000 = \$60,000$. From Equation 2, C_2 will be as follows:

$$C_2 = (1 + .04)(0) + \$52,000 = \$52,000$$

We plot the combination of $C_2 = \$52,000$ and $C_1 = \$60,000$ as point B in Figure 18.1. Point B is special because it is the point at which Carmencita is following the adage, "Neither a borrower nor a lender be."

Alternately, suppose Carmencita lives only for the present and wishes to consume as much as she can today, so that $C_2 = 0$. Solving for C_1, we get $C_1 = W + Y_1 + [Y_2/(1 + r)] = \$50,000 + \$10,000 + [\$52,000/(1 + .04)] = \$110,000$. In Figure 18.1, point C is the combination of $C_1 = \$110,000$ and $C_2 = 0$.

The line connecting these three points that satisfy the intertemporal budget constraint is the **intertemporal budget line,** marked as *IBL* in Figure 18.1. It is a straight line that is downward sloping, with a slope of $-(1 + r)$: i.e., at a real interest rate of 4% (.04), for every dollar consumed today there is $1.04 less consumption tomorrow, and for every dollar saved today there is $1.04 more consumption tomorrow. This line shows that there is a trade-off between current consumption and future consumption: the more you spend today, the less you have available to spend tomorrow. To the left and above point B, consumption in period 1, C_1, is less than $W + Y_1$, so Carmencita has excess funds to lend at the interest rate of r. To the right and below point B, C_1 is greater than $W + Y_1$, so Carmencita must borrow at the interest rate of r.

The Intertemporal Budget Constraint in Terms of Present Discounted Value

We can also determine the intertemporal budget constraint by rearranging the terms in Equation 2 to put all consumption on the left-hand side and all the other terms on the right-hand side. We do so by dividing both sides of Equation 2 by $(1 + r)$ and adding C_1 to both sides to get the following:

$$C_1 + \frac{C_2}{1 + r} = W + Y_1 + \frac{Y_2}{1 + r} \tag{3}$$

We will think of the two sides of the equation in terms of a concept called **present value** (or **present discounted value**), the common-sense notion that a dollar you will receive tomorrow is less valuable to you now than a dollar paid to you today. You can deposit a dollar today in a savings account that pays interest (that is, you can lend the dollar to the bank) and have more than a dollar in one year. If the interest rate is r, then $1 today will become $(1 + r)$ dollars next year: at an interest rate r of 4%, $1 today is worth $1.04 dollars next year. Alternatively, recognize that $1.04 dollars next year is the equivalent of $1 today. You can convert all next-period spending or income values into current values by dividing them by $(1 + r)$, a process called **discounting.** (The current [discounted] values of period 1 spending and income are C_1 and Y_1, respectively.) Adding up all these discounted values leads to the *present discounted value* of the spending, equal to wealth and income. Looked at in this way, the left-hand side of the intertemporal budget constraint in Equation 3 is the present discounted value of consumption spending, while the right-hand side is the present discounted value of initial wealth plus income, which we can refer to as lifetime resources. In other words, we can describe the intertemporal budget constraint in Equation 3 as follows:

Present value of consumption = present value of lifetime resources

Preferences

Preferences involve ranking different possible choices of consumption today and tomorrow. Putting aside budget constraints, we describe preferences by asking ourselves which combinations of spending today and spending tomorrow will make us equally happy. We can then plot these combinations to create an **indifference curve** that shows combinations of C_1 and C_2 that lead us to the same level of overall happiness (**utility** or **welfare**). Any point on a particular indifference curve represents the same level of utility as any other point on the curve. Carmencita's indifference curves are shown in Figure 18.2.

Indifference curves have three characteristics.[4]

1. *The farther an indifference curve is from the origin, the higher its utility.* Referring to Figure 18.2, consider point Z on the higher indifference curve IC_2, which is above and to the right of point X on the lower indifference curve IC_1. Point Z has higher consumption in both periods 1 and 2 than does point X ($C_1^Z > C_1^X$ and $C_2^Z > C_2^X$). Because we are assuming that more consumption is always better, it must be true that Carmencita is happier at point Z than

MyEconLab Mini-lecture

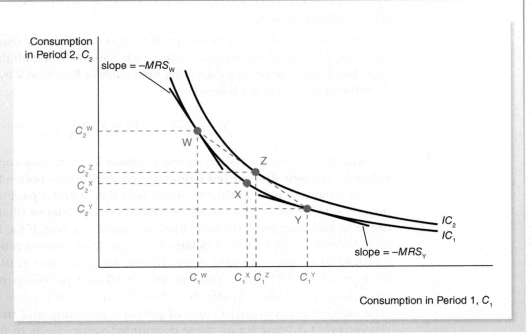

FIGURE 18.2

Indifference Curves

Indifference curves have three characteristics. As they go higher (moving from IC_1 to IC_2), they have higher utility; they are downward sloping; and they are bowed in toward the origin.

[4]Note also that indifference curves cannot cross because a particular combination of consumption today and consumption tomorrow cannot represent two different levels of utility. If indifference curves crossed, then the intersection point would imply that a particular combination of consumption today and consumption tomorrow could produce two different levels of utility.

point X. Because every point on IC_2 is above and to the right of every point on IC_1, the higher indifference curve IC_2 must have a higher utility than the lower indifference curve IC_1.

2. *Indifference curves slope down.* Consider points W and X in Figure 18.2. Since they sit on the same indifference curve IC_1, both points make Carmencita equally happy. Yet at point W, Carmencita spends C_2^W in the second period, while at point X, she spends less, C_2^X. How can she be equally happy at both points? To keep Carmencita just as happy, her loss of happiness from lower second-period consumption must be offset by higher consumption in period 1. Indeed, at point X, C_1^X is greater than C_1^W. For Carmencita to be indifferent, consumption in period 1 must rise as consumption in period 2 falls. Indifference curves are therefore downward sloping, illustrating the trade-off between consuming today versus consuming tomorrow, which we see as we move from points W to X to Y.

3. *Indifference curves are bowed in toward the origin.* The bowed-in shape of the indifference curves in Figure 18.2, which we refer to as **convexity,** results from the typical consumer's dislike of large fluctuations in consumption from one period to the next. In general, people prefer smooth consumption over time. Who wants to eat filet mignon and drive a Mercedes in one period, and then eat ramen noodles and take the bus in the other?

   Consider the three points W, Y, and Z in Figure 18.2. Point Z is halfway between points W and Y if we connect the three points with a straight line. That is, its consumption in both periods is an average of the consumption in both periods for points W and Y. Point Z thus has much smoother consumption than either point W or point Y. The preference for smooth consumption implies that point Z has higher utility than either point W or point Y. The preference for smooth consumption therefore implies that indifference curves are convex.

We can also describe the third characteristic through the concept of the **marginal rate of substitution,** also called the **intertemporal marginal rate of substitution,** the rate at which a consumer is willing to give up (substitute) consumption in period 2 for additional consumption in period 1. This rate, $(-\Delta C_2/\Delta C_1)$, is just the negative of the slope of the indifference curve at any given point. Because consumers prefer to smooth consumption over time (and thus become increasingly averse to giving up consumption in period 2), the marginal rate of substitution becomes smaller as second-period consumption falls, giving the indifference curve a convex shape. As we see in Figure 18.2, MRS_W is smaller than MRS_Y, so that the slope of the indifference curve becomes less negative.

Optimization

Using both an intertemporal budget line and a set of indifference curves, we can identify the optimal level of consumption for both periods. We all want to be as happy as possible, so we would like to get to the highest indifference curve that we can. On the other hand, we have to obey the intertemporal budget constraint. Figure 18.3, which plots Carmencita's budget line and a number of indifference curves, shows how we do this.

MyEconLab Mini-lecture

FIGURE 18.3

Consumer Optimization

The highest level of utility is reached at indifference curve IC_3, which is tangent to the intertemporal budget line at point O. At the optimal point O, the slope of IC_3, the negative of marginal rate of substitution, equals the slope of the intertemporal budget line, $-(1 + r)$, so that $MRS = 1 + r$.

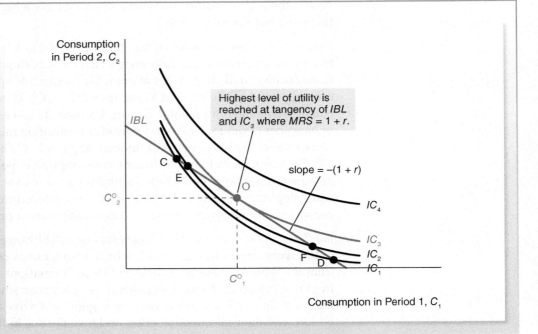

Carmencita can certainly achieve the level of utility associated with indifference curve IC_1 in Figure 18.3, since both points C and D on IC_1 are on her intertemporal budget constraint *IBL*. Indeed, she can achieve an even higher utility by moving to indifference curve IC_2, since points E and F also lie on the intertemporal budget line. On the other hand, she cannot get to a level of utility associated with the indifference curve IC_4, since no points on IC_4 *satisfy* the intertemporal budget constraint. The optimum indifference curve given her budget constraint is IC_3, which is tangent to the intertemporal budget line at point O. At point O, consumption in period 1 is C_1^O and consumption in period 2 is C_2^O. At point O, the optimum for Carmencita, the slope of the indifference curve (or the negative of the marginal rate of substitution) equals the slope of the intertemporal budget line, that is, $-MRS = -(1 + r)$. Multiplying both sides by -1 yields the following:

$$MRS = 1 + r \tag{4}$$

Equation 4 shows that Carmencita chooses her levels of consumption in periods 1 and 2 such that the marginal rate of substitution equals one plus the real interest rate, so that the slope of the indifference curve equals the slope of the intertemporal budget constraint IBL.

The Intertemporal Choice Model in Practice: Income and Wealth

Now that we understand how Carmencita makes her decisions about intertemporal choice, we can use this model to answer a set of questions about how consumption responds to changes in income and wealth. Later, we will turn to interest rates.

Response of Consumption to Income

We begin by analyzing what happens when income rises in either period 1 or period 2.

RISE IN CURRENT INCOME. Suppose Carmencita has done such a good job that her boss gives her a $1,000 bonus today. The present value of her lifetime resources has now gone up by $1,000, so Equation 3 indicates that she can raise her consumption in both periods. Indeed, because the real interest rate is unchanged, the slope of the intertemporal budget line remains the same, and so it shifts to the right in a parallel fashion from IBL_1 to IBL_2 in Figure 18.4. (More specifically, from Equation 3, the $1,000 increase in the present value of lifetime resources means that consumption in period 1 can increase by $1,000 for any given value of consumption in period 2, thereby shifting the intertemporal budget line to the right by $1,000.) The optimal point, where the indifference curve is tangent to the budget constraint, rises from point A to point B, where consumption in both periods has risen (from C_1^A to C_1^B and from C_2^A to C_2^B). Carmencita is certainly happier because she now is on a higher indifference curve, having jumped from IC_1 to IC_2.

RISE IN FUTURE INCOME. Suppose that Carmencita's boss tells her she has done a good job, but he can't afford to pay her the $1,000 bonus until next year. Instead, he will give her a bonus next year that has the same present value as a $1,000 bonus this year. (At a real interest rate of 4%, this means he will give her a bonus of $1,040 next year [$1,000 \times (1 + 0.04)$].) The outcome is then identical to that depicted in Figure 18.4: the present value of lifetime resources goes up by $1,000, the intertemporal budget line shifts to the right, and consumption in both periods rises.

MyEconLab Mini-lecture

FIGURE 18.4

Response to a Rise in Current Income, Future Income, or Wealth

A rise in current income, future income, or wealth leads to the intertemporal budget line rising in parallel from IBL_1 to IBL_2, because r is held constant and so the slope of the line does not change. The optimum moves from point A to point B, with the rise in consumption spread out over both periods, a phenomenon referred to as consumption smoothing.

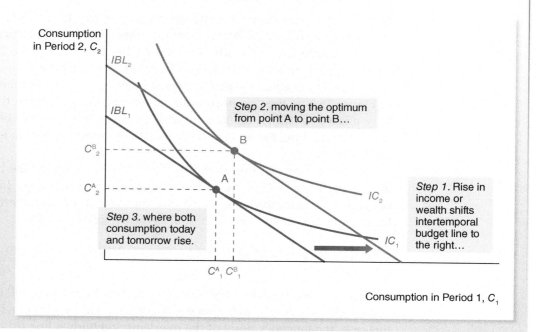

Response of Consumption to Wealth

Our analysis for income applies equally to evaluating the response of consumption to wealth. Suppose that Carmencita has some shares of Apple Computer that go up $1,000 in value. Now Carmencita finds that her wealth is $1,000 higher, and so the present value of her lifetime resources increases by $1,000, just as in Figure 18.4. The analysis is therefore identical: her intertemporal budget line shifts to the right and her consumption rises in both periods.

Consumption Smoothing

Our analysis of consumption and wealth reveals two important facts.

1. Consumption rises when the present value of lifetime resources increases, regardless of its source (current income, future income, or wealth).

2. Consumers will spread out any increase in consumption over today and tomorrow, even if the increase stems solely from an increase in current income. This characteristic is known as **consumption smoothing.**

Consumption smoothing is a logical consequence of two elements of the intertemporal choice model: the convexity of indifference curves and the ability of consumers to borrow or save. Indeed, consumption smoothing is a strong feature of the data because consumption fluctuates much less than GDP.

The Intertemporal Choice Model in Practice: Interest Rates

We will now consider the impact of a change in real interest rates on the intertemporal budget line and consumption.

Interest Rates and the Intertemporal Budget Line

To see what happens when the interest rate rises from r_1 to r_2, let's first look at Figure 18.5, at point B on the initial intertemporal budget line IBL_1, in which current consumption is equal to initial wealth plus first-period income, that is, $C_1 = W + Y_1$. In this special case, Carmencita is neither borrowing nor lending, so consumption in the second period is equal to second-period income, $C_2 = Y_2$. We therefore mark point B in Figure 18.5 as the "no borrowing or lending point." When the interest rate rises to r_2, point B is still on the new intertemporal budget line IBL_2 because, with no borrowing or lending, the level of the interest rate does not matter, leaving $C_1 = W + Y_1$ and $C_2 = Y_2$.

When the interest rate rises to r_2, however, the slope of the budget line becomes more negative at $-(1 + r_2)$, so the IBL_2 intertemporal budget line becomes steeper. Because it still goes through point B, this means that the new intertemporal budget line IBL_2 pivots clockwise around point B, as shown in Figure 18.5.

The Optimal Level of Consumption and the Intertemporal Budget Line

Because consumers on average save some of their income, we will look at the case when Carmencita's optimal consumption is at point I in Figure 18.5, in which $C_1^I < W + Y_1$. In this case, the tangency point of the intertemporal budget line IBL_1 and the indifference

MyEconLab Mini-lecture

FIGURE 18.5

Response to a Rise in the Interest Rate

When the interest rate rises from r_1 to r_2, the intertemporal budget line pivots clockwise around point B, the no borrowing or lending point, moving from IBL_1 to IBL_2. The optimum now moves from point I to point J. The substitution effect is larger than the income effect, so consumption in period 1 falls, while consumption in period 2 rises.

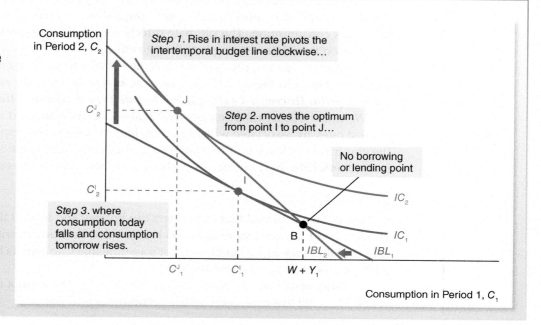

Step 1. Rise in interest rate pivots the intertemporal budget line clockwise...

Step 2. moves the optimum from point I to point J...

No borrowing or lending point

Step 3. where consumption today falls and consumption tomorrow rises.

Consumption in Period 2, C_2

Consumption in Period 1, C_1

curve IC_1, point I, is above and to the left of point B, the no borrowing or lending point. When the interest rate rises to r_2 and the intertemporal budget line pivots to IBL_2, we see that the optimal level of consumption at point J is on a higher indifference curve, IC_2. Consumption in period 1 has fallen to C_1^J, while consumption in period 2 has risen to C_2^J.

INCOME VERSUS SUBSTITUTION EFFECTS. We can differentiate two distinct effects on consumption when interest rates change: the **income effect,** the change in consumption due to changes in income, and the **substitution effect,** the change in consumption that occurs from the change in the relative price of consumption in the two periods. (You may recall a more general discussion of income and substitution effects from your microeconomics course. For a refresher, refer to an appendix to this chapter on the Companion Website at www.pearsonhighered.com/mishkin.)

In the scenario shown in Figure 18.5, Carmencita has savings, so she lends money (probably by depositing the funds in her bank account) from period 1 to period 2. At a higher interest rate, Carmencita earns more interest, which gives her more resources with which to consume. Thus, she can spend more in both periods. ***For savers, the income effect increases consumption in both periods when interest rates rise.***

With a higher interest rate, the present discounted value of consumption in the second period falls, so consumption in the second period becomes cheaper relative to consumption in the first period. As a result, Carmencita will choose to substitute away from and reduce first-period consumption to consume more in the second period. ***The substitution effect from higher interest rates leads to less consumption in period 1, but more consumption in period 2.***

We can also think of the substitution effect in terms of saving. When interest rates rise, the return to saving is higher and so a consumer will save more in the first period by reducing consumption, enabling her to spend more in the second period (consumption rises).

COMBINING INCOME AND SUBSTITUTION EFFECTS. When interest rates increase, both income and substitution effects shift second-period consumption higher. But in the first period, the substitution effect tamps down consumption while the income effect lifts consumption. The ultimate direction of the change in today's consumption depends on the relative strength of the two effects.

In practice, we usually assume that the substitution effect outweighs the income effect, as shown in Figure 18.5. In this case, *a rise in interest rates lowers today's consumption (increases saving), but boosts future consumption.*

We make this assumption because real-world data support the view that higher interest rates are associated with higher saving and lower consumption today. However, the empirical evidence on the relationship of interest rates to consumption and saving is not overwhelmingly strong. As we have seen here, theory does not settle this issue.[5]

Borrowing Constraints

So far we have assumed that consumers can borrow and lend at the same interest rate. However, not all consumers are good credit risks. Consumers with little or no wealth may find that they cannot get loans. Let's assume that Carmencita is one of those people and examine the effect on our analysis.

If Carmencita has no wealth and cannot borrow, she cannot spend more than she earns. We write this constraint on her spending as follows:

$$C_1 \leq Y_1$$

The equation indicates that consumption today must be less than or equal to income today. We refer to this constraint on Carmencita as a **borrowing constraint** (or a **liquidity constraint**). To see the implication for her consumption choices, let's first look at the effect of a borrowing constraint on her intertemporal budget line.

INTERTEMPORAL BUDGET LINE WITH A BORROWING CONSTRAINT. Suppose that without a borrowing constraint, Carmencita's intertemporal budget line is a straight line in panels (a) and (b) of Figure 18.6, connecting points A, B, and C with a slope of $-(1 + r)$. With a borrowing constraint, however, Carmencita cannot spend more than her current income. That is, C_1 cannot rise above Y_1. At point B, where $C_1 = Y_1$, the intertemporal budget line becomes vertical. The borrowing constraint gives an angle, or kink, to the intertemporal budget line at point B. We denote this line as IBL_{BC} in both panels of Figure 18.6.

OPTIMAL CONSUMPTION WITH A BORROWING CONSTRAINT. How will a borrowing constraint change Carmencita's consumption choices? We consider two cases.

In the first case, shown in panel (a) of Figure 18.6, Carmencita's optimal level of consumption in period 1 is less than Y_1. That is, she has no need to borrow. As a result,

[5]We can conduct the same analysis for a consumer who has no savings and thus borrows. In this case, the income effect is negative because a higher interest rate means that it is more costly to borrow, so a consumer has fewer resources to spend in period 1, and so will consume less in both periods. Because the income and substitution effects go in the same direction, there is no ambiguity about the effect of interest rates on today's consumption. A higher interest rate leads to lower consumption today because the income and substitution effects indicate that today's consumption falls. (On the other hand, there is ambiguity as to what happens to second-period consumption. In this case, the income and substitution effects work in the opposite direction. The income effect indicates that second-period consumption should fall, while the substitution effect indicates that it should rise.)

MyEconLab Mini-lecture

FIGURE 18.6

Optimization with a Borrowing Constraint

The intertemporal budget line with a borrowing constraint is kinked at point B and is denoted as IBL_{BC} in both panels of Figure 18.6. In panel (a), in which the borrowing constraint is not binding, the highest indifference curve that touches IBL_{BC} leads to a combination of consumption in periods 1 and 2 at point D, which lies on IBL_{BC} between points A and B. In panel (b), the budget constraint is binding, and the highest indifference curve that can be reached is IC_2, which touches IBL_{BC} at point B but is not tangent to IBL_{BC}.

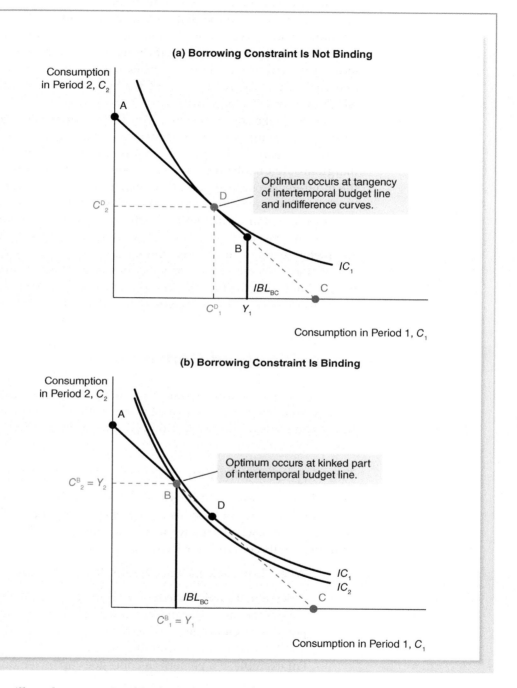

(a) Borrowing Constraint Is Not Binding

Optimum occurs at tangency of intertemporal budget line and indifference curves.

(b) Borrowing Constraint Is Binding

Optimum occurs at kinked part of intertemporal budget line.

she will not be constrained by her inability to borrow, and we can say that the *constraint is not binding*. Indeed, in panel (a), the highest indifference curve that touches IBL_{BC} leads to a combination of consumption in periods 1 and 2 at point D, which lies on IBL_{BC} between points A and B. The highest indifference curve she can reach is identical to the curve she could reach without a borrowing constraint, where $MRS = (1 + r)$, so the results are identical to the ones we developed in Figures 18.3 through 18.5. Just as in those figures, any increase in lifetime resources, regardless of its source, boosts consumption in both periods.

We now consider a case in which the *borrowing constraint is binding*. In panel (b) of Figure 18.6, we can see that with no constraints on borrowing, Carmencita's highest indifference curve is the one that touches the intertemporal budget line at point D, which is to the right of point B. Unfortunately for Carmencita, she can't get to this higher indifference curve at IC_2 because she cannot borrow. That is, she can't get consumption in period 1 that is above Y_1. Instead, the highest indifference curve she can reach is IC_2, which touches IBL_{BC} at point B.

We can make some important conclusions from this analysis. For consumers with binding borrowing constraints, consumption in any period is determined solely by the income they earn in that period. That is, after optimizing, it is no longer true that the marginal rate of substitution equals one plus the interest rate. Instead, the slope of the indifference curve at point B is steeper than $-(1 + r)$, so that $MRS > (1 + r)$.

In addition, we can see that borrowing constraints create two very different kinds of consumers. For a substantial fraction of consumers subject to binding borrowing constraints—perhaps as much as 20% of the U.S. population[6]—consumption is driven completely by current income, and so $C_1 = Y_1$ and $C_2 = Y_2$. The majority of the U.S. population, however, can engage in consumption smoothing, in which consumption both today and in the future will respond to any change in lifetime resources, even if it comes from a rise in future income rather than in current income.

The Keynesian Theory of Consumption

Now that we have outlined a basic intertemporal choice theory of consumption, we can use it to compare three of the most popular theories of consumption. We start with the Keynesian *consumption function* that we first discussed in Chapter 9 and now develop more fully here.

The Keynesian Consumption Function: Building Blocks

John Maynard Keynes, in his *General Theory of Employment, Interest and Money*, published in 1936, did not base his theory of consumption on the theory of intertemporal choice, but he reached somewhat similar conclusions. Keynes based his theory of consumption on three simple conjectures:

1. When disposable income, Y, rises, households spend more.

2. When a household's income goes up, its spending goes up by less than a one-to-one ratio with the increase in income. Formally, the **marginal propensity to consume,** the increase in consumption expenditure from an additional dollar of disposable income ($\Delta C/\Delta Y$), is between zero and one. For example, if a person's income goes up by ten dollars and his or her

[6]See, for example, Robert E. Hall and Frederic S. Mishkin, "The Sensitivity of Consumption to Transitory Income: Estimates from Panel Data on Households," *Econometrica* (March 1982): 461–481; and John Y. Campbell and N. Gregory Mankiw, "Consumption, Income, and Interest Rates: Reinterpreting the Time Series Evidence," in *NBER Macroeconomics Annual*, eds. Olivier Blanchard and Stanley Fischer (Cambridge, MA: MIT Press, 1989), 185–216.

spending rises by seven dollars, then the marginal propensity to consume is $0.7 = 7/10$.

3. The ratio of consumption to income (C/Y), the **average propensity to consume,** falls as income rises. For example, if a person's income rose from $25,000 to $50,000 and his consumption spending increased from $20,000 to $35,000, his average propensity to consume would fall from 0.8 ($20,000/$25,000) to 0.7 ($35,000/$50,000).

Keynes based the third conjecture on his observation that rich people save a higher fraction of their income than poor people. To use a term from microeconomics, saving is like a luxury good. This view suggests that the **average propensity to save,** also known as the **saving rate,** which is the ratio of saving to disposable income (S/Y), should rise with income. Dividing Equation 1 $(S = Y - C)$ by Y, we can write the average propensity to save as follows:

$$S/Y = (Y - C)/Y = 1 - (C/Y)$$

For the average propensity to save (S/Y) to rise with income, as Keynes believed, the average propensity to consume (C/Y) must fall as income rises.

Keynesian Consumption Function

Combining these three conjectures, Keynes wrote down a linear relationship between consumption expenditure and disposable income, which he called the **consumption function:**

$$C = \overline{C} + (mpc \times Y) \tag{5}$$

In Equation 5, mpc is a constant between zero and one $(0 < mpc < 1)$ and $\overline{C}$ is a constant, referred to as **autonomous consumption expenditure,** that is greater than zero $(\overline{C} > 0)$.

The linear consumption function in Equation 5 satisfies all three of Keynes's conjectures. First, since $mpc > 0$, as disposable income rises $(Y\uparrow)$, consumption also rises $(C\uparrow)$. Second, mpc, which is between zero and one, tells us how much consumption rises when disposable income, Y, rises by $1, and so it equals the marginal propensity to consume, which is therefore between zero and one, as Keynes conjectured. Third, dividing both sides of Equation 5 by Y yields

$$\frac{C}{Y} = \frac{\overline{C} + mpcY}{Y} = \frac{\overline{C}}{Y} + mpc$$

Because $\overline{C}$ and mpc are constants, as Y rises, $\overline{C}/Y$ falls and therefore the average propensity to consume, C/Y, also falls, which is consistent with Keynes's third conjecture that the saving rate, S/Y, rises as income rises.

The Relationship of the Keynesian Consumption Function to Intertemporal Choice

The consumption function outlined by Keynes indicates that consumption is solely related to current income and so does not display consumption smoothing. In this sense, it is consistent with the theory of intertemporal choice for borrowing-constrained households, but not for households without a binding borrowing constraint.

The Permanent Income Hypothesis

Since binding borrowing constraints apply only to a minority of households, Milton Friedman, in his monumental work published in 1957, *A Theory of the Consumption Function*,[7] argued that consumption smoothing was a key feature of consumption behavior. He drew on the theory of intertemporal choice to develop the **permanent income hypothesis,** which asserts that consumption depends on **permanent income,** the level of income that is expected to persist over a long period of time and is therefore representative of a consumer's lifetime resources. This differs from the Keynesian consumption function, in which consumption depends only on current income.

More specifically, Friedman divided income into two components, *permanent income,* denoted by Y_P, and *transitory income,* Y_T:

$$Y = Y_P + Y_T \qquad (6)$$

Transitory income, in contrast to permanent income, is the component of income that does not persist for a long period of time and so is subject to temporary fluctuations.

For example, if you pursue an MBA degree, you might expect to earn, say, an additional $10,000 a year over your whole career. Thus your permanent income and lifetime resources will be much higher than if you had not earned the MBA degree. On the other hand, if you go to Las Vegas and hit a $10,000 jackpot on a slot machine, you would expect this income to be temporary and so you would view it as transitory income, and it would add far less to your lifetime resources.

Milton Friedman drew from the consumption smoothing implication of intertemporal choice theory to reason that consumers would smooth out consumption spending in response to temporary fluctuations in income. In other words, they would not consume much more because of higher transitory income (like winning a jackpot) but would instead save most of it, and spend a little more over many years. On the other hand, if permanent income rose, say because of an advanced degree, consumption would be much higher.

The Permanent Income Consumption Function

The permanent income hypothesis implies that we can treat consumption as a function of permanent income:[8]

$$C = cY_P \qquad (7)$$

In Equation 7, c is a constant fraction that represents the marginal propensity to consume relative to permanent income. In other words, **the permanent income hypothesis indicates that consumption is proportional to permanent income.**

---

[7]Milton Friedman, *A Theory of the Consumption Function* (Princeton: Princeton University Press, 1957).

[8]Friedman assumed that the increase in lifetime resources from transitory income would be so small that it could be ignored and so would not lead to any increase in consumption. However, because transitory income can lead to a small increase in lifetime resources, the consumption function can be written as

$$C = c(Y_P + \theta Y_T)$$

where θ is a small number less than one, as intertemporal choice theory indicates.

Application

Consumer Confidence and the Business Cycle

Every month, the Conference Board, a private research organization, and the University of Michigan, with Thomson Reuters, publish measures of consumer confidence, which are described in the Macroeconomics in the News box that follows. These indices are among the most closely followed pieces of data distributed by economic forecasters. How does consumer confidence affect the business cycle? The permanent income hypothesis provides an answer.

As we have seen, permanent income is a forward-looking measure of future lifetime resources. When consumer confidence rises, consumers expect their income to be higher in the future, and so their lifetime resources and permanent income rise. The permanent income hypothesis tells us that autonomous consumption will then rise and the aggregate demand curve will shift to the right, as shown in the aggregate demand-aggregate supply (*AD/AS*) diagram in Figure 18.7. The result is that the economy moves from point 1 to point 2, where both aggregate output and inflation rise. The permanent income hypothesis thus gives consumer confidence a prominent role in explaining business cycle fluctuations, and this explains why announcements about the consumer confidence level are featured prominently in the news.

Relationship of the Permanent Income Hypothesis and Intertemporal Choice

Using the concept of permanent income, we can see how intertemporal choice theory comes to the same conclusion: that consumption responds more to a rise in permanent income than it does to a rise in transitory income. In the theory of intertemporal choice, consumption responds to the present value of future income streams, which in our two-period model was $Y_1 + Y_2/(1 + r)$. A permanent rise in income lifts both Y_1 and Y_2, lifting lifetime resources and increasing consumption both today and tomorrow.

FIGURE 18.7

Consumer Confidence and the *AD/AS* Diagram

A rise in consumer confidence shifts the *AD* curve to the right and moves the economy from point 1 to point 2, where output and inflation rise.

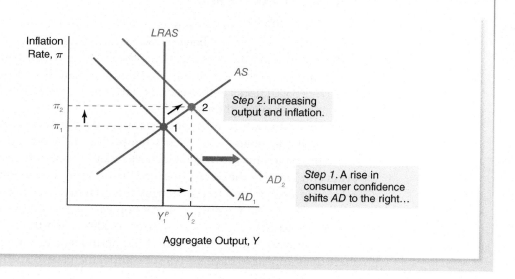

The Consumer Confidence and Consumer Sentiment Indices

The Conference Board's Consumer Confidence Index is derived from 5,000 U.S. households' responses to five questions about current business conditions, current employment conditions, and total family income for the next six months. A competing measure is the University of Michigan Consumer Sentiment Index, produced by the University of Michigan's Institute for Social Research and published by Thomson Reuters. This measure of consumer confidence is derived from responses from at least 500 households about their views of their own financial situations, the short-term general economy, and the long-term general economy. Both measures are announced monthly, receiving wide attention in the financial press, and are closely monitored by the Federal Reserve and other government agencies, along with manufacturers, retailers, financial institutions, and private economic forecasting firms.

On the other hand, a transitory hike in income will lift Y_1 but not Y_2, and boost lifetime resources (and today's consumption) by a much smaller amount.

Because the permanent income hypothesis is derived in a multi-period framework, using reasoning similar to that of intertemporal choice theory, it comes to an even stronger conclusion that consumption responds mostly to permanent income and hardly at all to transitory income. A rise in permanent income implies that income is higher for a very long time, so lifetime resources rise by a lot, indicating that consumption will also rise a lot. On the other hand, if the increase in income is transitory, then income rises for only one period, while it remains unchanged for many periods afterwards. In this case, lifetime resources will change by relatively little, implying that consumption will change minimally and most of the transitory income will be saved.

Policy and Practice

The 2008 Tax Rebate

In February 2008, Congress passed the Economic Stimulus Act to jump-start the U.S. economy, which had been weakened by the global financial crisis that began in the summer of 2007. The major provision of this legislation was the distribution of one-time tax rebates totaling $78 billion, accomplished by sending individual taxpayers $600 checks in the second quarter of the year. How big an impact should these rebates have had on spending?

The permanent income hypothesis suggests that the spending impact would be very small: the rebates were clearly temporary and were transitory income. In this situation, recipients of the rebate checks would spread their spending over many years and increase their current spending only slightly. In other words, the saving rate could be expected to rise sharply after a temporary tax rebate. This is exactly what seems to have transpired. As you can see in Figure 18.8, the saving rate jumped sharply in the second quarter of 2008 when the rebate checks were sent out. In contrast to the prediction of the permanent income hypothesis, however, there does appear to have been a substantial increase in spending as a result of the

FIGURE 18.8

Saving Rate and the 2008 Tax Rebate

The saving rate jumped sharply in the second quarter of 2008 when the tax rebate checks were distributed.

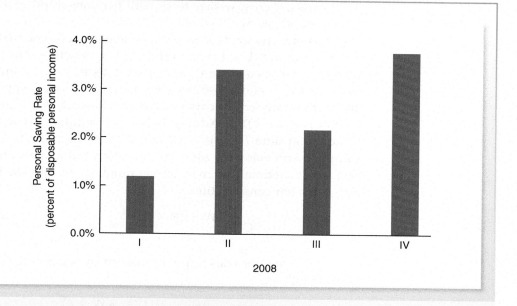

Source: Bureau of Economic Analysis. National Income and Product Accounts, available at www.bea.gov.

tax rebate. Some estimates suggest that 10%–20% of the rebate checks went into increased spending, while others suggest an even higher response, with 12%–30% of rebate checks going to consumption and 50%–90% going to consumer spending, including spending on durable goods. However, surveys of recipients of the rebate checks indicated that over half of recipients used the checks not to consume more but to pay off debt, as the permanent income hypothesis would predict.[9]

The Life-Cycle Hypothesis

Franco Modigliani, in a series of papers written with co-authors starting in the mid-1950s, extended the intertemporal choice model to many periods, developing the **life-cycle hypothesis.** For most people, income changes systematically over a lifetime, most notably when income declines at retirement. As the theory suggests, people tend to smooth consumption over their *life cycle.*

Life-Cycle Consumption Function

To illustrate the life-cycle hypothesis, we look at a very simple example in which Carmencita starts earning an income at time $T = 0$, the starting age of adulthood (say, age 20), and works until she retires R years later (say, $45 =$ age 65 $-$ age 20). She expects to live for L additional years after she becomes an adult (say, $60 =$ age 80 $-$ age 20).

[9]See Martin Feldstein, "The Tax Rebate Was a Flop. Obama's Stimulus Plan Won't Work Either," *Wall Street Journal,* August 6, 2009; Claudia R. Sahm, Matthew D. Shapiro, and Joel B. Slemrod, "Did the 2008 Tax Rebates Stimulate Spending?" *American Economic Review: Papers and Proceedings* 99, no. 2 (May 2009): 374–379; and Jonathan A. Parker, Nicholas S. Souleles, David S. Johnson, and Robert McClelland, "Consumer Spending and the Economic Stimulus Payments of 2008," *American Economic Review,* forthcoming, manuscript: March 2013, http://finance.wharton.upenn.edu/~souleles/research/papers/ESP2008_WP_Final.pdf.

Carmencita, like any optimizing consumer following the dictums of intertemporal choice theory, wishes to smooth her consumption over her lifetime. To keep things simple, we will assume that the interest rate is zero, so that all future income and consumption streams have the same present discounted value as current income or consumption. Until time period R, Carmencita earns a yearly salary of $\overline{Y}$, but when she retires at time R, her salary falls to zero. At any given point in time T, Carmencita's lifetime resources are made up of two components: 1) her wealth, W, and 2) the number of years she has left to work, $R - T$, multiplied by her salary, $\overline{Y}$, that is, $(R - T)\overline{Y}$.[10] Adding these two components together, her total lifetime resources at time T are $W + (R - T)\overline{Y}$. Since Carmencita wants to smooth her consumption and enjoy the same consumption throughout the rest of her life, she will divide her lifetime resources by the number of years she has left to live, $L - T$, to determine her consumption:

$$C = \left[\frac{W + (R - T)\overline{Y}}{L - T}\right] = \left[\frac{1}{L - T}\right]W + \left[\frac{R - T}{L - T}\right]\overline{Y} \tag{8}$$

We can rewrite this consumption function by separating out the wealth and income terms as follows:

$$C = \omega W + c\overline{Y} \tag{9}$$

where

$$\omega = [1/(L - T)] \tag{10}$$

$$c = [(R - T)/(L - T)] \tag{11}$$

The life-cycle hypothesis comes to the same conclusion that we already saw in our analysis of intertemporal choice: **changes in consumption are driven by changes in income and wealth.**

This life-cycle equation tells us several interesting things. First, let's suppose that Carmencita is pretty young, say, 25 years old, so that $T = 5$. Let's also suppose that she will retire at 65, so $R = 45$, and has a life expectancy of 80, so $L = 60$. Plugging these values into Equation 9 ($\omega = 1/55 = 0.02$, $c = 40/55 = 0.73$), we get the following:

$$C = 0.02 \times W + 0.73 \times \overline{Y}$$

When Carmencita is young, she will have a marginal propensity to consume of 2 cents out of every dollar of wealth and 73 cents out of every dollar of income.

What about when Carmencita is 60 years old ($T = 40$) and is only five years from retirement? Now, Equation 9 (with $\omega = 1/20 = 0.05$ and $c = 5/20 = 0.25$) yields the following consumption function:

$$C = 0.05 \times W + 0.25 \times \overline{Y}$$

She now has a marginal propensity to consume of 5 cents out of every dollar of wealth and 25 cents out of every dollar of income.

---

[10]As in the intertemporal choice model earlier, we are treating income Y as labor income only because it does not include interest payments, which in this example are zero anyway.

These two examples illustrate another important conclusion from the life-cycle hypothesis: *as consumers get older, the marginal propensity to consume out of wealth rises, while the marginal propensity to consume out of income falls*. The intuition behind this conclusion is the following: as consumers get older, they have fewer years to live and so will consume a higher fraction of their wealth each year, while their annual income will continue for fewer years, so the increase in their lifetime resources will be lower relative to their annual income and they will spend less of it.

Saving and Wealth Over the Life Cycle

The life-cycle hypothesis helps us see how saving and wealth evolve over people's lifetimes. To illustrate, let's look at a very simple example in which Carmencita has the same income $\overline{Y}$ every year that she works, the real interest rate is zero, and there are no capital gains or losses on her wealth, so that the change in wealth for any year is equal to the amount she has saved:

$$\Delta W = S = Y - C$$

Because Carmencita wants to smooth consumption, she will want her consumption to be the same every period at $\overline{C}$, which will be equal to the total resources that she has over her lifetime divided by the number of years she lives:

$$\overline{C} = [R/L] \times \overline{Y} = [45/60] \times \overline{Y} = 0.75 \times \overline{Y}$$

If Carmencita has a salary of $50,000, she will consume $37,500 every year.

Now let's look at what happens to saving and wealth over time. For the first forty-five years of her working life, Carmencita is saving $\overline{Y} - \overline{C} = \overline{Y} - 0.75\overline{Y} = 0.25\overline{Y}$ (i.e., a quarter of her salary), which is denoted by the blue shaded area in panel (a) of Figure 18.9. With a salary $\overline{Y}$ of $50,000 per year, Carmencita is saving $12,500 per year prior to retirement. Every year her wealth is increasing by that amount until she retires at age sixty-five, which is shown in panel (b) by wealth increasing linearly with a slope of $0.25\overline{Y} = 12,500$. At retirement, her total wealth (savings) has accumulated to $562,500, quite a little nest egg.

When Carmencita retires and is no longer earning a salary, she is dissaving. That is, she has negative saving equal to her consumption, $\overline{C}$, of $0.75\overline{Y}$, or $37,500, denoted by the red shaded area in panel (a) of Figure 18.9. But now every year her wealth is going down by this amount, as shown in panel (b), until at the end of her life she has exhausted all her savings. The life-cycle hypothesis has the following additional implication: *as people grow older before retirement, their wealth grows; after retirement, their wealth declines.* This result explains an important fact found in the data: older people tend to have higher holdings of assets (stocks, bonds, and housing) than do younger people.

FIGURE 18.9

Consumption, Saving, and Wealth over the Life Cycle

Carmencita's yearly salary income while working is $\overline{Y} = \$50,000$, while annual consumption over her entire lifetime is $\overline{C} = 0.75\overline{Y} = \$37,500$. For the first forty-five years of her working life, her saving is $0.25\overline{Y} = \$12,500$ per year, denoted by the blue shaded area in panel (a) of Figure 18.9. After retirement, she is dissaving: she has negative saving equal to her consumption, $\overline{C}$, of $0.75\overline{Y}$, or $\$37,500$, denoted by the red shaded area. Panel (b) shows what happens to wealth, which rises linearly until Carmencita retires, reaching a peak of $\$562,500$ and then declines to zero at the end of her life.

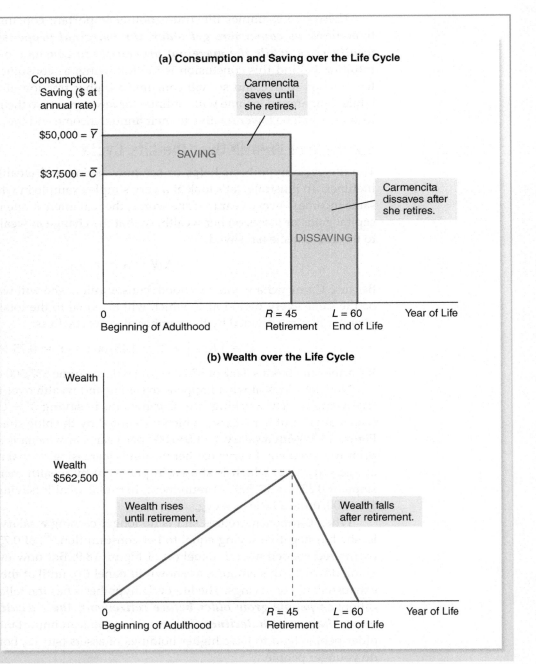

(a) Consumption and Saving over the Life Cycle

Carmencita saves until she retires.

SAVING

Carmencita dissaves after she retires.

DISSAVING

(b) Wealth over the Life Cycle

Wealth rises until retirement.

Wealth falls after retirement.

Application

Housing, the Stock Market, and the Collapse of Consumption in 2008 and 2009

The life-cycle hypothesis predicts a drop in consumption when wealth suddenly declines, as it did during the global financial crisis of 2007–2009. Over the course of the crisis, the stock market lost almost 50% of its value, and housing prices plummeted. Indeed, in 2008, U.S. consumers' wealth declined by $11.1 trillion, the largest drop ever recorded. The life-cycle hypothesis views wealth as an important component of lifetime resources. Changes in asset prices that cause wealth to fluctuate in value can be a major source of fluctuations in consumption. Indeed, estimates of the marginal propensity to consume out of wealth are in the neighborhood of 3.5 cents per dollar of wealth.[11] The life-cycle hypothesis therefore suggests that the $11.1 trillion decline in wealth in 2008 would lead to a nearly $400 billion decline in consumption. Indeed, as the life-cycle hypothesis predicts, consumption in the United States declined substantially in 2008 and 2009, making the recession the most severe since World War II.

Two Modifications of the Theory: The Random Walk Hypothesis and Behavioral Economics

Recent research has resulted in two adjustments to the theory of consumption: the *random walk hypothesis,* and the application of *behavioral economics* to consumption behavior.

The Random Walk Hypothesis

In 1978, Robert Hall, now of Stanford University, published a path-breaking paper based on the life-cycle and permanent income hypotheses that suggested that changes in consumption would be unpredictable.[12] When changes in a variable are unpredictable, the variable is said to follow a **random walk,** and that is why Hall's theory has become known as the **random walk hypothesis.**

The reasoning behind the random walk hypothesis starts with three steps.

1. The life-cycle and permanent income hypotheses (as well as the theory of intertemporal choice) imply that consumers are forward-looking. That is, they base their consumption decisions on their current expectations about future income that will determine their lifetime resources.

2. Only when expectations of future income change will expectations of lifetime resources change.

3. Since current consumption is determined by changes in expectations of lifetime resources, changes in consumption should only change when these expectations change.

[11]For example, see the survey in Frederic S. Mishkin, "Housing and the Monetary Transmission Mechanism," Federal Reserve Bank of Kansas City, *Housing, Housing Finance, and Monetary Policy, 2007 Jackson Hole Symposium* (Federal Reserve Bank of Kansas City, Kansas City, 2007): 359–413.

[12]Robert E. Hall, "Stochastic Implications of the Life Cycle-Permanent Income Hypothesis: Theory and Evidence," *Journal of Political Economy* 86 (December 1978): 971–987.

The fourth step is the assumption of a concept called *rational expectations*, which we explore in more detail in Chapter 21. This concept states that because expectations are derived from all available information, only new information, that is, unanticipated surprises, will cause expectations to change. Hence, ***expectations of lifetime resources and current consumption will change only when there is unanticipated new information, and so changes in consumption are unpredictable. That is, they follow a random walk.***

This implication of the random walk hypothesis suggests that tax policy cannot be used to manage fluctuations in consumption in order to soften swings in economic activity. Suppose Congress passes a tax cut when the economy is in recession, but this tax cut was already expected because Congress has always passed such tax cuts in previous recessions. The tax cut will not change expectations of lifetime resources and hence will not cause consumption to change. Only if the tax cut is a surprise will it work to raise consumption. Indeed, a tax cut that is smaller than the public expects could even cause consumption to fall, not rise. Because the public expected its disposable income to be higher as a result of a larger tax cut, the smaller tax cut would cause the public to revise downward its expectations of lifetime resources. The random walk hypothesis thus states that the effects of tax policy on consumption are highly uncertain because the effect on consumption depends on what the policy *is* relative to what it *was expected* to be.

Behavioral Economics and Consumption

In recent years, **behavioral economics,** which applies concepts from other social sciences, such as anthropology, sociology, and (in particular) psychology, to the study of economic behavior, has emerged as an important part of economic research. Recently, economists have applied these ideas to consumption behavior, suggesting that the optimizing behavior of consumers—which is a key assumption in all of the consumption theories we have discussed—may not be a completely accurate characterization of how consumers actually behave.

Because the field of behavioral economics is relatively young, we provide just a taste of its applications to the theory of consumption. One implication of behavioral economics is that consumers may be swayed by instant gratification, and so their decisions may not put enough weight on the future. David Laibson of Harvard University has labeled this phenomenon *hyperbolic discounting*, to capture the idea that consumers will not consistently discount the future over time, as is assumed in the theory of intertemporal choice.[13] Specifically, although they know that they should have a reasonably low discount rate and should not discount the future too heavily, when they make decisions, they just can't help themselves and instead seek instant gratification. The result is that consumers may act as though they have a very high discount rate, even though they know that their true discount rate should be much lower.

We experience this kind of behavior all the time. Even though we know that we should maintain a healthy diet and not overeat in order to live longer, many of us just can't help ourselves when we see that beautiful banana split, with hot fudge and whipped cream on top. Many of us end up far fatter than we would be if we were making optimal choices.

One result of succumbing to instant gratification and thereby making decisions with too high a discount rate is that consumers may overreact to current income and

---

[13]David Laibson, "Golden Eggs and Hyperbolic Discounting," *Quarterly Journal of Economics* 62 (May 1997).

not smooth consumption sufficiently. An additional problem that arises from seeking instant gratification is that consumers' saving rates may be way below what is considered optimal. This insight has led some behavioral economists to suggest that policy makers should help steer people into saving more, as we discuss in the following Policy and Practice case.

Policy and Practice

Behavioral Policies to Increase Saving

Insufficient saving has become a big worry in the United States. As we discussed in Chapters 4 and 6, saving that is too low leads to a dearth of investment, which can slow economic growth. Low saving can also lead to increasing indebtedness to foreigners, which can leave us poorer in the future. Furthermore, surveys indicate that most U.S. workers believe they are not saving enough for retirement.

Behavioral economists such as David Laibson and Richard Thaler of the University of Chicago believe that consumers are not making optimal decisions, and they have thus suggested that consumers' choices should be limited for their own good. This approach, which has been dubbed *libertarian paternalism*, takes the libertarian view that people should have free choice, but injects some paternalism by directing people to the right choice when decisions are overly complicated or subject to the pull of instant gratification.

One application of these ideas to increasing saving is to change the default options for savings plans to encourage more saving.[14] For example, many retirement savings plans that are tax-advantaged, such as 401k plans made available through employers, require workers to *choose* to enroll in the plan, that is, they have to *opt in* to the plan. Libertarian paternalists would advocate that workers should be automatically enrolled in the plan, so that there is some coercion to save more—this is the paternalistic part—but that they should be able to *opt out* if they so choose—the libertarian part. The idea is that consumers need to be nudged in the right direction by policy makers to save more, but should still be able to exercise choice by opting out.

The Obama administration has taken these ideas from behavioral economics to heart by adding provisions to the 2009 economic stimulus package that require employers that did not have retirement plans to enroll their workers into retirement accounts, with automatic payment deposits drawn from employees' salaries. Employees have the option of opting out of these direct deposit arrangements if they so choose.

Behavioral economics is a very young discipline, and it is still an open question whether proposals of this type will actually increase saving and living standards. Given the importance of saving, evaluating the best way to encourage more of it will be an active area of research in the future.

---

[14]For example, see James J. Choi, David I. Laibson, Brigitte Madrian, and Andrew Metrick, "Defined Contribution Pensions: Plan Rules, Participant Decisions, and the Path of Least Resistance," *Tax Policy and the Economy* 16 (2002), pp. 67–113, and Richard H. Thaler and Cass R. Sunstein, *Nudge: Improving Decisions on Health, Wealth, and Happiness* (New Haven, CT: Yale University Press, 2008).

SUMMARY

1. Because saving is the difference between disposable income and consumption, a theory of consumption is also a theory of saving, and vice versa.

2. The theory of intertemporal choice shows that consumers choose to maximize their utility by having the intertemporal budget line tangent to an indifference curve, where the marginal rate of substitution is equal to one plus the interest rate.

3. The theory of intertemporal choice indicates that no matter what the source of a rise in the present value of lifetime resources—whether it is from an increase in current income, future income, or wealth—the increase in consumption is spread out over both the present and future periods, a phenomenon that is referred to as consumption smoothing.

4. There are two effects on consumption from a rise in interest rates: the income effect for a consumer who has savings is a rise in consumption in both periods, while the substitution effect is a fall in consumption in period 1 but a rise in consumption in period 2. Because the usual assumption is that the substitution effect is stronger than the income effect, a rise in interest rates leads to a fall in today's consumption (a rise in saving) but a rise in future consumption. The presence of borrowing constraints implies that some consumers find this constraint binding, with their consumption determined by current income.

5. The Keynesian consumption function posits a linear relationship between consumption expenditure and disposable income. It is consistent with three conjectures by Keynes: 1) people spend more when they have more income; 2) the increase in spending is less than one-for-one when there is a rise in income; and 3) as income rises, the average propensity to consume, which is the ratio of consumption to income, falls.

6. The permanent income hypothesis indicates that consumption is proportional to permanent income, whereas it reacts little to transitory income.

7. The life-cycle hypothesis suggests that changes in consumption are driven by changes in income and by changes in wealth; furthermore, as consumers get older, the marginal propensity to consume out of income falls, while the marginal propensity to consume out of wealth rises.

8. The random walk hypothesis states that because expectations of lifetime resources and current consumption will change only when there is unanticipated, new information, changes in consumption are unpredictable, that is, they follow a random walk. Behavioral economics suggests that consumers may not fully optimize as is predicted in the theory of intertemporal choice, the permanent income hypothesis, and the life-cycle hypothesis. Some behavioral economists suggest that policy makers should help steer people to save more in order to counteract their tendency to pursue instant gratification.

KEY TERMS

autonomous consumption expenditure, p. 507

average propensity to consume, p. 507

average propensity to save, p. 507

behavioral economics, p. 516

borrowing constraint, p. 504

consumption function, p. 507

consumption smoothing, p. 502

convexity, p. 499

discounting, p. 497

disposable income, p. 494

income effect, p. 503

indifference curve, p. 498

intertemporal budget constraint, p. 495

intertemporal budget line, p. 497

intertemporal marginal rate of substitution, p. 499

life-cycle hypothesis, p. 511

liquidity constraint, p. 504

marginal propensity to consume, p. 506

marginal rate of substitution, p. 499

permanent income, p. 508

permanent income hypothesis, p. 508

present discounted value, p. 497

present value, p. 597

random walk, p. 515

random walk hypothesis, p. 515

saving, p. 494

saving rate, p. 507

substitution effect, p. 503

theory of intertemporal choice, p. 495

transitory income, p. 508

utility, p. 498

welfare, p. 498

REVIEW QUESTIONS

All Questions are available in MyEconLab *for practice or instructor assignment.*

The Relationship Between Consumption and Savings

1. Why is a theory of consumption also a theory of saving?

Intertemporal Choice and Consumption

2. What is the logic behind the intertemporal budget constraint? On what assumptions is it based, and how is its slope interpreted?

3. What do indifference curves show about current and future consumption? Why do they slope downward? Why are they convex?

4. Explain how the intertemporal budget constraint and indifference curves are used to derive a consumer's optimal choice of current and future consumption.

The Intertemporal Choice Model in Practice: Income and Wealth

5. What can shift the intertemporal budget line, *IBL*? What happens to current and future consumption when *IBL* shifts occur?

The Intertemporal Choice Model in Practice: Interest Rates

6. How do changes in the real interest rate affect the *IBL* and current and future consumption?

7. How do binding borrowing constraints affect the *IBL* and current and future consumption?

The Keynesian Theory of Consumption

8. On what assumptions did Keynes base his theory of consumption? How does his theory relate to intertemporal choice?

The Permanent Income Hypothesis

9. What is the permanent income hypothesis? How does its consumption function relate to intertemporal choice?

The Life-Cycle Hypothesis

10. Describe the life-cycle hypothesis and how it relates to intertemporal choice.

Two Modifications of the Theory: The Random Walk Hypothesis and Behavioral Economics

11. What modifications to the intertemporal choice theory have been suggested by the random walk hypothesis and behavioral economics?

PROBLEMS

All Problems are available in MyEconLab *for practice and assignment.*

Intertemporal Choice and Consumption

1. Suppose Prakash has an income today of $30,000, an expected income in period 2 of $35,000, and initial wealth of $5,000. Prakash faces an interest rate of 5%.
   a) Graph Prakash's intertemporal budget line. Denote the values of C_1 and C_2 at the intersection points with the horizontal and vertical axis, respectively.
   b) Identity the point on the intertemporal budget line at which Prakash has no money at the end of period 1 and is not borrowing from anyone.

2. Assume that Maria does not have a preference for smooth consumption. In particular, the average of two consumption points on the same indifference curve yields the same utility to Maria as either point (i.e., the average consumption point is on the same indifference curve as the other two points).
   a) Draw Maria's indifference curves.
   b) What is the implication of Maria's preferences for the marginal rate of substitution?

The Intertemporal Choice Model in Practice: Income and Wealth

3. Describe the effect of an increase in next period's income on the intertemporal budget constraint. If next year's income increases by $3,000 and the interest rate is 5%, by how much does the intertemporal budget line shift?

4. The following figure represents the optimization problem for a homeowner whose home is currently valued at $250,000.

   a) Identify the optimum consumption point (i.e., what are the values of C_1 and C_2 at which this individual's happiness is maximized?).
   b) If the value of the home decreases to $200,000, what is the optimum consumption point?

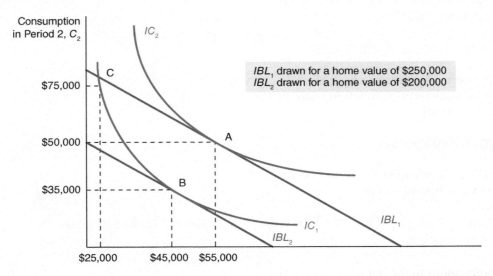

Consumption in Period 1, C_1

The Intertemporal Choice Model in Practice: Interest Rates

5. Describe the effects of a decrease in the interest rate on present and next period's consumption if the individual is a net lender (i.e., has sav-ings) after period 1 and the substitution effect is larger than the income effect. Show your answer graphically.

The Keynesian Theory of Consumption

6. Suppose Nicole's yearly income is $5,000 when she is fifteen, $35,000 when she is twenty-five, and $70,000 when she is fifty (these are all present value measures of future income). Assume that Nicole's autonomous consumption expenditure is $20,000 and that her marginal propensity to consume is 0.75.
   a) Plot Nicole's consumption function (measure income on the horizontal axis and consumption on the vertical axis) for every point in her life. Plot Nicole's consumption function if her autonomous consumption expenditure decreases to $15,000.
   b) Calculate Nicole's average propensity to consume when she is fifteen, twenty-five, and fifty (assuming autonomous consumption is $20,000).

7. What does the Keynesian consumption function imply about the average propensity to consume of a rich versus a poor country? Which country should have a higher average propensity to consume? How can you explain the relatively low levels of saving of rich countries?

The Life-Cycle Hypothesis

8. In May 2010, the size of Greece's budget deficit increased its probability of default and triggered a crisis across the Eurozone. To decrease the budget deficit, the Greek government proposed many measures. A few of them involved decreasing pension and/or benefits payments to retirees. Use the life-cycle hypothesis to evaluate the impact of an unexpected decrease in your income after you retire.

Two Modifications of the Theory: The Random Walk Hypothesis and Behavioral Economics

9. For each of the following situations, explain how current consumption will change according to the random walk hypothesis:
   a) The government increases taxes to close the budget deficit, but the size of the tax increase is smaller than expected.
   b) You receive your BS degree and find a job that increases your lifetime income.
   c) A stock market crash decreases a household's wealth.

10. Previous policies to increase saving in the United States have included fiscal policy measures to exempt a part of individuals' savings from income taxes (e.g., the creation of IRAs). According to the precepts of behavioral economics, do you think these measures could have a significant impact on the U.S. savings rate?

DATA ANALYSIS PROBLEMS

The Problems update with real-time data in MyEconLab *and are available for practice or instructor assignment.*

1. Go to the St. Louis Federal Reserve FRED database, and find data on real personal consumption expenditures (PCECCA) and a measure of real interest rates, the 10-year treasury inflation-indexed security (FII10). Convert the TIIS rate to "Annual" using the *frequency* setting. Download the data into a spreadsheet.

a) Report the level of consumption for the two most recent years of data available, and the average of the real interest rate over those two years.

b) Using the average real interest rate over the two years, calculate the value of consumption for the most recent period, in present discounted value terms to the prior year.

c) Using the average real interest rate over the two years, what is consumption for the earlier period worth in the most recent period?

2. Go to the St. Louis Federal Reserve FRED database, and find data on disposable personal income (DPI), personal saving (PSAVE), and personal consumption expenditures (PCEC). Download the data onto a spreadsheet. For each quarter, calculate the average propensity to consume, APC, and the average propensity to save, APS. Calculate the average of the APC and APS for the most recent four quarters of data available, and for the four quarters before that. Calculate the average disposable income over the most recent four quarters and over the four quarters before that. Do the data support Keynes' conjecture relating income to the APC and APS? Briefly explain.

3. Go to the St. Louis Federal Reserve FRED database, and find data on the civilian population (CNP16OV) and the civilian population 55 years old and over (LNU00024230). Convert the two population series to "Quarterly" using the *frequency* setting, and download the data. Create a series and calculate, for each quarter, the fraction of people 55 and older relative to the entire population. Express your result as a percentage.

a) For the decades of the 1980s, 1990s, and 2000s, and for the period from 2010 to the most recent quarter of data available, calculate the average of the 55-and-older population ratios, and report your results.

b) Based on the decade-by-decade results, what would you expect to happen to the marginal propensity to consume out of permanent income, assuming the life-cycle hypothesis holds? Briefly explain.

c) Suppose a shock resulted in declines of equal size in the wealth of households in the 1980s and today, but permanent income is unaffected. Based on your answer to part (a), how would such a decline impact consumption in each period, according to the life-cycle hypothesis? Briefly explain.

4. Go to the St. Louis Federal Reserve FRED database, and find data on the University of Michigan's consumer sentiment index (UMCSENT) and real personal consumption expenditures (PCECC96). Convert the consumer sentiment index to "Quarterly" using the *frequency* setting, and download the data. Using the most recent data available, calculate the level change in the consumer sentiment index from the same time a year earlier, and the percentage change in consumption from a year earlier. Do these values behave as you would expect? Based on the change in consumer sentiment, how should permanent income have changed? Briefly explain.

An online appendix, "Income and Substitution Effects: A Graphical Analysis," is available at the Companion Website, www.pearsonhighered.com/mishkin.

Investment

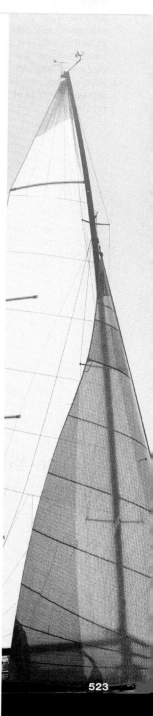

Preview

Investment spending comprises only around 15% of GDP, an economic pipsqueak next to consumption expenditure, which typically makes up 70% of total output. Yet investment spending is no pint-sized pushover. During recessions, changes in investment spending pack a bruising punch to the economy, accounting for well over half of the decline in total spending. When good times return, spending on business inventory, factories, and other investment items surges, shoving the economy back on course with some serious heft. During the business cycle expansion from 2001 to 2007, for example, investment spending rose at a 4% annual rate. Then, in December 2007, investment fell off a cliff, dropping at a 15% annual rate from December 2007 to December 2009.

What determines the economy's level of investment spending? Why did investment suddenly plummet starting in 2007?

In this chapter, we answer these questions by developing two models of investment behavior: the *neoclassical model*, which links investment to interest rates and tax policy, and *Tobin's q theory*, which considers the effects of asset prices. We then describe the tools available to policy makers to affect investment spending.

Data on Investment Spending

We open our discussion of investment by outlining the three basic components of investment spending (mentioned previously in Chapter 2).

1. **Business fixed investment,** which includes spending by businesses on equipment (computers, trucks, and machines) and structures (factories, shopping centers, and hospitals) that are used in production.

2. **Inventory investment,** which includes spending by businesses on additional holdings of raw materials and parts used in production, as well as finished goods.

3. **Residential investment,** which includes spending on new housing, whether it is occupied by owners or rented out by landlords.

MyEconLab Real-time data

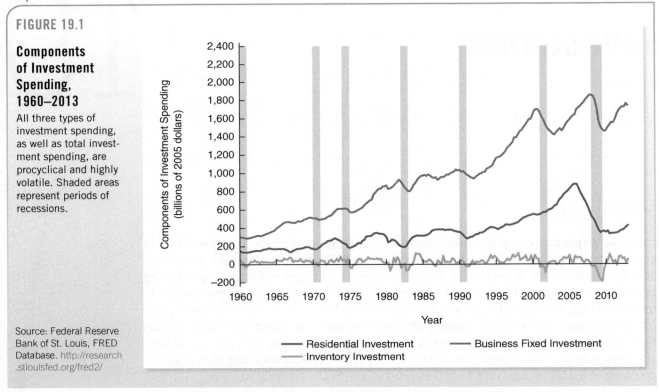

FIGURE 19.1

Components of Investment Spending, 1960–2013

All three types of investment spending, as well as total investment spending, are procyclical and highly volatile. Shaded areas represent periods of recessions.

Source: Federal Reserve Bank of St. Louis, FRED Database. http://research.stlouisfed.org/fred2/

Figure 19.1 plots these components from 1960 to 2013. Notice that all three are highly procyclical. That is, they rise during economic expansions and fall during economic contractions (denoted by the shaded areas). We will return to this important feature of investment as we develop our models.

The Neoclassical Theory of Investment

Dale Jorgenson of Harvard University developed the basic model for describing investment behavior, the **neoclassical theory of investment,** in the early 1960s. It takes its name from neoclassical microeconomic theory (which we discussed in Chapter 3), and builds on the neoclassical idea that the *user cost of capital* influences the desired stock of capital. Originally developed to explain business fixed investment, the theory applies equally, with appropriate modifications, to inventory and residential investment.

Determining the Level of Capital Stock

In our initial discussion of neoclassical theory in Chapter 3, we painted a rather simple picture of an economy with a fixed amount of workers and machines. Given those amounts, we determined the costs of those production inputs—the wage rate (for labor) and the rental cost of capital (for machines). Here, we loosen the assumption that the capital stock is fixed. We now ask how many machines will be desirable in the economy given a particular cost of renting those machines. In other words, what is the desired level of capital stock for a given rental cost of capital?

We established another important concept in Chapter 3: that a profit-maximizing firm will keep acquiring capital until the marginal product of capital—the output from one additional unit of capital—equals the real rental cost of capital.

$$MPK = R/P = r_c \tag{1}$$

In Equation 1, R/P is the rental cost of capital in terms of goods and services, that is, the real rental cost of capital, which we denote by r_c, to distinguish it from the real interest rate, r.

Why does Equation 1 hold? If MPK exceeds r_c, the benefits of adding an extra unit of capital outweigh its costs, and profit rises. Firms keep adding capital, but as they do, the marginal product of capital begins to fall, a result of diminishing returns. Eventually, the marginal product of capital declines to the level of the real rental cost of capital, and $MPK = r_c$. Similarly, if firms have too much capital, then the real rental cost of capital will exceed the marginal product of capital. As firms realize that they are losing money from holding too much capital, they will keep cutting the amount of capital until the marginal product of capital, MPK, rises to the real rental cost of capital, r_c.

User Cost of Capital

Jorgenson's insight was to develop a measure of the rental cost of capital using the concept of the **user cost of capital,** denoted by uc, the expected real cost of using a unit of capital over a particular period. Any owner of capital has to consider three possible costs of using that capital.

1. A user of capital who borrows to pay for the unit of capital must pay interest on a loan. The first component of the user cost is therefore the real interest rate, r,[1] multiplied by the real price of the unit of capital, p_k, that is, rp_k. Even if the user has enough cash on hand to pay for the capital, the user faces an opportunity cost equal to the real interest rate. The user could instead put his or her money into a savings account and earn a real interest rate of r, so the rental cost of the unit of capital is still rp_k.

2. The owner of the capital must take into account that the real price of the unit of capital can change. If the real price of capital is expected to rise, the owner will anticipate a gain in its real price of Δp_k^e. Because a gain is the negative of a cost, the effect on the user cost is $-\Delta p_k^e$.

3. When capital is used it is subject to wear and tear, so that it loses a fraction of its value, the depreciation rate δ, in each period. The real depreciation cost for a unit of capital is the depreciation rate multiplied by the real price of the unit of capital, or δp_k.

---

[1]Note that to keep the formulas simple, we are assuming here that there are no financial frictions, and so the real interest rate r is the real interest rate on investments.

Combining these three components, we write the user cost of capital, uc, as:

$$uc \quad = \quad rp_k \quad - \quad \Delta p_k^e \quad + \quad \delta p_k$$

which can be rewritten as:

$$uc \quad = \quad p_k \quad \times \quad [r \quad - \quad \Delta p_k^e/p_k \quad + \quad \delta] \qquad (2)$$

$$\text{user cost} = \text{real price} \times [\text{real interest} - \text{expected rate of} + \text{depreciation}]$$
$$\text{of capital} \qquad \text{rate} \qquad \text{change of real} \qquad \text{rate}$$
$$\text{price of capital}$$

For example, suppose a machine costs $p_k = \$1,000$ in constant dollars, the real interest rate is $r = 12\%$, the machine is expected to have a rate of increase in its real price of $\Delta p_k^e/p_k = 2\%$, and the rate of depreciation is $\delta = 5\%$. The user cost of capital for this machine over the year is $\$1,000 \times (0.12 - 0.02 + 0.05) = \$1,000 \times (0.15) = \$150$.

The user cost equation yields the following important conclusion: **the user cost of capital is positively correlated to the real interest rate and the depreciation rate, whereas it is negatively correlated to the expected rate of change of the real price of capital.**

Determining the Desired Level of Capital

Treating Jorgenson's user cost of capital as our measure of r_c, the desired level of capital is the capital stock that equates the marginal product of capital, MPK, with the user cost of capital, uc:

$$MPK = uc \qquad (3)$$

We show the determination of the desired level of the capital stock for period $t + 1$, K_{t+1}^*, in Figure 19.2. Here we assume that the output in the economy is expected to be $Y^e = \$10$ trillion; the price of capital is 1.0; and the values of r, $\Delta p_k^e/p_k$, and δ are the same as in the earlier example. The resulting user cost of capital is 0.15. Recall from Chapter 3 that the marginal product of capital from the Cobb-Douglas production function $Y = AK^{0.3}L^{0.7}$ is as follows:

$$MPK = 0.3Y/K$$

Because we are interested in determining the desired level of capital for the next period, K_{t+1}^*, the marginal product of capital we need to examine is the expected marginal product of capital for the next period, MPK^e:

$$MPK^e = 0.3Y_{t+1}^e/K_{t+1} = 0.3 (\$10 \text{ trillion}/K_{t+1}) \qquad (4)$$

This expected marginal product of capital curve, which is plotted in Figure 19.2, is downward sloping. K_{t+1} is in the denominator and therefore the marginal product of capital curve displays diminishing returns to capital, where the marginal product of capital falls as capital rises. The user cost of capital does not depend on the level of capital, so the user cost curve is a straight line at 0.15.

In Figure 19.2, the MPK^e curve and the user cost curve, uc, intersect at point E, where the desired level of capital K_{t+1}^* is \$20 trillion. If the amount of capital were instead \$15 trillion, the marginal product of capital would be 0.20, which is higher than the user cost of 0.15. In this case, adding more capital would increase firms' profits, so they would keep adding capital until the marginal product of capital fell to 0.15, which occurs at $K_{t+1}^* = \$20$ trillion. If, on the other hand, the amount of capital were \$25 trillion, the marginal product of capital would be 0.12, which is below the user cost of capital. Now firms would find the marginal

FIGURE 19.2

Determination of the Desired Level of the Capital Stock

The expected marginal product of capital curve is downward sloping, while the user cost of capital curve is a horizontal straight line. The curves intersect at point E, where the desired level of capital K^*_{t+1} is $20 trillion and firms are maximizing their profits.

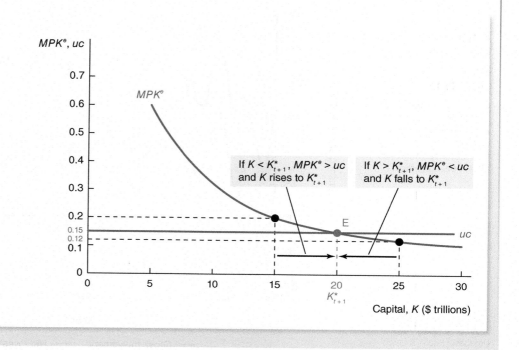

benefit of a unit of capital to be less than the cost, so they would shed capital until the marginal product rose back to 0.15 at $K^*_{t+1} = \$20$ trillion. The desired level of capital will therefore go to $20 trillion, the point at which firms are maximizing their profits.

From the Desired Level of Capital to Investment

Once we determine the desired level of capital, we can determine just how much needs to be invested to get there. Let's say we have $18 trillion today but desire $20 trillion of capital stock next year. To get there, we need to invest the desired change in capital stock, $2 trillion, which is known as **net investment.** Then, we need to replace the capital goods that we expect to wear out over the year (or to be scrapped because they are obsolete) through **depreciation.** The total spending on new capital goods, more precisely referred to as **gross investment,** equals net investment plus depreciation:

$$\text{Gross investment} = \text{net investment} + \text{depreciation} \qquad (5)$$

Figure 19.3 shows the relationship between gross investment and net investment from 1929–2012. Except for the years during the Great Depression, when gross investment was very low and less than depreciation, net investment has always been positive. (For simplicity, in this book the word "investment" refers to gross investment.)

We take depreciation to be proportional to the stock of capital at the beginning of the year, which we will denote by K_t, so that

$$\text{Depreciation} = \delta K_t \qquad (6)$$

where δ is called the **depreciation rate,** the fraction of capital that wears out every year.

MyEconLab Real-time data

FIGURE 19.3

Relationship Between Gross and Net Investment, 1929–2012

Except during the Great Depression, when gross investment was very low and less than depreciation, net investment has always been positive.

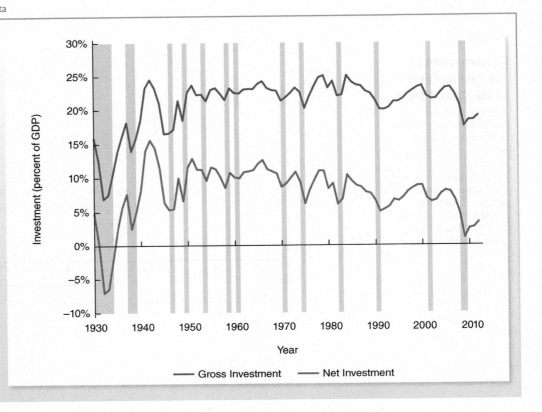

Source: Federal Reserve Bank of St. Louis, FRED Database. http://research .stlouisfed.org/fred2/

Net investment is the change in capital over the year, that is,

$$\text{Net investment} = K_{t+1} - K_t = \Delta K_t \qquad (7)$$

Substituting in for depreciation and net investment from Equations 6 and 7, we can write gross investment, I_t, as follows:

$$I_t = K_{t+1} - K_t + \delta K_t \qquad (8)$$

Suppose it is easy to put capital into place, so that a firm is able to immediately get the actual capital stock equal to the desired capital stock, which we will denote as K_{t+1}^*. Then we can replace K_{t+1} with K_{t+1}^* to produce Equation 9:[2]

$$I_t = K_{t+1}^* - K_t + \delta K_t \qquad (9)$$

---

[2]A more realistic assumption is that it takes time and money to put capital into place. For example, it can take years to build a factory or a shopping center. As a result, the capital stock adjusts slowly toward its desired level. We take account of adjustment costs to link the change in the capital stock to the desired level of capital using a so-called *partial-adjustment model*, which states that the capital stock moves only part of the way toward its desired level each period. We write the model algebraically as follows:

$$\Delta K_t = \phi(K_{t+1}^* - K_t)$$

This equation says that the change in the capital stock in period t is a fraction ϕ, less than one, of the desired change in the capital stock. Substituting this equation into Equation 8, we get the investment equation:

$$I_t = \phi(K_{t+1}^* - K_t) + \delta K_t$$

This equation, like Equation 9 in the text, also yields the conclusion that an increase in the desired capital stock leads to a rise in investment.

Equation 9 shows the link between desired capital and investment, and it displays the following important result: ***an increase in the desired capital stock leads to a rise in investment.***

Changes in the Desired Level of the Capital Stock

The desired level of the capital stock, K^*_{t+1}, changes when either the MPK^e or the uc curve shifts. Let's look at what happens in either case.

SHIFT IN THE MARGINAL PRODUCT OF CAPITAL CURVE. We show the effect of a shift in the marginal product of capital curve in Figure 19.4. As Equation 4 indicates, the expected marginal product curve shifts when expected future income, Y^e_{t+1}, changes. Suppose expected future income rises to $11 trillion. This could happen either because productivity is expected to go up or because the economy is booming and production is expected to be boosted by employing more labor. In this case, the MPK^e curve shifts up in Figure 19.4 from MPK^e_1 to MPK^e_2, so that at the old desired capital stock of $K^{*1}_{t+1} = \$20$ trillion, the marginal product of capital is at 0.165 (which is greater than the user cost at 0.15). Firms will therefore increase their profits by adding more capital until they reach point 2 at $K^{*2}_{t+1} = \$22$ trillion, where the marginal product of capital is back at 0.15 and equals the user cost of capital. Because a rise in the desired level of capital next period leads to a rise in investment today (as shown in Equation 9), we have the following result: ***a rise in expected future output, either because of a rise in productivity or a booming economy, leads to a higher desired level of capital and higher investment.***

MyEconLab Mini-lecture

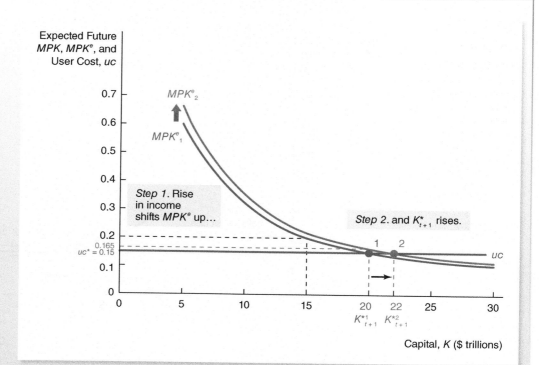

FIGURE 19.4

Shift in the Marginal Product of Capital Curve

A rise in expected future income causes the MPK^e curve to shift up from MPK^e_1 to MPK^e_2, and the desired level of capital increases from $K^{*1}_{t+1} = \$20$ trillion to $K^{*2}_{t+1} = \$22$ trillion, where the marginal product of capital is back at 0.15 and equals the user cost of capital, which has stayed constant.

The preceding result explains the procyclical nature of investment that we saw in Figure 19.1: when the business cycle is in an expansion phase, expected future output rises and so the desired capital stock and hence investment spending rise with it.

SHIFT IN THE USER COST OF CAPITAL. We show the result of a shift in the user cost of capital in Figure 19.5. The user cost Equation 2 indicates that the user cost of capital is determined by the real price of capital, the real interest rate, the expected rate of change of the real price of capital, and the depreciation rate. Suppose that, because of a tightening of monetary policy, the real interest rate rises by two percentage points from 12% to 14%. Holding everything else constant, the user cost of capital rises from 0.15 to 0.17, and the *uc* curve shifts up from uc_1 to uc_2. Now, at the original point 1, the marginal product of capital at 0.15 is less than the user cost at 0.17, so firms will want to reduce their capital because the benefit of a unit of capital is less than the cost. The desired capital stock will fall from K_{t+1}^{*1} = \$20 trillion to K_{t+1}^{*2} = \$17.6 trillion at point 2, where the expected marginal product of capital has risen to the new user cost of capital at 0.17. The user cost of capital is positively related to the real price of capital, the real interest rate, and the depreciation rate, whereas it is negatively related to the expected rate of change of the real price of capital. As a result, we come to the following conclusions: *a* ***rise in the real price of capital, the real interest rate, and the depreciation rate lead to a decline in the desired level of capital and a decline in investment, while a rise in the expected rate of change of the real price of capital leads to a rise in the desired level of capital and a rise in investment.***

MyEconLab Mini-lecture

FIGURE 19.5

Shift in the User Cost of Capital

An increase in the real interest rate from 12% to 14% raises the user cost of capital from 0.15 to 0.17, and so the *uc* curve shifts up from uc_1 to uc_2. The desired capital stock will fall from K_{t+1}^{*1} = \$20 trillion to K_{t+1}^{*2} = \$17.6 trillion at point 2, where the expected marginal product of capital has risen to the new user cost of capital at 0.17.

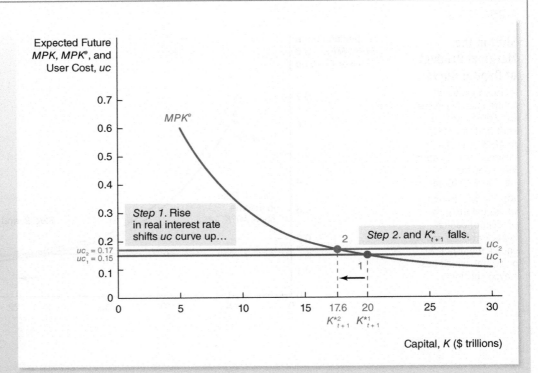

TAXES AND THE USER COST OF CAPITAL. Since the only sure things in life are death and taxes, firms must also take into account how taxes affect investment decisions.

To see how taxes affect investment, let's assume for simplicity that business taxes are levied as a percent of firm revenues. For example, firms might be taxed at a rate of 30%, so that the tax rate $\tau = 0.30$: a firm with revenue of $100 million would then pay $30 million in taxes. Now the after-tax revenue from a unit of capital is no longer the marginal product of capital, but is $1 - \tau$ times this amount, or 70% of the marginal product in our example. Instead of comparing the marginal product of capital to the user cost in order to decide on the desired level of capital, a firm will have to compare the after-tax marginal product, $(1 - \tau)MPK^e$, to the user cost, uc. Then the desired level of the capital stock will be the level at which

$$(1 - \tau)MPK^e = uc$$

that is, the level at which the after-tax marginal product equals the user cost.

Dividing both sides of the preceding equation by $(1 - \tau)$, we get the following:

$$MPK^e = \frac{uc}{1 - \tau} = p_k \frac{r - \Delta p_k/p_k + \delta}{1 - \tau} \tag{10}$$

The term $uc/(1 - \tau)$ in Equation 10 is called the **tax-adjusted user cost of capital:** it is the user cost of capital that the firm compares to the *before-tax* marginal product of capital to determine the desired level of capital. If the tax rate τ on firm revenue rises, then the tax-adjusted user cost of capital rises because the denominator in Equation 10 falls. The rise in the tax-adjusted user cost of capital then results in an upward shift in the user cost curve, as in Figure 19.5. As a result, the desired level of capital falls. We thus have an additional determinant for investment: *a rise in the tax rate on businesses leads to a decline in the desired level of capital and a decline in investment.*[3]

FINANCING CONSTRAINTS. In our derivation of the neoclassical model of investment, we assumed that firms are able to borrow freely. If the marginal product of capital is above the user cost, firms can go out and borrow from credit markets all they need to buy new capital. However, just as consumers can be subject to borrowing constraints, as we saw in Chapter 18, firms can be subject to **financing constraints,** wherein they are cut off from raising funds in financial markets because financial frictions have increased. When financing constraints are binding, even a firm with a profitable investment will not be able to get the financing to pay for it, and so investment will not occur. It is just as if the user cost of capital has risen. This reasoning suggests a modification to the neoclassical model: *the more binding the financing constraints, the lower the investment spending.*

---

[3]Taxation of business enterprises is actually far more complicated than a simple tax on revenues. The most important tax on businesses is the *corporate income tax*, which is a tax on a corporation's profits rather than its revenues. Since profits and revenues are generally positively related, a higher corporate income tax rate increases the taxes paid on revenues and hence raises the after-tax user cost of capital.

The definition of "profits" is not always straightforward and is a topic better left to accountants, but two items that affect profits are relevant to government policies aimed at encouraging investment spending. The first is *depreciation allowances*, the allowances for depreciation that firms deduct from profits. The second is the *investment tax credit*, which allows a firm to reduce its corporate taxes by a percentage of the amount spent on new capital. For example, an investment tax credit of 10% would enable a firm that buys a $100,000 machine to deduct $10,000 from its tax bill. Increases in either depreciation allowances or the investment tax credit lower taxes on businesses and thus lead to higher investment.

Summary: Neoclassical Theory of Investment

The neoclassical theory of investment indicates that investment decisions are affected by the following:

- expected future output (which is affected by future productivity and the business cycle)
- the real price of capital
- the real interest rate
- the expected rate of change of the real price of capital
- the depreciation rate
- the tax rate on businesses
- financing constraints (which reflect financial frictions)

Table 19.1 summarizes the impact of each of these determinants on the desired level of capital and investment.

TABLE 19.1   DETERMINANTS OF INVESTMENT

Note: only the effects of increases in the determinants are shown. The effects of decreases in the determinants on investment would be the opposite of those indicated in the third and last columns.

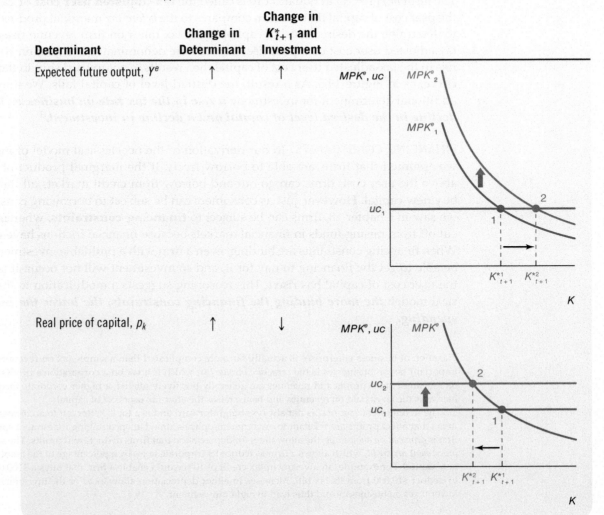

Determinant	Change in Determinant	Change in K^*_{t+1} and Investment	
Expected future output, Y^e	↑	↑	
Real price of capital, p_k	↑	↓	

TABLE 19.1	DETERMINANTS OF INVESTMENT (*Continued*)

Determinant	Change in Determinant	Change in K^*_{t+1} and Investment	
Real interest rate, r	↑	↓	
Expected rate of change of the real price of capital, $\Delta p_k / p_k$	↑	↑	
Depreciation rate, δ	↑	↓	

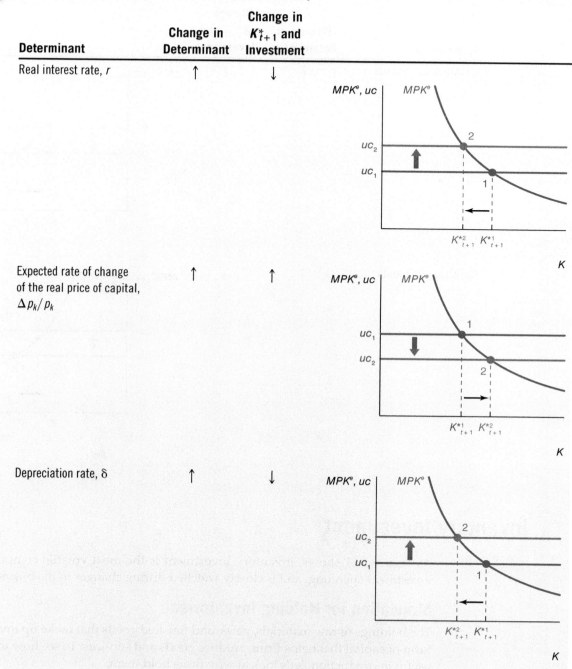

(*Continued*)

In neoclassical theory, monetary and fiscal policy play a prominent role in the determination of investment. Monetary policy affects investment through its impact on real interest rates, while fiscal policy affects investment spending through the tax rate on businesses.

TABLE 19.1	**DETERMINANTS OF INVESTMENT (*Continued*)**		
Determinant	**Change in Determinant**	**Change in K^*_{t+1} and Investment**	
Tax rate on businesses	↑	↓	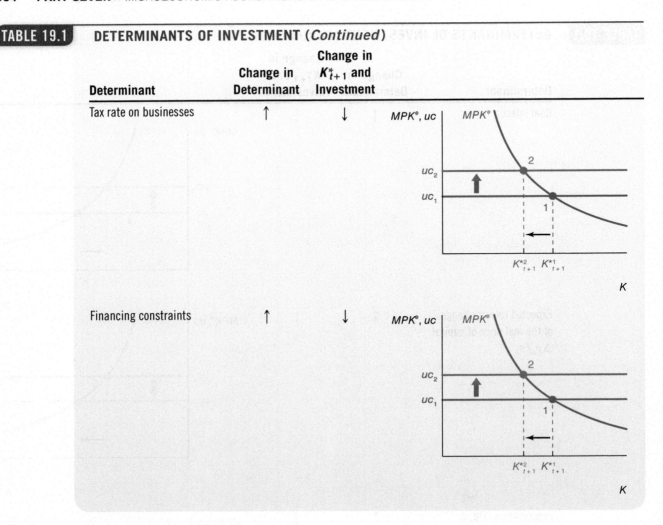
Financing constraints	↑	↓	

Inventory Investment

As Figure 19.1 shows, inventory investment is the most volatile component of total investment spending, and is closely watched during changes in the business cycle.

Motivation for Holding Inventories

The holdings of raw materials, parts, and finished goods that make up inventories are a form of capital that helps firms produce goods and services. To see how inventories are useful in production, let's look at why firms hold them.

INVENTORY AS A FACTOR OF PRODUCTION. Manufacturers need inventories of raw materials like steel to produce items such as automobiles. They also need spare parts, such as windshields, to produce items, such as cars. Retail stores stock shelves with finished goods to make sales.

Improvements in computer technology in recent years allow manufacturers to engage in **just-in-time production,** in which they order inventories for production just when they are needed. As a result, the level of inventories that are held by firms has declined substantially relative to production, making swings in inventory investment potentially less important in the business cycle.

WORK IN PROCESS. Production typically involves many steps. Firms have inventories of **work in process,** that is, holdings of partially finished components that will go into the final product. Firms hold inventories of work in process and have to store these components until they are ready to be used.

PRODUCTION SMOOTHING. It often makes sense for firms to smooth production over time. Many firms, like automobile manufacturers, experience large temporary fluctuations in demand. If they produced goods and services only when they were ordered, they would have huge swings in their production cycles, leaving workers and machines idle when sales were low and overworking them when sales were high. Overly large fluctuations in production are costly to the firm, so it would like to spread production out over time. Firms therefore engage in **production smoothing,** in which they keep on producing when sales are temporarily low, putting the goods produced into inventory, and then do not raise production when sales are temporarily high, instead drawing down these inventories to satisfy the higher demand. Car companies will produce cars and put them on their lots during times of the year when sales are low, say, in the summer, and then draw down these inventories at times when sales are high, as in the fall.

STOCK-OUT AVOIDANCE. The fourth reason for holding inventories is that firms cannot always predict how strong their sales will be. When sales are surprisingly high, a firm may run out of goods to sell and thereby lose sales, because the customer will go somewhere else to purchase the desired goods. To avoid losing these sales, firms hold inventories so that they don't stock out of goods, which is why this motive for holding inventories is known as **stock-out avoidance.** For example, car dealers often maintain a large number of automobiles on their lots so that they won't lose a sale to another dealer that has the make and model the customer wants.

The Theory of Inventory Investment

Because inventories play a similar role in production as a business fixed investment, the neoclassical theory that we developed previously applies equally to inventory investment, that is, the change in holdings of inventories over a given period. Specifically, there is a desired level of inventories that depends on the relationship of the marginal product of inventories to their user cost.

Let's consider the case of Carl the Car Dealer, who owns a Ford dealership. Carl has to decide how many Ford Mustangs he wants to keep on his lot. If he thinks sales are likely to be high in the future, then the marginal product of inventories becomes high because there is a greater likelihood that he will lose a sale if he has insufficient inventory. In this case, the marginal product curve for inventories will shift up, just as in Figure 19.4, and Carl will want to hold a larger number of Mustangs. The result will be higher inventory investment.

Alternatively, suppose the Federal Reserve tightens monetary policy to restrain inflation, so that Carl now faces a higher real interest rate. The cost of financing his inventory of Mustangs goes up, and therefore his user cost of inventories rises. As in

Figure 19.5, his user cost of capital curve rises, and he will now want to have fewer Mustangs on his lot. The result will be lower inventory investment.[4]

Tobin's *q* and Investment

Also in the 1960s, Nobel Laureate James Tobin of Yale University developed a model of investment closely related to the neoclassical theory, but which instead focuses on asset prices as a driver of investment spending.

Tobin's *q* Theory

Tobin began by considering two ways of measuring the amount of capital in a business. One approach uses the market value of the collection of capital that is embodied in the firm, that is, the overall market value of the firm as reflected in the stock market. The other approach is to consider the replacement cost of the firm's capital, or how much it would cost to install that capital today. The market value of the collection of capital in the firm can differ from the replacement cost of the capital because the firm's capital collectively can be worth more than the sum of its parts. We can take a ratio of the market value and the replacement cost, a concept that is now known as **Tobin's *q*:**

$$q = \frac{\text{Market Value of Firm}}{\text{Replacement Cost of Installed Capital}} \qquad (11)$$

Firms try to increase their market value. So, Tobin reasoned that if *q* is above 1, and the market price of capital is high relative to its replacement cost, the firm will benefit from increasing investment. Buying new capital increases the value of the firm because its market value is greater than the cost of acquiring it. Net investment will be positive.

On the other hand, if *q* is below 1, the market value of the capital is less than the cost of acquiring it, and so the firm will not want to buy any capital. In this case, the firm will want the level of its capital to shrink. It will want net investment to become negative, so it will let the existing capital in the firm wear out without replacing it.

The replacement cost of capital tends to move with the overall price level, which is relatively steady. Thus, most fluctuations in Tobin's *q* stem from changes in the market values of the firms as reflected in stock prices. When the stock market booms, Tobin's *q* rises and investment booms. On the other hand, when the stock market plummets, Tobin's *q* falls and so does investment spending. Tobin's *q* theory therefore yields the following result: *a rise in stock prices leads to a rise in Tobin's* **q** *and a rise in investment, while a decline in stock prices leads to a decline in Tobin's* **q** *and a fall in investment spending.*

Tobin's *q* Versus Neoclassical Theory

At first glance, Tobin's *q* theory looks quite different from the neoclassical theory developed earlier in the chapter, but actually they are quite closely related.

---

[4]Financing constraints can also affect inventory investment. If Carl would like to have more Mustangs on his lot, but his bank won't give him a loan to pay for them, Carl will just have to make do with less inventory, and inventory investment will fall. In 2008, during the most virulent phase of the 2007–2009 financial crisis, credit was extremely hard to get. Financing constraints then began to bind and inventory investment fell precipitously, by $25.9 billion (chained 2005 dollars) from 2007 to 2008. This sharp decline in inventory investment was one of the reasons why the recession of 2007–2009 ended up being so severe.

Because stock prices reflect the valuation of current and expected profits from capital, Tobin's q tells us whether installed capital is expected to yield high profits in the future, that is, whether the future marginal product of capital will be high relative to the user cost of capital. In neoclassical theory, when the future marginal product of capital is high relative to the user cost, the desired level of capital rises and investment is high. We get the same conclusion from Tobin's q theory.

With Tobin's q theory, we can reach the same conclusions as with the neoclassical theory:

1. A higher expected future marginal product of capital leads to a higher q and therefore higher investment.

2. A rise in the real interest rate or a rise in the effective tax rate, each of which increases the user cost of capital, lowers q and therefore causes investment to fall.

3. A higher price of capital increases the replacement cost of capital, which leads to a higher denominator, lowers q, and causes investment to fall.

However, Tobin's q theory adds to the neoclassical theory because it emphasizes that asset-price fluctuations, especially those in stock prices, can have an important independent effect on investment spending.

Application

Stock Market Crashes and Recessions

Tobin's q theory suggests that stock market crashes can be a major factor in economic downturns. We can see this by using the aggregate demand-aggregate supply (*AD/AS*) framework in Figure 19.6. When the stock market declines, Tobin's q theory indicates that autonomous investment will fall, which shifts the aggregate demand curve to the left in Figure 19.6. As a result, the economy moves from point 1 to point 2 in the figure, and output falls. Stock market crashes can thus play an important role in producing recessions. Indeed, stock market crashes are found to be a leading business cycle indicator, as discussed in Chapter 8. As Figure 19.6 suggests, the collapse of the stock market from 2007–2009 was an important factor in the decline in output and inflation during the Great Recession.

Residential Investment

The housing market is particularly relevant to U.S. consumers, since most of the U.S. population owns, or will own, a house or an apartment. This market is especially important because swings in residential investment often play a prominent role in business cycle fluctuations, particularly in recent years.

Residential housing is just another form of capital, and so residential investment can be explained by the neoclassical theory of investment, in which investment is determined by the marginal product of housing and the user cost of housing.[5]

---

[5]To further understand what determines housing prices and how they affect residential investment, see the appendix to this chapter, found on the Companion Website at www.pearsonhighered.com/mishkin.

FIGURE 19.6

Stock Market Crashes and the AD/AS Model

A stock market crash lowers Tobin's q and hence lowers investment spending, thereby shifting the AD curve to the left. The economy then moves from point 1 to point 2, where output falls, producing a recession.

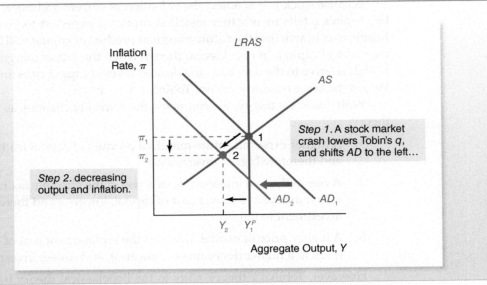

When more housing is needed (because of population growth or children leaving their parents' homes) or when households have higher expected income, the marginal product of houses rises, causing the desired stock of houses to rise. Hence, *a rise in household formation or expected income leads to higher residential investment.*

When mortgage rates rise or when house prices are expected to fall and so have a lower rate of expected appreciation, the user cost of capital rises, decreasing the desired stock of houses. Hence, *a rise in mortgage rates or lower expected appreciation of housing leads to lower residential investment.*

Financing constraints play a similar role in the housing market as in business fixed investment. When it is harder to get a mortgage, financing constraints are tighter, and so people will not be able to buy as much housing as they would like. *Tighter financing constraints lead to lower residential investment.*

Because owning a home is viewed by many American politicians as being on par with motherhood and apple pie, U.S. government policies have actively encouraged home ownership. The following Policy and Practice case discusses these policies and shows how they work through the user cost concept developed in the neoclassical theory of investment.

Policy and Practice

U.S. Government Policies and the Housing Market

American politicians often place home ownership up there with "motherhood and apple pie." As a result, the United States has done more to promote home ownership than almost any other country in the world.

The U.S. government has used tax policy to encourage home ownership. The interest paid on the first $1 million of a mortgage is tax deductible. So, if you have a mortgage at a 5% nominal interest rate and your tax bracket is 20%, this tax deduction lowers your taxes by 20% of your mortgage payment. In effect, your after-tax mortgage rate falls to 4%. The tax deductibility of mortgage interest therefore lowers the user cost of housing, making it cheaper for households to own houses, thereby encouraging home ownership.

The government also promotes home ownership through agencies that provide funds or guarantees for mortgage debt. The Federal Housing Administration (FHA) provides mortgage insurance that guarantees timely payment on individual mortgages so that lenders are not exposed to any credit risk. In addition, the Government National Mortgage Association (GNMA, or "Ginnie Mae") provides guarantees for mortgage-backed securities, described in Chapter 15, which are a standardized debt security that is made up of a bundle of individual mortgages. The U.S. government has also sponsored mortgage agencies that function as private corporations but have close ties to the government. These agencies, known as **government-sponsored enterprises (GSEs)**, include the Federal National Mortgage Association (FNMA, or "Fannie Mae") and the Federal Home Loan Mortgage Corporation (FHLMC, or "Freddie Mac"). These two GSEs provide funds to the mortgage market by selling bonds and then using the proceeds to buy mortgages or mortgage-backed securities. Another set of GSEs, the Federal Home Loan Banks, indirectly provide funds to the mortgage markets by selling bonds and then lending the proceeds to financial institutions that make mortgage loans. By providing guarantees and funds to the mortgage market, these government agencies and GSEs help lower mortgage rates, thereby further lowering the user cost of housing, which encourages home ownership.

Some economists say policies to encourage home ownership distort the markets and encourage too much home building. As discussed in Chapter 15, the two GSEs, Fannie Mae and Freddie Mac, required a bailout in the aftermath of the bursting of the housing bubble, costing the taxpayers billions of dollars.

SUMMARY

1. There are three basic components of investment: business fixed investment, inventory investment, and residential investment. All three types of investment are highly procyclical and volatile.

2. The neoclassical theory of investment derives the desired level of capital from the condition that the marginal product of capital equals the user cost of capital. It shows that the expected future desired level of capital and investment spending is positively related to expected future output, the expected rate of change of the real price of capital, depreciation allowances, and the investment tax credit. The expected future desired level of capital and investment spending is negatively related to the real price of capital, the real interest rate, and the depreciation rate.

3. There are four reasons for holding inventories: 1) they are a factor used in production;

2) they are a work in process; 3) they allow for production smoothing; and 4) they help firms avoid stock-outs. Because inventories play a role in production similar to the role of business fixed investment, the neoclassical theory applies equally to inventory investment, with the same results.

4. Tobin's q is the market value of installed capital divided by the replacement cost of this capital. A rise in stock prices leads to a rise in Tobin's q and a rise in investment, while a decline in stock prices leads to a decline in Tobin's q and a fall in investment spending.

5. Residential investment is positively related to expected future income, the rate of household formation, and the expected appreciation of housing prices. Residential investment is negatively related to real mortgage rates and tighter financing constraints.

KEY TERMS

business fixed investment, p. 523
depreciation, p. 527
depreciation rate, p. 527
financing constraints, p. 531
government-sponsored enterprises (GSEs), p. 539
gross investment, p. 527

inventory investment, p. 523
just-in-time production, p. 534
neoclassical theory of investment, p. 524
net investment, p. 527
production smoothing, p. 535
residential investment, p. 523

stock-out avoidance, p. 535
tax-adjusted user cost of capital, p. 531
Tobin's q, p. 536
user cost of capital, p. 525
work in process, p. 535

REVIEW QUESTIONS

All Questions are available in MyEconLab *for practice or instructor assignment.*

Data on Investment Spending

1. Identify and give examples of the three components of investment spending.

The Neoclassical Theory of Investment

2. What is the user cost of capital? What variables determine this cost, and how does a change in each variable affect it?

3. Explain how the user cost of capital and the expected marginal product of capital together determine the desired level of capital.

4. According to the neoclassical theory of investment, how do firms determine their optimal amount of investment spending once they have identified their desired level of capital?

5. Explain how the desired levels of capital and investment are affected by changes in the expected marginal product of capital, the user cost of capital, and taxes.

Inventory Investment

6. Why do firms hold inventories, and why is their inventory investment a matter of interest to macroeconomists?

Tobin's q and Investment

7. What is Tobin's q? How does it provide a theory of investment spending?

8. How are Tobin's q theory and the neoclassical theory of investment related?

Residential Investment

9. What are the determinants of residential investment?

10. What kinds of policies has the U.S. government pursued to encourage home ownership, and how do they achieve this goal?

PROBLEMS

All Problems are available in MyEconLab *for practice or instructor assignment.*

The Neoclassical Theory of Investment

1. Assume that Luke is considering investing in new equipment and computers for his construction company. The real interest rate is 5%, construction equipment is valued at $600,000, and computers are valued at $20,000. Neither type of capital is expected to change its price during the next year.
   a) Calculate the user cost of capital for construction equipment, assuming it depreciates at a 10% annual rate.
   b) Suppose the annual depreciation rate for computers is 35%. Calculate the user cost of capital for computers.

2. Using the expression for the expected marginal product of capital, $MPK^e = 3.6/K_{t+1}$, plot the MPK^e curve and determine the desired level of capital for the next period (measured in trillions) if the user cost equals 0.30 (assume the price of capital is normalized to 1.0).

3. Explain the consequences of each of the following events on the desired level of capital stock for the next period according to the neoclassical theory of investment:

a) An autonomous easing of monetary policy
b) Increase in the depreciation rate of capital
c) An increase in productivity

4. Discuss the effect of the investment tax credit implemented in the United States after the global financial crisis. What does empirical evidence suggest about the link between taxes and investment?

5. One common feature of developing countries is their relatively less-developed financial systems. What are the implications of a less efficient financial system for the level of investment in developing countries?

6. Oil leaks from offshore drilling platforms in the Gulf of Mexico have resulted in stricter regulations on this type of oil extraction.
   a) Discuss the effects of such regulations on the user cost of capital.
   b) Explain the effect of such regulations on the future desired level of capital stock and investment in this industry.

Inventory Investment

7. The following graph shows the quarterly change in private inventories in the United States from 2007 to 2010.

(Figures are billions of 2005 dollars.) Explain the changes in private inventories during this period.

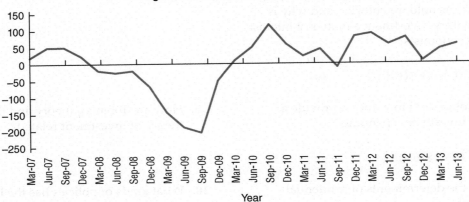

Change in Private Inventories (billions of dollars)

Source: BEA, Table 5.6.5B. www.bea.gov

Tobin's *q* and Investment

8. From 2009 to 2013, stock prices doubled in the United States. What was the likely effect of this stock market rise on business investment in the United States? Explain using Tobin's *q* theory.

Residential Investment

9. A relatively recent trend in most developed countries, including the United States, is the creation of single-person households. Discuss the short- and long-run consequences of this trend on residential investment.

10. The Federal Reserve has promised that at some future date, it will raise interest rates as part of its "exit strategy" from the expansionary monetary policy it pursued in the aftermath of the global financial crisis. What will be the impact of this "exit strategy" on residential investment?

DATA ANALYSIS PROBLEMS

The Problems update with real-time data in MyEconLab and are available for practice or instructor assignment.

1. Go to the St. Louis Federal Reserve FRED database, and find data on real private domestic investment (GPDIC96), real residential investment (PRFIC96), and real non-residential (business) fixed investment (PNFIC96).

a) Using these data, calculate inventory investment for the most recent quarter of data available.

b) For each quarter since 2000, calculate the percentage of inventory investment as a share of total investment, and then calculate, from 2000 to the most current quarter of data available, the average percent share of inventory investment relative to investment. Is this number zero? Does the average over this time support the idea that inventories have benefits? Why or why not?

2. Go to the St. Louis Federal Reserve FRED database, and find data on net domestic investment (A557RC1Q027SBEA) and gross domestic investment (W170RC1Q027SBEA).

    a) For each series, report the values for the most recent quarter of data available. Why are the values not equal? Comment on the relative sizes of the two values.

    b) Calculate depreciation for the most recent quarter of data available.

    c) Assuming the depreciation rate is 10%, calculate the current total size of the capital stock.

3. Go to the St. Louis Federal Reserve FRED database, and find data on the 30-year mortgage rate (MORTG), private residential fixed investment (PRFI), and the net percentage of bankers tightening credit standards on mortgages (DRTSPM). For the mortgage rate series, convert the data to "Quarterly" using the *frequency* setting, and download the data onto a spreadsheet. For each quarter, calculate the percentage change in residential investment from the same time one year prior.

    a) Report the most recent rate on the 30-year mortgage, and the rate one year prior. Compare these numbers to the percentage change in residential investment from one year earlier, and comment on the relationship as it relates to the user cost of capital.

    b) Using data from 2007:Q2 to the most recent data available, create a scatter plot with the net percentage of bankers tightening credit standards on the horizontal axis and the percent change in residential investment on the vertical axis. Comment on the relationship between the two variables.

    c) (Advanced) Using data from 2007:Q2 to the most recent data available, run a regression using the percentage change in residential investment as the dependent variable and the credit standards variable as the independent variable. Report the fitted equation, and comment on the goodness of fit. How does a 10-percentage-point increase in credit tightening by banks affect residential investment growth?

Online appendix, "A Model of Housing Prices and Residential Investment," is available at the Companion Website, www.pearsonhighered.com/mishkin

20 The Labor Market, Employment, and Unemployment

Preview

Few changes in U.S. society over the last half century are as striking as the entrance of women into the labor force. In the 1950s, young women, even college graduates, were expected to marry early and devote themselves to raising children and tending to household chores. Only a third of young women of prime working age—twenty-five to thirty-four—held or sought work outside the home in 1960. If this sounds unimaginable today, the change is a testament to the significance of shifts in the labor market, the most important market we interact with over our lifetimes. The labor market determines our wages, our ability to find work, and the time we have for leisure. Economists study the labor market to answer big-picture questions. Why has labor force participation of women increased so much? Why are unemployment rates in Europe typically higher than in the United States? Why does a college education today generate higher returns than it once did? Why has income inequality grown so much in recent years?

This chapter begins with a general look at the U.S. labor market over the last half-century. It then develops a supply and demand model of the labor market and examines the sources of unemployment. With this analysis, we then start answering many of the questions just posed.

Developments in the U.S. Labor Market

Among the many variables describing the U.S. labor market, economists pay particular attention to the *employment ratio*, the unemployment rate, and real wages.

Employment Ratio

One of the first key issues in labor market analysis is trends in the **employment-to-population ratio** (or more simply the **employment ratio**), the proportion of the civilian working-age population that is employed. As you can see in panel (a) of Figure 20.1, the U.S. employment-to-population ratio has had a slight upward trend over the last fifty years, rising from 56% of people over sixteen years of age working in 1960 to 59% in 2013.

The upward trend in the employment ratio is due entirely to the increased participation of women in the workforce. Notice in panel (b) of Figure 20.1 that the percentage of men working, the male employment ratio, fell from 79% in 1960 to 64% in 2013. Meanwhile, the percentage of women working, the female employment ratio, rose from

35% in 1960 to 53% in 2013. The data show clearly how women entered the labor force in increasing numbers over this same period.

Figure 20.1 demonstrates that employment fluctuates with the business cycle, rising during economic expansions and falling during recessions. As jobs became scarce during the most recent recession, the employment ratio tumbled. By the start of 2013, it stood at 58.6%, down 4.2 percentage points from the fourth quarter of 2007. We can quantify

MyEconLab Real-time data

FIGURE 20.1

Employment Ratios in the United States, 1960–2013

In panel (a), the employment ratio in the United States has an upward trend over the last fifty years and is subject to business cycle fluctuations, rising during economic expansions and falling during recessions (the shaded areas). Panel (b) shows that the upward trend for the overall employment ratio is due to the upward trend in the employment ratio for women.

Source: Federal Reserve Bank of St. Louis, FRED Database. http://research.stlouisfed.org/fred2/

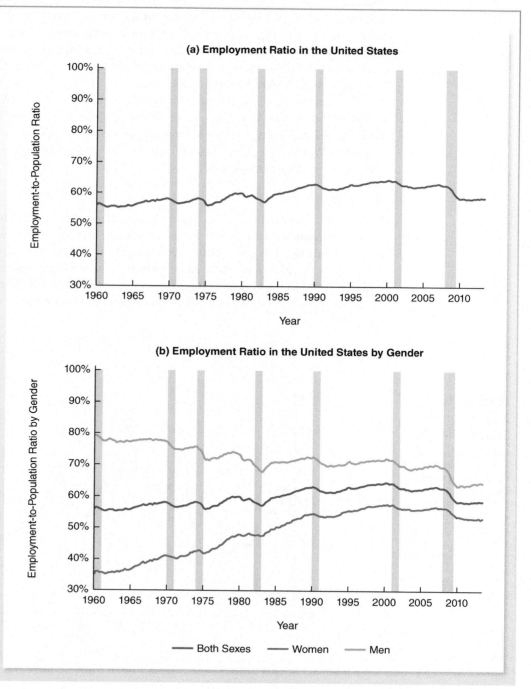

(a) Employment Ratio in the United States

(b) Employment Ratio in the United States by Gender

Both Sexes   Women   Men

this decline in the employment ratio in terms of the number of jobs lost. Because the total U.S. civilian working-age population in 2013 was around 245 million, the 4.2 percentage point decline translates into around 10 million jobs lost. The cost in terms of lost jobs during recessions, particularly the most recent severe one, can be high indeed.

Unemployment Rate

Not everyone who wants a job can find one. The *unemployment rate* measures the percentage of the labor force that is unemployed. As we discussed in Chapter 2, a person is considered an unemployed member of the labor force if he or she has no job but has been actively looking for a job over the prior four weeks. Figure 20.2 shows the U.S. unemployment rate from 1960 to 2013. The unemployment rate is always above zero; even in boom times, some people are unable to get work. We need a model of the labor market to explain this phenomenon.

The unemployment rate varies over the business cycle. In March 2007, before the recession began, the unemployment rate was 4.4%. By October 2009, it had peaked at 10.1%, a 5.7 percentage point increase. This dismal rate was the second-worst showing since World War II, surpassed only by the 10.8% unemployment rate reached in November and December 1982.

Real Wages

Up until the 1960s, the average worker grew richer over time. However, as Figure 20.3 shows, since then, average real wages for all workers have been essentially flat, growing at an annual rate of only 0.2% from 1965 to 2013. However, real wages for college-educated workers, particularly women, have grown substantially. Growing income disparities have emerged in the United States, disturbing many economists and politicians. Again, a model of the labor market will help explain the troubling trend of wage inequality.

MyEconLab Real-time data

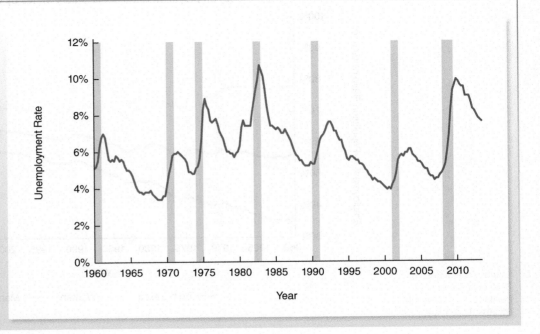

FIGURE 20.2

Unemployment Rate in the United States, 1960–2013

The unemployment rate varies over the business cycle, falling during business cycle expansions and rising during recessions (shaded areas). The unemployment rate is always above zero, indicating that even in boom times, some people are unable to get work.

Source: Federal Reserve Bank of St. Louis, FRED Database. http://research .stlouisfed.org/fred2/

Supply and Demand in the Labor Market

Building on the brief discussion of labor in Chapter 3, we derive a demand curve for labor, then we derive a supply curve, and finally we discuss the market equilibrium at which supply equals demand.

MyEconLab Real-time data

FIGURE 20.3

Real Wages in the United States, 1965–2013

Real wages for all workers do not have an upward trend, but college-educated workers' real wages have undergone substantial growth.

Sources: Panel (a) Real Wages for all Workers, Average hourly earnings, 1982–84 dollars, Federal Reserve Bank of St. Louis, FRED Database. http://research.stlouisfed.org/fred2/. Panel (b) Percentage changes in Real Wages by education. David Autor. "The Polarization of Job Opportunities in the U.S. Labor Market: Implications for Employment and Earnings," Working Paper, Center for American Progress and The Hamilton Project, April 2010.

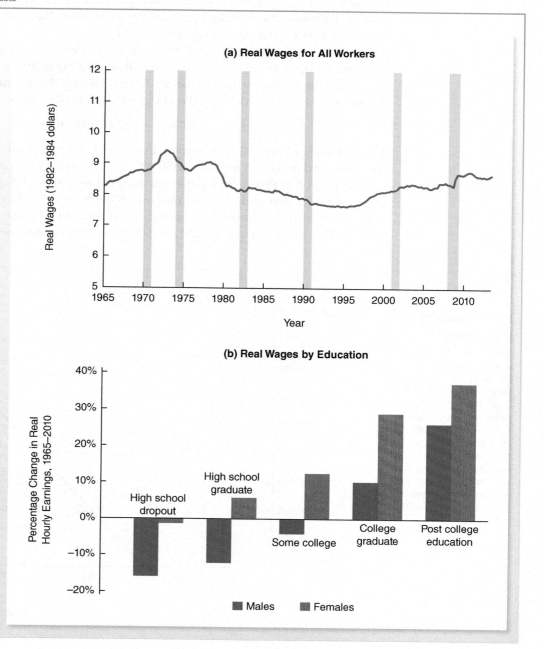

The Demand Curve for Labor

In Chapter 3, we learned that we can derive the demand curve for labor by analyzing profit maximization by firms. Firms will find it profitable to add new workers as long as the marginal product of labor, MPL, exceeds the cost of hiring workers—that is, the real wage rate, w. Firms will stop demanding additional labor only when the marginal product of labor falls to the real wage rate, so that hiring another worker does not add to profits. For any given real wage rate, we can find the quantity of labor demanded by looking at the intersection of the marginal product curve and the real wage line. In this sense, the marginal product of labor curve is the demand curve for labor, and we label this curve as D^L. Because the marginal product of labor displays diminishing returns—as labor increases, the marginal product declines—both the marginal product of labor curve and the demand curve slope downward.

Let's consider the numerical example we outlined in Chapter 3, in which the amount of output in the economy is $10 trillion and the quantity of labor is expressed in terms of the number of hired workers. There, we saw that for the Cobb-Douglas production function, $Y = AK^{0.3}L^{0.7}$, the marginal product of labor is

$$MPL = 0.7\,Y/L = 0.7 \times \$10 \text{ trillion}/L \qquad (1)$$

At a real wage of $140,000 per worker, Equation 1 indicates that the quantity of workers demanded will be 50 million ($140,000 = 0.7 \times$ $10 trillion/50 million), which we mark as point A in Figure 20.4. If the real wage is lower at $70,000 per worker, the quantity of workers demanded is 100 million ($70,000 = 0.7 \times$ $10 trillion/100 million), and this point is marked as point E. If the real wage falls even further to $35,000, then the quantity of workers demanded will be 200 million

MyEconLab Mini-lecture

FIGURE 20.4

Equilibrium in the Labor Market

The demand curve for labor is downward sloping, while the supply curve is upward sloping. Equilibrium in the labor market occurs at point E, where the quantity of labor demanded equals the quantity of labor supplied, the real wage $w^* = \$70,000$, and the quantity of labor used in production is $L^* = 100$ million workers.

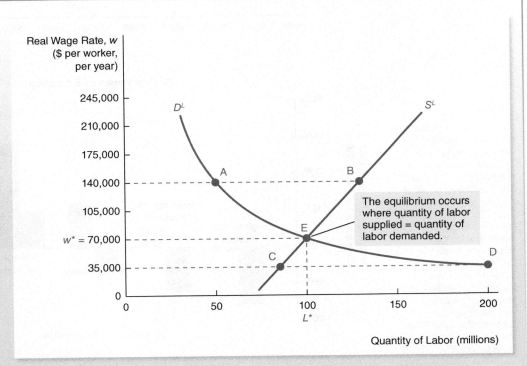

The equilibrium occurs where quantity of labor supplied = quantity of labor demanded.

($35,000 = 0.7 × $10 trillion/200 million), which we mark as point D in Figure 20.4. As you can see, the demand curve for labor is downward sloping.

The Supply Curve

Now let's turn to the supply curve for labor. In Chapter 3, to keep things simple, we assumed a fixed number of workers. However, in the real world, workers choose either to work or to take **leisure.** Economists define leisure as any activity that does not occur on the job—eating, sleeping, watching TV, partying, taking vacations, and taking care of children.[1] (College students are the real experts on the subject of leisure.) When real wages are high, so is the cost of leisure (not working). Thus, people are more willing to work and the quantity of labor supplied rises. The labor supply curve, S^L, that goes through points B, E, and C is therefore upward sloping.[2]

Equilibrium in the Labor Market

As always, the final step of supply and demand analysis is to study the market equilibrium, which occurs when the amount of labor that firms are willing to hire (*demand*) equals the amount of labor that workers are willing to offer (*supply*) at a given real wage rate. In the labor market, market equilibrium is achieved when the quantity of labor demanded equals the quantity of labor supplied, that is,

$$D^L = S^L \tag{2}$$

In Figure 20.4, the equilibrium in the labor market occurs at point E, the point at which the real wage rate $w^* = \$70,000$ per worker and the quantity of labor supplied $L^* = 100$ million workers.

Response of Employment and Wages to Changes in Labor Demand and Labor Supply

Any change that affects the amount of labor demanded or supplied at any given real wage rate leads to a new equilibrium in the labor market. We will look in detail at the impact of a change in the amount of labor demanded and supplied on our labor market model. We will then use our model in two applications.

Changes in Labor Demand

We begin by examining a change in the amount of labor demanded. As Equation 1 indicates, output growth, with the real wage held constant, will cause the marginal product of labor to go up. Output may grow because of a positive supply shock to production, such as a surge in productivity, or, alternatively, because of a positive demand shock to output, such as a boost in consumer spending that causes production to rise.

---

[1]Many activities that are classified as leisure include nonmarket work. Examples are child care and household chores.

[2]The upward-sloping labor supply curve assumes that the substitution effect of a higher real wage is larger than the income effect. (We discussed the income versus substitution effects in Chapter 18.) This is very likely to be the case if the labor supply curve is drawn under the assumption that future wages are held constant, so that movements of the current wage have only a small impact on long-run income, thereby making the income effect small.

FIGURE 20.5

Response to an Increase in the Demand for Labor

An increase in the demand for labor from a rise in output shifts the labor demand curve to the right from D_1^L to D_2^L, and the equilibrium moves from point 1 to point 2. At this new equilibrium, the real wage rises from w_1 to w_2 and the quantity of labor used in production rises from L_1 to L_2.

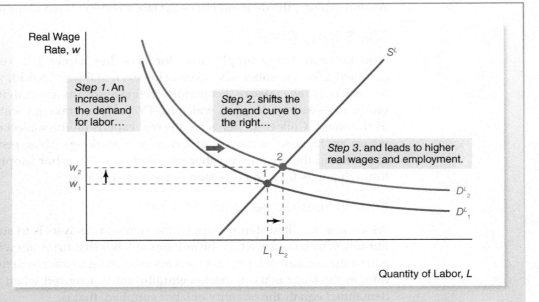

Whatever the cause, higher output increases the marginal product of labor and shifts the labor demand curve to the right from D_1^L to D_2^L, as shown in Figure 20.5. Equilibrium in the labor market therefore moves from point 1 to point 2: the real wage rises from w_1 to w_2 and the quantity of labor used in production rises from L_1 to L_2. Our supply and demand model of the labor market therefore yields the following result: *a rise in output, because of a positive supply or demand shock to production, leads to an increase in the demand for labor, higher real wages, and increased employment.*

Our supply and demand model of the labor market is therefore able to explain why employment is procyclical, as was shown in Figure 20.1. When the economy is booming and output is rising, employment will rise; if the economy contracts, output will fall, as will employment.[3]

Changes in Labor Supply

Anything that changes the amount of labor supplied at any given real wage rate causes the labor supply curve to shift and also leads to a new equilibrium in the labor market. Let's look at what happens when the supply of labor increases at any given real wage rate. One possible cause of this labor supply increase could be increased immigration, either from weakened enforcement of immigration laws or because immigration laws have changed to permit more legal immigrants. As shown in Figure 20.6, the increase in

---

[3]In Chapter 3, we looked at an application of a simplified version of the supply and demand model of the labor market and found that a negative supply shock from a surge in oil prices leads to a decline in real wages. The analysis using the model in this chapter would produce the same shift in the labor demand curve as in Chapter 3, but because the labor supply curve is upward sloping in the model in this chapter, it would also indicate that there would be a decline in employment from the oil price shock. Indeed, this is exactly what happened after oil prices surged in 1973–1974, 1979–1980, and 2007–2008.

MyEconLab Mini-lecture

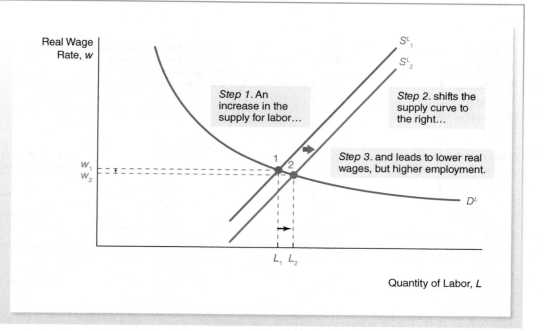

FIGURE 20.6

Response to an Increase in the Supply of Labor

An increase in the supply of labor, say from increased immigration, shifts the labor supply curve to the right from S_1^L to S_2^L, and the equilibrium moves from point 1 to point 2. As a result, the real wage rate falls from w_1 to w_2 and employment rises from L_1 to L_2.

immigration increases the quantity of labor supplied at any real wage rate and causes the labor supply curve to shift to the right from S_1^L to S_2^L. The labor market moves from point 1 to point 2. The real wage rate falls from w_1 to w_2 and employment rises from L_1 to L_2. We thus have the following result: ***anything that increases the labor supply (such as increased immigration) and shifts the labor supply curve to the right will cause real wages to fall and employment to rise.***

Armed with our supply and demand analysis of the labor market, we can answer a number of questions posed at the beginning of this chapter through a series of applications.

Application

Why Has Labor Force Participation of Women Increased?

Through the 1970s, a majority of women were not in the labor force. Put more technically, women had very low rates of **labor force participation,** the percentage of the adult population in the labor force. After marrying, women often left the work force and stayed home to care for children. As recently as 1970, women between the ages of twenty-five and thirty-four were less likely to work than women ten years their junior. By 2013, the employment ratio for women had increased dramatically, to 53%. Women today represent more than half of all managers and professionals, and they lead men in employment in many fields, including accounting and social work. Can our supply and demand model of the labor market explain this phenomenon?

The answer is yes, as Figure 20.7 demonstrates. With the advent of the birth control pill in the 1960s, women could choose to delay childbearing and have smaller families. The benefits of leisure (defined, perhaps unfairly, to include child care, a nonmarket activity) therefore decreased. Women were now willing to supply more labor at any given real wage

MyEconLab Mini-lecture

FIGURE 20.7

Why the Labor Force Participation of Women Has Increased

Post–1960s, the benefits of leisure (which includes child care) decreased, so women supplied more labor and the supply curve for labor shifted to the right from S_1^L to S_2^L. Improved technology and decreasing discrimination against women increased the demand for female labor, shifting the labor demand curve to the

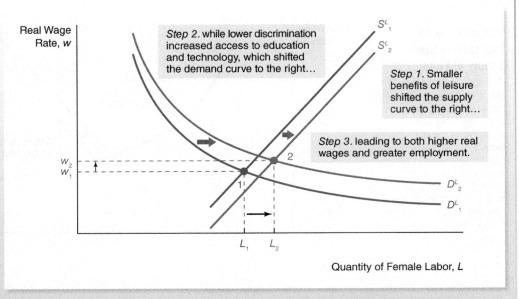

right from D_1^L to D_2^L. The rightward shift of both the labor supply and demand curves for women moved the economy from point 1 to point 2, and employment for women rose from L_1 to L_2.

rate, shifting the supply curve for labor rightward from S_1^L to S_2^L. Decreased discrimination against women that increased their access to education and technological advancements that favored brains rather than brawn further increased the demand for female labor, shifting the labor demand curve rightward from D_1^L to D_2^L. (To see how the workplace has changed since the early 1960s, just watch an episode of the television series *Mad Men*.) The rightward shift of both the labor supply and demand curves for women moved the economy from point 1 to point 2 in Figure 20.7, and employment for women rose from L_1 to L_2. (Note that as drawn, the labor demand curve shifts out more than the labor supply curve, with the result that real wages for women rise, which is exactly what has happened, with women's wages rising more quickly relative to men's.)

Application

Why Are Income Inequality and Returns to Education Increasing?

Another striking feature of U.S. labor markets is that wage growth for less educated workers has fallen behind wage growth for college-educated workers, increasing income inequality. How can our supply and demand model of the labor market explain these phenomena?

Figure 20.8 shows the **college wage premium**, the percentage difference between the average wage of a college-educated worker and that of a high-school graduate. In the early 1960s, the college wage premium was around 50%, indicating that a college-educated worker earned about 50% more than a high-school-educated worker. As you can see, the college wage premium has grown substantially in recent years, coming close to 100% (left vertical axis). The dramatic increase in the return to education demonstrates how important it is for you to stay in college and earn your degree. Figure 20.8 also plots the percentage of hours worked by college-educated workers, which has risen from around 20% in the early 1960s to nearly 50% today.

At first glance, the trend in Figure 20.8 seems to contradict our supply and demand framework for the labor market. The supply of college-educated workers has risen substantially, which should lower real wages. Yet their wages have risen relative to other workers' wages. To see why, consider the labor market for college graduates in Figure 20.9. (In this figure, wages are not given in absolute amounts, but are given as wages of college graduates relative to those of high-school graduates.) The increase in the supply of college graduates shown in Figure 20.9 would lead to a rightward shift of the labor supply curve from S_1^L to S_2^L. All else being equal, the relative wage of college graduates would decline. It must be that the demand for college-educated workers has also increased relative to the demand for high-school-educated workers. As depicted in Figure 20.9, the demand for college-educated labor rose by more than the increase in supply, so that the rightward shift of the labor demand curve from D_1^L to D_2^L is much greater than the rightward shift of the labor supply curve from S_1^L to S_2^L. The result is that the wages of college-educated workers rise relative to the wages of high-school graduates.

But why has the demand for college-educated labor increased so much? There are several plausible hypotheses. We refer to the first as **skill-biased technical change.** This is the idea that new technologies, such as computer hardware, software, and the Internet, have boosted the relative productivity of college-educated workers. The marginal product of labor has increased far more rapidly for college-educated graduates than for less educated workers, shifting the demand curve for college-educated labor sharply to the right.

FIGURE 20.8

The College Wage Premium and the Percentage of Hours Worked by College-Educated Workers

The college wage premium has grown substantially in recent years, rising from 50% in the 1960s to close to 100% in recent years (left vertical axis). The percentage of hours worked by college-educated workers has risen from around 20% in the early 1960s to nearly 50% today (right vertical axis).

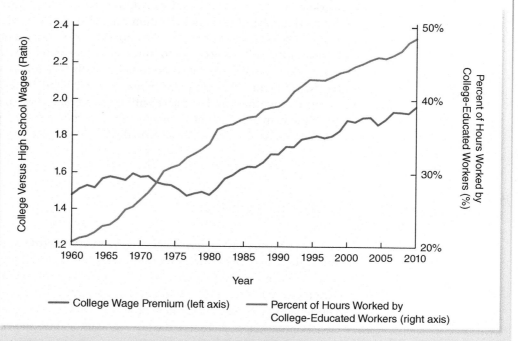

College Wage Premium (left axis)   Percent of Hours Worked by College-Educated Workers (right axis)

Source: Daron Acemoglu and David H. Autor, "Skills, Tasks and Technologies: Implications for Employment and Earnings," *Handbook of Labor Economics* Volume 4, Orley Ashenfelter and David E. Card (eds.), Amsterdam: Elsevier, 2010.

MyEconLab Mini-lecture

FIGURE 20.9

The Labor Market for College Graduates

The increase in the supply of college graduates resulted in a rightward shift of the labor supply curve from S_1^L to S_2^L, while the demand for college-educated labor rose as a result of skill-biased technical change and globalization, increasing demand by more than the increase in supply. The rightward shift of the labor demand curve from D_1^L to D_2^L is much greater than the

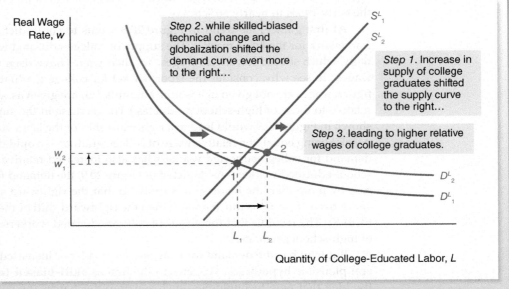

Step 2. while skilled-biased technical change and globalization shifted the demand curve even more to the right…

Step 1. Increase in supply of college graduates shifted the supply curve to the right…

Step 3. leading to higher relative wages of college graduates.

Quantity of College-Educated Labor, L

rightward shift of the labor supply curve from S_1^L to S_2^L. Equilibrium moved from point 1 to point 2, so the wages of college-educated workers rose relative to the wages of high-school graduates.

The second hypothesis is **globalization.** The opening up of markets internationally, both in finance and in trade, enables highly educated workers to work with a larger pool of uneducated workers in the less developed world, thereby making highly educated U.S. workers more productive. In addition, globalization can suppress the wages of low-skilled workers in the United States, who face increased competition from low-skilled workers abroad.

The rise in the college wage premium has increased income inequality. Since college-educated workers have higher income to begin with, when they do better relative to less educated workers, income inequality rises. In the United States, the wage premium for college-educated workers and workers with more advanced degrees has risen. The relative wage of people with high incomes, who are typically the most highly educated in our society, has risen so substantially that income inequality has become a serious political problem.[4]

Dynamics of Unemployment

So far, we have studied the labor market with a very useful supply and demand model framework that assumes that all workers who want to supply their labor at a given real wage rate can get a job. However, the model cannot explain the phenomenon of unemployment, when workers who want a job can't find one.

To understand why unemployment occurs, we first must delve deeper into the dynamics of the labor market, and observe the flow of workers into and out of the labor market.

---

[4]For further discussion of the link between returns to education and income inequality, see Claudia Goldin and Lawrence F. Katz, *The Race Between Education and Technology* (Cambridge, MA: Belknap Press, 2011).

Flows Into and Out of Employment Status

People of working age can be classified in one of three categories of employment status, shown in Figure 20.10:

1. *employed*, 144.3 million in July 2013;

2. *unemployed*, 11.5 million in July 2013 and

3. *not in the labor force*, 90.0 million in July 2013.

Workers move from one employment status to another all the time, as indicated in Figure 20.10 by the arrows pointing from each category to another. The number adjacent to each arrow indicates what percentage of workers in the category at the base of the arrow moved to the category at the tip of the arrow during July 2013. For example, 20% of the unemployed, 2.3 million workers, found new jobs and moved into the employed category in July. On the other hand, in July 2013, 1-1/2% of the employed, 2.0 million workers, lost jobs but stayed in the labor force and so moved into the unemployed category.

Workers also move in and out of the labor force. In July 2013, 23% of unemployed workers left the labor force. Some of these are **discouraged workers,** those who just stop looking for work. Another 3% of employed workers left the labor force in July, because of dissatisfaction or to pursue other activities such as going to school, raising children, or entering retirement. Some people rejoin the labor force. In July 2013, 4% of

FIGURE 20.10

Changes in Employment Status (July 2013)

There are three categories of employment status: *employed*, 144.3 million in July 2013; *unemployed*, 11.5 million in July 2013; and *not in the labor force*, 90.0 million in July 2013. The number adjacent to each arrow indicates what percentage of workers in the category at the base of the arrow moved to the category at the tip of the arrow during July 2013. For example, in July 2013, 20% of the unemployed found new jobs and moved into the employed category.

On the other hand, in July 2013, 1% of the employed lost jobs but stayed in the labor force and so moved into the unemployed category. Twenty-three percent of unemployed workers left the labor force in July 2013, and 3% of employed workers left the labor force. Workers also moved from out of the labor force back in: 4% of those not in the labor force got jobs and 3% started searching for jobs, moving themselves into the ranks of the unemployed.

Source: Bureau of Labor Statistics, www.bls.gov/cps/cps_flows_current.pdf

those not in the labor force got jobs and 3% started searching for jobs, moving themselves into the ranks of the unemployed.

Figure 20.10 suggests that even in a month in which the net change in jobs is small, there are a large number of new jobs created and jobs lost. For example, between 2000 and 2012, on average there were 29.6 million new jobs created and 29.5 million jobs lost, for an average net increase of 0.1 million jobs. The labor market is very dynamic: job creation and destruction is fundamental to understanding the roots of unemployment.

Duration of Unemployment

Two other key features of the labor market are important. In a typical month, around 20% of the unemployed find jobs. As a result, for most of the unemployed, **unemployment spells,** the length of time a worker remains unemployed, are shorter than three months. On the other hand, nearly 40% of the unemployed are **chronically unemployed;** that is, they have unemployment spells lasting more than six months.

A large fraction of unemployment comes from the chronically unemployed. Given that most unemployment spells are short, it seems counterintuitive that most unemployment comes from the chronically unemployed, who have long durations of unemployment. Consider a situation in which there are ten workers, eight of whom have been unemployed for two months, and two of whom have been unemployed for two years. The total number of months unemployed is sixty-four months (8 × 2 months + 2 × 24 months). However, despite the fact that 80% of workers have a short duration of unemployment, forty-eight of the sixty-four total months of unemployment—that is, three-quarters of the total months of unemployment—come from the chronically unemployed.

Causes of Unemployment

We will now use the dynamics of the labor market to understand why unemployment occurs. There are three basic sources of unemployment: frictional unemployment, structural unemployment, and wage rigidity.

Frictional Unemployment

With so many new jobs created and old jobs destroyed every year, it's no surprise that workers and firms have trouble making suitable job matches. Workers have different capabilities and different geographic preferences. Mary may be a math whiz, but she hates big cities, while George may be artistic and wants to live only in California. Jobs also have different characteristics that might not be apparent to potential workers. One firm may be supportive of its women employees, while another may not. Moreover, firms and workers have different search goals. Workers want an enjoyable, high-paying job, while firms search for a good employee who can do the particular job well at a reasonable wage. It takes time to achieve a job match, and in the meantime, workers who have either left their jobs voluntarily or have been let go will undergo a spell of unemployment.

We call unemployment related to the job search **frictional unemployment.** In a dynamic labor market such as the one we have in the United States, where workers are continually entering and leaving employment, there will always be some frictional unemployment. Importantly, some of this frictional unemployment is actually good for the economy. If workers and firms didn't conduct thorough searches, accepting instead the first job they saw or the first candidate they interviewed, a good match would be unlikely. When searches are insufficient, workers perform poorly and the economy suffers. The job search process can increase efficiency and sustain a better-performing economy. The conclusion is that *some frictional unemployment makes the economy better off and is thus desirable.*[5]

Policy and Practice

Unemployment Insurance and Unemployment

Unemployment insurance is a government program that provides unemployed workers with a percentage of their wages for a given period after they lose their jobs. In the United States, unemployment insurance is administered by each state and is typically around 50% of a worker's previous wages. Unemployment insurance is typically paid for twenty-six weeks, but during recessions this period is often extended, as it was during the most recent recession.

The important benefit of unemployment insurance is that it provides a safety net for workers, reducing hardship when they are fired from their jobs. (U.S. unemployment insurance benefits are paid only if an employer terminates the worker's employment, not when the worker quits.) Despite the desirability of a safety net for workers, there is a downside to unemployment insurance: higher unemployment.

To see why unemployment insurance increases unemployment, we use our analysis of frictional unemployment. Frictional unemployment occurs because the process of searching for a job takes time. Unemployment insurance gives back part of workers' salaries when they are unemployed, lowering the cost to workers of being unemployed and encouraging them to search longer and hold out for a higher-paying job. In addition, the lower cost of being unemployed encourages workers to turn down jobs that they think are less desirable. Both increased search time and workers' willingness to be pickier about the jobs they take result in workers experiencing a longer duration of unemployment spells, which then leads to more unemployment and a higher unemployment rate.

Empirical evidence strongly supports the view that unemployment insurance increases unemployment. Once workers become ineligible for unemployment insurance after twenty-six weeks, they become twice as likely to take a job. In a particularly striking experiment, new claimants to unemployment insurance in Illinois were randomly selected and were offered a $500 bonus if they found a job within eleven weeks. For those receiving the bonus, the average duration of unemployment fell by 7%.[6] Since this finding comes from what is known as a *controlled experiment*, it is quite likely that the bonus caused the lower unemployment duration and not the other way around. This experiment provides strong evidence that the

---

[5]However, measures aimed at lowering search frictions, such as government policies to facilitate good job matches, can not only improve the economy's efficiency but can also lower frictional unemployment.

[6]See Stephen A. Woodbury and Robert G. Spiegelman, "Bonuses to Workers and Employers to Reduce Unemployment: Randomized Trials in Illinois," *American Economic Review* 77 (September 1987): 513–530.

payments from unemployment insurance have an important impact on workers' decisions to stay unemployed rather than take a job and exit unemployment.

During the most recent recession, there was an active debate over whether the duration of unemployment benefits should be lengthened, especially because the duration of unemployment had shot through the roof, with the median duration of unemployment rising from around eight weeks to over twenty weeks. Concerns that extending unemployment benefits would lead to a higher unemployment rate led the Bush administration to desist from lengthening the period over which the unemployed could receive these benefits. The Obama administration, however, upon coming into office, extended unemployment benefits over a longer period, worried that the surge in unemployment was leading to too much hardship.

Structural Unemployment

There are two basic structural reasons why the chronically unemployed find it difficult to get a job. First, they may not have the skills to perform any job very well. They may be very uneducated or lack the life skills necessary to show up for work on time on a regular basis or dress appropriately for the job. These low-skilled workers will find it difficult to find good jobs and so may flit from job to job, or will be unwilling to take jobs that do not pay well. The result is that they will stay unemployed for long periods of time.

The second reason why the chronically unemployed may find it difficult to get a job is that they have acquired a specific set of skills or preferences while working in one industry. When the industry goes into decline and they lose their jobs, they may not have the skills or preferences to get work in growing industries in which jobs are plentiful. For example, an auto worker who loses his or her job when GM has to close down some of its operations is unlikely to have the computer skills to get a job in the rapidly expanding software industry. In addition, the worker in Michigan who worked for GM may be unwilling to move to California to work in the software industry.

Unemployment that arises from a lack of skills or a mismatch of skills with available jobs is a structural feature of the labor markets and is thus referred to as **structural unemployment.** Structural unemployment emerges during **sectoral shifts** in the economy, when new industries grow and old industries die off. Structural employment poses an even greater problem when emerging industries require workers to have skills that were uncommon in the old industries.

Wage Rigidity

One source of structural unemployment is **wage rigidity,** the inability of wages to adjust to the level that would equate supply and demand in the labor market and thus eliminate unemployment.

We show how wage rigidity can lead to unemployment using the supply and demand model of the labor market. Suppose the supply and demand curves for labor initially intersect at point A in Figure 20.11. At point A, the labor market is in equilibrium—the quantity of labor demanded equals the quantity supplied, so there is no unemployment—and the real wage is w_A. Now suppose the economy contracts and output falls, so that the demand curve for labor shifts to the left from D_1^L to D_2^L. If wages were flexible, the labor market would move to point B, the real wage would fall to w_B, the **market-clearing level**—the level at which the quantity of labor supplied equals

FIGURE 20.11

Wage Rigidity and Unemployment

Suppose that the demand curve for labor shifts to the left from D_1^L to D_2^L, but there is wage rigidity and so the real wage is fixed at $\overline{w} = w_A$ and cannot fall below this level. The quantity of labor demanded at this wage rate, L_C, will be less than the quantity supplied at this wage rate, L_A. Now, workers who want to supply L_A of labor will be unable to do so because firms will be willing to hire only L_C of labor, and there will be unemployment equal to $L_A - L_C$.

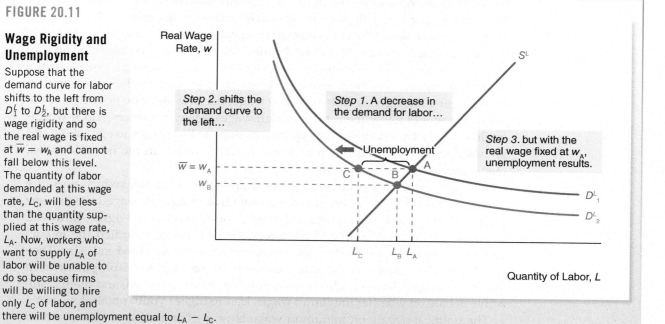

the quantity demanded—and unemployment would not occur. Note, however, that the quantity of labor used in production would fall from L_A to L_B.

Now suppose instead that there is wage rigidity, so that the real wage is fixed at $\overline{w} = w_A$ and cannot fall below this level. This could happen either because wages are slow to adjust and do not move in the current period, or because the government has set a floor on wages, called a **minimum wage,** that restricts employers from paying workers less than this amount. (We will discuss the impact of minimum wage laws in the following Policy and Practice case.) When the real wage stays at $\overline{w} = w_A$, the quantity of labor demanded at this wage rate, L_C, will be less than the quantity supplied at this wage rate, L_A. Now workers who want to supply L_A of labor will not be fully employed because firms will be willing to hire only L_C of labor. There will be unemployment equal to the difference between what firms are willing to hire, L_C, and the quantity of labor supplied at L_A. Wage rigidity can therefore be another source of unemployment.

Policy and Practice

Minimum Wage Laws

With the Fair Labor Standards Act of 1938, the U.S. federal government passed a minimum wage law that barred employers from paying less than a legal minimum wage to workers (initially set at 25 cents per hour). Since then, the federal government has continued to pass minimum wage laws and some states have followed with their own minimum wage legislation, in some cases with higher minimums than those set by federal law. The federal minimum wage has typically been between 30% and 50% of the average wage in manufacturing, and it is currently $7.25 per hour (although the Obama Administration has proposed raising it to at least $9 per hour). Because most hourly wages are above this minimum, the minimum wage laws affect only a small percentage of U.S. workers.

For low-wage workers, however, the minimum wage may be binding and prevent wages from adjusting downward, thereby causing unemployment, as the analysis in Figure 20.11 demonstrates. Minimum wage laws can have a big impact on teenagers. Teenagers tend to have low wages because many do not yet have the skills that would allow them to earn high wages. Many teenagers find it worthwhile to take jobs, internships, or apprenticeships at low wages to gain skills and knowledge that will help them earn much higher wages in the future. Indeed, many internships do not pay any salary at all.

As a group, teenagers have the highest unemployment rate, which typically averages over 15%. Many economists believe that minimum wage laws are one source of these high unemployment rates. Not all economists agree, however. Lawrence Katz of Harvard and Alan Krueger of Princeton studied the impact of minimum wage laws on teenage employment in the fast-food industry. They concluded that there were negligible effects on teenage unemployment from minimum wages. Their conclusion has, however, been contested, and there is still active debate on whether minimum wages lead to higher youth unemployment.

The political debate on minimum wage laws is often ferocious. Advocates of minimum wage laws believe that these laws help produce higher income for the working poor. Hence, even if they produce some unemployment, they are worthwhile because they help reduce poverty and reduce income inequality. Opponents of minimum wage laws argue that they hurt, rather than help, the working poor by keeping them out of jobs in which they could be gaining skills and earning promotions.

EFFICIENCY WAGES. There are two other sources of wage rigidity. The first is **efficiency wages,** which are wages that are above the market-clearing level at which supply equals demand, but that are efficient because they induce workers to work harder and be more productive. The classic example is Henry Ford's paying $5 per day in 1914 to his auto workers (see the box, "Efficiency Wages and Henry Ford"). Paying a high wage may cause the quantity of labor supplied to be greater than the quantity of labor demanded, leading to unemployment. However, employers may not want to lower the wage for fear of worker absenteeism, less work effort, and the possibly shoddy work that might result, particularly if workers feel the lower wage is unfair. Efficiency wages therefore imply that wages may be downwardly rigid and may not adjust to eliminate unemployment.

COLLECTIVE BARGAINING AND UNIONS. The second source of wage rigidity is unions, which can exert some monopoly power and prevent wages from adjusting to market-clearing levels. Unions set wages by **collective bargaining,** the process of bargaining for a common wage for a large group of workers at one time, rather than having each worker bargain individually for his or her wages. Unions can set wages above the market-clearing level and then let the firm decide on how much labor to employ. The amount of labor employed will be less than the quantity that workers will want to supply, thereby creating some unemployment.

Efficiency Wages and Henry Ford

In 1914, Henry Ford shook up the auto industry by raising the wages of his workers to $5 per day. Although $5 per day does not sound like much by today's standards, in those days it was a princely sum—double the prevailing wage in the industry. Was Henry Ford being altruistic? Although he knew that he could hire workers for less, he argued that paying $5 per day increased Ford Motor Company's bottom line. As he put it, "There was ... no charity involved.... We wanted to pay these wages so the business would be on a lasting foundation. We were building for the future. A low-wage business is always insecure... The payment of five dollars per day for an eight-hour day was one of the finest cost cutting moves we ever made."[*] In other words, deep down, Henry Ford understood the value of paying efficiency wages.

Ford seemed to be proved right: absenteeism fell by 75% and reports written at the time found that labor costs did indeed fall substantially. Estimates of the productivity rise at Ford's factory were between 30% and 50%. Ford Motor Company became wildly successful and changed the landscape of corporate America.

[*]Daniel G. Raff and Lawrence H. Summers, "Did Henry Ford Pay Efficiency Wages?" *Journal of Labor Economics*, Vol 5 (October 1987), pp. S57–86.

Natural Rate of Unemployment

Our analysis of why unemployment occurs suggests that unemployment is like death and taxes: it will always be with us. Frictional and structural unemployment, as well as some types of wage rigidity—such as minimum wage laws, efficiency wages, and unions—that are structural in nature lead to an unemployment rate that is above zero even in the long run, when wages have had time to adjust. The **natural rate of unemployment** is the level of the unemployment rate that remains even when wages in the labor market have fully adjusted.

As we discussed in Part 4 of this book, output and the unemployment rate fluctuate over the business cycle around the natural rate of unemployment. We refer to the difference between the actual unemployment rate and the natural rate of unemployment as the **cyclical unemployment rate** (also referred to as the *unemployment gap*). The actual unemployment rate is the sum of two components, the natural rate and the cyclical rate:

$$\text{Actual unemployment rate} = \text{natural rate of unemployment} + \text{cyclical rate of unemployment} \tag{3}$$

The use of the term "natural" in describing the full-employment level of unemployment is somewhat unfortunate: "natural" makes it sound as if this level of unemployment is an unchanging law of nature that cannot be influenced by government policies. In fact, the natural rate of unemployment can vary over time and across countries. In the United States, it appears to have been between 4% and 5% in the 1950s, around 6% in the 1980s and early 1990s, and slightly below 5% by the mid-2000s.

FIGURE 20.12

The *AD/AS* Model and a Rise in the Natural Rate of Unemployment

When the natural rate of unemployment rises, the long-run aggregate supply curve shifts to the left from $LRAS_1$ to $LRAS_2$, and the short-run aggregate supply curve shifts from AS_1 to AS_2. The economy moves from point 1 to point 2, where aggregate output falls to Y_2^P and inflation rises to π_2.

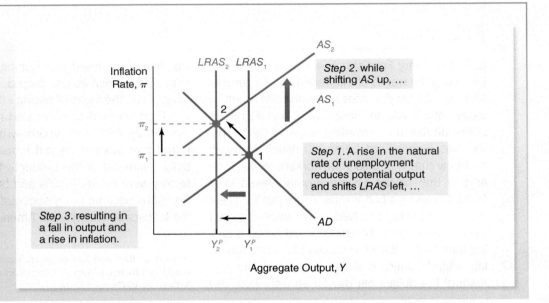

> *Step 2.* while shifting *AS* up, …
>
> *Step 1.* A rise in the natural rate of unemployment reduces potential output and shifts *LRAS* left, …
>
> *Step 3.* resulting in a fall in output and a rise in inflation.

The Role of the Natural Rate of Unemployment in the *AD/AS* Model

The natural rate of unemployment is an important concept because it plays a central role in the aggregate demand-aggregate supply (AD/AS) model that we make extensive use of in this book. When the natural rate of unemployment changes, both the short-run and long-run aggregate supply curves shift. For example, if the natural rate of unemployment rises, then, for a given level of the labor force, less labor will be available for production in the long run and so, from the production function developed in Chapter 3, the level of potential output will fall. As a result, the long-run aggregate supply curve will shift to the left as in Figure 20.12. The decline in potential output will cause the short-run aggregate supply curve to shift upward because, at the same level of output, $Y - Y^P$ will be higher and so inflation will be higher. Hence, as we see in Figure 20.12, the economy will move from point 1 to point 2, where inflation rises and the level of output falls. Changes in the natural rate of unemployment can therefore lead to fluctuations in both output and inflation.

Sources of Changes in the Natural Rate of Unemployment

The natural rate of unemployment varies over time for several reasons.

DEMOGRAPHICS. Some types of workers are more likely to become unemployed. Young workers, for instance, tend to move to and from jobs much more frequently than do older workers. Since moving from job to job involves search and thus leads to higher frictional unemployment, a growing percentage of young workers in the labor force will raise the natural rate of unemployment. From the 1940s until the 1960s, U.S. birth rates surged, leading to the "baby boom." Twenty years later, these young workers began to enter the labor force, increasing the percentage of workers aged sixteen to twenty-four in the labor force from 16.5% in 1960 to 24% in 1980. Many economists view this increase as explaining most of the increase in the natural rate of unemployment from 1960 to 1980. The percentage of young workers between the ages of sixteen and twenty-four began to decline starting in the 1980s, falling to below 14% by 2013. As a result, the natural rate of unemployment declined by a little over one-half percentage point.[7]

COMPOSITION OF THE LABOR FORCE. Three other important changes in the composition of the labor force have affected the natural rate of unemployment: increases in the prison population, increases in the number of workers taking disability, and the use of temporary workers.

Strong law enforcement and steeper sentences have increased the U.S. prison population, with the percentage of the U.S. population of working age in prison rising from 0.3% to 1% currently. People who end up in prison are generally less likely to have the skills required by firms and are therefore subject to higher structural unemployment. Taking such people off the streets and out of the labor force should therefore lower the natural rate of unemployment.

Since 1984, relaxation of federal rules that determine eligibility for disability insurance has led to a rise in the percentage of the working-age population dropping out of the labor force to obtain disability insurance, from 2.2% in 1984 to over 4% today. Because workers who apply for disability are likely to suffer higher structural unemployment, their removal from the labor force when they obtain disability insurance also lowers the natural rate of unemployment.

Another change in labor markets is the increasing use of temporary workers. The share of temporary workers hired by employment agencies has increased from 0.5% of total employment in 1980 to more than 2% currently. Rather than be unemployed, a worker can take temporary employment and still look for a job. Increasing opportunities for temporary employment lowers the natural rate of unemployment.

Combined together, increases in the prison population, the number of workers who go on disability insurance, and the number of temporary workers have had a large impact on the natural rate of unemployment, with estimates indicating that these factors have lowered the natural rate of unemployment since the 1980s by a little over one percentage point.

SURPRISES IN PRODUCTIVITY GROWTH. As we discussed in Chapter 6, the rate of productivity growth fell after 1973 and then rose in the mid-1990s with the advent of the new economy, the surge in firms' productivity due to the computer revolution. Did this fall and rise in productivity growth cause a similar rise and then fall in the natural rate of unemployment in the 1980s? The standard labor market supply and demand analysis indicates such a link.

Higher productivity growth leads to a higher demand for labor, which raises real wages. In theory, this should not lead to a lower natural rate of unemployment. In reality, however, it sometimes does. To see why, consider what happens when changes in productivity growth aren't immediately recognized by workers. In 1973, for example, productivity growth started to fall, but it took workers a long time to spot the decline. As a result, when firms (who could see their productivity growth declining) offered smaller wage increases, workers felt they were being stiffed. They became dissatisfied and sought work elsewhere, increasing the natural rate of unemployment, as occurred in the 1970s and 1980s. If, on the other hand, productivity growth accelerates (as occurred

---

[7]These estimates of the effects of demographics and the additional changes in the composition of labor on the natural rate of unemployment come from Lawrence Katz and Alan Krueger, "The High-Pressure U.S. Labor Market of the 1990s," *Brookings Papers on Economic Activity* 1 (1999: 1–87).

in the mid-1990s) but workers don't realize this, they won't expect big wage hikes. However, the actual higher productivity growth means that firms will be willing to pay higher real wages than workers expect, and the natural rate of unemployment will fall, as it did in the late 1990s.

Misperceptions by workers about the rate of productivity growth explain the rise of the natural rate of unemployment in the 1970s and 1980s, and then the fall of the natural rate of unemployment after the mid-1990s. There are concerns that the blows to the financial system and increased regulation in the aftermath of the recent financial crisis (discussed in Chapter 15) might cause the natural rate of unemployment to rise toward 6% again.

Although we worry about a high natural rate of unemployment in the United States, the natural rate of unemployment appears to be far higher in Europe, as we discuss in the following application.

Application

Why Are European Unemployment Rates Generally Much Higher Than U.S. Unemployment Rates?

Figure 20.13 shows the unemployment rates for several of the largest European countries and the United States over the period 1960–2013. Notice that average unemployment rates in Europe were typically lower than the U.S. unemployment rate before the 1980s, but in many countries in Europe typically are now appreciably higher than the U.S. unemployment rate. Why have unemployment rates risen in these European countries, and why are they generally so much higher than U.S. rates?

FIGURE 20.13

Unemployment Rates in Europe Versus the United States, 1960–2013

The average unemployment rates in Europe were typically lower than in the United States before 1980, but have been typically higher since then.

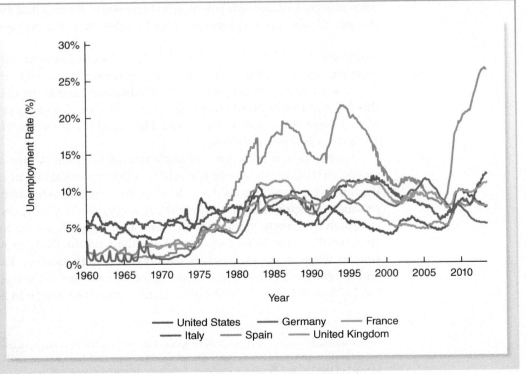

Source: Eurostat, available at http://epp.eurostat.ec.europa.eu/portal/page/portal/eurostat/home/.

First, since business cycles go up and down, we can say that over a long period the cyclical rate of unemployment on average should be close to zero. Because European unemployment rates have been on average higher than U.S. rates since the 1980s, this must reflect a corresponding rise in the natural rate of unemployment. Our analysis of what causes unemployment suggests three reasons why the natural rate of unemployment in European countries is now higher than the natural rate of unemployment in the United States.

1. *Generous European unemployment insurance benefits.* The percentage of European salaries paid out in benefits is much higher than in the United States, and workers are allowed to collect benefits for a much longer period of time, often years. These generous benefits in Europe reduce the cost of search, increasing the duration of unemployment spells and in turn boosting the natural rate of unemployment.

2. *Strong European unions.* Europe has much stronger unions than the United States, as shown by Table 20.1: less than 15% of U.S. workers are represented by unions in collective bargaining, whereas the percentage in many European countries, such as France, Germany, Italy, and Spain, is above 60%. Indeed, over time, unions have represented a smaller and smaller percentage of workers in the United States. Unions setting wage rates above market-clearing rates are likely to lead to a higher level of unemployment, just as is shown in Figure 20.11, in which the quantity of labor demanded falls short of the quantity supplied.

3. *Strict work rules.* European governments have imposed work rules on firms that can increase unemployment. For example, it is much harder for European firms to fire workers than it is for U.S. firms. As a result, European firms may be far more reluctant to create new jobs, even in growing industries. Structural unemployment is therefore higher in Europe because workers losing jobs in a declining industry will not find enough new jobs available in growing industries.

These three reasons explain why European unemployment rates are, on average, higher than those in the United States since the 1980s, but they do not explain why European unemployment rates were lower than those in the United States in the 1960s, since these three conditions already existed then, and why European unemployment rates rose so much starting in the 1980s. Some economists have speculated that the large rise in the natural rate of unemployment resulted from the shocks of the 1980s combined with the features of the European labor markets discussed previously.

TABLE 20.1　**PERCENT OF WORKERS REPRESENTED BY UNIONS IN DIFFERENT COUNTRIES**

COUNTRY	PERCENT (%)
France	92
Germany	61
Italy	85
Spain	73
United Kingdom	31
United States	13

Source: ICTWSS: Database on Institutional Characteristics of Trade Unions, Wage Setting, State Intervention and Social Pact at http://www.uva-aias.net/207. Data for 2011 for United Kingdom and United States; 2010 for Germany, Italy and Spain; and 2008 for France.

Starting in the 1980s, the demand for unskilled workers decreased relative to the demand for skilled workers because of new technologies associated with the development of cheap, high-speed computers. In the United States, this did not lead to higher unemployment, but as we have seen, it did lead to a fall in wages of unskilled workers relative to wages of skilled workers (the flip side of the higher return to education discussed earlier). The rigidities in the labor market induced by higher unemployment insurance benefits, greater union power, and restrictive work rules then meant that unskilled workers' wages could not adjust downward in Europe as in the United States, and so the natural rate of unemployment increased dramatically.

SUMMARY

1. The employment-to-population ratio has had an upward trend over the last fifty years because women have increased their labor force participation. Both the employment ratio and the unemployment rate are cyclical, with the employment ratio rising during economic expansions and falling during recessions, while the unemployment rate does the reverse. Although real wages have risen for the average worker, workers with more education have experienced much higher real-wage growth than workers with less education, leading to a growing college wage premium and higher income inequality.

2. The demand curve for labor is downward sloping, while the supply curve is upward sloping. Equilibrium in the labor market occurs when the quantity of labor demanded equals the quantity of labor supplied.

3. A rise in output, because of a positive supply or demand shock to production, causes an increase in the demand for labor and a rightward shift of the demand curve. The rightward shift of the demand curve then leads to higher real wages and higher employment. Anything that increases the supply of labor and shifts the labor supply curve out to the right will cause real wages to fall and employment to rise.

4. The labor market is very dynamic, with large flows in and out of unemployment. Most workers experience only short durations of unemployment spells, but the chronically unemployed, those who are unemployed for over six months, account for a large fraction of unemployment.

5. Unemployment is due to frictional unemployment, structural unemployment, and wage rigidities. Frictional unemployment occurs because matching up workers with suitable jobs through a search process takes time. Structural unemployment occurs because the chronically unemployed may not have the skills to get jobs in growing industries in which jobs are plentiful. Wage rigidities lead to unemployment because they prevent wages from going to market-clearing levels, so that the quantity demanded of labor remains below what workers are willing to supply. Wage rigidities occur because wages are slow to adjust, or because minimum wage laws, efficiency wages, or labor unions prevent wages from being adjusted downward.

6. The natural rate of unemployment is the level of the unemployment rate that remains when the labor market has had time to fully adjust, and it does vary over time. The actual unemployment rate is the natural rate of unemployment plus the cyclical rate of unemployment.

KEY TERMS

chronically unemployed, p. 556
collective bargaining, p. 560
college wage premium, p. 552
cyclical unemployment
  rate, p. 561
discouraged workers, p. 555
efficiency wages, p. 560
employment ratio, p. 544

employment-to-population
  ratio, p. 544
frictional unemployment, p. 556
globalization, p. 554
labor force participation, p. 551
leisure, p. 549
market-clearing level, p. 558
minimum wage, p. 559

natural rate of
  unemployment, p. 561
sectoral shifts, p. 558
skill-biased technical
  change, p. 553
structural unemployment, p. 558
unemployment insurance, p. 557
unemployment spells, p. 556
wage rigidity, p. 558

REVIEW QUESTIONS

All Questions are available in MyEconLab *for practice or instructor assignment.*

Developments in the U.S. Labor Market

1. What is the employment ratio? What notable trends in this ratio have occurred over the past fifty years?

Supply and Demand in the Labor Market

2. Why is the quantity of labor demanded inversely related to the real wage rate?

3. Is the quantity of labor supplied inversely related to the real wage rate? Why or why not?

Response of Employment and Wages to Changes in Labor Demand and Labor Supply

4. Identify three things that can change labor demand or supply and reduce employment. How would each of these affect real wages?

Dynamics of Unemployment

5. What are the three categories of employment status? What movement between categories results from the existence of discouraged workers?

Causes of Unemployment

6. What is frictional unemployment? Why can it be beneficial for workers, firms, and the economy?

7. Why does structural unemployment occur?
8. Why does real wage rigidity contribute to unemployment? What are its causes?

Natural Rate of Unemployment

9. What is the natural rate of unemployment? What has caused the natural rate to change over time?

10. What is cyclical unemployment?

PROBLEMS

All Problems are available in MyEconLab *for practice or instructor assignment.*

Supply and Demand in the Labor Market

1. Assume that the marginal product of labor is $MPL = 0.65 \times \$13/L$, where output is measured in trillions and L is the number of workers (in millions).
   a) Draw the *MPL* curve.
   b) Find the quantity of workers demanded if the real wage is $50,000 per worker.

2. Anthony currently earns $25 an hour and works forty hours a week. When his boss offers to pay him $28 per hour, Anthony decides to accept the offer and also decides to keep working forty hours. What is the effect of Anthony's decision on the labor supply curve?

Response of Employment and Wages to Changes in Labor Demand and Labor Supply

3. Using a graph, analyze the effect of techno-logical advances that have increased workers' productivity in the last few decades (e.g., the Internet) on the labor market. What will be the effect on the real wage and employment if the supply curve does not shift?

4. Using a graph, analyze the effect of a recession and an increase in day care costs on the real wage and employment.

Dynamics of Unemployment

5. For each of the following situations, explain how the labor force and the unemployment rate change.
   a) An individual quits his or her job and does not look for a job anymore.
   b) An individual who was not in the labor force now decides to look for a job.

6. During recessions, it becomes increasingly difficult to find a job. How do you think the number of "discouraged workers" would be affected by a recession?

Causes of Unemployment

7. Discuss the effects of the Internet on frictional unemployment. How do you think websites that allow employees to search for job oppor-tunities more efficiently impact frictional unemployment?

8. Suppose a country is rapidly making the tran-sition from an agricultural-based economy to an economy in which most of GDP comes from manufacturing.
   a) How do you think structural unemploy-ment will be affected?

   b) Can you think of any measure the govern-ment might undertake to affect structural unemployment in this case?

9. The following graph represents the labor mar-ket of a given country. Assuming the prevail-ing real wage is w_1,
   a) measure unemployment using the graph.
   b) list three factors that might prevent this market from clearing.

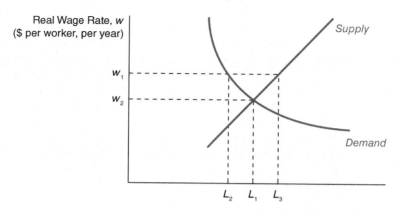

Natural Rate of Unemployment

10. The natural rate of unemployment is higher in France than in the United States. Suppose you are a recent college graduate and you are eager to find a job. Which country's labor market seems more promising to you? Can you identify the trade-off between a higher natural rate of unemployment and a more dynamic labor market?

DATA ANALYSIS PROBLEMS

The Problems update with real-time data in MyEconLab *and are available for practice or instructor assignment.*

1. Go to the St. Louis Federal Reserve FRED database, and find data on civilian employment (CE16OV) and a measure of real wages in the non-farm business sector (COMPRNFB). Convert the employment measure to "Quarterly" using the *frequency* setting, and download the data.
   a) Calculate the percentage change in real wages and employment from the previous quarter to the most current period. Based on your results, how have labor supply and labor demand changed, if at all?
   b) Calculate the percentage change in wages and employment between the most current period and the same time a year earlier. Based on your results, how have labor supply and labor demand changed, if at all?

2. Go to the St. Louis Federal Reserve FRED database, and find data on civilian employment (CE16OV), unemployed (UNEMPLOY), and not in the labor force (LNS15000000).
   a) Using the most recent data available, calculate the labor force, the working-age population, and the labor force participation rate.
   b) Use your answer from part (a) to calculate the employment-population ratio.

3. Go to the St. Louis Federal Reserve FRED database, and find data on labor force participation and the unemployment rate for the groups listed below. For each pair of demographic groups, calculate the difference in labor force participation and the difference in the unemployment rate between the two groups, using the most current data available, the data from one year prior, and the data from five years prior. Comment on the level and change in the gaps between the two demographic groups over time.
   a) Labor force participation rate of men (LNS11300001) and women (LNS11300002); unemployment rate of men (LNS14000001) and women (LNS14000002).
   b) Labor force participation rate of black or African American (LNS11300006) and white (LNS11300003); unemployment rate of black or African American (LNS14000006) and white (LNS14000003).
   c) Labor force participation rate of college graduates (LNS11327662) and high school only graduates (LNS11327660); unemployment rate of college graduates (LNS14027662) and high school only graduates (LNS14027660).

4. Go to the St. Louis Federal Reserve FRED database, and find data on the civilian unemployment rate (UNRATE) and a measure of the natural rate of unemployment (NROU).
   a) Calculate the cyclical unemployment rate for the most recent month available, and for one and two years prior.
   b) Given the changes in cyclical unemployment over these periods, what can you conclude about growth in the economy?

Part 8

Modern Business Cycle Analysis and Macroeconomic Policy

Part 8

Modern Business Cycle Analysis and Macroeconomic Policy

We end the book by discussing the latest developments in business cycle theory that have arisen from a greater focus on the microeconomic foundations of macroeconomic analysis. Chapter 21 describes the most widely used theory of expectations formation, the theory of *rational expectations*, and uses it to discuss how expectations influence macroeconomic policy. Chapter 22 describes the two competing business cycle theories that were developed in the wake of rational expectations theory: the *real business cycle model*, a classical model in which prices and wages are assumed to be flexible, and the *new Keynesian model*, which is Keynesian because it assumes that wages and prices are sticky. The epilogue outlines how these new approaches to business cycle theory, along with recent research on what drives economic development, have affected the topics on which macroeconomists agree and disagree regarding how macroeconomic policy should be conducted.

We will examine applications to make the critical connection between theory and real-world practice:

- "The Consumption Function"
- "A Tale of Three Oil Shocks"

In keeping with our focus on key policy issues and the techniques policy makers use in practice, we will also analyze the following specific examples in Policy and Practice cases:

- "The Political Business Cycle and Richard Nixon"
- "The Demise of Monetary Targeting in Switzerland"
- "Ben Bernanke and the Federal Reserve Adoption of Inflation Targeting"
- "The Appointment of Paul Volcker, Anti-Inflation Hawk"

The Role of Expectations in Macroeconomic Policy 21

Preview

When a supply shock sent oil prices surging higher during the 1970s, the inflation rate jumped to double-digit percentages. Yet three decades later, in 2008, a similar supply shock that sent the price of a barrel of crude oil surging to $140 led to a far more moderate increase in inflation. What made these episodes so different?

One crucial difference was public expectations about the effectiveness of monetary policy. In the 1970s, the Federal Reserve lacked credibility as an inflation fighter. In the 2000s, the central bank had earned that credibility, which helped keep inflation expectations much better grounded.

In this chapter, we look at how public expectations of the economy are formed and how they affect the economy. Over the last thirty years, the role of public expectations has moved to the front and center of thinking about how the economy works. We will first consider the theory of *rational expectations*, the most widely used theory to describe the formation of business and consumer expectations. After describing its roots in microeconomic theory, we will explore how this theoretical breakthrough has shaped current policy-making models and debates.

Rational Expectations and Policy Making

Before we outline the theory of *rational expectations*, we describe an earlier theory, the theory of *adaptive expectations*. Its shortcomings opened the door to a more robust theory more solidly grounded on microeconomic principles.

Adaptive Expectations

In the 1950s and 1960s, economists took the rather simplistic view that the public would form expectations from past experience only. If inflation had been rising at 5% a year for many years, they reasoned, the public would expect prices to keep rising by 5%. As times changed, the theory went, the public would adapt its expectations by taking an average of past events. For example, if inflation rose to a steady rate of 10%, expectations of future inflation would rise slowly toward 10%. In the first year, expected inflation might rise to only 6%; in the second year, to 7%; and so on. This view of expectation formation, called *adaptive expectations* (introduced in Chapter 11),

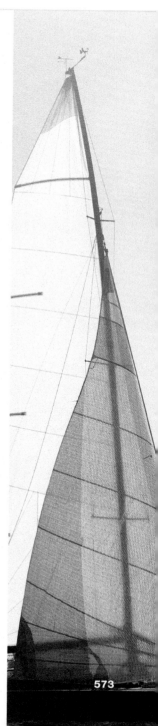

suggests that changes in expectations will occur slowly over time as past data accumulate.[1]

The theory of adaptive expectations, although intuitive, does not build on solid microeconomic foundations. It assumes that expectations are formed mechanically by averaging the past, and that people will ignore any new information about the future. This is unrealistic. Public expectations of inflation, for example, will almost surely be influenced by predictions of *future* monetary policy as well as by current and past monetary policy. In addition, people often change their expectations quickly in light of new information and so will not rely solely on past data to form their expectations.

Rational Expectations

To address these objections to adaptive expectations, John Muth, then of Carnegie-Mellon University, developed an alternative theory of expectations based on optimizing behavior, called **rational expectations,** which can be stated as follows:[2] *expectations will be identical to optimal forecasts (the best guess of the future) using all available information.*

To illustrate what we mean, consider the driving commute of Sammy the Student. In good weather, Sammy makes the trip between home and school in twenty minutes, on average. Depending on traffic, the trip can take as little as fifteen minutes or as much as twenty-five minutes. In a rainstorm, however, Sammy's best guess for his commute time—his **optimal forecast**—is twenty-five minutes. Based on the rational expectations theory, if Sammy's best guess for the future, given all he knows about the weather (and any other relevant information), is for a twenty-five-minute commute, then he should expect the commute to take twenty-five minutes.

If Sammy had adaptive expectations, and there was sunny weather three days in a row, looking at the past might lead him to expect another beautiful day, and he would expect it to take twenty minutes to get to school. However, if he listened to the weather report, which said it would be raining today, then the optimal forecast of his drive time would be twenty-five minutes, not twenty. His rational expectation of his driving time should be twenty-five minutes, while an adaptive expectation would give him the poor forecast of a driving time of twenty minutes.

Of course, even if Sammy has rational expectations, his expectation of the driving time is bound to be imperfect. On one rainy day, the commute might take thirty minutes because of a random car accident, and on another it might take twenty minutes. But is the expectation of twenty-five minutes irrational? No. In both cases, the forecast is off by five minutes. However, the forecast does not have to be perfectly accurate to be rational—it need only be the best possible given the available information. That is, it has to be correct *on average*, and the twenty-five-minute expectation meets this requirement. As there is bound to be some randomness to events, an optimal forecast will never be completely accurate.

The example makes the following important point about rational expectations: *even though a rational expectation equals the optimal forecast using all available information, a prediction based on it will not always be perfectly accurate.*

---

[1]More formally, adaptive expectations—say, of inflation—are written as a weighted average of past inflation rates:

$$\pi_t^e = (1 - \lambda) \sum_{j=1}^{\infty} \lambda^j \, \pi_{t-j}$$

where

π_t^e = adaptive expectation of inflation at time t

π_{t-j} = inflation at time $t - j$

λ = a constant between 0 and 1

[2]John Muth, "Rational Expectations and the Theory of Price Movements," *Econometrica* 29 (1961): 315–335.

Microeconomic Rationale Behind the Theory

Put simply, people match their expectations to their best possible guess of the future because it is costly for them not to do so. Sammy the Student has a strong incentive to be accurate in his expectations of the time it takes to drive to class. If his prediction underestimates his driving time, he may arrive late to class and be reprimanded, which may lower his grade. If his prediction overestimates his driving time, he will end up, on average, wasting time before class and will have given up leisure time unnecessarily. Accurate expectations are desirable, and there are strong incentives for making them equal to optimal forecasts by using all available information.

The same principle applies to businesses. Suppose that a car maker such as Ford knows that interest-rate movements affect the sales of cars. If Ford makes poor forecasts of interest rates, it will produce either too many cars or too few and thus earn less profit. Ford has strong incentives to acquire and apply all available information when forecasting interest rates.

Although it is desirable for households and businesses to have rational expectations, there is some controversy over whether households and businesses are completely rational in their expectations. After all, gathering and processing information to obtain optimal forecasts takes time and energy, which households and businesses may not have. Hence, although macroeconomic analysis assumes rational expectations, there is active research on alternative ways of describing how expectations are formed.[3]

Rational Expectations Theory and Macroeconomic Analysis

There are several important implications of the rational expectations theory for macroeconomic analysis.

1. ***Expectations that are rational use all available information, which includes any information about government policies, such as changes in monetary or fiscal policy.*** If households and businesses have information that government policy is likely to change in the future, their expectations will take this information into account. For example, if consumers think that a personal tax cut is imminent, they may start to spend more today, even before the tax cut is enacted.

2. ***Only new information causes expectations to change.*** If a piece of information is already anticipated, then when it is announced, it will have no effect on rational expectations. This anticipated information has already been incorporated into the expectations. Only announcements of unanticipated information cause expectations to change. If a personal tax cut had already been anticipated, then news of its implementation will have no effect on expectations. However, if new information emerges to suggest that an even larger tax cut is likely, expectations of disposable income will rise.

3. ***If there is a change in the way a variable moves, the way in which expectations of this variable are formed will change as well.*** To illustrate, suppose the Fed's policy interest rate, the federal funds rate, is set at an abnormally low level. How would we expect rates to move in the future?

[3]For a discussion of the evidence for and against rational expectations in financial markets, see the appendix to Chapter 7 on the Companion Website to Frederic S. Mishkin, *The Economics of Money, Banking, and Financial Markets*, 10th edition (Boston: Pearson Addison-Wesley, 2013), http://wps.aw.com/aw_mishkin_econmbfm_9/.

If the Fed's stated policy is to always restore its policy interest rate to "normal" levels, then an optimal forecast would assume that rates will eventually rise. Thus, a rational expectation would be for rates to rise in the future. But what if the Fed changes its stated policy, so that when the policy rate is low, it stays low? In this case, the optimal forecast of the future policy rate, and hence the rational expectation, is that rates will stay low. The change in the way the interest rate variable moves has therefore led to a change in the way that expectations of future policy rates are formed. We can generalize the rational expectations analysis here to expectations of any variable.

Rational Expectations Revolution

During the 1970s, the widespread adoption of the rational expectations theory into macroeconomic models reshaped how macroeconomists think. What is now called the **rational expectations revolution** was led by economists such as Robert Lucas of the University of Chicago; Thomas Sargent, formerly of the University of Minnesota and now at New York University; Robert Barro of Harvard University; and Bennet McCallum of Carnegie-Mellon University. We will look at how the rational expectations revolution affected macroeconomic thinking in the rest of this chapter.

Lucas Critique of Policy Evaluation

Economists have long used **macroeconometric models** to forecast economic activity and to evaluate the potential effects of policy options. In essence, the models are collections of equations that describe statistical relationships among many economic variables. Economists can feed data into such models, which then churn out a forecast or prediction.

In his famous paper "Econometric Policy Evaluation: A Critique," Robert Lucas spurred the rational expectations revolution by presenting a devastating argument against the value of the macroeconometric models used at the time for evaluating policy.[4]

Econometric Policy Evaluation

To understand Lucas's argument, we must first understand how econometric policy evaluation is done. Say, for example, that the Federal Reserve wants to evaluate the potential effects of changes in the federal funds rate from the existing level of, say, 5%. Using conventional methods, the Fed economists would feed different fed funds rate options—say, 4% and 6%—into a computer version of the model. The model would then predict how unemployment and inflation would change under the different scenarios. Then, the policy makers would select the policy with the most desirable outcomes.

Relying on rational expectations theory, Lucas identified faulty reasoning in the econometric approach if the model did not incorporate rational expectations, as was true for the macroeconometric models used by policy makers at the time. Lucas theorized that when policies change, public expectations will shift as well. For example, if the Fed raises the federal funds rate to 6%, this action might change the way the public forms expectations about where interest rates will be set in the future. Those changing expectations, as we've seen, can have a real effect on economic behavior and outcomes. Yet econometric models that do not incorporate rational expectations ignore any effects of changing expectations, and thus are unreliable tools for evaluating policy options.

[4]*Carnegie-Rochester Conference Series on Public Policy* 1 (1976): 19–46.

Application

The Consumption Function

Let's now apply Lucas's argument to a concrete example involving one influential macro-econometric model: the consumption function. As a review from Chapter 18, the permanent income hypothesis indicates that consumption is related to permanent income, which is a weighted average of future expected disposable income.

Suppose that disposable income has never before deviated far from its trend rate of growth. That is, if income has grown much faster or slower than normal in a particular year, it has always tended to return to normal growth rates in subsequent years. Rational expectations theory, then, suggests that any deviation from a trend will be only temporary, and an upward shock will have only a minimal effect on permanent income and hence on consumption. Looking only at past data, economists using the consumption function would predict only a weak effect on consumption from upward shocks to disposable income.

Now suppose that policy makers want to evaluate the effects of a permanent personal income tax cut. The consumption function estimated on past data will indicate that the tax cut and the resulting rise in disposable income will have only a small effect on consumption. But if policy makers make clear that the tax cut is permanent, rational expectations theory indicates that households will no longer expect the resulting rise in disposable income to be temporary. Instead, when the income tax cut goes into effect, they will expect disposable income to rise permanently, and will have a large spending response instead of the small one predicted by the estimated consumption function. Evaluating the likely outcome of the change in tax policy using a macroeconometric model based only on past statistical relationships between variables could thus be highly misleading.

The consumption function application demonstrates how the effects of a particular policy depend critically on the public's expectations about the policy. If the public expects the tax cut to be merely temporary, the spending response will be small. If, however, the public expects the tax cut to be permanent, the response of spending will be far greater. ***The Lucas critique points out not only that policy evaluation with conventional econometric models may be misleading, but also that the public's expectations about a policy will influence the public's response to that policy and the policy's ultimate outcomes.***

Policy Conduct: Rules or Discretion?

The Lucas critique exposed the need for new policy models that would reflect the insights of rational expectations theory. Here, we explore the implications of the critique on a long-running debate among economists: whether monetary policy makers should have the flexibility to adapt their policy to a changing situation, or whether they should adopt **rules,** binding plans that specify how policy will respond (or not respond) to particular data, such as data on unemployment and inflation.

Discretion and the Time-Inconsistency Problem

Policy makers operate with **discretion** when they make no commitment to future actions, but instead make what they believe in that moment to be the right policy decision for the situation. Empowering policy makers to shape policy "on the fly" introduces complexities. The *time-inconsistency problem*, first outlined in research by Nobel Prize winners Finn Kydland (University of California, Santa Barbara) and Edward Prescott (Arizona State University), and also by Guillermo Calvo of Columbia University, reveals the potential limitations of discretionary policy.[5] The **time-inconsistency problem** is the tendency to deviate from good long-run plans when making short-run decisions, and it is something we deal with continually in everyday life. We often have a plan that we know will produce a good outcome in the long run, but when tomorrow comes, we just can't help ourselves and we renege on our plan because doing so has short-run gains. For example, we make a New Year's resolution to go on a diet, but soon thereafter we can't resist having one more bite of that Snickers bar— and then another bite, and then another bite—and soon the weight begins to pile back on. In other words, we find ourselves unable to consistently follow a good plan over time; the good plan is said to be time-inconsistent and will soon be abandoned.

Policy makers are always tempted to pursue a policy that is more expansionary than firms or people expect, because such a policy will boost economic output and lower unemployment in the short run. The best policy, however, is *not* to pursue expansionary policy, because decisions about wages and prices reflect workers' and firms' expectations about policy (an implication of the rational expectations revolution). When workers and firms see a central bank, for example, pursuing discretionary expansionary policy, they will recognize that this action is likely to lead to higher inflation in the future. They will therefore raise their expectations about inflation, driving wages and prices up. The rise in wages and prices will lead to higher inflation, but may not result in higher output or lower unemployment on average.

A policy will have better inflation performance in the long run if it does not try to surprise people with an unexpectedly expansionary policy, but instead keeps inflation under control. However, even if a policy maker recognizes that discretionary policy will lead to a poor outcome (high inflation with little gain in output), he or she still may not be able to pursue the better policy of inflation control because politicians are likely to apply pressure on a policy maker to try to boost output in the short run with overly expansionary monetary policy.

How do we deal with the time-inconsistency problem? Good answers come from how-to books on parenting. Parents understand that they can spoil a child by always giving in to the child's demands. Nevertheless, when a child throws a tantrum, especially in public, many parents give the child whatever he or she wants, just to keep the child quiet. Because parents don't stick to their "do-not-give-in" plan, the child comes to expect that bad behavior will be rewarded, and throws tantrums over and over again. Parenting books suggest a solution to the time-inconsistency problem (although they don't call it that): set behavior rules for children, and then stick to them.

Types of Rules

In contrast to discretion, rules are essentially automatic. One famous type of rule, advocated by monetarists such as Milton Friedman, is the **constant-money-growth-rate rule,** in which the money supply is kept growing at a constant rate regardless of the state of the economy. Other monetarists, such as Bennett McCallum and Alan Meltzer, have

---

[5]Finn Kydland and Edward Prescott, "Rules Rather Than Discretion: The Inconsistency of Optimal Plans," *Journal of Political Economy* 85 (1977): 473–491; and Guillermo Calvo, "On the Time Consistency of Optimal Policy in the Monetary Economy," *Econometrica* 46 (November 1978): 1411–1428. The classic application to monetary policy is found in Robert J. Barro and David Gordon, "A Positive Theory of Monetary Policy in a Natural Rate Model," *Journal of Political Economy* 91 (August 1983): 589–610.

proposed variants of this rule that allow the rate of money supply growth to be adjusted for shifts in velocity, which has often been found to be unstable in the short run. Rules of this type are nonactivist because they do not react to economic activity. Monetarists advocate rules of this type because they believe that money is the sole source of fluctuations in aggregate demand, and because they believe that long and variable lags in the effects of monetary policy will lead to greater volatility in economic activity and inflation if policy actively responds to unemployment (as discussed in Chapter 13).

Activist rules, in contrast, specify that monetary policy should react to the level of output as well as to inflation. The most famous rule of this type is the *Taylor rule* that we discussed in Chapter 13. It specifies that the Fed should set its federal funds rate target by a formula that considers both the output gap $(Y - Y^P)$ and the inflation gap $(\pi - \pi^T)$.

The Case for Rules

As our discussion of the time-inconsistency problem suggests, discretionary monetary policy can lead to poor economic outcomes. If monetary policy makers operate with discretion, they will be tempted to pursue overly expansionary monetary policies that boost employment in the short run but generate higher inflation (and no higher employment) in the long run. A commitment to a policy rule like the Taylor rule or the constant-money-growth-rate rule solves the time-inconsistency problem because policy makers have to follow a set plan that does not allow them to exercise discretion and try to exploit the short-run trade-off between inflation and employment. By binding their hands with a policy rule, policy makers can achieve desirable long-run outcomes.

Another argument for rules is that policy makers and politicians cannot be trusted. Milton Friedman and Anna Schwartz's monumental work, *A Monetary History of the United States*,[6] documents numerous instances in which the Federal Reserve made serious policy errors, with the worst occurring during the Great Depression, when the Fed just stood by and let the banking system and the economy collapse (Chapters 5 and 15 discuss the Fed's actions during the Great Depression). Politicians are also not to be trusted because they have strong incentives to pursue policies that help them win the next election. They are therefore more likely to focus on increasing employment in the short run, without worrying that their actions might lead to higher inflation further down the road. Their advocacy for expansionary policies can then lead to the so-called **political business cycle,** discussed in the following Policy and Practice case, in which fiscal and monetary policy are expansionary right before elections, with higher inflation following.

Policy and Practice

The Political Business Cycle and Richard Nixon

You might know that Richard Nixon and his aides took some extraordinary actions to ensure a landslide victory in the 1972 presidential election, such as breaking into the offices of political rivals at the Watergate Hotel. Less well known are similar actions on the economic front prior to the election. The Nixon administration imposed wage and price controls on the economy, which temporarily lowered

---

[6]Milton Friedman and Anna Jacobson Schwartz, *A Monetary History of the United States, 1867–1960* (Princeton, NJ: Princeton University Press, 1963).

the inflation rate before the election. After the election, those same moves helped lead to a surge in inflation. Nixon also pursued expansionary fiscal policy by cutting taxes. And it has been rumored that the Chairman of the Federal Reserve, Arthur Burns, succumbed to direct pressure from Nixon to maintain low interest rates through Election Day. The aftermath was ugly. The economy overheated and inflation rose to over 10% by the late 1970s, which was abetted by the negative supply shocks during that period (see Chapter 12).

The Nixon episode led economists and political scientists to theorize that politicians would take steps to make themselves look good during election years. Specifically, the theory went, they would take steps to stimulate the economy before the election, leading to a boom and low unemployment that would increase their electoral chances. Unfortunately, the result of these actions would be higher inflation down the road, which then would require contractionary policies to get inflation under control, with a resulting recession in the future. The ups and downs of the economy would then be the result of politics and so could be characterized as a political business cycle. Although the Nixon episode provided support for the existence of a political business cycle, research has not come to a definitive answer as to whether this phenomenon is a general one.[7]

The Case for Discretion

Although policy rules have important advantages, they do have serious drawbacks. First, rules can be too rigid because they cannot foresee every contingency. For example, almost no one could have predicted that problems in one small part of the financial system, subprime mortgage lending, would lead to the worst financial crisis in over seventy years, with devastating effects on the economy. The unprecedented steps taken by the Federal Reserve during this crisis to prevent the crisis from creating a depression (described in Chapter 15) could not have been written into a policy rule ahead of time. Being able to act flexibly and use discretion can thus be key factors in a successful monetary policy.

The second problem with policy rules is that they do not easily incorporate the use of judgment. Monetary policy is as much an art as a science. Monetary policy makers need to look at a wide range of information in order to decide on the best course of action for monetary policy, and some of this information is not easily quantifiable. Judgment is thus an essential element of good monetary policy, and it is very hard to write it into a rule. Only with discretion can monetary policy bring judgment to bear.

Third, no one really knows what the true model of the economy is, and so any policy rule that is based on a particular model will prove to be wrong if the model is not correct. Discretion avoids the "straightjacket" that would lock in the wrong policy if the model that was used to derive the policy rule proved to be incorrect.

Fourth, even if the model were correct, structural changes in the economy would lead to changes in the coefficients of the model. The Lucas critique, which points out that changes in policies can change the coefficients in macroeconometric models, is just one example. Another is that the relationship of monetary aggregates, like M1 and M2, to aggregate spending broke down in the 1980s as a result of financial innovation. Following a

---

[7]The paper that launched research on the political business cycle was William Nordhaus, "The Political Business Cycle," *Review of Economic Studies* 42 (1975): 169–190.

Policy and Practice

The Demise of Monetary Targeting in Switzerland

In 1975, the Swiss National Bank (Switzerland's central bank) adopted monetary targeting when it announced a growth rate target for the monetary aggregate M1. Beginning in 1980, the Swiss switched their growth rate target to an even narrower monetary aggregate, the monetary base. Although monetary targeting was quite successful in Switzerland for many years, it ran into serious problems with the introduction of a new interbank payment system, the Swiss Interbank Clearing (SIC), and a wide-ranging revision of the commercial banks' liquidity requirements in 1988. These structural changes caused a severe drop in banks' desired holdings of deposits, which were the major component of the monetary base, at the Swiss National Bank. A smaller amount of the monetary base was now needed relative to aggregate spending, altering the relationship between the two, and so the 2% target growth rate for the monetary base was far too expansionary. Inflation subsequently rose to over 5%, well above that of other European countries.

High inflation rates horrified the Swiss, who have always prided themselves on maintaining a low-inflation environment even when the rest of Europe did not. These problems with monetary targeting led the Swiss to abandon it in the 1990s and adopt a much more flexible framework for the conduct of monetary policy.[8]

rule based on a constant growth rate of one of these aggregates would have produced bad outcomes. Indeed, this is what happened in the case of Switzerland in the late 1980s and early 1990s, when adherence to a rule using the growth rate of monetary aggregates led to a surge in inflation (discussed in the Policy and Practice case above). Discretion enables policy makers to change policy settings when an economy undergoes structural changes.

Constrained Discretion

The distinction between rules and discretion has strongly influenced academic debates about monetary policy for many decades. But the distinction may be too stark. As we have seen, both rules and discretion are subject to problems, and so the dichotomy between rules and discretion may be too simple to capture the realities that macroeconomic policy makers face. Discretion is a matter of degree. Discretion can be a relatively undisciplined approach that leads to policies that change with the personal views of policy makers or with the direction of political winds. Or, it might operate within a more clearly articulated framework, in which the general objectives and tactics of the policy makers—although not their specific actions—are committed to in advance. Ben Bernanke, now chairman of the Federal Reserve, along with the author of this textbook, came up with a name for this type of framework: **constrained discretion.**[9] Constrained discretion imposes a conceptual structure and inherent discipline on policy makers, but without eliminating all flexibility. It combines some of the advantages ascribed to rules with those ascribed to discretion.

[8]For a further discussion of monetary targeting in Switzerland, see Chapter 4 of Ben S. Bernanke, Thomas Laubach, Frederic S. Mishkin, and Adam S. Posen, *Inflation Targeting: Lessons from the International Experience* (Princeton, NJ: Princeton University Press, 1999).

[9]See Ben S. Bernanke and Frederic S. Mishkin, "Inflation Targeting: A New Framework for Monetary Policy?" *Journal of Economic Perspectives* 11 (Spring 1997): 97–116.

The Role of Credibility and a Nominal Anchor

An important way to constrain discretion is by committing to a **nominal anchor,** a nominal variable—such as the inflation rate, the money supply, or an exchange rate—that ties down the price level or inflation to achieve price stability. For example, if a central bank has an explicit target for the inflation rate, say 2%, and takes steps to achieve this target, then the inflation target becomes a nominal anchor. Alternatively, a government could commit to a fixed exchange rate between its currency and a sound currency like the dollar, and use this as its nominal anchor. If the commitment to a nominal anchor has **credibility,** that is, is believed by the public, it has important benefits.

Benefits of a Credible Nominal Anchor

First, a credible nominal anchor has elements of a behavior rule. Just as rules help prevent the time-inconsistency problem in parenting by helping adults resist pursuing the discretionary policy of giving in, a nominal anchor can help overcome the time-inconsistency problem by providing an expected constraint on discretionary policy. For example, if monetary policy makers commit to a nominal anchor of achieving a specific inflation objective, say a 2% inflation rate, then they know that they will be subject to public scrutiny and criticism if they miss this objective or pursue policies that are clearly inconsistent with this objective, such as an interest rate target that is too low. In order to avoid embarrassment and possible punishment, they will be less tempted to pursue overly expansionary, discretionary policies in the short run that will be inconsistent with their commitment to the nominal anchor.

Second, a credible commitment to a nominal anchor will help to anchor inflation expectations, which leads to smaller fluctuations in inflation. It thus contributes to price stability and also helps stabilize aggregate output. Credibility of a commitment to a nominal anchor is therefore a critical element in enabling monetary policy to achieve both of its objectives, price stability and stabilizing economic activity. In other words, credibility of a nominal anchor helps make monetary policy more efficient.

We will use the aggregate demand and supply framework to show why a credible nominal anchor helps produce this desirable outcome. First, we will look at the effectiveness of stabilization policy when it is responding to an aggregate demand shock, and then we will examine its effectiveness when it is responding to an aggregate supply shock.

Credibility and Aggregate Demand Shocks

We now examine the importance of credibility in the short run when there are positive and negative demand shocks.

POSITIVE AGGREGATE DEMAND SHOCK. Let's first look at what happens in the short run when there is a positive aggregate demand shock. For example, suppose businesses suddenly get new information that makes them more optimistic about the future, and so they increase their investment spending. As a result of this positive demand shock, the aggregate demand curve shifts to the right from AD_1 to AD_2 in panel (a) of Figure 21.1, moving the economy from point 1 to point 2. Aggregate output rises to Y_2, and inflation rises above the inflation target of π^T to π_2. As we saw in Chapter 13, the appropriate response that will stabilize inflation and economic activity is to tighten monetary policy and shift the short-run aggregate demand curve back down to AD_1 in order to move the economy back to point 1. However, because of the long lags until monetary policy has an effect on aggregate demand, it will take some time before the short-run aggregate demand curve shifts back to AD_1.

FIGURE 21.1

Credibility and Aggregate Demand Shocks

In panel (a), the positive aggregate demand shock shifts the aggregate demand curve to the right from AD_1 to AD_2, moving the economy from point 1 to point 2. If monetary policy is not credible, expected inflation will rise and so the short-run aggregate supply curve will rise and shift to the left to AS_3, sending the economy to point 3, where inflation has risen further to π_3. In panel (b), the negative aggregate demand shock shifts the aggregate demand curve left from AD_1 to AD_2, and the economy moves to point 2. If monetary policy is not credible, inflation expectations might rise and the short-run aggregate supply curve will rise and shift to the left to AS_3, sending the economy to point 3, where aggregate output has fallen even further to Y_3.

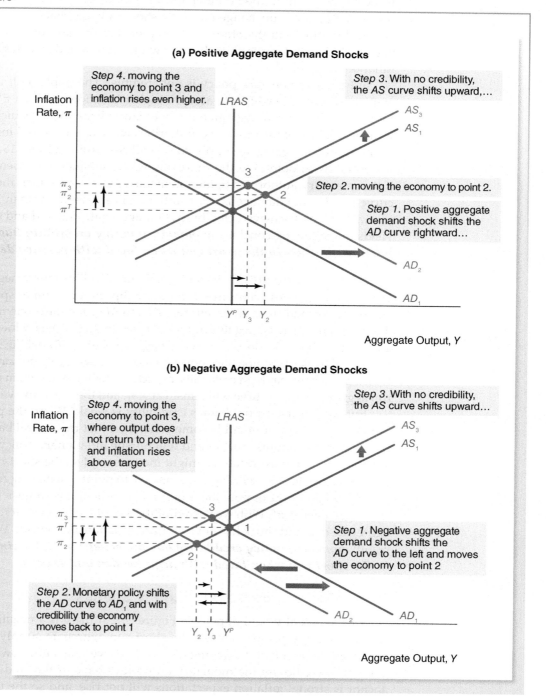

Now let's look at what happens to the short-run aggregate supply curve. Recall from Chapter 11 that the short-run aggregate supply curve is represented as follows:

$$\pi = \pi^e + \gamma(Y - Y^P) + \rho \qquad (1)$$

$$\text{Inflation} = \text{Expected Inflation} + \gamma \times \text{Output Gap} + \text{Price Shock}$$

If the commitment to the nominal anchor is credible, then the public's expected inflation π^e will remain unchanged and the short-run aggregate supply curve will remain at AS_1. Inflation will therefore go no higher than π_2, and over time, as the short-run aggregate demand curve shifts back down to AD_1, inflation will fall back down to the inflation target of π^T.

But what if monetary policy is not credible? The public will worry that the monetary authorities are willing to accept a higher inflation rate than π^T and are not willing to drive the short-run aggregate demand curve back to AD_1 quickly. In this case, the weak credibility of the monetary authorities will cause expected inflation π^e to rise and so the short-run aggregate supply curve will rise, shifting from AS_1 to AS_3 and sending the economy to point 3 in the short run, where inflation has risen further to π_3. Even if the monetary authorities tighten monetary policy and return the aggregate demand curve to AD_1, the damage is done: inflation has risen more than it would have if the central bank had achieved credibility. Our aggregate demand and supply analysis thus yields the following conclusion: ***monetary policy credibility has the benefit of stabilizing inflation in the short run when faced with positive demand shocks.***

NEGATIVE DEMAND SHOCK. Panel (b) of Figure 21.1 illustrates a negative demand shock. For example, suppose consumer confidence dips and consumer spending declines. The aggregate demand curve shifts left from AD_1 to AD_2, and the economy moves to point 2 in the short run, where aggregate output has fallen to Y_2, which is below potential output Y^P, and inflation has fallen to π_2, below the target level of π^T. To stabilize output and inflation, the central bank eases monetary policy to move the aggregate demand curve back to AD_1. If the central bank has high credibility, expected inflation will remain unchanged, the short-run aggregate supply curve will remain at AS_1, and the economy will return to point 1.

But what if the central bank's credibility is weak? When the public sees an easing of monetary policy, it might become concerned that the central bank is losing its commitment to the nominal anchor and will pursue inflationary policy in the future. In this situation, inflation expectations might increase, and so the short-run aggregate supply curve will rise to AS_3, sending the economy to point 3, where aggregate output goes to Y_3, which falls short of potential output Y^P, while inflation goes to π_3 which is above the target level of π^T. With weak credibility, monetary policy that responds to a negative aggregate demand shock has not stabilized inflation and output. We have the following result: ***monetary policy credibility has the benefit of stabilizing economic activity in the short run when faced with negative demand shocks.***

Credibility and Aggregate Supply Shocks

Now let's look at what happens in Figure 21.2 if there is a negative aggregate supply shock. If energy prices increase, the short-run aggregate supply curve shifts up and to the left. How much the aggregate supply curve will shift, however, depends on the amount of credibility the monetary authorities have. If the credibility of the nominal anchor is strong, inflation expectations will not rise, and so the upward and leftward shifts of the short-run aggregate supply curve to AS_2 will be small. When the economy moves to point 2 in the short run, the rise in inflation to π_2 will then be minor, and the fall in output to Y_2 will also be minor. If, on the other hand, the central bank's commitment to the nominal anchor is perceived as weak, then inflation expectations will rise substantially, and the upward and leftward shifts of the short-run aggregate supply curve will be much larger, moving it up to AS_3. Now the economy will move to point 3 in the short run, with worse outcomes on both inflation and output, that is,

MyEconLab Mini-lecture

FIGURE 21.2

Credibility and Aggregate Supply Shocks

If the credibility of monetary policy is high, the negative aggregate supply shock will shift the short-run aggregate supply curve only to AS_2 and the economy will move to point 2, where both the rise in inflation to π_2 and the fall in output to Y_2 will be minor. If credibility is weak, then inflation expectations will rise substantially and the upward shift of the short-run aggregate supply curve will be much larger, moving it up and to the left to AS_3. The economy will move to point 3, with worse outcomes on both inflation and output, that is, with inflation higher at π_3 and output lower at Y_3.

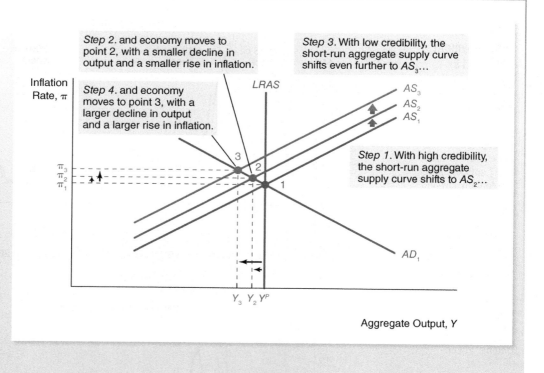

with inflation higher at π_3 and output lower at Y_3. We reach the following conclusion: ***monetary policy credibility has the benefit of producing better outcomes on both inflation and output in the short run when faced with negative supply shocks.***

The benefits of credibility when the economy is hit by negative supply shocks are exactly what we see in the data, as the following application illustrates.

Application

A Tale of Three Oil Price Shocks

In three different years, 1973, 1979, and 2007, the U.S. economy was hit by a major negative supply shock when the price of oil rose sharply. In the first two episodes, inflation rose sharply, whereas in the most recent episode, it rose by much less, as we can see in panel (a) of Figure 21.3. In the case of the first two episodes, monetary policy credibility was extremely weak because the Fed had been unable to keep inflation under control, which had resulted in high inflation. In contrast, when the third oil price shock hit in 2007–2008, inflation had been low and stable for quite a period of time, so the Fed had more credibility regarding its ability to keep inflation under control. Some economists think that credible monetary policy is the reason the most recent oil price shock appears to have had a smaller effect on inflation

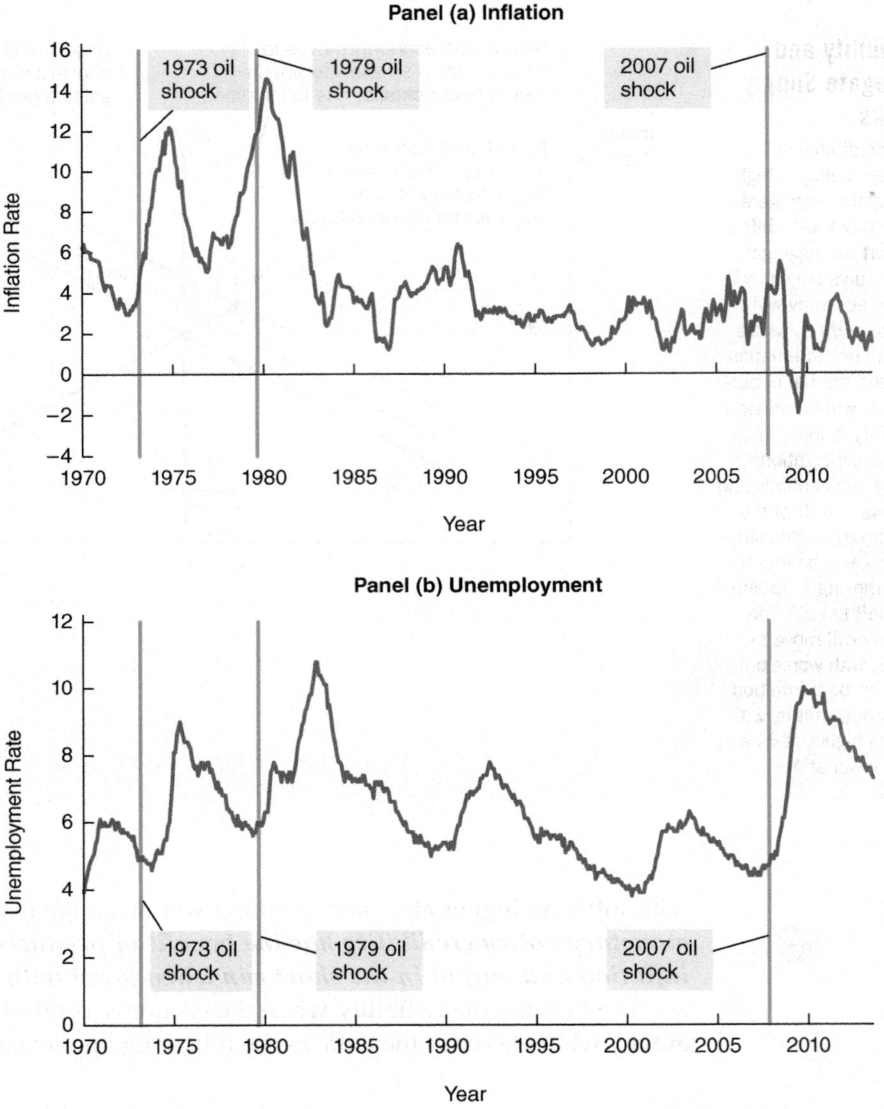

FIGURE 21.3

Inflation and Unemployment, 1970–2013

In the 1973 and 1979 oil shock episodes, inflation was initially high and the Fed's commitment to a nominal anchor was weak, while in the 2007 episode, inflation was initially low and the Fed's credibility was high. The result was that inflation and unemployment rose more in the first two episodes than in the latter episode, with unemployment rising sharply in the third episode only after the 2007–2009 crisis took a disastrous turn in October 2008.

Source: Bureau of Labor Statistics. www.bea.gov

Panel (a) Inflation

Panel (b) Unemployment

than the previous two shocks. Our aggregate demand and supply analysis provides the reasoning behind this view.

In the first two episodes, when the commitment to a nominal anchor and credibility were weak, the oil price shocks would have produced a surge in inflation expectations and a large upward and leftward shift in the short-run aggregate supply curve to AS_3 in Figure 21.2. Thus, the aggregate demand and supply analysis predicts there would be a sharp contraction in economic activity and a sharp rise in inflation. This is exactly what we see in panels (a) and (b) of Figure 21.3. The economic contractions were very severe, with unemployment rising to above 8% in the aftermath of the 1973 and 1979 oil price shocks. In addition, inflation shot up to double-digit levels.

In the 2007–2008 episode, the outcome was quite different. Through greater policy credibility established over many years, inflation expectations remained grounded when the oil price shock occurred. As a result, the short-run aggregate supply curve shifted up and to the left by much less, to only AS_2 in Figure 21.2. The aggregate demand and supply analysis predicts that there would be a much smaller increase in inflation from the negative supply shock, while the contraction in economic activity would also be less. Indeed, this is what transpired until the recent financial crisis entered its virulent phase in the fall of 2008. Inflation rose by much less than in the previous episodes, and the economy held up fairly well until the financial crisis took a disastrous turn in October 2008 (see Chapter 15). Only then did the economy go into a tailspin, but it is clear that this was not the result of the negative supply shock. Inflation actually fell quite dramatically, indicating that a massive negative demand shock was the source of the sharp contraction in economic activity.

Approaches to Establishing Central Bank Credibility

Our analysis has demonstrated that a credible nominal anchor that anchors inflation expectations is a key element in the success of monetary policy. But how is this credibility achieved? One approach is through continued success at keeping inflation under control through concerted policy actions. The preceding application shows that this approach proved successful for the Federal Reserve during the Greenspan and Bernanke years. Inflation targeting has not been the only approach to establishing central bank credibility. Another nominal anchor that some countries have successfully used to keep inflation under control is for a country to peg its exchange rate to an anchor country that already has a strong nominal anchor. We discussed this strategy, sometimes called *exchange rate targeting*, in Chapter 17. Here we explore several other approaches to establishing central bank credibility that have been suggested by economists.

Inflation Targeting

One approach to establishing central bank credibility involves a monetary policy strategy called **inflation targeting,** which involves several elements: (1) public announcement of medium-term numerical targets for inflation; (2) an institutional commitment to price stability as the primary, long-run goal of monetary policy and a commitment to achieving the inflation goal; (3) an information-inclusive approach in which policy makers use many variables (not just monetary aggregates) in making decisions about monetary policy; (4) increased transparency of the monetary policy strategy through communication with the public and the markets about monetary policy makers' plans and objectives; and (5) increased accountability of the central bank for attaining its inflation objectives.

Inflation targeting has been adopted by many countries throughout the world, particularly those that in the past were less successful at stabilizing inflation than the United States. The list of inflation-targeting countries includes New Zealand, Australia, Canada, Norway, Sweden, Switzerland, the United Kingdom, Brazil, Chile, Czech Republic, Hungary, Israel, Mexico, Peru, Philippines, Poland, South Africa, and South Korea, among others. Inflation targeting appears to have been able to strengthen the credibility of a nominal anchor in countries that have adopted it, with the benefits pointed out in the previous section. In these countries, inflation has fallen, inflation expectations appear to be more solidly grounded, and both inflation and aggregate output have been more stable.[10]

One country that was slow to adopt inflation targeting was the United States, but this changed in January of 2012, as the following Policy and Practice case indicates.

Policy and Practice

Ben Bernanke and the Federal Reserve Adoption of Inflation Targeting

Ben Bernanke, a former professor at Princeton University, became the new Federal Reserve chairman in February 2006, after serving as a member of the Board of Governors from 2002–2005 and then as the chairman of the president's Council of Economic Advisors. Bernanke is a world-renowned expert on monetary policy and, while serving as an academic, wrote extensively on inflation targeting, including articles and a book written with the author of this text.[11]

Bernanke's writings indicated that he was a strong proponent of inflation targeting and increased transparency in central banks. In an important speech given at a conference at the Federal Reserve Bank of St. Louis in 2004, he described how the Federal Reserve might move toward inflation targeting by announcing a numerical value for its long-run inflation goal.[12] Bernanke emphasized that announcing a numerical objective for inflation would be completely consistent with the Fed's dual mandate of achieving price stability and maximum employment (Chapter 13). Therefore, it might be called a *mandate-consistent inflation objective*, because the goal for measured inflation would be set above zero to avoid deflations, which have harmful effects on employment, and because measured inflation is likely to be biased upward. In addition, it would not be a short-run target that might lead to control of inflation that is too tight at the expense of overly high employment fluctuations.

After becoming Fed chairman, Bernanke made it clear that any movement toward inflation targeting must result from a consensus within the Federal Reserve and be consistent with the dual mandate given to the Fed by Congress. After Chairman Bernanke set up a subcommittee to discuss Federal Reserve communications, which included discussions about announcing a specific numerical inflation objective, the FOMC made partial steps in the direction of inflation targeting with its new communication strategy, first outlined in November of 2007 (with an amendment

[10]For surveys of the performance of inflation targeting, see Frederic S. Mishkin and Klaus Schmidt-Hebbel, "Does Inflation Targeting Matter?" in *Monetary Policy Under Inflation Targeting*, eds. Frederic S. Mishkin and Klaus Schmidt-Hebbel (Central Bank of Chile: Santiago, 2007), 291–372; and Carl E. Walsh, "Inflation Targeting: What Have We Learned?" *International Finance* 12 (Summer 2009): 195–234.

[11]Ben S. Bernanke and Frederic S. Mishkin, "Inflation Targeting: A New Framework for Monetary Policy," *Journal of Economic Perspectives*, vol. 11, no. 2 (1997); Ben S. Bernanke, Frederic S. Mishkin, and Adam S. Posen, "Inflation Targeting: Fed Policy After Greenspan," *Milken Institute Review* (Fourth Quarter, 1999): 48–56; Ben S. Bernanke, Frederic S. Mishkin, and Adam S. Posen, "What Happens When Greenspan Is Gone?" *Wall Street Journal*, January 5, 2000: p. A22; and Ben S. Bernanke, Thomas Laubach, Frederic S. Mishkin, and Adam S. Posen, *Inflation Targeting: Lessons from the International Experience* (Princeton, NJ: Princeton University Press, 1999).

[12]Ben S. Bernanke, "Inflation Targeting," Federal Reserve Bank of St. Louis, *Review*, vol 86, no. 4 (July/August 2004), pp. 165–168.

in January 2009), that provided FOMC participants' inflation projections for one, two, and three years ahead, as well as for the longer term. The inflation projections for the longer term were produced under an assumption of "appropriate policy" and so reflect each participant's long-run inflation objective. Because the long-run inflation projections of all the FOMC participants ended up being close to 2%, the FOMC finally moved to inflation targeting in January 2012 by agreeing to a single numerical value of the inflation objective, 2% on the PCE deflator. However, the FOMC also made it clear that it would be pursuing a flexible form of inflation targeting consistent with its dual mandate because it would seek not only to achieve its inflation target, but also to promote maximum sustainable employment.

Nominal GDP Targeting

A variant of inflation targeting that recently has received increased attention is **nominal GDP targeting,** in which the central bank announces an objective of hitting a particular level of nominal GDP (real GDP times the price level) that is growing over time. For example, if the inflation objective for the central bank was 2% and potential GDP was expected to grow at an annual rate of 3%, then nominal GDP targeting would imply a commitment to attaining a level of nominal GDP that is growing at 5% per year. Nominal GDP targeting has elements of an inflation targeting regime because the path of nominal GDP targeted reflects the chosen numerical inflation objective. However, in addition, nominal GDP targeting implies that the central bank will respond to slowdowns in the real economy even if inflation is not falling. To see this, note that with inflation unchanged, a slowdown in real GDP will result in a slowdown of nominal GDP, which will mean that the monetary authorities will want to pursue more expansionary policy.

Nominal GDP targeting has the possible advantage that it explicitly focuses on stabilizing real GDP and not only on controlling inflation. Another potential advantage is that either shortfalls of real GDP growth below potential or inflation below the inflation objective will encourage even more expansionary monetary policy, because actual nominal GDP will fall further below its target. Expectations of this more expansionary policy will help stimulate aggregate demand, and this could be particularly useful when the zero-lower-bound problem occurs, as discussed in Chapter 13, in which the monetary authorities are unable to lower the policy interest rate.

Two key disadvantages of nominal GDP targeting are cited by its critics. First, it requires accurate estimates of potential GDP growth, which are not easy to achieve. Second, nominal GDP targeting is more complicated to explain to the public than inflation targeting and thus might create confusion about the objectives of a central bank. At this time, no central bank has adopted nominal GDP targeting, but this could change in the future.

Appoint "Conservative" Central Bankers

Kenneth Rogoff of Harvard University has suggested that another way to establish central bank credibility is for the government to appoint central bankers who have a strong aversion to inflation.[13] He characterizes these central bankers as "conservative," although a better description might be "tough" or "hawkish on inflation."

---

[13]Kenneth Rogoff, "The Optimal Degree of Commitment to an Intermediary Monetary Target," *Quarterly Journal of Economics* (November 1985): 169–189.

When the public sees the appointment of a "conservative" central banker, it will expect that he or she will be less tempted to pursue expansionary monetary policy to exploit the short-run trade-off between inflation and employment, and will do whatever it takes to keep inflation under control. As a result, inflation expectations and realized inflation are likely to be more stable, with the benefits outlined previously.

The problem with this approach to solving credibility problems is that it is not clear that it will continue to work over time. If a central banker has more "conservative" preferences than the public, why won't the public demand that central bankers who are more in tune with their preferences be appointed? After all, in a democratic society, government officials are supposed to represent the will of the people.

Policy and Practice

The Appointment of Paul Volcker, Anti-Inflation Hawk

The quintessential example of the appointment of a "conservative" central banker occurred when President Jimmy Carter appointed Paul Volcker to be the chairman of the Federal Reserve in August 1979. Prior to Volcker's appointment, inflation had been climbing steadily and, by that month, the annual CPI inflation rate had reached 11.8%. Volcker was a well-known inflation hawk who had made it clear to the president that he would take on inflation and wring it out of the system. Shortly after Volcker took the helm of the Fed, in October 1979, the FOMC started raising interest rates dramatically, increasing the federal funds rate by over eight percentage points, to nearly 20% by April 1980. However, with a sharp economic contraction starting in January 1980, Volcker blinked and took his foot off the brake, allowing the federal funds rate to decline to around the 10% level by July, when the economy started to recover. Unfortunately, this monetary medicine had not done the trick and inflation remained very high, with CPI inflation still remaining above 13%. Volcker then showed his anti-inflation, hawkish mettle: the Fed raised the federal funds rate to the 20% level by January 1981 and kept it there until July. Then, in the face of the most severe recession of the post–World War II period up until then, which started in July 1981, the Fed kept the federal funds rate at a level around 15% until July 1982, despite a rise in the unemployment rate to nearly 10%. Finally, only when the inflation rate started to fall in July did the Fed begin to lower the federal funds rate.

Volcker's anti-inflation credentials had now been fully established, and by 1983 inflation had fallen below 4% and remained around that level for the rest of Volcker's tenure at the Fed through 1987. Volcker had reestablished the credibility of the Fed as an inflation fighter, with the result that inflation expectations had now stabilized, ending the period of high inflation in the United States that had become known as the "Great Inflation." Volcker became a monetary policy hero and has been lauded ever since as one of the greatest central bankers of all time.

Increase Central Bank Independence

Another approach to increasing central bank credibility is to give the central bank more independence from the political process. As was discussed earlier, the time-inconsistency problem may arise from politicians who are short-sighted because they focus on pursuing policies that will help them win the next election. A politically insulated central bank is more likely to be concerned with long-run objectives and thus be a defender of price stability.

A counterargument to increasing central bank independence is that it is inconsistent with democratic principles. It is undemocratic to have monetary policy (which affects almost everyone in the economy) controlled by an elite group of monetary policy makers who are responsible to no one. If we push the argument further, assuming that policy is always performed better by elite groups like the Fed, we might end up with such conclusions as "the Joint Chiefs of Staff should determine military budgets" or "the IRS should set tax policies with no oversight from the President or Congress."

Another argument against central bank independence is that an independent central bank has not always used its freedom successfully. For example, the Federal Reserve, which is one of the most independent of all U.S. government agencies, failed miserably in its policies during the Great Depression, and its independence certainly didn't prevent it from pursuing an overly expansionary monetary policy in the 1960s and 1970s that contributed to rapid inflation during this period.

Nonetheless, advocates of an independent central bank believe that macroeconomic performance will be improved by making the central bank more independent. Research by Alberto Alesina and Lawrence Summers, both of Harvard University, seems to support this conjecture:[14] when ranking central banks from 1 (least independent) to 4 (most independent), they found inflation performance to be the best in countries with the most independent central banks. As you can see in Figure 21.4, Germany

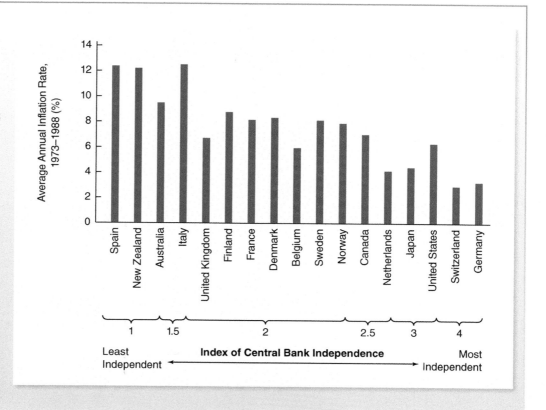

FIGURE 21.4

Central Bank Independence and Inflation Performance in Seventeen Countries

On the horizontal axis, the seventeen central banks are rated from least independent, 1, to most independent, 4. During the period 1973–1988, more independent central banks generally produced lower inflation than less independent central banks.

Source: Alberto Alesina and Lawrence H. Summers, "Central Bank Independence and Macroeconomic Performance: Some Comparative Evidence," *Journal of Money, Credit and Banking*, Vol. 25, No. 2 (May 1993), p. 154, Table 1.

[14]Alberto Alesina and Lawrence H. Summers, "Central Bank Independence and Macroeconomic Performance: Some Comparative Evidence," *Journal of Money, Credit and Banking* 25 (1993): 151–162.

and Switzerland, which had the two most independent central banks, were also the countries with the lowest inflation rates in the 1973–1988 period. By contrast, the countries with the highest inflation rates in those years—Spain, New Zealand, Australia, and Italy—were also the countries with the least independent central banks. (In recent years, there has been a trend toward much greater independence of central banks, so all of the banks that were considered to be least independent have since moved toward the more independent characterization.) Although a more independent central bank appears to lead to a lower inflation rate, this is not achieved at the expense of poor real economic performance. Countries with more independent central banks are no more likely to have high unemployment or greater output fluctuations than countries with less independent central banks.

SUMMARY

1. The theory of rational expectations states that expectations will be identical to optimal forecasts (the best guess of the future) using all available information. There are several important implications of rational expectations for macroeconomic analysis: 1) expectations that are rational use all available information, which includes any information about government policies, such as changes in monetary or fiscal policy; 2) only new information causes expectations to change; and 3) if there is a change in the way a variable moves, the way in which expectations of this variable are formed will change as well.

2. The simple principle (derived from rational expectations theory) that expectation formation changes when the behavior of forecasted variables changes led to the famous Lucas critique of econometric policy evaluation. Lucas argued that when policy changes, expectations formation changes; hence the relationships in an econometric model will change. An econometric model that has been formed on the basis of past data will no longer be the correct model for evaluating the effects of this policy change, and may prove to be highly misleading. The Lucas critique also points out that the effects of a particular policy depend critically on the public's expectations about the policy.

3. Policy makers are tempted to renege on a policy aimed at pursuing long-run objectives because there may be short-run gains from expansionary policy that produces bad long-run outcomes, a problem that has become known as the time-inconsistency problem. Advocates of rules to conduct monetary policy believe that rules solve the time-inconsistency problem because policy makers have to follow a set plan that enables them to stick to the plan and achieve desirable long-run outcomes. Advocates of discretion believe that rules are way too rigid because they cannot foresee every contingency and do not allow for the use of judgment. Constrained discretion imposes a conceptual structure and its inherent discipline on policy makers, but it does so without eliminating all flexibility, so that it combines some of the advantages ascribed to rules with some of those ascribed to discretion.

4. An important way of constraining discretion is to commit to a credible nominal anchor, a nominal variable such as the inflation rate, the money supply, or an exchange rate, which ties down the price level or inflation to achieve price stability. A credible nominal anchor helps solve the time-inconsistency problem and anchor inflation expectations. Credibility of a nominal anchor has the benefit of stabilizing both output and inflation fluctuations.

5. A popular approach to establishing a strong nominal anchor is inflation targeting, in which there is a commitment by policy makers to achieve medium-term numerical objectives for inflation. Countries that have adopted inflation targeting have achieved lower inflation, inflation expectations that are more solidly grounded, and more stable aggregate output and inflation. Other approaches to establishing central bank credibility include nominal GDP targeting, or appointing a "conservative" central banker (like Paul Volcker) who is hawkish on controlling inflation. Alternatively, more independence for the central bank can enable it to resist political influence and focus more on defending price stability.

KEY TERMS

constant-money-growth-rate rule, p. 578

constrained discretion, p. 581

credibility, p. 582

discretion, p. 577

inflation targeting, p. 587

macroeconometric models, p. 576

nominal anchor, p. 582

nominal GDP targeting, p. 589

optimal forecast, p. 574

political business cycle, p. 579

rational expectations, p. 574

rational expectations revolution, p. 576

rules, p. 577

time-inconsistency problem, p. 578

REVIEW QUESTIONS

All Questions are available in MyEconLab for practice or instructor assignment.

Rational Expectations and Policy Making

1. How does the theory of rational expectations differ from that of adaptive expectations?

Lucas Critique of Policy Evaluation

2. What is the significance of the Lucas critique of econometric policy evaluation?

Policy Conduct: Rules or Discretion?

3. What is the time-inconsistency problem, and what role does it play in the debate between advocates of discretion and advocates of rules in policy making?

4. What are the arguments for and against rules?

The Role of Credibility and a Nominal Anchor

5. What benefits does a credible nominal anchor provide?

6. How does a credible nominal anchor help improve the economic outcomes that result from a positive aggregate demand shock? How does it help if a negative aggregate supply shock occurs?

Approaches to Establishing Central Bank Credibility

7. What are the purposes of inflation targeting, and how does this monetary policy strategy achieve them?

8. What has been the general experience of countries that have adopted inflation targeting?

9. What are the arguments for and against central bank independence?

PROBLEMS

All Problems are available in MyEconLab for practice or instructor assignment.

Rational Expectations and Policy Making

1. Suppose that during the last ten years, Nicole tried to forecast future inflation rates to negotiate her salary. Every year, she used all available information and even incorporated news about the conduct of monetary policy. However, her forecasts were sometimes above and sometimes below the actual inflation rate. Was Nicole forming rational expectations?

2. Consider two individuals forming expectations about mortgage rates. Mark forms adaptive expectations, and looks only at past mortgage rates to form expectations about future rates. Gloria forms rational expectations. Suppose an individual who is well known for caring a lot more about unemployment than about inflation is appointed as chairperson of the Fed, and that mortgage rates have been constant during the last five years. How would expectations about future mortgage rates change for Mark and Gloria?

Lucas Critique of Policy Evaluation

3. Suppose an econometric model based on past data predicts a small decrease in domestic investment when the Federal Reserve increases the federal funds rate. Assume that the Federal Reserve is considering an increase in the federal funds rate target to fight inflation and promote a low-inflation economic environment that promotes investment and economic growth.

   a) Discuss the implications of the econometric model's predictions if individuals interpret the increase in the federal funds rate target as a sign that the Fed will keep inflation at low levels in the long run.

   b) What would be Lucas's critique of this model?

Policy Conduct: Rules or Discretion?

4. What are the benefits and costs of sticking to a set of rules in each of the following cases? How do each of these situations relate to the conduct of economic policy?

   a) Going on a diet

   b) Raising children

5. In some countries, the president chooses the head of the central bank. The same president can fire the head of the central bank and replace him or her with another director at any time. Explain the implications of such a situation for the conduct of monetary policy. Do you think the central bank will follow a monetary policy rule, or engage in discretionary monetary policy?

The Role of Credibility and a Nominal Anchor

6. Central banks that engage in inflation targeting usually announce the inflation target and the time period for which that target will be relevant. In addition, central bank officials are held accountable for their actions (e.g., they could be fired if the target is not reached), which are public information. Explain why transparency is such a fundamental ingredient of inflation targeting.

7. As part of its response to the global financial crisis, the Fed lowered the federal funds rate target to nearly zero by December 2008, a considerable easing of monetary policy. However, survey-based measures of five-to-ten-year inflation expectations remained low until February 2010. Comment on the Fed's credibility to fight inflation.

Approaches to Establishing Central Bank Credibility

8. Suppose the statistical office of a country does a poor job of measuring inflation and reports an annualized inflation rate of 4% for a few months, while the true increase in the price level has been around 2.5%. What will happen to the central bank's credibility if it is engaged in inflation targeting and its target is 2%, plus or minus 0.5%?

9. Immediately after the central bank of New Zealand adopted inflation targeting in 1989, economic growth was low and unemployment increased for some time (until 1992), but later, economic growth resumed and unemployment decreased. Comment on the relationship between inflation targeting and economic growth.

10. Comment on the impact on the Fed's credibility of the appointment of a majority of governors who are reluctant to increase interest rates to fight inflation for fears of causing too much unemployment in the short run.

DATA ANALYSIS PROBLEMS

The Problems update with real-time data in MyEconLab *and are available for practice or instructor assignment.*

1. Go to the St. Louis Federal Reserve FRED database, and find data on the personal consumption expenditure price index (PCECTPI). Download the data, then calculate a series for inflation. For each quarter, take the percentage change in the price index from the previous quarter. Multiply by 100 to represent the change in percentage form, and multiply by 4 to "annualize" the quarterly inflation figure. Now, create a new series representing adaptive inflation expectations. For each quarter, calculate inflation expectations as the simple average of the previous four quarters of inflation.

   a) How does expected inflation under the adaptive approach compare to actual inflation for the most recent quarter of data available?

   b) For each quarter, calculate the error, that is, the difference between actual inflation and expected inflation. Then, calculate and report the average of the error over the most recent 2-year period, and over the most recent 5-year period.

   c) If forecasters use rational expectations to form an "optimal" forecast, the implication is that forecasters will not make systematic errors. Thus, on average, the forecast errors should be close to zero. Comment on how your answers to part (b) would compare to a rational expectations forecast.

2. Go to the St. Louis Federal Reserve FRED database, and find data on the personal consumption expenditure price index (PCECTPI). Convert the *Units* setting to

"Percent Change from Year Ago" and download the data. Beginning in January 2012, the Fed formally announced a 2% inflation goal over the "longer term."

   a) Calculate the average inflation rate over the last four and the last eight quarters of data available. How does the rate compare to the 2% inflation goal?

   b) What, if anything, does your answer to part (a) imply about Federal Reserve credibility?

3. Go to the St. Louis Federal Reserve FRED database, and find data on the GDP deflator (GDPDEF) and the price of a barrel of oil (OILPRICE). For the GDP deflator, convert the *Units* setting to "Percent Change from Year Ago" and download the data.

   a) Calculate the average percent change in the price of oil over the most recent 5 years of data available. To do this, calculate the percentage change from beginning to end, and divide this number by 5. What is the change in the inflation rate over the same time period?

   b) Calculate the average percent change in the price of oil from January 1976 to January 1981. To do this, calculate the percentage change from beginning to end, and divide this number by 5. What is the change in the inflation rate over the same time period?

   c) Based on your answers to parts (a) and (b), what can you conclude about the credibility of current monetary policy compared to its credibility in the earlier period?

Modern Business Cycle Theory

22

Preview

After World War II, economists equipped with Keynesian models drew up the blueprints for new economic policies to reduce the severity of business cycle fluctuations without sparking inflation. But when they finally had the chance to implement these policies in the 1960s and 1970s, the results were unsatisfactory. As we saw in Chapter 13, not only did unemployment levels increase, but inflation actually accelerated to rates above 10%.

In the aftermath of these policy failures, economists set about building new models of the economy that, unlike the Keynesian model, incorporated the principles of microeconomics—that is, that individuals will act optimally based upon all available information. Two competing business cycle theories emerged: the *real business cycle model*, a classical model in which prices and wages are assumed to be flexible, and the *new Keynesian model*, which is Keynesian in that it assumes that wages and prices are sticky, but also assumes that expectations are rational.[1]

In this chapter, we examine these two theories and compare them with earlier Keynesian models. Both approaches provide very different answers to key questions of policy and practice in macroeconomics. Can the Federal Reserve boost economic activity by lowering interest rates? Do lower taxes always amount to expansionary policy? How can monetary and fiscal policy reduce fluctuations in output and unemployment? What are the costs to economic activity and employment of anti-inflation policies?

Real Business Cycle Model

The **real business cycle model,** originally developed by Nobel Prize winners Edward Prescott and Finn Kydland, begins with the assumption that all wages and prices are completely flexible. It argues that shocks to productivity or the willingness of workers to work, known as **real shocks,** cause fluctuations in potential output and long-run

---

[1]A precursor to the real business cycle and new Keynesian models is the *new classical model* in which expectations are rational and all wages and prices are completely flexible with respect to *expected* changes in the price level and expectations. The new classical model, which was developed in the early to mid-1970s by Nobel Prize winners Robert Lucas of the University of Chicago and Thomas Sargent, formerly of the University of Minnesota but now at New York University, among others, is discussed in a Web appendix to this chapter found at the Companion Website, www.pearsonhighered.com/mishkin.

aggregate supply.[2] With individual wages and prices completely flexible, the short-run and long-run aggregate supply curves are one and the same. Thus, in the aggregate demand and supply analysis of the real business cycle in Figure 22.1, there is only one aggregate supply curve, LRAS.

Productivity Shocks and Business Cycle Fluctuations

The complete wage and price flexibility of the real business cycle framework implies that aggregate output always equals potential output. Also, in such a model, business cycle fluctuations stem entirely from fluctuations in potential output. The key equation in real business cycle models is the aggregate production function introduced in Chapter 3:

$$Y^P = F(K, L) = AK_t^{0.3}L_t^{0.7} \tag{1}$$

where

$$A = \text{total factor productivity}$$
$$K = \text{capital stock}$$
$$L = \text{labor}$$
$$Y^P = \text{potential output}$$

MyEconLab Mini-lecture

FIGURE 22.1

The Real Business Cycle Model

In the real business cycle model, the short-run aggregate supply curve is always the same as the long-run aggregate supply curve; consequently, there is only one type of aggregate supply curve, LRAS, in the figure. Positive productivity shocks cause the long-run aggregate supply curve to shift to the right from $LRAS_1$ to $LRAS_2$, so that the economy moves to point 2, where aggregate output rises from Y_1^P to Y_2^P, while the inflation rate falls from π_1 to π_2. Negative supply shocks cause productivity to fall and the long-run aggregate supply curve to shift to the left from $LRAS_1$ to $LRAS_3$, and the economy then moves from point 1 to point 3, where aggregate output falls to Y_3^P and inflation rises to π_3.

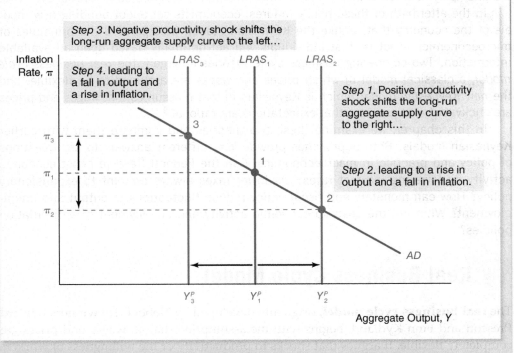

Step 3. Negative productivity shock shifts the long-run aggregate supply curve to the left...

Step 4. leading to a fall in output and a rise in inflation.

Step 1. Positive productivity shock shifts the long-run aggregate supply curve to the right...

Step 2. leading to a rise in output and a fall in inflation.

[2]Finn E. Kydland and Edward C. Prescott, "Time to Build and Aggregate Fluctuations," *Econometrica* 51 (November 1982): 1345–1370. For more detailed surveys of real business cycle research, see Charles Plosser, "Understanding Real Business Cycles," *Journal of Economic Perspectives* (Summer 1989): 51–78, and Sergio Rebelo, "Resuscitating Real Business Cycles," in *Handbook of Macroeconomics*, eds. J. Taylor and M. Woodford (Elsevier, 1999).

Real business cycle theorists see shocks to productivity, A, as the primary source of shocks to potential output and long-run aggregate supply. Positive productivity shocks, such as new inventions or government policies that make the economy more efficient, will increase A and cause the long-run aggregate supply curve to shift to the right from $LRAS_1$ to $LRAS_2$. Referring to Figure 22.1, if the aggregate demand curve does not shift, then the economy moves from point 1 to point 2, and aggregate output rises from Y_1^P to Y_2^P, while the inflation rate falls from π_1 to π_2.

A negative supply shock, such as permanent increases in the price of energy or strict government environmental regulations that cause production to fall, will reduce productivity A. The long-run aggregate supply curve shifts to the left from $LRAS_1$ to $LRAS_3$. Again referring to Figure 22.1, the economy then moves from point 1 to point 3, where aggregate output falls to Y_3^P and inflation rises to π_3.[3]

Solow Residuals and Business Cycle Fluctuations

How plausible is the view of real business cycle theorists that productivity shocks are the primary source of business cycle fluctuations? One way to assess the validity of the real business cycle model is to calculate estimates of productivity from the production function in Equation 1. Since, in the real business cycle model, aggregate output Y always equals potential output Y^P, we can solve Equation 1 for an estimate of A, $\hat{A}$:

$$\hat{A} = \frac{Y_t}{K_t^{0.3} L_t^{0.7}}$$

These estimates of productivity have become known as **Solow residuals,** and are named after Nobel Prize winner Robert Solow, who used this measure in his original research on the theory of economic growth we discussed in Chapter 6.

There is a close correspondence between the growth rate of the Solow residual and output growth. As shown in Figure 22.2, when recessions occur (the shaded portions of the graph), the growth rate of Solow residuals falls sharply. Real business cycle theorists take this co-movement of aggregate output and Solow residuals as strong confirmation that productivity shocks are the primary source of business fluctuations, as their theory predicts.

Employment and Unemployment in the Real Business Cycle Model

The real business cycle model explains fluctuations in employment and unemployment with the concept of **intertemporal substitution,** the willingness to shift work effort over time as real wages and real interest rates change. To illustrate the role of intertemporal substitution, let's say that you're a student deciding on a plan for summer vacation. You want to spend one of the next two summers traveling around the country to see all the national parks, but you need to work during the other summer to pay for your car. If you work this summer, you will earn a real wage of W_1. If you can earn a real interest rate of r, this translates into a real wage of $(1 + r)W_1$ next summer. To decide how much you should work, you would compare $(1 + r)W_1$ to the real wage of W_2 that you would earn next summer. When either your current wage W_1 is higher or the real

[3]Real business cycle models can also generate business cycle fluctuations from shifts in labor supply that might arise from, for example, changes in taxes that either encourage or discourage people from working more.

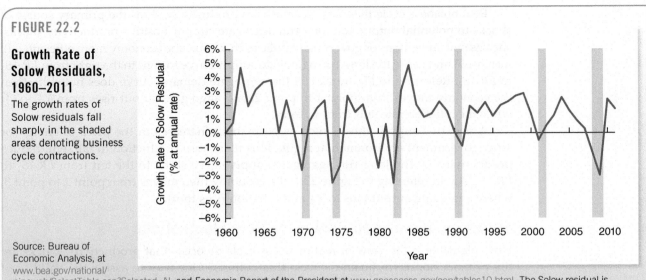

FIGURE 22.2

Growth Rate of Solow Residuals, 1960–2011

The growth rates of Solow residuals fall sharply in the shaded areas denoting business cycle contractions.

Source: Bureau of Economic Analysis, at www.bea.gov/national/ nipaweb/SelectTable.asp?Selected=N, and Economic Report of the President at www.gpoaccess.gov/eop/tables10.html. The Solow residual is computed using the same procedure used to produce Figure 6.13 in Chapter 6.

interest rate r is higher, you have a greater incentive to substitute work for leisure this summer; that is, you would choose to work this summer rather than next summer.

Now let's consider what happens when productivity rises and the economy moves to point 2 in Figure 22.1, where aggregate output has risen to Y_2^P. Because productivity is higher, workers are likely to get paid a higher real wage today, and intertemporal substitution tells us that they will be willing to work more.[4] The result is that employment will rise and unemployment will fall when output is rising. Similarly, when there is a negative productivity shock and the economy moves to point 3, where output is lower at Y_3^P, real wages will fall today, employment will fall, and unemployment will rise. Note that in both of these cases, the unemployment rate is changing with the natural rate of unemployment, so the economy remains at full employment and the unemployment gap is zero.

In the real business cycle model, unemployment is voluntary. It arises out of choices workers make to maximize their well-being. This does not mean that recessions are not costly to workers. Indeed they are, because workers' income has certainly fallen. In this model, workers will voluntarily work less because real wages have fallen.

Objections to the Real Business Cycle Model

There are several important criticisms of real business cycle analysis.

SOLOW RESIDUALS AND PRODUCTIVITY SHOCKS. Critics of real business cycle analysis dispute the evidence from Solow residuals. When the economy slows down and business dries up, the critics say, firms don't simply shutter every idle factory and lay off every unneeded worker. Instead, they tend to hoard capital and labor in preparation for the eventual return of business activity. With **labor hoarding,** workers sit idly by for a chunk of their workday, but are still counted in the government surveys as

---

[4]The effect of the productivity shock on real interest rates is ambiguous and so, depending on the model, the intertemporal substitution effect described here may be attenuated.

"employed." And idle capital is still on the books. As a result, the number of machines and workers in the economy that are actually producing output is overstated, and output per worker and per dollar of capital declines. Even though the idle workers and machines are just as productive as when there is work to do, hoarding of labor and capital gives the appearance of a negative productivity shock when none exists.

NEGATIVE PRODUCTIVITY SHOCKS. Critics of real business cycles also question whether productivity can ever be negative. Developments such as the Internet can cause a positive shock. But since technology typically advances over time, it can be hard to imagine why technology would regress. Proponents of real business cycle models point to examples of negative shocks, such as bad government policies that lower output or financial crises that temporarily decrease the efficiency of capital markets.

PROCYCLICAL INFLATION AND EMPLOYMENT. As we saw in Figure 22.1, the real business cycle model suggests that, with the aggregate demand curve unchanged, increases in aggregate output are associated with declines in inflation, while declines in output are associated with increases in inflation. As discussed in Chapter 8, we do not see this effect in the data. Inflation tends to rise during business cycle booms and fall during recessions. Procyclical inflation is the opposite of what the real business cycle model suggests. Proponents of the real business cycle model challenge the assertion that inflation is procyclical. Edward Prescott and Finn Kydland argue that procyclicality is not a feature of the post–World War II period. For example, inflation surged during the recessions that followed oil price shocks in the mid- and late 1970s.[5] (Their view, however, is not accepted by critics of real business cycle analysis.)

MARKET-CLEARING ASSUMPTION. Many economists are also skeptical of the market-clearing assumption in the real business cycle model. They interpret the empirical evidence as showing that wages and prices are far from flexible. In addition, they find the view of real business cycle analysis that unemployment is voluntary to be highly implausible. Try asking some unemployed workers if they are choosing to work less. You're likely to get some understandably unpleasant responses.

New Keynesian Model

As economists came to accept the proposition that theories about the business cycle should be grounded in solid microfoundations, they began to adopt the view that rational expectations provide a good benchmark for how expectations are formed. In addition, many economists found the analytic techniques of the real business cycle model to be attractive. However, a large number of economists remained unwilling to accept the classical view that wages and prices are fully flexible and that aggregate demand shocks play no role in the business cycle. This reasoning has led to a blending of much of the analysis of the rational expectations and real business cycle theorists, with models that build in wage and price stickiness derived from well-founded microeconomic reasoning. Keynesian economists offered the **new Keynesian model,** which is based on microeconomic foundations similar to those in real business cycle models, but embeds stickiness

---

[5]Finn Kydland and Edward C. Prescott, "Business Cycles: Real Facts and a Monetary Myth," *Quarterly Review,* Federal Reserve Bank of Minneapolis (Spring 1990): 3–18.

into the analysis. Such models are also referred to as **dynamic, stochastic, general equilibrium (DSGE) models** because they allow the economy to grow over time (*dynamic*), be subject to shocks (*stochastic*), and are based on *general equilibrium* principles.[6]

Building Blocks of the New Keynesian Model

There are three building blocks in the new Keynesian model: aggregate production, a new Keynesian short-run aggregate supply (Phillips) curve, and a new Keynesian aggregate demand (*IS*) curve.

AGGREGATE PRODUCTION. Just as in the real business cycle framework, a basic building block of the new Keynesian model is the aggregate production function we saw in Equation 1:

$$Y^P = F(K, L) = AK_t^{0.3}L_t^{0.7}$$

The new Keynesian model sees shocks to productivity, A, as an important source of fluctuations in potential output and hence in aggregate supply. Hence, just as in the real business cycle model, the long-run aggregate supply curve fluctuates. For example, if technological innovation causes A to rise, the long-run supply curve would shift from $LRAS_1$ to $LRAS_3$ in Figure 22.3. Although this feature of the new Keynesian model has much in common with the real business cycle model, it differs from the real business

MyEconLab Mini-lecture

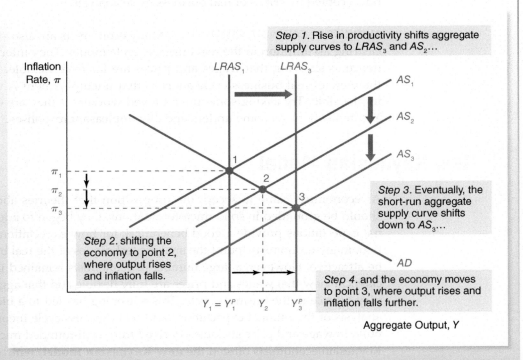

FIGURE 22.3

The New Keynesian Model

The new Keynesian model has short-run aggregate supply curves that are upward sloping, as AS_1, AS_2, and AS_3 indicate. If productivity rises, the long-run aggregate supply curve will shift to the right from $LRAS_1$ to $LRAS_3$. Because initially aggregate output at point 1 is now below potential output ($Y_1 < Y_3^P$), the short-run aggregate supply curve shifts down from AS_1 to AS_2 and the economy moves to point 2 at the intersection of AS_2 and AD, where aggregate output rises to Y_2 and inflation falls to π_2. At point 2, output remains below potential output, so eventually the short-run aggregate supply curve shifts down to AS_3 and the economy moves to point 3 at the intersection of $LRAS_3$ and AD.

Step 1. Rise in productivity shifts aggregate supply curves to $LRAS_3$ and AS_2...

Step 2. shifting the economy to point 2, where output rises and inflation falls.

Step 3. Eventually, the short-run aggregate supply curve shifts down to AS_3...

Step 4. and the economy moves to point 3, where output rises and inflation falls further.

[6]To be completely accurate, real business cycle models are also DSGE models, but of a much narrower form than new Keynesian models.

cycle model in that it allows for a short-run aggregate supply curve that is different from the long-run aggregate supply curve.

NEW KEYNESIAN SHORT-RUN AGGREGATE SUPPLY (PHILLIPS) CURVE. In contrast to the real business cycle model, the new Keynesian model views prices as being sticky, that is, they adjust infrequently. New Keynesians point to the concept of *staggered prices*, discussed in Chapter 8, in which firms fix their prices for a period of time and do not change them at the same time as other firms. Staggered prices imply that a firm sets its prices to reflect current and future demand for its products because it recognizes that other firms may change their prices in the future. When all firms operate in this way, we obtain a short-run aggregate supply curve that resembles the Phillips curve analysis we discussed in Chapter 11, with subtle changes. Instead of inflation depending on expected inflation today, the output gap and price shocks (which new Keynesians refer to as *markup shocks*), inflation depends on expected inflation *tomorrow*, the output gap and markup shocks, that is,

$$\pi_t = \beta E_t \pi_{t+1} + \gamma (Y_t - Y_t^P) + \rho_t \tag{2}$$

where

$$\begin{aligned} \beta &= \text{a parameter that indicates how expectations of future inflation} \\ &\quad \text{affect current inflation} \\ E_t \pi_{t+1} &= \text{the inflation rate next period, } t + 1, \text{ that is expected today at time } t \\ (Y_t - Y_t^P) &= \text{the output gap} \\ \gamma &= \text{a parameter describing the sensitivity of inflation to the output gap} \\ \rho_t &= \text{the price (markup) shock term}[7] \end{aligned}$$

Note that we have introduced time subscripts in describing the short-run aggregate supply curve in the preceding equation, which was not done in Chapter 11. We do this because timing becomes very important in understanding how the new Keynesian model differs from the aggregate demand and supply model we outlined in Chapter 12.

Through some algebraic manipulation, we can write the new Keynesian short-run aggregate supply (Phillips) curve in Equation 2 equivalently as:[8]

$$\pi_t = \sum_{j=0}^{\infty} \beta^j \left[\gamma(Y_{t+j} - Y_{t+j}^P) + \rho_{t+j} \right] \tag{3}$$

---

[7]Equation 2 is derived to describe deviations from a situation in which inflation is fixed at a given rate. In this interpretation, β can be thought of as a discount rate, that is, the rate at which future outcomes are discounted into the present, and so β is less than 1. Note that Equation 2 cannot be used to argue that there is a permanent trade-off between inflation and output as a result of the coefficient on expected inflation differing from 1, because it is only describing deviations around a stable inflation rate.

[8]To see how this equation is derived, first we advance Equation 2 by one period,

$$\pi_{t+1} = \beta E_{t+1} \pi_{t+2} + \gamma(Y_{t+1} - Y_{t+1}^P) + \rho_{t+1}$$

and then take expectations of both sides to yield the following:

$$E_t \pi_{t+1} = \beta E_t \pi_{t+2} + E_t \gamma (Y_{t+1} - Y_{t+1}^P) + E_t \rho_{t+1}$$

Now, substituting this expression for $E_t \pi_{t+1}$ into Equation 2, we get

$$\pi_t = \gamma (Y_t - Y_t^P) + \rho_t + \beta E_t \left[\gamma(Y_{t+1} - Y_{t+1}^P) + \rho_{t+1} \right] + \beta^2 E_t \pi_{t+2}$$

Continuing to solve this equation forward, we obtain the following equation:

$$\pi_t = \gamma (Y_t - Y_t^P) + \rho_t + \beta E_t \left[\gamma(Y_{t+1} - Y_{t+1}^P) + \rho_{t+1} \right] + \beta^2 E_t \left[\gamma(Y_{t+2} - Y_{t+2}^P) + \rho_{t+2} \right]$$
$$+ \beta^3 E_t \left[\gamma(Y_{t+3} - Y_{t+3}^P) + \rho_{t+3} \right] + \beta^4 E_t \left[\gamma(Y_{t+4} - Y_{t+4}^P) + \rho_{t+4} \right] + \dots$$

which, when written with a summation sign, is the same as Equation 3 in the text.

The new Keynesian short-run aggregate supply (Phillips) curve thus incorporates the effects of staggered prices: firms will set prices reflecting both current and future economic conditions as represented by expected future output gaps and markup shocks.

As you can see in Equation 2, the new Keynesian Phillips curve analysis implies that the short-run aggregate supply curve is upward sloping and is specific to a particular level of tomorrow's expected inflation rate. Notice in Figure 22.3 that inflation today and expected inflation tomorrow are initially at π_1. The short-run aggregate supply curve for this level of expected inflation, AS_1, passes through point 1 because $Y = Y^P$. Equation 2 then shows that actual inflation will be equal to π_1 and is not expected to change, so that expected inflation tomorrow will also be π_1. If Y rises above Y^P, then actual inflation will be higher than π_1, and so the short-run aggregate supply curve is upward sloping.

NEW KEYNESIAN *IS* CURVE AND THE AGGREGATE DEMAND CURVE. We observed from studying the microfoundations of consumer and firm behavior in Chapters 18 and 19 that consumers and firms are forward-looking. Forward-looking behavior suggests that consumption expenditure and investment spending depend on both current and future output. After all, if you are expecting good times in the future, you will be willing to buy more goods and services today. Similarly, if firms also expect good times, they know that the demand for their products will increase and therefore they will invest more today so that they can produce more goods to sell tomorrow.

The *IS* curve we derived in Chapter 9 lacks this dynamic feature but can be modified to incorporate expectations of future output and the real interest rate today. This reasoning leads to the following new Keynesian *IS* curve:

$$Y_t = \beta E_t Y_{t+1} - \delta r_t + d_t \tag{4}$$

where β is the parameter that indicates how much current output changes when future expectations of output change, δ describes how sensitive output is to the real interest rate, and d_t is a demand shock stemming from autonomous shifts in consumption expenditure, investment spending, net exports, or fiscal policy of the type we discussed in Chapter 9.

As with Equation 2, we can do some algebra and rewrite Equation 4 as follows:[9]

$$Y_t = \sum_{j=0}^{\infty} \beta^j (-\delta_{t+j} r_{t+j} + d_{t+j}) \tag{5}$$

[9]The β parameter can again be thought of as a discount rate and is the same β used in Equations 2 and 3. To see how Equation 5 is derived, first we advance Equation 4 by one period:
$$Y_{t+1} = \beta Y_{t+2} - \delta r_{t+1} + d_{t+1}$$
Advancing by one period and then taking expectations of both sides yields
$$E_t Y_{t+1} = \beta E_t Y_{t+2} + E_t[-\delta r_{t+1} + d_{t+1}]$$
Now substituting this expression for $E_t Y_{t+1}$ into Equation 4 we get,
$$Y_t = -\delta r_t + d_t + \beta E_t[-\delta r_{t+1} + d_{t+1}] + \beta^2 E_t Y_{t+2}$$
Doing this over and over again, we can rewrite Equation 4 as
$$Y_t = -\delta r_t + d_t + \beta E_t[-\delta r_{t+1} + d_{t+1}] + \beta^2 E_t[-\delta r_{t+2} + d_{t+12}]$$
$$+\beta^3 E_t[-\delta r_{t+3} + d_{t+3}] + \beta^4 E_t[-\delta r_{t+4} + d_{t+4}] + \beta^5 E_t[-\delta r_{t+5} + d_{t+5}] + \dots$$
which, when written with a summation sign, is the same as Equation 5 in the text.

This dynamic *IS* curve, in combination with the *MP* curve, implies that aggregate output depends not only on today's monetary policy (represented by the current real interest rate r_t) and today's demand shock (d_t), as it did in Chapter 9, but also on expectations of future monetary policy and demand shocks, that is, future real interest rates, r_{t+1}, r_{t+2}, etc., and future demand shocks, d_{t+1}, d_{t+2}, etc.

The *IS* curve in Equation 4 becomes the downward-sloping aggregate demand curve we see in Figure 22.3. With higher inflation rates, the monetary authorities raise real interest rates because they are following the Taylor principle, and the higher real interest rates then cause investment spending, consumption expenditure, and net exports to decline and equilibrium output to fall, as the aggregate demand curve AD_1 shows. Note, however, that the aggregate demand curve depends on expectations about the future output.

Business Cycle Fluctuations in the New Keynesian Model

We now look at what happens in the short run to output and inflation in the new Keynesian model when there are shocks to either aggregate supply or aggregate demand.

EFFECTS OF SHOCKS TO AGGREGATE SUPPLY. Just as in the real business cycle model, shocks to long-run aggregate supply can be an important source of business cycle fluctuations. Referring to Figure 22.3, suppose the economy is initially at point 1, with aggregate output at Y_1 and inflation at π_1. If there is a surge in productivity growth, say because new robotic technology makes the manufacturing sector more efficient, then the long-run aggregate supply curve will shift to the right from $LRAS_1$ to $LRAS_3$. Because initially aggregate output at point 1 is now below potential output and there is slack in the economy ($Y_1 < Y_3^P$), the short-run aggregate supply curve shifts down and to the right from AS_1 to AS_2 and the economy moves to point 2, where aggregate output rises to Y_2 and inflation falls to π_2.[10]

Because at point 2 there continues to be slack in the economy ($Y_2 < Y_3^P$), the short-run aggregate supply curve keeps on shifting downward until the economy settles at point 3, at the intersection of the new long-run aggregate supply curve, $LRAS_3$, and the aggregate demand curve AD. This long-run equilibrium point, at which output has risen and inflation has fallen even further, is the same one that was reached in the short run in the real business cycle model.

EFFECTS OF SHOCKS TO AGGREGATE DEMAND. Now let's consider what happens if consumer confidence suddenly rises and therefore consumers start to spend more. The positive demand shock shifts the aggregate demand curve to the right from AD_1 to AD_2 in Figure 22.4. If this shock is unanticipated, then expectations about future output and inflation remain unchanged, and so the short-run aggregate supply curve remains unchanged at AS_1. The economy would then move from point 1 to point 2, where aggregate output rises to Y_2 and inflation rises to π_2.

But what if the aggregate demand shock is anticipated? Now firms will expect inflation next period to be higher, and so the short-run aggregate supply curve will shift up. However, because prices are sticky, expected inflation next period will not rise to π_4, even though eventually the economy will move to point 4, which is the long-run equilibrium

---

[10]Note that if the productivity shock were anticipated, then the short-run aggregate supply curve would shift down even more, while the aggregate demand curve would shift to the right because future aggregate output would be higher. The result would be even higher output.

MyEconLab Mini-lecture

FIGURE 22.4

Shocks to Aggregate Demand in the New Keynesian Model

A positive demand shock from expansionary policy shifts the aggregate demand curve to the right from AD_1 to AD_2, but if the policy is unanticipated, the short-run aggregate supply curve remains at AS_1. The economy then moves from point 1 to point 2, where aggregate output rises to Y_2 and inflation rises to π_2. If the policy is anticipated, the short-run aggregate supply curve will shift up to AS_3 (but

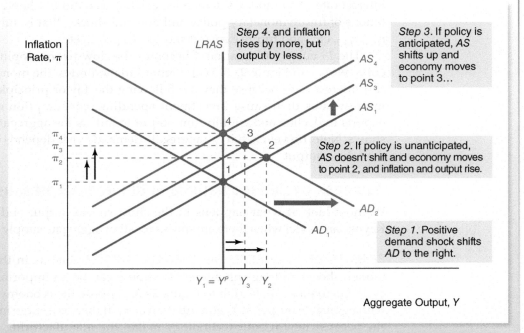

not all the way up to AS_4, which is where the short-run aggregate supply curve would shift if prices were completely flexible rather than sticky) and the economy moves to point 3, at which aggregate output rises to Y_3 (which is less than Y_2) and inflation rises to π_3 (which is higher than π_2).

at the intersection of the aggregate demand curve and the long-run aggregate supply curve. The slower adjustment of prices means that even though expectations are rational in the new Keynesian model, the short-run aggregate supply curve will not shift all the way up to AS_4, as it would if wages and prices were completely flexible. Instead, it will shift up to AS_3. Equilibrium is then reached at point 3, the point at which aggregate output still rises to Y_3, with inflation rising to π_3. We can see in Figure 22.4 that Y_2 is greater than Y_3, implying that the output response to unanticipated aggregate demand shocks is greater than the response to anticipated shocks. It is greater because the short-run aggregate supply curve does not shift when the aggregate demand shock is unanticipated, causing inflation to be lower and output to be higher. ***The new Keynesian model distinguishes between the effects of anticipated versus unanticipated aggregate demand shocks, with unanticipated shocks having a greater effect on output.***

Objections to the New Keynesian Model

One objection to the new Keynesian model is that prices may not be all that sticky. For example, empirical evidence finds that businesses change prices very frequently. It is not clear that the assumption of the slow adjustment of prices, a central element of the new Keynesian Phillips curve, is warranted. Other research, however, points out that even if prices are changed frequently, they may still adjust slowly to *aggregate* demand shocks. Businesses may find aggregate shocks less important than shocks to demand for the specific products they sell. Thus they may not find it worthwhile to pay attention to aggregate demand shocks in terms of their pricing decisions (and thus may have *rational inattention* along the lines described in Chapter 8). In this situation, there will be price stickiness with regard to aggregate demand shocks, and the new Keynesian model will remain valid.

The new Keynesian model is subject to some controversy, but it has become the dominant model in policy discussions in recent years.

A Comparison of Business Cycle Models

To provide a clear picture of the impact of the two new approaches to business cycle models discussed in this chapter, we compare them to the standard model of aggregate demand and supply outlined in Chapter 12, which we will call the **traditional Keynesian model.** We then compare each model's viewpoint as to how policy makers should respond to shortfalls in output as well as shape policies for reducing inflation.

How Do the Models Differ?

In the traditional Keynesian model, expectations are *not* rational but instead are adaptive and backward-looking. In addition, the traditional model is Keynesian because the Phillips curve, which is the basis of the short-run aggregate supply curve, assumes that prices do not immediately adjust and so are sticky. On the other hand, the real business cycle and new Keynesian models both assume that expectations are rational.

We can view the real business cycle model as a special case of the new Keynesian model in which prices become more and more flexible. As price flexibility increases, inflation responds more quickly to output gaps in the new Keynesian Phillips curve—in other words, the γ-coefficient in Equation 2 rises—and the short-run aggregate supply curve gets steeper, as we can see in Figure 22.5. Indeed, as γ rises more and more, the short-run aggregate supply curve keeps pivoting until it becomes the same as the long-run aggregate supply curve. Hence, as prices become more flexible in the new Keynesian model, it gets closer and closer to the real business cycle model.

The new Keynesian model also shares with the real business cycle model the view that long-run supply shocks can shape the business cycle. However, the new Keynesian model also suggests that demand shocks can be important too. The two models differ only in degree: the model you prefer depends on the extent to which you think business cycle fluctuations are due to supply shocks rather than demand shocks.

As a study aid, we outline the differences between business cycle models in Summary Table 22.1.

SUMMARY TABLE 22.1	**A COMPARISON OF THREE BUSINESS CYCLE MODELS**		
Model	**Expectations**	**Price Flexibility**	**Are Long-Run Supply Shocks a Source of Business Cycle Fluctuations?**
Real Business Cycle Model	Rational	Complete	Yes, they are the only source of business cycle fluctuations
New Keynesian Model	Rational	Sticky	Yes, but demand shocks are important too
Traditional Keynesian Model	Adaptive	Sticky	No

MyEconLab Mini-lecture

FIGURE 22.5

Comparison of New Keynesian and Real Business Cycle Models

As prices become more and more flexible, inflation responds more quickly to output gaps in the new Keynesian Phillips curve, the γ-coefficient rises, and the short-run aggregate supply curve gets steeper and steeper, pivoting from AS_1 to AS_2 to AS_3. With complete flexibility, the short-run aggregate supply curve becomes vertical and is the same as the long-run aggregate supply curve $LRAS$ in the real business cycle model.

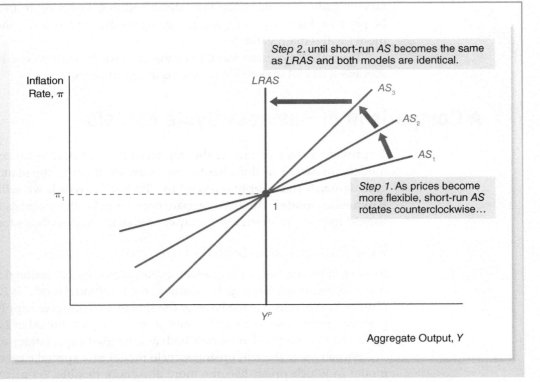

Short-Run Output and Price Responses: Implications for Stabilization Policy

To better understand the three models, we will first compare what each says about the short-run effects of expansionary policy on output and inflation, and the effects of policies to stabilize output, employment, and unemployment fluctuations. Then we will look at their implications for policies directed at reducing inflation. As a study aid, we summarize the different responses of output and inflation in the short run, and the resulting policy implications of the three models, in Summary Table 22.2.

The three panels of Figure 22.6 compare the responses of aggregate output and inflation to expansionary policy. The economy begins at point 1, the intersection of the aggregate demand curve AD_1 and the long-run aggregate supply curve $LRAS$, with aggregate output at $Y_1 = Y^P$. Now suppose that expansionary policy, such as an autonomous easing of monetary policy or an increase in government spending, shifts the aggregate demand curve to the right from AD_1 to AD_2.

REAL BUSINESS CYCLE MODEL. In the real business cycle depicted in panel (a), prices are completely flexible, so the short-run aggregate supply curve is identical to the long-run aggregate supply curve, $LRAS$. Expansionary policy therefore moves the economy to point 2, the intersection of the aggregate demand curve AD_2 with $LRAS$. Inflation immediately rises to π_2, while aggregate output remains unchanged at $Y_1 = Y^P$. **Hence, in the real business cycle model, expansionary policy only leads to inflation, but does not raise output.**

RESPONSE TO POLICY IN THE THREE BUSINESS CYCLE MODELS

Model	Response to Unanticipated Expansionary Policy	Response to Anticipated Expansionary Policy	Can Discretionary Policy Be Beneficial?	Response to Unanticipated Anti-Inflation Policy	Response to Anticipated Anti-Inflation Policy	Is Credibility Important to Successful Anti-Inflation Policy?
Real Business Cycle Model	Y unchanged, $\pi\uparrow$	Y unchanged, $\pi\uparrow$	No	Y unchanged, $\pi\downarrow$	Y unchanged, $\pi\downarrow$	No
Traditional Keynesian Model	$Y\uparrow$, $\pi\uparrow$	$Y\uparrow$, $\pi\uparrow$ by same amount as when policy is unanticipated	Yes	$Y\downarrow$, $\pi\downarrow$	$Y\downarrow$, $\pi\downarrow$ by same amount as when policy is unanticipated	No
New Keynesian Model	$Y\uparrow$, $\pi\uparrow$	$Y\uparrow$ by less than when policy is unanticipated, $\pi\uparrow$ by more than when policy is unanticipated	Yes, but designing a beneficial policy is difficult	$Y\downarrow$, $\pi\downarrow$	$Y\downarrow$ by less than when policy is unanticipated, $\pi\downarrow$ by more than when policy is unanticipated	Yes

MyEconLab Mini-lecture

FIGURE 22.6

Comparison of the Short-Run Responses to Expansionary Policy in the Three Models

Initially the economy is at point 1, as shown for all three models in panels (a) through (c). The expansionary policy shifts the aggregate demand curve from AD_1 to AD_2. In the real business cycle model in panel (a), the economy moves immediately to point 2 at the intersection of AD_2 and $LRAS$. In the traditional Keynesian model in panel (b), the expansionary policy moves the economy to point 1', whether the policy is anticipated or not. In the new Keynesian model in panel (c), the expansionary policy moves the economy to point 1' if it is unanticipated and to point 2' if it is anticipated.

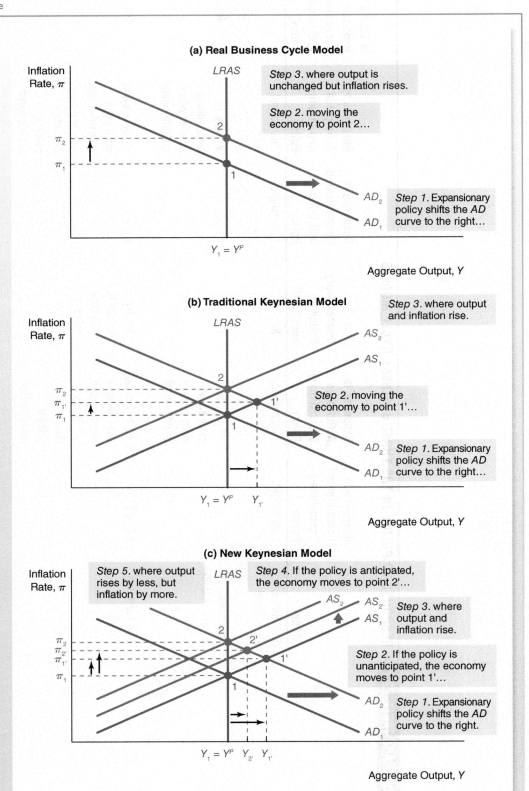

(a) Real Business Cycle Model

Inflation Rate, π

Step 3. where output is unchanged but inflation rises.

Step 2. moving the economy to point 2…

Step 1. Expansionary policy shifts the AD curve to the right…

$Y_1 = Y^P$

Aggregate Output, Y

(b) Traditional Keynesian Model

Step 3. where output and inflation rise.

Inflation Rate, π

Step 2. moving the economy to point 1'…

Step 1. Expansionary policy shifts the AD curve to the right…

$Y_1 = Y^P$ $Y_{1'}$

Aggregate Output, Y

(c) New Keynesian Model

Step 5. where output rises by less, but inflation by more.

Step 4. If the policy is anticipated, the economy moves to point 2'…

Inflation Rate, π

Step 3. where output and inflation rise.

Step 2. If the policy is unanticipated, the economy moves to point 1'…

Step 1. Expansionary policy shifts the AD curve to the right.

$Y_1 = Y^P$ $Y_{2'}$ $Y_{1'}$

Aggregate Output, Y

Policies to shift the aggregate demand curve therefore cannot affect aggregate output, which is determined by real shocks that cause potential output and the long-run aggregate supply curve to shift. In this view, traditional monetary and fiscal policies are powerless to stabilize output, employment, or unemployment fluctuations.[11]

What, then, is the role of macroeconomic policy makers? The real business cycle world is one in which the classical dichotomy we discussed in Chapter 5 holds exactly. Monetary policy has no effect on the real side of the economy and can be directed only at controlling inflation. As we found in Chapter 5, monetary policy makers will focus solely on controlling the money supply so that inflation remains low and stable.

TRADITIONAL KEYNESIAN MODEL. Adaptive expectations and sticky prices in the traditional Keynesian model imply that anticipated policy has no effect on expectations and hence on aggregate supply. In the traditional Keynesian model in panel (b), the short-run aggregate supply curve therefore remains at AS_1 whether the expansionary policy is anticipated or not. The economy still moves in panel (b) to point 1' at the intersection of AD_2 with $AS_{1'}$ whether the expansionary policy is anticipated or not, with output rising to $Y_{1'}$ and inflation rising to $\pi_{1'}$. *The traditional Keynesian model does not distinguish between the effects of anticipated and unanticipated policy: both have the same effect on output and inflation.*

NEW KEYNESIAN MODEL. In the new Keynesian model in panel (c), when expansionary policy is unanticipated, the short-run aggregate supply curve stays at AS_1 and the economy moves to point 1' at the intersection of AD_2 with AS_1, with output rising to $Y_{1'}$ and inflation rising to $\pi_{1'}$. Unlike the traditional Keynesian model, however, the new model recognizes that anticipated policy affects the short-run aggregate supply curve, just as the anticipated aggregate demand shock analyzed earlier does. The AS curve does not shift all the way to AS_2: price stickiness does not allow inflation to adjust fully to the anticipated policy in the short run. Instead, when expansionary policy is anticipated, the short-run aggregate supply curve shifts only to $AS_{2'}$, and the economy moves to point 2', where output increases to $Y_{2'}$ and inflation increases to $\pi_{2'}$. Notice that the $Y_{2'}$ level of output is lower than the $Y_{1'}$ level reached when the expansionary policy is unanticipated. The new Keynesian model distinguishes between the effects of anticipated and unanticipated policies. *In the new Keynesian model, anticipated policy has a smaller effect on output than unanticipated policy. On the other hand, in the new Keynesian model, anticipated policy has a larger effect on inflation than unanticipated policy.*

Unlike the real business cycle model, the new Keynesian model does not rule out beneficial effects from policy makers' attempts to stabilize economic activity. However, a policy maker who subscribes to the new Keynesian model has some big hurdles to overcome. First, the policy maker must consider public expectations. A new policy's outcomes hinge on whether the plans are anticipated or unanticipated. Second, the policy maker must consider how his or her actions will affect expectations about future policy. With the new Keynesian IS curve, aggregate demand is not only affected by current policy, but also by expectations about future policy.

---

[11]However, fiscal policy that focuses on affecting the long-run aggregate supply curve, such as some of the tax cuts discussed in Chapter 16, can be used to stabilize output and unemployment fluctuations.

Anti-Inflation Policy

A key issue for policy makers is whether it is worthwhile to pursue policies to reduce inflation. One way of measuring the cost of reducing inflation is with a concept called the **sacrifice ratio,** which is the percentage of real GDP that has to be given up to reduce inflation by one percentage point. For example, if it takes a cumulative decline of 15% of real GDP to achieve a 5% decline in inflation, then the sacrifice ratio is 3 (= 15/5). The higher the sacrifice ratio, the more costly it is for policy makers to pursue contractionary policies to lower inflation.

To see how high the sacrifice ratio is likely to be in each model, let's look at what happens when policy makers try to reduce inflation in Figure 22.7. Suppose the economy has a 10% inflation rate and is at point 1, at the intersection of the aggregate demand curve AD_1 and the long-run aggregate supply curve LRAS. A new Federal Reserve chairperson is appointed who decides that inflation must be reduced to the 2% level, a number that he or she believes is consistent with price stability. To get inflation down to that level, the aggregate demand curve has to shift to the left to AD_2 (by the Fed raising the real interest rate at any given inflation rate) so that the economy eventually moves to point 2 at the intersection of AD_2 and LRAS, where inflation is at $\pi_2 = 2\%$. We will examine the effects of pursuing this anti-inflation policy in each model.

REAL BUSINESS CYCLE MODEL. In the real business cycle model in panel (a), where prices are completely flexible, the short-run aggregate supply curve is the same as the long-run aggregate supply curve LRAS. The shift of the aggregate demand curve from AD_1 to AD_2 immediately moves the economy from point 1 to point 2, and aggregate output remains at Y^P. Hence, in the real business cycle model, anti-inflation policy decreases inflation but does not change real output. *The real business cycle therefore implies that reductions in inflation have no cost in terms of lower output, and so the sacrifice ratio is zero.*

TRADITIONAL KEYNESIAN MODEL. In the traditional Keynesian model in panel (b), the short-run aggregate supply curve does not change, whether the anti-inflationary policy is anticipated or not. Hence, when the aggregate demand curve shifts to the left from AD_1 to AD_2, the economy moves to point 2' (the intersection of the AD_2 and AS_1 curves). The inflation rate does decrease to $\pi_{2'}$, but output falls below potential output to $Y_{2'}$. *In the traditional Keynesian model, reducing inflation is costly and the sacrifice ratio is high, because achieving lower inflation requires a reduction in output.*

Of course, because output, Y, is below potential output at Y^P, eventually the slack in the economy will cause the short-run aggregate supply curve to shift down to AS_2, and inflation will fall to the 2% target.

NEW KEYNESIAN MODEL. In the new Keynesian model in panel (c), when the anti-inflation policy is unanticipated, the short-run aggregate supply curve remains at AS_1 and the economy moves to point 2', where AS_1 and AD_2 intersect. Aggregate output has now fallen to $Y_{2'}$, while inflation has fallen to $\pi_{2'}$. If, however, the anti-inflation policy is *expected*, the short-run aggregate supply curve will shift down from AS_1 to $AS_{2''}$, but not all the way down to AS_2 as would occur if wages and prices were completely flexible, as in the real business cycle model. The economy therefore moves to point 2'', the intersection of AD_2 and $AS_{2''}$. Inflation falls to $\pi_{2''}$, which is lower than $\pi_{2'}$, the inflation rate

FIGURE 22.7

Anti-Inflation Policy in the Three Models

Initially, the economy is in equilibrium at point 1 for all three models in panels (a) through (c). Inflation is at $\pi_1 = 10\%$ and the aggregate demand curve shifts to the left from AD_1 to AD_2, so that the economy eventually moves to point 2 at the intersection of AD_2 and $LRAS$, where inflation is at $\pi_2 = 2\%$. In the real business cycle model in panel (a), the economy immediately moves from point 1 to point 2 and aggregate output remains at Y^P. In the traditional Keynesian model in panel (b), the economy moves to point 2′ whether the anti-inflation policy is anticipated or not. In the new Keynesian model in panel (c), the economy moves to point 2′ if the policy is unanticipated and to 2″ if it is anticipated.

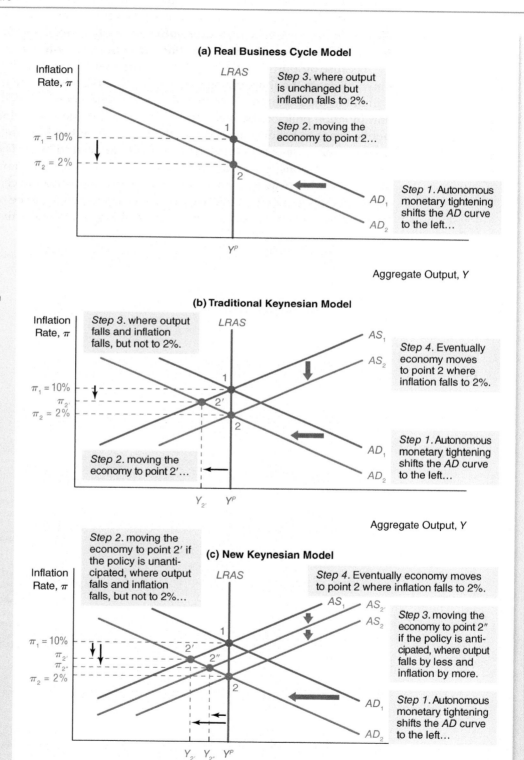

when the anti-inflation policy is unanticipated. Aggregate output falls to $Y_{2''}$, which is a smaller decline than to $Y_{2'}$, which occurs when the policy is unanticipated. ***In the new Keynesian model, anti-inflation policy is costly in terms of lost output. However, the sacrifice ratio is lower when the anti-inflation policy is anticipated.***

Because output, Y, is below potential output at Y^P, eventually the slack in the economy will cause the short-run aggregate supply curve to shift down to AS_2, and inflation will fall to the 2% target. However, the new Keynesian model has the view that for an anti-inflation policy to be successful in reducing inflation at the lowest output cost, the public needs to believe (expect) that the monetary authorities are serious about reducing inflation. Monetary policy makers therefore need to be *credible* when they pursue anti-inflation policies in order for these policies to have the maximum success. Thus adherents of the New Keynesian model view the approaches to central bank credibility, such as inflation targeting that we discussed in Chapter 21, to be of utmost importance for the effectiveness of policies aimed at stabilizing economic activity and inflation.

SUMMARY

1. The real business model is very classical because it assumes that wages and prices are completely flexible, whether shocks are anticipated or not. The real business cycle model sees business cycle fluctuations as coming solely from real shocks, shocks to productivity or the willingness of workers to work, that cause fluctuations in potential output and long-run aggregate supply.

2. The new Keynesian model assumes that expectations are rational but views wages and prices as sticky. The new Keynesian model distinguishes between the effects of anticipated and unanticipated policy: anticipated policy has a smaller effect on aggregate output than unanticipated policy. However, anticipated policy does matter to output fluctuations.

3. The real business cycle model views discretionary policy as counterproductive, while the traditional and new Keynesian models suggest that discretionary policy might be beneficial. However, the new Keynesian model indicates that there is uncertainty about the outcome of a particular policy, and so the design of a beneficial discretionary policy may be very difficult. A traditional Keynesian model in which expectations about policy have no effect on the short-run aggregate supply curve does not distinguish between the effects of anticipated and unanticipated policy. This model favors discretionary policy, in which the outcome of a particular policy is less uncertain. In addition, the traditional Keynesian model sees anti-inflation policy as very costly, while the new Keynesian model sees it as less costly. The real business cycle model does not see any cost associated with anti-inflation policy.

KEY TERMS

dynamic, stochastic, general equilibrium (DSGE) models, p. 602
intertemporal substitution, p. 599
labor hoarding, p. 600

new Keynesian model, p. 601
real business cycle model, p. 597
real shocks, p. 597

sacrifice ratio, p. 612
Solow residuals, p. 599
traditional Keynesian model, p. 607

REVIEW QUESTIONS

All Questions are available in MyEconLab *for practice or instructor assignment.*

Real Business Cycle Model

1. What are the key ideas of the real business cycle model? How does it explain business cycle fluctuations?
2. How does the real business cycle model explain fluctuations in employment and unemployment?

3. What objections to the real business cycle model have been raised?

New Keynesian Model

4. How do new Keynesian ideas about price setting and inflation expectations affect the short-run aggregate supply curve?
5. How do new Keynesian ideas about expectations affect the *IS* and aggregate demand curves?

6. In the new Keynesian model, what shocks cause business cycle fluctuations? Does it matter whether these shocks are anticipated or unanticipated? Explain.

Comparison of Business Cycle Models

7. Compare the traditional Keynesian, new Keynesian, and real business cycle models in terms of expectations, price flexibility, and potential sources of business cycle fluctuations.

8. How do the traditional Keynesian, new Keynesian, and real business cycle models differ in their analysis of the effects of expansionary policy?

9. How do the traditional Keynesian, new Keynesian, and real business cycle models differ in their analysis of the effects of anti-inflation policy?

10. How do the traditional, new Keynesian, and real business cycle models differ in their views about the efficacy of discretionary policy?

PROBLEMS

All Problems are available in MyEconLab *for practice or instructor assignment.*

Real Business Cycle Model

1. Assume the following production function: $Y_t = AK_t^{0.4}L_t^{0.6}$. The capital stock and output are measured in trillions of dollars, and the labor stock is measured in millions of people.

Variable	Period 1	Period 2	Period 3	Period 4	Period 5	Period 6
Capital (K)	1	1	1.1	1	0.95	1
Labor (L)	32	33	32	32	32	32
Output (Y)	10.0	10.6	11.6	10.8	10.4	10.8
Productivity (A)						

a) Using the value of output and the capital and labor stocks, calculate the Solow residual (productivity, A) and its growth rate for each period. Note: calculate growth rates for periods 2–6.

b) Plot the Solow residual (productivity) growth rate and the output growth rate for periods 2–6. Does this table constitute evidence in favor of real business cycle theory? Why or why not?

2. The graph on the next page is based on quarterly data on unemployment and real output growth in the United States between 2006 (q1) and 2013 (q2). Are these data consistent with the real business cycle theory hypothesis regarding the relationship between output and unemployment?

3. The Bureau of Labor Statistics (BLS) tracks the numbers of workers who are employed part-time for economic reasons. The number typically increases sharply at the beginnings of recessions and gradually declines at the ends of recessions. Is this behavior consistent with the real business cycle model? How do these workers help explain labor hoarding?

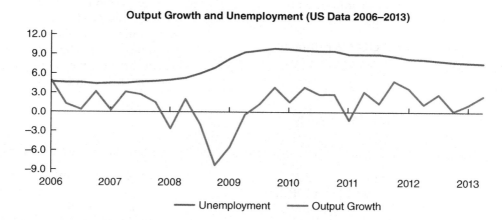

Source: Federal Reserve Bank of St. Louis, FRED Database.

New Keynesian Model

4. Using a graphical representation of the new Keynesian model, describe the effects of an unanticipated negative demand shock (label this equilibrium as point 2). Compare these effects to those of an anticipated negative demand shock (label this equilibrium as point 3).

5. Suppose consumer confidence surges, making consumers more willing to spend. Use the New Keynesian model to describe the effects on output and inflation depending on whether the surge in consumers' confidence was anticipated or unanticipated.

Comparison of Business Cycle Models

6. For each of the following cases, determine which would be the preferred macroeconomic model to analyze business fluctuations.
   a) Most wages are the result of collective bargaining and are therefore quite rigid. In addition, expectations are based mostly on past data.
   b) Few prices are rigid, and economic agents' expectations respond quickly to changes in variables and policy changes that affect how macroeconomic variables are determined.

7. Speeches made by Federal Reserve officials are an integral part of the Fed's management of expectations strategy. In a speech made in November 2002, then-Fed Governor Ben Bernanke, when trying to reassure the public that the Fed would try to avoid a general decrease in prices if needed, stated that the government might cut taxes, increase the federal deficit, and issue bonds that the Fed would buy by printing money. Comment on the effect of this speech on expectations about the Fed's credibility with regard to fighting inflation.

8. Suppose the U.S. Congress is forced to increase taxes to pay for the cost of health care reform in the United States. Describe the effects of such a policy, according to the three business cycle models, if this increase in taxes is fully anticipated by economic agents.

9. Transparency and communication with the public by the Federal Reserve have increased significantly over the last decade. What does this say about the Federal Reserve's view of the relevance of the three business cycle models?

10. The table below shows the inflation rate and the level of real GDP under the anti-inflation policy known as the Volcker disinflation for two periods in the early 1980s.

Date	Inflation	Real GDP ($ billions)
1981:Q1	10.1%	6628.6
1982:Q4	5.3%	6486.2

a) Use the data in the table to calculate the sacrifice ratio.
b) Leading up to the Volcker disinflation, the Federal Reserve had little credibility with the public. With this backdrop and given the data above, what can you conclude about the relevance of the three business cycle models at that time?

DATA ANALYSIS PROBLEMS

The Problems update with real-time data in MyEconLab *and are available for practice or instructor assignment.*

1. Go to the St. Louis Federal Reserve FRED database, and find data on real GDP (GDPC1), the labor force (CLF16OV), and a measure of the capital stock, real consumption of fixed capital (A262RX1Q020SBEA). Download all of the data onto a spreadsheet. For (CLF16OV), change the frequency setting to "Quarterly" before downloading. For each quarter, calculate the Solow residual; then, using those values, calculate the percentage change in the Solow residual and real GDP from the previous quarter. Multiply these numbers by 4 to annualize the quarterly numbers.
   a) For the most recent quarter of data available, what is the growth rate of real GDP? How does it compare to the Solow residual growth rate?
   b) When was the last time this measure of the Solow residual growth rate was negative? How did it compare with GDP growth?
   c) Use the " = *correl()*" function to calculate the correlation coefficient between GDP growth and Solow residual growth over the most recent five years of data.
   d) Do your calculations support or refute the real business cycle model? Briefly explain.

2. Go to the St. Louis Federal Reserve FRED database, and find data on civilian employment (CE16OV) and the personal consumption expenditure price index (PCEPI). For both series, change the *Units* setting to "Percent Change from Year Ago."

   a) Report the inflation rate and the growth rate in employment for the most recent period.
   b) At the end of the last recession, what were the inflation rate and the employment growth rate?
   c) Based on your answers to parts (a) and (b), do the data support or refute the real business cycle model? Briefly explain.

3. Go to the St. Louis Federal Reserve FRED database, and find data on real GDP (GDPC1) and the GDP deflator (GDPDEF). Convert the deflator to the inflation rate by setting the *Units* setting to "Percent Change from Year Ago," and download the data.
   a) Based on data from the last 10 years, identify the period of lowest inflation. Prior to that period (but within the last 10 years), identify the period of highest inflation. What is the total change in the inflation rate over these two periods?
   b) Using the dates identified in part (a), calculate the percent change in real GDP over the two periods.
   c) Use your answers to parts (a) and (b) to calculate the sacrifice ratio.
   d) From 1981:Q1 to 1982:Q4, GDP fell by 2.1% and inflation decreased by 4.8 percentage points. How does the sacrifice ratio for this prior period compare to your calculations in part (c) for the most recent period?

Online appendix, "The New Classical Model," is available at the Companion Website at www .pearsonhighered.com/mishkin.

Policy and Practice: Where Do Macroeconomists Agree and Disagree?

Preview

Economists are a contentious lot, and this is particularly true of macroeconomists. Regarding the global financial crisis and the Great Recession of 2007–2009, macroeconomists of different persuasions, classical versus Keynesian, have had very different views on what policy makers should have done. Keynesian economists argued that both the Federal Reserve and the U.S. government should have pursued aggressive expansionary policies to stimulate the economy, with some arguing that the measures taken were not aggressive enough, while classical economists saw the actions taken by the Fed and the U.S. government as counterproductive: they would not help much in getting output and employment to increase but would likely lead to higher inflation.

With the rational expectations revolution, the new approaches to business cycle theory, and new research on what drives economic development, there have been dramatic changes in the way macroeconomists think about the conduct of macroeconomic policy. Although there are some important differing viewpoints among macroeconomists on how policy should be conducted, there has been a remarkable amount of convergence on some of the key principles of macroeconomic policy making. We will discuss where the field of macroeconomics stands today and the areas in which macroeconomists agree and disagree.

Where Macroeconomists Agree

Modern classical and Keynesian theories of the business cycle have much in common. Not surprisingly, their development and the additional research in macroeconomics that we have discussed throughout this book have led to a set of principles with regard to policy and practice. These principles, on which almost all modern macroeconomists agree, have been given the name "the **new neoclassical synthesis**." Here

we look at how the macroeconomics field has developed in recent decades and examine each of the principles of the new neoclassical synthesis in turn.[1]

Inflation Is Always and Everywhere a Monetary Phenomenon

In the wake of the Great Depression and the publication of Keynes's *The General Theory of Employment, Interest and Money* in 1936, the majority of economists in the 1950s and 1960s had become Keynesians who did not view monetary policy as a key factor in developments in the aggregate economy. Research by Milton Friedman and his followers, who later became known as monetarists, argued that the growth in the money supply was a key determinant of aggregate economic activity and particularly inflation, along the lines we discussed in Chapter 5. This led Milton Friedman to opine, as discussed in Chapter 5, that "Inflation is always and everywhere a monetary phenomenon." Although the majority of the macroeconomics profession has not come to the view that money growth is always the most critical piece of information about where inflation will head in the short run, the profession has reached a consensus agreeing with Friedman's adage, because, as we saw in Chapter 13, monetary policy determines the inflation rate in the long run.[2]

The Benefits of Price Stability

With the rise of inflation in the 1960s and 1970s, not only economists, but also politicians and the public, began to discuss the high costs of inflation. A high inflationary environment leads to overinvestment in the financial sector, which expands because it can earn profits by helping individuals and businesses escape some of the costs of inflation. High inflation, which is generally accompanied by high volatility of inflation, leads to uncertainty about the future price level, making it harder for firms and individuals to plan and make appropriate decisions, thereby decreasing economic efficiency. The interaction of the tax system with inflation also increases distortions that adversely affect economic activity.[3] The recognition of the high costs of inflation led to the view that *price stability*, that is, low and stable inflation, can increase the level of resources productively employed in the economy and can help increase the rate of economic growth.

No Long-Run Trade-off Between Unemployment and Inflation

The dominance of Keynesian thinking in the 1950s and 1960s stemmed from the view that the Great Depression was the direct result of policy inaction when adverse shocks hit the economy. This insight led to an era of policy activism in the 1960s, in which

---

[1]The term "new neoclassical synthesis" was invented by Marvin Goodfriend and Robert G. King in "The New Neoclassical Synthesis and the Role of Monetary Policy," *NBER Macroeconomics Annual* 12 (1997): 231–283. For an excellent recent survey on the new neoclassical synthesis and where macroeconomists agree, see Michael Woodford, "Convergence in Macroeconomics: Elements of the New Synthesis," *American Economics Journal: Macroeconomics* 1 (2009): 267–279.

[2]Although inflation is always and everywhere a monetary phenomenon, fiscal policy can be the ultimate source of expansionary monetary policy, as we saw in Chapter 16. If the government is running large budget deficits, the central bank may be forced to buy this debt, which leads to an expansion of the money supply, which in turn results in inflation.

[3]For excellent surveys of the cost of inflation, see Stanley Fischer, "The Role of Macroeconomic Factors in Growth," *Journal of Monetary Economics* 32 (December 1993): 485–512; and Palle Anderson and David Gruen, "Macroeconomic Policies and Growth," in *Productivity and Growth: Proceedings of a Conference Held at the H.C. Coombs Centre for Financial Studies, Kirribilli, Australia, July 10-11,* eds. Palle Anderson, Jacqueline Dwyer, and David Gruen (Sydney: Reserve Bank of Australia, 1995), 279–319.

Keynesian economists argued that they could fine-tune the economy to produce maximum employment with only slight inflationary consequences. Particularly influential in this thinking was a paper published in 1960 by Nobel Prize winners Paul Samuelson and Robert Solow,[4] who argued that the Phillips curve suggested a long-run trade-off between unemployment and inflation, and that this trade-off should be exploited. Indeed, Samuelson and Solow even mentioned that a nonperfectionist goal of a 3% unemployment rate could be attained at what they considered to be a low inflation rate of 4–5% per year. This thinking, not only by Samuelson and Solow but also by the then-dominant Keynesian economists, led to increased monetary and fiscal policy activism to push the economy to full employment and keep it there. However, the subsequent economic record was not a happy one: inflation accelerated, with the inflation rate in the United States and other industrialized countries eventually climbing above 10% in the 1970s, leading to the "Great Inflation," which we discussed in Chapter 13. In the meantime, the unemployment rate rose from the level it had been at in the 1950s.

In 1967 and 1968, Milton Friedman, as well as his fellow Nobel Prize winner Edmund Phelps of Columbia University, argued that there was no long-run trade-off between unemployment and inflation; rather, the economy would gravitate to some natural rate of unemployment in the long run no matter what the rate of inflation was.[5] In other words, the long-run Phillips curve would be vertical, and attempts to lower unemployment below the natural rate (or output above potential) would only result in higher inflation. Eventually, empirical research confirmed that there was no long-run trade-off between unemployment and inflation, and so macroeconomists came to assume that the long-run aggregate supply curve is vertical, as we assumed in the aggregate demand and supply analysis used throughout this book.

The Crucial Role of Expectations

Starting in the early 1970s, in a series of papers discussed in Chapter 21, Robert Lucas launched the rational expectations revolution, which demonstrated that the public and the markets' expectations of policy actions have important effects on almost every sector of the economy. The theory of rational expectations emphasized that economic agents should be driven by optimizing behavior and therefore their expectations of future variables should be optimal forecasts (the best guess of the future) using all available information. Because the optimizing behavior posited by rational expectations indicates that expectations should respond immediately to new information, rational expectations theory suggests that it might not take very long to get to the long run. Therefore, attempting to lower unemployment below the natural rate could lead to higher inflation very quickly. In addition, the rational expectations revolution implies that the impact of monetary policy on the economy is substantially influenced by whether or not it is anticipated. This proposition has become widely accepted and is a feature of all the modern business cycle theories we discussed in Chapter 22.

Another key result from the rational expectations revolution is that expectations about what monetary policy will be in the future have an important impact on the evolution of economic activity, as is emphasized in the new Keynesian model. This result

---

[4]Paul A. Samuelson and Robert M. Solow, "Analytical Aspects of Anti-Inflation Policy," *American Economic Review* 50 (May 1960): 177–194.

[5]Milton Friedman, "The Role of Monetary Policy," *American Economic Review* 58 (March 1968): 1–17; and Edmund Phelps, "Money-Wage Dynamics and Labor-Market Equilibrium," *Journal of Political Economy* 76 (July/August 1967, Part 2): 687–711.

implies that the conduct of monetary policy needs to involve the current setting of policy instruments, as well as management of expectations about future policy. The crucial role of management of expectations, discussed in Chapter 22, has been emphasized by Michael Woodford of Columbia University, one of the leading new Keynesian theorists. The recognition that management of expectations is a central element of monetary policy making brings to the forefront the credibility of monetary policy authorities. Furthermore, it highlights the importance of actions by the monetary authorities because "actions speak louder than words": monetary authorities will be believed only if they take actions that are consistent with how they want expectations to be managed.

The Taylor Principle

The recognition that economic outcomes depend on expectations of monetary policy suggests that policy evaluation requires the comparison of economic performance under different monetary policy rules. The Taylor rule that we discussed in Chapter 13 has received enormous attention in the literature on monetary policy. It advises that monetary policy set the policy interest rate (the federal funds rate) in response to the deviation of inflation from its desired level or target (the inflation gap) and the deviation of output from potential output (the output gap). Taylor emphasized that a rule of this type had desirable properties and, in particular, would stabilize inflation only if the coefficient on inflation exceeded unity. This conclusion came to be known as the "Taylor principle," establishing the view that monetary policy must raise the nominal interest rate by more than the rise in inflation, so that real interest rates will rise in response to a rise in inflation. Although the Taylor principle now is followed by almost all central banks, during the late 1960s and 1970s many central banks, including the Federal Reserve, violated the Taylor principle, resulting in the "Great Inflation" that so many countries experienced in the 1970s and early 1980s. Indeed, as inflation rose in the United States during this period, real interest rates fell. With the adoption of the Taylor principle by central banks in recent years, inflation has remained low throughout the world.

The Time-Inconsistency Problem

Another important development in macroeconomics that emanated from the rational expectations revolution was the discovery of the importance of the time-inconsistency problem, developed and discussed in papers by Finn Kydland, Edward Prescott, Guillermo Calvo, Robert Barro, and David Gordon.[6] As we discussed in Chapter 21, the time-inconsistency problem arises because monetary policy conducted on a discretionary, day-by-day basis may lead to poor long-run outcomes. However, even if a central bank recognizes that discretionary policy will lead to a poor outcome—high inflation with no gains in output—and so renounces it, the time-inconsistency problem is likely to arise nonetheless from political pressure. In the view of many observers, politicians in a democratic society are shortsighted because they are driven by the need to win their next election, so they are unlikely to focus on long-run objectives such as promoting a stable price level. Instead, they will seek short-run solutions to problems like high

---

[6]Finn Kydland and Edward Prescott, "Rules Rather Than Discretion: The Inconsistency of Optimal Plans," *Journal of Political Economy* 85 (1977): 473–491; and Guillermo Calvo, "On the Time Consistency of Optimal Policy in the Monetary Economy," *Econometrica* 46 (November 1978): 1411–1428. The classic application to monetary policy is found in Robert J. Barro and David Gordon, "A Positive Theory of Monetary Policy in a Natural Rate Model," *Journal of Political Economy* 91 (August 1983): 589–610.

unemployment or high interest rates by calling on the central bank to lower interest rates and unemployment with overly expansionary monetary policy.

Central Bank Independence

Making central banks independent can help insulate them from political pressures to pursue overly expansionary policy and thus help them to avoid the time-inconsistency problem. Independence should lead to better policy outcomes because it insulates the central bank from the myopia that is frequently a feature of the political process, arising from politicians' concerns about getting elected in the near future. As we saw in Chapter 21, evidence supports the conjecture that macroeconomic performance is improved when central banks are more independent. When ranking central banks in industrialized countries from least independent to most independent, inflation performance is the best in countries with the most independent central banks.

Commitment to a Nominal Anchor

The inability of monetary policy to boost employment in the long run, the importance of expectations, the benefits of price stability, and the time-inconsistency problem provide the rationale for why commitment to a nominal anchor—that is, stabilization of a nominal variable such as the inflation rate, the money supply, or an exchange rate—is so crucial to successful macroeconomic policy outcomes.

As we saw in Chapter 21, an institutional commitment to price stability via establishment of a nominal anchor provides a counterbalance to the time-inconsistency problem because it makes it clear that the central bank must focus on the long run and thus resist the temptation to pursue short-run expansionary policies that are inconsistent with the nominal anchor. Commitment to a nominal anchor can also encourage the government to be more fiscally responsible, which also makes high inflation less likely, as we saw in Chapter 16. When a government has committed to a nominal anchor, it is difficult for it to run large budget deficits. Politicians may be more likely to recognize that eventually they will have to pay for current deficit spending by raising taxes and will not be able to resort to the so-called inflation tax, the printing of money to pay for goods and services that leads to more inflation and is thus inconsistent with the price stability goal.

Commitment to a nominal anchor also leads to policy actions that promote price stability, which helps promote economic efficiency and growth. The commitment to a nominal anchor helps stabilize inflation expectations, which in turn reduces fluctuations in actual inflation. Commitment to a nominal anchor is therefore a crucial element in successfully managing expectations, and a successful commitment to a nominal anchor has been found to produce not only more stable inflation, but lower volatility of output as well.[7]

Credibility

With the advent of rational expectations, macroeconomists have come to understand that credibility is central to successful policy making. In Chapters 21 and 22, we saw that monetary policy credibility has the benefit of stabilizing inflation and also business cycle fluctuations. In Chapter 22, we saw that credibility of anti-inflation policies is crucial to decreasing the cost of reducing inflation in terms of lost output.

[7]For a survey of the empirical research that supports this conclusion, see Frederic S. Mishkin and Klaus Schmidt-Hebbel, "Does Inflation Targeting Matter?" in *Monetary Policy Under Inflation Targeting*, eds. Frederic S. Mishkin and Klaus Schmidt-Hebbel (Santiago: Central Bank of Chile, 2007), 291–372.

Institutions Rule

Research over the last twenty or so years, described in Chapter 7, has led macroeconomists to recognize that fundamental institutions, such as well-defined property rights and the absence of corruption, are crucial to achieving high economic growth. This view has been described by Dani Rodrik of Harvard University as "Institutions Rule." But how do you get institutions to change in a positive direction? Institutional reform is not an easy task, and how to achieve it is one of the most difficult problems facing economists who study economic development and growth.

Where Macroeconomists Disagree

Although the macroeconomics profession now agrees on a large number of principles, as this epilogue and earlier chapters indicate, substantial disagreements remain, particularly with regard to business cycle analysis and policy and practice. (Indeed, this is what keeps the field so dynamic and interesting.) There are six basic areas of disagreement: 1) how flexible wages and prices are, 2) how long it takes to get to the long run, 3) the sources of business cycle fluctuations, 4) whether stabilization policy is worthwhile, 5) how costly it is to reduce inflation, and 6) how dangerous budget deficits are. Economists generally fall into two camps on these issues, classical or Keynesian. We discuss how views from each of these camps differ for each of these issues.

Flexibility of Wages and Prices

Classicals and Keynesians have very different views on the subject of the flexibility of wages and prices.

CLASSICAL VIEW. As we have seen, classical economists, such as real business cycle theorists, view wages and prices as being very flexible. The assumption of complete wage and price flexibility in the real business cycle model leads to the classical dichotomy that real variables are not affected by monetary policy and so aggregate output is always at its potential level. Classicals are comfortable analyzing macroeconomic issues from a perspective of optimizing agents in which markets clear very quickly. They use frameworks in which wages and prices are very flexible, like those described in Part 2 of this book. They even use them to think about short-run business cycle fluctuations.

KEYNESIAN VIEW. In contrast, Keynesian economists, including new Keynesians, see wages and prices as sticky in the short run. They do not accept the classical dichotomy and see monetary policy as having important real effects on the economy in the short run. They are comfortable using flexible price frameworks for long-run analysis only.

How Much Time It Takes to Get to the Long Run

Classical and Keynesian macroeconomists disagree over how much time it takes to get to the long run.

CLASSICAL VIEW. Because they assume that wages and prices are flexible, classical economists believe that it takes only a very short time to get to the long run. Flexible wages and prices move the economy to the long run very quickly. As a result, classical economists are comfortable using classical, long-run frameworks to think about macro-economic issues.

KEYNESIAN VIEW. Some Keynesian economists, on the other hand, believe that it takes a long time indeed to get to the long run, because they subscribe to Keynes's adage that "in the long run we are all dead." Because wages and prices adjust only slowly over time, these Keynesians believe that the economy may take a very long time to reach its long-run equilibrium. However, with the advent of rational expectations and the focus on macroeconomic modeling that is solidly grounded on microeconomic foundations, new Keynesian economists see the economy as moving to the long run far more quickly than traditional Keynesians, who adopt the view that expectations may be slow to adjust because they are adaptive. Further, traditional Keynesians are skeptical of some of the microfoundations employed in dynamic, stochastic, and general equilibrium models, and reject the use of long-run models to analyze short-run effects of discretionary policies.

Hence different Keynesian economists can have different views of how much time it takes to get to the long run. Some Keynesian economists are more comfortable using classical frameworks like those outlined in Part 2 because they believe it doesn't take very long to get to the long run. Others are less comfortable using classical models and prefer using models like the aggregate demand and supply model to analyze what is happening to the economy.

Sources of Business Cycle Fluctuations

The sources of business cycle fluctuations is another polarizing area for classical and Keynesian economists.

CLASSICAL VIEW. Real business cycle theorists see fluctuations in economic activity as coming solely from shocks to long-run aggregate supply. Because they do not attribute economic fluctuations to aggregate demand shocks, they are perfectly comfortable with analyzing business cycle fluctuations with little regard to aggregate demand.

KEYNESIAN VIEW. Keynesian economists, on the other hand, see demand shocks as an important source of business cycle fluctuations because the short-run aggregate supply curve is not vertical. Here again, there are different types of Keynesians. New Keynesian economists see the short-run aggregate supply curve as shifting faster than traditional Keynesians because they embed the concept of rational expectations in their models. This suggests that expectations of inflation adjust quickly, causing the short-run aggregate supply curve to shift more rapidly. As we just discussed, different Keynesians also have diverging views on the flexibility of prices and therefore on how much time it takes to get to the long run.

Even new Keynesians differ in their views on how flexible prices are; depending on their beliefs regarding price flexibility, they may have views that are closer to those of real business cycle theorists than to those of traditional Keynesians. Indeed, we have seen that the real business cycle model is actually a special case of the new Keynesian model. If prices become completely flexible, the short-run aggregate supply curve becomes identical to the long-run aggregate supply curve. New Keynesians can therefore have very different views on how much business cycle fluctuations are due to demand shocks versus supply shocks. Some new Keynesian models give a prominent role to fluctuations in long-run aggregate supply in explaining business cycle fluctuations, while others see fluctuations in aggregate demand as being far more important.

Effectiveness of Stabilization Policy

Classical and Keynesian economists also debate the value of active policy making on the health of the macroeconomy.

CLASSICAL VIEW. Classical economists see almost no role for policy makers in trying to stabilize real economic activity. Since classical models fix the economy at full employment, there is obviously no need to stimulate aggregate demand by using discretionary policy. In real business cycle models, policy to stabilize the economy has no effect on the real economy because aggregate output is solely determined by the position of the long-run aggregate supply curve and not on the position of the aggregate demand curve. Macroeconomic policy that shifts the aggregate demand curve simply causes inflation to fluctuate. Adherents of the real business cycle model therefore take the view that the self-correcting mechanism described in Chapter 12 is rapid, and so policies used to stabilize real economic activity are likely to do little good. They oppose stabilization policy that is both active and discretionary because it can adversely impact inflation.

KEYNESIAN VIEW. Traditional Keynesian economists see stabilization policy as having benefits. Their view that it takes a long time to get to the long run implies that the self-correcting mechanism is very slow. Activist policies to stabilize economic fluctuations are highly beneficial because they can reduce economic fluctuations and reduce the severity of the business cycle. Because traditional Keynesians do not view expectations as changing rapidly, they view time inconsistency as less of a problem. They thus see less of a problem with discretionary policies than do classical economists.

The new Keynesian model does allow a role for active policies aimed at stabilizing real economic activity because anticipated policy *does* matter to economic fluctuations. Policy makers can count on some output response from their anticipated policies and can use them to stabilize the economy. However, because new Keynesians believe in rational expectations, which imply that expectations can change rapidly, they recognize that designing activist policies to stabilize the economy is far from easy. The effects of anticipated and unanticipated policy will not be the same. Policy makers will encounter more uncertainty about the outcome of their actions because they cannot be sure to what extent policy is anticipated. Hence an activist policy is unlikely to operate as intended and fully achieve its goals. Furthermore, their acceptance of rational expectations means that new Keynesians take the time-inconsistency problem very seriously and are not enamored of discretionary policies. Again, because new Keynesians have different views on wage and price flexibility, they can disagree on how active stabilization policy should be.

Cost of Reducing Inflation

By the end of the 1970s, the high inflation rate (over 10%) made the reduction of inflation the primary concern of policy makers. The cost, in terms of output, of reducing inflation is described by the concept of the *sacrifice ratio*, the percentage reduction of real GDP that is necessary to reduce the inflation rate by one percentage point. The higher the sacrifice ratio, the higher the cost of reducing inflation, and the more reluctant policy makers will be to pursue contractionary policies to lower inflation. Classical and Keynesian economists, however, have quite different views on how costly it is to reduce inflation.

CLASSICAL VIEW. As we saw in the analysis of anti-inflation policies, classical models with flexible prices see sacrifice ratios and the costs of anti-inflation policies as quite low. In the real business cycle model, the sacrifice ratio is even zero: contractionary policy to lower inflation has no cost at all, since contractionary policy has no impact on aggregate output.

KEYNESIAN VIEW. The traditional Keynesian view sees the aggregate supply curve as shifting down only slowly over time because prices are sticky and expectations of inflation adjust slowly. Thus, as we saw earlier, anti-inflation policies are likely to lead to large losses of output. Traditional Keynesian estimates of sacrifice ratios in the late 1970s and early 1980s put them at around 5; that is, it would take a 5% reduction of output to lower the inflation rate by one percentage point.[8] Reducing inflation would then be very costly indeed. New Keynesian models, however, are far more sanguine about the cost of anti-inflation policies because they assume that expectations are rational. If anti-inflation policies are credible, the rational expectations assumption in new Keynesian models suggests that there will be a small decline in output from their implementation.

However, in New Keynesian models, if anti-inflation policies are not credible, then they can be very costly and the sacrifice ratio will be high. But how do you establish credibility for these policies? You might think that an announcement by policy makers at the Federal Reserve that they plan to pursue an anti-inflation policy would do the trick. The public would expect this policy and would act accordingly. However, such a conclusion implies that the public will believe the policy makers' announcement. Unfortunately, that is not how the real world works. The Federal Reserve, for example, has not always done what it set out to do. In fact, during the 1970s, the Chairman of the Federal Reserve Board, Arthur Burns, repeatedly announced that the Fed would pursue a vigorous anti-inflation policy. The actual policy pursued, however, had quite a different outcome. Money growth during the Burns era was very high and real interest was very low, even turning negative for several years. The result of this easy monetary policy was a soaring inflation rate. Such episodes reduced the credibility of the Federal Reserve in the eyes of the public, and as predicted by the New Keynesian model, the reduction of inflation from 1980 to 1983 was bought at a very high cost.

The Dangers of Budget Deficits

With the massive government budget deficits in the United States and so many other countries throughout the world in recent years, amounting to over 10% of GDP in many cases, government fiscal imbalances have become one of the most talked-about topics among both macroeconomists and the general public. In Chapter 16, we saw that two groups of macroeconomists have very different views about whether or not budget deficits are a big problem.

The majority of macroeconomists see budget deficits as highly dangerous. They believe that government budget deficits lead to a reduction of national saving, which

[8]For example, see Arthur M. Okun, "Efficient Disinflationary Policies," *American Economic Review* 68 (May 1978): 348–352; and Robert J. Gordon and Stephen R. King, "The Output Cost of Disinflation in Traditional and Vector Autoregressive Models," *Brookings Papers on Economic Activity* 1 (1982): 205–245.

leads to lower investment and a greater burden on future generations, since budget deficits raise future taxes and increase indebtedness to foreigners. The majority of economists also believe that budget deficits are inflationary because at some point they can drive the monetary authorities to monetize the debt, leading to an expansion of the money supply, which then produces a rise in the inflation rate.

A significant minority of macroeconomists, those who believe in Ricardian equivalence, are much more sanguine about government budget deficits. Ricardian equivalence suggests that larger budget deficits resulting from tax cuts just induce greater private saving today, because taxpayers understand that they will be paying higher taxes in the future and so they save now to pay for them. The higher personal saving then results in no decline in national saving, and so tax cuts do not crowd out private investment or lead to lower net exports that must be financed by greater indebtedness to foreigners. Ricardian equivalence therefore implies that budget deficits that arise from tax cuts do not impose any burden on future generations.

Advocates of Ricardian equivalence also see less of an inflationary danger from budget deficits arising from tax cuts. Because lower taxes today induce more private saving, households are induced to purchase more government bonds, so that the government does not have to monetize the debt and print money to finance the resulting budget deficit. Cutting taxes therefore does not lead to higher money supply growth and so does not produce inflation.

The Future of Business Cycle Theory

Our discussion of where macroeconomists agree and disagree suggests that a key topic of future research in business cycle theory will be understanding the sources of price stickiness. Two issues—why price stickiness occurs and how long it takes prices to adjust—are at the core of disagreements between classical and Keynesian business cycle analysis. Indeed, research on price stickiness has been exploring what costs to adjusting prices may lead to slow adjustment. Other research has focused on *rational inattention*, or how it may be rational for firms to adjust prices infrequently because it is costly for them to figure out how much they should change their prices.

Because the formation of expectations is at the core of business cycle analysis and discussions of policy and practice, macroeconomists are delving deeper into understanding expectations formation. One drawback of the theory of rational expectations is that it assumes people can update their expectations costlessly. An alternative view is that people take a while to learn how to best update their expectations. The role of learning in expectations has therefore become an area of active research.

The recent global financial crisis, which we studied in Chapter 15, made it clear that financial crises can have disastrous effects on economic activity. Another area of active research is examining how disruptions to the financial system affect the macroeconomy. An urgent task for the macroeconomics profession is to analyze how financial frictions can be included in general equilibrium macroeconomic models, so that episodes like the recent 2007–2009 financial crisis and recession can be better understood.

Although business cycle theory has come a long way, with a growing consensus on many issues, there are still many unanswered questions that will keep macroeconomists busy in the coming years. Successful models must be able to forecast outcomes and explain why modern, market-based economies experience substantial economic fluctuations.

SUMMARY

1. There is a set of principles with regard to policy and practice that most macroeconomists agree on, and these principles are referred to as the "new neoclassical synthesis." They are: 1) inflation is always and everywhere a monetary phenomenon, 2) price stability has important benefits, 3) there is no long-run trade-off between inflation and unemployment, 4) expectations play a critical role in the policy and practice of macroeconomics, 5) central banks must follow the Taylor principle of raising real interest rates as inflation rises, 6) the time-inconsistency problem has important implications for how policy should be conducted, 7) central banks should be independent, 8) commitment to a nominal anchor is crucial for good policy outcomes, 9) credibility is central to successful policy making, and 10) fundamental institutions, such as well-defined property rights and the absence of corruption, are crucial to achieving high economic growth.

2. Macroeconomists disagree on the following issues: 1) the flexibility of wages and prices, 2) how much time it takes to get to the long run, 3) the sources of business cycle fluctuations, 4) the effectiveness of stabilization policy, 5) the cost of reducing inflation, and 6) the dangers of budget deficits.

3. Key topics of future business cycle research will be: 1) understanding the sources of price stickiness, 2) understanding expectations formation, and 3) examining how disruptions to the financial system affect the macroeconomy.

KEY TERMS

new neoclassical synthesis,
   p. 619

Glossary

accelerationist Phillips curve   A formulation of the Phillips curve equation where the natural rate of unemployment can be interpreted as the non-accelerating inflation rate of unemployment (NAIRU). 287

activists   People who regard the self-correcting mechanism through wage and price adjustment as very slow because wages and prices are sticky. 343

acyclical   When a variable's ups and downs do not consistently coincide with those of the business cycle. 211

adaptive expectations   Expectations that are formed by looking at the past and therefore change only slowly over time. 286

adverse selection   The problem that arises because the party who is most eager to engage in a transaction is the one most likely to produce an undesirable (adverse) outcome for you. 376

adverse supply shock   See *negative supply shock*. 57

agency problem   See *principal-agent problem*. 401

agency theory   The analysis of how asymmetric information problems can generate adverse selection and moral hazard problems. 392

aggregate demand   The total amount of output demanded in the economy. 231

aggregate demand curve   The relationship between the inflation rate and aggregate output when the goods market is in equilibrium. 257

aggregate production function   A description of how much output is produced for any given amounts of factor inputs. 51

aggregate supply curve   Represents the relationship between the total quantity of output that firms are willing to produce and the inflation rate. 287

anchor currency   In a fixed exchange rate regime, the currency to which the value of another currency is pegged. 477

"animal spirits"   Emotional waves of optimism and pessimism. 235

appreciation   When a currency increases in value. 460

asset-price bubble   The rise of asset prices above their fundamental economic values. 395

assets   Property that includes bonds, stocks, art, land, etc. 13

asymmetric information   A situation in which one party to a transaction has much less accurate information than the other. 374

autonomous consumption   The amount of consumption expenditure that is unrelated to either disposable income or the real interest rate. 82

autonomous consumption expenditure   The amount of consumption expenditure that is exogenous (independent of variables in the model, such as disposable income or interest rates). 233, 507

autonomous easing of monetary policy   The action of a central bank to decrease the autonomous real interest rate resulting in a decrease in the real interest rate. 254

autonomous investment   A component of planned investment spending that is completely exogenous (unexplained by variables in the model such as the real interest rate). 84, 235

autonomous net exports   The level of net exports that is treated as exogenous. 236

autonomous spending   Exogenous spending that is unrelated to variables in the model such as output or real interest rates. 245

autonomous tightening of monetary policy   An autonomous increase in the real interest rate by the central bank. 253

average propensity to consume   The ratio of consumption to income. 507

average propensity to save   The ratio of saving to disposable income. 507

backward-looking expectations   See *adaptive expectations*. 286

balance of payments accounts   A bookkeeping system for recording all receipts and payments that have a direct bearing on the movement of funds between a nation (private sector and government) and foreign countries. 77

balance sheet   A list of the household's or institution's assets and liabilities. 375

balanced growth path   Growth at a constant rate. 192

bank failures   When banks cannot pay off depositors and other creditors and thus go out of business. 220

bank panic   Simultaneous failures of multiple banks. 396

banks   Financial institutions that acquire funds by issuing deposits and use the proceeds to make loans. 375

behavioral economics   A field that applies concepts from other social sciences such as anthropology, sociology, and (particularly) psychology to the study of economic behavior. 516

Board of Governors of the Federal Reserve System: A board of seven governors (including the chair) that plays an essential role in decision making within the Federal Reserve System. 105

bonds Debt securities that offer a stream of payments for a fixed period of time. 40, 373

boom See *business cycle expansion.* 208

borrowed reserves A bank's borrowings from the Fed. 129

borrowing constraint The constraint prevents people from borrowing the full amount they would like, so that consumption today must be less than or equal to income today. 452, 504

budget surplus The government's tax receipts minus its outlays. 75

business cycle contraction The period from a peak P to a trough T as illustrated on a chart of economic activity. 208

business cycle expansion The period from a trough T to a peak P as illustrated on a chart of economic activity. 208

business cycles Fluctuations in aggregate economic activity in which many economic activities expand and contract together in a recurring, but not a periodic, fashion. 6, 207

business fixed investment Includes spending by businesses on equipment (computers, trucks, and machines) and structures (factories, shopping centers, and hospitals) that are used in production. 523

capital The quantity of structures and equipment—such as factories, trucks, and computers—that workers use to produce goods and services. It also refers to assets minus liabilities on a balance sheet. 50, 375

capital-accumulation equation An equation that says that the change in the capital stock equals investment minus depreciation. 151

capital controls Restrictions on the free movement of capital across the borders of a country. 480

capital dilution Growth in the labor force that leads to less capital per worker. 159

capital good A good that is produced in the current period to be used in the production of other goods that is not used up in the stages of production. 22

capital-labor ratio The amount of capital per worker; plays a very prominent role in the Solow model. 149

capital mobility When assets are traded freely between countries. 466

central banks The government agencies that oversee banking systems. 12

chain-weighted measures A method of calculating income measures in which the base year prices are updated perpetually. 33

chronically unemployed People who have unemployment spells lasting more than six months. 556

classical dichotomy The view that in the long run there is a complete separation between the real side of the economy and the nominal side. 111

classical models Business cycle models that make use of a flexible price framework and are preferred by economists who believe that prices adjust quickly to their long-run equilibria. 222

classicals (classical economists) Economists who assumed that wages and prices are completely flexible—that is, they completely and quickly adjust to the long-run equilibrium at which supply equals demand. 109

closed economy An economy that is closed to international trade with zero net exports. 81

Cobb-Douglas production function A production function in which the shares of labor and capital income are constant. 51

coincident variable A macroeconomic variable that reaches its peaks and troughs at the same time the business cycle reaches its peaks and troughs. 211

collateral Property the borrower promises in the loan contract to the lender if it defaults on its debt. 380

collective bargaining The process of bargaining for a large group of workers at one time rather than have each worker bargain individually for their wages. 560

college premium A higher wage for college graduates relative to high-school graduates. 180

college wage premium The percentage difference between the average wage of a college-educated worker and a high-school graduate. 552

common law A legal system that came from English law, in which the law is continually reinterpreted by judges. 184

constant-money-growth-rate rule The money supply is kept growing at a constant rate regardless of the state of the economy. 578

constant returns to scale If you increase all the factor inputs by the same percentage, then output increases by exactly the same percentage. 54

constrained discretion A conceptual structure and inherent discipline on policy makers, but without eliminating all flexibility. 581

consumer price index (CPI) A measure of the average prices of consumer goods and services. 34

consumption See *consumption expenditure.* 25

consumption expenditure   The total spending for currently produced consumer goods and services (e.g., hamburgers, iPods, rock concerts, visits to the doctor, etc.). 25, 232

consumption function   The relationship between disposable income and consumption expenditure. 232, 507

consumption smoothing   The fact that consumers will spread out any increase in consumption over today and tomorrow, even if it the increase stems solely from an increase in current income. 502

contributions for social insurance   Primarily Social Security taxes that are assessed upon a fixed percentage of a worker's wages, up to a fixed ceiling (or cap). 430

convergence   Countries with different initial levels of per capita income will gravitate to a similar level of per capita income. 147

convexity   The bowed-in shape of an indifference curve, which results from the typical consumer's dislike of large fluctuations in consumption from one period to the next. 499

corporate taxes   Primarily taxes on the profits on businesses. 430

cost-push inflation   Results either from a temporary negative supply shock or a push by workers for wage hikes beyond what productivity gains can justify. 351

cost-push shocks   Where workers push for wages higher than productivity gains, thereby driving up costs and inflation. 286

countercyclical   When economic variables move opposite to aggregate economic activity—that is, down during expansions and up during contractions. 211

crawling peg   When a currency is allowed to depreciate at a steady rate so that the inflation rate in the pegging country can be higher than that of the anchor country. 482

credibility   Believed by the public. 582

credit boom   When financial institutions to go on a lending spree. 393

credit default swaps   Financial insurance contracts that provide payments to holders of bonds if they default. 401

credit markets   The markets where households and businesses get funds (credit) from each other. 42

credit spread   The difference between the interest rate on loans to businesses and the interest rate on completely safe assets. 392

crowding out   A phenomenon that occurs when a rise in government spending, which reduces national saving and increases the budget deficit, reduces private investment. 86, 438

currency   Money in the form of bills and coins. 102

currency board   A fixed exchange rate regime in which the domestic currency is backed 100% by the anchor currency, and the government or central bank stands ready to exchange domestic currency for the anchor currency at a fixed rate whenever the public requests it. 477

cyclical unemployment rate   The difference between the actual unemployment rate and the natural rate of unemployment. 561

data lag   The time it takes for policy makers to obtain data indicating what is happening in the economy. 343

debt deflation   Occurs when a substantial unanticipated decline in the price level sets in, leading to a further deterioration in firms' net worth because of the increased burden of indebtedness. 397

debt intolerance   When countries are unable to sell their debt at relatively low levels of government debt to GDP and so are far more likely to default on their government debt at much lower levels of debt to GDP. 439

debt repudiation   Default and failure to pay back debt by a government. 439

debt-to-GDP ratio   A indicator of a country's indebtedness—the amount of debt relative to the available income to pay it back, measured by the amount of debt in nominal terms relative to nominal GDP. 431

deflation   A situation where the inflation rate is negative and the price level is decreasing.

deleveraging   When financial institutions cut back on their lending to borrower-spenders. 393

demand for money   The quantity of money that people want to hold. 110

demand-pull inflation   Results from policy makers pursuing policies that increase aggregate demand. 351

demand shocks   Shocks that cause the aggregate demand curve to shift. 307

dependency ratio   The ratio of retirees to workers who make Social Security contributions. 433

depreciation   The loss of capital because capital goods wear out (or will be scrapped because they are obsolete). 150

depreciation   When a currency falls in value and is worth fewer U.S. dollars. 460, 527

depreciation rate   The fraction of capital that wears out each year. 150, 527

depression   A recession where the decline in real GDP is severe. 6

devaluation   When a country's central bank resets the par exchange rate at a lower level. 479

diminishing marginal product As the amount of one factor input increases, holding other inputs constant, the increased amount of output from an extra unit of the input (its *marginal product*) declines. 55

discount rate The interest rate the Fed charges banks for loans. 126

discounting The process of converting all next-period spending or income into current values by dividing them by $(1 + r)$ raised to the power T where T is the number of years in the future. 497

discouraged workers Those who would like to work but have given up looking. 37, 555

discretion When policy makers make no commitment to future actions, but instead make what they believe in that moment to be the right policy decision for the situation. 577

disposable income The total income available for spending; this equals total (gross) income net of (minus) taxes. 232, 494

distortions Departures from the most efficient economic outcomes. 439

divine coincidence No conflict between the dual objectives of stabilizing inflation and economic activity. 336

dominated assets Assets such as currency and checkable deposits that are perceived to be poor investments because investors can hold other assets that pay higher returns and yet are perceived to be just as safe. 276

dual mandate Co-equal objectives of price stability and maximum sustainable employment. 330

dynamic, stochastic, general equilibrium (DSGE) models Models that allow the economy to grow over time (dynamic), be subject to shocks (stochastic), and are based on general equilibrium principles. 602

economic model A simplified representation of the economic phenomenon that takes a mathematical or graphical form. 4

economic profits The revenue from selling goods and services, minus the costs of the inputs. 60

economic theory A logical framework to explain a particular economic phenomenon. 3

effectiveness lag The time it takes for the policy actually to have an impact on the economy. 344

efficiency wages Wages that are above the market-clearing level where supply equals demand, but which are efficient because they induce workers to work harder and be more productive. 560

employment ratio The percentage of the adult civilian population employed. 38, 544

employment-to-population ratio The proportion of the civilian working-age population that is employed. 544

endogenous growth theory A theory that explains why advances in technology *endogenously* (from within the system) fuel sustained economic growth. 189

endogenous variables A variable that a macroeconomist wants to explain inside his or her model. 4

entitlements Transfer payments made by a government not on a discretionary basis, but are locked in by earlier legislation. 429

equation of exchange The equation $MV = PY$, which relates nominal income to the quantity of money. 109

equilibrium real interest rate When the economy is producing at its potential and the inflation rate is consistent with price stability. 330

equities A share of ownership of a corporation. 373

excess demand A condition where the quantity demanded of the factor is above the quantity supplied. 64

excess reserves Any additional reserves the banks choose to hold. 126

excess supply A condition where the quantity demanded of a factor is less than the quantity supplied. 62

exchange rate The price of one currency, say, the dollar, in terms of other currencies, say, the euro. 235

exchanges Where buyers and sellers of securities (or their agents or brokers) meet in one central location to conduct trades. 373

excludability The ability of the owner of a piece of property to deny its use to others unless they pay for it. 179

exogenous variables A set of factors not explained by the model that are used to explain the endogenous variables. 4

expectations-augmented Phillips curve An equation for the Phillips curve that indicates that inflation is negatively related to the difference between the unemployment rate and the natural rate of unemployment. 284

expected return The return that is expected on an asset, which includes payments from an asset, such as interest, and any expected change in its value, as a fraction of its price. 275, 467

expenditure approach A technique for computing GDP by measuring the total spending on currently produced final goods and services in the economy. 24

expenditure multiplier The change in equilibrium output from a change in government purchases. 441

factor accumulation Growth in labor and capital. 169

factors of production   The inputs that go into the production process. 50

favorable supply shock   See *positive supply shock*. 57

federal funds rate   The interest rate charged on overnight loans between banks. 220

Federal Open Market Committee   The committee that makes decisions regarding the conduct of open market operations; composed of the seven members of the Board of Governors of the Federal Reserve System, the president of the Federal Reserve Bank of New York, and the presidents of four other Federal Reserve banks on a rotating basis. 104

Federal Reserve System   The central banking authority responsible for monetary policy in the United States; composed of twelve Federal Reserve banks and the Board of Governors of the Federal Reserve System. 104

final goods and services   The end goods in the production process. 21

finance companies   Raise funds by selling commercial paper (a short-term debt instrument) and by issuing stocks and bonds. 375

financial crisis   A large-scale disruption in financial markets characterized by business failures and sharp declines in the prices of assets. 12, 392

financial deepening   Financial development that improves firms' access to external sources of funds and has strong links to economic growth. 384

financial engineering   The development of new, sophisticated financial instruments products. 400

financial frictions   Impairments to the efficient functioning of financial markets. 584

financial innovation   When an economy introduces new types of loans or other financial products. 393

financial instruments   See *securities*. 373

financial intermediary   A type of financial institution such as a bank, insurance company, finance company, mutual fund, or pension fund. 374

financial intermediation   The process of linking borrower-spenders and lender-savers through financial intermediaries. 374

financial liberalization   Countries eliminating restrictions on financial institutions and markets domestically. 393

financing constraints   When firms are cut off from raising funds in financial markets because credit markets have dried up. 531

fire sales   When banks sell off assets quickly. 396

fiscal policy   Policy makers' decisions to change government spending or taxes. 11

Fisher effect   The outcome that when expected inflation occurs, interest rates will rise; named after economist Irving Fisher. 116

Fisher equation   Defines the real interest rate in precise terms by stating that the nominal interest rate i equals the real interest rate plus the expected rate of inflation π^e. 40

fixed exchange rate regime   An exchange rate regime in which the value of a currency is pegged relative to the value of one other currency (called the anchor currency) so that the exchange rate is fixed. 447

fixed investment   Planned spending by firms on equipment (machines, computers, airplanes) and structures (factories, office buildings, shopping centers) and planned spending on new residential housing. 233

floating (flexible) exchange rate regime   An exchange rate regime in which the value of a currency is determined by supply and demand in the foreign exchange market. 477

flow   An amount per a given unit of time. 23

foreign exchange interventions   International financial transactions that central banks regularly engage in to influence exchange rates. 475

foreign exchange market   Market for determining exchange rates and the trading of currencies and bank deposits denominated in particular currencies. 459

forward exchange rate   The exchange rate for the forward transaction. 460

forward transaction   A type of exchange rate transaction that ensures the exchange of bank deposits at some specified future date. 460

free-rider problem   Where private investors who do not spend their resources on collecting information can take advantage of (get a *free ride* on) the information that other investors collect. 377

frictional unemployment   Occurs because workers and firms need time to search and make suitable matchups. 328, 556

fundamental economic values   Values based on realistic expectations of the assets' future income streams. 394

fundamental identity of national income accounting   Defines GDP as the sum of consumption expenditure, investment, government purchases, and net exports, that is, $Y = C + I + G + NX$. 20

GDP deflator   Nominal GDP divided by real GDP. 33

general equilibrium   When all markets are simultaneously in equilibrium at the point where the quantity of aggregate output demanded equals the quantity of aggregate output supplied. 303

globalization   The opening up of markets internationally, both in finance and in trade. 554

government budget constraint   The requirement that the government budget deficit equal the sum of the change in the monetary base and the change in government bonds held by the public. 431

government budget deficits   An excess of government spending relative to revenue. 11

government capital   Physical assets such as highways, broadband networks, or schools. 437

government consumption   Government purchases for current goods and services like health care and police. 26, 74

government investment   Spending on capital goods like highways and schools that add to the capital stock and promote economic growth. 26, 74

government purchases   Spending by the government—whether federal, state, or local—on currently produced goods and services. 26, 232, 428

government saving   Equals net government income less government consumption. 74

government-sponsored enterprises (GSEs)   Sponsored agencies that function as private corporations, but have close ties to the government. 539

grants in aid   Reflect federal assistance to state and local governments. 429

Great Inflation   A period in the 1970s of high inflation, peaking at over 14%. 220

Great Moderation   The period from the mid-1980s to the mid-2000s during which the volatility of real GDP and its components, as well as in inflation, declined both in the United States and abroad. 221

gross domestic product (GDP)   The total value of goods and services produced in an economy. 19

gross investment   Total spending on new capital goods. 527

gross national product (GNP)   Measures the total income earned by U.S. residents. 30

growth accounting equation   The growth version of the production function, which states that the growth rate of output equals the growth rate of total factor productivity plus the contribution from the growth of both capital and labor. 167

haircuts   When lenders require larger amounts of collateral. 404

hedge funds   A special type of mutual fund that acquires funds by selling shares but only to very wealthy people, so they are less regulated than mutual funds. 375

hierarchical mandates   Mandates for a central bank that require stable prices as a condition of pursuing other goals. 329

high-powered money   See *monetary base*. 126

human capital   Investments in knowledge and skills, such as education and training programs, that increase worker productivity and in turn increase wages. 180, 437

hyperinflation   Extremely high inflation rates. 9, 115

implementation lag   The time it takes for policy makers to change policy instruments once they have decided on the new policy. 343

implicit price deflator for GDP   See *GDP deflator*. 33

impossible trinity   See *policy trilemma*. 480

imputed value   An estimate of what the price of the good or service would be if it were traded in a market. 21

income   The flow of earnings per unit of time. 102

income approach   A way of measuring GDP that involves adding up all the incomes received by households and firms in the economy, including profits and tax revenue to the government. 28

income effect   The change in consumption due to changes in income. 503

index of leading indicators   A combination of ten variables that some economists use to forecast changes in the economy. 211

indifference curves   A curve showing all possible combinations of current and future consumption that lead us to the same level of overall happiness (utility or welfare). 498

inflation   The condition of a continually rising price level. 7

inflation gap   The difference between inflation and the inflation target. 329

inflation hedges   Assets whose real returns are less affected than that of money when inflation varies. 276

inflation rate   The rate of change of the price level, usually measured as a percentage change per year. 7

inflation target   A target level of inflation used by a central bank to pursue a price stability objective. 329

inflation targeting   A monetary policy strategy that involves public announcement of a medium-term numerical target for inflation. 587

inflation tax   Seignorage that results in higher inflation and leads to a tax on holders of money balances, which lose value in real terms. 450

institutions   A set of rules, organizations, and customs that govern the behavior of individuals and firms. 183

insurance companies   Companies that acquire funds from premiums paid by policyholders and in turn insure policyholders against financial hazards like death or against loss from theft, fire, or accidents. 375

interest rate   The cost of borrowing, or the price paid for the rental of funds. 40

intermediate goods and services   Goods and services used up entirely in the stages of production. 21

international reserves   A central bank's foreign-currency denominated asset holdings. 475

intertemporal budget constraint How much a person can consume today versus tomorrow, given a consumer's total resources. 495

intertemporal budget line A curve that shows the tradeoff between current consumption and future consumption: The more you spend today, the less you have available to spend tomorrow. 497

intertemporal marginal rate of substitution See *marginal rate of substitution*. 499

intertemporal substitution The willingness to shift work effort over time as real wages and real interest rates change. 599

inventories Firms' holdings of raw materials, unfinished goods, and unsold finished goods. 22

inventory investment Spending by firms on additional holdings of raw materials, parts, and finished goods, calculated as the change in holdings of these inventory items in a given time period—say, a year. 22, 233, 523

investment Spending on currently produced capital goods that are used to produce goods and services over an extended period of time. 26, 150

investment banks Banks that both trade securities and help corporations issue securities by guaranteeing a price for the securities and then selling them. 373

investment function A function that shows the relationship between per capita investment and the per capita capital stock when investment equals saving. 150

investment tax credit Gives businesses a tax break when they make an investment in physical capital. 89

IS curve Shows the relationship between aggregate output and the real interest rate when the goods market is in equilibrium. 238

just-in-time production Where manufacturers order inventories for production just when they are needed. 534

Keynesian models Economic models with slowly adjusting (sticky) prices. 223

Keynesians Followers of John Maynard Keynes, who argue that the government should pursue active policies to stabilize economic fluctuations. 221

labor The sum of the number of hours people work. 50

labor force The combined number of people employed and unemployed. 38

labor force participation The percentage of the adult population in the labor force. 551

labor-force participation rate The percentage of the adult civilian population in the labor force. 38

labor hoarding Where workers sit idly for a chunk of their workday, but are still counted in the government surveys as "employed." 600

labor productivity The amount of output produced per unit of labor. 52

lagging variable A macroeconomic variable whose turning points occur after the business cycle changes course. 211

large open economy An economy that is open to trade and capital flows, but is sufficiently large that its saving and investment decisions do influence the world real interest rate. 90

law of one price States that if two countries produce an identical good and transportation costs and trade barriers are very low, the price of the good should be the same in both countries no matter which country produces it. 463

leading variable A macroeconomic variable that reaches a peak or trough before the turning points of a business cycle. 211

legislative lag Represents the time it takes to pass legislation to implement a particular policy. 343

leisure Any activity that does not occur on the job—eating, sleeping, watching TV, partying, taking vacations, and taking care of children. 549

leverage cycle A lending boom and then a lending crash. 393

liabilities Debts or IOUs such as those belonging to an individual or firm that sells (issues) securities. 373

life-cycle hypothesis A theory that suggests that people tend to smooth consumption over their life cycle. 511

liquid Easily converted into cash. 103

liquidity The ease and speed with which an asset can be turned into cash relative to other assets. 275

liquidity constraint See *borrowing constraint*. 504

liquidity preference framework Determines the equilibrium nominal interest rate by equating the supply and demand for money. 263

liquidity preference function A function that shows that as the nominal interest rate rises the demand for real money balances falls, and that as income rises the demand for real money balances also rises. 263

liquidity trap An extreme case of ultrasensitivity of the demand for money to interest rates in which conventional monetary policy has no direct effect on aggregate spending, because a change in the money supply has no effect on interest rates. 277

logarithmic scale See *ratio scale*. 192

long-run Phillips curve The line connecting all possible long-run relationships between the inflation rate and the unemployment rate. 285

M1 A measure of money that includes currency, traveler's checks, and checkable deposits. 106

M2 A measure of money that adds to M1: money market deposit accounts, money market mutual fund shares, small denomination time deposits, savings deposits, overnight repurchase agreements, and overnight Eurodollars. 106

macroeconometric models Models used to forecast economic activity and to evaluate the potential effects of policy options. 579

macroeconomics The study of economic activity and prices in the overall economy of a nation or a region. 3

macroprudential regulation Regulatory policy to affect what is happening in credit markets in the aggregate. 418

managed float regime (dirty float) An exchange rate regime in which countries attempt to influence their exchange rates by buying and selling currencies. 477

management of expectations Communication with the public and the markets to influence their expectations about what policy actions will be taken in the future. 361

marginal product The increased output from an extra unit of the input. 55

marginal product of capital The slope of the production function that indicates how much output increases for each additional unit of capital. 55

marginal product of labor The slope of the production function that indicates how much output increases for each additional unit of labor. 56

marginal propensity to consume The increase in consumption expenditure from an additional dollar of disposable income. 233, 506

marginal rate of substitution The rate at which a consumer is willing to give up (substitute) consumption in period 2 for additional consumption in period 1. 499

market-clearing The level at which the quantity of labor supplied would equal the quantity demanded and unemployment would not occur. 558

medium of exchange Anything that is used to pay for goods and services. 102

menu costs The costs a firm bears when it changes the price of its goods. 118, 223

microcredit Programs that offer very small loans, often less than $100. 374

microeconomics Looks at the behavior of individual firms, households, or markets. 3

minimum wage A floor on wages set by the government. 559

monetary aggregate The measure of the money supply used by the Federal Reserve System (M1 and M2). 106

monetary base The sum of the Fed's monetary liabilities and the U.S. Treasury's monetary liabilities. 125

monetary (currency) union Situation in which a group of countries decides to adopt a common currency, thereby fixing their exchange rates relative to each other. 480

monetary policy The management of the amount of money in the economy and interest rates. 12

monetary policy (MP) curve Indicates the relationship between the real interest rate the central bank sets and the inflation rate. 252

monetary transmission mechanisms The ways monetary policy affects aggregate demand. 382

monetizing the debt Issuing money to finance the debt. 449

money Defined by economists as an asset that is generally accepted as payment for goods and services or in the repayment of debts. 102

money multiplier Tells us how much the money supply changes for a given change in the monetary base. 136

money supply The amount of money in the economy. 104

monopolistic competition The condition of a market when firms set prices, even if there is substantial competition in their market. 223

moral hazard The risk (hazard) that the other party will engage in activities that are undesirable (immoral) from your point of view. 376

mortgage-backed securities Securities that cheaply bundle mortgages into a standardized debt security. 400

multiple deposit creation When a central bank supplies the banking system with $1 of additional reserves, deposits increase by a multiple of this amount. 129

mutual funds Acquire funds by selling shares to individuals and use the proceeds to buy securities such as stocks and bonds. 375

national income The value determined by combining the compensation of employees, other income (such as from the self-employed), and corporate profits for an economy. 30

national income accounting An accounting system to measure economic activity and its components. 20

national income identity See *fundamental identity of national income accounting.* 24

national saving The sum of private saving and government saving. 75

national saving rate The share of national income saved by the government and households. 75

national wealth A country's holdings of assets minus its liabilities at a particular point in time. 74

natural rate of output The level of aggregate output supplied at the natural rate of unemployment. 287

natural rate of unemployment The level of the unemployment rate that remains even when wages in the labor market have fully adjusted, which can be interpreted as the full-employment level of unemployment. 283, 561

natural real interest rate See *equilibrium real interest rate*. 330

negative supply shock A shock that leads to a decline in the quantity of output produced from given quantities of capital and labor. 57

neoclassical theory of investment Theory that builds on the neoclassical idea that the user cost of capital influences the desired stock of capital to explain business fixed investment, inventory, and residential investment.

net capital outflow The difference between saving and investment. 77

net capital outflow identity See *net capital outflow*. 77

net domestic product A measure equal to the GDP of an economy less that economy's depreciation. 30

net exports Exports minus imports: that is, the value of currently produced goods and services exported, or sold to other countries, minus the value of goods and services imported, or purchased from abroad. 27, 232

net foreign assets The net holdings of foreign assets (American-owned foreign stocks, bonds, bank accounts, factories, etc., minus foreign-owned U.S. assets). 78

net government income The government's disposable income that is available to spend. 31

net interest payments Interest payments made to holders of government debt such as U.S. Treasury bonds, less the interest paid to the government for debts, such as student loans. 429

net investment The desired change in capital stock. 527

net worth See *capital*. 375

neutrality of money The implication that adjustments in the money supply have no impact on real variables. 111

new Keynesian model Based on similar microeconomic foundations as in real business cycle models, but embeds stickiness into the analysis. 601

new neoclassical synthesis A set of principles, on which almost all modern macroeconomists agree. 619

nominal anchor A nominal variable—such as the inflation rate, the money supply, or an exchange rate—that ties down the price level or inflation to achieve price stability. 582

nominal exchange rate The relative price of one currency in terms of another. 460

nominal GDP A measure of GDP that has not been adjusted to accurately reflect changes in the price level. 31

nominal GDP targeting A variant of inflation targeting in which the central bank announces an objective of hitting a particular level of nominal GDP that is growing over time. 589

nominal interest rate An interest rate you read about in the newspaper that makes no allowance for inflation. 41

nominal variables Variables that are measured at current market prices. 31

non-accelerating inflation rate of unemployment (NAIRU) The rate of unemployment where inflation stops accelerating (changing). 287

nonactivists People who believe wages and prices are very flexible, so the self-correcting mechanism is very rapid. 343

nonborrowed monetary base The monetary base minus the banks' borrowing from the Fed. 129

nonconventional monetary policy Non-interest-rate tools used to stimulate aggregate demand when a central bank faces the zero-lower-bound problem. 358

nonrival Something that can be used by multiple people in more than one activity simultaneously. 179

nontradable Refers to items that are not traded across borders. 464

Okun's law Describes the negative relationship between the unemployment gap and the output gap. 288

open economy An economy open to trade and flows of capital across its borders. 89

open market operations The Fed's buying and selling of bonds in the open market. 105, 126

open market purchase A purchase of bonds by the Fed. 127

open market sale A sale of bonds by the Fed. 127

opportunity cost The amount of income forgone (sacrificed) by holding money rather than alternative assets such as bonds. 263

optimal forecast The best guess of the future using all available information. 574

originate-to-distribute A practice used by mortgage brokers of making loans and quickly selling them to investors in the form of security. 401

output gap The difference between output and potential output. 209, 275

patents Legal rights that give inventors the sole right to use, make, or sell licensing rights to others for a set period of time, typically around twenty years. 182

payment technology Newer methods for payment, such as credit cards, that could affect the demand for money. 273

payroll tax Taxes on wages, such as Social Security taxes. 444

peaks High points of economic activity. 208

pension funds Acquire funds through contributions from employees and their employers and provide retirement income to the employees covered by the pension plan. 375

perfect capital mobility A situation where an open economy does not have any restrictions on flows of capital between domestic and foreign residents or vice versa. 89

perfect competition A market where buyers and sellers are price takers because they are not large or powerful enough to charge more than the market price for their goods or services. 59, 223

permanent income The level of income that is expected to persist over a long period of time and is therefore representative of a consumer's lifetime resources. 508

permanent income hypothesis A hypothesis that asserts that consumption depends on permanent income. 508

personal consumption expenditure See *consumption expenditure*. 25

personal consumption expenditure (PCE) deflator Nominal PCE divided by real PCE. 34

personal taxes Taxes composed of income taxes and property taxes that are a major source of total government revenue. 430

Phillips curve The negative relationship between unemployment and inflation. 281

planned expenditure The total amount of spending on domestically produced goods and services that households, businesses, the government, and foreigners want to make. 231

planned investment spending The total planned spending by businesses on new physical capital (e.g., machines, computers, factories) plus planned spending on new homes. 232

policy trilemma The fact that a country (or monetary union like the Eurozone) can't pursue the following three policies at the same time: 1) free capital mobility, 2) a fixed exchange rate, and 3) an independent monetary policy. 488

political business cycle When fiscal and monetary policy is expansionary right before elections, with higher inflation following. 579

portfolio theories Where people decide how much of an asset, such as money, they want to hold as part of their overall portfolio of assets. 275

positive supply shock Results in an increase in the quantity of output produced for given combinations of capital and labor. 57

potential output The natural rate of output, the level of production that an economy can sustain in the long run. 208, 274

present discounted value See *present value*. 497

present value The common-sense notion that a dollar you will receive tomorrow is less valuable to you now than a dollar paid to you today. 497

price indexes Different measures of the price level. 33

price level The average level of prices in the economy. 32

price shocks Shifts in inflation that are independent of the tightness in the labor markets or of expected inflation. 286

price stability Low and stable inflation. 329

principal-agent problem Where individuals or institutions act as agents for investors (the principals) but do not have the investors' best interests at heart. 401

printing money Use of new government-printed money to purchase goods and services. 449

private disposable income Equals the income received by the private sector, plus payments made to the private sector by the government, minus taxes paid to the government. 31

private saving Equals private disposable income minus consumption expenditure. 74

private saving rate The proportion of private disposable income that is saved. 74

procyclical When a variable moves up during expansions and down during contractions—that is, in the same direction as aggregate economic activity. 211

production approach A technique for computing GDP as the current market value of all final goods and services newly produced in the economy during a fixed period of time. 20

production function See *aggregate production function*. 51

production smoothing When firms keep on producing when sales are temporarily low, putting the goods produced into inventory, and then do not raise production when sales are temporarily high, instead drawing down these inventories to satisfy the higher demand. 535

productivity How productive capital and labor are. 51

property rights The protection of property from expropriation by the government or other parties. 183

prudential regulation   Rules set by the government to prevent banks from taking on too much risk. 384

prudential supervision   Where the government monitors banks by examining them on a regular basis. 384

quantitative easing   An expansion of the balance sheet that leads to a huge increase in liquidity in the economy. 360

quantity theory of money   View that nominal income (spending) is determined solely by movements in the quantity of money M. 110

random walk   When changes in a variable are unpredictable. 515

random walk hypothesis   Theory based on the life-cycle and permanent income hypotheses that suggests that changes in consumption will be unpredictable. 515

ratio scale   A scale in which equal distances reflect the same percentage change. 192

rational expectations   Expectations that are identical to optimal forecasts (the best guess of the future) using all available information. 574

rational expectations revolution   The widespread adoption of the rational expectations theory into macroeconomic models. 576

rational inattention   The act of only making decisions about prices at infrequent intervals because it is rational to do so given the time and effort that is required to make these decisions. 223

real business cycle model   A business cycle model that begins with the assumption that all wages and prices are completely flexible and argues that real shocks cause fluctuations in potential output and long-run aggregate supply. 597

real exchange rate   The relative price of goods in two countries, that is, the rate at which you can exchange domestic goods for foreign goods. 460

Real Gross Domestic Product (GDP)   Measures the output of actual goods and services produced in an economy over a fixed period, usually a year. 5

real interest rate   The amount of extra purchasing power a lender must be paid for the rental of his or her money. 41

real money balances   The quantity of money in real terms. 263

real rental price (cost) of capital   The rental price of capital in terms of goods and services. 60

real shocks   Shocks to productivity or the willingness of workers to work that affect aggregate supply. 597

real variable   A measure of an economic variable in terms of quantities of actual goods and services. 32

real wage rate   The wage in terms of goods and services. 60

recession   When economic activity declines and real GDP per person falls. 6

recognition lag   The time it takes for policy makers to be sure of what the data are signaling about the future course of the economy. 343

rental price (cost) of capital   The price paid to rent a unit of capital. 60

repurchase agreements (repos)   Short-term borrowing which, in effect, use assets like mortgage-backed securities as collateral. 404

required reserve ratio   The fraction of deposits that the Fed requires be kept as reserves. 126

required reserves   Reserves that the Fed requires banks to hold. 126

reserves   Banks' holding of deposits in accounts with the Fed plus currency that is physically held by banks (vault cash). 126, 265

residential investment   Includes spending on new housing, whether it is occupied by owners or rented out by landlords. 523

restrictive covenants   Debt contracts that restrict borrowers' activities. 379

revaluation   When a country's central bank resets the par value of its exchange rate at a higher level. 479

Ricardian equivalence   An argument that suggests that tax cuts have no effect on spending and national saving. 450

risk   The degree of uncertainty associated with the return on the asset relative to other assets. 275

risk averse   When most people do not like risk and so find riskier assets less desirable. 262

rival   Something that if used in one activity, cannot be used in another. 179

Romer models   Models of economic growth developed by Paul Romer that explain why advances in technology endogenously (from within the model) fuel economic growth. 189

rules   Binding plans that specify how policy will respond (or not respond) to particular data such as unemployment and inflation. 577

sacrifice ratio   The percentage reduction of real GDP that is necessary to reduce the inflation rate by one percentage point. 612

saving   The difference between the amount of income a person has to spend and his or her current spending. 494

saving-investment diagram   A graphical analysis of the equilibrium in the goods market. 84

saving rate   The fraction of consumer's income that is saved each year. 149, 507

screening   Collecting information about potential borrowers before a transaction occurs to avoid adverse selection problems. 378

seasonally adjusted The process by which economists adjust the data to subtract out the usual seasonal fluctuations using advanced statistical techniques. 32

sectoral shifts When new industries grow and old industries die off. 558

securities Claims on the borrowers' future income or assets in the form of common stock or bonds. 373

securitization The bundling together of smaller loans (like mortgages) into standard debt securities. 400

seignorage The revenue the government generates by issuing the currency. 449

self-correcting mechanism A feature that occurs because the short-run aggregate supply curve shifts up or down to restore the economy to full employment (aggregate output at potential) over time. 307

shadow banking system Hedge funds, investment banks, and other non-depository financial firms, which are not as tightly regulated as banks. 404

shoe-leather costs Term economists use to denote the time and fuel spent on trips to the bank. 118

skill-biased technical change The idea that new technologies such as computer hardware, software, and the Internet have boosted the relative productivity of college-educated workers. 553

small open economy An economy that is open to trade and to flows of capital across its borders and that is "small" relative to the world economy, so that whatever happens in this economy has no effect on the world real interest rate. 90

Solow diagram A diagram based on the Solow growth model showing the steady-state level of investment and capital-labor ratio graphically. 152

Solow growth model Explains how saving rates and population growth determine capital accumulation, which in turn determine economic growth. 148

Solow residual Economic growth that is not explained by capital growth or labor growth, which is an estimate of total factor productivity. 167, 599

sovereign debt crisis A collapse in the market for a country's debt. 435

speculative attacks Massive sales of a weak currency that lead to a sharp decline in the exchange rate. 483

spot exchange rate The exchange rate for the spot transaction. 460

spot transaction The predominant exchange rate transaction, which affects the immediate (two-day) exchange of bank deposits. 459

stabilization policy An important goal for macroeconomic policy to minimize business cycle fluctuations and stabilize economic activity. 13

stagflation A situation of rising inflation but a falling level of aggregate output. 312

staggered price setting When competitors adjust prices at different intervals. 224

steady state Where capital per worker comes to rest and stops changing. 151

sticky prices Prices that adjust slowly over time to their long-run equilibrium. 222

stock A quantity at a given point in time. 23

stock-out avoidance The motivation for holding inventories to avoid running out of goods and thereby losing sales. 535

store of value A repository of purchasing power that lasts over time. 103

structural unemployment Unemployment that arises from lack of skills or a mismatch of skills with available jobs. 328, 558

structured credit products Financial instruments that pay out income streams from a collection of underlying assets. 400

subprime mortgages Mortgages offered to borrowers with less-than-stellar credit records. 400

substitution effect The change in consumption that occurs from the change in the relative price of consumption in two periods. 503

supply shock A shift in the production function so that there is a different level of output produced from given quantities of capital and labor. 57

supply-siders Economists who focus on the favorable effects of tax cuts on aggregate supply. 445

T-account A simplified balance sheet that shows only changes in the balance sheet. 127

tariffs Taxes on imported goods. 430

tax-adjusted user cost of capital The user cost of capital that the firm compares to the before-tax marginal product of capital to determine the desired level of capital. 531

tax multiplier The change in equilibrium output from a change in taxes that is always less in absolute value than the expenditure multiplier because the initial change in spending occurs through consumption expenditure. 441

tax smoothing A policy of keeping tax rates fairly stable when government spending fluctuates. 439

tax wedges The difference between what people earn after taxes on their labor or investments and what they are paid before they make their tax payments. 439

taxes on production and imports Primarily sales taxes, but they also include taxes on imported goods, known as *tariffs*. 430

Taylor principle Where monetary policy makers raise *nominal* rates by more than any rise in expected inflation so that *real* interest rates rise when there is a rise in inflation. 253

Taylor rule A rule that provides a guide for how to set the real federal funds rate, the policy instrument, which equals its historical average of 2%, plus a weighted average of the inflation gap and the output gap. 345

technological spillover The spread of technology to its creators' neighbors and eventually around the world due to the nonrivalry of ideas. 196

terms of trade See *real exchange rate*. 460

theory of intertemporal choice Irving Fisher's theory, published in 1930, which describes consumption decisions in a simplified world with only two periods of time—today (period 1) and the future (period 2). 495

theory of purchasing power parity (PPP) A theory that states that exchange rates between any two currencies will adjust to reflect changes in the price levels of the two countries. 464

time-inconsistency problem The tendency to deviate from good long-run plans when making short-run decisions. 578

Tobin's *q* A ratio of the market value and replacement cost. 536

total factor productivity See *productivity*. 51

trade balance The difference between merchandise exports and imports. 27

trade deficit A situation where net exports is negative in an economy. 77

trade surplus A situation where net exports is positive in an economy. 77

traditional Keynesian model The standard model of aggregate demand that assumes expectations are not rational and prices are sticky. 607

transaction costs The time and money spent trying to exchange goods or services. 102

transfer payments Direct payments to individuals—such as unemployment insurance benefits, Social Security benefits, Medicare, or welfare payments—where goods or services are not provided in return. 428

transfers Government payments for Social Security, Medicare, and unemployment insurance benefits. 26

transitory income The component of income that does not persist for a long period of time, and so is subject to temporary fluctuations. 508

troughs Low points of economic activity as illustrated on a chart. 208

twin deficits The phenomenon of a simultaneous trade deficit and government budget deficit. 94

underground economy Good and services produced that are hidden from the government, either because they are illegal or because the person producing the goods and services is avoiding paying taxes on the income he or she receives. 21

unemployment gap The difference between the unemployment rate and the natural rate of unemployment. 284

unemployment insurance A government program that provides unemployed workers with a percentage of their wages for a given period after they lose their job. 557

unemployment rate Measures the percentage of workers looking for work, but who do not have jobs, at a particular point in time. 7

unemployment spells The length of time a worker remains unemployed. 556

unit of account Anything used to measure value in an economy. 103

user cost of capital The expected real cost of using a unit of capital over a particular period. 525

uses-of-saving identity Tells us that saving either goes into investment—acquiring capital goods and boosting the capital stock—or, alternatively, into net exports—selling goods to foreigners in exchange for foreign currency assets. 77

utility A measure of overall happiness. 498

value added The value of a firm's output minus the cost of the intermediate goods purchased by the firm. 22

value-added tax A tax that is paid by a producer on the difference between what it receives for its goods and services minus the costs. 76

velocity of money The rate of turnover of money, the average number of times per year that a dollar is spent in buying the total amount of final goods and services produced in the economy. 109

wage rate The price of labor. 60

wage rigidity The inability of wages to adjust to the level that would equate supply and demand in the labor market and thus eliminate unemployment. 558

wealth A person's holdings of assets (such as bonds, stocks, houses, and fine art) minus his or her liabilities. 73, 102

welfare See *utility*. 498

work in process Holdings of partially finished components that will go into the final product. 535

world real interest rate The real interest rate found in world markets. 89

zero lower bound The zero floor on the policy rate. 355

zero-lower-bound problem The limit on monetary policy when nominal rates are zero. 382

Index

Italicized *t* refers to tables, *f* refers to figures. Footnotes are indicated by *n*.